Climbing
Man's Family Tree

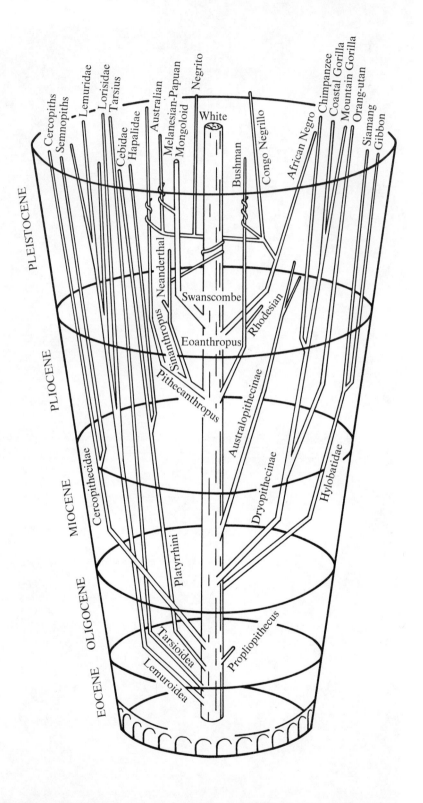

Climbing
Man's Family Tree

*A Collection of Major Writings
on Human Phylogeny, 1699 to 1971*

Edited by

Theodore D. McCown

Department of Anthropology
University of California at Berkeley

and

Kenneth A. R. Kennedy

Department of Anthropology
Cornell University

Prentice-Hall, Inc., Englewood Cliffs, New Jersey

To our colleagues in the Department of Anthropology,
University of California at Berkeley,
this book is respectfully dedicated.

Dr. Theodore D. McCown died August 17, 1969, while
this book was being prepared. His students and colleagues
remember him as a scholar of profound erudition and a
gentleman of impeccable courtesy. This final published work
of Dr. McCown reflects the broad scope of his interests
in human paleontology and his own major contribution
to the study of Neanderthal Man.

Kenneth A. R. Kennedy
Cornell University

ISBN: 0–13–137638–1
Library of Congress Catalog Card No.: 75–172944
Printed in the United States of America
10 9 8 7 6 5 4 3 2 1

Frontispiece after Hooton 1946

Contents

Part Three: 1890 to 1925   189

Part Four: 1925 to 1959   241

Preface

This collection of scientific papers represents material used by the editors at their respective institutions in university courses on human evolution. All of the papers deal with some facet of the problem of the biological relationships of modern man to his prehistoric progenitors as these affinities are documented by the fossil record. This study is called paleoanthropology, one of a number of subfields within the discipline of physical anthropology. In their study of fossil man, paleoanthropologists have frequently used a biological device called the phylogenetic tree, a diagrammatic representation of living and extinct biotic forms arranged on trunks and branches to define their degrees of genealogical affinity and lines of descent. The articles selected for this book broadly outline how man's phylogenetic tree has been conceived over the past three centuries of scientific inquiry.

In an effort to relate in a meaningful historical framework some of the major concepts described in the articles, the editors have prepared the essays that introduce each of the five parts of the volume. It is hoped that these will prove useful to students in anthropology and the biological sciences as well as to the reader interested in the history of science. There can be no substitute for reading original sources in the study of any scientific field; the essays are merely guides toward greater appreciation of the selected articles.

The editors wish to acknowledge with deep appreciation the assistance they have received from Dr. Adrienne Zillman of the University of California at Santa Cruz, Miss Kathleen Gibson of the University of California at Berkeley, Dr. Mary C. Marino of the University of Saskatchewan,

Mrs. Carolyn McGory and Mr. and Mrs. Evans Young of Cornell University, Mrs. Beverly Bammel of Syracuse, New York, and Mrs. Audrey Dejournette of Oakland, California. Special gratitude is expressed to Mrs. Margaret C. Fairlie Kennedy, whose encouragement and enthusiastic assistance made possible the completion of the manuscript.

Introduction

The idea of fossil man is very recent in Western thought. That particular mineralized bones found in caves and river gravels are the corporeal vestiges of our own kind who lived many thousands of years ago is an idea that was not only unfamiliar to thinkers of classical antiquity and the European Middle Ages, but was even greeted with considerable scorn when it was suggested in the early years of the eighteenth century. It is remarkable that the idea of fossil man was conceived at all, so humiliating to the human ego are its implications of our affinities with anthropoid apes and monkeys. No wonder that denials of the existence of human fossils have been delivered with emotion. Even the self-appointed disciples of the "scientific method" have not always been free from strong biases when faced with the problems of human biological history: some who could accept the paleontological evidence for non-human manifestations of life on this earth have denied the applicability of that evidence to theories concerned with their own species.

In the study of the intellectual development of paleo-anthropology, as in the examination of the history of any other body of scientific knowledge, the investigator must be aware of three important factors: (1) the kinds of questions that the discipline asks, which set its sphere of inquiry apart from the concerns of other disciplines; (2) the concepts already current in the intellectual background of Western culture at any given period of time which have found their way into the framing of the questions which the discipline asks; (3) the trends that the discipline has pursued through time, as a result of the introduction of new concepts.

With regard to the first consideration, it is not possible within the compass of this book to examine in detail all of the problems involved in the science of paleoanthropology. As was noted in the preface, the focus of interest that has been selected is human phylogeny as interpreted from an examination of the fossil record. The classic papers dealing with the initial discoveries and descriptions of the human fossils, the ideas concerning human antiquity and place of origin, and the philosophical speculations about man's place in nature are other focuses of investigation that merit the kind of attention that the question of human phylogeny receives in this book. All of these questions are intimately related and attention cannot be directed at one without implicating the others. Thus the periods of time on which the divisions of this book are based are determined by initial fossil discoveries of crucial importance.

Turning next to the identification of those concepts in Western thought which have become most intimately involved in the problem of human phylogeny and the human fossil record, the historian is immediately aware that they are to be sought in the spheres of the physical sciences of astronomy and geology; in the biological sciences of taxonomy, comparative anatomy, and paleontology; and in religious concepts and social philosophies. Most of these ideas originated in the minds of thinkers of classical antiquity, but other concepts do not make their first appearance before the last three centuries. A discussion of the older concepts is the subject of the remainder of the introduction, their later developments and the concepts of more recent times being relegated to the portions of the text where they are relevant.

The third factor for consideration—the trends of paleoanthropology through time—is a theme that is apparent throughout this collection of papers and one that develops from an examination of the material itself. A brief summary at the end of the book attempts to point out the more obvious turns in the road of paleoanthropological thought since its initial conception in the early years of the eighteenth century.

All of these factors have a special significance when examined by the paleoanthropologist, for in tracing the history of ideas concerning human paleontology, he is in a position to discover where in the material that confronts him daily current biases and preconceptions may be entrenched. Yet this is an aspect of his profession that he has failed to regard as important until very recently. A century has passed since the recognition and acceptance of the first fossil specimens of man within the scientific community. With the awareness that paleoanthropology has attained maturity through its immense accumulation of data, the development of schools of instruction as well as schools of interpretation, the wide circulation of its technical journals, its frequent scientific convocations, and the development of its methodologies, the students of man are now facing the problems of the intellectual development of their discipline.

Cosmos and Man

From a comparison of the concepts about nature that were entertained in classical antiquity with like concepts in the Middle Ages, it is apparent that there is a greater similarity of belief in the realm of biology than in the realms of the cosmic system and man's place in it. Most earlier thinkers of the Greco-Roman cultural tradition held a multi-world view conditioned by the precept that time was cyclical and that nature was an entity analogous in its behavior to the life cycle of the human body. Such a temporal concept satisfied the canon of classical aesthetics, that only an orderly and finite universe could be virtuous and real. Cycles were the dynamics of perpetual and beneficent change that reflected the nature of a Cosmic Intelligence. Man was of course implicated in this system, for as the seeds of decay were intrinsic in each new world, so man himself gradually became corrupted as the cycle in which he lived progressed. As each cycle neared its end and as man descended to the nadir of his degeneration, the earth and all of its living things were doomed to destruction in a vast cataclysm of fire and flood, until saved at the critical moment by the intervention of the Deity. This event was followed by another cycle. The duration of a completed cycle ranged from Plato's estimate of 72,000 years to Cassander's 360,000, but Phythagoras lamented that no man might know the number of the cycle in which he now lived. The doctrine of the Five Ages of human history was synchronized with these concepts of cycle, degeneration, catastrophism, and divine intervention, the earliest and most felicitous period being the Golden Age at the commencement of each cycle. The Greeks themselves were curious as to where the cyclic concept had originated, various thinkers attributing it to the Egyptian priesthood, to Hesiod, or to Heraclitus. Aristotle's assertion that there was only one world rather than many and that alternate generation and destruction meant no more than that the elements of nature combine now into one form and then into another received as little popular favor in this period as the mechanistic world view of Democritus, whose philosophy also gave no place to cycles.

The Church Fathers were faced with the problem of synthesizing the prestigious pagan literature with the Scriptures of Christian tradition. While many of the pagan concepts did survive in the single-world view of Christianity, the notion of cycle was a threat to belief in the One Creation, the single Atonement through Christ, and the Final Day of Judgment. Saint Augustine declared that the cyclic concept was incompatible with orthodoxy, in reaction to some of his theological predecessors who had favored the incorporation of the idea into Christian doctrine. The world view of the Middle Ages was of a universe created by God in the manner described in Genesis. The world was subject to His constant intervention, as witnessed by the occurrence of natural catastrophes and miracles which were the manifestations of divine wrath and approbation. The earth, whose existence extended back in time but a few millenia, was destined for imminent dissolution. Whereas the thinkers of the ancient world saw an orderliness and an intelligence inherent in the cycles of nature herself, the Christian philosophers considered that these qualities were imposed on the world by a supernatural Cause beyond the physical limits of nature. In the Ptolemaic universe, man, the reason for its existence, was set to the task of working out his salvation—if, by the grace of God, he were to escape the everlasting damnation incurred through the indiscretion of the very first member of his species. Thus while degeneration and divine intervention were pagan concepts congenial to Christian philosophy, cyclic time was inadmissible and catastrophes were limited to the biblical Deluge and to the Day of Judgment.

If a single factor can be isolated as contributing most to the genesis of a new world view in the sixteenth century, it is the idea of the expansion of spatial horizons from the circumscribed universe of the Middle Ages to the greater world view, both celestial and geographical, that was perceived by the late Renaissance scholars. The Copernican system revealed that the earth was a decentralized planet adrift in a limitless sea of other astral bodies. Newton's demonstration that these points of light, and indeed all matter, were influenced by the same laws of nature complemented Descartes' application of mathematical techniques to the description of the cosmos. The sciences of astronomy, physics, and mathematics succeeded in suggesting to philosophers that while final causes might forever remain unknown to man, the pursuit of "natural philosophy" could make credible the dynamics of nature through the discovery of natural laws which had originated with the Creator and were constantly being maintained by Him. Such laws were within the power of the human mind to understand; thus it fell to these scholars to explain through their investigations what the plan of Creation might be. This plan is reflected in nature—God's artifact and the device for revealing God's purpose. To study nature was to become familiar with divine effort, an attitude that was later to bear the label of providentialism. During the sixteenth century and much of the seventeenth there was little conflict between science and religion per se; instead, disagreements were entertained within the community of scientists themselves. Atheism was ascribed to individuals' moral lapses and not to their contamination from too close proximity to science.

What then were the ideas that threatened belief in a world with an antiquity of only a few thousand years, a world with one global catastrophe in the past and one yet to be fulfilled, a world that was unique because of its single creation and occupancy by man, a degenerate creature? As the researchers in the developing fields of the astral and geological sciences were piously laboring to elucidate the divine plan of nature, during this period from the sixteenth to the eighteenth centuries, the outcomes of their efforts were such as to strain the credibility of the accepted traditions. The pioneer investigations of nature undermined these venerable traditions and led directly to the notion of fossil man and the ultimate discovery of his osseous remains. The perfection of God's creation came into debate when the early telescopes revealed lunar craters and sun spots, and nature's permanency could hardly be maintained when the heavenly bodies were recognized as having the properties of motion and physical alteration. As the concept of unlimited time emerged from the theories of the formation of the universe, the concept of limited space appeared incongruous beside it. Furthermore, while the astronomers and physicists of this period were gently ushering out by the back door the concepts of the immutable heavens and the limited age of the earth since its creation, they were introducing through the front doors of their disciplines the notion of cosmic evolution, an idea that was to be wed to the biological sciences by the middle of the nineteenth century. At first the speculations on the nature of the universe which were founded on the Cartesian and Newtonian methodologies did not seem pertinent to the history of the earth insofar as its creation and development are recorded in Genesis. For while the scanners of the heavens were becoming progressively more concerned with the discernment of process of the natural world, the religious philosophers of these times were intent on demonstrating design in nature, and traditional doctrines seemed unassailable. But questions concerning the operation of natural laws on the earth could not exist independently of speculations already current in astronomical theory, questions about the origin of the earth as one of many such astral bodies and suggestions for an explanation of the Deluge. The science of geology may be said to have emerged from these late seventeenth century speculations, whose reasoned hypotheses rather than empirical investigation of the earth itself occasioned many fantastic "Theories of the Earth," as the cosmogonical writings of the period were frequently called. These were the vehicles that brought the concepts of geological antiquity and change into the forefront of Western thought in the eighteenth century, and in the century that followed those concepts were recognized as having biological implications.

The Chain of Being

In harmony with the idea of an orderly cyclic system as the creation of a beneficent and intelligent Being was the belief that the Platonic World of Forms, while cyclical, was an exhaustive replica of the World of Ideas, which had but a single creation. Hence the former World was fully stocked with all possible things, for the virtuous Deity could not begrudge existence to anything that could conceivably exist. These existants were imperceptibly graded in their structures and properties one from another so that there was a logical sequence of biotic phenomena—a unilinear graduation—based on each element's possessing certain qualities of "perfection" and "privation," according to Aristotle. Such a chain of being was composed of an indefinite number of links ranging in hierarchical order from the lowest sorts of existants through every possible grade of life up to the Absolute Being. Each element of the graduated series differed from the element above and below it in the least possible degree. Aristotle's "classification" of organic nature was a product of medieval scholasticism, for he did not formulate the "Scala Natura," or Ladder of Nature, beyond some eleven grades of animals—the "genos"—that originated with the zoophytes and terminated with man. But he recognized the significance of grouping together animals that were interfertile and similar in their morphology as members of the same "eidos"—the category known to later naturalists as the species. All specific groups were regarded as immutable entities of the chain of being, and since their ordering in the scale was static, phylogenetic affinities were not suggested. There is no historicity in this classic world view where immutability and finitude were nature's most perfect qualities. As to man's place in this system of nature, there was no question but that he stood between the known infra-human primates and the legendary near-men of travellers' accounts, and the epic heroes and demi-gods, a place that he maintained in every cycle.

The Neoplatonists had perpetuated the concept of the chain of being and introduced it into the biological concepts of the Middle Ages. The chain of being gained the sanction of Saint Augustine and Saint Thomas Aquinas because of its relevance to their theological struggles with the problems of inequality and evil in nature. The ideas of Aristotle became crystallized into an academic dogma under a scholastic regime, and original research was superceded by elaborate commentaries on the works of the ancient philosophers. During the Middle Ages knowledge of the organic world was contained in the beautifully illustrated "herbals" and "beastiaries" describing the medicinal and magical properties of various biotic forms.

The study of living things did not develop in Europe until motivated by the importation of myriad types of hitherto unknown flora and fauna from the New World and from newly explored portions of Asia, Oceania, and Africa. The classification and description of biotic nature, a discipline called then as now by the name "natural history," was a less prestigious science than physics and astronomy in the sixteenth century. Its methodology seemed less reliable and its research was neither dramatic nor utilitarian, but out of such humble beginnings came the first taxonomic systems. Taxonomy developed from botany, in which field de l'Obel, Caselpino, and Jung classified plants in their state-supported gardens according to various criteria—leaf form, type of stem, configuration of the reproductive parts of the flower. Basing his classification on the last criterion, Jung devised a binomial system where a plant identified by a noun (its genus) was modified by an adjective (its species), which followed the noun in good Latin form. His was a "natural classification" since it was based upon the traits of living things that were independent of their utilitarian value to man, the basis for many of the earlier "artificial classifications." The total morphological pattern of plants, rather than the selection of a single feature, was also considered important by these taxonomists who sought to describe all of living nature. Jung's classification was influential in zoology, where his binomial system was introduced by the seventeenth century naturalist John Ray. Ray's *Synopsis methodica animalium quadreupedum et serpentini generes* (1698) was the first synthetic arrangement of animals according to a natural system. Influenced by Ray in his efforts to arrive at a classification of all living things according to a system that would be subject to a strict discipline of observation and description, Linnaeus prepared in 1736 the first edition of his *Systema Naturae,* of which the tenth edition, which appeared in 1758, became the standard taxonomic treatise.

The Nature of Fossils

To the thinkers of the ancient Greco-Roman world, the recognition of marine fossils on the tops of mountains and in the sediments of deposits far from the sea and the discovery of gigantic bones encased in rocks supported the cyclic concept. The waters of the present world had once been higher than they now were, having receded as the Great Summer phase of the Annus Magnus advanced following the zenith of an age, after which the world approached the brink of another disaster. The fossils were frequently explained as the remains of animals that had been generated in the deposits in which they were found in a former cycle or in an earlier period of the present one. Human bones became the remains of epic heroes, and massive reptilian and mammal bones were the vestiges of Titans. The interest in finding fossil animals and plants continued into the Middle Ages, but it was an interest generated not by their curiosities as biological specimens but rather by their supposed properties of a magical and quasi-religious nature. Two interpretations of fossils were entertained before their true explanation was offered in the sixteenth century, and the relationship between the fossilized remains of animals and plants found by geologists to the existing forms of life on the earth was not appreciated until the middle of the eighteenth century. To be sure, Tertullian and other early Christian writers, aware of pagan explanations for these phenomena, recognized that fossils were the vestiges of once living things, and the suggestion that fossils had been transported to their present inaccessible reaches of the earth and to the peaks of high mountains by the agency of the Deluge was a popular belief of the Middle Ages. But contemporary with this explanation was the idea that fossils were unrelated to any biotic causes, their origin being ascribed to various celestial causes of occult import. When the prehistoric artifacts of early man were encountered, they were lumped with the fossils of sea urchins, belemnites, and true meteorites into a category called "ceraunia," all of which were valued for their medicinal and auspicious qualities.

The rejection of the notion that the fossils were associated with the Deluge by da Vinci, Fracastoro, and Palissy in the sixteenth century did not answer the question of where the survivors of the fossilized organisms might be today. For in a world view that maintained the immutability of living things and precluded the extinction of any of God's creatures, the discovery of these strange animals and plants seemed imminent. In what regions of the world not yet explored by the naturalists were they to be found, or had some of them sought refuge in the mysterious depths of the sea? As new regions were opened up for discovery, however, the student of nature became confounded by the multitude of unfamiliar organisms that had to be described and classified. Yet few of these new creatures resembled anything that could represent the descendant of a European fossil. Rather, the newly discovered regions yielded their own distinctive fossil specimens that were unmatched by those forms, either living or fossil, already known to the naturalist. This dilemma was further aggravated because neither the fossil record nor the collections of organisms from foreign parts assisted in filling in the gaps between recognized forms in the chain of being. To admit that the fossils themselves were the missing links was only to beg the question of where the transitional forms might be today. Resistance to the idea of species extinction was strong; as late as the final half of the eighteenth century Thomas Jefferson claimed that the American and Siberian mammoths were extinct only in the minds of the unphilosophical: "Such is the economy of nature, that no instance can be produced, of her having permitted any one of her animals to become extinct; or her having formed any link in her great work so weak as to be broken."

While the fossil record was an incipient threat to the concept of nonextinction of species, the question of specific immutability, later to become the refuge of providentialism in the latter part of the eighteenth century, seemed to be beyond the possibility of attack. To most naturalists of the seventeenth century, species were assumed to be the natural entities of the biotic world, the fixed representations of their Platonic types. Individual organisms might deviate from the ideally perfect morphological models representative of their species, but such variations were regarded as insignificant aberrations within the chain of being. Variations were considered useful in explaining the apparent gaps between adjacent species in the chain, for these variations were the bridges between distinct species. This view gained favor with the realization that the missing links were not to be found in the fossil record or among the unfamiliar organisms imported from afar. Common descent constituted the fullest criterion of an individual species, but observation of the morphology of organisms was also considered to give confirmation of unification of the members of a species through descent. Spontaneous generation was not disproven with finality until the nineteenth century, but it had lost its biological respectability two centuries earlier through the experiments of Swammerdam, Redi, and Leeuwenhoek as well as through the work of other microscopists in the latter part of the sixteenth century. The idea of generation by descent strengthened the concept of continuity and immutability of species, for comparative anatomists had yet to discover the implications of their researches.

As we have noted, the concept of evolution was not confined exclusively to the biological sphere of Western thought, for it was already present in the ideas of the sixteenth century cosmogonists. But when evolution was applied to the question of the origin and development of the living things, it was viewed as a threat by some conservative thinkers aware of the growing tendency of seventeenth century scientific observers to remove divine supervision and Scriptural interpretation even further from the phenomena of nature. If biotic forms were subject to processes analogous to those that determined the composition of astronomical and geological phenomena, then how could God's concern for His universe be demonstrated?

Interestingly enough, Christian theology had already attacked the matter of the immutability of species in the writings of Saint Augustine and Saint Thomas Aquinas. Saint Augustine interpreted the creation story of the Bible by saying that in the day when the plants and animals were created, God had infused into the earth the necessary energy or potency so that it could thereafter produce living things by a process of a natural unfolding of His plan. The earth was the giver of life, since God had given it the power to produce a natural evolution of forms. However, these writings did not receive the attention of the opponents of organic evolution in the nineteenth century, and in the period before the dawn of the eighteenth century, the question of organic evolution was not an issue of consideration.

The Problem of Natural Affinities between Species

Genealogical trees have their origin in areas of human activity far removed from evolutionary theory. On the atrium walls of Roman patrician homes were "stemma," or genealogical exhibits consisting of small shrines, each containing a painted mask to represent a deceased member of the family. Pliny the Elder and Seneca inform us that these niches were connected to one another by bands indicating the degrees of affinity between the various ancestors. Sometimes the stemma was a chart painted on the wall in which the names of the ancestors were connected by similar lines.

It is not clear what relation these pre-Christian genealogical trees had to the "arbor iuris" of medieval law, a diagram showing degrees of affinity within which marriage between members of families was permissible. The central part of the arbor iuris represented the status of the person with respect to whom the relatives were listed. Above this point, in two central connected columns, were the ancestors in the direct line of ascent to the seventh degree. While the point of relativity was the center of the tree, the point of family origin was at the top. These diagrams suggest the shape of a tree, but it is unknown whether their designers thought of a tree while compiling them. The arbor iuris was first devised in the sixth or seventh century A.D., and by A.D. 874 it had received the name by which it became known.

The earliest chronological charts of genealogy known to historians are represented in a manuscript dated A.D. 1100. This manuscript illustrates the Carolingian pedigree with a series of circles that contain the names of heads of families. The circles are connected by lines indicating descent. Another chart from this period shows a Saxon line and is of the same general type. Both trees are reproduced in a work called *Monumenta Germaniae Historica,* an edition of the *Chronicon.*

Appearing shortly after these family pedigrees are the Jesse-trees of medieval altar pieces, stained glass, and religious carvings which were most popular from the twelfth to the fourteenth centuries. These illustrate the genealogy of Christ. A typical one is the illumination in a Bible copied in England during this period, now in the possession of a private anonymous owner in London. It depicts a stem commencing at the top of the page and continuing downward. A number of circles on the stem bear the names of the direct ancestors of the House of Jesse in their degrees of affinity to Christ. The last circle on the page represents Christ; circles to the left and right of the main stem bear the names of collateral relatives. These genealogies are based on the first chapter of Matthew. Another common motif is the reclining Adam from whose side springs an upward-directed leafy stem along whose length appear the names of the relatives of the Holy Family, Christ's name being at the top of the tree.

The historical relationship between the arbor iuris, the circle and line genealogical trees, and the Jesse-trees is uncertain before the thirteenth century, but when Boccaccio began the writing of his *Genealogia deorum gentilium* in about 1350, the ideas of the legal and biblical diagrams were combined. Boccaccio's six years as a student of canon law made him familiar with the arbor iuris, and the Jesse-trees that were by this time common motifs may have suggested to him the creation of a diagram that would illustrate the degrees of affinity between the various pagan gods. In Boccaccio's trees the lines of descent branch downward from some ancestor, as in the arbor iuris, and the use of a pictorial stem, branches, and leaves may have been suggested by the name of the legal diagrams. It is interesting to note Boccaccio's sense of conflict between the downward growth of his genealogical trees and the upward growth of an actual tree, as indicated in his explanations, "versa in celum radice," and "in celum versa radice." His use of circles and lines reveals his familiarity with the genealogical trees of the same pattern. By 1370 a single copy of his trees had been made and from this some thirty to forty reproductions were available by the fifteenth century. The *Genealogia* was printed in Venice in 1472, the editions that followed depicting the trees in varying degrees of accuracy. In the Italian translation of 1547 the diagrams have been stylized into the form of a real tree, the trunk containing the name of the primal divinity, Demogorgon. The later progeny of his line are set on the uppermost branches of the tree at the top of the pages.

The tree diagram was not used in biology until the eighteenth century. Pallas, the German naturalist and student of Linnaeus who travelled to Siberia and the Crimea, included in a communication to Blumenbach a biological tree depicting the degrees of morphological affinity that he perceived between various animals. This revision of the chain-of-being representation of animals placed in juxtaposition to one another reflected Pallas's private belief in organic evolution. But with Blumenbach the phylogenetic tree was without issue.

In 1766 the French botanist, Duchesne, produced a small opus on the strawberry plants that he had been investigating: *Histoire naturelle des fraisiers, contenant les vues d'économie rénuies a la botanique.* The author illustrated the similarity of a particular strawberry plant to other kinds of strawberry plants in a diagram in which the parent plant was placed at the top of the page and its progeny at the bottom. These examples of the first biological trees are curiosities that preceded the arboreal jungles that flourished after Lamarck's researches in the early years of the nineteenth century. It is to Lamarck that the first full description of phylogenetic trees and the problems of phylogenetic descent must be attributed. In his *Recherches sur l'organisation des corps vivant* (1802) Lamarck described the evolutionary views that he held of the tree of life as a linear series of species or genera with shaded gradations between them, with lateral ramifications from the main stem, and with the extremities of the branches forming isolated points. His idea was further developed in his 1809 opus, *Philosophie Zoologique,* where his phylogenetic tree is described as having branches ramifying from a common root in the ancient past: "The existing animals . . . form a branching series irregularly graduated, the gaps having been filled by lost forms. It follows that the species which terminate each branch of the series are related, upon the side at least, with others that shade into them."

The introduction of the phylogenetic tree into the study of man's biological history took place exactly a century after the appearance of Duchesne's. diagram. In 1866 the German naturalist Haeckel published his *Generelle Morphologie*, which included a series of phylogenetic trees as illustrations of his evolutionary ideas. A linear arrangement of the hominid fossils had been suggested by Huxley three years before, but a diagrammatic scheme did not exist in the scientific literature until the close of the nineteenth century.

The phylogenetic tree must be distinguished from the genealogical tables of the different races of domestic animals and plants already known to eighteenth century biologists. Animal breeders had long been aware of the particular lines of descent of the stocks that they had crossed, and the practice of pollenization of different varieties of plants was not a recent one. Buffon included a genealogical table of the various races of dogs derived from the wolf-dog in his *Natural History* (1753). Like the phylogenetic trees, these tables employed the concepts of mutability of biotic forms and their descent from common ancestors, but since the new races were all derivatives of a single species and since they had been brought into existence only through the agency of human selectivity, they could not represent the patterns of an organic evolution operating on separate species in nature. Buffon believed that if the domestic breeds were permitted to return to feral conditions, they would revert to their original types within a few generations, for to him they were degenerate forms that marred the pristine perfection of nature as a consequence of man's interferences. So long as natural species were conceived as permanent, and artificially selected species were regarded as unstable outside of man's attendance upon them, the genealogical diagrams were not phylogenetic.

A comparison of a phylogenetic tree with the genealogical tree of a family pedigree, with which the reader is no doubt already familiar, may prove helpful. While the growth of the family tree is generally downward from the top of the diagram to the bottom, the phylogenetic tree is most frequently depicted beginning its growth from a basal trunk or root. The phylogenetic tree may be accompanied by a geological time scale parallelling the upward growth of the tree, reflecting the ideal stratigraphic succession from lower and earlier deposits to later and more recent ones. The temporal significance of a family pedigree is limited to the dates of birth and death of its individual members; the phylogenetic tree cannot be so specific in its temporal aspects since it involves the origin, evolution, and extinction of species or higher taxonomic categories through long eons of time. In the family tree new members are always being added to the stems or branches of the last members; the phylogenetic tree grows at such a slow rate in terms of our present time concepts that we have no hope of observing new branches forming from the uppermost levels. Rather, ramification is observed within the central or lower portions of the tree, where it reflects the discoveries of new species of living organisms or the discovery of hitherto unknown fossil forms. This type of growth is particularly well represented in the phylogenetic tree for man, for while there are no new forms recognized as evolving from the species *sapiens* already existing today, the accumulations of new fossil evidence necessitate the addition and readjustment of the lower branches of our tree. Furthermore, the family pedigree does not imply any theoretical principle (save the assumption of legitimacy respecting its most noble members!), but the phylogenetic tree is more than a record of births, deaths, and consanguinal lines. It may also imply such ideas as progression and direction along a specific path of adaptation, and by its very construction it may imply certain notions with respect to the survival values of certain lines. Finally, the kind of back-crossing or over-crossing that is not unknown in the genealogical pedigrees of families is absent in biological trees where contemporaneity of species precludes their interbreeding with members of their "grandparental" generation.

No two biological trees are alike since their creators are seldom in complete agreement as to how the various branches should be arranged. Nevertheless certain rules apply to them all. Names of biotic forms ranged across the same horizontal plane may be interpreted as those forms that are contemporary. The length of the stem or branch indicates the amount of time elapsed in the evolution of an organism represented by an arm of the tree. Branches or off-shoots from the parental stem may move horizontally to indicate that lapse of the time element is not important, or the branches may ascend vertically to indicate a temporal progression. When two organisms are represented by two branches leaving a parent stem, the organism that separates first is that one believed by the designer of the tree to be closest to the parent in its retention of the parental morphological pattern. Organisms sharing similarities with regard to specific traits which are of interest to an author may be drawn as branches which converge toward one another. Extinction of a species is noted by the termination of a branch, just as the continuation of a branch represents the survival and continued evolution of a species through time. The basic stock of a phylogenetic group is represented by the main trunk or main stem, and from this central base radiate the stems and branches, branchlets, and twigs of progressively finer taxonomic divisions. There is no convention with regard to the particular meaning of these subdivisions of the tree, for a stem may stand for a family, a genus, a race, or a species.

The names of organisms which are of taxonomic import do not reflect any particular phylogenetic position that the organisms hold *vis-à-vis* one another, save in the mind of their discoverer or their initial describer who named them. The name is seldom greeted by all scholars as the logical and necessary one for a newly discovered species, especially in the discipline of paleoanthropology. The original name nevertheless becomes incorporated into the literature according to the rules of taxonomy, which may lead the unwary to suppose that its phylogenetic position has been settled by calm scholarly agreement. Anthropologists are not the only natural historians guilty of the invention of novel taxonomic categories for their fossil discoveries. Revisions in the naming of fossil hominids have frequently been proposed, and several attempts have been made to adjust them to the chaos that already exists in scientific nomenclature. Weidenreich rejected the literal interpretation of the hominid fossil names but recommended a continuation of their use since the names were universally understood. Howells completely drops the use of the traditional names and replaces them with colloquial terms, thus transforming *Sinanthropus pekinensis* to Peking Man. The practice of letting a special name stand only when it can be backed by a full description of the differences which set it apart from its adjacent forms is a condition recommended by Le Gros Clark. Thus *Pithecanthropus* consists of a single genus with two species which are set off from other hominids by their small brain size, certain cranial specializations, type of dentition, and other traits. The resolution of this problem is not in sight, and the invention of hypothetical varieties of fossil men has not led to the clarifications that one might anticipate.

Part One

By the year 1800, scholars were forced to admit something foreseen centuries earlier: the sketchy Scriptural account of Adam and his immediate descendants could not resolve timely questions concerning man's place in nature, his precivilized condition, and his biological origin. Data for the elucidation of their conjectures about early man were of two sorts: (1) speculations which might or might not be supported by empirical investigation and (2) the direct evidence of prehistoric human bones and cultural artifacts. To properly appreciate the concepts of man's primitive condition that were entertained in the period beginning at the close of the seventeenth century, it is necessary to trace very briefly the coincidental changes in the spheres of geology, biology, and social philosophy as well as to note the shifting focus of providentialism within these spheres.

In the eighteenth century there occurs a change in the orientation of the interests of natural philosophers. The term *science* appears more frequently in the writings of the period, and it is applied to the study of the physical nature of the universe, a study that had become divorced from the theological focus that characterized it earlier. Researches in astronomy, physics, and chemistry were now less spectacular, being confined in large part to refinements and demonstrations of Newtonian principles. Providentialism, finding the physical sciences preoccupied, sought refuge in natural history. While analogous to the physical sciences in its concern for a description of nature rather than an investigation into the problems of the origins, processes, and developments of natural phenomena, natural history presented to the

1699 to 1856

15

scholar some enigmas that Newtonian physics could not resolve and that seemed to involve supernatural intervention. To include both science and natural history the term *natural theology* or *divine theology* was now employed, with a broader meaning than the expression "natural philosophy" of the previous century. The natural theologian sought to integrate the data of science and natural history with current theology and Scriptural interpretation. The plan and design of nature rather than nature's history and processes were the concerns of Paley and Pluche, who found analogies of the natural creation in chronometers and other mechanical devices. Historical events in nature were limited to the Creation, the Deluge, and the eventual dissolution of the universe on the Final Day of Judgment. The earth and its creatures were held to have been immutable since the day of their creation, although celestial change could no longer be ruled out. While the Deists might argue that once the Creator had constructed the universe He did not tamper with it through periodic interventions, the natural theologians and Theists were assured that God was actively working in the world, the immanent manipulator of historical and natural processes, the initiator of revelations, and a Being personally interested in the universe He had wrought.

Within this philosophical matrix the earliest developments of geology, referred to above as the "Theories of the Earth," had their inception. The proposers of these theories either sought to keep within the traditional framework of theology, as did Thomas Burnet and William Whiston, or, like de Maillet, Comte de Buffon, and von Holbach, they were indifferent or antagonistic to it. The latter group of writers emphasized geological antiquity and change. Both kinds of cosmogonists were operating outside any systematic method of direct research in the field of nature itself, but the iconoclastic scholars, with their interest in the roles of time and change, brought upon geology the stigma of heresy and atheism. Their position evoked further criticism for its materialistic connotations, particularly in France where the intellectuals were markedly hostile to the established social order, then under considerable ecclesiastical domination. Those who were tradition-oriented reasoned that if the age of the earth could be strictly correlated with the biblical chronology, divergent opinions would be authoritatively silenced. Concern for a true understanding of natural geological processes became important to the supporters of Genesis.

A similar dichotomy between traditional beliefs and novel explanations for the origin and history of the earth also existed within a group of thinkers who were now turning to first-hand examination of their planet. Some of these empiricists, such as Hooke and Woodward, tried to synchronize their observations and interpretations with Scripture, as when Woodward noted that while the earth did indeed reveal signs of having become modified from its pristine condition, such alteration was neither unfortunate nor fortuitous but part of a divine plan for the preparation of a realm suitable for fallen creatures. But to other observers, equally impressed by the fact that the earth does not present today its original aspect but bears the scars of a series of igneous and aqueous events of varying intensities over longer periods of time than could be met by traditional interpretation, the theories of the earth were unsatisfactory. The role of fire and flood, the causes of stratification, the presence of marine fossils on the tops of mountains far removed from the sea, and other puzzling geological phenomena outside the bounds of revelation and human historical records demanded investigation. Among pioneers of field geology in the middle part of the eighteenth century were Desmarest, who mapped the volcanic regions of France after Guettard discovered the ancient cinder cones, and Arduino, who classified mountains according to their composition and supposed order of development.

As geological theory began to move along the path earlier trod by astronomy in its emancipation from literal Scriptural interpretation, the upholders of the belief in the "eternal hills" found themselves siding with Werner, the professor of mining at Freiberg, whose theories could easily be correlated with Scripture. On the basis of work conducted in the Hartz Mountains of Germany, Werner fashioned a worldwide geological theory founded on the idea that water was the prime agent of geological activity. A vast primal ocean covered the globe at the time of Creation, diminishing in volume coincidentally with the formation of the rocky strata from sedimentation. Werner's stages of geological formation could be synchronized with the Six Days of Creation, and his theory of periodic floods did not clash with the precepts of the champions of the Deluge, the so-called Diluvialists, or Floodists. Animal fossils were arranged in the strata that Werner described in a sequence that paralleled the order of mention of the fauna in Genesis. Nor was a lengthy time scale necessary for this theory, providing that the Six Days of Creation were interpreted allegorically as periods of geological development. Deluc and other scholars supported such a "Mosaic geology" at the turn of the eighteenth century. Another of Werner's disciples, Kirwan, noted that he was led into the study of Scriptural geology ". . . by observing how fatal the suspicion of the high antiquity of the globe has been to the credit of Mosaic history, and consequently to religion and morality. . . ."

The geologists who were impressed less with the role of water than with that of fire and heat in the formation and history of the earth greatly offended tradition by their insistence on the great antiquity of the earth, their neglect of the geological importance of the Deluge, and their failure to hypothesize supernatural intervention where direct geological evidence was not discernible for the explanation of a given problem. The opinions of these Vulcanists—so called to mark their opposition to the aqueous theories of the Wernerian Neptunists—underwent refinement by the

Scottish geologist Hutton. The greatest contribution of this scholar is his perception of the continuation in the past of present-day geological processes of deposition, uplift, and erosion, all of which are working gradually and continuously on the earth, all of which produce, given adequate time, the kinds of changes to which the Neptunists and Vulcanists attributed their cataclysms. The Uniformitarianism which emerged from Hutton's research did not become a contender with Neptunism for academic respectibility, for Werner's theories were already being superceded during the first two decades of the nineteenth century by another geological school called Catastrophism. The latter resulted from a wedding of the cataclysmic elements of earlier geological theories with the Huttonian concept of a generous time scale for earth history and the importance of both fire and flood in the operation of nature's laws. The shift that now occurred to support Catastrophism rather than Neptunism was a logical one, for as Catastrophism was defined by its chief spokesman, Cuvier, it was best suited to conservative views of natural processes. Catastrophism maintained that a series of cataclysmic events had occurred on the earth with remarkable periodicity and that the last of these holocausts was the biblical Deluge. A special creation was not necessarily coincident with the termination of each catastrophe. But while admitting change, Catastrophists did not tolerate the suggestion of the mutability of living species. The events that led to the destruction of life at the end of each catastrophe were regarded as signs of God's beneficent intervention in His Creation, a process that was progressive since it was directed toward preparing the world for human occupancy. It was a cyclic process, but one not directed in its orientation to the maintenance of the status quo. In opposition to these views stood the Uniformitarians, now marshalled behind Charles Lyell. They regarded the Deluge as having played a negligible role in geology, and their views concerning divine intervention were essentially agnostic.

By the close of the third decade of the nineteenth century Catastrophism was losing its hold among the scientifically minded body of intellectuals, and the discovery of the vestiges of an Ice Age, though drawing attention as a possible catastrophe, was submitted to Uniformitarian interpretation as simply another geological process that had been far from sudden or unprecedented in earth history. The Uniformitarians demonstrated that geology could be self-sufficient outside the realm of theological interpretation, just as the physical sciences had shown themselves to be a century earlier. The "Mosaic geologists," deprived of the geological verification of the Deluge—that most precious of Catastrophist holocausts —forced to surrender their hopes that the Six Days of Creation would similarly receive literal confirmation, and made to recognize that the six thousand years of earth history were not sufficient for geological theory and consequently that the age of life on the earth was greater than this brief time allotment, were now forced to find support for their premises outside of geology. They took their next stand in the biological sciences.

Natural historians of the early eighteenth century had not reached any agreement on the questions of the possibility of the extinction of species, their immutability, and the origin of new species since the Fifth Day of Creation. Therefore, biology seemed a safe refuge for those who ridiculed such speculation. But the hopes of the latter were short-lived. The recognition that species could become extinct made its way into biology largely through the work of Cuvier, who regarded fossils as the inhabitants of a former world that was separated from the present one by a catastrophic episode. That most fossils were of animals no longer existing, and that the fossils of known existing forms were rare, did indeed support his thesis, particulary when he was able to reconstruct their morphology by his broad knowledge of comparative osteology. While similarities in structure between fossil and living organisms are explained today on the basis of evolutionary parallelism or of their phylogenetic affinities, to Cuvier and his disciples each species was the result of a special creation. The Catastrophists observed that there appeared throughout the succession of geological time, as revealed in the stratigraphic sequences, a progression of biotic forms of increasing complexity in morphological organization. Progressionism became the biologiocal complement of the geological theory of Catastrophism and so gave unity to the chaotic history of life that the Catastrophists preached. The chain of being had become temporalized, but its elements remained immutable. This philosophy was popular as a reaction to the tenets of Uniformitarianism, which now responded with its own interpretation of how life was to be correlated with geology : instead of asserting that biotic forms showed an increase in anatomical organization through time, as their antagonists held, Lyell argued that complex organisms were to be found in ancient strata along with the less complex ones, and that all forms of life came into existence simultaneously. By so believing, the Uniformitarians thought they had rid natural history of any implications of Catastrophist supernaturalism. This non-Progressionist theory exempted mankind from original creation, since his arrival on earth seemed to be late. The observation that the different geological strata contained forms of ancient life that were unique to the particular deposits laid down in the past was made in the last decades of the eighteenth century by William Smith, a drainage engineer who used this observation in his work of identifying those deposits and soils best suited for the construction of canals and sumps. His contribution led to the development of a descriptive methodology for paleontology. The concepts of progressive change and continuity of process were to lend support to the notion of organic evolution already forming in the minds of many naturalists.

But while paleontology forced the conservators of tradition into admitting that some species had become extinct in the past, the question of specific mutability appeared safe from attack. By the fourth decade of the nineteenth century it became apparent that the role of providentialism was to be judged by a biological question—the nature of species—rather than by a geological question—the origin and history of the earth—as the case had been stated earlier. Each new theory of the earth and its living inhabitants came dangerously near to upsetting accepted concepts, but the crisis that was feared was consistently prevented by the assurance that the next step in the argument could not be taken. A definitive article of faith in support of Catastrophism, the demonstration of nature's benevolence and utilitarianism, and arguments for the divine design of nature were proposed in the *Bridgewater Treatises* of 1829. Seven leading British scholars summarized in these volumes the main branches of natural science with which they were familiar, to clarify for the general reader the divine scheme of nature. Appearing when Uniformitarianism was just rising on the intellectual horizon, such a concerted effort was an important landmark in the history of concepts affecting the interpretation of the human fossil record, one that was next to become the heated issue in both providentialist and non-providentialist camps. These treatises were representative of the strides made in the biological sciences after 1700.

The popularity that greeted Linnaeus's taxonomic system was sustained by de Candolle, who applied the classification to plants that were unknown to his mentor, and by Lamarck, who divided the animal kingdom into some fourteen classes ranging along an ascending scale from invertebrates to animals with backbones. Into the system Cuvier introduced the fossil fauna, an innovation continued by Owen, who classified the paleontological specimens of the British Museum. Linnaeus saw his generic and specific groups as the true reflections of the natural world, but admitted that the higher classifications, such as orders and classes, were more artificial because they contained elements of man's subjectivity imposed on nature. This question of the relationship of human rationalization to the true nature of the biotic realm caused skepticism on the part of Kant, Buffon, Goldsmith, and other thinkers of the period. Was taxonomy a legitimate method for viewing the organic world? There were two ways out of this apparent impasse: (1) the admission that when the chain of being is broken up the segments cannot be other than artificial, hence species are not conceptually valid; or (2) the centering of interest only on the idealized prototype which represents the species for which individual organisms might be better or worse examples. If they were worse examples, they were variations, or "unnatural" distortions from the norm or prototype, and hence of no real significance in the plan of nature. A key issue in the debate over this problem of the validity of systematics was the evidence for missing links. Critics of taxonomy stressed that such phenomena could not be provided by their classifying colleagues, for transitional forms had never come from the geographical regions then under exploration. But to systematists this was not an important question, since the absence of such organisms could not upset their rational deductions as to what the plan of nature must be. Furthermore, certain organisms were considered to represent missing links, particularly at the lower and upper extremities of the chain of being. Was not the freshwater *Hydra* the long-sought-for link between the plant and animal kingdoms? And was not the biological zone between man and the anthropoid apes and near-men of travelers' tales rather hazy? For those who were dissatisfied with these possibilities there was the venerable notion that the variations themselves represented transitional forms: two species occupying adjacent loci on the chain of being were united by their more variable and atypical members.

The concept of the prototype was well entrenched in the discipline of comparative anatomy, handmaiden of the taxonomists. After the revitalization of comparative anatomy in the nineteenth century, largely through the efforts of Hunter in England, Cuvier in France, and the Naturphilosophen in Germany, the discipline shifted from an isolated interest in the physiology of organisms to a concern for morphology. Human anatomy, which had become a specialized study since the sixteenth century and one independent of comparative anatomy, now became incorporated into the researches of Hunter, Cuvier, and the Naturphilosophen. Of these the Naturphilosophen best illustrate the attention that comparative anatomists gave to the concept of the prototype. Along with teleology and Kantian idealism they held the notion that the existing forms of life are the products of numerous variations around central archetypes. Members of a species are merely variations of a common plan or theme called the "archetype" which is basic to the group to which the organism is assigned by the taxonomist. Unknown laws of nature produce the variations around the archetype, but the archetypes are nevertheless deductible. It was the task of the comparative anatomist to discover these true elements of nature. Goethe went even farther and deduced the nature of the archetypical plant, an ideal organism that contained the basic features of all individual species of plants. Every group of organisms, Goethe reasoned, possessed some organ that represented the archetype of the group. He sought on the basis of this precept to reconstruct it for vertebrate creatures. His selection of the individual spinal vertebra as the archetype for the skull and the remainder of the vertebrate animal illustrates well this practice of selecting an anatomical part representative of the whole organism. Some of the naturalists who were faced with the first fossil hominid discoveries by the middle of the century were thinking of species in terms of archetypal patterns. But while there were differences in the interpretation of the philosophical implications of the prototype and the archetype, biologists almost universally agreed that these entities were stable through time. Into this static arrangement of biotic forms was introduced the serious speculation that such immutable products of a special creation might be vulnerable to relatively permanent morphological changes. Many factors contributed to this notion. Linnaeus suggested that new plant species might arise from fertile hybrids; thus while genera were stable, species were potentially subject to change. Indeed, species are but the results of various crossings in the past of different members of a genus. Such a circumstance was regarded by Linnaeus as fortuitous, but this did not deliver the great classifier of living nature from the disgrace of having some of his writings excluded from the Church's sanction for a brief period since such notions of immutability were not in accord with biblical botany. Buffon later noted that when a species is forced to change its habitat because of changes in the environment to which it is adapted, alterations appear in its physical morphology. Such changes ensure its survival in the new habitat, and in time these changes become hereditary constituents of the species. Furthermore, if man can alter a species through artificial selection, what more can nature do through long eons of time? Change, therefore, according to Buffon, depended on the circumstance of the environmental stimulus, the productivity of the species, and a sufficient amount of time for the mutability of species to occur. For Erasmus Darwin specific mutability was a consequence of the progressive transformations organisms had to undergo to meet new internal and external environmental pressures. To Lamarck, also, a changing environment seemed to be correlated with the mutability of the living things in it: the environment was not an incidental background to life, but rather life's determinant, since all living things must adapt to it.

The environmental theories of specific mutability became incorporated in an anonymous work that appeared in 1844, *The Vestiges of the Natural History of Creation*. Its true author was the Scottish publisher Robert Chambers, whose interests in natural history led him to combine the Catastrophist notion of Progressionism, the Uniformitarian doctrine of the continuity of operation of natural processes, and the concept of the mutability of species in a theory of transformism, or organic evolution. Rejecting Lyell's non-Progressionism, Chambers argued that living things had ascended the chain of being through time from simple to more complex forms, the fossils being the ancestors of organisms now living or the vestiges of extinct lines. Characteristics that organisms acquired in their adjustments to changing environments were passed on to future generations, which were also adapted to meet new environmental pressures. Mutability of species thus found favor with the biologists, whom the supporters of tradition had assumed were best able to maintain the tenets of a static chain of being and of special creation.

Out of these heresies matured the concept of organic evolution, which culminated in the middle of the nineteenth century in the work of Charles Darwin. The question now posed by certain naturalists was this: if species are mutable, what are the mechanisms in nature that control mutability and determine which species shall become extinct and which shall pass on their traits to future generations? It seemed obvious to the early organic evolutionists that once an animal or plant had acquired a specific type of structure that would help it to survive, that new feature would become incorporated into the species through some hereditary process. What was not clear was how the adaptation could be acquired. The inheritance of such characteristics must somehow be under the control of nature; Lamarck hypothesized that they appeared as a consequence of the "felt needs" of the adapting animals.

Charles Darwin was influenced very little by the French and German writers of natural history, and therefore he was less involved than many of his colleagues in the problems of comparative anatomy and taxonomy. Embryology was only slightly more important to him, and what ideas he held on that subject were derived in large part from the writings of von Baer. Darwin was freed from the French preoccupation with Progressionism and the German tenets of Naturphilosophie. His knowledge of Lamarck came from a familiarity with Lyell's discussion of this biologist in the *Principles of Geology,* a work that converted Darwin to Uniformitarianism. During his South American voyage Darwin noticed how species differ geographically and how the Galapagos fauna resembled species from the mainland but maintained their own characteristics. Such a circumstance could be explained only by the supposition that species were capable of being modified through time. Darwin's later observations of the changes brought about through artificial selection practiced by stock breeders afforded him the data for a comparison with the problem of how physical features in animals could be produced in nature. Even before reading Malthus's paper on population, Darwin saw that struggle for existence in nature was a normal condition and not simply nature's way of keeping the populations of different species in perfect balance, as struggle in nature had been conceived during the previous century. Under the conditions of struggle for survival, Darwin noted that favorable variations would tend to be preserved and unfavorable ones rejected, the result being the formation of a new species. Darwin had arrived at his theory of natural selection as early as 1838, but did not reveal his ideas formally until twenty years later, at which time they were presented in conjunction with a paper by Wallace that was brought to his attention. Darwin appreciated the importance of individual variation as an explanation for species formation, although like all naturalists before the discovery of the Mendelian laws of inheritance he was unable to explain how variation arose. This forced him to accept Lamarck's beliefs concerning the inheritance of acquired characteristics. Variations which had been relegated to the role of the aberrant and defective in nature were now elevated by Darwin to a position where they were recognized as the integral units of organic evolution. Darwin was fully aware of the formidable implications contained in his philosophy, for here indeed lay the most vital point of nineteenth century providentialism: surely mankind, the inheritor of the Kingdom of Heaven, was exempt from the normal processes of nature and was the focal interest of the Deity. That life in general should be a reflection of a selective process operating in nature rather than the result of a predetermined system regulated and periodically adjusted by its Creator was hardly the world view that the devout might prefer, but that such a process was also operating on mankind was a suggestion as intolerable as it was impious. Characteristically, Darwin avoided controversy in the *Origin of Species* with the brief comment that by the pursuit of his theory of natural selection, "Light will be thrown on the origin of man and his history."

Among the concepts that evolved in the sphere of social philosophy during the eighteenth and early nineteenth centuries that have influenced the interpretation of the human fossil record, none is more important than the idea of progress. That this idea could not have been part of medieval philosophy is obvious from an examination of its precepts: (1) there is a process of progressive development inherent in the psychical and social nature of man which can operate independently of supernatural intervention; (2) this process will continue indefinitely for as long as man exists, and man's future is not threatened by any foreseeable limitation; (3) happiness on earth is the goal of social progress and the end toward which the individual should strive, regarding the goal as worthy for its own sake; (4) man may aspire to this goal since he is both morally and socially a perfectable creature; (5) the means by which progress is to be realized is man's knowledge and control of his social environment. Those are notions hardly compatible with the world views of the ancient and medieval periods, although Christianity had prepared the way by its rejection of cyclic time and by assuring that human history was unique, significant, and relevant to a universal world community that was distinct from the circumscribed social unit of the city-state. When the idea of progress was formulated during the late Renaissance, it was in part a reaction to the then popular belief among non–theologically oriented intellectuals that the brightest period of human history—the Golden Age—was to be sought only in antiquity, for the minds of that period were of a degree of excellence unequalled in subsequent times. But as respect for the ancients was jarred by the recognition that many of their interpretations of nature were incorrect, as demonstrated by the substitution of Copernican for Ptolemaic astronomy and by the ascendency of Vesalius over Galen in the study of anatomy, natural philosophers began to speculate about a progressive acquisition of human knowledge. By the early part of the seventeenth century it became a truism that in the course of human history there had been advances in technology and that further improvements could be anticipated in the future. But this attitude did not constitute a theory of human progress until the mechanistic aspects of Cartesianism became transferred to ideas about the human psyche; the human mind was conceived mechanistically but as controlled by environmental determinants, which if modified for good, could impel the psychological betterment that was essential to social and moral progress. Divine intervention was excluded as a factor in the human condition. The Humanistic movement placed man in the center of all speculative interests, hence it is not surprising that his social life was regarded as the proper exemplar of intellectual progress. Since all minds were equal until molded for better or worse by the social environment, the task of the philosophically inclined was to discover through rationalism what the favorable conditioning agents might be, to hasten progress.

The quest was pursued along two related lines of inquiry: (1) the proposing of various social controls such as radical political reform, improvement of education, acceleration of utilitarian and industrial projects in the economic sphere, or the improvement of medical and hygienic measures; and (2) the study of the laws of society which, under the hand of Comte, promised to elevate the concept of progress to a scientific discipline. The French Revolution marks the popularity of the first approach apart from the second, although both were inseparable in the minds of later adherents of progress. In France the rational arguments for reform preached by Condorcet were manifested in the holocaust of the Revolution, misinterpreted by people of all classes. That circumstance goes far to explain the subsequent retreat of progress as a theory into the realm of the positivism set forth by Comte. The threat of the Revolution to the English reverence for the status quo precluded the liberals of that country from asserting a program of progress along French lines. The English, with their revolution well behind them, accepted the idea of progress during the eighteenth century but combined it with a well-entrenched providentialism, preferring to postpone their utopias until the distant future where they could not inconvenience the social order of this world, with which the middle and upper social classes were then satisfied. That social reforms did not take place in England until well into the nineteenth century is a reflection of this philosophy, although economic conditions received attention from Adam Smith and his successors. By the nineteenth century when social utopias were deserving of concern, they were not of a revolutionary nature. Progress was the rationale for these utopias, be they closed systems where all the members were assigned to their proper functions by a powerful and enlightened political control or less rigid societies where the liberty of the individual allowed him to exploit his particular capacities for the betterment of his neighbors. German interpretation of the concept of progress was along French lines at the time of its introduction in the late eighteenth century through the writings of Herder, but it was not divorced from providentialism. Under the influence of Hegel, progressive theory became embodied in a closed social system in which the final stage of man's struggle was to be found in the Germany of his period, following of course the necessary political reforms. By 1850 the idea of progress was understood at all levels of society in the countries mentioned above. It became a stand for political propagandists and is manifested in the literature of the period. Goals of progress varied, but the predominant theme was human happiness, variously interpreted.

The most formidable critics of the idea of progress were some Christian philosophers. To the Christian, man had become a degenerate creature through his Fall, and evidence of this decline could be sought in the records of human immorality. To the inheritor of Renaissance tradition, the Golden Age was not to be sought in the Garden of Eden, but in the classical world. Varying opinions about degeneration led to the literary battles during the Renaissance over the question of whether ancient or contemporary scholars were superior. Renaissance Degenerationists argued that while we might be superior to Europeans who lived during the tenth century, how could the latter be conceived as superior to the classical thinkers of antiquity? The Middle Ages became the battle ground between the supporters and opponents of the theory of progress. As the concept of progress gained popularity, the problem was resolved by the belief in a progressive process that operated by means of alternating periods of decline and ascent in human history with a gradually rising inclination all along the course of the progressive trend, relegating the undesirable aspects of human behavior to the function of necessary determinants of progressive change. Furthermore, an unfavorable social environment could be used to justify an age that did not appear to be conducive to social betterment. One Degenerationist who could hope for human improvement was Rousseau, who while pessimistic about the course of human history, was optimistic about man himself as a perfectible animal who could attain happiness through the practice of reason and the application of the resulting rules of social action. Both kinds of Degenerationists, the Christian and the "philosophe," based their theses on the idea of man having been happier in the past than in his present circumstances. But the Christian doctrine of human degeneration was more intimately involved in the problems of interpreting the bones of early men once these were discovered and recognized. Christian tenets found support in a complex body of ideas denoted by the term *Romanticism*, that return of interest to the High Middle Ages, the ceremonies and traditions of the Church, Classical and Germanic folklore, and a revitalization of the doctrine of man's Fall, degeneration, and dependency on divine intervention. Other attacks on the idea of progress came from those who saw the implications of Malthus's thesis on the nature of human population. Surely, if what the good curate said was true, the unrestricted realization of Enlightenment ideals would lead to the extinction of the human species. Increase in population was regarded as one of the anticipated improvements by the supporters of progress. Yet Malthus maintained that in the absence of those checks that were operating coincidentally with the tendency of populations to increase in a geometric ratio, the food supply on which the population depended, which increases arithmetically, could not be sufficient to prevent the death by famine of vast numbers of individuals. The checks operating to prevent this condition were the very social evils that the upholders of progress were attempting to eliminate—vice, misery, and fear of want.

While the development of the idea of progress was independent of the growth of the natural sciences, by the nineteenth century "evidence" for progress was being sought in the research studies of physicists and biologists. When Herbert Spencer published his *Social Statics* in 1851, readers found in his book a social theory supporting progress and employing the tenets of Comte's positivism, to which was added as supportive evidence the theory of biological evolution. Spencer supplied his readers with a world view of such comprehensive scope that it could contain the entire gamut of phenomena in nature. As soon as Charles Darwin had enunciated the principle of natural selection, Spencer recognized that it supported the theory of social selection that he had earlier conceived from a reading of Malthus's essay. To Spencer all nature was evolving, and social progress was but an expected ramification of this universal principle. By officiating as high priest at this unholy marriage of biological theory and social progress, Spencer facilitated the notion that the offspring of their union—biological progress—was legitimate. The reading public of Spencer's time was receptive to his ideas and their response helped support considerable research into problems that might otherwise have been held in greater reserve, such as Darwin's theory of natural selection and the results of paleontological investigation involving human material. With the emergence of a human fossil record in the latter half of the nineteenth century, the followers of Spencer, impressed with the evidence for the antiquity of man, were led to remark that since man was so venerable a species he must have undergone significant progressive developments through time, just as the men of today were guaranteed the continuation of biological progress in the future. For while the individual finds his end in death, society points to the eventual establishment of a perfect social order and of a superior biological condition commensurate with it. Thus the idea of progress has pertained to the idea of fossil man through the attempts that were made to reconstruct the condition of man before he attained the plateaus of civilization of the ancient and modern worlds; historicity, when applied to the idea of progress, led to speculations on the biological and social condition of early man.

This brief survey of scientific and social thought during the eighteenth and first half of the nineteenth centuries is prefatory to the analysis of particular speculations about early man. Taking first those concepts that were purely hypothetical and unrelated to the empirical evidence of man's osseous remains, the student of the history of ideas is faced with arguments about the human social condition at the brute level prior to man's ascent along the ladder of progress, that is, in the "state of nature." This primeval stage could be discerned through the pursuit of four avenues of investigation: (1) the psychological constitutions of feral children; (2) behavior and receptivity to planned education among the anthropoid apes; (3) the cultures of so-called primitive peoples; and (4) the substitution for these three kinds of research by the sober application of inductive reason by the qualified Enlightenment intellectual.

Granted that the "state of nature" did not mean the same thing to all eighteenth century philosophers, among those who were optimistic about the trends of human culture, the discernment of the precivilized mind of man in the psychology of such famous feral children as Wild Peter of Hanover, the Wild Girl of Labrador, and the Wild Boy of Aveyron seemed a reasonable hypothesis. Linnaeus had classified ten so-called feral children, known during the period of 1544–1731 as members of the species *sapiens,* although their quadrupedal habits, unkempt hairy appearance, and mute condition were recognized to be distinctive traits marking them as a race apart from the other phenotypic subdivisions of mankind. Many of these feral children were mental defectives who had been abandoned shortly before their discovery, as Blumenbach was able to demonstrate for Wild Peter, but others had a history of life in the wilderness of European countrysides that could not be reconstructed. Jean Itard attempted to educate the child from Aveyron, believing that its lack of socialization was the explanation for its retarded state. While his charge never learned to speak, there was considerable speculation concerning its possession of the psychology of man in the state of precivilized life in the remote past, when such depravity was a universal human condition.

The discovery of the anthropoid apes had a greater influence on the social philosophy of the eighteenth century than it did on the biological disciplines of that time. The first hint of the existence of the gorilla dates to the publication in 1625 of the account of English explorer Andrew Battell, who was held captive by the Portuguese in Angola when he saw the gigantic "pongo." While Battell's account was known to Buffon, it was not mentioned in the writings of Cuvier, and the first anatomical description of the gorilla did not appear until 1847. The chimpanzee was first anatomically described by Claes Pieterszoon Tulp in 1641. The later description of this primate by Tyson in 1699 was known to Linnaeus, who classified the ape as *Simia satyrus* in the tenth edition of the *Systema Naturae*. Linnaeus was also aware of an anthropoid ape first described in 1658 by the Dutch physician in Batavia, Jakob da Bondt, but he was misled by an illustration of the creature reproduced in a work by Tyson. The latter anatomist had placed a leaf on the figure for purposes of decency in the publication, thus adding emphasis to da Bondt's description of the extreme modesty of the primate. Therefore, Linnaeus placed this specimen in a separate human genus—*Troglodytes*—with two subspecies—*Homo nocturnus* and *Homo sylvestris orang outang*. By the latter specific name, meaning in Malay "man of the woods," this anthropoid is known to us today. The gibbon was seen by early Dutch explorers in Southeast Asia and was described by Buffon. Its small size and specialized arboreal adaptation precluded its interest to discussants of the social and biological affinities of the anthropoid apes to man. There was considerable confusion regarding the specific differences among the four known anthropoid apes and their ranges of habitat. These problems were largely resolved through the researches of Cuvier and Owen, who recognized the distinction between the African and Asiatic apes. Much of the confusion relating to the behavior and physical character of the infra-human primates and their nearness to man stemmed from the exaggerated accounts of travelers. The human and infra-human inhabitants of regions remote from Europe were frequently not distinguished by explorers, and it was a common suggestion in the eighteenth century that both monkeys and apes interbred with men in certain primitive societies, the results of such unions being fertile offspring. Lord Monboddo, on the basis of similar unreliable accounts, concluded that the orang-utan represented a stage of human social evolution advanced over that demonstrated by such feral children as Wild Peter of Hanover. All that inhibited the orang-utan from speaking was a lack of the rudiments of a sound Scottish education, for once so improved, the anthropoid would be well along the road to acquisition of the basic constituents of civilization.

While the Degenerationists regarded the primitive peoples of the newly discovered areas of the globe as the degenerate progeny of Adam who had sunk into barbarism since the abandonment of the Tower of Babel, the adherents of the concept of progress saw human history as an ascent from savagery rather than as a decline from an original state of perfection, the ethnic populations representing therefore that once universal human condition. This interpretation led to the question of just how low on the cultural scale man might fall before effecting contact with the brute creation. That ill-defined zone between the most enlightened ape and the most brutish man led to speculation as to which of the known tribal groups of mankind were best representative of this twilight region. Hottentots,

American Indians, Australian aborigines, African Negroes, hill tribes of the Indian subcontinent, and the Ceylonese Veddas were frequently pointed out as illustrative of this stage. The holding of such a position was a dubious honor according to those philosophers, not infrequent among the English, who did not believe that native peoples could be improved and made worthy of civilization. But many French scholars did not relegate these societies to the limbo of detestable cultural and moral fossils of a bygone era, for if the savage was capable of improvement, then his nobility as a human creature was assured. Particular ethnic groups such as Voltaire's Hurons, Diderot's Tahitians, and Raynal's East and West Indians were cited as examples of the comparative advantages of the "state of nature" over the civilization of politically corrupted European man. Since such elaborations of the concept of progress implied historicity, it is not surprising that the determination of the "state of nature" became identified with the attempts of early anthropologists to discern the prehistoric social condition of mankind. The comparative method in sociology and anthropology was based on the assumption that if primitive peoples were nearer to man's prehistoric condition, then a study of the social institutions of such peoples would reveal the various stages of prehistory. When such peoples were examined cross-culturally, the level of progress for human institutions was outlined, which in turn indicated the cultural level of the population studied. All stages of institutions were considered to be of universal scope in the remote past. The problem was to determine their order of cultural evolution.

To Rousseau, however, the study of primitive people was useless in reconstructing the "state of nature," for a past condition could not be discerned from present data. Hence a reasonable hypothesis of man's primal state must be formulated. Even if such a state had no historical validity, it was politically a necessary concept. Rousseau defined man as the perfectable creature, and he described natural man as living alone, without speech, ignorant of death, and organizing bands only in periods of stress. Great amounts of time were essential to realize the gradual change from the natural to the civilized state. However, the happiest time for man was not at the brute level, but rather after the formulation of the social contract yet before he had developed the arts of husbandry that led to the desire for the acquisition of property. Primitive peoples were not survivors of natural man, but the links between the savage and civilized human condition. The primal stage admittedly had certain advantages in terms of its freedom from evil, but once transcended it could never be recalled; man's reason must now dictate to him the methods for attaining perfection in a civilized society adjusted to his needs.

Implicit in the concepts of the social condition of early man were questions about the biological nature of our progenitors and the position that early man occupied in the taxonomic scheme, problems that were foreseen prior to the discovery of the actual fossilized bones of our ancestors. In the eighteenth century man's relative position in the chain of being was debated: did he stand in the middle of the ladder that extended from zoophyte to the Absolute, or was he at one of the extremes? Regardless of the number and magnitude of the spiritual beings arranged above man, there was no question but that man stood above the anthropoidal creatures that occupied an adjacent position in the chain. The taxonomist could seek for the missing links between ape and man either at the lower end of the human class, that is, among primitive peoples, or at the upper end of the anthropoid class, namely, among the newly described apes and in travelers' accounts of creatures that were nearmen. So long as the chain of being was devoid of historicity and formed a logical unilinear gradation of the prototypes that exemplified the principles of continuity and plentitude of forms in the natural world, there could be no suggestion that any link of the chain bore any generic relationship to similar elements above and below it. As we have already seen, this taxonomic assumption became reflected in paleontology with the idea of Progressionism. But once people began to doubt that the species in the chain of being were not immutable and to believe that transformation of species had been in operation for vast eons of time, indeed since the appearance of the first living things, the species and their real and supposed missing links took on the role of historical stages in a biological progression of types through time. Furthermore, if the fossils of nonhuman creatures were the remains of creatures now extinct or with descendants whose morphology was greatly modified from that of their fossil progenitors, the possibility could not be ruled out that fossils of our human ancestors would in time be resurrected by the geologist's pick. These might be the missing links between the hypothetical primal human ancestor with his anthropoidal characteristics and the type of humanity on the earth today.

Comparative anatomists since the foundation of early Greek medical schools had recognized that there were structural resemblances between man and the infra-human primates. Indeed, Galen's thesis on human anatomy in the second century B.C. was based on dissections of the Barbary ape. Such a morphological likeness was to be anticipated as a logical concomitant of the chain of being. With von Baer's declaration in the early nineteenth century that within a phylum the organisms show greater degrees of similarity in the early stages of their life history than in the later stages (for example, the observation that a tadpole is more like a fish than a frog), the static interpretations of comparative anatomy were threatened. The Naturphilosophen could hardly maintain their definition of archetypes in the light of such embryological researches. Not until the latter part of the century were the evolutionary implications of these observations formulated by Haeckel, the biologist who found comparative anatomy ripe for the suggestion that man's morphological affinities with the infra-human primates might be of a phylogenetic as well as of an anatomical nature.

It was an equally short step from the assumption that certain ethnic populations were culturally primitive and reflective of a state of nature to the assumption that they were physically and racially primitive as well. Racial gradation was implicit in the chain of being, and if this kind of seriation was converted from a stationary stairway of prototypes to a mobile escalator of transitional forms through the catalytic agents of the mechanism of progress and organic evolution, then these uncivilized populations should possess primitive morphological traits reminiscent of a condition common to all of mankind in the ancient past. Logically, the morphological stage of biological progress of a population should be commensurate with its cultural level, according to the stricter adherents of this early anthropology. While this notion would seem to be upheld only if one adopted the Hebraic-Christian tenet of the single origin of man—the monogenetic hypothesis—those thinkers who supported the thesis that mankind had had separate centers of creation—the polygenetic theorists—could accept biological and cultural progress by emphasizing the principle of parallelism in human history.

Monogenesis was not a sharply defined view in the early part of the Christian era. The emperor Julian in the fourth century speculated about the number of creative centers there may have been at the time of the biblical Creation, and his pagan predecessors generally believed that different peoples had originated in the lands that they occupied at the time of their discovery by the Western world, for racial differences were explained environmentally. Saint Augustine discussed the question of the single origin of man in his *City of God*, a dictum that became perpetuated in Church tradition:

> No believer can doubt that all men (whatever their color, stature, voice, proportions or other national character) have the same origin. No one should accept the idea of the Antipodes, that is of dried up continents inhabited by man on the opposite side of the earth we tread. No one should believe that the world existed thousands of years before the 6,000 years which Holy Scripture teaches us.

When the discovery of the American Indians demanded an explanation, Pope Julius in 1512 decreed that these hitherto unknown peoples were descendants of Adam and Eve. Heretics now became a problem to the supporters of this dogma; many heretics were members of the clergy as well as secular natural philosophers. The French writer La Peyrère produced the *Prae-Adamitae* in 1655; it was publicly burned in Paris for its insidious use of Scripture to support the thesis that not all of mankind, but only the Jews, had sprung from Adam. Like Paracelsus, La Peyrère's ideas on multiple human origins placed him in danger of the Inquisition.

To Enlightenment philosophers, polygenesis seemed the common-sense answer to the question of racial variation and gradation, Voltaire, Desmoulins, and Bory de Saint-Vincent all accepting the arguments for environmentalism. In the early nineteenth century polygenesis had a popular vogue in the United States where, apart from the scientifically oriented treatment that it received from Samuel Morton, it became a conceptual tool of the political movement supporting Negro slavery. In the attempt to justify slavery, some monogenecists were no less biased and backed their position with Scriptural interpretation. Nevertheless, monogenesis had a greater scientific respectability during the eighteenth and early part of the nineteenth centuries, and was the philosophy of Linnaeus, Blumenbach, de Quatrefages, and Prichard. Even Agassiz, who posited separate centers of creation for animals and plants, concurred with his colleagues in biology that man had a single time and place of origin. Man had developed his particular morphological variations during a period of time subsequent to this event as a result of distinctive environmental pressures operating on isolated populations.

Related to the problems of the biological nature of man, his place in the taxonomic scheme in relation to both the infra-human primates and the various racial entities that made up his species, was the question repeatedly asked of the comparative anatomist: what are the structural and morphological characteristics that differentiate man from the rest of animal creation? This question was asked afresh with each discovery of the living apes of Africa and Southeast Asia and primitive peoples of those and other regions of the world. But while they accorded deference to the principle of continuity in the chain of being by asserting that biologically man and ape were adjacent to one another in the ladder of life, naturalists tended to define man's intellectual and psychic capacities as the hallmark for this species' unique place in nature. Thus Tyson, who discovered that the infant chimpanzee that he dissected in 1699 resembled man in more traits than it resembled the adult orang-utan and monkey with which he compared it, did not call his "pygmy" human since the similarities he described were all of a physical nature; man was distinct from this connecting link between the rational and animal biotic forms because of his nobler faculties, especially his power of speech. Tyson could discern no physiological reason why his chimpanzee could not speak, since its larynx so closely resembled the human vocal apparatus. Also its brain seemed as large in proportion to its body size as did the brain of man in the brain–body size ratio. Therefore Tyson concluded that human faculties must arise from a higher, nonphysiological cause, which proved that man's place was between ape and angel (a view that ran counter to the tenet of natural theology that organ structure was perfectly adapted to function in animals and that this relationship could be perceived by the natural historian). Buffon also recognized the structural similarities between man and ape, but did not regard man as a primate because of the development of man's mental faculties and his power of speech, features that were unrelated to the organization of matter and that partook of some "superior principle" which he left to the readers of his *Natural History* to define for themselves. Linnaeus asked, "Show me a generic character by which to distinguish man and ape: I myself know of none," and he supported this viewpoint by placing man in the order of the primates. His followers were not at a loss to attempt to answer this question for him.

The Dutch naturalist von Camper criticized Buffon and Tyson for their anthropomorphic descriptions of the anthropoids. The latter were all quadrupeds, he said, and elevating them to the status of erect walkers was belittling to man, whose place in nature was unique. A quantitative attempt to distinguish the human species from the monkeys and apes resulted in the development of von Camper's anthropometric "facial line" and "facial angle," for which the modal values for mankind differed from those for the creatures beneath him in the taxonomic hierarchy. Later pioneers in anthropometry used other body measurements to support or reject von Camper's thesis. One of the scholars influenced by von Camper was the German anatomist Blumenbach. He placed man apart from the primates in an order of his own—*Bimanes*—which reflected a functional specialization of the human group. He substituted for the facial line his own method of comparing the conformation of the human skull when viewed occipitally and superiorly, and classified the various races of mankind according to this feature, his standard of human excellence being the skull of a Georgian female. Blumenbach assured his readers that this basic Caucasian type originated with the first human pair, but that the narrower- and broader-headed races were degenerate departures from this classic norm. Cuvier adopted Buffon's classification of the primates and Blumenbach's criteria of humanity. Thus man was placed in the order *Bimanes* and his special features were revealed in the proportions based on measurements of facial and cranial size; man has a smaller face and larger brain case than the ape, and these ratios are reversed as one descends the taxonomic system.

In addition to such quantitative attempts to distinguish man from the anthropoids that resembled him, there were efforts to isolate specific anatomical structures whose presence or absence in these creatures would solve once and for all the question of man's unique place in nature. The classic example is von Camper's contention that man differed anatomically from the beasts by his lack of an intermaxillary or premaxillary bone. This statement was based on his observation of the face of an adult orangutan. The amateur naturalist Goethe, seeking correspondences in the structures of various animals, noted that the human maxilla is formed of two pieces of bone on each side of the face only in the embryonic stage, but that in adult life only one piece on each side of the face is observable. The human intermaxillary had in fact been known since the time of Vesalius and was recognized then as an embryonic structure. The observed presence of this bone in the adult orang-utan but not in the adult human being was exactly as von Camper had claimed. Goethe was led to believe that he had discovered the bone in the human species, for in the anatomical tests to which he referred it was not distinguished as a separate element in illustrations of the human maxilla. When von Camper received from Goethe's friend Johann Marck a paper entitled "On the Intermaxillary in Man and Animals," in which Goethe contended that in animals the incisor teeth had their roots in the intermaxillary but that in man this bone had merely atrophied from its prenatal development, he accepted the author's evidence for the presence of the bone in the walrus and other animals, but on the subject of its presence in man von Camper remained true to his beliefs and kept silent. A more frequent argument for the anatomical uniqueness of man concerned his cerebral development as reflected in the large cranial size and particular structural features of the human brain. Richard Owen's insistence on the presence of the hippocampus major and other cerebral features in man but not in the infra-human primates was attacked by Thomas Huxley and lampooned by Charles Kingsley in his tale The Water Babies (1864). The quest for human features that were more than qualitative was carried on into the late nineteenth century, and its ultimate resolution has been assumed by most laymen today. Nevertheless, this naïve quest, along with the insistence by some naturalists that all these speculations about the nature of early man really applied only to events that had transpired since our fall from Adam's pristine state, served the purpose of allowing the young discipline of paleoanthropology that now emerged to escape somewhat the accusation of heresy and so to mature until the time when the accumulation of immense data in the fossil record rendered its critics impotent.

From this review of the main hypotheses concerning man's history and place in nature it should be apparent that the idea that man had a substantial antiquity was entertained by naturalists and intellectuals of the eighteenth century before the discovery and recognition of any empirical evidence regarding that early creature by researchers in the century that followed. We now invite the reader's attention toward an understanding of the empirical evidence of man's past estate. This evidence is of three types: (1) the prehistoric stone artifacts found in association with extinct fauna in ancient geological deposits; (2) the fossils of certain infra-human primates in deposits that were recognized as geologically ancient; and (3) the fossils of men uncovered in similar kinds of geological contexts and in frequent association with prehistoric stone artifacts and an extinct fauna. The last kind of evidence, which to us today seems an irrefutable proof of the presence of ancient man, was the weakest argument for that concept during the nineteenth century when it was directed at the critics of the idea of fossil man. The reasons for the resistance on the part of some scientists against recognizing our ancient kin as they emerged from the caves and gravel beds where they had been encased for millenia merit further scrutiny.

In the early years of the eighteenth century the artifacts of stone and iron manufactured by early man were still being classified as "ceraunia." Objects recognized as having regular shapes and perforations, like hafted axes and hammers, were called "Donnerkeil" or "Stralhammer" in German, reflecting the popular notion that such objects were generated during electrical storms. Indeed, certain of these prehistoric implements were directly associated with specific meteorological events recorded in historical accounts and in folktales. The suggestions of Mercati, de Boot, Aldrovandus, and other Renaissance scholars that these objects were products of human manufacture gained recognition only after the belief in man's brief history on the earth had been called into serious question. In 1715 Conyers, a London apothecary and antique dealer, noted the discovery of a stone axe in association with the bones of a mammoth which were dredged from the Thames. His interpretation that the implement, later recognized as Acheulian in age and type, was that of an ancient Britisher who had slain the mammoth was rejected; his critics argued that Roman elephants imported to England during the reign of Claudius had drowned in the Thames, and that the axe itself had no relevance. Similarly in 1797 John Frere discovered at Hoxne in Suffolk some dressed flints at a depth of thirteen feet, in close proximity to a deposit containing bones of extinct mammals. While Frere recognized these flints as belonging to the "Ante-Diluvial Period," his published account was refuted by the Catastrophist camp. Somewhat later a British clergyman, John McEnery, investigated the caves along the southern coast of England where the bones of extinct fauna were abundant. At Kent's Cavern in Devonshire he discovered in such a paleontological association of extinct mammoth, rhino, horse, and cave bear bones a workshop of stone tools. McEnery's view that here indeed was evidence of antediluvian man was rejected by Buckland on Catastrophist principles, and the cleric thereafter tactfully remained quiet on this issue. However, the British became receptive to the notion of early man largely on the basis of the archaeological evidence at Brixham Cave near the harbor of the same name. Here a committee of naturalists under the sponsorship of the Royal Society and the Geological Society of London recognized the evidence for associating the stone artifacts with extinct fauna that William Pengelly, the director of archaeological operations, was uncovering. This conversion was promoted by the acceptance of the committee of the similar kinds of evidence from France where Boucher de Perthes, since his publication of 1838, *Antiquites celtiques et antediluviennes,* had championed the belief in the validity of his prehistoric discoveries. The British scholars Prestwich, Lyell, Evens, and Flower in 1858–59 visited the sites where de Perthes had found stone artifacts, and their reports as well as the evidence from Brixham Cave convinced many of the skeptics who had not been satisfied earlier with the data from Kent's Cavern. The latter site was reexcavated by Pengelly from 1865 to 1883 and the interpretations of McEnery were verified, his record being published posthumously.

Apart from such somewhat heterodox studies of the stone artifacts from fossiliferous deposits, there was considerable interest during the early part of the nineteenth century in the antiquarian monuments, barrows, and hill forts that were being uncovered in England, France, and the countries of Scandinavia. In Scandinavia interest in these relics of the past was intense for nationalistic reasons. Unlike the nations to the south of them, the Scandinavian countries had a recorded history of but one thousand years, which was recognized as only partially representative of their greater ethnic background. In England such nationalistic motivation was matched by the enthusiasm aroused for classical archaeology and the recovery of the Elgin marbles. Those antiquarians less able to carry out foreign expeditions found contentment in the discovery of the vestiges of the ancient past that were conveniently scattered about their island. To these classically oriented pursuits, the prehistoric archaeology that now developed was complementary.

In the Scandinavian countries the problems of dating the prehistoric past were first investigated. There was no way to resolve the apparent contemporaneity of prehistoric remains and the pioneers of prehistory used the terms *Celtic, Anglo-Saxon, Druidical*, and so on to cover all pre-Roman artifacts. To break through the problem of dating things prehistoric it was necessary to demonstrate that some arrangement of pre-Roman artifacts in a chronological sequence was possible and that any temporal series accepted could be supported by geologically stratigraphical data. The problem of a chronological sequence of artifacts was attacked by scholars associated with the National Danish Museum of Antiquities, where Thomsen arranged the collection according to their material of manufacture: stone artifacts, bronze artifacts, and iron artifacts. This system was described in the museum's guidebook in 1836. It was a scheme readily adapted by other scholars beginning with the Swede Nilsson and by Thomsen's student Worsaae, the author of *The Primeval Antiquities of Denmark* (1847) and later director of the Museums of Ethnography and Northern Antiquities in Copenhagen. To these scholars the Three-Age System was not evolutionary, since the appearances of the stages were sudden and were so interpreted as indicative of migrations of new peoples into Europe, each bearing the equipment of novel cultures. However the comparative method that was part of nineteenth century theories of cultural evolution was used by Nilsson and others as a means of determining what the function of the artifacts might have been, as the knowledge of tool use among primitive peoples might illuminate this problem. In 1840 the study of prehistory can hardly be said to have existed, save for the efforts of a few intellectuals in Scandinavia, but by 1860 their ideas had diffused to other European scholars and the ground had been prepared for the discovery of the remains of the actual manufacturers of the stone artifacts. The union of prehistoric research with human paleontology was imminent.

The discovery of the first fossil infra-human primates would be a circumstance unrelated to the problem of the acceptance of the fossil record for man but for the fact that Catastrophists were convinced that monkeys and apes as well as man had appeared simultaneously after the last great cataclysmic episode. The finding of fossil anthropoids in deposits that were geologically dated as Tertiary intensified the problem of whether man might have a similar antiquity. The Catastrophists rejected the fossil anthropoid record for the same reason that they disregarded the claims that man-made stone tools were contemporary with the fauna of extinct mammals. The eventual acceptance of the fossil anthropoids by paleontologists dealt a severe blow to the prestige of Catastrophism with its tenet of man's recent appearance on the earth. Lartet was the discover of one and the describer of two important fossil finds of nonhuman primates: the mid-Miocene *Pliopithecus* from the deposit of Sansan in Gers that he found in 1832, and the *Dryopithecus* of similar antiquity, uncovered in 1856 by Fontan in Saint-Guardens in Haut-Garonne. With his colleague Gaudry, Lartet described the latter specimen as closer in its morphology to man than to any known living primate. The skull and long bones of a Miocene monkey that had been found in 1838 in Pikermi, Greece by a German soldier found their way into the hands of the German anatomist Wagner who described them in 1862. This was the *Mesopithecus* specimen whose early Tertiary date was verified by Gaudry when he visited the site at Pikermi.

Between 1700 and 1856 a number of genuine fossil man sites were investigated, from which the bones were preserved and about which some published account was written. There were of course many cases where the care of the osseous remains was not the concern of the discoverer and for which no published records were ever kept. Of those specimens that were recorded, over a third have been lost, in certain cases purposefully destroyed since their presence was an offense to the conservative opinion of the times. All of these specimens were at one time or other rejected as legitimate vestiges of early man, half of them falling under the judgment of the Catastrophists Cuvier and Buckland, who sentenced them to the limbo of inadequate scientific evidence of early man. These specimens were rejected on any one of three grounds: (1) the bones were not human but belonged to some other creature; (2) the bones were human but had become mixed with the osseous remains of the extinct fauna with which they were reportedly found through the carelessness of the individual who uncovered them (a frequent verdict if this discoverer should be so unfortunate as to be an amateur paleontologist); or (3) the mixture of human with extinct faunal remains was a consequence of an intrusive burial of a recently deceased human being into a geologically ancient bone pit. Some examples of each of these cases may help to clarify the question of why this evidence of our early ancestors was resisted so successfully by those skeptical of the idea of fossil man.

A fragment of cranium from Cannstadt near Stuttgart, which was picked up from a deposit without any attention to its association with the remains of extinct fauna in the vicinity, is the earliest human fossil find made in Europe. Soon after its date of discovery in 1700 it became lost among the natural history collections of the princes of Würtemberg and was not recovered until 1835, at which time a description of the fragment was published. But already by 1812 Cuvier had become aware of its existence and categorically rejected it as being a fragment of human bone. This obscure section of a right parietal bone was to become very important to de Quatrefages, who supported the humanity of the specimen in the latter part of the nineteenth century. But Cuvier was justified in his rejection of the human nature of that famous specimen, *Homo diluvii testis*, the "old sinner" of the Swiss naturalist whose paper appeared in 1726: *A Most Rare Memorial of That Accursed Generation of Men in the First World, the Skeleton of a Man Drowned in the Flood.* Scheuchzer had long been searching for ante-Diluvian Man before he described the bones found by workmen at Oenigen. An initial discovery of some bones at Altdorf in Franconia he had heralded as the remnants of such a Noahcian Man, although these bones were later discovered to be the vertebrae of an extinct *Ichthyosaurus*. The specimen from Oenigen was rejected by Cuvier, who correctly identified the bones of this "old sinner" as those of a giant salamander, the extinct *Andrias scheuchzeri*, as it was named in honor of its finder. Scheuchzer's enthusiasm for the discovery of the victims of the Deluge was shared by the Diluvialists, and while the possibility of such discoveries was never denied by the Catastrophists, none of the specimens brought to the museums and other centers of learning by earnest amateur paleontologists were ever identified as such. Instead, these bones turned out to be the remnants of mammoths, *Dinotheria*, and other large vertebrates.

While the Diluvialists were seeking evidence of Noahcian Man, a priest and naturalist by the name of Esper was searching the caves of Franconia for such fossil material. He found the complete skeleton of a human specimen as well as various bones of other human beings in the caverns of Gailenreuth in 1774. These bones were in association with vestiges of extinct animals, a circumstance that led to the rejection by his colleagues of any idea that the human and faunal remains were contemporary in time, for that could not be possible in view of the geological and biological history prevailing at that time. Cuvier suggested that the human bones had fallen into the deeper and earlier deposit as a result of local geological changes, but Esper's immediate associates rejected the find as being the careless bumble of an amateur who had mixed his paleontological specimens while working the deposit. The Geilenreuth specimens disappeared after Esper's death, and their true significance is unknown today.

A classic case of an early man discovery that was dismissed as an intrusive burial is that of the "Red Lady of Paviland." This specimen, actually a male whose bones had been painted with red ochre for funeral purposes and whose skull was missing from the deposit, came from a cave in Wales where the human bones were directly associated with those of extinct mammals. Buckland, who described the fossil in 1824, rejected it as an ante-Diluvial Man and claimed that it dated to the time of the Roman occupation of western England. What time has proven to be a good upper Paleolithic fossil hominid, Buckland slandered as a lady of dubious reputation who had yielded her favors to the garrison of an ancient Roman camp, whose walls stood nearby, then crawled into the cave at Paviland to die. The "Red Lady" was deposited in the University Museum at Oxford, where it was lost and forgotten until its resurrection by Sollas in 1913. Buckland rejected the antiquity of other fossil man discoveries, such as the fifty or more skeletons from Aveline's Hole (Burrington Cave) that had been known since 1797. The argument for intrusive burial was applied by Cuvier to the fossil human finds disclosed by Schlotheim since 1820 at Kostritz and Bilzingsleven in Thuringia and at the Rhine Valley site of Lahr, investigated by Ami Boué in 1823. Lyell rejected the human fossil evidence that the Belgian paleontologist Schmerling had been uncovering at Engis and Engihoul since 1828 until finally convinced of its validity after some thirty years of skepticism. Similar reservations were held regarding Tournal's finds in Bize in 1828, de Cristol's finds at Pondres and Souvignarques in Gard in 1829, and the caves of Herault, explored by de Serres in 1838.

Before closing, it may be rewarding to note an obscure and now all but forgotten work by the British naturalist Philip Henry Gosse, the father of Sir Edmond William Gosse and the parent represented in Sir Edmond's *Father and Son* (1907). The work of the elder Gosse was written as a reaction to the Uniformitarian concept of Lyell that was now finding a hold in popular thought. *Omphalos: an Attempt to Untie the Geological Knot* (1857) was an effort to make compatible the Scriptural and geological evidence of the age of the earth and man's place in it. Gosse argued that God's creative act was "prochronic"—all things and all living beings on the earth were created instantaneously at a particular and arbitrary moment in their life cycle. All the signs of previous phases of existence are found in the things of the earth, although among these first phenomena no such prior stages ever had taken place. Adam was created as an adult, yet he possessed a navel just as if he had been born in the natural manner. The geological record shows truly what would have happened if God had chosen to fix the creative moment at an earlier point in the history of the universe; the fossils represent God's conception of this history, although the fossils themselves were never living things. What is important about this thesis is not any scientific benefit it may have afforded the naturalist or philosopher, for its scientific significance was nil: rather it is important for the very fact that it was rejected at the time of its appearance in 1857 as a theory that could not answer the significant problems of human biological history. That it received this kind of negative reception from scientists as well as amateurs in natural history reflects the degree of sophistication that had been reached by the middle of the nineteenth century concerning man's origin, history, and place in nature. But this does not infer a decrease in concern over man's primal estate. Rather it is in the human fossil record that providentialism was to marshal its forces for its final stand against the skeptics of traditional attitudes about the human animal.

Orang-Outang sive *Homo sylvestris:* or the Anatomy of a Pygmie

Edward Tyson
1699

That the *Pygmies* of the Antients were a sort of *Apes,* and not of *Humane Race,* I shall endeavour to prove in the following *Essay.* And if the *Pygmies* were only *Apes,* then in all probability our *Ape* may be a

"Orang-Outang sive *Homo sylvestris:* or the Anatomy of a Pygmie." *Orang-Outang: or the Anatomy of a Pygmy Compared with That of a Monkey, an Ape, and a Man. To which is Added a Philosophical Essay Concerning the Pygmies, the Cynocephalie, the Satyrs, and Sphinges of the Antients. Wherein it will Appear that They are All either Apes or Monkeys and not Men, as Formerly Pretended.* Pp. 1–3, 25, 36–37, 54–57. Printed for T. Bennet, London, 1699.

Pygmie; a sort of *Animal* so much resembling *Man,* that both the Antients and the Moderns have reputed it to be a *Puny Race* of Mankind, call'd to this day, *Homo Sylvestris,* The *Wild Man*; *Orang-Outang,* or a *Man* of the *Woods*; by the *Africans Quoias Morrou;* by others *Baris,* and by the *Portugese,* the *Salvage.* But observing that under these Names, they describe different *Animals;* for Distinction-sake, and to avoid Equivocation, I shall call the Subject, of which I am about to give the *Anatomy,* a *Pygmie,* from its Stature; which I find to be just the same with the Stature of the *Pygmies* of the Antients. *Tulpius* 'tis true, and *Bontius,* and *Dapper* do call it, *Satyrus.* And tho' I am of Opinion, that the *Satyrs* of the Antients were of the *Ape,* or rather *Monkey-kind*; yet for the Reasons alledged in the following *Essay,* I cannot think our *Animal* a *Satyr.* The *Baris* or *Barris,* which they describe to be much taller than our *Animal,* probably may be what we call a *Drill.* But I must confess, there is so great Confusion in the Description of this sort of Creature, which I find is a very large Family (there being numerous *Species* of them) that in Transcribing the Authors that have wrote about them, 'tis almost impossible but to make mistakes; from the want of their well distinguishing them. I shall endeavour therefore in my Account of this, so to discriminate it, that it may be easily known again, where-ever 'tis met with. Not that I think in a single Observation I can be so exact, but that I may be liable to

make Errors my self, how careful soever I have been.

I will not urge any thing more here, why I call it a *Pygmie:* 'Tis necessary to give it a Name; and if what I offer in the ensuing Essay, does not sufficiently Account for the *Denomination,* I leave it to others to give it one more proper. What I shall most of all aim at in the following Discourse, will be to give as particular an Account as I can, of the formation and structure of all the Parts of this wonderful *Animal;* and to make a *Comparative* Survey of them, with the same Parts in a *Humane Body,* as likewise in the *Ape* and *Monkey*-kind. For tho' I own it to be of the *Ape* kind, yet, as we shall observe, in the *Organization* of abundance of its Parts, it more approaches to the Structure of the same in *Men:* But where it differs from a *Man,* there it resembles plainly the Common *Ape,* more than any other *Animal.*

And tho' I may seem too tedious in discoursing so long upon a single subject, yet I have this to offer, that if we had an accurate and particular *History* of any *one Species* of *Animal,* it might in a great measure serve for the *whole kind.* Wherein they differ, might easily be taken notice of, and there would be no need of repeating any thing, wherein they all agreed. So formerly dissecting a Young *Lion* and a *Cat* at the same time, I wondered to find so very great Resemblance of all the Parts, both in the one and the other; that the *Anatomy* of the one might serve for the other, allowing for the Magnitude of the Parts, with very little other alteration: And not only for this, but for several other *Animals,* that belong to the same Family. I could have wished I had had the like Opportunity, when I was dissecting our *Pygmie,* of comparing the same Parts with those of an *Ape* and a *Monkey:* For want of it, I have referred all along to the Accounts given us of the *Anatomy* of these Creatures by other Authors; which, tho' it renders my Discourse more prolix, yet I thought it would not be unacceptable to the Curious. But I shall take care to draw up in a shorter view, wherein our *Pygmie* more resembled a *Man,* than an *Ape* and *Monkey,* and wherein it differ'd.

Now notwithstanding our *Pygmie* does so much resemble a *Man* in many of its Parts, more than any of the *Ape-kind,* or any other *Animal* in the World that I know of: Yet by no means do I look upon it as the Product of a *mixt* Generation; 'tis a *Brute-Animal sui generis,* and a particular *Species of Ape.* For when I was dissecting it, some Sea-Captains and Merchants who came to my House to see it, assured me, that they had seen a great many of them in *Borneo, Sumatra,* and other Parts, tho' this was brought from *Angola* in *Africa;* but was first taken a great deal higher up in the Country, and in Company with it there was a *Female* of the same kind.

I shall have hereafter occasion to make my Remarks on several Particulars, relating to it's way of Living, it's Sagacity, Actions, and the like. I shall now therefore first of all describe its *outward* shape and

figure; then look within, and observe the *Mechanism* there. But meeting with a *Text* in *Aristotle,* wherein he gives a general Description of the *Ape-kind,* I think it not amiss to Transcribe it; and by Commenting upon it, to shew wherein our present Subject agrees with or differs from it; and what I have besides to Remark, I shall afterwards take notice of, and then proceed to the *Anatomy* of the *Inward* Parts.

•　•　•

We shall now proceed to the *Anatomy,* which in a *History* of *Animals,* is certainly the most Necessary, most Significant, and Instructive Part. Nor can I see, how an *History* of *Animals* can be well wrote without giving the *Dissection* of the *Inward Parts:* 'Tis as if one should undertake to describe a *Watch,* and at the same time, take notice only of the *Case* or Cover, and tell what fine Garniture there is about it; but inform us nothing of the admirable Contrivances of the *Wheels* and *Springs within,* which gives it Life and Motion. *Galen*[1] thought the *Dissection* of *Apes* very useful for the understanding the Structure of the *Parts* in *Humane Bodies;* and recommends it to his Scholars to Practice themselves herein. Not that he only dissected *Apes,* (as Vesalius oftentimes charges him with) or preferred it before the Dissection of *Humane Body:* But where that could not be had, he advises them to get *Apes,* and dissect them; especially those that come nearest to

1 *De Anat. Administr. lib.* 1. *cap.* 2. p. m. 27.

a *Man.* Had he known our *Pygmie,* no doubt but he would have preferred it, for this purpose, as much beyond the *Ape,* as he does the *Ape* beyond the *Cynocephalus,* and all other *Animals.* For, as we shall observe, there is no *Animal,* I have hitherto met with, or heard of, that so exactly resembles a *Man,* in the Structure of the *Inward Parts,* as our *Pygmie*: But where it differs, (as I have remark'd) there it resembles an *Ape;* being different both from a *Man* and an *Ape*: And in many things agreeing with both of them.

• • •

I shall conclude by observing to you, that this having been the Common Error of the Age, in believing the *Pygmies* to be a sort of *little Men,* and it having been handed down from so great Antiquity, what might contribute farther to the confirming this Mistake, might be, the Imposture of the Navigators, who sailing to these Parts where these Apes are, they have embalmed their Bodies, and brought them home, and then made the People believe that they were the *Men* of those Countries from whence they came. This *M. P. Venetus* assures us to have been done; and 'tis not unlikely: For, saith he *Abundat quoque Regio ipsa (sc.* Basman in Java in majori) *diversis Simiis magnis & parvis, hominibus simillimis, hos capiunt Venatores & totos depilant, nisi quòd in barba & in loco secreto Pilos relinquunt, & occisos speciebus Aromaticis condiunt, & postea desiccant, venduntque Negociatoribus,*

qui per diversas Orbis Partes Corpora illa deferentes, homines persuadent Tales Homunciones in Maris Insulis reperiri. Joh. Jonston relates the same thing, but without quoting the Author; and as he is very apt to do, commits a great mistake, in telling us, *pro Homunculis marinis venditant.*

I shall only add, That the Servile Offices that these Creatures are observed to perform, might formerly, as it does to this very day, impose upon Mankind to believe, that they were of the same *Species* with themselves; but that only out of sullenness or cunning, they think they will not *speak,* for fear of being made Slaves. *Philostratus* tells us, That the *Indians* make use of the *Apes* in gathering the Pepper; and for this Reason they do defend and preserve them from the *Lions,* who are very greedy of preying upon them. And altho' he calls them *Apes,* yet he speaks of them as *Men,* and as if they were the Husbandmen of the *Pepper Trees.* . . . And he calls them the People of *Apes.* . . . *Dapper* tells us, *That the* Indians *take the* Baris *when joung, and make them so tame, that they will do almost the work of a Slave; for they commonly go erect as Men do. They will beat Rice in a Mortar, carry Water in a Pitcher,* &c. And *Gaffendus* in the Life of *Pieresky,* tells us, *That they will play upon a Pipe or Cittern, or the like Musick, they will sweep the House, turn the Spit, beat in a Mortar, and do other Offices in a Family.* And *Acosta,* as I find him quoted by *Garcilasso de la Vega.*

...tells us of a *Monkey* he saw at the Governour's House at *Cartagena,* whom they sent often to the Tavern for Wine, with Money in one hand, and a Bottle in the other; and that when he came to the Tavern, he would not deliver his Money, until he had received his Wine. If the Boys met with him by the way, or made a houting or noise after him, he would set down his Bottle, and throw Stones at them; and having cleared the way, he would take up his Bottle, and hasten home. And tho'he loved Wine excessively, yet he would not dare to touch it, unless his Master gave him License.

A great many Instances of this Nature might be given that are very surprising. And in another place tells us, That the Natives think that they can speak, but will not, for fear of being made to work. And *Bontius* mentions that the *Javans* had the same Opinion concerning the *Orang-Outang, Loqui verò eos, easque Javani aiunt, sed non velle, ne ad labores cogerentur.*

We proceed now to the *upper Venter,* the *Head,* where at present we shall examine the *Brain;* that Part, which if we had proceeded according to the *Method of Nature* in forming the Parts, we must have began with. For I can't but think, as 'tis the first Part we observe formed, so that the whole of the Body, *i. e.* all the *Containing Parts,* have their rise from it. But I shall not enlarge upon this Argument here; it would be too great a digression, to give my Reasons for such an *Hypothesis.* From what is generally received, *viz.* That the *Brain* is reputed the more immediate Seat of the *Soul* it self; one would be apt to think, that since there is so great a disparity between the *Soul* of a *Man,* and a *Brute,* the *Organ* likewise in which 'tis placed should be very different too. Yet by comparing the *Brain* of our *Pygmie* with that of a *Man;* and, with the greatest exactness, observing each Part in both; it was very surprising to me to find so great a resemblance of the one to the other, that nothing could be more. So that when I am describing the *Brain* of our *Pygmie,* you may justly suspect I am describing that of a Man, or may think that I might very well omit it wholly, by referring you to the accounts already given of the *Anatomy* of an *Humane Brain,* for that will indifferently serve for our *Pygmie,* by allowing only for the magnitude of the Parts in *Man.* Tho' at the same time I must observe, that proportionably to the Bulk of the Body, the *Brain* in our *Pygmie,* was extreamly large; for it weighed (the greatest part of the *Dura Mater* being taken off) twelve Ounces, wanting only a Dram. The *Parisians* remark, that in their *Monkeys* the Brain *was large in proportion to the Body, it weighing two Ounces and a half:* which nevertheless was inconsiderable to ours; since our *Pygmie* exceeded not the Stature and Bulk of the Common *Monkey* or *Ape;* so that herein, as in a great many other Circumstances, our *Pygmie* is different from the Common *Monkey* and *Ape,* and more resembles a *Man.*

I can't agree with *Vesalius,* that the Structure of the *Brain* of all

Quadrupeds, nay all *Birds,* and of some *Fishes* too, is the same as in Man. There is a vast difference to be observed in the formation of the Parts, that serve to compose the *Brain* in these various *Animals.* And tho' the *Brain* of a *Man,* in respect of his Body, be much larger than what is to be met with in any other *Animal* (for *Vesalius* makes the *Brain* of a *Man* to be as big as those of three Oxen) yet I think we can't safely conclude with him, that *Animals,* as they excell in the largeness of the *Brain,* so they do likewise in the Principal Faculties of the *Soul:* For if this be true, then our *Pygmie* must equal a *Man,* or come very near him, since his *Brain* in proportion to his Body, was as large as a *Man's. Vesalius*[2] his words are these;

Cerebri nimirùm constructione Simia, Canis, Equus, Felis, & Quadrupeda quœ hactenùs vidi omnia, & Aves etiam universœ, plurimaque Piscium genera, omni propemodùm ex parte Homini correspondeant: neque ullum secanti occurrat discrimen, quod secùs de Hominis, quàm illorum Animalium functionibus statuendum esse prœscribat. Nis forte quis meritò dicat Cerebri molem Homini, Perfectissimo sanè quod novimus Animali, obtigisse maximam, ejusque Cerebrum etiam tribus Boum Cerebris grandius reperiri: & dein secundum Corporis proportionem mox Simiœ, dein Cani magnum quoque non secus obtingere Cerebrum, quàm si Animalia Cerebri tantum prœstarent mole, quanto Principis Animœ viribus apertius viciniùsve donata videntur.

2 *And. Vesalij de Corporis Humanis fabrica,* lib. 7. cap. 1. p. 773, 774.

Since therefore in all respects the *Brain* of our *Pygmie* does so exactly resemble a *Man's,* I might here make the same Reflection the *Parisians* did upon the *Organs* of *Speech, That there is no reason to think, that Agents do perform such and such Actions, because they are found with Organs proper thereunto:* for then our *Pygmie* might be really a *Man.* The *Organs* in *Animal* Bodies are only a regular *Compages* of Pipes and Vessels, for the *Fluids* to pass through, and are passive. What actuates them, are the *Humours* and *Fluids:* and *Animal Life* consists in their due and regular motion in this *Organical* Body. But those *Nobler Faculties* in the *Mind* of *Man,* must certainly have a *higher Principle;* and *Matter organized* could never produce them; for why else, where the *Organ* is the same, should not the *Actions* be the same too? and if all depended on the *Organ,* not only our *Pygmie,* but other *Brutes* likewise, would be too near akin to us. This Difference I cannot but remark, that the *Antients* were fond of making *Brutes* to be *Men:* on the contrary now, most unphilosophically, the *Humour* is, to make *Men* but meer *Brutes* and *Matter.* Whereas in truth *Man* is part a *Brute,* part an *Angel;* and is that *Link* in the *Creation,* that joyns them both together.

This *Digression* may be the more pardonable, because I have so little to say here, besides just naming the *Parts;* and to tell you (what I have already) that they were all like to those in a *Man:* For the *Dura Mater,* as a *Common Membrane,* firmly secured the situation of the whole *Brain,* strictly adhering to the *Sutures* of the *Cranium* above; before to the *Crista Galli;* and at the *basis* so strongly, that it was not easily to be separated. By it's *anterior Process* of the *Falx,* it divided the two *Hemispheres* of the *Cerebrum;* by it's *transverse Process,* which descended deep, just as in a *Man,* it separated the *Cerebrum* and *Cerebellum:* it enjoyed the same *Sinus's,* and in all Particulars 'twas conformable to what is in a *Man.*

The *Pia Mater* in our *Pygmie* was a fine thin Membrane which more immediately covered the Substance of the *Brain,* and may be reckoned it's *proper Membrane;* insinuating it's self all along between the *Anfractus* of the *Cerebrum* and the *Circilli* of the *Cerebellum;* being copiously furnished with numerous Branches of *Blood Vessels,* but they appear'd more on the *Convex* Part, then at the *Basis.*

The *figure* of the whole *Brain* in our *Pygmie* was globous; but by means of a greater jutting in of the Bones of the *Orbit* of the *Eye,* there was occasioned a deeper depression on the *Anterior Lobes* of the *Brain* in this place, than in a *Man.* As to other Circumstances here, I observed all Parts the same. The *Ansractus* of the *Cerebrum* were alike; as also the *Substantia Corticalis* and *Medullaris.* On the *basis* of the *Brain,* we may view all the *Ten pair* of *Nerves* exactly situated and placed as in a *Humane Brain;* nor did I find their Originations different, or any Particularity that was so. I shall therefore refer to the *figures* I have caused

to be made of the *Brain,* and their Descriptions; where we may observe the *Arteriœ Carotides, Vertebrales,* and *Communicans,* and the whole of the *Blood Vessels* in our *Pygmie* to be the same as in a Man. Here was the *Infundibulum,* the *Glandulœ duœ albœ ponè Infundibulum,* the *Medulla Oblongata* with it's *Annular Protuberance,* and the beginning of the *Medulla Spinalis,* just as in *Man.* I am here only a *Nomenclator,* for want of Matter to make particular Remarks upon. And the Authorrs that have hitherto furnished me with Notes, how the same *Parts* are in *Apes* and *Monkeys,* do fail me now; it may be, finding here nothing new or different, they are therefore silent. All the *Parisians* do tell us of the *Brain* in their *Monkeys* is this:

The Brain *was large in proportion to the Body: It weighed two Ounces and an half. The* Dura Mater *entered very far to form the* Falx. *The Anfractuosities of the External part of the Brain were very like those of Man in the Anteriour part; but in the inward parts before the Cerebellum, there was hardly any: they in requital were much deeper in proportion. The* Apophyses, *which are called* Mamillares, *which are great Nerves that do serve to the smelling, were not soft, as in Man, but hard and membranous. The* Optick *Nerves were also of a Substance harder and firmer than ordinary. The* Glandula Pinealis *was of a Conical figure, and it's point was turned towards the hinder part of the Head. There was no* Rete Mirabile: *for the* Carotides *being entered into the Brain, went by one single Trunk on each side* of the edge of the seat of the Sphenoides *to pierce the* Dura Mater, *and to be distributed into the basis of the Brain.* In our Subject I thought the *Anfractus* of the Brain much the same, both in the anteriour and hinder part. Nor did I observe any difference in the *Mamillary Processes* or *Optick Nerves,* or *Rete Mirabile,* but all, as in a *Man.*

The *Cerebellum* in our *Pygmie* was divided by *Circilli,* as in *Man.* It had likewise the *Processus Vermiformes.* Dr. *Willis*[3] makes this Remark upon this Part: *Cerebellum autem ipsum, in quibusvis ferè Animalibus, ejusdem figuræ & proportionis, nec non ex ejusmodi lamellis conflatum reperitur. Quæ Cerebrum diversimodè ab homine configuratum habent, uti* Volucres & Pisces, *item inter Quadrupedes* Cuniculi & Mures, *quorum Cerebra bra gyris seu convolutionibus carent; his Cerebelli species eadem, similis plicarum dispositio & Partium cæterarum composituræ existunt.* 'Tis from hence he forms his noted *Hypothesis,* How that the *Animal Spirits* that are bred in the *Cerebrum,* do serve for *Voluntary Motions;* and those in the *Cerebellum* for *involuntary.*

3 *Willis Cerebri Anat.* cap. 3. p. 22.

If we survey the inward Parts of the *Brain* in our *Pygmie,* we shall here likewise find all exactly as in a *Humane Body; viz.* The Merullary Substance running up between the *Cortical;* The *Concameration,* the *Corpus Callosum,* the *Fornix* and it's *Crura* the *same.* The *Ventricles* large and spatious. The *Corpora Striata,* the *Thalami Nervorum Opticorum* all alike. The *Plexus Choroides* the same; as were also the three *Foramina* as in *Man;* The *Glandula Pinealis* proportionably large. The *Protuberantiæ Orbiculares;* i.e. The *Nates* and *Testes* in our *Pygmie* were the same as in *Man;* whereas in *Brutes* (as Dr. *Willis* well observes) the *Nates* are always proportionably larger than in *Man;* but it was not so in our *Pygmie.* The *Valvula major* here was very plain. The *Cerebellum* being divided, the *Medullary* Parts represented the Branches of Trees, as a *Man*'s does. The *Medulla Oblongata* and *Medulla Spinalis* the same as the *Humane;* and all Parts being so conformable here to a *Humane Brain,* I thought it sufficient just to name them, since I have caused to be made two *figures* of the *Brain* in our *Pygmie* from the Life, and in its Natural Bigness, where all the Parts are plainly represented to the Eye.

The Nomenclature of Apes

Georges Louis Leclerc, Comte de Buffon
1749–1767

To teach children, and to address men, are two very different offices. Children receive without examination, and even with avidity, the arbitrary and the real, the true and the false, whenever they are presented to them under the form of precepts. Men, on the contrary, reject with contempt all precepts which are not founded on solid principles. We shall, therefore, adopt none of those methodical distributions by which, under the appellation of *ape,* a multitude of animals, belonging to very different species, have been huddled together in one indiscriminate mass.

What I call an *ape* is an animal without a tail, whose face is flat, whose teeth, hands, fingers, and nails, resemble those of man, and which, like him, walks erect on two feet. This definition, derived from the nature of the animal itself, and from its relations to man, excludes all animals that have tails; all those that have prominent faces or long muzzles; all those that have crooked or sharp claws; and all those that walk more willingly on four than on two legs. According to this precise idea, let us examine how many species of animals ought to be ranked under the denomination of *ape.* The ancients knew only one. The *pithecos* of the Greeks, and the *simia* of the Latins, is a true *ape,* and was the subject upon which Aristotle, Pliny, and Galen instituted all the physical relations they discovered between that animal and man. But this ape, or pigmy of the ancients, which so strongly resembles man in external structure, and still more strongly in its internal organization, differs from him, however, by a quality, which, though relative in itself, is not the less essential. This quality is magnitude. The stature of man, in general, exceeds five feet; that of the *pithecos,* or pigmy, never rises above one-fourth of this height. Hence, if this ape had been still more similar to man, the ancients would have been justified for regarding it only as an *homunculus,* an imperfect dwarf, a

"The Nomenclature of Apes." *Natural History, General and Particular.* Translated by W. Smellie. Vol. 10, pp. 1–36. T. Cadell and M. Davis, London, 1791. "Nomenclature des singes." *Histoire Naturelle, Générale et Particulière.* Imprimerie royale, Paris, 1749–1767.

pigmy, capable of combating with cranes; while man knew how to tame the elephant and conquer the lion.

But, since the discovery of the southern regions of Africa and India, we have found another ape, possessing this quality of magnitude; an ape as tall and strong as man, and equally ardent for woman as for its own females; an ape who knows how to bear arms, to attack his enemies with stones, and to defend himself with clubs. Besides, he resembles man still more than the pigmy; for, independent of his having no tail, of his flat face, of the resemblance of his arms, hands, toes, and nails to ours, and of his walking constantly on end, he has a kind of visage with features which approach to those of the human countenance, a beard on his chin, and no more hair on his body than men have, when in a state of nature. Hence the inhabitants of his country, the civilized Indians, have not hesitated to associate him with the human species, under the denomination of *orang-outang,* or *wild man;* while the Negroes, almost equally wild, and as ugly as these apes, who imagine not that civilization exalts our nature, have given it the appellation of *pongo,* which is the name of a beast, and has no relation to man. This orang-outang, or pongo, is only a brute, but a brute of a kind so singular, that man cannot behold it without contemplating himself, and without being thoroughly convinced that his body is not the most essential part of his nature.

Thus, we have discovered two animals, the pigmy and the orang-outang, to which the name of *ape* ought to be applied. There is a third, to which, though more deformed both in relation to man and to the ape, this appellation cannot be refused. This animal, which till now was unknown, and was brought from the East Indies, under the name of *gibbon,* walks on end, like the other two, and has a flat face. He likewise wants a tail. But his arms, instead of being proportioned to the height of his body, like those of man, the orang-outang, or the pigmy, are so enormously long, that, when standing on his two feet, he touches the ground with his hands, without bending either his body or limbs. This ape is the third and last to which the name ought to be applied: in this genus, he constitutes a singular or monstrous species, like the race of thick-legged men, said to inhabit the island of St. Thomas.

After the apes, another tribe of animals present themselves, to which we shall give the generic name of *baboon.* To distinguish them more accurately from the other kinds, let it be remarked, that the baboon has a short tail, a long face, a broad high muzzle, canine teeth, proportionally larger than those of man, and callosities on his buttocks. By this definition, we exclude from the baboon tribe all the apes that have no tail; all the monkeys, with tails as long or longer than their bodies; and all those which have thin, sharp pointed muzzles. The ancients had no proper names for these animals. Aristotle alone seems to have pointed out one of the baboons under the name *simia porcaria*,[1] though he has given but a very imperfect idea of the animal. The Italians first called it *babuino;* the Germans, *bavion;* the French, *babouin;* the British, *baboon;* and all the modern writers of Latin, *papio.* We shall call it *baboon,* to distinguish it from the other species which have since been discovered in the southern regions of Africa and India. We are acquainted with three species of these animals:

1. The *baboon* properly so called, which is found in Lybia, Arabia, &c., and is probably the *simia porcaria* of Aristotle.
2. The *mandrill,* or *ribbed nose,* is still larger than the baboon, has a violet-coloured face, the nose and cheeks ribbed with deep oblique furrows, and is found in Guinea and in the warmest provinces of Africa.
3. The *ouanderou,* which is smaller than the baboon and mandrill; its body is thinner, its head and face are surrounded with a kind of long bushy mane, and it is found in Ceylon, Malabar, and other southern regious of India.

Thus we have properly defined three species of apes, and three species of baboons, which are all very different from one another.

But, as Nature knows none of our definitions, as she has not

---

1 The denomination *simia porcaria,* which is employed by no other author but Aristotle, was not improperly applied to denote the baboon; for I find in the works of several travellers, who probably never read Aristotle, the muzzle of the baboon compared to the snout of a hog. Besides, these animals have same resemblance in the form of their bodies.

classed her productions by bundles or genera, and as her progress is always gradual and marked by minute shades, some intermediate animal should be found between the ape and baboon. This intermediate species actually exists, and is the animal which we call *magot,* or the *Barbary ape.* It occupies a middle station between our two definitions. It forms the shade between the apes and baboons. It differs from the first by having a long muzzle and large canine teeth; and from the second, because it actually wants the tail, though it has an appendix of skin, which has the appearance of a very small tail. Of course, it is neither an ape nor a baboon, but, at the same time, partakes of the nature of both. This animal, which is very common in Higher Egypt, as well as in Barbary, was known to the ancients. The Greeks and Romans called it *cynocephalus,* because its muzzle resembled that of a dog. Let us now arrange these animals in their proper order: the *orang-outang* is the first ape; the *pigmy* the second; and the *gibbon,* though different in figure, the third; the *cynocephalus,* or *magot,* the fourth ape, or the first baboon; the *papio* is the first baboon; the *mandrill* the second; and the *ouanderou,* or little baboon, the third. This order is neither arbitrary nor fictitious, but agreeable to the scale of Nature.

After the apes and baboons, come the *guenons,* or *monkeys;* that is, animals resembling the apes and baboons, but which have tails as long, or longer than their bodies. The word *guenon* has, for some ages, had two acceptations different from that we have here given: it is generally employed to signify small apes, and sometimes to denote the female of the ape. But more anciently, we called *singes,* or *magots,* the apes without a tail, and *guenons,* or *mones,* those which had long tails. This fact appears from the works of some travellers[2] in the sixteenth and seventeenth centuries. The word *guenon* is probably derived from *kébos,* which the Greeks employed to denote the long-tailed apes. These *kébes,* or *guenons,* are smaller and weaker than the apes and baboons. They are easily distinguishable from one another by this difference, and particularly by their long tail. With equal ease they may be distinguished from the *makis* or *maucaucos;* because they have not a sharp muzzle, and, instead of six cutting teeth, like the makis, they have only four, like the apes and baboons. We know eight species of guenons; and, to prevent confusion, we shall bestow on each a proper name:

1. The *macaque,* or hare-lipped monkey;
2. The *patas,* or red monkey;
3. The *malbrouk;*

4. The *mangabey,* or monkey with the upper eyelids of a pure white colour;
5. The *mone,* or varied monkey;
6. The *callitrix,* or green monkey;
7. The *moustac,* or whiskered monkey;
8. The *talapoin;*
9. The *douc,* or monkey of Cochinchina.

The ancient Greeks knew only two of these *guenons,* or long-tailed monkeys, namely, the mone and the callitrix, which are natives of Arabia and the northern parts of Africa. They had no idea of the other kinds; because these are found only in the southern provinces of Africa and the East Indies, countries entirely unknown in the days of Aristotle. This great philosopher, and the Greeks in general, were too wise to confound beings by common, and therefore, equivocal names. They call the ape without a tail *pithecos,* and the monkey with a long tail, *kébos.* As they knew these animals to be distinct species, they gave to each a proper name, derived from their most striking characters. All the apes and baboons which they knew, namely, the *pigmy,* the *cynocephalus,* or *magot,* and the *simia porcaria,* or *papio,* have their hair nearly of a uniform colour. But the monkey, which we have called *mone,* and the Greeks *kébos,* has hair of different colours, and is generally known by the name of the *varied ape.* This species of monkey was most common, and best known in the days of Aristotle; and, from its most distinguished character, he calls it *kébos,* which, in Greek, signifies *varieties in colour.* Thus all the animals belonging to the class of

2 In Senegal there are several species of apes, as the *guenons,* with a long tail; and the *magots,* who have no tail. *Voyage de la Maire,* p. 101. In the mountains of South America, there is a kind of *mones,* or long-tailed monkeys, which the Savages call *cacuyen.* They are of the same size with the common kind, from which they differ only by having a beard on their chin. . . . Along with these *mones,* there are found a number of small yellow animals, called *sagouins. Singularités de la Fr. Antarct. par Thevet,* p. 103.

apes, baboons, and monkeys, mentioned by Aristotle, are reduced to four, the *pithecos,* the *cynocephalus,* the *simia porcaria,* and the *kébos;* which we believe to be the *pigmy,* the *magot,* or Barbary ape, the *baboon,* and the *mone,* or varied monkey, not only because they agree with the characters given of them by Aristotle, but likewise because the other species must have been unknown to the ancients, since they are natives of countries into which the Greek travellers had never penetrated.

Two or three centuries after Aristotle, we find, in the Greek writers, two new names, *callithrix* and *cercopithecos,* both relative to the *guenons,* or long-tailed monkeys. In proportion as discoveries were made of the southern regions of Africa and Asia, we found new animals, and other species of monkeys; and, as most of these monkeys had not, like the *kébos,* various colours, the Greeks invented the generic name *cercopithecos,* or *tailed ape,* to denote all the species of monkeys or apes with long tails; and, having remarked, among these new species, a monkey with hair of a lively greenish colour, they called it *callithrix,* which signifies *beautiful hair.* This callithrix is found in the south part of Mauritania, and in the neighbourhood of the Cape de Verd, and is commonly known by the name of the *green ape.*

With regard to the other seven species of monkeys, mentioned above under the appellations of *makaque, patas, malbrouk, mangabey, moustac, talapoin,* and *douc,* they were un-known to the Greeks and Latins, The makaque is a native of Congo; the patas, of Senegal; the mangabey, of Madagascar; the malbrouk of Bengal; the moustac, of Guinea; the talapoin of Sinam; and the douc, of Cochinchina. All these territories were equally unknown to the ancients.

As the progress of Nature is uniform and gradual, we find between the baboons and monkeys an intermediate species, like that of the magot between the apes and baboons. The animal which fills this interval has a great resemblance to the monkeys, particularly to the makaque; its muzzle, at the same time, is very broad, and its tail short, like that of the baboons. Being ignorant of its name, we have called it *maimon,* or *pig-tailed baboon,* to distinguish it from the others. It is a native of Sumatra. Of all the monkeys or baboons, it alone has a naked tail; and, for this reason, several authors have given it the denomination of the *pig-tailed* or *rat-tailed ape.*

We have now enumerated all the animals of the Old World, to whom the common name of *ape* has been applied, though they belong not only to different species, but to different genera. To augment the confusion, the same names of *ape, cynocephalus, kébos,* and *cercopithecos,* which had been invented by the Greeks fifteen centuries ago, have been bestowed on animals peculiar to the New World, though so recently discovered. They never dreamed that none of the African or East Indian animals had any existence in the southern regions of the New Continent. In America, we have discovered animals with hands and fingers. This similarity was alone sufficient to procure to them the name of *apes*, without considering that, for the transference of a name, identity of genus, and even of species, is necessary. Now, these American animals, of which we shall make two classes, under the appellations of *sapajous*, or monkeys with prehensile tails; and *sagoins*, or monkeys with long tails, which are not prehensile, or want the faculty of laying hold of any object, are very different from the apes of Asia and Africa; and, in the same manner, as no apes, baboons, or monkeys, are to be found in the New World, there are neither sapajous nor sagoins in the Old. Though we have already given a general view of these facts, in our Dissertation concerning the animals of both continents, we can now prove them in a more particular manner, and demonstrate, that, of seventeen species, to which all the animals of the Old World called *apes*, may be reduced, and of twelve or thirteen in the New World, to which this name has been transferred, none of them are the same, or to be found equally in both worlds; for, of the seventeen species in the Old Continent, three or four apes must first be retrenched, which certainly exist not in America, and to which the sapajous and sagoins have no resemblance. In the second place, three or four baboons must ilkewise be retrenched: they are larger than the sapajous and sagoins, and also very different in figure.

There remain only nine monkeys with which any comparison can be instituted. Now, all these monkeys, as well as the apes and baboons, have general and particular characters, which separate them entirely from the sapajous and sagoins. The first of these characters is to have naked buttocks, and natural callosities peculiar to these parts. The second is to have *abajoues*, or pouches under the cheeks, in which they can keep their victuals. The third is to have a narrow partition between the nostrils, and the apertures of the nostrils themselves placed in the under part of the nose, like those of man. The sapajous and sagoins have none of these characters. The partition between their nostrils is always very thick; the apertures of their nostrils are situated in the sides of the nose, and not in the under part of it. They have hair on their buttocks, and no callosities. They have no pouches under the cheeks. Hence they differ from the monkeys not only in species, but in genus, since they possess none of the general characters which are common to the whole tribe of monkeys. This difference of genus necessarily implies greater differences in species, and shows that these animals are very remote from each other.

It is with much impropriety, therefore, that the names *ape* and *monkey* have been applied to the *sapajous* and *sagoins*. We must preserve their names, and, instead of associating them with the apes, we should begin by comparing them with one another. These two tribes differ from each other by a remarkable character: all the sapajous use their tail as a finger to hang upon branches, or to lay hold of any object they cannot reach with their hand. The sagoins, in the contrary, have not the power of employing their tail in this manner. Their face, ears, and hair are also different: we may, therefore, separate them into two distinct genera. In giving the history of the species, I shall avoid all those denominations which can apply only to the apes, baboons, and monkeys, and preserve the names they receive in their native country.

We are acquainted with six or seven species of sapajous, and six of sagoins, most of which have some varieties. We have carefully searched all the writings of travellers in order to discover the proper name of each species; because the names they receive in the places they inhabit generally point out some peculiar characteristic, which alone is sufficient to distinguish them from one another.

With regard to the varieties, which, in this class of animals, are perhaps more numerous than the species, we shall endeavour to refer each of them to their proper kinds. We have had forty of these animals alive, each of which differed more or less from one another; and to us it appears that the whole may be reduced to thirty species, namely, three apes, and an intermediate species between them and the baboons; three baboons, and an intermediate species between them and the monkeys; nine monkeys; seven sapajous; and six sagoins. All the others, or at least most of them,

ought to be regarded as varieties only. But, as we are uncertain whether some of these varieties may not be distinct species, we shall endeavour to give all of them proper names.

On this occasion, let us consider terrestrial animals, some of which have a great resemblance to man, in a new point of view. The whole have improperly received the general name of *quadrupeds*. If the exceptions were few, we would not have found fault with the application of this name. It was formerly remarked, that our definitions and denominations, however general, never comprehend the whole; that beings always exist which elude the most cautious definitions which ever were invented; that intermediate beings are always discovered; that several of them, though apparently holding a middle station, escape from the list; and that the general names, under which we mean to include them, are incomplete; because Nature should be considered by unities only, and not by aggregates; because man has invented general denominations with the sole view of aiding his memory, and supplying the defects of his understanding; and because he afterwards foolishly considered these general names as realities; and, in fine, because he has endeavoured to comprehend under them beings, and even whole classes of beings, which required different appellations. I can give an example, without departing from the class of quadrupeds, which, of all animals, we are best acquainted with, and, of course, were in a condition to have bestowed on them the most precise denominations.

The name *quadruped* supposes that the animal has *four feet*. If it wants two feet, like the manati; if it has arms and hands, like the ape; or if it has wings, like the bat; it is not a quadruped. Hence this general term, when applied to these animals, is abused. To obtain precision in words, the ideas they present must be strictly true. If we had a term for two hands similar to that which denotes two feet, we might then say that man was the only biped and *bimanus,* because he alone has two hands and two feet; that the manati is a *bimanus;* that the bat is only a biped; and that the ape is a *quadrimanus,* or four-handed animal. Let us now apply these new denominations to all the particular beings to which they belong, and we shall find, that, from about two hundred animals, who go under the common name of *quadrupeds,* thirty-five species of apes, baboons, monkeys, sapajous, sagoins, and makis, must be retrenched, because they are *quadrimanus,* or four-handed; and that to these thirty-five species, the loris, or tailless maucauco, the Virginian, murine, and Mexican opossum, the Egyptian and woolly jerboas, &c., should be added, because they are four-handed, like the apes and monkeys. Thus the list of four-handed animals being at least forty species, the real number of quadrupeds is one fifth diminished. We must likewise retrench twelve or fifteen species of bipeds, namely, the bats, whose fore-feet are rather wings

than feet, and likewise three or four jerboas, because they can walk on their hind-feet only, the fore-feet being too short. If we substract also the manati, which has no hind-feet, the arctic and Indian walrus, and the seals, to whom the hind-feet are useless; and, if we still retrench those animals which use their fore-feet like hands, as the bears, the marmots, the coatis, the agoutis, the squirrels, the rats, and many others, the denomination of *quadruped* will appear to be applied improperly to more than one half of these animals. The whole and cloven-hoofed are indeed the only real quadrupeds. When we descend to the digitated class, we find four-handed, or ambiguous quadrupeds, who use their fore-feet as hands, and ought to be separated or distinguished from the others. Of whole-hoofed animals, there are three species, the horse, the ass, and the zebra. If to these we add the elephant, the rhinoceros, the hippopotamus, and the camel, whose feet, though terminated by nails, are solid, and serve the animals for walking only, we shall have seven species to which the name of *quadruped* is perfectly applicable. The number of cloven-hoofed animals greatly exceeds that of the whole-hoofed. The oxen, the sheep, the goats, the antelopes, the bubalus, the lama, the pacos, the giraffe, the elk, the rein-deer, the stag, the fallow deer, the roebuck, &c., are all cloven-footed, and constitute about forty species. Thus we have already fifty animals, ten whole and forty cloven-hoofed, to whom the name *quadruped* is properly applied. In the digitated animals, the lion, tiger, panther, leopard, lynx, cat, wolf, dog, fox, hyæna, badger, polecat, weesels, ferret, porcupines, hedgehogs, armadillos, ant-eaters, and hogs, which last constitute the shade between the digitated and cloven-footed tribes, form a number consisting of more than forty species, to which the term of *quadruped* applies with perfect precision; because, though their fore-feet be divided into four or five toes, they are never used as hands. But all the other digitated species, which use their fore-feet in carrying food to their mouths, are not, in strict propriety of language, quadrupeds. These species, which likewise amount to forty, make an intermediate class between quadrupeds and four-handed animals, being neither the one nor the other. Hence, to more than a fourth of our animals, the name of *quadruped* does not apply; and to more than a half of them, the application of it is incomplete.

The four-handed animals fill the interval between man and the animals; and the two-handed species constitute a mean term in the distance between man and the cetaceous tribes. The bipeds with wings form the shade between quadrupeds and birds; and the digitated species, which use their fore-feet as hands, fill the whole space between the quadrupeds and the four-handed kinds. But I will pursue this subject no farther: however useful it may be for acquiring a distinct knowledge of animals, it is still more so by affording a fresh proof, that all our definitions or general terms

want precision, when applied to the objects of beings which they represent.

But why are these definitions and general terms, which appear to be the most brilliant exertions of the human intellect, so defective in their application? Does the error necessarily arise from the narrow limits of our understanding? Or, rather, does it not proceed solely from our incapacity of combining and perceiving at one time a great number of objects? Let us compare the works of Nature with those of man. Let us examine how both operate, and inquire whether the mind, however acute, can follow the same route, without losing itself in the immensity of space, in the obscurity of time, or in the infinity of related beings. When man directs his mind to any object, if his perceptions be accurate, he takes the straight line, runs over the smallest space, and employs the least possible time in accomplishing his end. What an expense of thought, how many combinations are necessary to avoid those deceitful and fallacious roads which at first present themselves in such numbers, that the choice of the right path requires the nicest discernment? This path, however, is not beyond the reach of the human intellect, which can proceed without deviating from the straight line. The mind is enabled to arrive at a point by means of a line; and, if another point must be gained, it can only be attained by another line. The train of our ideas is a delicate thread, which extends in length, without any other dimensions. Nature, on the contrary, never moves a step which extends not on all sides, and runs at once through the three dimensions of length, breadth, and thickness. While man reaches but one point, Nature accomplishes a solid, by penetrating the whole parts which compose a mass. In bestowing form on brute matter, our statuaries, by the union of art and time, are enabled to make a surface which exactly represents the outside of an object. Every point of this surface requires a thousand combinations. Their genius is directly exerted upon as many lines as there are strokes in the figure. The smallest deviation would be a deformity. This marble, so perfect that it seems to breathe, is, of course, only a multitude of points at which the artist arrives by a long succession of labour; because human genius, being unable to seize more than one dimension at the same time, and our senses reaching no farther than surfaces, we cannot penetrate matter: but Nature, in a moment, puts every particle in motion. She produces forms by exertions almost instantaneous. She at once developes them in all their dimensions. As soon as her movements reach the surface, the penetrating forces with which she is animated operate internally. The smallest atom, when she chooses to employ it, is instantly compelled to obey. Hence she acts, at the same time, on all sides, before, behind, above, below, on the right and left; and, consequently, she embraces not only the surface, but every particle of the mass. How different likewise

is the product? What comparison is there between a statue and an organized body? How unequal, at the same time, are the powers, how disproportioned the instruments? Man can employ only the power he possesses. Limited to a small quantity of motion, which he can only communicate by the mode of impulsion, his exertions are confined to surfaces; because, in general, the impulsive force is only transmitted by superficial contact. He neither sees nor touches more than the surfaces of bodies; and, when he wishes to attain a more intimate knowledge, though he opens and divides, still he sees and touches nothing more than their surfaces. To penetrate the interior parts of bodies, he would require a portion of that force which acts upon the mass, or of gravity, which is Nature's chief instrument. If man could employ this penetrating force as he does that of impulsion, or if he had a sense relative to it, he would be enabled to perceive the essence of matter, and to arrange small portions of it, in the same manner as Nature operates at large. It is owing to the want of instruments, therefore, that human art cannot approach that of Nature. His figures, his pictures, his designs, are only surfaces, or imitations of surfaces; because the images he receives by his senses are all superficial, and he has no mode of giving them a body.

What is true with regard to the arts, applies likewise to the sciences. The latter, however, are not so much limited; because the mind is their chief instrument, and because, in the former, it is subordinate to the senses. But, in the sciences, the mind commands the senses as often as it is employed in thinking and not in operating, in comparing and not in imitating. Now, the mind, though bound up by the senses, though often deceived by their fallacious reports, is neither diminished in its purity nor activity. Man, who naturally loves knowledge, commenced by rectifying and demonstrating the errors of the senses. He has treated them as mechanical instruments, the effects of which must be submitted to the test of experiment. Proceeding thus with the balance in one hand, and the compass in the other, he has measured both time and space. He has recognised the whole outside of Nature; and, being unable to penetrate her internal parts by his senses, his deductions concerning them have been drawn from comparison and analogy. He discovered that there exists in matter a general force, different from that of impulsion, a force which falls not under the cognisance of our senses, and which, though we are incapable of using it, Nature employs as her universal agent. He has demonstated, that this force belongs equally to all matter, in proportion to its mass or real quantity; and that its action extends to immense distances, decreasing as the spaces augment. Then, turning his views upon living beings, he perceived that heat was another force necessary to their production; that light was a matter endowed with infinite elasticity and activity; that the formation and expansion of organized bodies were

effects of a combination of all these forces; that the extension and growth of animals and vegetables follow the laws of the attractive force, and are effected by an augmentation in the three dimensions at the same time; and that a mould, when once formed, must, by these laws of affinity, produce a succession of other moulds perfectly similar to the original. By combining these attributes, common to the animal and vegetable, he recognised, that there existed in both an inexhaustible, circulating store of organic substance; a substance equally real as brute matter; a substance which continues always in a live, as the other does in a dead state; a substance universally diffused, which passes from vegetables to animals by means of nutrition, returns from animals to vegetables by the process of putrefaction, and maintains a perpetual circulation for the animation of beings. He perceived, that these active organic particles existed in all organized bodies; that they were combined, in smaller or greater quantities, with dead matter; that they were more abundant in animals, in which every thing is alive, and more rare in vegetables, in which death predominates, and life seems to be extinct, organization being surcharged with brute matter; and that plants are, of course, deprived of progressive motion, of heat, and of life, exhibiting no other quality of animation but expansion and reproduction. Reflecting on the manner in which these last are accomplished, he discovered that every living being is a mould that has the power of assimilating the substances with which it is nourished; that growth is an effect of this assimilation; that the development of a living body is not a simple augmentation of volume, but an extension in all dimensions, a penetration of new matter through all parts of the mass; that these parts, by increasing proportionally to the whole, and the whole proportionally to the parts, the form is preserved, and continues always the same, till growth is completed; that, when the body has acquired its full expansion, the same matter, formerly employed in augmenting its volume, is returned, as superfluous, from all the parts to which it had been assimilated, and, by uniting in a common point, forms a new being perfectly similar to the first, and, to attain the same dimensions, requires only to be developed by the same mode of nutrition. He perceived that man, quadrupeds, cetaceous animals, birds, reptiles, insects, trees, and herbs, were nourished, expanded, and reproduced by the same law; and that the mode of their nutrition and generation, though depending on the same general cause, appeared to be very different, because it could not operate but in a manner relative to the form of each particular species of being. Proceeding gradually in his investigation, he began, after a succession of ages, to compare objects. To distinguish them from each other, he gave them particular names; and, to unite them under one point of view, he invented general terms. Taking his own body as the physical model of all animated

beings, he measured, examined, and compared all their parts, and he discovered that the form of every animal which breathes is nearly the same; that, by dissecting an ape, we may learn the anatomy of a man; that, taking another animal, we always find the same fund of organization, the same senses, the same viscera, the same bones, the same flesh, the same motion of the fluids, the same play and action of the solids. In all of them he found a heart, veins, and arteries, and the same organs of circulation, respiration, digestion, nutrition, and secretion; in all of them he found a solid structure composed of the same pieces, and nearly situated in the same manner. This plan proceeds uniformly from man to the ape, from the ape to quadrupeds, from quadrupeds to cetaceous animals, to birds, to fishes, and to reptiles: this plan, I say, when well apprehended by the human intellect, exhibits a faithful picture of animated nature, and affords the most general, as well as the most simple view under which she can be considered: and, when we want to extend it, and to pass from the animal to the vegetable, we perceive this plan, which had at first varied only by shades, gradually degenerating from reptiles to insects, from insects to worms, from worms to zoophytes, from zoophytes to plants; and, though changed in all its external parts, still preserving the same character, the principal features of which are nutrition, growth, and reproduction. These features are common to all organized substances. They are eternal and divine; and, instead of being effaced by time, it only renews and renders them more conspicuous.

If, from this grand picture of resemblances exhibited in animated nature, as constituting but one family, we pass to that of the differences, where each species claims a separate apartment, and a distinct portrait, we shall find, that, with the exception of a few large kinds, such as the elephant, the rhinoceros, the hippopotamus, the tiger, and the lion, which ought to have particular frames, all the others seem to unite with their neighbours, and to form groups of degraded similarities, or genera, represented by our nomenclators in a net-work of figures, some of which are supported by the feet, others by the teeth, by the hair, and others by relations still more minute: and even the apes, whose form seems to be most perfect, or approaches nearest to that of man, present themselves in a group, and require the utmost attention to be distinguished from each other; because the privilege of separate species depends less on figure than magnitude; and man himself, though a distinct species, and infinitely removed from that of all other animals, being only of a middle size, has a greater number of neighbouring species than the very large kinds. In the history of the orang-outang, we shall find, that, if figure alone be regarded, we might consider this animal as the first of apes, or the most imperfect of men; because, except the intellect, the orang-outang wants nothing that we possess, and, in his body, differs less from man than from the other animals which receive the denomination of *apes*.

Hence mind, reflection, and language, depend not on figure nor the organization of the body. These are endowments peculiar to man. The orang-outang, though he neither thinks nor speaks, has a body, members, senses, a brain, and a tongue, perfectly similar to those of a man: he counterfeits every human movement; but he performs no action that is characteristic of man. This imperfection is perhaps owing to want of education, or to an error in our judgment. You compare, it may be said, an ape in the woods with a man in polished society. But, in order to form a proper judgment of them, a savage man and an ape should be viewed together; for we have no just idea of man in a pure state of nature. The head covered with bristly hair, or with curled wool; the face veiled with a long beard; two crescents of hairs still grosser, by their length and prominency, contract the front, and not only obscure the eyes, but sink and round them like those of the brutes; the lips thick and protruded; the nose flat; the aspect wild and stupid; the ears, the body, and the members covered with hair; the breasts of the female long and flabby, and the skin of her belly hanging down as far as her knees; the children wallowing in filth, and crawling on their hands and feet; the father and mother sitting squat on their hams, both hideous, and besmeared with corrupted grease. This sketch, drawn from a savage Hottentot, is a flattering portrait; for the distance between man in a pure state of nature and a Hottentot, is greater than between a Hottentot and us. But, if we want to compare the ape to man, we must add the relations of organization, the conformities of temperament, the vehement appetite of the males for the females, the same structure of genitals in both sexes, the periodic courses of the female, the voluntary or forced intermixture of the Negresses with the apes, the produce of which has entered into both species; and then consider, on the supposition that they are not the same, how difficult it is to perceive the interval by which they are separated.

If our judgment were limited to figure alone, I acknowledge that the ape might be regarded as a variety of the human species. The Creator has not formed man's body on a model absolutely different from that of the mere animal. He has comprehended the figure of man, as well as that of all other animals, under one general plan. But, at the same time that he has given him a material form similar to that of the ape, he has penetrated this animal body with a divine spirit. If he had conferred the same privilege, not on the ape, but on the meanest, and what appears to us to be the worst constructed animal, this species would soon have become the rival of man; it would have excelled all the other animals by thinking and speaking. Whatever resem-

blance, therefore, takes place between the Hottentot and the ape, the interval which separates them is immense; because the former is endowed with the faculties of thought and of speech.

Who will ever be able to ascertain how the organization of an idiot differs from that of another man? Yet the defect is certainly in the material organs, since the idiot is likewise endowed with a soul. Now, as between one man and another, where the whole structure is perfectly similar, a difference so small that it cannot be perceived is sufficient to prevent thought, we should not be surprised that it never appears in the ape, who is deprived of the necessary principle.

The soul, in general, has a proper action totally independent of matter. But, as its Divine Author has been pleased to unite it to the body, the exercise of its particular acts depends on the state of the material organs. This dependence is apparent, not only from the case of idiots, but from people affected with delirium, from sleep, from new-born infants, who cannot think, and from very old men, whom the power of thinking has forsaken. It is even probable, that the chief effect of education consists not so much in instructing the mind, or maturing its operations, as in modifying the material organs, and bringing them into the most favourable state for the exercise of the sentient principle. Now, there are two kinds of education, which ought to be carefully distinguished, because their effects are extremely different; the education of the individual, which is common to man and the other animals; and the education of the species, which appertains to man alone. A young animal, both from natural incitements and from example, learns, in a few weeks, to do every thing its parents can perform. To an infant, several years are necessary before it acquires this degree of perfection; because, when brought forth, it is incomparably less advanced, weaker, and more imperfectly formed, than the smaller animals. In early infancy, the mind is nothing, when compared to the powers it will afterwards acquire. In receiving individual education, therefore, the infant is much slower than the brute; but, for this very reason, it becomes susceptible of that of the species. The multiplicity of succours, the continual cares, which the state of imbecility for a long time requires, cherish and augment the attachment of the parents. In training the body, they cultivate the mind. The time employed in strengthening the former gives an advantage to the latter. The bodily powers of most animals are more advanced in two months than those of the infant in two years. Hence the time employed in bestowing on the infant its individual education, is as twelve to one, without estimating the fruits of what follows after this period, without considering that animals separate from their parents as soon as they can provide for themselves, and that, not long after this separation, they know each other no more. All

education ceases the moment that the aid of the parents becomes unnecessary. This time of education being so short, its effects must be very limited: it is even astonishing that the animals acquire, in two months, all that is necessary for them during the rest of life: if we suppose that a child, in an equal period, were strong enough to quit his parents, and never return to them, would there be any perceptible difference between this infant and a brute? However ingenious the parents, they would not have time sufficient to modify and prepare his organs, or to establish the smallest communication of thought between their minds and his. They could not excite his memory by impressions frequently enough reiterated. They could not even mollify or unfold the organs of speech. Before a child can pronounce a single word, his ears must be struck many thousand times with the same sound; and, before he can make a proper application of it, the same combination of the word and the object to which it relates, must be many thousand times presented to him. Education, therefore, which alone can develope the powers of the mind, must be uninterruptedly continued for a long time. If stopt, not at two months, as in the animals, but even at the age of one year, the mind of the infant, having received no instruction, would remain inactive like that of the idiot, the defect of whose organs prevents the reception of knowledge. This reasoning would acquire redoubled strength, if the infant were born in a pure state of nature, if it were confined to the sole tutorage of a Hottentot mother, and were enabled by its bodily powers to separate from her at the age of two months. Would it not sink below the condition of an idiot, and, with regard to its material part, be entirely levelled with the brutes? But in this condition of nature, the first education requires an equal time as in the civilized state; for, in both, the infant is equally feeble, and equally slow in its growth; and, consequently, demands the care of its parents during an equal period. In a word, if abandoned before the age of three years, it would infallibly perish. Now, this necessary, and so long continued intercourse between the mother and child, is sufficient to communicate to it all that she possesses: and though we should falsely suppose that a mother, in a state of nature, possesses nothing, not even the faculty of speech, would not this long intercourse with her infant produce a language? Hence a state of pure nature, in which man is supposed neither to think nor speak, is imaginary, and never had an existence. This necessity of a long intercourse between parents and children produces society in the midst of a desert. The family understand each other both by signs and sounds; and this first ray of intelligence, when cherished, cultivated, and communicated, unfolds, in process of time, all the germs of cogitation. As this habitual intercourse could not subsist so long,

without producing mutual signs and sounds, these signs and sounds, always repeated and gradually engraven on the memory of the child, would become permanent expressions. The catalogue of words, though short, forms a language which will soon extend as the family augments, and will always follow, in its improvement, the progress of society. As soon as society begins to be formed, the education of the infant is no longer individual, since the parents communicate to it not only what they derive from Nature, but likewise what they have received from their progenitors, and from the society to which they belong. It is no longer a communication between detached individuals, which, as in the animals, would be limited to the transmission of simple faculties, but an institution of which the whole species participate, and whose produce constitutes the basis and bond of society.

Even among brute animals, though deprived of the sentient principle, those whose education is longest, appear to have most intelligence. The elephant, which takes the longest time in acquiring its full growth, and requires the succour of its mother during the whole first year of its existence, is also the most intelligent of all animals. The Guinea-pig, which is full grown, and capable of generating at the age of three weeks, is, for this reason alone, perhaps one of the most stupid species. With regard to the ape, whose nature we are endeavouring to ascertain, however similar to man, he is so strongly marked with the features of brutality, that it is distinguishable from the moment of his birth. He is then proportionally stronger and better formed than the infant: he grows faster: the support of his mother is necessary for a few months only: his education is purely individual, and, consequently, as limited as that of the other animals.

Hence the ape, notwithstanding his resemblance to man, is a brute, and, instead of approaching our species, holds not the first rank among the animals; because he is by no means the most intelligent. The relation of corporeal resemblance alone has given rise to the prejudice in favour of the great faculties of the ape. He resembles man, it has been said, both externally and internally; and, therefore, he must not only imitate us, but do every thing which we perform. We have seen, that all the actions which ought to be denominated *human,* are relative to society; that they depend, at first, on the mind, and afterwards on education, the physical principle of which is the long intercourse that necessarily subsists between the parents and children; that, in the ape, this intercourse is very short; that, like the other animals, he receives only an individual education; and that he is not susceptible of that of the species. Of course, he can perform no human actions, since no action of the ape has the same principle, or the same design. With regard to imitation, which appears to be the most striking character of the ape kind, and which

the vulgar have attributed to him as a peculiar talent, before we decide, it is necessary to inquire whether this imitation be spontaneous or forced. Does the ape imitate us from inclination, or because, without any exertion of the will, he feels the capacity of doing it? I appeal to all those who have examined this animal without prejudice, and I am convinced that they will agree with me, that there is nothing voluntary in this imitation. The ape, having arms and hands, uses them, as we do, but without thinking of us. The similarity of his members and organs necessarily produces movements, and sometimes successions of movements, which resemble ours. Being endowed with the human structure, the ape must move like man. But the same motions imply not that he acts from imitation. Two bodies which receive the same impulse, two similar pendulums or machines, will move in the same manner. But these bodies or machines can never be said to imitate each other in their motions. The ape and the human body are two machines similarly constructed, and necessarily move nearly in the same manner. But parity is not imitation. The one depends on matter, and the other on mind. Imitation presupposes the design of imitating. The ape is incapable of forming this design, which requires a train of thinking; and, consequently, man, if he inclines, can imitate the ape; but the ape cannot even incline to imitate man.

This parity is only the physical

part of imitation, and by no means so complete as the similitude, from which, however, it proceeds as an immediate effect. The ape has a greater resemblance to us in his body and members, than in the use he makes of them. By observing him attentively, we easily perceive, that all his movements are brisk, intermittent, and precipitous; and that, in order to compare them with those of man, we must adopt another scale, or rather a different model. All the actions of the ape are derived from his education, which is purely animal. To us they appear ridiculous, inconsequent, and extravagant; because, by referring them to our own, we assume a false scale, and a deceitful mode of measuring. As his nature is vivacious, his temperament warm, his dispositions petulant, and none of his affections have been softened or restrained by education, all his habitudes are excessive, and resemble more the movements of a maniac than the actions of a man, or even of a peaceable animal. It is for this reason that we find him indocile, and that he receives with difficulty the impressions we wish to make on him. He is insensible to caresses, and is rendered obedient by chastisement alone. He may be kept in captivity, but not in a domestic state. Always melancholy, stubborn, repugnant, or making grimaces, he may be said to be rather conquered than tamed. The species, of course, have never been rendered domestic in any part of the world, and, consequently, is farther removed from man than

most other animals: for docility implies some analogy between the giver and the receiver of instruction. It is a relative quality, which cannot be exerted but when there is a certain number of common faculties on both sides, that differ only between themselves, because they are active in the master and passive in the scholar. Now, the passive qualities of the ape have less relation to the active qualities of man than those of the dog or elephant, who require no more than good treatment to communicate to them the delicate and gentle sensations of faithful attachment, voluntary obedience, grateful service, and unreserved devotion.

In relative qualities, therefore, the ape is farther removed from the human race than most other animals. His temperament is also very different. Man can inhabit every climate. He lives and multiplies in the northern as well as the southern regions of the earth. But the ape exists with difficulty in temperate countries, and can multiply only in those which are warm. This difference of temperament implies others in organization, which, though concealed, are not the less real: it must likewise have a great influence on his natural dispositions. The excess of heat, which is necessary to the constitution and vigour of this animal, renders all his qualities and affections inordinate. No other cause is requisite to account for his petulance, his salaciousness, and his other passions, which appear to be equally violent and disorderly.

Thus the ape, which philosophers,

as well as the vulgar, have regarded as a being difficult to define, and whose nature was at least equivocal, and intermediate between that of man and the animals, is, in fact, nothing but a real brute, endowed with the external mark of humanity, but deprived of thought, and of every faculty which properly constitutes the human species; a brute inferior to many others in his relative powers, and still more essentially different from the human race by his nature, his temperament, and the time necessary to his education, gestation, growth, and duration of life; that is, by all the real habitudes which constitute what is called *Nature* in a particular being.

Order I: Bimanus. Order II: Quadrumana

Johann Friedrich Blumenbach
1779, 1780

Order I.—*Bimanus*

1. Homo.
   Erectus bimanus.
   Mentum prominulum.
   Dentes æqualiter approximati; incisores inferiores erecti.

Species 1.—Sapiens. Man.[1] Among the external characters by which Man is distinguished, not only from animals in general, but from the Apes which most closely resemble him, are the power of *walking erect* (for which his whole form, but particularly the basin-like shape of his hip-bones, the relative proportion of his thighs and arms, and the wide soles of his feet, are calculated); the facility with which he uses two *perfect hands;* and the prominence of his chin, with the perpendicular direction of the lower incisor teeth.

The female, beside the peculiar form of the bosom in the bloom of life, possesses two other characters of distinction from the male, and all other animals, viz. a periodical

[1] See Lawrence's *Lectures on the Natural History of Man.* London, 1819. 8vo. with 12 plates.

"Order I: Bimanus. II: Quadrumana." *A Manual of the Elements of Natural History.* Translated by R.T. Gore. Section 4, pp. 34–42. W. Simpkin and R. Marshall, London, 1825. "I. Ordn. Bimanus. II. Quadrumana." *Handbuch der Naturgeschichte.* Dietrich, Göttingen, 1779, 1780.

discharge of blood during a certain number of years; and a particular part in the sexual organs, the absence or destruction of which forms a physical sign of loss of virginity, and which, at least as far as regards its form and position, has not been remarked in any other animal.

As to the mental faculties of man, excepting the sexual propensity, he presents few traces of instinct, and of the mechanical kind none. On the other hand, he is exclusively in possession of reason, and of speech, which he has invented, and which must not be confounded with the voice, existing from birth, and even in those born dumb. From these two exclusive privileges is derived the peculiar perfectibility by which he is elevated above the rest of the animal creation.

Man is, in himself, a defenceless, helpless, creature. No other animal continues so long in a state of infancy; no other is so long before it obtains its teeth; no other is so long before it can stand; no other arrives so late at puberty. Even his greatest advantages, Reason and Speech, are but germs, developed, not spontaneously, but by external assistance, cultivation, and education. This necessity of assistance, and his numerous urgent wants, prove the natural destination of man for *social connexion*. On the contrary, it is not so easy at once to decide, whether the proportion in all parts of the world of the number of males to females born, and the relative proportion of the periods during which both sexes are capable of propagating the species, be such as to render

it certain that man is destined elsewhere for monogamy, as well as in Europe.

His residence and his diet are both unrestricted; he inhabits the whole habitable earth, and feeds upon the varied materials derived from the organized creation. Relatively to his moderate bulk, and in comparison with other mammifera, he reaches a very advanced age.

There is but one species of the genus Man; and all people of every time and every climate with which we are acquainted, may have originated from one common stock.[2] All national differences in the form and colour of the human body are not more remarkable nor more inconceivable than those by which varieties of so many other organized bodies, and particularly of domestic animals, arise, as it were, under our eyes. All these differences too, run so insensibly, by so many shades and transitions one into the other, that it is impossible to separate them by any but very arbitrary limits. I conceive, however, that the whole human species may be most conveniently divided into the following five *Races*[3]:

1. THE CAUCASIAN RACE

(*Abbild. Nat. Hist. Gegenst. Tab. 3 and 51.*) Colour more or less

[2] I have spoken of this subject in my Treatise *de Generis Humani Varietate Nativâ*. 3d Edition.

[3] Compare the Charts of the World, coloured according to this division, in the 1st Vol. of *Archivs für Ethnographie und Linguistick*. Von J.F. Bertuch und J.S. Vater.

white, with florid cheeks; hair long, soft, and brown (running on the one hand into white, on the other into black); according to the European ideas of beauty, the form of the face and skull most perfect. It includes all the Europeans, with the exception of the Laplanders; the western Asiatics on this side of the Ob, the Caspian Sea, and the Ganges; lastly, the northern Africans; altogether the inhabitants of the world known by the ancient Grecians and Romans.

2. THE MONGOLIAN RACE

(*Abbild. Nat. Hist. Gegenst. Tab. 1.*) Mostly of a pale yellow (sometimes like a boiled quince, or dried lemon peel); with scanty, harsh, black hair; with half closed, and apparently tumid eyelids; a flat face, and lateral projections of the cheek bones. This race includes the remaining Asiatics, excepting the Malays; in Europe, the Laplanders; and, in North America, the Esquimaux, extending from Behring's Strait to Labrador.

3. THE ETHIOPIAN RACE

(*Abbild. Nat. Hist. Gegenst. Tab. 5.*) Black in a greater or less degree; with black frizzly hair; jaw projecting forwards; thick lips and flat nose. Composed of the remaining Africans, viz. the Negroes who pass into the Moors by means of the Foulahs, in the same manner as other varieties merge into one another in consequence of their intercourse with a neighbouring people.

4. THE AMERICAN RACE

(*Abbild. Nat. Hist. Gegenst. Tab. 2.*) Mostly tan colour or cinnamon brown (sometimes like rust of iron or tarnished copper); with straight, coarse, black hair; with a wide, though not a flat face, and strongly marked features. Comprises all the Americans, except the Esquimaux.

5. THE MALAYAN RACE

(*Abbild. Nat. Hist. Gegenst. Tab. 4.*) Of a brown colour, from a clear mahogany to the darkest clove or chesnut brown; with thick, black, bushy hair, a broad nose, and wide mouth. To this class belong the South Sea Islanders, or inhabitants of the fifth part of the world; of the Marianne, Philippine, Molucca, and Sunda Isles, &c., with the true Malays.[4]

The Caucasian must, on every physiological principle, be considered as the primary or intermediate of these five principal Races. The two extremes into which it has deviated, are on the one hand the Mongolian, on the other the Ethiopian. The other two Races form transitions between them; the Amer-

[4] "Each of these five Races includes two kinds of people, which are more or less strikingly distinguished by their form. Thus, for instance, the Hindoos may be considered as a subdivision or secondary Race, distinct from the Caucasian; the Chinese and Japanese from the Mongolian; the Hottentots from the Ethiopian; the North Americans from those in the Southern part of the New World; and the black Papoos of New Holland, &c. from the brown Otaheitans and other Islanders of the Pacific Ocean." *Beytr. zur Natur. Geschichte,* 1 Th. p. 72 of the 2d Edition.

ican between the Caucasian and Mongolian; and the Malayan between the Caucasian and Ethiopian.[5]

It is unnecessary to recount all the fabulous imaginations with which the Natural History of the human species has been burdened; to notice a few however:—The supposed Patagonian giants have sunk in the relations of travellers, from Magellan's times down to our own, from twelve feet to seven and a half, and at last are but little taller than any other men of good stature.

It is also rendered more than probable by pathological considerations, that the *Quimos of* Madagascar, set forth by Commerson as a nation of pygmies, are nothing else than a kind of cretins, or idiots, with big heads and long arms, such as are met with in the district of Salzburgh, in the Pays du Vaud, and in Piedmont.

So also the Albinoes, Kackerlacken, or white Ethiopians,[6] are not even a variety, much less a species; but rather specimens of disease, coming more within the range of Pathology than of Natural History.

The homo *troglodytes* of Linnæus, is an incomprehensible combination of the history of the Albino resulting from disease, and of the Ourangoutang: his homo *lar,* on the contrary, is a true Ape.

The children[7] who have lived in a savage state among brutes are wretched monsters in intellect, which can no more be considered as perfect specimens of the master-piece of the Creation, than other men disfigured by accident or disease.

The fables of men with tails, of the natural apron of the Hottentot women, of the supposed natural deficiency of beard in the Americans,[8] Syrens, Centaurs, and others of the

---

[5] It is allowable to suppose that the people dispersed through the various parts of the world have, according to the differences in the degree and duration of the influence of climate and other causes of degeneration, either deviated still more from the form of the primary race, or approximated more closely to it. Thus, for example, the Jakuts, Koraks, Esquimaux, and other nations of the Mongolian Race, have deviated considerably from the Caucasian Race; whilst on the other hand, the American, placed at a greater distance, but in a milder climate, has in an equal degree approximated; and it is only at the Southern extremity of the Continent, in the frozen Tierra del Fuego, that it again recedes to the Mongolian. So also the Ethiopian Race has passed to the extreme of variation in the burning regions of Africa, but passes into the Malayan in the milder climate of New Holland, the New Hebrides, &c. It is unnecessary to point out the influence of the mixture of different Races, which accidentally come in contact with each other in their emigrations.

[6] These white Ethiopians, or Negroes as they are called, must be distinguished from the *Negroes spotted white*. One of these whom I saw in London, and a specimen of whose black and white wooly hair I possess, is represented in my *Abbild. Nat. Hist. Gegenst.* Tab. 21. from the life.

[7] I have treated of this matter more fully in my *Beytr. zur Natur. Geschichte,* 2 Th. p. 13, 14.

[8] I have admitted a difference in the strength of the growth of hair in the Mongolian and Malayan Races; but the want of beard in many American nations is artificial, as much as the small feet of the Chinese women, (the Struthopodes of the Eudoxus of Pliny.).

same stamp, can only be excused by the simple easy credulity of our ancestors.

II. Quadrumana

Mammifera with four hands, which are required by their mode of life and residence in trees. They are originally natives only of the countries between the Tropics— (*Histoire Naturelle des Singes, peints d'après Nature*, par J. D. Audebert. Paris, 1797. Gr. fol.)

2. Simia.—Ape. *Ger.* Affe. *Fr.* Singe.
Habitus plus minus anthropomorphus, auriculæ et manus fere humanæ, nares anteriores.
Dentes *primores* incisores, supra et infra 4; *laniarii* solitarii, reliquis longiores.

Confined to the Old World; more nearly approaching to man than the animals of the succeeding genera, but easily distinguished from him, not only by the characters already pointed out, but also by the entire form, and particularly by the flatness of the loins and smallness of the hips.

(*a.*) WITHOUT TAILS

1. Satyrus. The Ourang-outang.— S. rufa, pilis longis raris, capite globoso, fronte tumida, auriculis minoribus.
(*Abbild. Nat. Hist. Gegenst. Tab. 12. and 22.*) Confined apparently to the island of Borneo, and even there

in small number;[9] when taken young it can, as well as the chimpansé and other apes, be taught to perform a variety of actions, which however must not be confounded with its natural habits.

As Camper has proved by dissection, it is not capable either of speech or of walking naturally in an upright posture.

2. Troglodytes. The Chimpansé. —S. nigra, macrocephala, torosa, auriculus magnis.
(*Abbild. Nat. Hist. Gegenst. Tab. 11.*) In the interior of Angola, Congo, &c., like the preceding species, about the size of a child of three years.

3. Lar. The Gibbon. (Homo *Lar* of Linnæus.)—S. brachiis longissimis, talos attingentibus.
(*Schreber. Tab. 3.*) In both the Indian Peninsulas, and in the Moluccas: has a round face tolerably like that of man, with very long arms, and is of a black colour.

4. Sylvanus. The Barbary Ape.— S. brachiis corpore brevioribus, natibus calvis, capite subrotundo.
(*Schreber. Tab. 4.*) In North Africa, the East Indies, &c., the strongest and the most common of all the tail-less apes; it also readily breeds in Europe, and is very docile. Scarcely different from the *Inuus*, (Buffon's *Magot*). It has become wild at Gibraltar, and breeds there in a state of freedom.

9 Consequently a very small species; whilst the human, on the contrary, amounting to about a thousand millions, is certainly the largest among mammiferous animals.

(b.) WITH TAILS

5. *Rostrata. The long-nosed Ape. Ger. der langnasige. Affe. Fr. la Guenon à long nez.—S. cauda mediocri, naso elongato, rostrato.*

(*Abbild. Nat. Hist. Gegenst. Tab. 13.*) From the Sunda Isles. It is *simia,* but not *sima;* being remarkable for its long proboscis-like nose.

6. *Silenus. The Wanderow. Ger. der Bartaffe.—S. caudata, barbata, nigra, barba incana prolixa.*

(*Schreber. Tab. 11.*) From Ceylon, &c.: old and scarcely recognizable representations[10] of this ape have been transformed by the embellishments of subsequent copyists[11] into the supposed men with tails.

7. *Cynomolgus. The Macaco. Ger. die (insgemein so gennante,) Meerkatze. Fr. le Macacque.—S. cauda longa, arcuata, naribus bifidis elatis.*

(*Schreber. Tab. 12.*) From Guinea, Angola, &c.: nearly olive green. Of true Apes with tails, that which is most frequently brought to Europe.

3. Papio.—Baboon. *Ger.* Pavian. *Fr.* Babouin.—Facies prolongata, minus anthropomorpha, nasus utrinque tuberosus, nates nudæ, coccineæ, cauda *(plerisque)*[12] abbreviata. Dentes ut in simiis.

Also confined to the Old World. The head has little resemblance to that of man; on the contrary, in many is more like that of the hog, particularly in the snout. In general, they are very untameable and lascivious.

1. *Hamadryas. (Cynocephalus.) Ger. der Hundskopf. Fr. le Tartarin. —P. cinereus, auriculis comosis, unguibus acutiusculis.*

(*Schreber. Tab. 10.*) In Egypt and Africa to the Cape of Good Hope. It is often represented in the hieroglyphics of the ancient Egyptians.[13]

2. *Mormon. The ribbed faced Baboon. Ger. der Choras.—P. naso miniato ad latera cærulescente.*

(*Schreber. Tab. 8 A. 8 B.*) From Ceylon, &c.: is near five feet high; has a singular appearance, from the bright coloured streaks upon and at the sides of the nose.

3. *Maimon. The Mandrill.—P. facie violacea, glabra, profunde sulcata.*

(*Schreber. Tab. 7.*) From Guinea, the Cape, &c., where whole droves of them often plunder the vineyards and orchards; much smaller than the preceding species.

4. Cercopithecus.—Monkey. *Ger.* Meerkatze

Auriculæ et manus humanæ.

Nares laterales.

Nates tectæ.

Dentes ut in simiis.

The whole genus is confined to the warmer parts of South America, where the Indians commonly use it as game.

---

[10] Originally in Bernh. Von Breydenbach *Reyss in das gelobt Land.* Mainz, 1486. folio.

[11] For instance, in Vol. VI. of Martini's *Translation* of Buffon.

[12] For the formidable baboon of Borneo (papio *pongo*) is tail-less, whilst the cynocephalus may be said to be long-tailed.

[13] See the *Rouleau de Papyrus* publiée par Cadet, 1805.

(*a*) CAUDA PREHENSILI—
SAPAJOUS.

1. Seniculus. Ger. der rothe Brül-laffe. Fr. l'Alouate.—C. barbatus rufus, gutture tumido.
(*Abbild. Nat. Hist. Gegenst. Tab. 91.*) In troops in the great forests of Guiana, &c., where it, together with another species, (Cereop. *Belzebub.*) emits a deafening noise, principally on change of weather, and which is produced by a remarkable bony cavity in the larynx, placed between the unusually large lateral portions of the lower jaw.

2. Paniscus. The Coaita.—C. ater, palmis tetradactylis, absque pollice.
(*Schreber. Tab. 26 A. 26 B.*) Extremely dexterous in the use of its long prehensile tail.[14]

(*b*) CAUDA NON PREHENSILI—
SAGOUINS.

3. Jacchus. The Ouistiti. Ger. Uistiti.—C. juba pilosa alba ad genas ante aures, cauda villosa annulata.

(*Schreber. Tab. 33.*) Brown, and so small that it will fit in the shell of a cocoa nut.

5. Lemur.—Makis.
Nasus acutus, dentes *primores* superiores 4; per paria remoti; inferiores 4–6, porrecti, compressi, incumbentes: *laniarii* solitarii, approximati.[15]

1. Tardigradus. The Lori.—L. ecaudatus.
(*Schreber. Tab. 38.*) From Ceylon; of the size and colour of a squirrel; with slender legs, and together with the next species, has a pointed claw on the index toe of the hinder foot, but on all the other toes a flat nail.

2. Mongoz. The Mongoz.—L. facie nigra, corpore et cauda griseis.
(*Schreber. Tab. 39 A. 39 B.*) Together with some similar species in Madagascar and the neighbouring isles. The hinder are much longer than the fore feet. Its skin, like that of many apes, has a peculiar smell, nearly resembling that of an ant hill.

---

14 The singular manner in which they hang together, so as to form a chain, for the purpose of swinging themselves from one tree to another on the opposite banks of a river, is represented in the original edition of Ant. de Ulloa's

Viage, &c. Madrid, 1748. fol. Vol. I. p. 144–49.
15 Gotth. Fischer's *Anatomie der Makic.* 1 B. Frankf. 1804. 4to. with plates.

Of the Several Steps of the Human Progression from the Brute to the Man

James Burnett, Lord Monboddo
1779–1799

Of the several steps of the human progression from the brute to the man

The subject of this chapter will be to mark some of the first steps of this wonderful progression of man. Of these I have seen with mine own eyes three, which I believe is what very few now living can say. The first I saw, was in the pure natural state when he was catched in the woods of Hanover, walking on all four. It was Peter the Wild Boy, as he was called, whom I have mentioned above. I saw him twice, and I had a very particular account of him from an Oxford gentleman, who, at my desire, went to see him; which account I have published.[1] He had learned to articulate but few words, though he was put to school, and no doubt a great deal of pains bestowed to teach him to

[1] Vol. III. p. 368. See also p. 58 of the same volume, where I have given the accounts of him that were published in the newspapers, immediately after he was brought to England.

speak. But this we should not wonder at, when we consider what trouble it requires to teach deaf men to speak, though born and brought up among us. Of his being a man, there never was the least doubt entertained; and that he was not an idiot, or defective in natural capacity, I think is evident from the several accounts of him which I have published in the passages above quoted. And indeed, from what I saw of him myself, I think I can attest, that he had as much understanding as could be expected in a man who had learned none of our arts, not even the use of his own body so as to walk erect, till he was 15 years of age; for till then he was a quadruped.

The next step of this progression is the Ourang Outang, or *Man of the Woods,* as the name imports, by which he is called by the people of Africa, where he is to be seen, and who do not appear to have the least doubt that he is a man; which, as they live in the country with him, they should know better than we

"Of the Several Steps of the Human Progression from the Brute to the Man, Etc." *Ancient Metaphysics: or the Science of Universals.* Book 1, Chapter 2, pp. 25–34. J. Balfour and Company, Edinburgh, 1779–1799.

can do. Two of them I saw in London some years ago, and one of them I could have purchased for £. 50; which money, poor as I am, I would have given for him, and been at the expence of his education, if I had not been convinced, not only that *he* was a man, but that it was of absolute necessity that, in the progress of the human species, man should at some time or another be such an animal: For, if he was originally a quadruped, as I think I have proved by facts incontestible, with only a natural aptitude, more than any other animal, to walk on two, as Aristotle has said, the first step in his progression was to become a biped, to which, by nature, he was so much adapted. I will not here repeat what I have elsewhere said at so great length, in proof of the humanity of the Ourang Outang,[2] where I think I have demonstrated that he is a man, both in mind and body, and

particularly as to his mind, by which, as I have observed, Aristotle has chiefly distinguished animals: For I have shown that he has the sense of what is decent and becoming,[3] which is peculiar to man, and distinguishes him from the brute as much as any thing else. And he has a sense of honour, which is really surprising, and such as is not to be found in many men among us; for he cannot bear to be exposed as a show, nor to be laughed at; and travellers mention examples of some of them having died of vexation, for being so treated.[4] He has also the feeling of humanity in a strong degree; and a sense of justice, as is evident, from a remarkable example given.[5] Further, he has made some progress in the arts of life; for he builds huts,[6] and he has got the use of a stick for attacking or defending, which, as Horace observes,[7] was the first artificial weapon man used, after he had ceased to use his native weapons, his nails and fists. He has learned also the use of fire,[8] which is more than the inhabitants of the Ladrone Islands had learned, when they were discovered by the Portuguese; and lastly, he buries his dead.[9]

---

[2] See chap. 4th of book 2d of vol. I. of the Origin of Language, 2d edition, and particularly p. 289. of that chapter, where I have summed up the evidence of his being a man: In which there is one circumstance deserving particular notice, that he carries off negro boys and girls to make servants of them, and keeps them for years, using them with great gentleness and humanity; a thing of which we cannot conceive any brute animal capable. See also what I have said in the Appendix to vol. III of this work, and particularly what I have there stated from a French Book of Travels, lately published, where there is a fact related, p. 360. which, if true, puts an end to the question, viz. that the Ourang Outang not only copulates with females of our species, and produces children, but that the offspring of that copulation does likewise produce.

[3] Vol. I. of Origin of Language, 2d edit. p. 273. 279. and 291. From which passages, it appears, that both the males and females there mentioned had a sense of modesty, which made them conceal their nudities.

[4] Ibid. p. 282.–284.

[5] Ibid. p. 204.–288.

[6] Ibid. p. 274.–277.–283.

[7] *Sermonum,* lib. 1. Sat. 3.

[8] Origin of Language, p. 285.

[9] Ibid. p. 274.

Thus I have proved, that the Ourang Outang is not only a man, with respect to his body, but also in mind, the principal part of man and of all other animals. As the reader, however, may be desirous to know still more of this wonderful phenomenon of human nature I will add here some information concerning him, which I have lately received from a gentleman of the name of Begg, who was captain of a Liverpool ship, employed in the slave trade on the coast of Africa. He was promised, he told me, a handsome reward, if he could bring home an Ourang Outang from Angola, where he saw herds of them, and was at great pains, with the assistance of his crew, to get hold of one of them; but to no purpose. He therefore resolved, that as he could get none of them alive, he would try to get one or more of them dead: And accordingly he fired upon them, and killed some of them, which I am persuaded he would not have done, if he had been as fully convinced, as I am, that they were of the human species. But in this, too, he was likewise disappointed; for, before he and his crew could get to the place where they fell, they were carried off by their companions, for the purpose, as he supposes, of burying them, which, we are informed by others, they practice.[10]

I have corresponded with this gentleman likewise by letters, in one of which he says, that

10 Vol. I. of Origin of Language, p. 274.

In a voyage to Old Callabar in Africa, I purchased a female Ourang Outang from one of the natives. She was, as I was informed, about eight months old, four foot fix inches high, of a dark brown colour, but white about the breasts; of a gentle disposition, walked generally upright on her hind feet, sometimes on all four; but the latter seemed to me not to be her natural motion. Palm nuts, roots, and subacid fruits were her favourite food. She would not eat beef or any animal substance. Water, and wine drawn from the palm tree (very much esteemed by the natives), were her constant drink. She would often drink a tumbler glass of wine and water, and always put the glass softly down on its bottom, and never broke one. She was very fond of the girls and boys, but more particularly of the latter, and would weep and cry like a child when she was vexed; but never shewed any signs of great ferocity, and was easily appeased. I gave her a blanket for a bed, which she would take great pains to spread in such a manner as to make it smooth and easy, and then would lie down. She always slept with her hands (if I may use the expression) under her head, and would snore when asleep, resembling the human species. She lived three months, and died of the dysentery.

The following is the information I have been able to collect from the inhabitants of Africa, where I have been, on whose veracity we cannot altogether depend; but having compared different accounts, I always found them in a great measure to correspond.

That they have been seen in separate great bodies, attacking each other with sticks with great animosity. That they generally build their nests or houses together in great numbers, a single

Ourang Outang being but seldom or never seen separately. That they often have been known to beat and bruise the negroes, and even to kill them, when fired at by them. That the common size of an Ourang Outang is from five and half to six feet. That they have great strength in their arms, and run with great agility. That they have a kind of chattering guttural noise they make, but whether they can communicate their ideas or not to each other, I cannot say; but it is the received opinion among the natives that they can. That dead Ourang Outangs have been found covered with leaves of trees, but whether from accident or design could not be ascertained. This is what Information I could acquire from the negroes; but I can by no means vouch for the truth of any part of it. What I say from my own observation you may depend on for fact.

From this account of Mr Begg, it is evident that they are so far advanced towards the political life, as to herd together, and to communicate together, by a chattering guttural noise, which, I am persuaded, led the way among all people to articulation and the use of speech. And the Bristol merchant, with whom I have corresponded, and whose communications I have mentioned in the 1st volume of the Origin and Progress of Language,[11] says, that he heard that they were so far advanced in the political life, as to have a king or governor.[12] It appears also, from Mr Begg's account, that they have so much of the social spirit in them, and

are so much attached to their herd, as not to neglect them even when they are dead, but to carry off their bodies for burial.

This animal, it is to be observed, lives entirely upon the fruits of the earth; for the carnivorous diet I hold to be unnatural to man, and that he was first driven to it by necessity, which could not be the case of the Ourang Outang, who lives in a fruitful country, very thinly peopled. Further, he has not the use of water, except to drink it; for swimming or sailing, I hold to be likewise unnatural to man, and that it was also necessity that first drove him to it.

There is another observation I have to make, which is, that the Ourang Outang sometimes walks upon all four. And the Bristol merchant, above mentioned, says, that the smallest class of this species, called *Chimpenza* by the natives, walks oftener on all four, than upright.[13] And there is a French writer, La Brosse, who has made a collection of voyages in the South Seas, one of which gives an account of an island, where the people, though they be so far advanced in the arts of life, as to have the use of speech, yet walk sometimes upon *all four*. This, I think, shews very clearly, that originally they walked upon all four, as well as the Ourang Outang; and that they have not been very long from that primaeval state, any more than the Ourang Outang. These examples, I think, prove very clearly what I have laid down in

11 Page 281.
12 Ibid. p. 282.

13 Ibid. p. 282.

the preceding chapter, that man, in the first stage of his natural life, was a quadruped; so that it was very natural he should retain that way of walking, in the first stages of his civilized life.

This account I have given of the Ourang Outang, agrees perfectly with the description which Horace gives us of man, in the first stage of his existence on this earth. I quoted it above, p. 27.; but I will give it here entire.

Cum prorepserunt primis animalia
  terris,
Mutum ac turpe pecus, glandem
  atque cubilia propter,
Unguibus et pugnis, dein fustibus,
  atque ita porro
Pugnabant armis, quae post
  fabricaverat usus:
Donec verba, quibus voces
  sensusque notarent,
Nominaque invenere: Dehinc
  absistere bello, &c.

This account of man, in his first state, applies so exactly to the Ourang Outang, that it may be said to be a description of him; for man is said first to creep, that is, to go upon all four, and then he is very properly denominated *mutum ac turpe pecus*. After that, he is erected, and gets the use of an artificial weapon, such as the Ourang Outang uses. Next, he invents rude and barbarous cries, which Mr Begg calls chattering guttural sounds, *quibus voces sensusque notarent,* that is, by which men communicated their sensations, appetites, and desires to one another. And, last of all, they formed ideas, and in-

vented words to express them, which Horace calls *nomina*. But this is a step in the progress towards the civilized life, which the Ourang Outang has not yet made. This history of man, I am persuaded, Horace learned from the philosophers with whom he conversed in Athens; and I hold it to have been the general opinion of the Greek philosophers at that time, and particularly of the Epicureans, who studied facts of natural history very much.[14] Of this sect Horace was, though not wholly addicted to it;

(Nullius addictus (as he says) jurare in verba magistri:)

but getting all the information he could from the other sects of philosophy.

There are, I know, many, who will think this progress of man, from a quadruped and an Ourang Outang to men such as we see them now a days, very disgraceful to the species. But they should consider their own progress as an individual. In the womb, man is no better than a vegetable; and, when born, he is at first more imperfect, I believe, than any other animal in the same state, wanting almost altogether that comparative faculty, which the brutes, young and old, possess. If, therefore, there be such a progress in

14 Epicrus was a diligent inquirer into facts of natural history, particularly concerning the progress of men in the invention of arts. And accordingly Lucretius tells us, that he discovered that men learned music from the singing of birds, which, as I shall presently shew, is confirmed by what I learned from the savage girl I saw in France.

the individual, it is not to be wondered that there should be a progress also in the species, from the mere animal up to the intellectual creature: But, on the contrary, I should think it not agreeable to that wonderful order and progression of things that we observe in nature, if it were otherwise; for the species, with respect to the genus, is to be considered as an individual.

The last step of this progression I likewise saw, and it was a great one. It was the wild girl, or *fille sauvage,* as the French called her, who came from a country where the people had learned to articulate very imperfectly indeed, but sufficiently to communicate their wants and desires. I saw her in Paris about 26 years ago, and conversed with her much, as she had been then in Paris for several years, and spoke French well enough. She was taken up by a French ship somewhere upon the coast of Labradore, and was carried to one of the West India islands, from whence she sailed in a ship, which was wrecked upon the coast of Flanders, and only she and a negro girl were saved. Her first appearance in France was at a village called Songe, near to Chalon in Champagne, whither I went to inquire about her. She was first seen there swimming a river, and coming out of it with a fish in her hand, which she had caught: For she told me, that in her country they lived like beavers, always near water, and caught the fish with their hands, by diving, as the people of the Ladrone Islands do. They were hunters, too; and she and the negro girl, in their journey from Flanders, subsisted on game, which they caught by speed of foot. She said, that in her country, besides language, they had a certain music, which they had formed in imitation of birds. But they had no use of fire, and in that, too, they resembled the people of the Ladrone Islands; and she told me, that, when she first came to France, a fire in a room was her terror and abhorrence; and the eating of flesh, dressed by fire, threw her into a very bad disease, of which she recovered with much difficulty. She was wonderfully swift of foot, and could overtake, in that way, almost any animal, and then knock it on the head with a bludgeon she wore, which she called a *boutou,* a name given, by the inhabitants of the Carribbee Islands, to a bludgeon; from which it appears she had been in one of those islands, in her way from America to France. She could climb a tree, too, like a squirrel, and leap from one tree to another; but all these bodily faculties, she told me, with much regret, she had lost at the time I saw her. Who would desire to know more of her, may read her life, published at Edinburgh in the year 1768, translated from the French by a clerk of mine, who was with me in France. The facts contained in the French work, I was assured, might be depended on, by M. la Condamine, who knew the lady that wrote it. In the preface prefixed to the translation, I have related several facts concerning her, which I learned from the girl herself: And if the reader be desirous to know still more concerning her, he may read a con-versation that. I had with her, which I have printed from a pocket book that I then kept in Paris, and have published in the appendix to this volume.

Degradation and Simplification of Organization from One Extremity to the Other of the Animal Chain, Proceeding from the Most Complex to the Simplest. Bimana

Jean Baptiste Pierre Antoine de Monet, Chevalier de Lamarck
1809

Degradation and simplification of organisation from one extremity to the other of the animal chain, proceeding from the most complex to the simplest

AMONG the problems of interest for zoological philosophy, one of the most important is that which concerns the degradation and simpli-fication observed in animal organi-sation on passing from one extreme to the other of the animal chain, from the most perfect animals to those whose organisations are the simplest.

Now the question arises wheth-er this is a fact that can be established; for, if so, it will greatly enlighten us as to nature's plan and will set us on the way to dis-cover some of her most important laws.

I here propose to prove that the fact in question is true, and that it is the result of a constant law of nature which always acts with uni-formity; but that a certain special and easily recognised cause produces variations now and again in the results which that law achieves throughout the animal chain.

We must first recognise that the general series of animals arranged according to their natural affinities is a series of special groups which result from the different systems of

"Degradation and Simplification of Organization from One Extremity to the Other of the Animal Chain, Proceeding from the Most Complex to the Simplest." "Bimana." *Zoological Philosophy.* Translated by H. Elliot. Chapter 6, pp. 68–72; Chapter 8, pp. 169–73. Macmillan and Company, London, 1914. Reprinted with permission from the publisher. "Dégradation et simpli-fication de l'organisation d'une extrémite à l'autre de la châine animale, en procédant du plus composé vers le plus simple." "Les Bimanes." *Philosophie Zoologiques.* Dentu, Paris, 1809.

organisation employed by nature; and that these groups are themselves arranged according to the decreasing complexity of organisation, so as to form a real chain.

We notice then that except for the anomalies, of which we shall ascertain the cause, there exists from one end to the other of this chain a striking degradation in the organisation of the animals composing it, and a proportionate diminution in the numbers of these animals' faculties. Thus if the most perfect animals are at one extremity of the chain, the opposite extremity will necessarily be occupied by the simplest and most imperfect animals found in nature.

This examination at length convinces us that all the special organs are progressively simplified from class to class, that they become altered, reduced and attenuated little by little, that they lose their local concentration if they are of the first importance, and that finally they are completely and definitely extinguished before the opposite end of the chain is reached.

As a matter of fact, the degradation of which I speak is not always gradual and regular in its progress, for often some organ disappears or changes abruptly, and these changes sometimes involve it in peculiar shapes not related with any other by recognisable steps.

Often again some organ disappears and re-appears several times before it is definitely extinguished. But we shall see that this could not have been otherwise; for the factor which brings about the progressive complexity of organisation must have had varied effects, owing to its liability to modification by a certain other factor acting with great power. We shall however see that the degradation in question is none the less real and progressive, wherever its effects can be seen.

If the factor which is incessantly working towards complicating organisation were the only one which had any influence on the shape and organs of animals, the growing complexity of organisation would everywhere be very regular. But it is not; nature is forced to submit her works to the influence of their environment, and this environment everywhere produces variations in them. This is the special factor which occasionally produces in the course of the degradation that we are about to exemplify, the often curious deviations that may be observed in the progression.

We shall attempt to set forth in full both the progressive degradation of animal organisation and the cause of the anomalies in the progress of that degradation, in the course of the animal series.

It is obvious that, if nature had given existence to none but aquatic animals and if all these animals had always lived in the same climate, the same kind of water, the same depth, etc., we should then no doubt have found a regular and even continuous gradation in the organisation of these animals.

But the power of nature is not confined within such limits.

It first has to be observed that even in the waters she has established considerable diversity of conditions: fresh-water, set water, still or stagnant water, running water the water of hot climates, of cold climates, and lastly shallow water and very deep water; these provide as many special conditions which each act differently on the animals living in them. Now the races of animals exposed to any of these conditions have undergone special influences from them and have been varied by them all the while that their complexity of organisation has been advancing.

After having produced aquatic animals of all ranks and having caused extensive variations in them by the different environments provided by the waters, nature led them little by little to the habit of living in the air, first by the water's edge and afterwards on all the dry parts of the globe. These animals have in course of time been profoundly altered by such novel conditions; which so greatly influenced their habits and organs that the regular gradation which they should have exhibited in complexity of organisation is often scarcely recognisable.

These results which I have long studied, and shall definitely prove, lead me to state the following zoological principle, the truth of which appears to me beyond question.

Progress in complexity of organisation exhibits anomalies here and there in the general series of animals, due to the influence of environment and of acquired habits.

An examination of these anoma-lies has led some to reject the obvious progress in complexity of animal organisation and to refuse to recognise the procedure of nature in the production of living bodies.

Nevertheless, in spite of the apparent digressions that I have just mentioned, the general plan of nature and the uniformity of her procedure, however much she varies her methods, are still quite easily distinguished. We have only to examine the general series of known animals and to consider it first in its totality and then in its larger groups; the most unequivocal proofs will then be perceived of the gradation which she has followed in complexity of organisation; a gradation which should never be lost sight of by reason of the aforementioned anomalies. Finally, it will be noticed that whenever there have been no extreme changes of conditions, that gradation is found to be perfectly regular in various portions of the general series to which we have given the name of families. This truth becomes still more striking in the study of species; for the more we observe, the more difficult, complicated and minute become our specific distinctions.

The gradation in complexity of animal organisation can no longer be called in doubt, when once we have given positive and detailed proof of what we have just stated. Now since we are taking the general series of animals in the opposite direction from nature's actual order when she brought them successively into existence, this gradation becomes for us a remarkable degradation which prevails from one end to the other of the animal chain, except for the gaps arising from objects which are not yet discovered and those which arise from anomalies caused by extreme environmental conditions.

Let us now cast an eye over the complexity and totality of the animal series, in order to establish positively the degradation of organisation from one extremity to the other; let us consider the facts presented and let us then pass rapidly in review the fourteen classes of which it is primarily composed.

The general arrangement of animals set forth above is unanimously accepted as a whole by zoologists: who dispute only as to the boundaries of certain classes. In examining it I notice a very obvious fact which would in itself be decisive for my purpose; it is as follows:

At one extremity of the series (that namely which we are accustomed to consider as the anterior) we find the animals that are most perfect from all points of view, and have the most complex organisation; while at the opposite extremity of the same series we find the most imperfect that exist in nature—those with the simplest organisation and to all appearances hardly endowed with animality.

This accepted fact, which indeed cannot be questioned, becomes the first proof of the degradation which I propose to establish; for it is a necessary condition of it.

Another fact brought forward by an examination of the general series of animals and furnishing a second proof of the degradation prevailing in their organisation from one extremity to the other of their chain, is the following:

The first four classes of the animal kingdom contain animals that are in general provided with a vertebral column, while the animals of all the other classes are absolutely destitute of it.

It is known that the vertebral column is the essential basis of the skeleton, which cannot exist without it; and that wherever there is a vertebral column there is a more or less complete and perfect skeleton.

It is also known that perfection of faculties is a proof of perfection of the organs on which they rest.

Now although man may be above his rank on account of the extreme superiority of his intelligence as compared with his organisation, he assuredly presents the type of the highest perfection that nature could attain to: hence the more an animal organisation approaches his, the more perfect it is.

Admitting this, I observe that the human body not only possesses a jointed skeleton but one that is above all others the most complete and perfect in all its parts. This skeleton stiffens his body, provides numerous points of attachment for his muscles and allows him an almost endless variation of movement.

Since the skeleton is a main feature in the plan of organisation of the human body, it is obvious that every animal possessed of a skeleton has a more perfect organisation than those without it.

Hence the invertebrate animals are more imperfect than the vertebrate animals; hence, too, if we place the most perfect animals at the head of the animal kingdom, the general series exhibits a real degradation in organisation; since after the first four classes all the animals of the following classes are without a skeleton and consequently have a less perfect organisation.

But this is not all: Degradation may be observed even among the vertebrates themselves; and we shall see finally that it is found also among the invertebrates. Hence this degradation follows from the fixed plan of nature, and is at the same time a result of our following her order in the inverse direction; for if we followed her actual order, if, that is to say, we passed along the general series of animals from the most imperfect to the most perfect, instead of a degradation in organisation we should find a growing complexity and we should see animal faculties successively increasing in number and perfection. In order to prove the universal existence of the alleged degradation, let us now rapidly run through the various classes of the animal kingdom.

. . .

Bimana

MAMMALS WITH DIFFERENTIATED
UNGUICULATE LIMBS; WITH
THREE KINDS OF TEETH AND
OPPOSABLE THUMBS ON THE
HANDS ONLY

MAN

Varieties
{
Caucasian
Hyperborean
Mongolian
American
Malayan
Ethiopian or Negro
}

This family has received the name of Bimana, because in man it is only the hands that have a separate thumb opposite to the fingers while in the Quadrumana the hands and feet have the same character as regards the thumb.

SOME OBSERVATIONS WITH
REGARD TO MAN

If man was only distinguished from the animals by his organisation, it could easily be shown that his special characters are all due to longstanding changes in his activities and in the habits which he has adopted and which have become peculiar to the individuals of his species.

As a matter of fact, if some race of quadrumanous animals, especially one of the most perfect of them, were to lose, by force of circumstances or some other cause, the habit of climbing trees and grasping the branches with its feet in the same way as with its hands, in order to hold on to them; and if the individuals of this race were forced for a series of generations to use their feet only for walking, and to give up using their hands like feet; there is no doubt, according to the observations detailed in the preceding chapter, that these quadrumanous animals would at length be transformed into bimanous, and that the thumbs on their feet would cease to be separated from the other digits, when they only used their feet for walking.

Furthermore, if the individuals of which I speak were impelled by the desire to command a large and distant view, and hence endeavoured to stand upright, and continually adopted that habit from generation to generation, there is again no doubt that their feet would gradually acquire a shape suitable for supporting them in an erect attitude; that their legs would acquire calves, and that these animals would then not be able to walk on their hands and feet together, except with difficulty.

Lastly, if these same individuals were to give up using their jaws as weapons for biting, tearing or grasping, or as nippers for cutting grass and feeding on it, and if they were to use them only for mastication; there is again no doubt that their facial angle would become larger, that their snout would shorten more and more, and that finally it would be entirely effaced so that their incisor teeth became vertical.

Let us now suppose that a quadrumanous race, say the most perfect, acquired through constant habit among all its individuals the conformation just described, and the faculty of standing and walking upright, and that ultimately it gained the supremacy over the other races of animals, we can then easily conceive:

1. That this race having obtained the mastery over others through the higher perfection of its faculties will take possession of all parts of the earth's surface, that are suitable to it;

2. That it will drive out the other higher races, which might dispute with it the fruits of the earth, and that it would compel them to take refuge in localities which it does not occupy itself;

3. That it will have a bad effect on the multiplication of allied races, and will keep them exiled in woods or other deserted localities, that it will thus arrest the progress of their faculties towards perfection; whereas being able itself to spread everywhere, to multiply without obstacle from other races and to live in large troops, it will create successively new wants, which will stimulate its skill and gradually perfect its powers and faculties;

4. Finally, that this predominant race, having acquired an absolute supremacy over all the rest, will ultimately establish a difference between itself and the most perfect animals, and indeed will leave them far behind.

The most perfect of the quadrumanous races might thus have become dominant; have changed its habits as a result of the absolute sway exercised over the others, and of its new wants; have progressively acquired modifications in its organisation, and many new faculties; have kept back the most perfect of the other races to the condition that they had reached; and have wrought very striking distinctions between these last and themselves.

The orang of Angola (*Simia troglodytes,* Lin.) is the most perfect of animals: it is much more perfect than the orang of the Indies (*Simia satyrus,* Lin.), called the orangoutang; yet they are both very inferior to man in bodily faculties and intelligence.[1] These animals often stand upright; but as that attitude

[1] See in my *Recherches sur les corps vivants,* p. 136, some observations on the orang of Angola.

is not a confirmed habit, their organisation has not been sufficiently
modified by it, so that the standing
position is very uncomfortable for
them.

We know from the stories of
travellers, especially as regards the
orang of the Indies, that when it
has to fly from some pressing danger
it immediately falls on to its four
feet. Thus, it is said, the true origin
of this animal is disclosed, since it
is obliged to abandon a deceptive
attitude that is alien to it.

No doubt this attitude is alien to
it, since it adopts it less when moving about, and its organisation is
hence less adapted to it; but does
it follow that, because the erect position is easy to man, it is therefore
natural to him?

Although a long series of generations has confirmed the habit of
moving about in an upright position,
yet this attitude is none the less
a tiring condition in which man
can only remain for a limited period,
by means of the contraction of some
of his muscles.

If the vertebral column were the
axis of the human body, and kept
the head and other parts in equilib-
rium, man would be in a position
of rest when standing upright. Now
we all know that this is not the
case; that the head is out of relation with the centre of gravity; that
the weight of the chest and belly,
with their contained viscera, falls
almost entirely in front of the vertebral column; that the latter has
a slanting base, etc. Hence it is
necessary as M. Richerand observes,

to keep a constant watch when
standing in order to avoid the falls
to which the body is rendered liable
by the weight and arrangement of
its parts.

After discussing the questions with
regard to the erect position of man,
this observer expresses himself as
follows: "The relative weight of the
head, and of the thoracic and abdom-
inal viscera, gives a forward inclination to the axial line of the
body, as regards the plane on which
it rests; a line which should be
exactly perpendicular to this plane,
if standing is to be perfect. The
following fact may be cited in support of this assertion: I have observed that children, among whom
the head is bulky, the belly protruding and the viscera burdened
with fat, find it difficult to get
accustomed to standing upright; it
is only at the end of their second
year that they venture to trust their
own strength; they continue liable
to frequent falls and have a natural
tendency to adopt the position of a
quadruped" (*Physiologie,* vol. ii., p.
268).

This arrangement of parts, as a
result of which the erect position is
a tiring one for man, instead of
being a state of rest, would disclose
further in him an origin analogous
to that of the other mammals, if
his organisation alone were taken
into consideration.

In order to follow out the hypothesis suggested at the beginning of
these observations, some further
considerations must now be added.

The individuals of the dominant

race in question, having seized all the places of habitation which were suitable to them and having largely increased their needs according as the societies which they formed became larger, had to multiply their ideas to an equivalent extent, and thus felt the need for communicating them to their fellows. We may imagine that this will have compelled them to increase and vary in the same degree the signs which they used for communicating these ideas; hence it is clear that the individuals of this race must have made constant efforts, and turned all their resources towards the creation, multiplication and adequate variation of the signs made necessary by their ideas and numerous wants.

This is not the case with other animals; for although the most perfect of them such as the Quadrumana mostly live in troops, they have made no further progress in the perfection of their faculties subsequent to the high supremacy of the race named; for they have been chased away and banished to wild and desert places where they had little room, and lived a wretched, anxious life, incessantly compelled to take refuge in flight and concealment. In this situation these animals contract no new needs and acquire no new ideas; their ideas are but few and unvaried; and among them there are very few which they need to communicate to others of their species. Very few different signs therefore are sufficient to make themselves understood by their fellows; all they require are a few movements of the body or parts of it, a few hissings and cries, varied by simple vocal inflections.

Individuals of the dominant race already mentioned, on the other hand, stood in need of making many signs, in order rapidly to communicate their ideas, which were always becoming more numerous and could no longer be satisfied either with pantomimic signs or with the various possible vocal inflections. For supplying the large quantity of signs which had become necessary, they will by various efforts have achieved the formation of articulate sounds. At first they will only have used a small number, in conjunction with inflexions of the voice; gradually they will have increased, varied and perfected them, in correspondence with the growth in their needs and their gain of practice. In fact, habitual exercise of their throat, tongue and lips in the articulation of sounds will have highly developed that faculty in them.

Hence would arise for this special race the marvellous faculty of speaking; and seeing that the remote localities to which the individuals of the race would have become distributed, would favour the corruption of the signs agreed upon for the transmission of each idea, languages would arise and everywhere become diversified.

In this respect, therefore, all will have been achieved by needs alone: they will have given rise to efforts, and the organs adapted to the articulation of sounds will have become developed by habitual use.

Such are the reflections which might be aroused, if man were distinguished from animals only by his organisation, and if his origin were not different from theirs.

The Fossil Remains of the Animal Kingdom

Edward Pidgeon
1830

. . .

We have now to notice a fact connected with fossil osteology of the most singular and striking kind. We find, as has been seen, quadrupeds of different genera, cetacea, birds, reptiles, fishes, insects, mollusca, and vegetables, in the fossil state. But to the present moment no human remains have been found, nor any traces of the works of man in those particular formations where these different organic fossils have been discovered. What is meant by this assertion is, that no human bones have been found in the regular strata of the surface of the globe. In turf-bogs, alluvial beds, and ancient burying-grounds, they are disinterred as abundantly as the bones of other living species. Similar remains are found in the clefts of rocks, and sometimes in caves, where stalactite is accumulated upon them; and the stage of decomposition in which they are found, and other circumstances, prove the comparative recentness of their deposition; but not a fragment of human bone has been found in such situations as can lead us to suppose that our species was contemporary with the more ancient races,—with the palæotheria, the anoplotheria, or even with the elephants and rhinoceroses of comparatively a later date. Many authors, indeed, have asserted, that debris of the human species have been found among the fossils, properly so called; but a careful examination of the facts on which such assertions were founded, have proved that these authors were utterly mistaken. We refer our readers to the preliminary discourse

"The Fossil Remains of the Animal Kingdom." *The Animal Kingdom Arranged in Conformity with its Organization by the Baron Cuvier, Member of the Institute of France, Etc. with Additional Descriptions of All of the Species hitherto Named, and Many Not Noticed. Supplementary Volume on the Fossils.* Pp. 21–25, 38–40. Whittaker and Company, London, 1830.

of the Baron to his "Ossemens Fossiles," for the most complete satisfaction on this question. The same may be asserted of all articles of human fabrication. Nothing of that description has ever been found indicating the existence of the human race at an era antecedent to the last general catastrophe of this globe, in those countries where the strata have been examined, and the fossil discoveries we are treating of been made. Yet there is nothing in the composition of human bones that should prevent their being preserved as well as any others. There is no principle of premature decomposition in their texture. They are found in ancient fields of battle equally well preserved with those of horses, whose bones we know are found abundantly in the proper fossil state. Neither can it be said that the comparative smallness of human bones has any thing to do with the question, when it is recollected, that fossil remains of some of the smallest of the rodentia are to be found in a state of preservation.

The result, then, of all our investigations serves to prove that the human race was not coeval with the fossil genera and species: for no reason can be assigned why man should have escaped from the revolutions which destroyed those other beings, nor, if he did not escape, why his remains should not be found intermingled with theirs. His bones are found occasionally in sufficient abundance in the latest and most superficial depositions of our globe, where their bones are never found: their bones are in immense quantities

in some of the ancient strata of the earth, where no traces of him exist. Human remains in caverns and fissures, along with some of those more ancient debris, prove nothing for the affirmative of man's coeval existence with the lost species. Their freshness proves the lateness of their origin; their fewness, the impossibility that mankind could have been established in the adjacent regions at the period when those other animals lived there; and their situation and general circumstances, the accident of their introduction.

It is a fact not less remarkable, that no remains of the quadrumanous races, which occupy the next rank in creation to man, at least in physical conformation, are to be found in the strata of which we have been speaking. Nor will this fact be deemed less remarkable when it is considered that the majority of the mammifera there found have their congenitors at present in the warmest regions of the globe, in the intertropical climates where those anthropomorphous animals are almost exclusively located.

Where, then, was the human species during the periods in question? Where was this most perfect work of the Creator, this self-styled image of the divinity? If he existed any where, was he surrounded by such animals as now surround him, and of which no traces are discoverable among the organic fossils? Were the countries which he and they inhabited overwhelmed by some desolating inundation, at a time when his present abodes had been left dry by the retreating waters?

These are questions, says the Baron, to which the study of the extraneous fossils enables us to give no reply.

It is not meant, however, to deny that man did not exist at all in the eras alluded to—he might have inhabited a limited portion of the earth, and commenced to extend his race over the rest of its surface, after the terrible convulsions which had devastated it were passed away. His ancient country, however, remains as yet undiscovered. It may, for aught we know, lie buried, and his bones along with it, under the existing ocean, and but a remnant of his race have escaped to continue the human population of the globe. All this, however probable, is but conjecture. But one thing is certain, that in a great part of Europe, Asia, and America, countries where the organic fossils have been found, man did not exist previously to the revolutions which overwhelmed these remains, nor even previously to those by which the strata containing such remains have been denudated, and which were the latest by which this earth has been convulsed.

It only remains for us now to give a summary view of the succession of strata, and an enumeration of the different fossil genera and species in the respective strata, by the order of which we are enabled to calculate to a certain extent the number of revolutions the globe has undergone. In doing this, we shall pursue the order observed by the Baron in his great work.

In speaking of the strata of which this globe is composed, we must be understood to mean here nothing more recent than that formation which is proved to have resulted from the last grand catastrophe by which the earth was overwhelmed. The strata then formed, the most superficial of the regular strata, consisting of beds of loam and argillaceous sand, mixed with rolled pebbles from remote regions, and filled with debris of land animals unknown, or foreign to the places in which they are found, appear to have covered all the plains, and the floors of the caverns, and choked up the fissures of the rocks within their reach. To such formations, Dr. Buckland has given the name of *diluvium,* and described them with his usual clearness and accuracy. They must be considered as totally distinct from the other strata, which, like them, are equally loose, but have been continually deposited, by streams and rivers, in the usual course of nature, since the last great convulsion of the globe, and which contain no fossil remains, but such as are indigenous to the country where they are found. These last depositions Dr. Buckland distinguishes by the term *alluvium,* and they must be considered as entering for nothing into the question of the grand revolutions of the earth. But in the *diluvial* strata, all modern geologists have discovered the clearest evidence of that tremendous inundation, which constituted the last general catastrophe by which the surface of our planet has been modified. It may not be amiss to inform our readers here, that both these formations agreeing in their character of uncompactness, but differing in their antiquity, are alike termed loose, or *alluvial,* by Cuvier and other geologists.

It is the study of fossil osteology alone which has led to any precise notions concerning the theory of the earth. Had organic fossils been totally neglected, no one would have imagined that successive eras, and a series of different operations, had taken place in the formation of the globe. By them alone are we certified that the covering of this planet has not always been the same, as it is obvious that, before they were buried in its depths, they must have existed on its surface. We have extended, by analogy to the primitive formations, the conclusion with which the fossils have supplied us for the secondary; and, had the strata of the earth been destitute of organic remains, it would have been impossible to maintain that their production had not been simultaneous.

It is also to the fossils, slight as our acquaintance is with them even yet, that we are indebted for the little that we know concerning the nature of the revolutions of the globe. By them we learn that certain strata have been tranquilly deposited in a fluid mass; that the variations in the strata have corresponded with those of the fluid; that their denudation was occasional by the translation of this fluid; and that this denudation has taken place more than once. Nothing of all this could have been learned with any certainty, but for the study of the organic remains.

What an immense field for reflection is opened to the mind of the philosopher, by a survey of the discoveries to which fossil osteology has conducted us! We read, in the successive strata, the successive efforts of creative energy, from the sterile masses of primitive formation, up to the fair and fertile superficies of the globe, enriched with animal and vegetable decomposition. We find that there was a time when life did not exist on this planet; we are enabled clearly to draw the line between inanimate and organized matter, and to perceive that the latter is the result of a distinct principle,—of something superadded to, and not inherent in, the former. We also contemplate a progressive system of organic being, graduating towards perfection through innumerable ages. We find the simplest animals in the earliest secondary formations; as we ascend, the living structure grows more complicated—the organic development becomes more and more complete, until it terminates in man, the most perfect animal we behold. And shall we say that this march of creation has yet arrived at the farthest limit of its progress? Are the generative powers of nature exhausted, or can the Creator call no new beings from her fertile womb? We cannot say so. Revolution has succeeded revolution—races have been successively annihilated to give place to others. Other revolutions may yet succeed, and man, the self-styled lord of the creation, be swept from the surface of the earth, to give place to beings as much superior to him as he is to the most elevated of the brutes.

The short experience of a few thousand years—a mere drop in the ocean of eternity—is insufficient to warrant a contrary conclusion. Still less will the contemplation of past creations, and the existing constitution of nature, justify the proud assumption that man is the sole end and object of the grand system of animal existence.

In surveying the different species whose remains are found in the fossil state, it will be expedient to deviate from the order of the Animal Kingdom, and to follow that which the Baron has observed in the *Ossemens Fossiles,* as by this means the reader will be better enabled to understand the order of succession, and the respective geological positions of the species described.

Note.—As, in our earlier part of this essay, we have stated, in deference to the opinion of Baron Cuvier, that the existing causes which now modify the earth's surface are insufficient to produce catastrophes on such a scale as that of those we have been surveying, it is but justice to mention that this point has been mooted, with much force of argument, in a very able article on the present subject in the *Quarterly Review* for September, 1826. Some very strong facts are there adduced relative to the action of earthquakes and volcanoes to a very great extent, and also proofs of derangement in comparatively recent strata, which, though partial, was evidently so violent as to prove that the disturbing forces still existed in all their pristine vigour. We must, however, waive any further discussion of this kind, and content ourselves with referring our readers to the article in question, which, for its extent, contains as lucid an epitome of all the latest information on this interesting topic as we have ever had the pleasure to peruse.

Part Two

In 1856 a human skullcap and some postcranial bones were found by workmen quarrying the Feldhof grottoes in the Neander Valley near Düsseldorf, Germany. The bones were collected by the foreman and given to Johann Karl Fuhlrott, the teacher of natural science at the school in Elberfeld. Recognizing these remains as human, Fuhlrott searched the deposit from which they had been taken for additional bones. Later he brought the specimens to the attention of Hermann Schaafhausen, a naturalist and professor at the University at Bonn. This is how the most famous of human fossils, the Neanderthal Man, was introduced to the realm of scientific inquiry.

If the meager number of genuine fossil man sites identified in the century and a half preceding the discovery of the Neander Valley specimen is compared with the number of sites identified in the subsequent thirty-five year period, the degree of increase of the fossil record is found to be about 500 percent. What are the causes for this sudden influx of osseous specimens into the European museums and research centers which had for so long been rejecting them?

The discovery of the Neanderthal specimen itself is certainly one of the reasons for this turn of events. Here was an undoubted hominid, but one whose morphology was unusual indeed : a low skullcap with very pronounced brow ridges in association with postcranial bones that were like those of modern man. Such an association of pithecoid and hominid traits in a single individual puzzled the gentlemen of the scientific conference held at Kassel in 1857 when they examined the bones brought by Fuhlrott and Shaafhausen. Resistive to the concept of a primitive

1856
to
1890

93

hominid progenitor, their explanations of the bones were ingenious. Rudolf Wagner, the anatomist, suggested that here were the remains of an elderly and recently living Dutchman. His colleague, von Mayer, believed that they were the bones of a Cossack who had crossed the Rhineland in 1814 and had died in the service of the czar; the soldier's body had been washed into the cave at Neanderthal soon after his death. Another visitor suggested that the bones were the vestiges of a wild man who had once occupied the woods near the cave. The French prehistorian, Pruner-Bey, called them the bones of an ancient Celt. The final words was said by the great pathologist, Rudolf Virchow, who assured the conference that these were merely the remnants of a recent sufferer of rickets and arthritis. To Virchow, early human progenitors could not be contemporary with extinct fauna; nor could he support the idea that our prehistoric ancestors were physically primitive. He was correct, however, in observing the evidence of disease in the remains of this fossil hominid. In the face of such derision, Fuhlrott and Schaafhausen nevertheless published an essay on their fossil man. This paper appeared in 1859 and attracted the attention of Huxley and Lyell, who were receptive to the Germans' evidence. To Huxley this "most bestial of all known human skulls" supported his belief in man's evolution. The specimen was christened *Homo neanderthalensis* by the British anatomist King in 1864, the same year that his colleague George Busk revealed to the attendants of a meeting at the British Association in London that a similar skull had been excavated at Forbes' Quarry on the Rock of Gibraltar during construction operations there as early as 1849. This second neanderthaloid specimen had been forgotten, but it attained prominence when it was hailed as supportive evidence for the Neander Valley discovery.

The first widely circulated publications concerning these fossil specimens and their relevance to the concepts of organic evolution appeared in the year 1863. These were Thomas Huxley's essays, *Evidence as to Man's Place in Nature*, and Lyell's *Geological Evidences of the Antiquity of Man*. The popularity of both was another cause for increasing interest in the idea of fossil man. Huxley was converted from the non-Progressionism once preached by Lyell, to Darwinian evolution after reading Darwin's opus of 1859. The small volume of essays that Huxley produced four years later directly faced the issues that his mentor had been too reticent to discuss. What Huxley accomplished by pointing out the marks of evolution on the human organism as attested by the fossil record, Lyell accomplished by converting many of his readers to the acceptance of prehistoric artifacts as the handiwork of our fossil antecedents. But both writers were limited by the small number of fossil and archaeological sites that were then available as evidence for their interpretations. Consequently, Huxley had recourse to the anthropoid apes for his illustrations of man's primate status, a circumstance that goes far to explain how he

came to be misunderstood as maintaining that our ancient human progenitors were "missing links" standing morphologically between modern
man and modern ape. In 1863 the only fossil human specimens accepted
as worthy of serious consideration were those from the Neander Valley
in Germany and from the cave sites in Belgium, plus a handful of fossils
of doubtful significance. As the number of fossil hominid specimens increased in the period between the discovery of Neanderthal Man to the
discovery of *Pithecanthropus*—that is, until 1890—it became more and
more difficult for the critics of human evolution to deny the factors of
change and the great antiquity in human biological history.

The amplification of the human fossil record forced the supporters
of these newer concepts to ask whether more than a single type of fossil
hominid might be involved in human history. Of the seventy or so genuine
fossil hominid specimens that were discovered and described in the
scientific literature of this period, three morphological types came to be
recognized: (1) specimens that resembled the original Neanderthal Man,
as did those from the sites at Gibraltar, Spy, and La Naulette in Belgium;
Schipka in Moravia; and possibly Taubach in Germany, although the
evidence from the latter site was dubious; (2) specimens that resembled
modern Europeans but retained certain so-called "primitive traits," as did
those from the sites of Cro-Magnon, Laugerie-Basse, and Chancelade in
France; Engis in Belgium; and the Grimaldi caves of Monaco; (3)
specimens that were in all their physical features identical with the bones
of modern Europeans, as were those from Furfooz in Belgium and Grenelle
and La Truchere in France. None of these ancient men were exactly the
missing links that had been anticipated by the supporters of the idea of
human evolution. Consequently, the special simian features of the neanderthaloid specimens became emphasized and were compared with the
analagous physical traits of the infra-human primates, just as the special
hominid phenotypic traits of the Cro-Magnon specimens were sought in
certain of the races living in Europe at the present time or during early
historic periods. It was not unusual for the early students of fossil man to
compare their ancient specimens with non-European phenotypic patterns,
and on the basis of superficial similarities of morphology to suggest phylogenetic affinities. The Chancelade fossil was compared with that of a
living Eskimo on the basis of certain parallels of cranial structure.

The tendency to think of the first discovered fossil specimens in terms
of their physical affinities to living races reflected the hesitancy on the part
of nineteenth century biologists like de Quatrefages to ascribe to mankind
an antiquity measurable in hundreds of thousands of years. These supporters of human evolution were not upholding the traditional notions of
the 6,000 years of human history, but they lacked any method of accurate
dating of the sites from which their fossil discoveries came. The faunal
and archaeological associations made possible only a relative type of

dating. Therefore classification of the specimens was based primarily on their morphological features according as those were understood to be "primitive," and hence earlier in time, or "modern," and so of more recent date.

That the Pleistocene was the period of significant hominization was not questioned, but when claims were made that both fossil human bones and paleolithic tools were being found in geological deposits dating to the Tertiary, the champions of fossil man were forced into two different camps. Part of this controversy was resolved in the twentieth century when the lower limits of the Pleistocene were extended backward in time to include the Villafranchian, a geological period that was formerly put in the Pliocene and now constitutes one-half the time of the Pleistocene. But at the end of the nineteenth century the supposed vestiges of Tertiary Man from Foxhall in Suffolk, Savona in Liguria, Castenedolo in Brescia, and Calaveras County in California as well as the supposed examples of the tools of Tertiary Man at Saint-Prest and Thenay in France were assertions of human antiquity not always accepted by scholars still thinking within the framework of a restricted time scale of human history.

The earliest attempt to arrange the fossils onto a true phylogentic tree was made by Huxley in his essay of 1863. Implicit in this and subsequent phylogenetic studies were two basic questions of interpretation: (1) what are the genetic affinities between the human line and the anthropoid lines and how might the paleoanthropologist determine which of the infra-human primates were phylogenetically closest to man; and (2) what are the genetic relationships of the various fossil hominid specimens to each other and to modern man. In the attempts of Huxley and his colleagues to answer these questions are to be discovered the foundations of the various schools of paleoanthropology that have since developed.

Darwin, Huxley, and Haeckel regarded the ape and hominid lines as autonomous branches that had separated from the mother branch of the *Catarrhini* early in the Mid-Tertiary. The common human ancestor who appeared at this point of divergence was called *Eohomo* by Huxley, who in a moment of felicity sketched him riding astride an *Eohippus*. Neither Darwin nor Huxley designated a phylogenetic tree illustrative of their conception of the path of man's evolution, but Huxley did suggest a phylogenetic sequence in which were used for the first time the newly recognized fossil hominid discoveries. His unilinear gradation, based on the comparative morphology of the available specimens, started from a purely hypothetical ape-man to Neanderthal Man, to the Borreby specimens of Denmark (an assemblage of post-Pleistocene fossils believed to be morphologically primitive by several biologists of the time during which Huxley was writing), then on to the Engis specimen, and finally to certain representatives of modern man which Huxley regarded as primitive in their physical constitutions—the Veddas of Ceylon, African Bushmen, Australian aborigines, Papuans, and the pygmy groups of Asia and Africa. *Homo sapiens* was not a new phenomenon, and Huxley viewed the first Neanderthal specimen as morphologically close to modern man in spite of the frequent exaggeration of its simian features.

Huxley's phylogenetic scheme is the classic example of the so-called "Unilinear School" of paleoanthropology. Such a system favors the concept of a direct evolutionary line from a supposed human ancestor, often hypothetical and unrelated to any specific fossil specimens, through a few fossil types which are considered representative of universal stages of hominization. This scheme does allow for some broadening, as when the fossils found after Huxley were added as branches shooting off the main human stem. The intellectual affinities of this concept with the chain of being are obvious. Its elements, the particular fossil specimens that represent the stages of human biological evolution, are the eighteenth century prototypes as seen through the lens of evolutionary theory. Monogenetic racial theorists had little difficulty in embracing this school of thought. The Unilineal School is very much a part of physical anthropology today, being closest in its tenets to popular concepts of the course of human evolution.

When Haeckel published the first diagrams of his phylogenetic trees, beginning in 1866, he adhered to this uniserial system for the hominid line. As he came to question that man had acquired his ape-like traits independently, and favored more and more an ape-human pattern of divergence, he hypothesized a speechless ape—*Pithecanthropus alalus*—a true missing link that was a balanced blending of pongid and hominid physical traits. For Haeckel language was the hallmark of humanity. Since he failed to question a then current philological dogma that all human languages could not have been ultimately derived from a common mother tongue, that is, that languages were originally polyidiomatic, he concluded that the races of man that spoke these diverse languages must have possessed different evolutionary lines; human races were polyphyletic. Therefore, he said that from the seed of the linguistically predisposed but mute *Pithecanthropus* grew two races, the Ulotrichi and the Lissotrichi. These in turn underwent further evolutionary ramifications in the process of becoming the living races of man. Haeckel saw the Indo-Germanic- (Indo-European-) speaking peoples of the world as making up the human type furthest removed from *Pithecanthropus* both intellectually and morphologically, a situation that the great anatomist regarded as proven by the fact that this favored group of mankind was demonstrating the warmest hospitality to his own theories of human evolution! Within Haeckel's phylogenetic scheme are contained the tenets of the "Polyphyletic School." The followers of this interpretation, such as Karl Vogt, see human evolution and race formation occurring independently in different corners of the world. Yet the end results of such local evolution are the same, considering that man is of a single species with interfertile races. Such an interpretation places a heavy burden on parallelism as an evolutionary process, and its acceptance by the adherents of racial polygenesis is consequently understandable.

While the nineteenth century supporters of human evolution might disagree on the merits of the Unilinear or Polyphyletic interpretation of fossil data, there was no question but that the human animal had evolved from some past less well endowed primate from one particular locality. Darwin suggested Africa as the place of man's origin because that continent contained the primates that most closely resembled man. The "mysterious East" had always been a favorite locus for human cultural and historical origins, and its prestige as the birthplace of man at least had the merit of not being contradicted by Scripture. Because the fossil hominids were then being discovered in Europe (as a consequence of their being sought first and more throughly there) it was asked if this part of the earth might not have been the home of our species. Indeed, certain local areas of western Europe were seriously regarded by some prehistorians as the very spots of man's origin, an idea encouraged as much by the finding of increasingly greater numbers of hominid fossils, infra-human primate fossils, and paleolithic tools as it was by nationalistic hopes that one's country or district might offer to the world evidence of having been the cradle of human evolution. Such enthusiasm in turn encouraged further investigation.

It must be recalled that these discoveries and interpretations of the human fossil record were taking place in the light of the reception of Darwin's two great works of this period, *The Origin of Species* in 1859 and *The Descent of Man* in 1871. Criticisms of Darwin's ideas were of two sorts: (1) of his failure to support nonevolutionary concepts by his theory of natural selection; and (2) of his inability to explain all biological problems of origin and affinity of structure in terms of his theory. Many of the problems raised as criticisms against Darwin were resolved in the following century with the development of the science of genetics. Without a knowledge of the mechanism of inheritance, Darwin was frequently perplexed by the problem of the great amount of time that must be presupposed if natural selection was to play its role as the principal process in the rise of new species. Many of Darwin's critics had supported the idea of organic evolution before or after reading his opus of 1859, but not all of them could appreciate the significance of natural selection. Mivart, among others, relegated natural selection to a minor role in the evolution of mankind. Instead of natural selection, many of Darwin's critics argued for the effects of macromutation, Lamarckian inheritance, and various theologically oriented theories as fundamental to the process by which species were modified. Darwinism itself underwent modification during the decade that followed the first edition of the *Origin of Species*, and the so-called Neo-Darwinists maintained that Lamarckian precepts should be rigorously excluded from all ideas about organic evolution. This contention made them lean even more heavily on the role of natural selection as the most important mechanism of evolution, save perhaps in the case of man where macromutation from an infra-human primate ancestor might seem a more comforting explanation of human origins. During this period a number of evolutionary mechanisms supplementary to natural selection were suggested. Darwin himself considered sexual selection to be one such process. Other scholars were concerned with the results of geographical isolation of biotic forms which might lead to the formation of new species, with the concept of organic selection, or with the idea that innate potentials for variation existing within an organism might become manifested under certain adaptive conditions, a compromise between Darwinism and elements of Lamarck's transformism. Still other theories were offered as possible replacements for the factor of natural selection. Samuel Butler's theory of racial memory, Neo-Lamarckism, orthogenesis, and macromutation were some of the concepts entertained by those unconvinced of the potency of natural selection in the history of the biotic universe. But in spite of formidable critics, Darwin also had vigorous and loyal supporters.

Even those who were ignorant of or indifferent to the subtleties of Darwin's biological arguments appreciated the backing that his theory seemed to lend to the idea of progress. As fossil men were recovered from the earth, their remains seemed to add to the evidence for human development and to support the tenets of Spencerian progress: here were the vestiges of those men lower on the scale of nature than ourselves, but like us, a part of a cultural and biological progression that seemed guaranteed to continue in the future. Human progress seemed incontestible from the evidence of archaeology that was now forthcoming. The cultural sequences that were encountered in the Dordogne Valley of France and elsewhere in Europe were held to represent universal stages through which all of mankind had passed on the way to attaining civilization.

When the Degenerationists and the Special Creationists realized that their next stand was to be taken at the frontiers of the new area of speculation on man and his origin, that is, in paleoanthropology as this discipline came to be called, they offered two arguments that seemed to them to be invulnerable to scientific contradiction or refutation. The Degenerationists correctly observed that the discoveries of the Cro-Magnon types of hominids had not given the evolutionists the kind of missing link that they had promised; rather, these large-brained fossils had crania not intermediate between man and ape in size but within the range of cranial capacities found in certain living races. Therefore, ancient man was just a common savage in his phenotype and not morphologically primitive or unique. Such an ancestor was like Adam, save that he had lost his God-given cultural institutions after Adam's Fall. Those who maintained that modern primitive peoples could not attain civilization through their own efforts went on to suggest that civilization was a revealed gift from the Deity to those favored peoples who were deserving of it at some period subsequent to the Fall. A second attack from the upholders of traditional concepts of human origins involved the idea of macromutation: man is the result of a divinely directed and sudden genetic leap from an animal that was morphologically an anthropoid to a creature endowed with human powers of cerebration, culture, and language. It is ironic that the concept of mutation, once believed to give the *coup de grace* to theories of human evolution, should today hold a necessary place in genetic interpretation of this problem.

The final sallies of the anti-evolutionists were somewhat resolved to the satisfaction of both parties through Wallace's hypothesis of human cerebral evolution. Like de Quatrefages and Topinard, Wallace recognized that the fossil discoveries made thus far in Europe were morphologically not very different from various kinds of living hominids of different racial groups in the world today. Even the more unusual Neanderthal Man had a cranial capacity within the range of modern racial norms. Wallace suggested that man's physical development had been very slow in its evolution, but that once man was morphologically differentiated from his apish kin he remained physically stable for all time. However, he argued, the human brain was a new feature in biological history that evolved since the Mid-Tertiary, any further physical development in man being unnecessary and so impossible. Thus freed from the process of natural selection, man became a very special creature in the biotic realm, but since, in Wallace's view, intellectual development does not have any physical manifestation, it is not surprising that the cranial capacities of certain fossil specimens should fall within the same size range as the capacities of man today. The Degenerationists appreciated this theory since it distinguished man from the other creatures of the natural world. The evolutionists liked it for its generous time allowance for human evolution, particularly at a time when physicists were seeking to estimate scientifically the age of the earth and the duration of man's life on it. But after the discovery of *Pithecanthropus* in 1890–91, these arguments for a large-brained human progenitor lost their vitality.

On Some Fossil Remains of Man

Thomas Henry Huxley
1863

I have endeavoured to show in the preceding Essay, that the Anthropini, or Man Family, form a very well defined group of the Primates, between which and the immediately following Family, the Catarhini, there is, in the existing world, the same entire absence of any transitional form or connecting link, as between the Catarhini and Platyrhini.

It is a commonly received doctrine, however, that the structural intervals between the various existing modifications of organic beings may be diminished, or even obliterated, if we take into account the long and varied succession of animals and plants which have preceded those now living and which are known to us only by their fossilized remains. How far this doctrine is well based, how far, on the other hand, as knowledge at present stands, it is an overstatement of the real facts of the case, and an exaggeration of the conclusions fairly deducible from them, are points of grave importance, but into the discussion of which I do not, at present, propose to enter. It is enough that such a view of the relations of extinct to living beings has been propounded, to lead us to inquire, with anxiety, how far the recent discoveries of human remains in a fossil state bear out, or oppose, that view.

I shall confine myself, in discussing this question, to those fragmentary Human skulls from the caves of Engis in the valley of the Meuse, in Belgium, and of the Neanderthal near Düsseldorf, the geological relations of which have been examined with so much care by Sir Charles Lyell; upon whose high authority I shall take it for granted, that the Engis skull belonged to a contemporary of the Mammoth (*Elephas primigenius*) and of the woolly Rhinoceros (*Rhinocerus tichorhinus*), with the bones of which it was found associated; and that the Neanderthal skull is of great, though uncertain, antiquity. Whatever be the geological age of the latter skull,

"On Some Fossil Remains of Man." *Man's Place in Nature.* Essay 3, pp. 139–41, 165–67, 180–84. University of Michigan, Ann Arbor, 1959. "On Some Fossil Remains of Man." *Evidence as to Man's Place in Nature.* Essay 3. Williams and Norgate, London and Edinburgh, 1863.

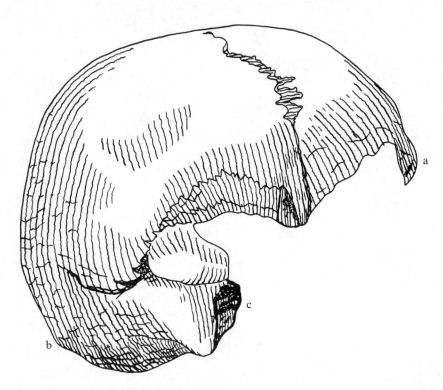

Fig. 1. The skull from the cave of Engis—viewed from the right side. One half the size of nature *a* glabella, *b* occipital protuberance. (*a* to *b* glabello-occipital line), *c* auditory foramen.

I conceive it is quite safe (on the ordinary principles of paleontological reasoning) to assume that the former takes us to, at least, the further side of the vague biological limit which separates the present geological epoch from that which immediately preceded it. And there can be no doubt that the physical geography of Europe has changed wonderfully since the bones of Men and Mammoths, Hyænas and Rhino-ceroses were washed pell-mell into the cave of Engis.

. . .

Such are the two best known forms of human cranium, which have been found in what may be fairly termed a fossil state. Can either be shown to fill up or diminish, to any appreciable extent, the structural interval which exists between Man and the man-like apes?

Or, on the other hand, does neither depart more widely from the average structure of the human cranium, than normally formed skulls of men are known to do at the present day?

It is impossible to form any opinion on these questions, without some preliminary acquaintance with the range of variation exhibited by human structure in general—a subject which has been but imperfectly studied, while even of what is known, my limits will necessarily allow me to give only a very imperfect sketch.

The student of anatomy is perfectly well aware that there is not a single organ of the human body the structure of which does not vary, to a greater or less extent, in different individuals. The skeleton varies in the proportions, and even to a certain extent in the connexions, of its constituent bones. The muscles which move the bones vary largely in their attachments. The varieties in the mode of distribution of the arteries are carefully classified, on account of the practical importance of a knowledge of their shiftings to the surgeon. The characters of the brain vary immensely, nothing being less constant than the form and size of the cerebral hemispheres, and the richness of the convolutions upon their surface, while the most changeable structures of all in the human brain, are exactly those on which the unwise attempt has been made to base the distinctive characters of humanity, viz. the posterior cornu of the lateral ventricle, the hippocampus minor, and the degree of projection of the posterior lobe beyond the cerebellum. Finally, as all the world knows, the hair and skin of human beings may present the most extraordinary diversities in colour and in texture.

So far as our present knowledge goes, the majority of the structural varieties to which allusion is here made, are individual. The ape-like arrangement of certain muscles which is occasionally met with[1] in the white races of mankind, is not known to be more common among Negroes or Australians: nor because the brain of the Hottentot Venus was found to be smoother, to have its convolutions more symmetrically disposed, and to be, so far, more ape-like than that of ordinary Europeans, are we justified in concluding a like condition of the brain to prevail universally among the lower races of mankind, however probable that conclusion may be.

We are, in fact, sadly wanting in information respecting the disposition of the soft and destructible organs of every Race of Mankind but our own; and even of the skeleton, our Museums are lamentably deficient in every part but the cranium. Skulls enough there are, and since the time when Blumenbach and Camper first called attention to the marked and singular differences which they exhibit, skull collecting and skull measuring has been a zealously pursued branch of Natural History, and the results obtained

[1] See an excellent Essay by Mr. Church on the Myology of the Orang, in the Natural History Review, for 1861.

have been arranged and classified by various writers, among whom the late active and able Retzius must always be the first named.

. . .

And now, to return to the fossil skulls, and to the rank which they occupy among, or beyond, these existing varieties of cranial conformation. In the first place, I must remark, that, as Professor Schmerling well observed in commenting upon the Engis skull, the formation of a safe judgment upon the question is greatly hindered by the absence of the jaws from both the crania, so that there is no means of deciding, with certainty, whether they were more or less prognathous than the lower existing races of mankind. And yet, as we have seen, it is more in this respect than any other, that human skulls vary, towards and from, the brutal type—the brain case of an average dolichocephalic European differing far less from that of a Negro, for example, than his jaws do. In the absence of the jaws, then, any judgment on the relations of the fossil skulls to recent Races must be accepted with a certain reservation.

But taking the evidence as it stands, and turning first to the Engis skull, I confess I can find no character in the remains of that cranium which, if it were a recent skull, would give any trustworthy clue as to the Race to which it might appertain. Its contours and measurements agree very well with those of some Australian skulls which I have examined—and especially has it a tendency towards that occipital flattening, to the great extent of which, in some Australian skulls, I have alluded. But all Australian skulls do not present this flattening, and the supraciliary ridge of the Engis skull is quite unlike that of the typical Australians.

On the other hand, its measurements agree equally well with those of some European skulls. And assuredly, there is no mark of degradation about any part of its structure. It is, in fact, a fair average human skull, which might have belonged to a philosopher, or might have contained the thoughtless brains of a savage.

The case of the Neanderthal skull is very different. Under whatever aspect we view this cranium, whether we regard its vertical depression, the enormous thickness of its supraciliary ridges, its sloping occiput, or its long and straight squamosal suture, we meet with apelike characters, stamping it as the most pithecoid of human crania yet discovered. But Professor Schaaffhausen states that the cranium, in its present condition, holds 1033.24 cubic centimetres of water, or about 63 cubic inches, and as the entire skull could hardly have held less than an additional 12 cubic inches, its capacity may be estimated at about 75 cubic inches, which is the average capacity given by Morton for Polynesian and Hottentot skulls.

So large a mass of brain as this, would alone suggest that the pithecoid tendencies, indicated by this skull, did not extend deep into the organization; and this conclusion is borne out by the dimensions of the other bones of the skeleton given by Professor Schaaffhausen, which show that the absolute height and relative proportions of the limbs were quite those of an European of middle stature. The bones are indeed stouter, but this and the great development of the muscular ridges noted by Dr. Schaaffhausen, are characters to be expected in savages. The Patagonians, exposed without shelter or protection to a climate possibly not very dissimilar from that of Europe at the time during which the Neanderthal man lived, are remarkable for the stoutness of their limb bones.

In no sense, then, can the Neanderthal bones be regarded as the remains of a human being intermediate between Men and Apes. At most, they demonstrate the existence of a Man whose skull may be said to revert somewhat towards the pithecoid type—just as a Carrier, or a Pouter, or a Tumbler, may sometimes put on the plumage of its primitive stock, the *Columba livia*. And indeed, though truly the most pithecoid of known human skulls, the Neanderthal cranium is by no means so isolated as it appears to be at first, but forms, in reality, the extreme term of a series leading gradually from it to the highest and best developed of human crania. On the one hand, it is closely approached by the flattened Australian skulls, of which I have spoken, from which other Australian forms lead us gradually up to skulls having very much the type of the Engis cranium. And, on the other hand, it is even more closely affined to the skulls of certain

ancient people who inhabited Denmark during the 'stone period,' and were probably either contemporaneous with, or later than, the makers of the 'refuse heaps,' or 'Kjokkenmöddings' of that country.

The correspondence between the longitudinal contour of the Neanderthal skull and that of some of those skulls from the tumuli at Borreby, very accurate drawings of which have been made by Mr. Busk, is very close. The occiput is quite as retreating, the supraciliary ridges are nearly as prominent, and the skull is as low. Furthermore, the Borreby skull resembles the Neanderthal form more closely than any of the Australian skulls do, by the much more rapid retrocession of the forehead. On the other hand, the Borreby skulls are all somewhat broader, in proportion to their length, than the Neaderthal skull, while some attain that proportion of breadth to length (80:100) which constitutes brachycephaly.

In conclusion, I may say, that the fossil remains of Man hitherto discovered do not seem to me to take us appreciably nearer to that lower pithecoid form, by the modification of which he has, probably, become what he is. And considering what is now known of the most ancient Races of men; seeing that they fashioned flint axes and flint knives and bone-skewers, of much the same pattern as those fabricated by the lowest savages at the present day, and that we have every reason to believe the habits and modes of living of such people to have remained the same from the time of the Mammoth and

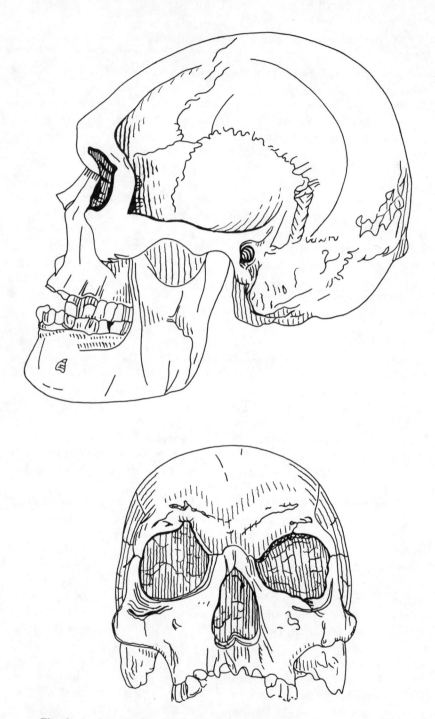

Fig. 2. Ancient Danish skull from a tumulus at Borreby; one-third of the natural size. From a camera lucida drawing by Mr. Busk.

the tichorhine Rhinoceros till now, I do not know that this result is other than might be expected.

Where, then, must we look for primæval Man? Was the oldest *Homo sapiens* pliocene or miocene, or yet more ancient? In still older strata do the fossilized bones of an Ape more anthropoid, or a Man more pithecoid, than any yet known await the researches of some unborn paleontologist?

Time will show. But, in the meanwhile, if any form of the doctrine of progressive development is correct, we must extend by long epochs the most liberal estimate that has yet been made of the antiquity of Man.

Post-Pliocene Period: Bones of Man and Extinct *Mammalia* in Belgian Caves.
Post-Pliocene Period: Fossil Human Skulls of the Neanderthal and Engis Caves

Charles Lyell
1863

Post-Pliocene period—bones of man and extinct mammalia in Belgian caves

Having hitherto considered those formations in which both the fossil shells and the mammalia are of living species, we may now turn our attention to those of older date, in which the shells being all recent, some of the accompanying mammalia are extinct, or belong to species not known to have lived within the times of history or tradition.

DISCOVERIES OF MM. TURNAL AND CHRISTOL IN 1828, IN THE SOUTH OF FRANCE

In the Principles of Geology, when treating of the fossil remains found in alluvium, and the mud of caverns, I gave an account in 1832 of the investigations made by MM. Tournal and Christol in the South of France.[1]

M. Tournal stated in his memoir, that in the cavern of Bize, in the

[1] 1st ed. vol. ii. ch. xiv., 1832; and 9th ed. p. 738, 1853.

"Post-Pliocene Period: Bones of Man and Extince Mammalia in Belgian Caves." "Post-Pliocene Period: Fossil Human Skulls of the Neanderthal and Engis Caves." *The Geological Evidences of the Antiquity of Man with Remarks on Theories of the Origin of Species by Variation.* Chapter 4, pp. 59–74; Chapter 5, pp. 75–80, 92. John Murray, London, 1863.

department of the Aude, he had found human bones and teeth, together with fragments of rude pottery, in the same mud and breccia cemented by stalagmite in which land-shells of living species were embedded, and the bones of mammalia, some of extinct, others of recent species. The human bones were declared by his fellow-labourer, M. Marcel de Serres, to be in the same chemical condition as those of the accompanying quadrupeds.[2]

Speaking of these fossils of the Bize cavern five years later, M. Tournal observed, that they could not be referred, as some suggested, to a 'diluvial catastrophe,' for they evidently had not been washed in suddenly by a transient flood, but must have been introduced gradually, together with the enveloping mud and pebbles, at successive periods.[3]

M. Christol, who was engaged at the same time in similar researches in another part of Languedoc, published an account of them a year later, in which he described some human bones, as occurring in the cavern of Pondres, near Nismes, in the same mud with the bones of an extinct hyæna and rhinoceros.[4] The cavern was in this instance filled up to the roof with mud and gravel, in which fragments of two kinds of pottery were detected, the lowest

and rudest near the bottom of the cave, below the level of the extinct mammalia.

It has never been questioned that the hyæna and rhinoceros found by M. Christol were of extinct species; but whether the animals enumerated by M. Tournal might not all of them be referred to quadrupeds which are known to have been living in Europe in the historical period seems doubtful. They were said to consist of a stag, an antelope, and a goat, all named by M. Marcel de Serres as new; but the majority of paleontologists do not agree with this opinion. Still it is true, as M. Lartet remarks, that the fauna of the cavern of Bize must be of very high antiquity, as shown by the presence, not only of the Lithuanian aurochs (*Bison europæus*), but also of the reindeer, which has not been an inhabitant of the South of France in historical times, and which, in that country, is almost everywhere associated, whether in ancient alluvium or in the mud of caverns, with the mammoth.

In my work before cited,[5] I stated that M. Desnoyers, an observer equally well versed in geology and archæology, had disputed the conclusion arrived at by MM. Tournal and Christol, that the fossil rhinoceros, hyæna, bear, and other lost species, had once been inhabitants of France contemporaneously with Man. 'The flint hatchets and arrowheads' he said, 'and the pointed bones and coarse pottery of many French and English caves, agree pre-

[2] Annales des Sciences Naturelles, tom. xv. p. 348: 1828.

[3] Annales de Chimie et de Physique, p. 161: 1833.

[4] Christol, Notice sur les Ossements humains des Cavernes du Gard. Montpellier, 1829.

[5] Principles, 9th ed. 739.

cisely in character with those found in the tumuli, and under the dolmens (rude altars of unhewn stone) of the primitive inhabitants of Gaul, Britain, and Germany. The human bones, therefore, in the caves which are associated with such fabricated objects, must belong not to antediluvian periods, but to a people in the same stage of civilization as those who constructed the tumuli and altars.'

'In the Gaulish monuments,' he added, 'we find, together with the objects of industry above mentioned, the bones of wild and domestic animals of species now inhabiting Europe, particularly of deer, sheep, wild boars, dogs, horses, and oxen. This fact has been ascertained in Quercy, and other provinces; and it is supposed by antiquaries that the animals in question were placed beneath the Celtic altars in memory of sacrifices offered to the Gaulish divinity Hesus, and in the tombs to commemorate funeral repasts, and also from a superstition prevalent among savage nations, which induces them to lay up provisions for the manes of the dead in a future life. But in none of these ancient monuments have any bones been found of the elephant, rhinoceros, hyæna, tiger, and other quadrupeds, such as are found in caves, which might certainly have been expected, had these species continued to flourish at the time that this part of Gaul was inhabited by Man.'[6]

After giving no small weight to

the arguments of M. Desnoyers, and the writings of Dr. Buckland on the same subject, and visiting myself several caves in Germany, I came to the opinion that the human bones mixed with those of extinct animals, in osseous breccias and cavern mud, in different parts of Europe, were probably not coeval. The caverns having been at one period the dens of wild beasts, and having served at other times as places of human habitation, worship, sepulture, concealment, or defence, one might easily conceive that the bones of Man and those of animals, which were strewed over the floors of subterranean cavities, or which had fallen into tortuous rents connecting them with the surface, might, when swept away by floods, be mingled in one promiscuous heap in the same ossiferous mud or breccia.[7]

That such intermixtures have really taken place in some caverns, and that geologists have occasionally been deceived, and have assigned to one and the same period fossils which had really been introduced at successive times, will readily be conceded. But of late years we have obtained convincing proofs, as we shall see in the sequel, that the mammoth, and many other extinct mammalian species very common in caves, occur also in undisturbed alluvium, embedded in such a manner with works of art, as to leave no room for doubt that Man and the mammoth coexisted. Such discoveries have led me, and other geologists, to reconsider the evidence

---

[6] Desnoyers, Bulletin de la Société Géologique de France, tom. ii. p. 252; and article on Caverns, Dictionnaire.

[7] Principles, 9th ed. p. 740.

previously derived from caves brought forward in proof of the high antiquity of Man. With a view of re-examining this evidence, I have lately explored several caverns in Belgium and other countries, and re-read the principal memoirs and treatises treating of the fossil remains preserved in them, the results of which inquiries I shall now proceed to lay before the reader.

RESEARCHES, IN 1833–1834, OF
DR. SCHMERLING IN THE CAVERNS
NEAR LIEGE

The late Dr. Schmerling of Liége, a skilful anatomist and paleontologist, after devoting several years to the exploring of the numerous ossiferous caverns which border the valleys of the Meuse and its tributaries, published two volumes, descriptive of the contents of more than forty caverns. One of these volumes consisted of an atlas of plates, illustrative of the fossil bones.[8]

Many of the caverns had never before been entered by scientific observers, and their floors were encrusted with unbroken stalagmite. At a very early stage of his investigations, Dr. Schmerling found the bones of Man so rolled and scattered, as to preclude all idea of their having been intentionally buried on the spot. He also remarked that they were of the same colour, and in the same condition as to the amount of animal matter contained in them, as those of the accompanying animals,

some of which, like the cave-bear, hyæna, elephant, and rhinoceros, were extinct; others, like the wild cat, beaver, wild boar, roe-deer, wolf, and hedgehog, still extant. The fossils were lighter than fresh bones, except such as had their pores filled with carbonate of lime, in which case they were often much heavier. The human remains of most frequent occurrence were teeth detached from the jaw, and the carpal, metacarpal, tarsal, metatarsal, and phalangial bones separated from the rest of the skeleton. The corresponding bones of the cave-bear, the most abundant of the accompanying mammalia, were also found in the Liége caverns more commonly than any others, and in the same scattered condition. Occasionally, some of the long bones of mammalia were observed to have been first broken across, and then reunited or cemented again by stalagmite, as they lay on the floor of the cave.

No gnawed bones nor any coprolites were found by Schmerling. He therefore inferred that the caverns of the province of Liége had not been the dens of wild beasts, but that their organic and inorganic contents had been swept into them by streams communicating with the surface of the country. The bones, he suggested, may often have been rolled in the beds of such streams before they reached their underground destination. To the same agency the introduction of many land-shells dispersed through the cave-mud was ascribed, such as *Helix nemoralis, H. lapicida, H. pomatia,* and others of living species.

[8] Recherches sur les Ossements fossiles découverts dans les Cavernes de la Province de Liége. Liége, 1833–1834.

Mingled with such shells, in some rare instances, the bones of fresh-water fish, and of a snake (*Coluber*), as well as of several birds, were detected.

The occurrence here and there of bones in a very perfect state, or of several bones belonging to the same skeleton in natural juxtaposition, and having all their most delicate apophyses uninjured, while many accompanying bones in the same breccia were rolled, broken, or decayed, was accounted for by supposing that portions of carcasses were sometimes floated in during floods while still clothed with their flesh. No example was discovered of an entire skeleton, not even of one of the smaller mammalia, the bones of which are usually the least injured.

The incompleteness of each skeleton was especially ascertained in regard to the human subjects, Dr. Schmerling being careful, whenever a fragment of such presented itself, to explore the cavern himself, and see whether any other bones of the same skeleton could be found. In the Engis cavern, distant about eight miles to the south-west of Liége, on the left bank of the Meuse, the remains of at least three human individuals were disinterred. The skull of one of these, that of a young person, was embedded by the side of a mammoth's tooth. It was entire, but so fragile, that nearly all of it fell to pieces during its extraction. Another skull, that of an adult individual (see fig. 2), and the only one preserved by Dr. Schmerling in a sufficient state of integrity to enable

the anatomist to speculate on the race to which it belonged, was buried five feet deep in a breccia, in which the tooth of a rhinoceros, several bones of a horse, and some of the reindeer, together with some ruminants, occurred. This skull, now in the museum of the University of Liége, is figured in [the next section], where further observations will be offered on its anatomical character, after a fuller account of the contents of the Liége caverns has been laid before the reader.

On the right bank of the Meuse, on the opposite side of the river to Engis, is the cavern of Engihoul. Both were observed to abound greatly in the bones of extinct animals mingled with those of Man; but with this difference, that whereas in the Engis cave there were several human crania and very few other bones, in Engihoul there occurred numerous bones of the extremities belonging to at least three human individuals, and only two small fragments of a cranium. The like capricious distribution held good in other caverns, especially with reference to the cave-bear, the most frequent of the extinct mammalia. Thus, for example in the cave of Chokier, skulls of the bear were few, and other parts of the skeleton abundant, whereas in several other caverns these proportions were exactly reversed, while at Goffontaine skulls of the bear and other parts of the skeleton were found in their natural numerical proportions. Speaking generally, it may be said that human bones, where any were met with, occurred at all depths in the cave-mud and gravel, sometimes above and sometimes below those of the bear, elephant, rhinoceros, hyæna, &c.

Some rude flint implements of the kind commonly called flint knives or flakes, of a triangular form in the cross section were found by Schmerling dispersed generally through the cave-mud, but he was too much engrossed with his osteological inquiries to collect them diligently. He preserved some few of them, however, which I have seen in the museum at Liége. He also discovered in the cave of Chokier, two and a half miles south-west from Liége, a polished and jointed needle-shaped bone, with a hole pierced obliquely through it at the base; such a cavity, he observed, as had never given passage to an artery. This instrument was embedded in the same matrix with the remains of a rhinoceros.[9]

Another cut bone and several artificially shaped flints were found in the Engis cave, near the human skulls before alluded to. Schmerling observed, and we shall have to refer to the fact in the sequel, that although in some forty fossiliferous caves explored by him human bones were the exception, yet these flint implements were universal, and he added that 'none of them could have been subsequently introduced, being precisely in the same position as the remains of the accompanying animals.' 'I therefore,' he continues, 'attach great importance to their presence; for even if I had not found the human bones under conditions

entirely favourable to their being considered as belonging to the antediluvian epoch, proofs of Man's existence would still have been supplied by the cut bones and worked flints.'[10]

Dr. Schmerling, therefore, had no hesitation in concluding from the various facts ascertained by him, that Man once lived in the Liége district contemporaneously with the cave-bear, and several other extinct species of quadrupeds. But he was much at a loss when he attempted to invent a theory to explain the former state of the fauna of the region now drained by the Meuse; for he shared the notion, then very prevalent among naturalists, that the mammoth and the hyæna[11] were beasts of a warmer climate than that now proper to Western Europe. In order to account for the presence of such 'tropical species,' he was half-inclined to imagine that they had been transported by a flood from some distant region; then again he raised the question whether they might not have been washed out of an older alluvium, which may have pre-existed in the neighbourhood. This last hypothesis was directly at variance with his own statements, that the remains of the mammoth and hyæna were identical in appearance, colour, and chemical condition with those of the bear and other associated fossil animals, none of which exhibited signs of having been previously enveloped in any dissimilar matrix. Another enigma which led

9 Schmerling, part ii. p. 117.

10 Schmerling, part ii. p. 179.
11 Ibid. part ii. pp. 70, 96.

Schmerling astray in some of his geological speculations was the supposed presence of the agouti, a South-American rodent, 'proper to the torrid zone.' My friend M. Lartet, guided by Schmerling's figures of the teeth of this species, suggests, and I have little doubt with good reason, that they appertain to the porcupine, a genus found fossil in post-pliocene deposits of certain caverns in the south of France.

In the year 1833, I passed through Liége, on my way to the Rhine, and conversed with Dr. Schmerling, who showed me his splendid collection, and when I expressed some incredulity respecting the alleged antiquity of the fossil human bones, he pointedly remarked, that if I doubted their having been contemporaneous with the bear or rhinoceros, on the ground of Man being a species of more modern date, I ought equally to doubt the coexistence of all the other living species, such as the red deer, roe, wild cat, wild boar, wolf, fox, weasel, beaver, hare, rabbit, hedgehog, mole, dormouse, field-mouse, water-rat, shrew, and others, the bones of which he had found scattered everywhere indiscriminately through the same mud with the extinct quadrupeds. The year after this conversation I cited Schmerling's opinions, and the facts bearing on the antiquity of Man, in the 3rd edition of my Principles of Geology (p. 161, 1834), and in succeeding editions, without pretending to call in question their trustworthiness, but at the same time without giving them the weight which I now consider they were entitled to. He had accumulated ample evidence to prove that Man had been introduced into the earth at an earlier period than geologists were then willing to believe.

One positive fact, it will be said, attested by so competent a witness, ought to have outweighed any amount of negative testimony, previously accumulated, respecting the non-occurrence elsewhere of human remains in formations of the like antiquity. In reply, I can only plead that a discovery which seems to contradict the general tenor of previous investigations is naturally received with much hesitation. To have undertaken in 1832, with a view of testing its truth, to follow the Belgian philosopher through every stage of his observations and proofs, would have been no easy task even for one well-skilled in geology and osteology. To be let down, as Schmerling was, day after day, by a rope tied to a tree, so as to slide to the foot of the first opening of the Engis cave,[12] where the best-preserved human skulls were found; and, after thus gaining access to the first subterranean gallery, to creep on all fours through a contracted passage leading to larger chambers, there to superintend by torchlight, week after week and year after year, the workmen who were breaking through the stalagmitic crust as hard as marble, in order to remove piece by piece the underlying bone-breccia nearly as hard; to stand for hours with one's feet in the mud, and with water dripping from the roof on one's

12 Schemerling, part i, p. 30.

head, in order to mark the position and guard against the loss of each single bone of a skeleton; and at length, after finding leisure, strength, and courage for all these operations, to look forward, as the fruits of one's labour, to the publication of unwelcome intelligence; opposed to the prepossessions of the scientific as well as of the unscientific public;—when these circumstances are taken into account, we need scarcely wonder, not only that a passing traveller failed to stop and scrutinise the evidence, but that a quarter of a century should have elapsed before even the neighbouring professors of the University of Liége came forth to vindicate the truthfulness of their indefatigable and clear-sighted countryman.

In 1860, when I revisited Liége, twenty-six years after my interview with Schmerling, I found that several of the caverns described by him had in the interval been annihilated. Not a vestige, for example, of the caves of Engis, Chokier, and Goffontaine remained. The calcareous stone in the heart of which the cavities once existed, had been quarried away, and removed bodily for building and lime-making. Fortunately, a great part of the Engihoul cavern, situated on the right bank of the Meuse, was still in the same state as when Schmerling delved into it in 1831, and drew from it the bones of three human skeletons. I determined, therefore, to examine it, and was so fortunate as to obtain the assistance of a zealous naturalist of Liége, Professor Malaise, who accompanied me to the cavern, where

we engaged some workmen to break through the crust of stalagmite, so that we could search for bones in the undisturbed earth beneath. Bones and teeth of the cave-bear were soon found, and several other extinct quadrupeds which Schmerling has enumerated. My companion, continuing the work perseveringly for weeks after my departure, succeeded at length in extracting from the same deposit, at the depth of two feet below the crust of stalagmite, three fragments of a human skull, and two perfect lower jaws with teeth, all associated in such a manner with the bones of bears, large pachyderms, and ruminants, and so precisely resembling these in colour and state of preservation, as to leave no doubt in his mind that Man was contemporary with the extinct animals. Professor Malaise has given figures of the human remains in the bulletin of the royal academy of Belgium for 1860.[13]

The rock in which the Liége caverns occur belongs generally to the carboniferous or mountain limestone, in some few cases only to the older Devonian formation. Whenever the work of destruction has not gone too far, magnificent sections, sometimes 200 and 300 feet in height, are exposed to view. They confirm Schmerling's doctrine, that most of the materials, organic and inorganic, now filling the caverns, have been washed into them through narrow vertical or oblique fissures, the upper extremities of which are choked up with soil and gravel, and

13 Tom. x. p. 456.

would scarcely ever be discoverable at the surface, especially in so wooded a country. Among the sections obtained by quarrying, one of the finest which I saw was in the beautiful valley of Fond du Forêt, above Chaudefontaine, not far from the village of Magnée, where one of the rents communicating with the surface has been filled up to the brim with rounded and half-rounded stones, angular pieces of limestone and shale, besides sand and mud, together with bones, chiefly of the cave-bear. Connected with this main duct, which is from one to two feet in width, are several minor ones, each from one to three inches wide, also extending to the upper country or table-land, and choked up with similar materials. They are inclined at angles of 30° and 40°, their walls being generally coated with stalactite, pieces of which have here and there been broken off and mingled with the contents of the rents, thus helping to explain why we so often meet with detached pieces of that substance in the mud and breccia of the Belgian caves. It is not easy to conceive that a solid horizontal floor of hard stalagmite should, after its formation, be broken up by running water; but when the walls of steep and tortuous rents, serving as feeders to the principal fissures and to inferior vaults and galleries are encrusted with stalagmite, some of the incrustation may readily be torn up when heavy fragments of rock are hurried by a flood through passages inclined at angles of 30° or 40°.

The decay and decomposition of the fossil bones seem to have been arrested in most of the caves by a constant supply of water charged with carbonate of lime, which dripped from the roofs while the caves were becoming gradually filled up. By similar agency the mud, sand, and pebbles were usually consolidated.

The following explanation of this phenomenon has been suggested by the eminent chemist Liebig. On the surface of Franconia, where the limestone abounds in caverns, is a fertile soil in which vegetable matter is continually decaying. This mould or humus, being acted on by moisture and air, evolves carbonic acid, which is dissolved by rain. The rainwater, thus impregnated, permeates the porous limestone, dissolves a portion of it, and afterwards, when the excess of carbonic acid evaporates in the caverns, parts with the calcareous matter and forms stalactite. So long as water flows, even occasionally, through a suite of caverns, no layer of pure stalagmite can be produced; hence the formation of such a layer, is generally an event posterior in date to the cessation of the old system of drainage, an event which might be brought about by an earthquake causing new fissures, or by the river wearing its way down to a lower level, and thenceforth running in a new channel.

In all the subterranean cavities, more than forty in number, explored by Schmerling, he only observed one cave, namely that of Chokier, where there were two regular layers of stalagmite, divided by fossiliferous cave-mud. In this instance, we may suppose that the stream, after flowing for a long period at one level, cut its way down to an inferior suite of caverns, and, flowing through them for centuries, choked them up with debris; after which it rose once more to its original higher level: just as in the mountain limestone district of Yorkshire some rivers, habitually absorbed by a 'swallow hole,' are occasionally unable to discharge all their water through it; in which case they rise and rush through a higher subterranean passage, which was at some former period in the regular line of drainage, as is often attested by the fluviatile gravel still contained in it.

There are now in the basin of the Meuse, not far from Liége, several examples of engulfed brooks and rivers: some of them, like that of St. Hadelin, east of Chaudefontaine, which reappears after an underground course of a mile or two; others, like the Vesdre, which is lost near Goffontaine, and after a time re-emerges; some, again, like the torrent near Magnée, which, after entering a cave, never again comes to the day. In the season of floods such streams are turbid at their entrance, but clear as a mountain-spring where they issue again; so that they must be slowly filling up cavities in the interior with mud, sand, pebbles, snail-shells, and the bones of animals which may be carried away during floods.

The manner in which some of the large thigh and shank bones of the rhinoceros and other pachyderms are rounded, while some of the smaller bones of the same creatures, and of the hyæna, bear, and horse, are reduced to pebbles, shows that they were often transported for some distance in the channels of torrents, before they found a resting-place.

When we desire to reason or speculate on the probable antiquity of human bones found fossil in such situations as the caverns near Liége, there are two classes of evidence to which we may appeal for our guidance. First, considerations of the time required to allow of many species of carnivorous and herbivorous animals, which flourished in the cave period, becoming first scarce, and then so entirely extinct as we have seen that they had become before the era of the Danish peat and Swiss lake dwellings: secondly, the great number of centuries necessary for the conversion of the physical geography of the Liége district from its ancient to its present configuration; so many old underground channels, through which brooks and rivers flowed in the cave period, being now laid dry and choked up.

The great alterations which have taken place in the shape of the valley of the Meuse and some of its tributaries are often demonstrated by the abrupt manner in which the mouths of fossiliferous caverns open in the face of perpendicular precipices 200 feet or more in height above the present streams. There appears also, in many cases, to be such a correspondence in the openings of caverns on opposite sides of some of the valleys, both large and small, as to incline one to suspect that they originally belonged to a series of tunnels and galleries which were continuous before the present system of drainage came into play, or before the existing valleys were scooped out. Other signs of subsequent fluctuations are afforded by gravel containing elephant's bones at slight elevations above the Meuse and several of its tributaries. The loess also, in the suburbs and neighbourhood of Liége, occurring at various heights in patches lying at between 20 and 200 feet above the river, cannot be explained without supposing the filling up and re-excavation of the valleys at a period posterior to the washing in of the animal remains into most of the old caverns. It may be objected that, according to the present rate of change, no lapse of ages would suffice to bring about such revolutions in physical geography as we are here contemplating. This may be true. It is more than probable that the rate of change was once far more active than it is now. Some of the nearest volcanoes, namely, those of the Lower Eifel about sixty miles to the eastward, seem to have been in eruption in post-pliocene times, and may perhaps have been connected and coeval with repeated risings or sinkings of the land in the basin of the Meuse. It might be said, with equal truth, that according to the present course of events, no series of ages would suffice to reproduce such an assemblage of cones and craters as those of the Eifel (near Andernach for example); and yet some of them may be of sufficiently modern date to belong to the era when Man was contemporary with the mammoth and rhinoceros in the basin of the Meuse.

But, although we may be unable to estimate the minimum of time required for the changes in physical geography above alluded to, we cannot fail to perceive that the duration of the period must have been very protracted, and that other ages of comparative inaction may have followed, separating the post-pliocene from the historical periods, and constituting an interval no less indefinite in its duration.

Post-pliocene period—fossil human skulls of the neanderthal and engis caves

FOSSIL HUMAN SKELETON OF THE NEANDERTHAL CAVE NEAR DUSSELDOLF

Before I speak more particularly of the opinions which anatomists have expressed respecting the osteological characters of the human skull from Engis, near Liége, mentioned in the last chapter and described by Dr. Schmerling, it will be desirable to say something of the geological position of another skull, or rather skeleton, which, on account of its peculiar conformation, has excited no small sensation in the last few years. I allude to the skull found in 1857, in a cave situated in that part of the valley of the Düssel, near Düsseldorf, which is called the Neanderthal. The spot is a deep and narrow ravine about seventy English miles north-east of the region of the Liége caverns treated of in the last chapter, and close to the village and railway station of Hochdal between Düsseldorf and Elberfeld. The cave occurs in the precipitous southern or left side of the winding ravine, about sixty feet above the stream, and a hundred feet below the top of the cliff. The accompanying section will give the reader an idea of its position.

When Dr. Fuhlrott of Elberfeld first examined the cave, he found it to be high enough to allow a man to enter. The width was seven or eight feet, and the length or depth fifteen. I visited the spot in 1860, in company with Dr. Fuhlrott, who had the kindness to come expressly from Elberfeld to be my guide, and who brought with him the original fossil skull, and a cast of the same, which he presented to me. In the interval of three years, between 1857 and 1860, the ledge of rock, *f*, on which the cave opened, and which was originally twenty feet wide, had been almost entirely quarried away, and, at the rate at which the work of dilapidation was proceeding, its complete destruction seemed near at hand.

In the limestone are many fissures, one of which, still partially filled with mud and stones, is represented in the section at *a c* as continuous from the cave to the upper surface of the country. Through this passage the loam, and possibly the human

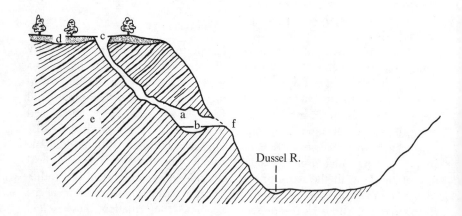

Fig. 1. Section of the Neanderthal Cave near Düsseldorf. *a* Cavern 60 feet above the Düssel, and 100 feet below the surface of the country at *c*. *b* Loam covering the floor of the cave near the bottom of which the human skeleton was found. *b, c* Rent connecting the cave with the upper surface of the country. *d* Superficial sandy loam. *e* Devonian limestone. *f* Terrace, or ledge of rock.

body to which the bones belonged, may have been washed into the cave below. The loam, which covered the uneven bottom of the cave, was sparingly mixed with rounded fragments of chert, and was very similar in composition to that covering the general surface of that region.

There was no crust of stalagmite overlying the mud in which the human skeleton was found, and no bones of other animals in the mud with the skeleton; but just before our visit in 1860 the tusk of a bear had been met with in some mud in a lateral embranchment of the cave, in a situation precisely similar to *b,* fig. 1, and on a level corresponding with that of the human skeleton. This tusk, shown us by the proprietor of the cave, was two and a half inches long and quite perfect; but whether it was referable to a recent or extinct species of bear, I could not determine.

From a printed letter of Dr. Fuhlrott we learn that on removing the loam, which was five feet thick, from the cave, the human skull was first noticed near the entrance, and, further in, the other bones lying in the same horizontal plane. It is supposed that the skeleton was complete, but the workmen, ignorant of its value, scattered and lost most of the bones, preserving only the larger ones.[14]

The cranium, which Dr. Fuhlrott showed me, was covered both on its outer and inner surface, and especially on the latter, with a profu-

[14] Letter to Professor Schaaffhausen, cited Natural History Review, No. 2, p. 156.

sion of dendritical crystallisations, and some other bones of the skeleton were ornamented in the same way. These markings, as Dr. Hermann von Meyer observes, afford no sure criterion of antiquity, for they have been observed on Roman bones. Nevertheless, they are more common in bones that have been long embedded in the earth. The skull and bones, moreover, of the Neanderthal skeleton had lost so much of their animal matter as to adhere strongly to the tongue, agreeing in this respect with the ordinary condition of fossil remains of the post-pliocene period. On the whole, I think it probable that this fossil may be of about the same age as those found by Schmerling in the Liége caverns; but, as no other animal remains were found with it, there is no proof that it may not be newer. Its position lends no countenance whatever to the supposition of its being more ancient.

When the skull and other parts of the skeleton were first exhibited at a German scientific meeting at Bonn, in 1857, some doubts were expressed by several naturalists, whether it was truly human. Professor Schaaffhausen, who, with the other experienced zoologists, did not share these doubts, observed that the cranium, which included the frontal bone, both parietals, part of the squamous, and the upper third of the occipital, was of unusual size and thickness, the forehead narrow and very low, and the projection of the supra-orbital ridges enormously great. He also stated that the absolute and relative length of the thigh bone, humerus, radius, and ulna, agreed well with the dimensions of a European individual of like stature at the present day; but that the thickness of the bones was very extraordinary, and the elevation and depression for the attachment of muscles were developed in an unusual degree. Some of the ribs, also, were of a singularly rounded shape and abrupt curvature, which was supposed to indicate great power in the thoracic muscles.[15]

In the same memoir, the Prussian anatomist remarks that the depression of the forehead is not due to any artificial flattening, such as is practised in various modes by barbarous nations in the Old and New World, the skull being quite symmetrical, and showing no indication of counter-pressure at the occiput; whereas, according to Morton, in the Flat-heads of the Columbia, the frontal and parietal bones are always unsymmetrical.[16] On the whole, Professor Schaaffhausen concluded that the individual to whom the Neanderthal skull belonged must have been distinguished by small cerebral development, and uncommon strength of corporeal frame.

When on my return to England I showed the cast of the cranium to Professor Huxley, he remarked at once that it was the most ape-like skull he had ever beheld. Mr. Busk, after giving a translation of Professor Schaaffhausen's memoir in the Natural History Review,[17] added some valuable comments of his own on the characters in which this skull approached that of the gorilla and chimpanzee.

Professor Huxley afterwards studied the cast with the object of assisting me to give illustrations of it in this work, and in doing so discovered what had not previously been observed, that it was quite as abnormal in the shape of its occipital as in that of its frontal or superciliary region. Before citing his words on the subject, I will offer a few remarks on the Engis skull which the same anatomist has compared with that of the Neanderthal.

FOSSIL SKULL OF THE ENGIS CAVE NEAR LIEGE

Among six or seven human skeletons, portions of which were collected by Dr. Schmerling from three or four caverns near Liége, embedded in the same matrix with the remains of the elephant, rhinoceros, bear, hyæna, and other extinct quadrupeds, the most perfect skull, as I have before stated, was that of an adult individual found in the cavern of Engis. This skull, Dr. Schmerling figured in his work, observing that it was too imperfect to enable the anatomist to determine the facial angle, but that one might infer, from the narrowness of the frontal portion, that it belonged to an individual of small intellectual development. He speculated on its

---

[15] Professor Schaaffhausen's Memoir, translated, Natural History Review, No. 2, April 1861.

[16] Natural History Review, No. 2, p. 160.

[17] No. 2, 1861.

Ethiopian affinities, but not confidently, observing truly that it would require many more specimens to enable an anatomist to arrive at sound conclusions on such a point. M. Geoffroy St. Hilaire and other osteologists, who examined the specimen, denied that it resembled a negro's skull. When I saw the original in the museum at Liége, I invited Dr. Spring, one of the professors of the university, to whom we are indebted for a valuable memoir on the human bones found in the cavern of Chauvaux near Namur, to have a cast made of this Engis skull. He not only had the kindness to comply with my request, but rendered a service to the scientific world by adding to the original cranium several detached fragments which Dr. Schmerling had obtained

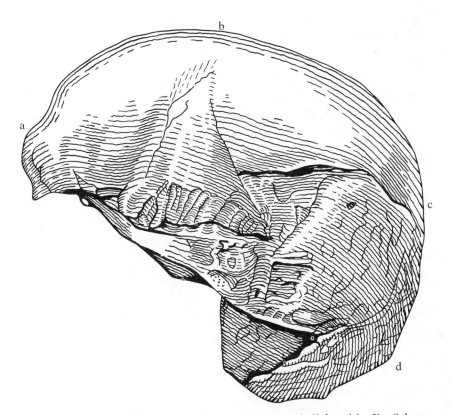

Fig. 2. Side view of the cast of part of a human skull found by Dr. Schmerling embedded amongst the remains of extinct mammalia in the cave of Engis, near Liége. *a* Superciliary ridge and glabella. *b* Coronal suture. *c* The apex of the lambdoidal suture. *d* The occipital protuberance.

from Engis, and which were found to fit in exactly, so that the cast represented at fig. 2 is more complete than that given in the first plate of Schmerling's work. It exhibits on the right side the position of the auditory foramen, which was not included in Schmerling's figure. Mr. Busk, when he saw this cast, remarked to me that, although the forehead was, as Schmerling had truly stated, somewhat narrow, it might nevertheless be matched by the skulls of individuals of European race, an observation since fully borne out by measurements.

· · ·

The direct bearing of the apelike character of the Neanderthal skull on Lamarck's doctrine of progressive development and transmutation, or on that modification of it which has of late been so ably advocated by Mr. Darwin, consists in this, that the newly observed deviation from a normal standard of human structure is not in a casual or random direction, but just what might have been anticipated if the laws of variation were such as the transmutationists require. For if we conceive the cranium to be very ancient, it exemplifies a less advanced stage of progressive development and improvement. If it be a comparatively modern race, owing its peculiarities of conformation to degeneracy, it is an illustration of what the botanists have called 'atavism,' or the tendency of varieties to revert to an ancestral type, which type, in proportion to its antiquity, would be of lower grade. To this hypothesis, of a genealogical connection between Man and the lower animals, I shall again allude in the concluding chapters.

Origin of Organic Nature

Karl Christoph Vogt
1863

Gentlemen,—The desire of man to inquire into the origin of all things produces daily fresh attempts of ascending the scale leading in that direction. Faith has in this respect an easy task; it builds upon some old myth a system which points to an unknown beyond. The path of science is more rugged, as it must steadily keep to the principle, not to depart from the facts and the limits fixed by observation and experiment. The further back science proceeds, the more necessary is it to use caution in drawing inferences from the facts, and the greater should be the candour in confessing the gaps which are every where met with; not for the reason that no created being can penetrate into the sanctuary of Nature, but simply because the facts and observations are so numerous that they cannot be mastered by one individual.

. . .

The existing materials for bridging over the gulf between man and ape I have placed before you. I have shown in what points the three anthropoid apes establish the similarity; in what respects the races of mankind, and especially the Negro, approach the ape-type, without, however, completely reaching it. I have demonstrated that the oldest cave-skulls known to us decidedly approach the ape-type, both by the elongated form and the low arching of the skull. I have, finally, directed your attention to the microcephali, those congenital idiots, not as constituting a separate species, as some of my detractors make me say, but as a morbid arrest of development, which indicates one of the stages which the human embryo must necessarily pass through, and which now in its abnormity represents that intermediate form, which at a remote period may have been normal. I remind you on this occasion of what I said concerning these microcephali, together with Gaudry's remark on the Greek monkey. Just as Gaudry observed that the whole

"Origin of Organic Nature." *Lectures on Man: His Place in Creation, and in the History of the Earth.* Lecture 16, pp. 443, 462–69. Longman, Green, Longman and Roberts, London, 1863. *Vorlesungen über den Menschen, seine Stellung in der Schöpfung und in der Geschichte der Erde.* Vorlesung 16. Ricker, Giessen, 1863.

skull of the Greek monkey would constitute it a *Semnopithecus* had not the limbs been found, which present the type of the macacus, so, I remarked, might the skull of a microcephalus, found in a fossil state, in the absence of the jaws be mistaken for that of an ape, until the discovery of the limbs should establish the human type. But as it is certain that the microcephalus, with his arrested development, is not suited for propagation, it is neither the only possible nor the only imaginable intermediate form between man and ape. But this arrest which the brain experienced in its forward march, is the simian stage. This abnormal creature, this arrested monstrosity of the present creation, fills up the gap which cannot be bridged over by normal types in the present creation, but may be so by some future discoveries.

We are told that intermediate forms have not been found, and we admit this. But when it is added that none can be found, the history of the last ten years, with all its discoveries relating to man and the ape, tells a different tale. Twenty years ago fossil monkeys were unknown, now we know nearly a dozen; who can tell that we may not in a few years know fifty? A year ago no intermediate form between *Semnopithecus* and *Macacus* was known, now we possess a whole skeleton; who can assert that in ten, twenty, or fifty years we may not possess intermediate forms between man and ape?

But whilst we assume the actual descent of the human race from the apes, and believe that the differences between both, which will become greater by the further development of man, are the result of selection and intermixture, we must, on the other hand, decidedly repudiate an inference we are charged with, and which consists in this, that we must necessarily come back to the original unity of mankind, and consider Adam as an intermediate form between ape and man. "The changes in the history of science," says Councillor R. Wagner, "have a remarkable, almost comic, aspect, when we look at the fierce contest now raging between mono-genists and poly-genists, as they call in France the advocates for one or many parent stocks of mankind. Three years ago, just before Darwin's book appeared, the theory of the possibility or probability of the different races of mankind having descended from a single pair was considered as perfectly antiquated, and as having lagged behind all scientific progress, whilst now, to judge from the applause with which Darwin's theory is received, there is nothing more certain than the inference that both ape and man had for their single progenitor a form intermediate between ape and man."[1]

We crave pardon, Sir Councillor; never was there a more incorrect inference, and when you advise us "to let this question rest for the present, as it cannot be scientifically solved," you should not have been the first to raise it; for as far as I

[1] Since the above was written, Prof. Rud. Wagner has departed this life.— Ed.

know, no Darwinist, if we must call them so, has either raised that question or drawn the above inference, for the simple reason that it neither accords with the facts nor their consequences.[2]

It is easy to prove our assertion as regards man and ape.

The ape-type does not culminate in one, but in three anthropoid apes, which belong to at least different genera. Two of these genera, the orang and the gorilla, must at all events be divided into different species; there are perhaps some varieties of them which form dispersive circles, like some around certain races of man. Be this as it may, this much is certain, that each of these anthropoid apes has its peculiar characters by which it approaches man; the chimpanzee, by the cranial and dental structure; the orang, by its cerebral structure; the gorilla, by the structure of the extremities. None of these stands next to man in all points,—the three forms approach man from different sides without reaching him.

I say "from different sides." For, in point of fact, these three anthropoid apes do not rise above the same fundamental form from which they branch off; but they sprang from different ape families which we must consider as having run parallel. Gratiolet has, as regards cerebral structure, followed up this subject. I shall not enter into details which must be studied in his treatise, but

I shall give here the conclusions he arrived at.

"On comparing the brain of the orang with that of other brains," says Gratiolet, "we are bound, on account of the size of the anterior lobe, the relative smallness of the posterior lobe, and the development of the superficial transition convolution *(plis de passage),* to place the orang at the head of the gibbons and the Semnopitheci, of which any one may easily convince himself on comparing the respective brains drawn with scrupulous exactness.

"These analogies are the more remarkable, as they lead to the same result as the examination of external characters."

The orang, considered as the highest gibbon, has a "gibbon's brain, only richer, more developed, in a word, brought nearer perfection."

Of the chimpanzee, Gratiolet remarks, "On comparing his brain with that of the true Macacus, and specially of the magot, it is impossible for us to reject the analogies presented by this comparison. The examination of the skull and face confirms these analogies by new ones.

"When, therefore, we put aside every preconceived theory, and keep solely to the facts, we are irresistibly led to the conclusion: The chimpanzee brain is a perfected Macacus brain.

"In other words: the chimpanzee stands in the same relation to the Macacus and the baboon, as the orang to the gibbon and the Semnopithecus." Of the gorilla, finally, he

---

2 This is quite true, although the author is mistaken respecting there being no Darwinist advocates for unity: I have alluded to this in the Preface.—Ed.

says: "The gorilla is a mandrill, just as the chimpanzee is a Macacus and the orang a gibbon. The absence of a tail, the existence of a broad sternum, the peculiar locomotion, not upon the palmar surface of the fingers, but upon the dorsal surface of the second phalanx, are indeed characters they possess in common; but however important these may be, they do not permit the approximation of these three genera. As heads of three different series, these apes still preserve the characters of the groups to which they belong, although they possess, if I may so express myself, common insignia of their high dignity."

No valid objection can be raised to these deductions of Gratiolet, in presence of the facts; but these facts prove our assertions, that the higher developed forms of different parallel series of apes approach man from different sides. Let us imagine the three anthropoid apes continued to the human type,—which they do not reach and, perhaps, never will reach; we shall then see developed from the three parallel series of apes, three different primary races of mankind, two dolichocephalic races descended from the gorilla and chimpanzee, and one brachycephalic descended from the orang;—that descended from the gorilla is, perhaps, distinguished by the development of the teeth and the chest; that descended from the orang by the length of the arms and light-red hair; and that issued from the chimpanzee, by black colour, slender bones, and less massive jaws.

When, therefore, we look upon the apes and their development as proceeding from different parallel series, the assumption of only one intermediate form between man and ape is unjustifiable, inasmuch as we know in our present creation three different sources for such intermediate forms.

Schröder van der Kolk and Vrolik agree with us in this respect, although they are opposed to Darwin's theory. "We know," they say, "no species of apes which forms a direct transition to man. If man is to be derived from the ape, we must search for his head amongst the small monkeys which group themselves around the Cebus and the Ouistitis; for his hand we must go to the chimpanzee; for his skeleton, to the Siamang; for his brain, to the orang, [and I add, for his foot, to the gorilla]. Putting aside the difference in the teeth, it is manifest that the general aspect of the skull of a Cebus, of a Ouistiti, or some other cognate monkeys, resembles, though in miniature, more the skull of man than the skull of an adult gorilla, chimpanzee, or orang. The *carpus* of the chimpanzee, [and of the gorilla], has the same number of bones as that of man, whilst that of the orang is distinguished by those singular intermediary bones found in all other monkeys. The skeleton of the Siamang resembles by its sternum, the shape of the thorax, the ribs, and the pelvis, much more that of man, than that of the gorilla, chimpanzee, and the orang; and our researches have also shown that the brain of the orang stands nearer to that of man than the brain of the chimpanzee. It would thus be requisite to collect the human characters from five different apes, from one of America, from two of Africa, from one of Borneo, and from one of Sumatra; the primitive relations of man are accordingly so scattered, that we can hardly believe in one common stock."

It is just this plurality of characters which confirms us in our view. If the Macaci in the Senegal, the baboons on the Gambia, and the gibbons in Borneo could become developed into anthropoid apes, we cannot see why the American apes should not be capable of a similar development; If in different regions of the globe anthropoid apes may issue from different stocks, we cannot see why these different stocks should be denied the further development into the human type, and that only one stock should possess this privilege; in short, we cannot see why American races of man may not be derived from American apes, Negroes from African apes, or Negritos, perhaps, from Asiatic apes!

On examining the species of mankind and their history, we arrive at similar results. We have traced the plurality of species, not merely in the historic, but also in the prehistoric period; we have shown that no existing species present a greater contrast than did, *e.g.*, the cave-men of Belgium and the Rhenish provinces, and the Lapps of the stone-period. This plurality and diversity which we find in the primitive races of Europe—that is to say, upon a very limited space, will also be found in the primitive races of other parts

of the world. At all events, all the facts which carry us back to the oldest history of Asia, Africa, and America admit of no other inference.

But if this plurality of races be a fact, as well established as their constancy of characters, despite of the many inter-mixtures through which the natural primitive races had to pass; if this constancy be another proof for the great antiquity of the various types, for their occurrence in the diluvium, or even in older strata —then all these facts do not lead us to one common fundamental stock, to one intermediate form between man and ape, but to many parallel series, which, more or less locally confined, might have been developed from the various parallel series of the apes.

It is not unworthy of notice that the fossil apes of the tertiary period, from which man perhaps might have issued, are much more widely spread than the present monkeys, and that they follow in their distribution the same laws as at present. The monkeys found in Europe, as high up as England, are all narrow-nosed, whilst those found in American caves are all flat-nosed. The difference between the Fauna of the Old, and that of the New World, as now observed, existed already then—there was no road which led from South America to Europe. But if apes became developed into men, they had in the Old World a range from the equator up to England, and could thus form the autochthonic races upon the various spots, where we have found the oldest species of mankind. This assumption equally leads us to an original plurality of mankind, not to their derivation from a single stock, but from the various twigs of that tree, so rich in branches, which we surround with the order of primates or apes.

Here again, gentlemen, you will observe the agreement in demeanour of the now distinct types. The simian type parts in various directions; it first divides into two chief branches —monkeys of the old, monkeys of the new world—each of these main branches produces twigs which seem more and more to part from each other. But on arriving at perfection the ends of the twigs turn again towards each other, so that from the fundamentally distinct families of the gibbons, Macaci, and baboons are developed the three anthropoid apes, which, by a number of common characters stand considerably nearer each other than the groups of which they are the heads. Does not the history of man present something similar? The further back we go in history the greater is the contrast between individual types, the more opposed are the characters— the most decided longheads immediately by the side of the most decided shortheads. Our savage ancestors stand opposed to each other—stock against stock, race against race, species against species. By the constant working of his brain man gradually emerges from his primitive barbarism; he begins to recognise his relation to other stocks, races, and species, with whom he finally intermixes and interbreeds. The innumerable mongrel races gradually fill up the spaces between originally so distinct types, and, notwithstanding the constancy of characters, in spite of the tenacity with which the primitive races resist alteration, they are by fusion slowly led towards unity.

My task is finished, believing that I have, as far as was in my power, attained the object I had in view. But before concluding, I feel bound to address a few words to friends and opponents.

The lamentation over the destruction of all faith, morality, and virtue; the woeful cry about the endangered existence of society, which years ago forced me to take up my pen, is heard again—but this time it is in the French tongue. The pulpits of the orthodox churches, the pews of the pietistic oratories, the platforms of the missions, the chairs of the consistories, resound with the pretended attacks on the foundations of human existence made by materialism and Darwinism. They feel surprised, that people with such views can be good citizens, honest men, good husbands and fathers. There are priests, who, while defrauding the state of taxes, mount the pulpit and preach: that when materialists and Darwinists do not commit all sorts of crimes, it is not from righteousness but from hypocrisy.

Let them rage! *They* require the fear of punishment, the hope of reward in a dreamt-of beyond, to keep in the right path—for us suffices the consciousness of being men amongst men, and the acknowledgment of their equal rights. We have no other hope than that of receiving the acknowledgments of our fellow-men;

no other fear than that of seeing our human dignity violated—a dignity we value the more, since it has been conquered with the greatest labour by us and our ancestors, down to the ape.

To our friends we return thanks for their support, and conclude with an anecdote.

In a satirical journal, edited by my late friend, Fritz Jenni, called *Der Guckkasten* (The Show-box), there is a picture of a cowkeeper with his milk-cans, and before him a cur, barking furiously. Says the milkman, "Thou barkest! Thou always barkest! Thou barkest at all the dogs! Thou barkest at me, and barkest till thou hast done barking, and canst bark no more!"

Then let them bark, till they can bark no more.

On the Anthropology of Linnaeus

Thomas Bendysche
1863

The publication of the first edition of the *Systema Naturæ* took place in 1735. It is difficult at the present day to form an idea of the courage that must have been necessary to put forth those few folio pages, at the end of which Man, for the first time, was classed as one with the rest of the animal creation. As I shall have to make constant reference to the various editions of the *Systema Naturæ,* and the changes made in them by the author, according to the changes which naturally took place in his views from time to time, I shall commence by giving the tabular view of these editions, printed by Linnæus himself in the twelfth, as he calls it, and last edition which he issued.

EDITIONS OF THE SYSTEMA
NATURE

1 Leydæ,   1735
2 Holmiæ, 1740, 8vo, p. 80.
3 Halle,   1740, *id. cum* 1.
4 Paris,   1744, *id. cum* 2.
5 Halle,   1747, p. 88, *id. cum* 2.
7 Lips.,   1748, *id. cum* 6.
8 Holmiæ, 1753, p. 136.
9 Leydæ,   1756, *id. cum* 6.
10 Holmiæ, 1758, 8vo, *auc. à me ipso.*
11 Lips.,   1762, *prodiit vitiosa.*
12 Holmiæ, 1760, ult.

I have examined all these edi-

"On the Anthropology of Linnaeus: 1735–1776." The History of Anthropology. *Memoires of the Anthropological Society of London.* Vol. 1, pp. 421–26. 1863.

CLASSIS I. QUADRUPEDIA (*Corpus* hirsutum. *Pedes* quatuor. Feminæ vivipar., lactiferæ.)

ANTHROPOMORPHA. *Dentes* primores utrinque, vel nulli.	Homo. Simia. Bradypus.	Nosce to ipsum.	
		Anteriores. *Digiti* 5.	Posteriores. 5.
		Posteriores anterioribus similes. *Digiti* 3 vel 2.	3.

tions, except the eighth, which I have not been able to find, with these results:

In the first edition, man is thus treated[1] (1735):

PARADOXON

The satyr, tailed, hairy, bearded, with a human body, much given to gesticulations, extremely lascivious, is a species of ape, if one has ever been seen. The *tailed men,* also, of whom modern travellers relate so much, is of the same genus.

Here we see that man is not only considered as an animal, but even a quadruped, and placed in the same Order with the ape and the sloth; and by the motto, *Nosce te ipsum,* the task of distinguishing him further is wittily cast upon the reader. The second edition was published in 1740. In it, man is treated thus:

SYSTEMA NATURE. ED. 1740
CLASSIS I. QUADRUPEDIA. ORDO I.
ANTHROPOMORPHA. DENTES
PRIMORES UTRINQUE QUATUOR,
AUT NULLI.

1. Homo. *Nosce te ipsum.—Homo* variat.: Europæus albus, Americanus rubescens, Asiaticus fuscus, Africanus niger.

1 I give the original Latin of the text throughout.

2. Simia. *Os. dentatum. Pedes pentactyli scandentes.* Mammæ *pectorales.*
   Simia mammis quaternis; capite ad aures crinito. Animal cynocephalum, tardigradum dictum, simii species. Seb. 1, p. 55, t. 35, f. 1, 2.
   Simiarum species descriptæ non sunt, nec earum differentiæ detectæ. E. gr. *Papio, Satyrus, Cercopithecus, Cynocephalus.*

3. Bradypus. *Os dentatum. Pedes scandentes.* Mammæ II, *pectorales.*
   Bradypus manibus tridactylis, cauda brevi. Ai s. ignavus gracilis Americanus. Seb. 1, p. 53.
   Bradypus manibus didactylis, cauda nulla. Tardigradus ceylanicus. Seb. 1, p. 54.

4. Myrmecophaga. Os edentulum. Pedes incedentes. Mammæ viii, abdominales: ventrales 6, pectorales 2.
   Myrmecophaga manibus tridactilis, plantis pentadactylis.
   Tamandua-guacu Brasiliensibus. Raj. 241.
   Myrmecophaga manibus monodactilis, plantis tetradactylis.

Here we have the four geographical varieties, whilst the ant-eater is added to the Order; the *paradoxon* is the same. The third edition was published in the same year at Halle, in Latin and German. It is so far like the first that the anteater is not included in the Order; and like the second, because the varieties of man are given. It was issued with the goodwill of the author. The fourth edition was published at Paris in 1744, with the *Fundamenta botanica*. It scarcely differs from the second as regards man. The fifth is the same as the second. The sixth was published at Stockholm in 1748. In it the ant-eater is no longer included in the first Order of quadrupeds, which contains, as in the first, man, the ape, and the sloth. The arrangement is, in fact, the same; but there is added this quaint note upon man:

Know thyself, theologically; *that you are created with an immortal soul, after the image of God.*

Morally; *that you alone are blessed with a rational soul for the glory of your great Creator.*

Naturally; *that you are the lord of animals, and the ultimate end of creation, for whose sake all other things have been made.*

Physiologically; *that you are a most perfect and wonderful machine.*

Dietetically; *that the Parent of nature has given you kindred animals to be to you for use and food.*

Pathologically, *what a fragile bubble you are, and exposed to a thousand calamities.*

If you understand these things, you are man, *and a genus very distinct from all others.*

The *Paradoxa* are dropped in this edition. The seventh, published at Leipzig in the same year, appears to be the same. The eighth, of 1753, as I have already said, I have never

seen, but it cannot differ much from the last two, for the ninth, of 1756, is exactly the same. We now come to the tenth, which was so much enlarged by Linnæus as to be almost a new work. In it the famous *observations* are dropped, and the *Imperium Naturæ* takes their place. I mention this, but only to say that the consequent reflections would rather find place in a work on general zoology than on anthropology. What relates to man in the tenth edition, I give at full length; and may say here, that the edition reckoned as the eleventh by Linnæus himself, is also stated by him to be spurious and faulty; whilst the *principal* additions made in the twelfth, and last (1760), have been inserted in the notes; the others, consisting only of one or two additional notes in the original from the classics.

TENTH EDITION, 1758. GENERUM
CHARACTERES COMPENDIOSI

I. PRIMATES:

  1. Homo, *Nosce te ipsum.*

  2. Simia, *Dentes laniarii, hinc remoti.*

  3. Lemur, *Dentes primores inferiores.*

  4. Vespertilio *Manus palmatæ volatiles.*

I. PRIMATES.

Dentes primores superiores IV, paralleli. Mammæ pectorales II.

1. Homo, *Nosce te ipsum.*

  Sapiens. 1. H. diurnus; *varians cultura, loco.*

  Ferus tetrapus, mutus, hirsutus. *Juvenis ursinus Lithuanus.* 1661. *Juvenis lupinus Hessensis.* 1344. *Juvenis ovinus Hibernus.* Tulp. *obs.* iv, 9. *Juvenis Hannoveranus. Pueri*

2 *Pyrenaici.* 1719. *Johannes Leodi-censis.*[2]

Americanus. a. rufus, cholericus, rectus.

Pilis nigris, rectis crassis; *Naribus* patulis; *Facie* ephelitica; *Mento* subimberbi. *Pertinax,* hilaris, liber. *Pingit* se lineis dædalis rubris. *Regitur* consuetudine.

Europœus. β. albus, sanguineus, torosus.

Pilis flavescentibus prolixis. *Oculis* cœruleis. *Levis,* acutissimus, inventor. *Tegitur* vestimentis arctis. *Regitur, Ritibus.*

Asiaticus. γ. luridus, melancholicus, rigidus.

Pilis nigricantibus *Oculis.* fuscis. *Severus,* fastuosus, avarus. *Tegitur* indumentis laxis. *Regitur* opinionibus.

Afer. δ. niger, phlegmaticus, laxus. *Pilis* atris, contortuplicatis. *Cute* holoserica. *Naso,* simo. *Labiis* tumdus. *Feminis* sinus pudoris, *Mammœe* lactantes prolixæ *Vafer,* segnis, negligens. *Unguit se pingui.* Regitur arbitrio.

Monstrosus. ϵ. solo (*a*) arte (*b, c*).

a. *Alpini* parvi, agiles, timidi. *Patagonici* magni, segnes.

b. *Monorchides* ut minus fertiles: Hottentotti. *Junceœ* puellæ abdomine attenuato: Europæ.

c. *Macrocephali,* capite conico: Chinenses.

Plagiocephali, capite anticæ compresso: Canadenses.

2 To these are added in the twelfth ed., *Juvenisb ovinus Bambergensis.* Camerar., *Puella Campanica,* 1731. *Puella Transisalana,* 1717.

Habitat inter Tropicos[3] *sponte gratisque: per relipuam* Telluris *totam continentem coactœ.*

[Here follows a long *description.*]

Differt itaque a reliquis corpore erecto nudo, et piloso capite, superciliis, ciliisque, tandem pube, axillis, maribusque mento. Feminis nymphæ et clitoris: mammæ 2 pectorales. Caput cerebro omnium maximo: uvula: facies abdomini parallela, nuda: naso prominente: compresso, brevior: mento prominente: cauda nulla. Pedes talis incedentes.

Troglodytes 2. H. nocturnus.

Homo sylvestris Orang Outang. *Bont. Jav.,* 84, s. 84. Kakurlacko, *Kjœp. itin.,* c. 86. Dalin, *Orat.* 5. *Habitat in* Æthiopiæ *conterminis* (Plin.) *in* Javæ, Amboinæ, Ternatæ, *speluncis.* Corpus *album, incessu erectum, nostro dimidio minus.* Pili *albi, contortuplicati.* Oculi *orbiculati:* iride, pupillaque *aurea.* Visus *lateralis, nocturnus.* Ætas xxv annorum. Die *cœcutit, latet;* Noctu, *videt, exit, furatur.* Loquitur *sibilo: Cogitat, credit sui causa factam tellurem, se aliquando iterum fore imperantem, si fides peregrinatoribus.*

2. Simia.

3. Lemur.

4. Vespertilio.[4]

3 In ed. xii, *Palmis lotophagus. Hospitatur extra* tropicos *sub novercante Cerere, carnivorus.*

4 Here we meet for the first time with the word *Primates;* under this are included man, the ape, the lemur, and the bat. The Sloth at last disappears.

Origin and Pedigree of Man. Migration Distribution of Mankind. Human Species and Human Races

Ernst Heinrich Haeckel
1868

Origin and pedigree of man

Of all the individual questions answered by the Theory of Descent, of all the special inferences drawn from it, there is none of such importance as the application of this doctrine to Man himself. As I remarked at the beginning of this treatise, the inexorable necessity of the strictest logic forces us to draw the special deductive conclusion from the general inductive law of the theory, that Man has developed gradually, and step by step, out of the lower Vertebrata, and more immediately out of Ape-like Mammals. That this doctrine is an inseparable part of the Theory of Descent, and hence also of the universal Theory of Development in general, is recognized by all thoughtful adherents of the theory, as well as by all its opponents who reason logically.

But if the doctrine be true, then the recognition of the animal origin and pedigree of the human race will necessarily affect more deeply than any other progress of the human mind the views we form of all human relations, and the aims of all human science. It must sooner or later produce a complete revolution in the conception entertained by man of the entire universe. I am firmly convinced that in future this immense advance in our knowledge will be regarded as the beginning of a new period of the development of Mankind. It can only be compared to the discovery made by Copernicus, who was the first who ventured distinctly to express the opinion, that it was not the sun which moved round the earth, but the earth round the sun. Just as the *geocentric conception* of the universe—namely, the false opinion that the earth was the centre of the universe, and that all

"Origin and Pedigree of Man." "Migration and Distribution of Mankind. Human Species and Human Races." *The History of Creation: or the Development of the Earth and its Inhabitants by the Action of Natural Causes. A Popular Exposition of the Doctrine of Evolution in General, and That of Darwin, Goethe, and Lamarck in Particular.* Translated by E. Ray Lankester. Chapter 22, pp. 263–77, Chapter 23, pp. 325–33. D. Appleton, New York, 1868. *Natürliche Schöpfungsgeschichte. Gemeinverständliche wissenschaftliche Vorträge über die Entwicklungslehre im allgemeinen und diejenige von Darwin, Goethe und Lamarck im Besonderen.* Chapters 22–23. G. Reimer, Berlin, 1868.

its other portions revolved round the earth—was overthrown by the system of the universe established by Copernicus and his followers, so the *anthropocentric conception* of the universe—the vain delusion that Man is the centre of terrestrial nature, and that its whole aim is merely to serve him—is overthrown by the application (attempted long since by Lamarck) of the theory of descent to Man. As Copernicus' system of the universe was mechanically established by Newton's theory of gravitation, we see Lamarck's theory of descent attain its causal establishment by Darwin's theory of selection. This comparison, which is very interesting in many respects, I have discussed in detail elsewhere.

In order to carry out this extremely important application of the Theory of Descent to man, with the necessary impartiality and objectivity, I must above all beg the reader (at least for a short time) to lay aside all traditional and customary ideas on the "Creation of Man," and to divest himself of the deep-rooted prejudices concerning it, which are implanted in the mind in earliest youth. If he fail to do this, he cannot objectively estimate the weight of the scientific arguments which I shall bring forward in favour of the animal derivation of Man, that is, of his origin out of Ape-like Mammals. We cannot here do better than imagine ourselves with Huxley to be the inhabitants of another planet, who, taking the opportunity of a scientific journey through the universe, have arrived upon the earth and have there met

with a peculiar two-legged mammal called Man, diffused over the whole earth in great numbers. In order to examine him zoologically, we should pack a number of the individuals of different ages and from different lands (as we should do with the other animals collected on the earth) into large vessels filled with spirits of wine, and on our return to our own planet we should commence the comparative anatomy of all these terrestrial animals quite objectively. As we should have no personal interest in Man, in a creature so entirely different from ourselves, we should examine and criticise him as impartially and objectively as we should the other terrestrial animals. In doing this we should, of course, in the first place refrain from all conjectures and speculations on the nature of his soul, or on the spiritual side of his nature, as it is usually called. We should occupy ourselves solely with his bodily structure, and with that natural conception of it which is offered by the history of his individual development.

It is evident that in order correctly to determine Man's position among the other terrestrial organisms we must, in the first place, follow the guidance of the natural system. We must endeavour to determine the position which belongs to Man in the natural system of animals as accurately and distinctly as possible. We shall then, if in fact the theory of descent be correct, be able from his position in the system to determine the real primary relationship, and the degree of consanguinity connecting Man with the animals most like him. The hypo-thetical pedigree of the human race will then follow naturally as the final result of this anatomical and systematic inquiry.

Now if, by means of comparative anatomy and ontogeny, we seek for man's position in that Natural System of animals which formed the subject of the last two chapters, the incontrovertible fact will at once present itself to us, that man belongs to the tribe, or phylum, of the Vertebrata. Every one of the character-istics, which so strikingly distinguish all the Vertebrata from all Inver-tebrata, is possessed by him. It has also never been doubted that of all the Vertebrata the Mammals are most closely allied to Man, and that he possesses all the characteristic features distinguishing them from all the characteristic features distin-guishing them from all other Verte-brata. If then we further carefully examine the three different main groups or sub-classes of Mammals—the inter-connections of which were discussed in our last chapter—there cannot be the slightest doubt that Man belongs to the Placentals, and shares with all other Placentals, the important characteristics which dis-tinguish them from Marsupials and from Cloacals. Finally, of the two main groups of placental Mammals, the Deciduata and the Indeciduata, the group of Deciduata doubtless in-cludes Man. For the human embryo is developed with a genuine decidua, and is thus absolutely distinguished from all the Indeciduata. Among the Deciduata we distinguish two legions, the Zonoplacentalia, with girdle-

shaped placenta (Beasts of Prey and Pseudohoofed animals), and the Discoplacentalia, with disc-shaped placenta (all the remaining Decid-uata). Man possesses a disc-shaped placenta, like all Discoplacentalia; and thus our next question must be, What is man's position in this group?

In the last chapter we distin-guished the following five orders of Discoplacentalia: (1) Semi-apes; (2) Rodents; (3) Insectivora; (4) Bats; (5) Apes. The last of these five orders, that of Apes, is, as every one knows, in every bodily feature far more closely allied to Man than the four others. Hence the only re-maining question now is, whether, in the system of animals, Man is to be directly classed in the order of genuine Apes, or whether he is to be considered as the representative of a special sixth order of Discoplacen-talia, allied to, but more advanced than, that of the Apes.

Linnæus in his system classed Man in the same order with genuine Apes, Semi-apes, and Bats, which he called *Primates;* that is, lords, as it were the highest dignitaries of the animal kingdom. But Blumenbach, of Göttingen, separated Man as a special order, under the name of *Bimana,* or two-handed, and con-trasted him with the Apes and Semi-apes under the name of *Quadrumana,* or four-handed. This classification was also adopted by Cuvier and, consequently, by most subsequent zoologists. It was not until 1863 that Huxley, in his excel-lent work, the "Evidence as to Man's Place in Nature," showed that this classification was based upon erroneous ideas, and that the so-called "four-handed" Apes and Semi-apes are "two-handed" as much as man is himself. The difference between the foot and hand does not consist in the *physiological* peculiarity that the first digit or thumb is opposable to the four other digits or fingers in the hand, and is not so in the foot, for there are wild tribes of men who can oppose the first or large toe to the other four, just as if it were a thumb. They can therefore use their "grasping foot" as well as a so-called "hinder hand," like Apes. The Chinese boatmen row with it. The Negro, in whom the big toe is especially strong and freely moveable, when climbing seizes hold of the branches of the trees with it, just like the "four-handed" Apes. Nay, even the newly born children of the most highly developed races of men, during the first months of their life, grasp as easily with the "hinder hand" as with the "fore hand," and hold a spoon placed in its clutch as firmly with their big toe as with the thumb! On the other hand, among the higher Apes, especially the gorilla, hand and foot are differentiated as in man.

The essential difference between hand and foot is therefore not physiological, but *morphological,* and is determined by the characteristic structure of the bony skeleton and of the muscles attached to it. The ankle-bones differ from the wrist-bones in arrangement, and the foot possesses three special muscles not existing in the hand (a short flexor muscle, a short extensor muscle, and

a long fibular muscle). In all these respects, Apes and Semiapes entirely agree with man, and hence it was quite erroneous to separate him from them as a special order on account of the stronger differentiation of his hand and foot. It is the same also with all the other structural features by means of which it was attempted to distinguish Man from Apes; for example, the relative length of the limbs, the structure of the skull, of the brain, etc. In all these respects, without exception, the differences between Man and the higher Apes are less than the corresponding differences between the higher and the lower Apes. Hence Huxley, for reasons based on the most careful and most accurate anatomical comparisons, arrives at the extremely important conclusion —"Thus, whatever system of organs be studied, the comparison of their modifications in the Ape series leads to one and the same result, that the structural differences which seperate Man from the Gorilla and Chimpanzee are not so great as those which separate the Gorilla from the lower Apes." In accordance with this, Huxley, strictly following the demands of logic, classes Man, Apes, and Semi-apes in a single order, *Primates,* and divides it into the following seven families, which are of almost equal systematic value: (1) Anthropini (Man); (2) Catarrhini (genuine Apes of the Old World); (3) Platyrrhini (genuine American Apes); (4) Arctopitheci (American clawed Apes); (5) Lemurini (short-footed and long-footed Semi-apes);

(6) Chiromyini; (7) Galepithecini (Flying Lemurs).

If we wish to arrive at a natural system, and consequently at the pedigree of the Primates, we must go a step further still, and entirely separate the Semi-apes, or Prosimiae, (Huxley's last three families), from Genuine Apes, or Simiae (the first four families). For, as I have already shown in my General Morphology, and explained in the last chapter, the Semi-apes differ in many and important respects from Genuine Apes, and in their individual forms are more closely allied to the various other orders of Discoplacentalia. Hence the Semi-apes must probably be considered as the remnants of the common primary group, out of which the other orders of Discoplacentalia, and, it may be, all Deciduata, have developed as two diverging branches. (Gen. Morph. ii. pp. 148 and 153.) But man cannot be separated from the

Systematic Survey of the Families and Genera of Apes

Sections of Apes	Families of Apes	Genera of Apes	Systematic Name of the Genera
I. APES OF THE NEW WORLD (Hesperopitheci), OR FLAT-NOSED APES (Platyrrhini)			
A. Platyrrhini with claws Arctopitheci	I. Silky apes *Hapalida*	1. Brush ape 2. Lion ape	1. Midas 2. Jacchus
B. Platyrrhini with blunt nails Dysmopitheci	II. Flat-nosed, without prehensile tail *Aphyocerca*	3. Squirrel ape 4. Leaping ape 5. Nocturnal ape 6. Tail ape	3. Chrysothrix 4. Callithrix 5. Nyetipithecus 6. Pithecia
	III. Flat-nosed, with prehensile tail *Labidocerca*	7. Rolling ape 8. Climbing ape 9. Woolly ape 10. Howling ape	7. Cebus 8. Ateles 9. Lagothrix 10. Mycetes
II. APES OF THE OLD WORLD (Heopitheci), OR NARROW-NOSED APES (Catarrhini).			
C. Tailed Catarrhini Menocerca	IV. Tailed Catarrhini, with cheek-pouches *Ascoparea*	11. Pavian 12. Macaque 13. Sea cat	11. Gynocephalus 12. Inuus 13. Cereopithecus
	V. Tailed Catarrhini, without cheek-pouches *Anasca*	14. Holy ape 15. Short ape 16. Nose ape	14. Semnopithecus 15. Colobus 16. Nasalis
D. Tailless Catarrhini Lipocerca	VI. Human apes *Anthropoides*	17. Gibbon 18. Orang-Ontan 19. Chimpanzec 20. Gorilla	17. Hylobates 18. Satyrus 19. Engeco 20. Gorilla
	VII. Men *Erecti* (*Anthropi*)	21. Ape-like man, or speechless man 22. Talking man	21. Pithecanthropus (Alalus) 22. Homo

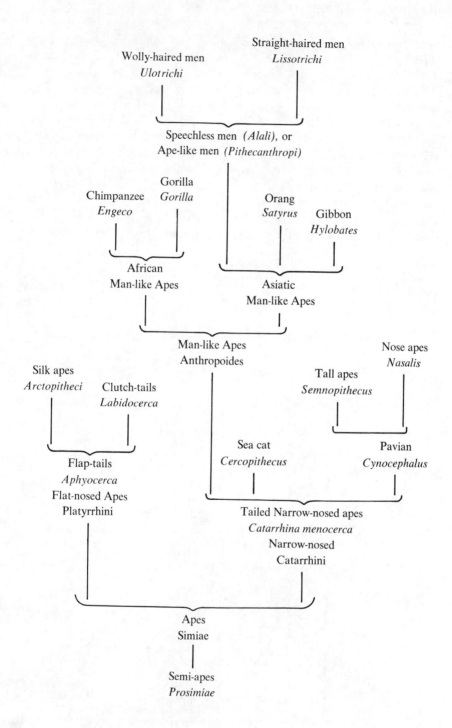

Straight-haired men
Lissotrichi

Wolly-haired men
Ulotrichi

Speechless men *(Alali)*, or
Ape-like men *(Pithecanthropi)*

Gorilla
Gorilla

Chimpanzee
Engeco

Orang
Satyrus

Gibbon
Hylobates

African
Man-like Apes

Asiatic
Man-like Apes

Man-like Apes
Anthropoides

Nose apes
Nasalis

Silk apes
Arctopitheci

Clutch-tails
Labidocerca

Tall apes
Semnopithecus

Sea cat
Cercopithecus

Pavian
Cynocephalus

Flap-tails
Aphyocerca
Flat-nosed Apes
Platyrrhini

Tailed Narrow-nosed apes
Catarrhina menocerca
Narrow-nosed
Catarrhini

Apes
Simiae

Semi-apes
Prosimiae

138

order of Genuine Apes, or Simiæ, as he is in every respect more closely allied to the higher Genuine Apes than the latter are to the lower Genuine Apes.

Genuine Apes (Simiæ) are universally divided into two perfectly natural groups, namely, the Apes of the New World, or American Apes, and the Apes of the Old World, which are indigenous to Asia and Africa, and which formerly also existed in Europe. These two classes differ principally in the formation of the nose, and they have been named accordingly. American Apes have flat noses, so that the nostrils are in front, not below; hence they are called *Flat Noses* (Platyrrhini). On the other hand, the Apes of the Old World have a narrow cartilaginous bridge, and the nostrils turned downwards, as in man; they are, therefore, called *Narrow Noses* (Catarrhini). Further, the jaw, which plays an important part in the classification of Mammals, is essentially distinct in these two groups. All Catarrhini, or Apes of the Old World, have exactly the same jaws as Man, namely, in each jaw four incisors above and below, then on each side a canine tooth and five cheek teeth, of which two are pre-molars and three molars; altogether thirty-two teeth. But all Apes of the New World, all Platyrrhini, have four more cheek teeth, namely, three pre-molars and three molars on each side, above and below: they consequently possess thirty-six teeth. Only one small group forms an exception to this rule, namely, the *Arctopitheci,* or *Clawed Apes,* in whom the third molar has degenerated, and they accordingly have on each half of their jaw three pre-molars and two molars. They also differ from the other Platyrrhini by having claws on the fingers of their hands and the toes of their feet, not nails like Man and the other Apes. This small group of South American Apes, which includes among others the well-known pretty little Midas-monkey and the Jacchus, must probably be considered only as a peculiarly developed lateral branch of the Platyrrhini.

Now, if we ask what evidence can be drawn, as to the pedigree of Apes, from the above facts, we must conclude that all the Apes of the New World have developed out of one tribe, for they all possess the characteristic jaw and the nasal formation of the Platyrrhini. In like manner it follows that all the Apes of the Old World must be derived from one and the same common primary form, which possessed the same formation of nose and jaw as all the still living Catarrhini. Further, it can scarcely be doubted that the Apes of the New World, taken as an entire tribe, are either derived from those of the Old World, or (to express it more vaguely and cautiously) both are diverging branches of one and the same tribe of Apes. We also arrive at the exceedingly important conclusion—which is of the utmost significance in regard to Man's distribution on the earth's surface—that Man *has developed out of the Catarrhini.* For we cannot discover a zoological character distinguishing him in a higher degree from the allied Apes of the Old World than that in which the most divergent forms of this group are distinguished from one another. This is the important result of Huxley's careful anatomical examination of the question, and it cannot be too highly estimated. The anatomical differences between Man and the most human-like Catarrhini (Orang, Gorilla, Chimpanzee) are in every respect less than the anatomical differences between the latter and the lowest stages of Catarrhini, more especially the Dog-like Baboon. This exceedingly important conclusion is the result of an impartial anatomical comparison of the different forms of Catarrhini.

If, therefore, we recognise the natural system of animals as the guide to our speculations, and establish upon it our pedigree, we must necessarily come to the conclusion that *the human race is a small branch of the group of Catarrhini, and has developed out of long since extinct Apes of this group in the Old World.* Some adherents of the Theory of Descent have thought that the American races of Men have developed, independently of those of the Old World, out of American Apes. I consider this hypothesis to be quite erroneous, for the complete agreement of all mankind with the Catarrhini, in regard to the characteristic formation of the nose and jaws, distinctly proves that they are of the same origin, and that they developed out of a common root after the Platyrrhini, or American Apes, had already branched off from

them. The primæval inhabitants of America, as is proved by numerous ethnographical facts, immigrated from Asia, and partly perhaps from Polynesia (or even from Europe).

There still exist great difficulties in establishing an accurate pedigree of the Human Race; this only can we further assert, that the nearest progenitors of man were tail-less Catarrhini (Lipocerca), resembling the still living Man-like Apes. These evidently developed at a late period out of tailed Catarrhini (Menocerca), the original form of Ape. Of those tail-less Catarrhini, which are now frequently called Man-like Apes, or Anthropoides, there still exist four different genera containing about a dozen different species.

The largest Man-like Ape is the famous Gorilla (called Gorilla engena, or Pongo gorilla), which is indigenous to the tropics of western Africa, and was first discovered by the missionary, Dr. Savage, in 1817, on the banks of the river Gaboon. Its nearest relative is the *Chimpanzee* (Engeco troglodytes, or Pongo troglodytes), also indigenous to western Africa, but considerably smaller than the Gorilla, which surpasses man in size and strength. The third of the three large Man-like Apes is the *Orang,* or *Orang Outang,* indigenous to Borneo and the other Sunda Islands, of which two kindred species have recently been distinguished, namely, the large Orang (Satyrus orang, or Pithecus satyrus) and the small Orang (Satyrus morio, or Pithecus morio). Lastly, there still exists in southern Asia the genus

Gibbon (Hylobates), of which from four to eight different species are distinguished. They are considerably smaller than the three first-named Anthropoides, and in most characteristics differ more from Man.

The tail-less Man-like Apes—especially since we have become more intimately acquainted with the Gorilla, and its connection with Man by the application of the Theory of Descent—have excited such universal interest, and called forth such a flood of writings, that there is no occasion for me here to enter into any detail about them. The reader will find their relations to Man fully discussed in the excellent works of Huxley, Carl Vogt, Büchner, and Rolle. I shall therefore confine myself to stating the most important general conclusion resulting from their thorough comparison with Man, namely, that each one of the four Man-like Apes stands nearer to Man in one or several respects than the rest, but that no one of them can in every respect be called absolutely the most like Man. The Orang stands nearest to Man in regard to the formation of the brain, the Chimpanzee in important characteristics in the formation of the skull, the Gorilla in the development of the feet and hands, and, lastly, the Gibbon in the formation of the thorax.

Thus, from a careful examination of the comparative anatomy of the Anthropoides, we obtain a similar result to that obtained by Weisbach, from a statistical classification and a thoughtful comparison of the very

numerous and careful measurements which Scherzer and Schwarz made of the different races of Men during their voyage in the Austrian frigate *Novara* round the earth. Weisbach comprises the final result of his investigations in the following words:

The ape-like characteristics of Man are by no means concentrated in one or another race, but are distributed in particular parts of the body, among the different races, in such a manner that each is endowed with some heirloom of this relationship—one race more so, another less, and even we Europeans cannot claim to be entirely free from evidences of this relationship.[1]

I must here also point out, what in fact is self-evident, that not one of all the still living Apes, and consequently not one of the so-called Man-like Apes, can be the progenitor of the Human Race. This opinion, in fact, has never been maintained by thoughtful adherents of the Theory of Descent, but it has been assigned to them by their thoughtless opponents. The Ape-like progenitors of the Human Race are long since extinct. We may possibly still find their fossil bones in the tertiary rocks of southern Asia or Africa. In any case they will, in the zoological system, have to be classed in the group of *tail-less Narrow-nosed Apes* (Catarrhini Lipocerci, or Anthropoides.

The genealogical hypotheses, to

[1] Weisbach: "Novara-Reise," Anthropolog. Theil.

which we have thus far been led by the application of the Theory of Descent to Man, present themselves to every clearly and logically reasoning person as the direct results from the facts of comparative anatomy, ontogeny, and palæontology. Of course our phylogeny can indicate only in a very general way the outlines of the human pedigree. Phylogeny is the more in danger of becoming erroneous the more rigorously it is applied in detail to special animal forms known to us. However, we can, even now, with approximate certainty distinguish at least the following twenty-two stages of the ancestors of Man. Fourteen of these stages belong to the Vertebrata, and eight to the Invertebrate ancestors of Man (Prochordata.)

. . .

In now turning to the equally interesting and difficult question of the relative *connection, migration,* and *primæval home* of the twelve species of men, I must premise the remark that, in the present state of our anthropological knowledge, any answer to this question must be regarded only as a provisional hypothesis. This is much the same as with any genealogical hypothesis which we may form of the origin of kindred animal and vegetable species, on the basis of the "Natural System." But the necessary uncertainty of these special hypotheses of descent, in no way shakes the absolute certainty of the general theory of descent. Man, we may feel certain, is descended from Catarrhini, or narrow-nosed apes, whether we

agree with the polyphylites, and suppose each human species, in its primæval home, to have originated out of a special kind of ape; or whether, agreeing with the monophylites, we suppose that all the human species arose only by differentiation from a single species of primæval man (Homo primigenius).

For many and weighty reasons we hold the monophyletic hypothesis to be the more correct, and we therefore assume a *single primæval home* for mankind, where he developed out of a long since extinct anthropoid species of ape. Of the five now existing continents, neither Australia, nor America, nor Europe can have been this primæval home, or the so-called "Paradise," the "cradle of the human race." Most circumstances indicate southern Asia as the locality in question. Besides southern Asia, the only other of the now existing continents which might be viewed in this light is Africa. But there are a number of circumstances (especially chorological facts) which suggest that the primæval home of man was a continent now sunk below the surface of the Indian Ocean, which extended along the south of Asia, as it is at present (and probably in direct connection with it), towards the east, as far as further India and the Sunda Islands; towards the west, as far as Madagascar and the south-eastern shores of Africa. We have already mentioned that many facts in animal and vegetable geography render the former existence of such a south Indian continent very probable. Sclater has given this continent the name of

Lemuria, from the Semi-apes which were characteristic of it. By assuming this Lemuria to have been man's primæval home, we greatly facilitate the explanation of the geographical distribution of the human species by migration.

We as yet know of no fossil remains of the hypothetical primæval man (Homo primigenius) who developed out of anthropoid apes during the tertiary period, either in Lemuria or in southern Asia, or possibly in Africa. But considering the extraordinary resemblance between the lowest woolly-haired men, and the highest man-like apes, which still exist at the present day, it requires but a slight stretch of the imagination to conceive an intermediate form connecting the two, and to see in it an approximate likeness to the supposed primæval men, or ape-like men. The form of their skull was probably very long, with slanting teeth; their hair woolly; the colour of their skin dark, of a brownish tint. The hair covering the whole body was probably thicker than in any of the still living human species; their arms comparatively longer and stronger; their legs, on the other hand, knock-kneed, shorter and thinner, with entirely undeveloped calves; their walk but half erect.

This ape-like man very probably did not as yet possess an actual human language, that is, an articulate language of ideas. Human speech, as has already been remarked, most likely originated after the divergence of the primæval species of men into different species.

The number of primæval languages is, however, considerably larger than the number of the species of men above discussed. For philologists have hitherto not been able to trace the four primæval languages of the Mediterranean species, namely, the Basque, Caucasian, Semitic, and Indo-Germanic to a single primæval language. As little can the different Negro languages be derived from a common primæval language; hence both these species, Mediterranean and Negro, are certainly *polyglottonic,* that is, their respective languages originated after the divergence of the speechless primary species into several races had already taken place. Perhaps the Mongols, the Arctic and American tribes, are likewise polyglottonic. The Malayan species is, however, *monoglottonic;* all the Polynesian and Sundanesian dialects and languages can be derived from a common, long since extinct primæval language, which is not related to any other language on earth. All the other human species, Nubians, Dravidas, Australians, Papuans, Hottentots, and Kaffres are likewise monoglottonic.

Out of speechless primæval man, whom we consider as the common primary species of all the others, there developed in the first place— probably by natural selection—various species of men unknown to us, and now long since extinct, and who still remained at the stage of speechless ape-men (Alalus, or Pithecanthropus). Two of these species, a woolly-haired and a straight-haired, which were most strongly divergent, and consequently overpowered the others in the struggle for life, became the primary forms of the other remaining human species.

The main branch of woolly-haired men (Ulotrichi) at first spread only over the southern hemisphere, and then emigrated partly eastwards, partly westwards. Remnants of the eastern branch are the Papuans in New Guinea and Melanesia, who in earlier times were diffused much further west (in further India and Sundanesia), and it was not until a late period that they were driven eastwards by the Malays. The Hottentots are the but little changed remnants of the western branch; they immigrated to their present home from the north-east. It was perhaps during this migration that the two nearly related species of Caffres and Negroes branched off from them; but it may be that they owe their origin to a peculiar branch of ape-like men.

The second main branch of primæval straight-haired men (Lissotrichi), which is more capable of development, has probably left a but little changed remnant of its common primary form—which migrated to the south-east—in the ape-like natives of Australia. Probably very closely related to these latter are the South Asiatic *primæval Malays,* or *Promalays,* which name we have previously given to the extinct, hypothetical primary form of the other six human species. Out of this unknown common primary form there seem to have arisen three diverging branches, namely, the true Malays, the Mongols, and the Euplocomi; the first spread to the east, the second to the north, and the third westwards.

The primæval home, or the "Centre of Creation," of the Malays must be looked for in the south-eastern part of the Asiatic continent, or possibly in the more extensive continent which existed at the time when further India was directly connected with the Sunda Archipelago and eastern Lemuria. From thence the Malays spread towards the south-east, over the Sunda Archipelago as far as Borneo, then wandered, driving the Papuans before them, eastwards towards the Samoa and Tonga Islands, and thence gradually diffused over the whole of the islands of the southern Pacific, to the Sandwich Islands in the north, the Mangareva in the east, and New Zealand in the south. A single branch of the Malayan tribe was driven far westwards and peopled Madagascar.

The second main branch of primæval Malays, that is, the Mongols, at first also spread in Southern Asia, and, radiating to the east, north, and north-west, gradually peopled the greater part of the Asiatic continent. Of the four principal races of the Mongol species, the Indo-Chinese must perhaps be looked upon as the primary group, out of which at a later period the other Coreo-Japanese and Ural-Altaian races developed as diverging branches. The Mongols migrated in many ways from western Asia into Europe, where the species is still represented in northern Russia and Scandinavia by the Fins and Lapps, in Hungary by the kindred Magyars, and in Turkey by the Osmanlis.

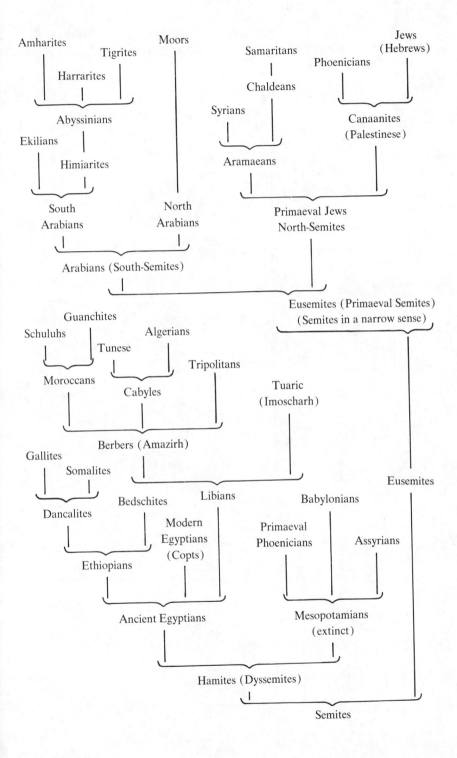

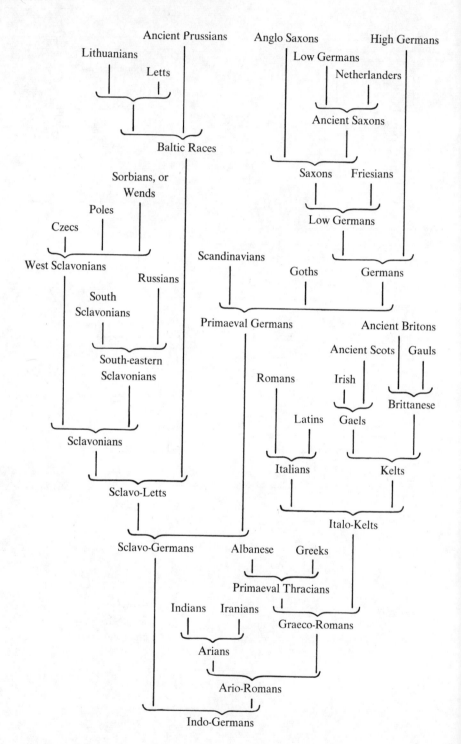

Systematic Survey of the Twelve Human Species

Tribe	Human Species	A.	B.	C.	Home
TUFT-HAIRED Lophocomi (about 2 millions)	1. PAPUAN	2	Re	Mn	New Guinea and Melanesia, Philippine Islands, Malacca
	2. HOTEN-TOT	$\frac{1}{20}$	Re	Mn	The extreme south of Africa (The Cape)
FLEECY-HAIRED Eriocomi (about 150 millions)	3. KAFFRE	20	Pr	Mn	South Africa (between 30° S. Lat. and 5° N. Lat.)
	4. NEGRO	130	Pr	Pl	Central Africa (between the Equator and 30° N. Lat.)
STRAIGHT-HAIRED Euthycomi (about 600 millions) lions)	5. AUSTRA-LIAN	$\frac{1}{12}$	Re	Mn	Australia
	6. MALAY	30	Co	Mn	Malacca, Sundanesia, Polynesia, and Madagascar
	7. MONGOL	550	Pr	Mn?	The greater part of Asia and and northern Europe
	8. ARCTIC	25	Co	Pl?	The extreme north-east of Asia and the extreme north of America
	9. AMERI-CAN	12	Re	Mn?	The whole of America with the exception of the extreme north
CURLY-HAIRED Euplocomi (about 600 millions)	10. DRAVI-DAS	34	Co	Mn	South Asia (Hindostan and Ceylon)
	11. NUBIAN	10	Co	Mn?	Central Africa (Nubia and Fula-land)
	12. MEDI-TERRANEAN	550	Pr	Pl	In all parts of the world, having migrated from South Asia to North Africa and South Europe
	13. HYBRIDS OF THE SPECIES	11	Pr	Pl	In all parts of the world but predominating in America and Asia
	TOTAL	1350			

N. B.—Column A denotes the Average Number of the Population in millions. Column B shows the Degree of the Phyletic Development of the Species, thus Pr = Progressive Diffusion; Co = Comparative stability; Re = Retrogression and Extinction. Column C denotes the Character of the Primæval Language; Mn (Monoglottonic) signifies that the Species had one Simple Primæval Language; Pl (Polyglottonic) a Compound Primæval Langeage.

On the other hand, a branch of the Mongols migrated from northeastern Asia to America, which was probably in earlier times connected with the former continent by a broad isthmus. The Arctic tribes, or Polar men, the Hyperboreans of north-eastern Asia, and the Esquimaux of the extreme north of America, must probably be regarded as an offshoot of this branch, which became peculiarly degenerated by unfavourable conditions of existence. The principal portion of the Mongolian immigrants, however, migrated to the south, and gradually spread over the whole of America, first over the north, later over South America.

The third and most important main branch of primæval Malays, the curly-haired races, or Euplocomi, have probably left in the Dravidas of Hindostan and Ceylon, that species of man which differs least from the common primary form of the Euplocomi. The principal portion of the latter, namely, the Mediterranean species, migrated from their primæval home (Hindostan?) westwards, and peopled the shores of the Mediterranean, south-western Asia, north Africa, and Europe. The Nubians, in the north-east of Africa, must perhaps be regarded as an off-shoot of the primæval Semitic tribes, who migrated far across central Africa almost to the western shores.

The various branches of the Indo-Germanic race have deviated furthest from the common primary form of ape-like men. During classic antiquity and the middle ages, the Romanic branch (the Græco-Italo-Keltic group), one of the two main branches of the Indo-Germanic species, outstripped all other branches in the career of civilization, but at present the same position is occupied by the Germanic. Its chief representatives are the English and Germans, who are in the present age laying the foundation for a new period of higher mental development, in the recognition and completion of the theory of descent. The recognition of the theory of development and the monistic philosophy based upon it, forms the best criterion for the degree of man's mental development.

On the Affinities and Genealogy of Man. General Summary and Conclusion

Charles Robert Darwin
1871

On the affinities and genealogy of man

Even if it be granted that the difference between man and his nearest allies is as great in corporeal structure as some naturalists maintain, and although we must grant that the difference between them is immense in mental power, yet the facts given in the previous chapters declare, as it appears to me, in the plainest manner, that man is descended from some lower form, notwithstanding that connecting links have not hitherto been discovered.

Man is liable to numerous, slight, and diversified variations, which are induced by the same general causes, are governed and transmitted in accordance with the same general laws as in the lower animals. Man tends to multiply at so rapid a rate that his offspring are necessarily exposed to a struggle for existence, and consequently to natural selection. He has given rise to many races, some of which are so different that they have often been ranked by naturalists as distinct species. His body is constructed on the same homological plan as that of other mammals, independently of the uses to which the several parts may be put. He passes through the same phases of embryological development. He retains many rudimentary and useless structures, which no doubt were once serviceable. Characters occasionally make their reappearance in him, which we have every reason to believe were possessed by his early progenitors. If the origin of man had been wholly different from that of all other animals, these various appearances would be mere empty deceptions; but such an admission is incredible. These appearances, on the other hand, are intelligible, at least to a large extent, if man is the co-descendant with other mammals of some unknown and lower form.

. . .

"On the Affinities and Genealogy of Man." "General Summary and Conclusion." *The Descent of Man, and Selection in Relation to Sex.* Chapter 6, pp. 178–79, 191–93; Chapter 21, pp. 368–78, 386–87. John Murray, London, 1871.

On the Birthplace and Antiquity of Man. We are naturally led to inquire where was the birthplace of man at that stage of descent when our progenitors diverged from the Catarhine stock. The fact that they belonged to this stock clearly shows that they inhabited the Old World; but not Australia nor any oceanic island, as we may infer from the laws of geographical distribution. In each great region of the world the living mammals are closely related to the extinct species of the same region. It is therefore probable that Africa was formerly inhabited by extinct apes closely allied to the gorilla and chimpanzee; and as these two species are now man's nearest allies, it is somewhat more probable that our early progenitors lived on the African Continent than elsewhere. But it is useless to speculate on this subject, for an ape nearly as large as a man, namely, the Dryopithecus of Lartet, which was closely allied to the anthropomorphous Hylobates, existed in Europe during the Upper Miocene period; and since so remote a period the earth has certainly undergone many great revolutions, and there has been ample time for migration on the largest scale.

At the period and place, whenever and wherever it may have been, when man first lost his hairy covering, he probably inhabited a hot country; and this would have been favorable for a frugiferous diet, on which, judging from analogy, he subsisted. We are far from knowing how long ago it was when man first diverged from the Catarhine stock; but this may have occurred at an epoch as remote as the Eocene period; for the higher apes had diverged from the lower apes as early as the Upper Miocene period, as shown by the existence of the Dryopithecus. We are also quite ignorant at how rapid a rate organisms, whether high or low in the scale, may under favorable circumstances be modified: we know, however, that some have retained the same form during an enormous lapse of time. From what we see going on under domestication, we learn that within the same period some of the co-descendants of the same species may be not at all changed, some a little, and some greatly changed. Thus it may have been with man, who has undergone a great amount of modification in certain characters in comparison with the higher apes.

The great break in the organic chain between man and his nearest allies, which cannot be bridged over by any extinct or living species, has often been advanced as a grave objection to the belief that man is descended from some lower form; but this objection will not appear of much weight to those who, convinced by general reasons, believe in the general principle of evolution. Breaks incessantly occur in all parts of the series, some being wide, sharp, and defined, others less so in various degrees; as between the orang and its nearest allies—between the Tarsius and the other Lemuridæ—between the elephant and in a more striking manner between the Ornithorhynchus or Echidna, and other mammals. But all these breaks depend merely on the number of related forms which have become extinct. At some future period, not very distant as measured by centuries, the civilized races of man will almost certainly exterminate and replace throughout the world the savage races. At the same time the anthropomorphous apes, as Prof. Schaaffhausen has remarked, will no doubt be exterminated. The break will then be rendered wider, for it will intervene between man in a more civilized state, as we may hope, than the Caucasian, and some ape as low as a baboon, instead of as at present between the negro or Australian and the gorilla.

With respect to the absence of fossil remains, serving to connect man with his ape-like progenitors, no one will lay much stress on this fact, who will read Sir C. Lyell's discussion, in which he shows that in all the vertebrate classes the discovery of fossil remains has been an extremely slow and fortuitous process. Nor should it be forgotten that those regions which are the most likely to afford remains connecting man with some extinct ape-like creature, have not as yet been searched by geologists.

. . .

General summary and conclusion

A brief summary will here be sufficient to recall to the reader's mind the more salient points in this work. Many of the views which have been advanced are highly speculative, and some no doubt will prove erroneous; but I have in every case given the reasons which have led me to one view rather than to another. It seemed worth while to try how far the principle of evolution would throw light on some of the more complex problems in the natural history of man. False facts are highly injurious to the progress of science, for they often long endure; but false views, if supported by some evidence, do little harm, as every one takes a salutary pleasure in proving their falseness; and when this is done, one path toward error is closed, and the road to truth is often at the same time opened.

The main conclusion arrived at in this work, and now held by many naturalists who are well competent to form a sound judgment, is that man is descended from some less highly-organized form. The grounds upon which this conclusion rests will never be shaken, for the close similarity between man and the lower animals in embryonic development, as well as in innumerable points of structure and constitution, both of high and of the most trifling importance—the rudiments which he retains, and the abnormal reversions to which he is occasionally liable—are facts which cannot be disputed. They have long been known, but until recently they told us nothing with respect to the origin of man. Now, when viewed by the light of our knowledge of the whole organic world, their meaning is unmistakable. The great principle of evolution stands up clear and firm, when these groups of facts are considered in connection with others, such as the mutual affinities of the members of the same group, their geographical distribution in past and present times, and their geological succession. It is incredible that all these facts should speak falsely. He who is not content to look, like a savage, at the phenomena of Nature as disconnected, cannot any longer believe that man is the work of a separate act of creation. He will be forced to admit that the close resemblance of the embryo of man to that, for instance, of a dog—the construction of his skull, limbs, and whole frame, independently of the uses to which the parts may be put, on the same plan with that of other mammals— the occasional reappearance of various structures, for instance, of several distinct muscles, which man does not normally possess, but which are common to the Quadrumana— and a crowd of analogous facts— all point in the plainest manner to the conclusion that man is the co-descendant with other mammals of a common progenitor.

We have seen that man incessantly presents individual differences in all parts of his body and in his mental faculties. These differences or variations seem to be induced by the same general causes, and to obey the same laws as with the lower animals. In both cases similar laws of inheritance prevail. Man tends to increase at a greater rate than his means of subsistence; consequently he is occasionally subjected to a severe struggle for existence, and natural selection will have effected whatever lies within its scope. A succession of strongly-

marked variations of a similar nature are by no means requisite; slight fluctuating differences in the individual suffice for the work of natural selection. We may feel assured that the inherited effects of the long-continued use or disuse of parts will have done much in the same direction with natural selection. Modifications formerly of importance, though no longer of any special use, will be long inherited. When one part is modified, other parts will change through the principle of correlation, of which we have instances in many curious cases of correlated monstrosities. Something may be attributed to the direct and definite action of the surrounding conditions of life, such as abundant food, heat, or moisture; and lastly, many characters of slight physiological importance, some indeed of considerable importance, have been gained through sexual selection.

No doubt man, as well as every other animal, presents structures which, as far as we can judge with our little knowledge, are not now of any service to him, nor have been so during any former period of his existence, either in relation to his general conditions of life, or of one sex to the other. Such structures cannot be accounted for by any form of selection, or by the inherited effects of the use and disuse of parts. We know, however, that many strange and strongly-marked peculiarities of structure occasionally appear in our domesticated productions, and if the unknown causes which produce them were to act more uniformly, they would probably become common to all the individuals of the species. We may hope hereafter to understand something about the causes of such occasional modifications, especially through the study of monstrosities: hence the labors of experimentalists, such as those of M. Camille Dareste, are full of promise for the future. In the greater number of cases, we can only say that the cause of each slight variation and of each monstrosity lies much more in the nature or constitution of the organism, than in the nature of the surrounding conditions; though new and changed conditions certainly play an important part in exciting organic changes of all kinds.

Through the means just specified, aided perhaps by others as yet undiscovered, man has been raised to his present state. But since he attained to the rank of manhood, he has diverged into distinct races, or, as they may be more appropriately called, subspecies. Some of these, for instance, the Negro and European, are so distinct that, if specimens had been brought to a naturalist without any further information, they would undoubtedly have been considered by him as good and true species. Nevertheless all the races agree in so many unimportant details of structure and in so many mental peculiarities, that these can be accounted for only through inheritance from a common progenitor; and a progenitor thus characterized would probably have deserved to rank as man.

It must not be supposed that the divergence of each race from the other races, and of all the races from a common stock, can be traced back to any one pair of progenitors. On the contrary, at every stage in the process of modification, all the individuals which were in any way best fitted for their conditions of life, though in different degrees, would have survived in greater numbers than the less well fitted. The process would have been like that followed by man, when he does not intentionally select particular individuals, but breeds from all the superior and neglects all the inferior individuals. He thus slowly but surely modifies his stock, and unconsciously forms a new strain. So with respect to modifications, acquired independently of selection, and due to variations arising from the nature of the organism and the action of the surrounding conditions, or from changed habits of life, no single pair will have been modified in a much greater degree than the other pairs which inhabit the same country, for all will have been continually blended through free intercrossing.

By considering the embryological structure of man—the homologies which he presents with the lower animals—the rudiments which he retains—and the reversions to which he is liable, we can partly recall in imagination the former condition of our early progenitors; and can approximately place them in their proper position in the zoological series. We thus learn that man is descended from a hairy quadruped, furnished with a tail and pointed ears, probably aboreal in its habits, and an inhabitant of the Old World.

This creature, if its whole structure had been examined by a naturalist, would have been classed among the Quadrumana, as surely as would the common and still more ancient progenitor of the Old and New World monkeys. The Quadrumana and all the higher mammals are probably derived from an ancient marsupial animal, and this through a long line of diversified forms, either from some reptile-like or some amphibian-like creature, and this again from some fish-like animal. In the dim obscurity of the past we can see that the early progenitor of all the Vertebrata must have been an aquatic animal, provided with branchiæ, with the two sexes united in the same individual, and with the most important organs of the body (such as the brain and heart) imperfectly developed. This animal seems to have been more like the larvæ of our existing marine Ascidians than any other known form.

The greatest difficulty which presents itself, when we are driven to the above conclusion on the origin of man, is the high standard of intellectual power and of moral disposition which he has attained. But every one who admits the general principle of evolution, must see that the mental powers of the higher animals, which are the same in kind with those of mankind, though so different in degree, are capable of advancement. Thus the interval between the mental powers of one of the higher apes and of a fish, or between those of an ant and scale-insect, is immense. The development of these powers in animals does not offer any special difficulty; for with our domesticated animals, the mental faculties are certainly variable, and the variations are inherited. No one doubts that these faculties are of the utmost importance to animals in a state of nature. Therefore the conditions are favorable for their development through natural selection. The same conclusion may be extended to man; the intellect must have been all-important to him, even at a very remote period, enabling him to use language, to invent and make weapons, tools, traps, etc.; by which means, in combination with his social habits, he long ago became the most dominant of all living creatures.

A great stride in the development of the intellect will have followed, as soon as, through a previous considerable advance, the half-art and half-instinct of language came into use; for the continued use of language will have reacted on the brain, and produced an inherited effect; and this again will have reacted on the improvement of language. The large size of the brain in man, in comparison with that of the lower animals, relatively to the size of their bodies, may be attributed in chief part, as Mr. Chauncey Wright has well remarked[1] to the early use of some simple form of language—that wonderful engine which affixes signs to all sorts of objects and qualities, and excites trains of thought which would never arise from the mere impression of the senses, and if they

[1] On the "Limits of Natural Selection," in the 'North American Review,' Oct. 1870, p. 295.

did arise could not be followed out. The higher intellectual powers of man, such as those of ratiocination, abstraction, self-consciousness, etc., will have followed from the continued improvement of other mental faculties; but without considerable culture of the mind, both in the race and in the individual, it is doubtful whether these high powers would be exercised, and thus fully attained.

The development of the moral qualities is a more interesting and difficult problem. Their foundation lies in the social instincts, including in this term the family ties. These instincts are of a highly-complex nature, and in the case of the lower animals give special tendencies toward certain definite actions; but the more important elements for us are love, and the distinct emotion of sympathy. Animals endowed with the social instincts take pleasure in each other's company, warn each other of danger, defend and aid each other in many ways. These instincts are not extended to all the individuals of the species, but only to those of the same community. As they are highly beneficial to the species, they have in all probability been acquired through natural selection.

A moral being is one who is capable of comparing his past and future actions and motives—of approving of some and disapproving of others; and the fact that man is the one being who with certainty can be thus designated makes the greatest of all distinctions between him and the lower animals. But in our third chapter I have endeavored to show that the moral sense follows, firstly, from the enduring and always present nature of the social instincts, in which respect man agrees with the lower animals; and secondly, from his mental faculties being highly active and his impressions of past events extremely vivid, in which respects he differs from the lower animals. Owing to this condition of mind, man cannot avoid looking backward and comparing the impressions of past events and actions. He also continually looks forward. Hence after some temporary desire or passion has mastered his social instincts, he will reflect and compare the now weakened impression of such past impulses with the ever-present social instinct; and he will then feel that sense of dissatisfaction which all unsatisfied instincts leave behind them. Consequently he resolves to act differently for the future—and this is conscience. Any instinct which is permanently stronger or more enduring than another, gives rise to a feeling which we express by saying that it ought to be obeyed. A pointer dog, if able to reflect on his past conduct, would say to himself, I ought (as indeed we say of him) to have pointed at that hare, and not have yielded to the passing temptation of hunting it.

Social animals are partly impelled by a wish to aid the members of the same community in a general manner, but more commonly to perform certain definite actions. Man is impelled by the same general wish to aid his fellows, but has few or no special instincts. He differs also from the lower animals in being able to express his desires by words, which thus become the guide to the aid required and bestowed. The motive to give aid is likewise somewhat modified in man: it no longer consists solely of a blind instinctive impulse, but is largely influenced by the praise or blame of his fellowmen. Both the appreciation and the bestowal of praise and blame rest on sympathy; and this emotion, as we have seen, is one of the most important elements of the social instincts. Sympathy, though gained as an instinct, is also much strengthened by exercise or habit. As all men desire their own happiness, praise or blame is bestowed on actions and motives, according as they lead to this end; and, as happiness is an essential part of the general good, the greatest-happiness principle indirectly serves as a nearly safe standard of right and wrong. As the reasoning powers advance and experience is gained, the more remote effects of certain lines of conduct on the character of the individual, and on the general good, are perceived; and then the self-regarding virtues, from coming within the scope of public opinion, receive praise, and their opposites receive blame. But with the less civilized nations reason often errs, and many bad customs and base superstitions come within the same scope, and consequently are esteemed as high virtues, and their breach as heavy crimes.

The moral faculties are generally esteemed, and with justice, as of higher value than the intellectual powers. But we should always bear in mind that the activity of the mind in vividly recalling past impressions is one of the fundamental though secondary bases of conscience. This fact affords the strongest argument for educating and stimulating in all possible ways the intellectual faculties of every human being. No doubt a man with a torpid mind, if his social affections and sympathies are well developed, will be led to good actions, and may have a fairly sensitive conscience. But whatever renders the imagination of men more vivid and strengthens the habit of recalling and comparing past impressions, will make the conscience more sensitive, and may even compensate to a certain extent for weak social affections and sympathies.

The moral nature of man has reached the highest standard as yet attained, partly through the advancement of the reasoning powers and consequently of a just public opinion, but especially through the sympathies being rendered more tender and widely diffused through the effects of habit, example, instruction, and reflection. It is not improbable that virtuous tendencies may through long practice be inherited. With the more civilized races, the conviction of the existence of an all-seeing Deity has had a potent influence on the advancement of morality. Ultimately man no longer accepts the praise or blame of his fellows as his chief guide, though few escape this influence, but his habitual convictions controlled by reason afford him the safest rule. His conscience then becomes his supreme judge and monitor. Nevertheless the first foundation or origin of the moral sense lies in the social instincts, including sympathy; and these instincts no doubt were primarily gained, as in the case of the lower animals, through natural selection.

The belief in God has often been advanced as not only the greatest, but the most complete, of all the distinctions between man and the lower animals. It is, however, impossible, as we have seen, to maintain that this belief is innate or instinctive in man. On the other hand, a belief in all-pervading spiritual agencies seems to be universal; and apparently follows from a considerable advance in the reasoning powers of man, and from a still greater advance in his faculties of imagination, curiosity, and wonder. I am aware that the assumed instinctive belief in God has been used by many persons as an argument for His existence. But this is a rash argument, as we should thus be compelled to believe in the existence of many cruel and malignant spirits, possessing only a little more power than man; for the belief in them is far more general than of a beneficent Deity. The idea of a universal and beneficent Creator of the universe does not seem to arise in the mind of man, until he has been elevated by long-continued culture.

He who believes in the advancement of man from some lowly-organized form, will naturally ask, "How does this bear on the belief in the immortality of the soul?" The barbarous races of man, as Sir J. Lubbock has shown, possess no clear belief of this kind; but arguments derived from the primeval beliefs of savages are, as we have just seen, of little or no avail. Few persons feel any anxiety from the impossibility of determining at what precise period in the development of the individual, from the first trace of the minute germinal vesicle to the child either before or after birth, man becomes an immortal being; and there is no greater cause for anxiety because the period in the gradually-ascending organic scale cannot possibly be determined.[2]

I am aware that the conclusions arrived at in this work will be denounced by some as highly irreligious; but he who thus denounces them is bound to show why it is more irreligious to explain the origin of man as a distinct species by descent from some lower form, through the laws of variation and natural selection, than to explain the birth of the individual through the laws of ordinary reproduction. The birth both of the species and of the individual are equally parts of that grand sequence of events, which our minds refuse to accept as the result of blind chance. The understanding revolts at such a conclusion, whether or not we are able to believe that every slight variation of structure, the union of each pair in marriage, the dissemination of each seed, and other such events, have all been ordained for some special purpose.

· · ·

The main conclusion arrived at in this work, namely, that man is descended from some lowly-organized form, will, I regret to think, be highly distasteful to many persons.

[2] The Rev. J. A. Picton give a discussion to this effect in his 'New Theories and the Old Faith,' 1870.

But there can hardly be a doubt that we are descended from barbarians. The astonishment which I felt on first seeing a party of Fuegians on a wild and broken shore will never be forgotten by me, for the reflection at once rushed into my mind—such were our ancestors. These men were absolutely naked and bedaubed with paint, their long hair was tangled, their mouths frothed with excitement, and their expression was wild, startled, and distrustful. They possessed hardly any arts, and, like wild animals, lived on what they could catch; they had no government, and were merciless to every one not of their own small tribe. He who has seen a savage in his native land will not feel much shame, if forced to acknowledge that the blood of some more humble creature flows in his veins. For my own part, I would as soon be descended from that heroic little monkey, who braved his dreaded enemy in order to save the life of his keeper; or from that old baboon, who, descending from the mountains, carried away in triumph his young comrade from a crowd of astonished dogs—as from a savage who delights to torture his enemies, offers up bloody sacrifices, practises infanticide without remorse, treats his wives like slaves, knows no decency, and is haunted by the grossest superstitions.

Man may be excused for feeling some pride at having risen, though not through his own exertions, to the very summit of the organic scale; and the fact of his having thus risen, instead of having been aboriginally placed there, may give him hopes for a still higher destiny in the distant future. But we are not here concerned with hopes or fears, only with the truth as far as our reason allows us to discover it. I have given the evidence to the best of my ability; and we must acknowledge, as it seems to me, that man with all his noble qualities, with sympathy which feels for the most debased, with benevolence which extends not only to other men but to the humblest living creature, with his godlike intellect which has penetrated into the movements and constitution of the solar system—with all these exalted powers—Man still bears in his bodily frame the indelible stamp of his lowly origin.

Questions of Affinity and Origin

St. George Jackson Mivart
1873

. . .

Having completed our survey and summary of the structural resemblances and differences presented by the different forms of Primates, we may now consider and endeavour to appraise their value, as bearing upon the question of the "Origin of Species," and especially upon the asserted "descent of man" from some "non-human" ape ancestor. The question, that is, as to man's body; for as to the totality of his nature no mere anatomical examinations will enable us to decide—that is the task of psychology and philosophy generally.

In the first place, it is manifest that man, the apes, and Half-apes cannot be arranged in a single ascending series of which man is the term and culmination.

We may, indeed, by selecting one organ, or one set of parts, and confining our attention to it, arrange the different forms in a more or less simple manner. But, if all the organs be taken into account, the cross relations and interdependencies become in the highest degree complex and difficult to unravel.

This has been more or less generally recognised; but it has been put forward by Mr. Darwin,[1] and widely accepted, that the resemblances between man and apes are such that man may be conceived to have descended from some ancient members of the broad-breastboned group of apes, and the Gorilla is still popularly credited with the closest relationship to him which is to be found in all existing apes.

As to the latter opinion, evidence has been here adduced to show that it is quite untenable.

As to Mr. Darwin's proposition, much remains to be said. But it is certainly true that on the whole the anatomical characters of man's body have much more resemblance to those common to the latisternal group than to those presented by

[1] 'Descent of Man,' vol. i. p. 197.

"Questions of Affinity and Origin." *Man and Apes: an Exposition of Structural Resemblances and Differences Bearing upon the Questions of Affinity and Origin.* Part 3, pp. 171–93. Hardwicke, London, 1873.

any other section of the order Primates.

But, in the first place, we should consider what evidence of common origin does community of structure afford.

The human structural characters are shared by so many and such diverse forms, that it is impossible to arrange even groups of genera in a single ascending series from the Aye-Aye to man (to say nothing of so arranging the several single genera), if all the structural resemblances are taken into account.

On any conceivable hypothesis there are many similar structures, each of which must be deemed to have been independently evolved in more than one instance.

If the number of wrist-bones be deemed a special mark of affinity between the Gorilla, Chimpanzee, and man, why are we not to consider it also a special mark of affinity between the Indris and man? That it should be so considered, however, would be deemed an absurdity by every evolutionist.

If the proportions of the arms speak in favour of the Chimpanzee, why do not the proportions of the legs serve to promote the rank of the Gibbons?

If the "bridging convolutions" of the Orang go to sustain its claim to supremacy, they also go far to sustain a similar claim on the part of the long-tailed, thumbless Spider Monkeys.

If the obliquely-ridged teeth of *Simia* and *Troglodytes* point to community of origin, how can we deny a similar community of origin, as

thus estimated, to the Howling Monkeys and Galagos?

The liver of the Gibbons proclaims them almost human; that of the Gorilla declares him comparatively brutal.

The ear lobule of the Gorilla makes him our cousin; but his tongue is eloquent in his own dispraise.

The slender Loris, from amidst the Half-apes, can put in many a claim to be our shadow refracted, as it were, through a Lemurine prism.

The lower American apes meet us with what seems "the front of Jove himself," compared with the gigantic but low-browed denizens of tropical Western Africa.

In fact, in the words of the illustrious Dutch naturalists, Messrs. Schroeder van der Kolk, and Vrolik,[2] the lines of affinity existing between different Primates construct rather a network than a ladder.

It is indeed a tangled web, the meshes of which no naturalist has as yet unravelled by the aid of natural selection. Nay, more, these complex affinities form such a net for the use of the teleological retiarius as it will be difficult for his Lucretian antagonist to evade, even with the countless turns and doublings of Darwinian evolutions.

But, it may be replied, the spontaneous and independent appearance of these similar structures is due to "atavism" and "reversion"— to the reappearance, that is, in modern descendants, of ancient and sometimes long-lost structural char-

2 'Nat. Hist. Review,' vol. ii. p. 117.

acters, which formerly existed in more or less remote hypothetical ancestors.

Let us see to what this reply brings us. If it is true, and if man and the Orang are diverging descendants of a creature with certain cerebral characters, then that remote ancestor must also have had the wrist of the Chimpanzee, the voice of a long-armed ape, the blade-bone of the Gorilla, the chin of the Siamang, the skull-dome of an American ape, the ischium of a slender Loris, the whiskers and beard of a Saki, the liver and stomach of the Gibbons, and the number of other characters before detailed, in which the various several forms of higher or lower Primates respectively approximate to man.

But to assert this is as much as to say that low down in the scale of Primates was an ancestral form so like man that it might well be called an *homunculus;* and we have the virtual pre-existence of man's body supposed, in order to account for the actual first appearance of that body as we know it—a supposition manifestly absurd if put forward as an explanation.

Nor if such an *homunculus* had really existed, would it suffice to account for the difficulty. For it must be borne in mind that man is only one of many peculiar forms. The body of the Orang is as exceptional in its way as is that of man in another. The little Tarsier has even a more exceptional structure than has man himself. Now, all these exceptional forms show cross relations and

complex dependencies as involved and puzzling as does the human structure, so that in each several case we should meet with a similar network of difficulties, if we sought to account for existing structural characters through the influence of inheritance and "natural selection."

It may be replied that certain of these characters have arisen in total independence, and this reply is no doubt true; but how are we to discriminate between those which are inherited and those which are independently acquired? Structures like strong teeth or powerful claws, obviously useful in the struggle for life, may well be supposed to have independently appeared, and been preserved time after time; but what characters could well be thought, *à priori,* less likely to be independently acquired than a more or less developed chin, such as man shares with the Siamang alone, or a slightly aquiline nose, such as that found in the Hoolock Gibbon and often in the human species? Can either character be thought to have preserved either species in the struggle for life, or have persistently gained the hearts of successive generations of female Gibbons? Certainly seductiveness of this sort will never explain the arrangement of the lobes of the liver, or the presence of an oblique ridge on the grinding surfaces of the back teeth.

Again, can this oblique ridge of the grinding teeth be supposed to have arisen through life necessities? and yet, if it is a real sign of genetic affinity, how comes it to be absent from the man-like Gibbons, and to reappear for the first time in American apes, and among others in the aberrant and more or less baboon-like Howling Monkeys?

The same remark applies to the condition of wrist-bones of man, the Chimpanzee, and Indris. If this condition arises independently, and is no mark whatever of genetic affinity, what other single character can with certainty be deemed to be valid evidence of affinity of the kind?

But if the foregoing facts and considerations tell against a belief in the origin of man and apes, by the purely accidental preservation in the struggle of life of minute and fortuitous structural variations, do they tell against the doctrine of evolution generally?

To this question it must be replied that, if we have reason to think an innate law has been imposed upon nature, by which new and definite species, under definite conditions, emerge from a latent and potential being into actual and manifest existence, then the foregoing facts do not in the least tell against such a conception—a conception, that is, of a real and true process of "evolution" or "unfolding."

For there is no conceivable reason why these latent specific forms should not have the most complex and involved relationships one to another; similar structures independently appearing in widely different instances.

Analogy drawn from the inorganic world is all in favour of such latent potentialities, and the process of development of every individual animal is the unmistakable manifestation of actual organic evolution and emergence of real from potential existence in each separate case.

It has recently been strongly asserted by Dr. H. Charlton Bastian,[3] that organic nature does manifestly contain within it these innate powers of developing new and definite forms, more or less like those existing in inorganic nature, as evidenced by crystallisation.

He has given detailed descriptions[4] of the most strange and startling direct transformations amongst the lower animals, including the direct evolution of Rotifers and Nematoid worms. Moreover, the evidence of the occurrence of sudden and direct transformations does not repose on Dr. Bastian's observations alone. Similar phenomena have been observed by M. Pineau, M. Jules Haime, M. T. C. Hildyard, M. Metcalf Johnson, Dr. Gros, and M. Nicolet.[5]

It would be difficult and eminently unscientific summarily to reject such an accumulation of evidence. To do so simply on an account of à priori prejudice, reposing upon nothing better than negative testimony, would be in the highest degree unphilosophical.

Moreover, we have of late years become acquainted with the remarkable fact of the occasional sudden transformation of a certain large Mexican Eft with external gills—

[3] 'The Beginnings of Life,' 1872.

[4] L. c. vol. ii. pp. 307–540.

[5] For an account of their observations and references to their original statements, see 'Bastian.' Op. cit. vol. ii. pp. 493–527.

the Axolotl—into an animal not only of a different species but of a different genus. Here the whole structure, the arrangement even of certain bones and distribution of the teeth in the jaws, becomes transformed without the most careful observations having as yet enabled us to discover what conditions determine in these exceptional cases such a marvellous metamorphosis.

It is true that the Axolotl has characters of immaturity, and that the form ultimately attained by it is probably the fully-developed condition; but the wonder is thus only increased, since while the ordinary and immature Axolotls breed freely, the rarely-developed adults are absolutely sterile.

To revert from this digression, however, to the question of the cause and mode of specific origin. I have elsewhere[6] endeavoured to show, by many different facts, what is the teaching of nature as to such origin —namely, that very frequently indeed similarity of structure may arise without there being any genetic affinity between the resembling forms,[7] as also that it is much rather to an internal cause or principle than to any action of surrounding external conditions that the origin of new specific forms is due.[8]

The characters and relations exhibited to us by the history of the highest order of mammals—the order Primates, common to us and to the apes—seems then not only fully to corroborate, but to accentuate and intensify the arguments advanced in the 'Genesis of Species' in support of what the author believes to be the more philosophical conception of the cause and nature of "specific genesis" generally.

Not only is there abundant reason to believe that apes and Half-apes have little, if any, closer genetic affinity than they have either with Lions or with Whales, but there is some evidence to support the belief that the apes of the Old and of the New Worlds respectively (the *Simiadæ* and *Cebidæ*) have been created independently one of the other, and that the various common characters they exhibit are but parallel adaptive modifications, due simply to similarity as to the exigencies of life to which they are respectively exposed.

Fossil remains, as yet unknown, may bridge over the gulf at present existing between these families. It would be a bold thing to positively affirm that such will not be discovered, when we reflect how very few are the extinct animals known to us compared with the vast multitudes which have existed, how very rarely animal remains are fossilised, and how very rarely again such fossils are both accessible and actually found. Nevertheless, the author believes that it is far more likely that tropical geological explorations may reveal to us latisternal apes more human than any now existing, rather than that they will bring to our

6 'Genesis of Species,' 2nd edition, 1872.

7 'Genesis of Species,' p. 71, chap. iii., on the co-existence of closely similar structures of diverse origin.

8 Op. cit. p. 251. chap. xi., on Specific Genesis.

knowledge forms directly connecting the *Simiadæ* and *Cebidæ*.

To return from this subordinate question, it may be asked, "What is the bearing of all the foregoing facts on the origin and affinities of man?"

Man being, as the mind of each man may tell him, an existence not only conscious, but conscious of his own consciousness; one not only acting on inference, but capable of analysing the *process* of inference; a creature not only capable of acting well or ill, but of understanding the ideas "virtue" and "moral obligation," with their correlatives freedom of choice and responsibility —man being all this, it is at once obvious that the principal part of his being is his mental power.

In nature there is nothing great
    but man,
In man there is nothing great
    but mind.

We must entirely dismiss, then, the conception that mere anatomy by itself can have any decisive bearing on the question as to man's nature and being as a whole. To solve this question, recourse must be had to other studies; that is to say, to philosophy, and especially to that branch of it which occupies itself with mental phenomena— psychology.

But if man's being as a whole is excluded from our present investigation, man's body considered by itself, his mere "massa corporea," may fairly be compared with the bodies of other species of his zoological order, and his corporeal affinities thus estimated.

Let us suppose ourselves to be purely immaterial intelligences, acquainted only with a world peopled like our own, except that man had never lived on it, yet into which the dead body of a man had somehow been introduced.

We should, I think, consider such a body to be that of some latisternal ape, but of one much more widely differing from all the others than such others differ one from another amongst themselves. We should be especially struck with its vast brain, and we should be the more impressed by it when we noted how bulky was the body to which that brain belonged. We should be so impressed because we should have previously noted that, as a general rule, in back-boned animals, the larger the bulk of the body the less the relative size of the brain. From our knowledge of the habits and faculties of various animals in relation to their brain structure, we should be led to infer that the animal man was one possessing great power of co-ordinating movements, and that his emotional sensibility would have been considerable. But above all, his powers of imagination would have been deemed by us to have been prodigious, with a corresponding faculty of collecting, grouping, and preserving sensible images of objects in complex and coherent aggregations to a degree much greater than in any other animal with which we were before acquainted. Did we know that all the various other kinds of existing animals had been developed one from another by evolution; did we know that the numerous species had been evolved from potential to actual existence by implanted powers in matter, aided by the influence of incident forces; then we might reasonably argue, by analogy, that a similar mode of origin had given rise to the exceptional being, the body of which we were examining.

If, however, it were made clear to us—immaterial intelligences—that the dead body before us had been, in life, animated, not by a merely animal nature, but by an active intelligence like our own, so that the difference between him and all other animals was not a difference of degree but of *kind*—if we could be made to understand that its vast power of collecting and grouping sensible images served but to supply it with the materials made use of by its intelligence to perceive, not merely sensible phenomena, but also abstract qualities of objects—if we became aware that the sounds uttered by it in life were not exclusively emotional expressions, but signs of general conceptions (such as predominate in the language of even the lowest savage), then the aspect of the question would be entirely altered for us.

We should probably decide that if the body before us seemed to us to be so little related to the informing rational soul that its existence anterior to and independent of such rational soul was quite conceivable and possible, then its origin by process of natural evolution would, indeed, also be conceivable and indeed *à priori* probable.

But if, on the other hand, we were convinced, from whatever reason, that it was inconceivable and impossible for such a body to be developed or exist without such informing soul, then we should, with perfect reason and logic, affirm that as no natural process would account for the entirely different kind of soul—one capable of articulately expressing general conceptions[9]—so no merely natural process could account for the origin of the body informed by it—a body to which such an intellectual faculty was so essentially and intimately related.

Dropping now the metaphor of immaterial spirits, it seems that the answers supposed to be given by such spirits must be the answers really given by sincere and unbiassed investigators in the combined spheres of Zoology and Anthropology.

But however near to apes may be the body of man, whatever the kind or number of resemblances between them, it should be always borne in mind that it is to no one kind of ape that man has any special or exclusive affinities—that the resemblances between him and lower forms are shared in not very unequal proportions by different species; and be the preponderance of resem-

9 "It is not emotional expressions or manifestations of sensible impressions, however exhibited, which have to be accounted for, but the enunciation of distinct deliberate judgments as to 'the what,' 'the how,' and 'the why,' by definite articulate sounds; and for these Mr. Darwin not only does not account, but he does not adduce anything even tending to account for them." 'Quarterly Review,' July 1871. Article, 'The Descent of Man,' p. 79.

blance in which species it may, whether in the Chimpanzee, the Siamang, or the Orang, there can be no question that at least such preponderance of resemblance is *not* presented by the much vaunted Gorilla, which is essentially no less a brute and no more a man than is the humblest member of the family to which it belongs.

The Origin of Man

Paul Topinard
1876

With regard to the position of Man in the Mammalian series, and the dignity of his races, we come to the general conclusion that they are distinct from the other problems which the knowledge of that Man implies. It matters but little whether at a particular moment, sooner or later, the physical types had been *genera, species,* or *varieties,* and whether it is still so. What philosophers are curious to know is how they took their origin, whether suddenly and spontaneously at all points, or progressively and naturally from things which had pre-existed.

At first naturalists and anthropologists took but little interest in all these questions. They worked without listening to dogmas taught outside their own sphere, their methods of investigation were carried on in temperate regions. According as the science of facts progressed, it became impossible for them any longer to be uninterested in the lofty views which gave to Newton and Humboldt so great a reputation, and which is not forbidden in any other branch of human knowledge.

Two currents therefore are established regarding the Origin of Man leading to two different doctrines— the one orthodox, *monogenistic,* affirming that all the human races are derived from one and the same stock, and have been produced by the influence of climate and external circumstances in the brief space of time that has elapsed since the creation of the world, according to the biblical version; the other revolu-

"Monogenism of M. De Quatrefages. Polygenism of Agassiz. Transformism of Lamarck. Selection of Mr. Darwin. Their Application to Man. His Genealogy, His Place in Nature." *Anthropology.* Chapter 1, pp. 515–35. Chapman and Hall, London, 1890. *L'Anthropologie.* Chapter 1. C. Reinwald, Paris, 1876.

tionary, *polygenistic,* maintaining that this lapse of time is insufficient, that the types are permanent under present conditions and as we now see them, and, consequently, that they must originally have been multiple. But the horizon has now changed; it is no longer a question of 5877 years, but of an incalculable number of ages, and what was false in the former case may be true in the latter. It is with the telescope that we must now search for the origin of man. Let us then look at the doctrines before us. We shall be brief, this work professing merely to be a *résumé* of facts and of the methods of study relating to Anthropology. This Third Part does not strictly come within our plan, and is only supplementary.

We shall say nothing respecting the dissertations of metaphysicians on the essence of Man, the pre-established harmony between the body and mind, or the intelligent intervention of nature; nor as regards the philosophers of a higher order. The following quotation will form the exception: "In the necessary course of things," said Epicurus and Lucretius, "all possible combinations take place, sooner or later, in the midst of complex conditions, which sometimes are more or less favourable to them, and sometimes contradict them, so that the results are as variable as can be according to the conditions of times and places, and the combination of those conditions."[1]

We would willingly pass over in silence the explanations which we find at the foundation of all religious systems, if one of them—our own—had not been disputed by eminent anthropologists. In that concerning the book of Genesis, such as we find from the compilation of Esdras after the Babylonian captivity, two opinions present themselves to our notice. Some, believing themselves to be thoroughly orthodox, affirm that it is merely a question relating to the Semitic peoples, and particularly to the Jews; they revive the arguments upon which, in 1655, Isaac de la Peyrère founded his doctrine of the Pre-Adamites,[2] and bid us to remember, for example, that God "set a mark upon Cain, lest any finding him should kill him," and go on to remark that, in chapter vi., the "sons of God" are represented as races of Adam, and the "sons of men" as non-Adamic races. Others, radical in their orthodoxy, declare, on the contrary, that all races originally descended from a single pair—Adam and Eve—and consecutively from the three pairs saved from the Deluge; that all the animal species are derived in the same way from pairs saved at the same time; that the influence of climate and external circumstances soon manifested itself, and that subsequently came the diversity of languages. But Linnæus had some doubts on the subject; he was dissatisfied with regard to the exceptional character of the country which had supplied the wants of zoological species as opposed to one

[1] "Sur le Transformisme," by Paul Broca, in "Bull. d'Anthrop.," 2nd series, vol. iv., 1870.

[2] "Præadamitæ," by Isaac de la Peyrère: Ed. Elzevied, Amsterdam, 1655.

another as the polar bear and the tropical hippopotamus. Prichard replied that it had to do with the supernatural, and hence, that a little more or a little less made no difference. This must be repeated to those who inquire whether Adam was white, black (*Prichard*), or red (*Eusebius de Salles*), or who make him a dolichocephale, while the Pre-Adamites should have been brachycephales (*Staniland Wake*).

We pass on to the scientific doctrines. In the first place, we have that of M. de Quatrefages, who, without allowing himself to be disturbed by influences foreign to science, strongly defends the doctrine of the unity of the human species, while thoroughly acknowledging its very great antiquity. He considers that zoological species are unchangeable in their physical type, and circumscribed by their character of homogenesis within their own area, and of heterogenesis outside it.[3] Human races are only varieties arising from the influence of climate and external circumstances (*milieux*), and of crossing, and may be reduced to a small number, all of which come from one and the same stock. Man was created in the beginning, in conditions to us unknown, by the intervention of an extraneous force, or by a supreme will. M. de Quatrefages, therefore, recognises but one human species,

---

[3] "De l'Unité de l'Espèce Humaine," 1 vol., Paris, 1869; "Rapport sur les Progrès de l'Anthropologie," Paris, 1869; "Leçons Professées au Muséum," in "Revue des Cours Scientifiques," 1864–65, 1867–68, &c., by M. de Quatrefages.

and in deference to man's elevated rank, and his character for religiousness, he concedes to him a place apart in the zoological series, under the name, proposed by Isidore G. Saint-Hilaire, of *règne humain*.

The various arguments in favour of this doctrine have been examined in the course of this work. We merely remark that religiousness is not really peculiar to Man; and that among men, whether individuals or races, many do not possess it; that the influence of external circumstances is but little, and does not—as far as we can see, and in the present state of things, as Geoffroy Saint-Hilaire said—succeed in producing a new physical character indefinitely transmissible; that fecundity exclusively taking place between individuals of the same species is not the criterion of the species; and, lastly, that the interval which physically separates the principal *human types* is equal to, if not sometimes greater than, that which separates and determines *zoological species*. The origin of species, Agassiz maintained, is lost in the obscurity of the first establishment of the present state of things. Species are not strictly fixed within certain limits, nor determined by the faculty of individuals of being fertile only *inter se*. Human races differ as much as certain families, certain genera, or certain species. They were produced, in some independent way, on eight different points of the globe, or centres, which are as distinct in their fauna as in their flora. Agassiz admitted, nevertheless, the intervention, at every phase of the history of the world, of a superior will, operating by virtue of a preconceived plan.[4]

The third of these propositions, coming from a naturalist of such world-wide renown, has considerable weight; and agrees with our own conclusions as anthropologists. As to his centres of creation, which he calls realms (*des royaumes*), their particular localisation is only justified, as regards some of them, by the flora and fauna generally, but not by Man: the Australian realm for example. To his Arctic realm, apparently so proper, it may be objected that it is now entirely peopled by men and animals which have been imported there, and that their conditions of existence were precisely identical at one time in the centre of France. The doctrine of M. de Quatrefages is *classical monogenism,* which must be distinguished from the new monogenism of which we shall speak presently: that of Agassiz is a *special polygenism.* Both are allied to each other, in that they search into the secret of the formation of Man outside the known natural laws which regulate the universe. It is otherwise with the doctrine we are now about to speak of, namely—

TRANSFORMISM

This is of French origin. The entire honour of its introduction is due to A. Lamarck, although De Maillet and Robinet had previously sketched out some of its traits. A species, Lamarck wrote in 1809,[5] varies infinitely, and, *considered as regards time,* does not exist. Species pass from one to the other by an infinity of transitions, both in the animal and vegetable kingdom. They originate either by transformation or divergence. By going back for ages, we thus come to a small number of primordial germs, or monads, the offspring of spontaneous generation. Man is no exception to this; he is the result of the slow transformation of certain apes. The ladder to which we before compared the organic kingdoms only exists, he says, as regards the principal masses. Species, on the contrary, are, as it were, the isolated extremities of the branches and boughs which form each of these masses.

This striking hypothesis was the offspring of Lamarck's brain, at a time when the knowledge of natural history, palæontology, and embryology was very imperfect, and upon which so vivid a light has since been shed. Nothing has been added to its principle: the ways and methods of transformation have been discussed, facts of observation have been supplied, genealogical tables of animated beings have been proposed; but the foundation has remained intact both in France, in Germany, and in England. Lamarck, in that

---

[4] "Sketch of the Natural Provinces of the World," by Professor Agassiz, in "Types of Mankind," by Nott and Gliddon. Philadelphia, 1854.

[5] "Philosophie Zoologique," by J. B. A. Lamarck, Professeur de Zoologie au Muséum, Paris; 1st edition 1809, 2nd edition 1873, in two volumes.

he was in advance of his time, and stood forward firmly in advocacy of his theory, showed himself to be a man of genius. The ways and methods of Lamarck may be summed up in a single sentence—the adaptation of organs to conditions of existence. Change in external circumstances, he says, obliges the animal placed in the presence of animals of greater strength, or in new conditions of life, to contract different habits, which produce an increased activity in certain organs, a diminution, or a want of exercise, in others. By virtue of the physiological law inherent in every organism, that the organ, or a certain part of the organ, diminishes or increases in proportion to the work that it performs, these organs become modified when submitted to new conditions. The internal power of the organism, dependent on the general function of nutrition which is called forth, is immense. The wants induced by external changes brought it into play.

The doctrine in its entirety was too far in advance of the age to have the success which was its due. Cuvier, the advocate of the orthodox opinions of the time, had but little difficulty in stifling it in the cradle—Cuvier, who ridiculed the idea of the foundation of the Normal school, as well as the honorary title of *élève* granted by the Convention to Lacépède. Notwithstanding this, however, the doctrine had its adepts. In France—Poiret, Bory de Saint-Vincent, Geoffroy Saint-Hilaire; abroad—Treviranus, Oken, Gœthe. From the year 1818 Geoffroy Saint-

Hilaire became its champion, and laid particular stress on the immediate effects on the body of external circumstances. Cuvier a second time resumed the discussion, and, in opposition to him, propounded his own doctrine on the periodical revolutions of the earth, of the renewal each time of the Flora and Fauna, and of the incessant and miraculous intervention of a creative will. The contention between these two powerful geniuses had to do with the movement which ended in the Revolution of 1830. Authority at last had the advantage, and in France *transformism* was vanquished. But the number of its proselytes increased from far and wide. The last work of Gœthe was favourable to it. Botanists, especially, accepted the new doctrine—W. Herbert, P. Mathews, Lecoq, Hooker, Rafinesque, Naudin. Then the geologists—Omalius d'Halloy, Keysserling, and other *savants*. L. Buch, Schaffhauser, Herbert Spencer, and Lyell had already cleared the way, by sapping at the foundation the theory of the periodical catastrophes of Cuvier, when Charles Darwin made his appearance, in 1859.

This great naturalist was not vividly impressed by the views of Lamarck. His own ideas passed through his mind during his voyage round the world in the *Beagle*.[6] On his return to London, six years afterwards, he studied the results which

[6] "Voyage d'un Naturaliste autour du Monde, à bord du Navire le *Beagle*, de 1831 à 1836," by Charles Darwin. Traduction de E. Barbier-Reinwald.

were obtained by breeders on animals, and he devoted himself to make experiments, especially on pigeons. The subject of artificial selection most occupied him, when one day he stumbled on the work "On Population," by Malthus. This was a streak of light; the word which was to make the fortune of his theory was found—"the struggle for existence."

By a singular coincidence, another English *savant,* Richard Wallace, who had taken up his abode in Malaisia, forwarded to him at that moment a memoir, supported by facts, in which the same ideas were set forth. But Mr. Wallace, with his task hardly entered upon, recoiled before the consequences of his labours when he perceived that they, of necessity, applied to Man. Charles Darwin, on the contrary, persevered, and it is with justice that his countrymen gave to his theory the name of Darwinism, a theory which should be thus defined: "Natural selection, by the struggle for existence, applied to the transformism of Lamarck."

We know that breeders and horticulturists obtain, almost at will, the new forms which they desire, by first selecting from one and the same species, then from the offspring of a first cross, then from those of the next crosses, and so on, individuals posessing in the highest degree the variety required. A new species is thus developed, and by dint of perseverance, fixed. The divergences from the primitive type which are obtained are very strange. They have to do with colour, form of the head, the proportions of the skeleton, the configuration of the muscles, and even with the habits (*mœurs*) of the animal. Sir John Sebright undertook to produce in three years a certain feather in a bird, and in six years a certain form of beak or head. In this consists "artificial selection," as it is effected by the intelligent hand of Man on animals in a state of domestication. But is not the same result sometimes produced naturally in wild animals? Mr. Darwin affirms it, by substituting for the hand of Man the chance circumstance derived from vital competition (*concurrence*).

Competition is a general law of the universe—it is exerted between physical forces, between beings of the two kingdoms, between men, between peoples. Under the name of "struggle for existence" it is even useful; without that, there would soon be a retardation of everything upon the face of the earth. It has been calculated that a single pair of elephants—the slowest of all animals to breed—would produce, barring all restraints, fifteen millions of young in five hundred years. Derham, quoted by Boudin, speaks of a woman, who died at 93 years of age, as having 1298 children, grandchildren, and great-grandchildren. Malthus has proved that population increases in a geometrical ratio, while the resources of that population only augment in an arithmetical ratio. The law of the stronger predominates everywhere—the large devour the small; those the best protected by their organisation, the best provided with means of attack or of resistance to external agencies, survive the longest; the more numerous they are, and the longer they live, the more they multiply and establish a stock in preference to those who are less favoured.

Spontaneous variability is another element of the Darwinian theory. Two individuals of the same species, or of the same family, do not resemble each other in every respect; they differ by characters of no value, or by characters which give them an advantage in the struggle over those whose wants, or conditions of climate, food, and external circumstances of every sort are the same. The animal with a protective-colored skin, that is one like the ground upon which he is moving, will better escape his enemies. In one of Darwin's works there is a very curious example of this kind in butterflies. The animal with the thick fur will be under more favourable circumstances at the poles, the one with the sleek skin at the equator. Every advantage acquired from birth, and therefore more easily transmissible in consequence, places the individual in a better condition for resistance to causes of destruction and to sterility. It follows, then, that certain individuals are, as it were, selected, chosen by a natural process which replaces the agency of Man in artificial selection; and that these individuals are precisely those who are separated the most from others by some new character. The thing being repeated for many generations, the divergences become marked, the tendency to inheritance

increases, and new types are formed, farther and farther removed from the point of departure. It follows, also, that wherever an *ensemble* of conditions exhibits itself, which allows a divergence to be developed without being stifled by rival divergences, it will take its place in the series of beings, and possibly form one for the occupation of a zoological species. One difference between artificial and natural selection is in the time they require for a transformation to become confirmed. In the former nothing is left to chance; matters progress rapidly, but the types are not thoroughly fixed, and readily revert to the primitive type. In the latter we must reckon by ages, chance also intervening, for the destruction of that which has commenced only to be completed. The results once obtained are more stable. Between the methods set forth by Lamarck and those of Darwin there are important differences. As regards the former, the point of departure of transformation is in the external circumstance which modifies the way of living and creates new habits, new wants, which induce a change in the nutrition and structure of organs. For the latter, the point of departure is in the superiority that procures for the individual some advantage in the daily struggle. Lamarck considers that variation is effected gradually in the course of existence. Darwin, that it appears spontaneously at birth, or rather during embryonic life. To the process of selection by vital competition, Mr. Darwin adds selection by sexual competition, which depends on the will, on the choice and vitality of the individuals, and especially affects the males.[7]

The Germans, who have vigorously espoused the cause of transformism, particularly Hæckel, recognise two orders of methods. They give to those of the French school, including changes of life and habits, of food and climate, training, the excess or want of use of organs, the name of *phenomena of direct adaptation;* and to those of the English school, that is to say, to congenital characters, the name of *phenomena of indirect adaptation.* Endeavours have been made to see whether there may not be other processes of formation of species. According to the doctrine of Darwin, the new character pre-exists in the germ, and depends on the influence of the parents even before conception. According to Geoffroy Saint-Hilaire, the action of climate and external circumstances is not confined to its exercise upon the individual in the course of existence, it may equally make itself felt in the germ in progress of development, and produce varieties, sometimes monstrosities. Such would be the origin of the race of gnato oxen of La Plata. In the above processes it is only a question as to slow transformations. We might also have sudden transformations. "An accident which it is not neces-

sary to mention," writes E. Geoffroy Saint-Hilaire, "trifling at its origin, but of incalculable importance in its effects, has been sufficient to change the inferior type of oviparous vertebrata into an ornithological type. The process of M. Kölliker would be equally an accident, taking for his *point de départ* the various degrees of geneagenesis and the succession of forms in the development of the embryo. He thinks that beings may produce other beings separated from their parents by characters of species, genus, and even of class. He bases his theory on that which takes place sometimes in inferior forms, and supposes, as regards the superior, that a normal egg may go past the period of its ordinary development, and give origin to a higher organisation. These theories and processes concern the two organic kingdoms. The limits of this work do not allow of our entering into the subject further, and we must confine ourselves to Man. Do they apply to Man, as well as to animals? Evidently they do, or they are false: laws are uniform. As we said in the early part of this work, the Primates form the first natural group of the order of Mammalia, thanks to a certain number of characters common to them and to the succeeding orders. Moreover, this group presents numerous points of contact with the latter, and, in the series of families of which it is composed, an ascending gradation of types is observed, becoming more and more perfect. Thus, at the bottom of the scale we have the Lemurs, some of which are allied to the Insectivora, others to the

---

7 "La Descendance de l'Homme et la Sélection Sexuelle," by Ch. Darwin; translated into French, 2nd edition, Paris, 1873. See also "L'Origine des Espèces et de la Variation des Animaux et des Plantes sous l'Action de la Domestication," by the same.

Cheiroptera, and even to the Marsupialia; above them the Cebians, many of whose genera are lemurs in a state of transition; then the Pithecians, some species of which seem derived from Cebians. Afterwards, the anthropoid apes make their appearance, separated by a sensible interval, if one of them, the Gibbon, did not diminish it, owing to his numerous features of resemblance to the Pithecians. At the summit is Man, many of whose types approximate in many of their features to the Anthropoids.

Their differences, indeed, may be thus summed up: (1) There are modifications of form connected with the decidedly vertical attitude of Man and the oblique attitude of the Anthropoid; (2) The more perfect adaptation of the foot and hand to their respective functions of locomotion and prehension in Man; (3) The volume of the brain, which is three times as large, or more, in Man, thus causing a corresponding activity of the organ, and a proportionate development of all its functions; namely, language, observation, judgment, &c. The continuity, on the one hand, of the inferior order of Mammalia with the superior order of Primates, and in this latter of its inferior family of Lemurs with its superior family of Man passing through the Anthropoids more nearly akin to Man than to the Pithecians; and, on the other hand, the continuity of certain human races with others rising higher and higher in the scale are clearly the result of this. Moreover, between one type and another, sufficiently recognised

for naturalists to make them the representatives of special groups, whether of order, family, genus, or species, some variation of the organ, or some bastard species, almost always comes in to establish the transition. *Natura non facit saltum.* It might be said that a creative force had been at work, step by step, leaving its track behind it, and that groups are due to the periods of repose during which that force was in operation on a certain spot, with a view the better to increase the number of forms. When Lamarck supposed that Man was the issue of the chimpanzee, his mind was attentively engaged in observing both the family of Primates in particular and the animal kingdom in general. The rudimentary organs in Man, or vestiges of perfectly useless organs—like the ilio-cæcal appendix—which are well developed in other species among the Mammalia, and the unusual appearance of organs, like the supplementary mammæ, or conformations peculiar to other animal species, furnish so many arguments in favour of transformation. On no other hypothesis are they to be explained. They may be phenomena of atavism, of remote reminiscences, of facts of reversion. Embryology would also be favourable to the doctrine. "The series of diverse forms which every individual of a species passes through," says Hæckel, "from the early dawn of his existence, is simply a short and rapid recapitulation of the series of specific multiple forms through which his progenitors have passed, the ancestors of the existing species, during the enormous duration of the geological periods."[8] A series of teratological cases, entering into the arrests, and even into the perversions of development, of the embryo, are thus explained. Hare-lip, polydactilia, microcephaly, are, as it were, hesitations of the principles of evolution, attempts on its part to stop at points where it had rested in anterior forms, or to progress in other previously-followed directions. Human palæontology does not reach back sufficiently far for us to found any arguments upon it: it should pass beyond the last or quaternary period. The most ancient human fossil of this period, however, is favourable to the idea of a derivation of man from the anthropoid.

Direct proofs as to transformism are not wanting. In so far as Man is concerned, the matter is clear; but rational proofs, as Geoffroy Saint-Hilaire said, are abundant. Transformism imposes itself as a necessity: everything is *as if* things had thus taken place; or man was created out of nothing, by enchantment; or he proceeds from that which existed previously. But what are we to think as to the mode? Those of direct adaptation of organs to life are so rational, they are so conformable to the general laws of physiology, that it would be unwise to reject them positively. Of course we have never seen a White changed into a Black, nor smooth hair into woolly; but in time, by passing through intermediate races produced

by crossing, there is no proof that the phenomena might not have taken place. We are too exacting. Prichard was anxious to prove that Whites might make their appearance spontaneously among Negroes. All his arguments were wrong, in that he entirely left out of sight the way in which races have become removed from place to place. But we are not at all sure that his aspirations, if better supported, might not now triumph. The brain increases in volume, and its convolutions increase in richness, in proportion to the degree of activity of which they are the seat, bringing in their train a series of subordinate craniological characters. Nutrition and external circumstances may in the same way cause the stature and colour of individuals to vary as well as the proportions of the body. *La fonction fait l'organe* of Lamarck is a demonstrative fact. When a muscle is paralysed, it becomes atrophied, the osseous eminences in which it is inserted disappear, the skeleton becomes deformed. In persons who have lost a limb by amputation, the nerves, having become useless, progressively become atrophied from their extremity to their central point in the brain (*Luys*). The digestive tube is dilated, and the belly becomes large in those who are large eaters of vegetable food. All the difficulty is in the transmission of the acquired individual character; clearly, facts are at fault here. There is no proof, however, that the tribe of Akkas is not indebted for its diminutiveness to the fact of inheritance fixing accidental characters. If the albinos are as common among the Mon-

---

8 "Histoire de la Création des Etres Organisés d'après les Lois Naturelles," by E. Hæckel. French translation. Paris, 1874.

bouttous as Dr. Schweinfürth states, the question is, whether circumstances being favourable, a new species may not some day start up. Supposing in that country, through some catastrophe, the temperature and radiation should be suddenly lowered, many would die, but the survivors would have a better chance of thriving. In poly-dactilia, supposing crossing outside the family did not counteract inheritance, transmission, now limited to five generations, according to the facts hitherto mentioned, would certainly go beyond.

Let us pass on to the methods of indirect adaptation of Mr. Darwin. Vital competition is a thing which must not be confounded with selection. It exists, no matter how we apply it, between individuals, as between societies and races. We have before us the fact of races inferior in the struggle becoming extinct. The Charruas, the Caribs, the ancient Californians, the Tasmanians, no longer exist; the Australians, the Negritos, the Esquimaux, are fast following them. The Polynesian, the American Indians, will soon be in their wake, if they have no chance of surviving except by crossing. The superior races, on the contrary, thrive and increase. It is easy to foretell the moment when the races which now decrease the interval between the White man and the Anthropoid shall have entirely disappeared.

There is nothing mysterious in this extinction; its mechanism is altogether natural. The result will be the survivance of those most adapted to benefit the superior races. But at one time, in Australia, in Malaisia, in America, and in Europe it was not so. These very races which now are succumbing, were superior relatively to others which no longer exist. The Australians of the present, whom we look upon as savages, have a civilisation conformable to their external condition, a certain social organisation—in relation to the Negritos of the interior of the Philippines, for example. We think we have proved that they have ejected a negro race inferior to themselves, as we now eject them. The wandering aborigines of Western Australia, described by Scott Nind, are the remnants of this race. In our own country, the races of the Périgord, which have disappeared before, or become absorbed into, the brachycephalic races from the East and the blondes from the North, have played the same part before the races anterior to the Neanderthal as these probably did to the Miocene races of Thenay and Saint-Prest. In these successive extinctions, which exhibit to us series of generations, strata of more and more perfect races succeeding and replacing each other, do we not recognise the selection by vital competition of Mr. Darwin? But where is the character which gives the advantage in the struggle? Among animals, and during the first ages of the human race, the power which enabled them the better to defend themselves against other living beings, and against changes of climate and external conditions, was necessarily of a physical kind, such as quick-sightedness, more acute smell, more vigorous muscles, a constitution better adapting itself to cold or heat, to marsh miasm, or to certain kinds of diet. If Man acclimates tolerably well now, it must not be forgotten that he owes the power, in a great measure, to the processes which he makes use of. Formerly he must have succumbed, or his constitution must have been modified. We speak here especially of sudden acclimation. But from the period when societies were formed, and moral force took its legitimate supremacy over brute force, the advantage remained with the most skilful, the most industrious —in a word, with the most intelligent. Selection, from henceforth, was made to the advantage of a single organ. The largest brains—those with the richest convolutions, and with the most delicate structure, with the most appropriate histological elements—were the most favoured. Hence a state of progress which is undeniable. The process of Mr. Darwin has, therefore, had its effect in the past, as it has now in the present. With appropriate institutions we might direct it, and accelerate its already so remarkable results.

The external circumstances of Lamarck must, in fact, have an action of whose mechanism we know nothing. The selection of Mr. Darwin has one of which we are certain. With the latter we reckon by strata of races, with the former we must do the same. The characters which we now see permanent in a given race are not the more so when we compare a succession of races.

Absolute immobility nowhere exists, and fixity of species is only relative. May there not be other processes contributing to gradual transformation? Certainly not. There are three orders of characters which *transformism* explains, says M. Broca, some of *evolution,* others of *improvement,* a third *serial.* But there is a fourth, the unimportant, the key to which he does not give. Such are the presence of the *os intermedium* of the carpus, the absence of a nail on the great toe, and the absence of a round ligament in the hip-joint, peculiar to the orangoutang among Anthropoids. Why, how, and when, did these characters take their origin?

Another objection is that, in going back in the past, we do not find human races differing much from the races of the present; that we do not find, for example, men with half the cranial capacity of those of the present. But do we discover the Pliocene Man and the Miocene Man by the flint implements of Saint-Prest and Thenay? The former made use of fire, the latter did not: is not this a reason for suspecting that the fact of the volume of his brain being less was the cause? If he was unacquainted with fire he ought not to have the sense to bury his dead. The Anthropoids are in this condition, and we have none of their remains. Probably also, human bones do not last for so immeasurably prolonged a period. However, on surveying the road travelled over, and the discoveries made during the last fifteen years, we must not despair. Is it not by chance, when making a road or a railway cutting, or after a land-slip, or an earthquake, that discoveries of this kind are made? Here a man of intellect, and one interested in the subject, should be at hand.

Now, Africa, Asia, Oceania, and even the greater part of Europe, are still as it were virgin soils. Perhaps, also, the stratum in which is now lying the *précurseur,* not possessing language, announced by G. de Mortillet and Hovelacque is at present submerged; perhaps he has only existed on a very limited point of the globe. Some day or other he may present himself before us under the form of a skeleton stranded upon some bank of time, as at Grenelle; crushed under a rock, as at Langerie-Haute; or embedded in lava, as at Denise.

The derivation of Man from some previously-existing form being admitted, the question is what this form may have been. Lamarck believed it to have been a chimpanzee. We have seen that each of the three great Anthropoids approaches more or less to Man in certain characters, but not one possesses them all. So in the inferior races; no one race, not even the Bosjesman, is specially marked out as descending from an anthropoid—they are only made to approach more or less by such or such a character. The precursor of Man, then, is only analogous to the Anthropoids. The human type is an improvement upon the general type of their family, but not of one of their known species in particular.

M. Hæckel does not express an opinion on this point. He asks whether the dolichocephales of Eu-

rope and Africa are not derived from the chimpanzee and the gorilla of the coasts of Guinea, both of which are dolichocephales; and whether the brachycephales of Asia do not descend, on the contrary, from the brachycephalic orangs of Borneo and Sumatra. Many reasons lead to the belief, indeed, that all the dolichocephales are originally from Europe and Africa, and the brachycephales from Eastern Asia, not to speak of the old continent of Asia. M. Vogt thinks otherwise. He thinks that Man is only cousin-german to the anthropoid, and that the ancestor common to them both is farther off still. Here M. Hæckel speaks positively. He says that this very remote ancestor is an ape of the old continent, a Pithecian, which was itself derived from a Lemur, and this in its turn from a Marsupial. He even gives it the name of *Lémurien*—a term borrowed from Mr. Sclater; and, as the focus of this series of transformations, a continent now submerged, of which Madagascar, Ceylon, and the Sunda islands are the remains.

But what becomes, in all this, of the old dispute between monogenists and polygenists? It no longer has any interest, and, to be brief, may be summed up as follows: As to the question of the most elementary human types to which we might go back, types utterly irreducible, whatever their value of genera or species, in the sense usually applied to those words, are they the issue of many Anthropoid ancestors, Pithecoids or others; or are they derived from a single stock, represented by a single individual of their genera now known, or not? The anthropological data given in this work appear to us more favourable to the former opinion, if we accept the transformation theory. The most characteristic races, whether living or extinct, do not form one single ascending series, such as may be compared to a ladder or a tree, but, reduced to their simplest expression, to a series of frequently parallel lines.

We shall conclude by giving a *résumé* of the possible genealogy of Man, according to Hæckel. Equally relying on comparative anatomy, palæontology, and embryology, the learned professor of zoology at the University of Jena thus gives his views on the subject of *evolution*:

At the commencement of what geologists call the *Laurentian* period of the earth, and of the fortuitous union of certain elements of carbon, oxygen, hydrogen, and nitrogen, under conditions which probably took place only at that epoch, the first albuminoid clots were formed. From them, and by spontaneous generation, the first cellules or *cleavage-masses* took their origin. These cellules were then subdivided and multiplied, and arranged themselves in the form of organs, and after a series of transformations, fixed by M. Hæckel at *nine* in number, gave origin to certain vertebrata of the genus *Amphioxus lanceolatus*. The division into sexes was marked out, the spinal marrow and *chorda dorsalis* became visible. At the *tenth* stage, the brain and the skull made their appearance, as in the lamprey; at the *eleventh*, the limbs and jaws

were developed, as in the dogfish: the earth was then only at the Silurian period. At the *sixteenth*, the adaptation to terrestrial life ceased. At the *seventeenth*, which corresponds to the Jurassic phase of the history of the globe, the genealogy of Man is raised to the kangaroo among the Marsupials. At the *eighteenth*, he becomes a Lemurian: the Tertiary epoch commences. At the *nineteenth*, he becomes Catarrhinian, that is to say an ape with a tail, a Pithecian. At the *twentieth*, he becomes an Anthropoid continuing so throughout the whole of the Miocene period. At the *twenty-first*, he is the man-ape, he does not yet possess language, nor, in consequence, the corresponding brain. Lastly, at the *twenty-second*, Man comes forth, as we now see him, at least in his inferior forms. Here the enumeration stops. M. Hæckel forgets the *twenty-third* stage, that in which the Lamarcks and Newtons make their appearance. Although having attained so lofty an eminence, Man must have had a very low origin, in no way differing from that of the first and most simple organic corpuscles. What he is now in the womb, he would have been permanently on making his appearance in the animal series.

This theory is painful and revolting to those who delight to surround the cradle of humanity with a brilliant aureole; and if we were to boast of our genealogy and not of our actions, we might indeed consider ourselves humiliated. But what is this new restraint to our *amour-propre* in comparison with that which astronomy has already imposed? When the earth was fixed in the centre of the system, and it was thought that the universe was created for the earth, and the earth for Man, our pride ought to have been satisfied. This doctrine, called by the Germans "geocentric," as applied to the earth, and "anthropocentric," as applied to Man, was perfectly co-ordinate; but it fell to the ground the moment it was demonstrated that the earth is only the humble satellite of a sun which itself is but one of the luminous points in space. It was then, and not now, that Man was truly recalled to humility. It was no longer for him that the sun rose each morning, that the celestial vault was nightly bespangled with innumerable resplendent orbs. Out of all this Macrocosm there was but one lowly planet left to Man. Like that peasant who dreamt that he was ruler of the world, and woke up to find himself in a simple cottage, it was not without regret that he saw himself thus degraded. Long the remembrance of his vanished dream troubled his thoughts; but he was obliged to be resigned, to become accustomed to the reality; and now he consoles himself, as he is no longer this monarch of creation, with the thought that he is really sovereign of the earth. This undoubted royalty he has a right to be proud of. But in what way is it threatened or diminished by the *transformation theory?* Would it be less real if he had brought it under subjugation by himself or inherited it from his first ancestors? Far from depreciating

Man and his origin, the doctrine of Lamarck dignifies and ennobles them, by substituting for the theory of the supernatural the theory of the mutability and natural evolution of organic forms.

But, after all, what matter to science the regret or complacency of some people? Its aims and designs are beyond their comprehension. Man is not at liberty to put or not to put a curb upon the functional activity of his brain; his spirit of inquiry is the most noble, the most irresistible of his attributes; and as M. Gabriel de Mortillet said at the meeting of the Association for the Advancement of Science, his characteristic is here, and not in religiousness. For want of knowledge the imagination muses upon the unknown, and forms it to our own ideal. But to true observers the reality is sufficient; they contemplate the magnificent spectacle which is opening out before them; they even worship nature in its beauty, its grandeur, its harmony, and its thousand varieties of form and movement. The animal has the simple notion of cause and effect, and sees that the boundary of his faculties and senses is limited. Man alone investigates and wills; his horizon is indefinite, like his intellectual faculties when they are exercised without trammel.

Let us not, therefore, seek to contract the circle of knowledge. Is it not knowledge which has conducted us step by step, age after age, to the degree of prosperity we now enjoy? Is it not this which engenders civilisation, which adds to our well-being, brings to us the purest satisfaction, instructs us in philosophy, and secures our supremacy over everything on our planet? Each one has his task to perform in this immense sphere. To some is given subjects of study relating to the progress of life; to others its realities. Let the former have for their object the development in society of ideas of justice, honour, and morality, without which it cannot exist. The means are within their power. Our part is to ascertain facts, to deduce from them laws, and to look at them calmly, without allowing ourselves to be carried away by our feelings. Whatever may be his origin, whatever his future destiny, Man, to the anthropologist, is but a Mammifer, whose organisation, wants, and diseases are in the highest degree complex; whose brain, with its admirable functions, have reached the highest development. As such, he is subject to the same laws as the rest of the animal creation; as such, he is a participator in their destinies.

Darwinism Applied to Man

Alfred Russell Wallace
1889

Our review of modern Darwinism might fitly have terminated with the preceding chapter; but the immense interest that attaches to the origin of the human race, and the amount of misconception which prevails regarding the essential teachings of Darwin's theory on this question, as well as regarding my own special views upon it, induce me to devote a final chapter to its discussion.

To any one who considers the structure of man's body, even in the most superficial manner, it must be evident that it is the body of an animal, differing greatly, it is true, from the bodies of all other animals, but agreeing with them in all essential features. The bony structure of man classes him as a vertebrate; the mode of suckling his young classes him as a mammal; his blood, his muscles, and his nerves, the structure of his heart with its veins and arteries, his lungs and his whole respiratory and circulatory systems,

"Darwinism Applied to Man." *Darwinism*. Chapter 15, pp. 445–46, 454–61. Macmillan and Company, London and New York, 1889.

all closely correspond to those of other mammals, and are often almost identical with them. He possesses the same number of limbs terminating in the same number of digits as belong fundamentally to the mammalian class. His senses are identical with theirs, and his organs of sense are the same in number and occupy the same relative position. Every detail of structure which is common to the mammalia as a class is found also in man, while he only differs from them in such ways and degrees as the various species or groups of mammals differ from each other. If, then, we have good reason to believe that every existing group of mammalia has descended from some common ancestral form—as we saw to be so completely demonstrated in the case of the horse tribe, —and that each family, each order, and even the whole class must similarly have descended from some much more ancient and more generalised type, it would be in the highest degree improbable—so improbable as to be almost inconceivable—that man, agreeing with them so closely in every detail of his structure, should have had some quite distinct mode of origin. Let us, then, see what other evidence bears upon the question, and whether it is sufficient to convert the probability of his animal origin into a practical certainty.

Summary of the animal characteristics of man

The facts now very briefly summarised amount almost to a demonstration that man, in his bodily structure, has been derived from the lower animals, of which he is the culminating development. In his possession of rudimentary structures which are functional in some of the mammalia; in the numerous variations of his muscles and other organs agreeing with characters which are constant in some apes; in his embryonic development, absolutely identical in character with that of mammalia in general, and closely resembling in its details that of the higher quadrumana; in the diseases which he has in common with other mammalia; and in the wonderful approximation of his skeleton to those of one or other of the anthropoid apes, we have an amount of evidence in this direction which it seems impossible to explain away. And this evidence will appear more forcible if we consider for a moment what the rejection of it implies. For the only alternative supposition is, that man has been specially created —that is to say, has been produced in some quite different way from other animals and altogether independently of them. But in that case the rudimentary structures, the animal-like variations, the identical course of development, and all the other animal characteristics he possesses are deceptive, and inevitably lead us, as thinking beings making use of the reason which is our noblest and most distinctive feature, into gross error.

We cannot believe, however, that a careful study of the facts of nature leads to conclusions directly opposed to the truth; and, as we seek in vain, in our physical structure and the course of its development, for any indication of an origin independent of the rest of the animal world, we are compelled to reject the idea of "special creation" for man, as being entirely unsupported by facts as well as in the highest degree improbable.

The geological antiquity of man

The evidence we now possess of the exact nature of the resemblance of man to the various species of anthropoid apes, shows us that he has little special affinity for any one rather than another species, while he differs from them all in several important characters in which they agree with each other. The conclusion to be drawn from these facts is, that his points of affinity connect him with the whole group, while his special peculiarities equally separate him from the whole group, and that he must, therefore, have diverged from the common ancestral form before the existing types of anthropoid apes had diverged from each other. Now, this divergence almost certainly took place as early as the Miocene period, because in the Upper Miocene deposits of Western Europe remains of two species of ape have been found allied to the gibbons, one of them, Dryopithecus, nearly as large as a man, and believed by M. Lartet to have approached man in its dentition more than the existing apes. We seem hardly, therefore, to have reached, in the Upper Miocene, the epoch of the common ancestor of man and the anthropoids.

The evidence of the antiquity of man himself is also scanty, and takes us but very little way back into the past. We have clear proof of his existence in Europe in the latter stages of the glacial epoch, with many indications of his presence in interglacial or even pre-glacial times; while both the actual remains and the works of man found in the auriferous gravels of California deep under lava-flows of Pliocene age, show that he existed in the New World at least as early as in the Old.[1] These earliest remains of man have been received with doubt, and even with ridicule, as if there were some extreme improbability in them. But, in point of fact, the wonder is that human remains have not been found more frequently in pre-glacial deposits. Referring to the most ancient fossil remains found in Europe—the Engis and Neanderthal crania,—Professor Huxley makes the following weighty remark: "In conclusion, I may say, that the fossil remains of Man hitherto discovered do not seem to me to take us appreciably nearer to that lower pithecoid form, by the modification of which he has, probably, become what he is." The Californian remains and works of art, above referred to, give no indication of a specially low form of man; and it remains an unsolved problem why no traces of the long line of man's ancestors, back to the remote period when he first branched off from the pithecoid type, have yet been discovered.

It has been objected by some

[1] For a sketch of the evidence of Man's Antiquity in America, see *The Nineteenth Century* for November 1887.

writers—notably by Professor Boyd Dawkins—that man did not probably exist in Pliocene times, because almost all the known mammalia of that epoch are distinct species from those now living on the earth, and that the same changes of the environment which led to the modification of other mammalian species would also have led to a change in man. But this argument overlooks the fact that man differs essentially from all other mammals in this respect, that whereas any important adaptation to new conditions can be effected in them only by a change in bodily structure, man is able to adapt himself to much greater changes of conditions by a mental development leading him to the use of fire, of tools, of clothing, of improved dwellings, of nets and snares, and of agriculture. By the help of these, without any change whatever in his bodily structure, he has been able to spread over and occupy the whole earth; to dwell securely in forest, plain, or mountain; to inhabit alike the burning desert or the arctic wastes; to cope with every kind of wild beast, and to provide himself with food in districts where, as an animal trusting to nature's unaided productions, he would have starved.[2]

It follows, therefore, that from the time when the ancestral man first walked erect, with hands freed from any active part in locomotion, and when his brain-power became sufficient to cause him to use his hands in making weapons and tools, houses and clothing, to use fire for cooking, and to plant seeds or roots to supply himself with stores of food, the power of natural selection would cease to act in producing modifications of his body, but would continuously advance his mind through the development of its organ, the brain. Hence man may have become truly man—the species, Homo sapiens—even in the Miocene period; and while all other mammals were becoming modified from age to age under the influence of ever-changing physical and biological conditions, he would be advancing mainly in intelligence, but perhaps also in stature, and by that advance alone would be able to maintain himself as the master of all other animals and as the most widespread occupier of the earth. It is quite in accordance with this view that we find the most pronounced distinction between man and the anthropoid apes in the size and complexity of his brain. Thus, Professor Huxley tells us that "it may be doubted whether a healthy human adult brain ever weighed less than 31 or 32 ounces, or that the heaviest gorilla brain has exceeded 20 ounces," although "a full-grown gorilla is probably pretty nearly twice as heavy as a Bosjes man, or as many an European woman."[3] The average human brain, however, weighs 48 or 49 ounces, and if we take the average ape brain at only 2 ounces less

[2] This subject was first discussed in an article in the *Anthropological Review*, May 1864, and republished in my *Contributions to Natural Selection*, chap. ix, in 1870.

[3] *Man's Place in Nature*, p. 102.

than the very largest gorilla's brain, or 18 ounces, we shall see better the enormous increase which has taken place in the brain of man since the time when he branched off from the apes; and this increase will be still greater if we consider that the brains of apes, like those of all other mammals, have also increased from earlier to later geological times.

If these various considerations are taken into account, we must conclude that the essential features of man's structure as compared with that of apes—his erect posture and free hands—were acquired at a comparatively early period, and were, in fact, the characteristics which gave him his superiority over other mammals, and started him on the line of development which has led to his conquest of the world. But during this long and steady development of brain and intellect, mankind must have continuously increased in numbers and in the area which they occupied—they must have formed what Darwin terms a "dominant race." For had they been few in numbers and confined to a limited area, they could hardly have successfully struggled against the numerous fierce carnivora of that period, and against those adverse influences which led to the extinction of so many more powerful animals. A large population spread over an extensive area is also needed to supply an adequate number of brain variations for man's progressive improvement. But this large population and long-continued development in a single line of advance renders it the more difficult to ac-

count for the complete absence of human or pre-human remains in all those deposits which have furnished, in such rich abundance, the remains of other land animals. It is true that the remains of apes are also very rare, and we may well suppose that the superior intelligence of man led him to avoid that extensive destruction by flood or in morass which seems to have often overwhelmed other animals. Yet, when we consider that, even in our own day, men are not unfrequently overwhelmed by volcanic eruptions, as in Java and Japan, or carried away in vast numbers by floods, as in Bengal and China, it seems impossible but that ample remains of Miocene and Pliocene man do exist buried in the most recent layers of the earth's crust, and that more extended research or some fortunate discovery will some day bring them to light.

The probable birthplace of man

It has usually been considered that the ancestral form of man originated in the tropics, where vegetation is most abundant and the climate most equable. But there are some important objections to this view. The anthropoid apes, as well as most of the monkey tribe, are essentially arboreal in their structure, whereas the great distinctive character of man is his special adaptation to terrestrial locomotion. We can hardly suppose, therefore, that he originated in a forest region, where fruits to be obtained by climbing are the chief vegetable food. It is more probable that he began his existence on the open plains or high plateaux of the temperate or subtropical zone, where the seeds of indigenous cereals and numerous herbivora, rodents, and game-birds, with fishes and molluscs in the lakes, rivers, and seas supplied him with an abundance of varied food. In such a region he would develop skill as a hunter, trapper, or fisherman, and later as a herdsman and cultivator, —a succession of which we find indications in the palæolithic and neolithic races of Europe.

In seeking to determine the particular areas in which his earliest traces are likely to be found, we are restricted to some portion of the Eastern hemisphere, where alone the anthropoid apes exist, or have apparently ever existed.

There is good reason to believe, also, that Africa must be excluded, because it is known to have been separated from the northern continent in early tertiary times, and to have acquired its existing fauna of the higher mammalia by a later union with that continent after the separation from it of Madagascar, an island which has preserved for us a sample, as it were, of the early African mammalian fauna, from which not only the anthropoid apes, but all the higher quadrumana are absent.[4] There remains only the great Euro-Asiatic continent; and its enormous plateaux, extending from Persia right across Tibet and Siberia to

[4] For a full discussion of this question, see the author's *Geographical Distribution of Animals,* vol. i. p. 285.

Manchuria, afford an area, some part or other of which probably offered suitable conditions, in late Miocene or early Pliocene times, for the development of ancestral man.

It is in this area that we still find that type of mankind—the Mongolian—which retains a colour of the skin midway between the black or brown-black of the negro, and the ruddy or olive-white of the Caucasian types, a colour which still prevails over all Northern Asia, over the American continents, and over much of Polynesia. From this primary tint arose, under the influence of varied conditions, and probably in correlation with constitutional changes adapted to peculiar climates, the varied tints which still exist among mankind. If the reasoning by which this conclusion is reached be sound, and all the earlier stages of man's development from an animal form occurred in the area now indicated, we can better understand how it is that we have as yet met with no traces of the missing links, or even of man's existence during late tertiary times, because no part of the world is so entirely unexplored by the geologist as this very region. The area in question is sufficiently extensive and varied to admit of primeval man having attained to a considerable population, and having developed his full human characteristics, both physical and mental, before there was any need for him to migrate beyond its limits. One of his earliest important migrations was probably into Africa, where, spreading westward, he became modified in colour and hair in correlation with physiological changes adapting him to the climate of the equatorial lowlands. Spreading north-westward into Europe the moist and cool climate led to a modification of an opposite character, and thus may have arisen the three great human types which still exist. Somewhat later, probably, he spread eastward into North-West America and soon scattered himself over the whole continent; and all this may well have occurred in early or middle Pliocene times. Thereafter, at very long intervals, successive waves of migration carried him into every part of the habitable world, and by conquest and intermixture led ultimately to that puzzling gradation of types which the ethnologist in vain seeks to unravel.

.   .   .

Part Three

In the thirty-five years following the discovery of the bones of *Pithecanthropus* the discipline of paleoanthropology grew into a mature program of research marked by an increase in discoveries of fossil hominid specimens, the development of new techniques for analyzing the fossils, the establishment of research centers for human paleontology, the teaching of university courses on this subject, the formulation of new theories to interpret the fossil record, and an increasing awareness among scholars that the discipline of genetics could shed light on the problems of the origin of man and his history. A major feature in this coming of age of paleoanthropology was not only the discovery of fossil hominids in deposits beyond the borders of Europe, but also the realization that the European, Asiatic, and African fossil specimens now known were of varieties that could not be classified within the narrow dichotomy of the Neanderthal or Cro-Magnon types.

The realization that ancient man might be discovered in Africa, Asia, and Australia was initiated by Dubois's discovery in 1890–91. From a fluvial deposit at Trinil in Java Dubois recovered a skullcap and long bones of a hominid that could not be matched by any specimen in the European fossil record at that time. At the meeting of the Royal Dublin Society in 1895 the discoverer stressed that his *Pithecanthropus erectus* occupied a phylogenetic position between the anthropoid and human stems, as Haeckel had conceived of his hypothetical *Pithecanthropus*. Immediately differences of interpretation arose over the question of whether this specimen was an ape, a transitional ape-man form, a *Homo sapiens,* or at least a

1890 to 1925

creature more closely akin to man than to the anthropoids. Had Dubois not been offended by his colleagues' speculations and by the hesitancy with which his fossil man was received by some of them, he might have brought forth additional specimens which he had discovered in Southeast Asia. Instead he did not reveal the mandibular fragment from Kedung Brubus until 1924, although it had been found twenty-six years earlier, and the four femora that he had recovered from the Trinil beds in 1900 did not come to scientific attention until 1932. The bones from Wadjak, also in Java, were resurrected in 1921 through the intercession of the American anthropologist, Aleš Hrdlička.

That early man had a wider range of phenotypic variation than could be represented by the Neanderthal and Cro-Magnon types of fossils found in Europe was supported by new evidence from Asia, Africa, and Australia, and especially by the discovery of the Heidelberg mandible from Germany. The type of hominid represented by *Pithecanthropus* had not been found outside the island of Java during this period of paleoanthropological research. But the morphological affinities of the European Neanderthal specimens with the Broken Hill fossil from Northern Rhodesia suggested that here was a fossil form with a wider geographical distribution. It is curious to note that during this period when the fossil record for Europe was being considerably amplified, morphological variation for the Neanderthal specimens was hardly admitted, whereas for the later Cro-Magnon fossils the paleoanthropologists were eager to isolate sub-types and racial entities on the basis of individual specimens. Of the Neanderthal specimens from La Ferrassie, Le Moustier, La Quina, and La Chapelle-aux-Saintes it was the complete male specimen from La Chapelle-aux-Saintes that was set up by Boule as the prototype of Neanderthal Man. The other Neanderthal specimens were better or worse examples of this type of ancient humanity in accordance with the degree of their resemblance to this ideal form. Among the Cro-Magnon specimens thus far discovered, Verneau claimed the male and female burial at the Grotte des Enfants as indicative of a negroid racial element in this population, just as the specimen from Combe Capelle was accorded a sub-specific classification by Klaatsch. With the eskimoid specimen from Chancelade and the Cro-Magnon specimen proper, the Upper Paleolithic hominids of Europe became divided further into racial sub-types while the Neanderthals tended to be lumped into a single phenotype.

While the discovery of *Pithecanthropus* provided paleoanthropologists with a hominid fossil that seemed similar in some of its physical features to the anthropoid apes, it was recognized nevertheless as being a hominid very different from Haeckel's *Pithecanthropus alalus,* that medley of simian and human physical conditions. Scientists continued to be embarrassed for the lack of a convincing missing link. Then, among the discoveries of this period, came a series of remarkable finds from Piltdown and Sheffield Park in Sussex between 1908 and 1915. Here was a fossil to jar the anti-evolutionists out of their complacency and scepticism about the possibility of discovering missing links. Piltdown Man, or *Eoanthropus dawsoni,* sported a modern-like skullcap and a simian mandible. Was he not the true representative of that transitional form between man and ape? This happy discovery seemed at first to answer many of the needs of those paleoanthropologists harassed by embarassing questions. It was remarkable that the different anatomical portions of this fossil turned up in deposits at Piltdown and Sheffield Park in an order that paralleled chronologically the succession of questions asked about the specimen by interested scholars. In the light of our present knowledge that Piltdown was a fraud, it has been suggested that the hoax was a sincere attempt on the part of its manufacturer to hasten the day when human evolution could no longer be a matter of doubt. Interestingly, the *Eoanthropus* specimen had outlived its service some quarter of a century before its fraudulency was ascertained, and the fossil was frequently described in the textbooks and scientific papers of the early twenties of this century as an aberrant type of hominid whose very nature precluded its serious consideration in the construction of man's phylogenetic tree.

How were the differences in the physical type of early man and the great geographical dispersions of some of these types to be explained in terms of human phylogeny? To answer this question the early twentieth century paleoanthropologists needed to know two things: the relative ages of the specimens that they considered the prototypes of the different kinds of early men, and the loci of human evolution from whence these types began their adaptive radiation.

The dating by geological stratification and faunal association of the deposits at Trinil and Heidelberg demonstrated that the antiquity of man could be extended as far back as the Mid-Pleistocene. Dubois's dating of the *Pithecanthropus* bones to the Early Pleistocene or Pliocene was rejected by the members of the Selenka expedition who visited Trinil in 1906, but reports from other regions of discoveries of Tertiary Man were still current. However, during this period the claims for Tertiary Man were not as enthusiastically received as they had been in the earlier part of the second half of the nineteenth century. Ameghino's assertions of a South American origin for man, which were based on his studies of osteological series of New World monkeys, were appreciated only by a limited number of scholars in Europe. By 1927 the revelation that a supposed early American hominid progenitor, *Hesperopithecus haroldcooki,* was nothing but the tooth of an extinct peccary did much to undermine the prestige of claims for the fossils of Tertiary Man, especially in the New World. Support for this notion was stronger in the field of prehistoric archaeology, where it was asserted that pre-Paleolithic tools called "eoliths" were to be found in Tertiary deposits in western Europe and India. The eolithic controversy of the 1890s had no sooner subsided when Moir revived interest in the so-called rostrocariante tools from the Pliocene beds of East Anglia. The eolithic and rostrocarinate controversies became less intense when it was realized that such "tools" could be produced by natural agents, for example water activity working with an abrasive agent on stones. It came to be recognized that eoliths were not confined to Tertiary deposits, that they were found in obvious pre-hominid deposits, and that they were never found in regions where the materials of which they were composed were not already present.

The venerable idea that man had originated somewhere in Asia now seemed confirmed by the discovery of *Pithecanthropus*. This thesis found further support when in the Siwalik Hills of northern India the fossils of Miocene and Pliocene apes were uncovered by Pilgrim. Some of these fossils were immediately recognized as possessing morphological features similar to those represented in the hominid stem, various scholars favoring one fossil anthropoid over another as nearest to man. Although fossil anthropoids from the Tertiary were being found in Egypt at this time, the idea that Africa might be the birthplace of man, as Darwin had earlier suggested, was overshadowed by opinions that favored Asia as the place of human beginnings, as seen in the writings of Richard Swan Lull.

During this period the major theories of human phylogeny became defined. Many interpretations of the fossil human record appearing before 1925 persisted to the present, but with some striking modifications. Some tenets that once seemed unassailable have had to be abandoned. Thus while the thesis of a catarrhine origin for the human stem was not entirely rejected, the discovery of fossil primates from India and Egypt lent much support to the hypothesis of a pongid ancestry for man. Gregory was at this time the recognized American authority on the comparative anatomy of the higher primates. On the basis of similarities of dental form between the fossil apes and the fossil men then known he championed *Dryopithecus* as nearest to the human stem. Pilgrim also accepted an ape ancestry for man, and he saw osteological and dental features in the fossil ape *Sivapithecus* that led him to hail it as the Miocene progenitor. Indeed, he placed *Sivapithecus* in the family *Hominidae* with man, the other large anthropoids falling under the family *Simiidae*. In reaction to these concepts of an anthropoid human ancestor, several anatomists argued that the human line had its origins in primate forms much lower on the taxonomic scale. Thus Wood-Jones suggested that the distinctively human line originated at the beginning of the Tertiary without ever having been directly connected with the anthropoid stem. Rather, man had evolved from a tarsioid stock whose only living representative today is the small arboreal *Tarsius* of Madagascar. Wood-Jones admitted that no fossil form of such a human ancestor was yet known, but he based his thesis on data from comparative anatomy and embryology. Tate Regan, on the other hand, placed *Tarsius* and *Homo* at the ends of two lines that began to diverge in Cretaceous times. Others students of primate phylogency asserted that the nonhuman progenitor of man was to be found in the lemuroid line or among the platyrrhines of South America, theories that never found the same degree of acceptance that was accorded the anthropoid ape and tarsioid hypotheses. The writings of Boule kept alive the notion that man's closest relatives in the phylogenetic tree were to be sought among the catarrhines. Finally, there is the bizarre notion of the German prehistorian Hermann Klaatsch, who believed that the human species is older than either the anthropoid or the infra-anthropoid lines, the apes being degenerate forms of humanity. Klaatsch maintained that the human stem arose from a now extinct being which was already human rather than simian, and that after it had reached the evolutionary stage represented by *Pithecanthropus* it ramified into various primate forms which continued to evolve as the living races of man as well as the living kinds of great apes. Klaatsch reflected certain eighteenth century ideas that apes were degenerate forms of humanity, founding his interpretation on the premise that the human body is more primitive in its structure than that of any of the apes, the latter being specialized deviants pointing in a direction of evolution different from that of the more generalized catarrhine and human stocks. Klaatsch was the chief representative of the Polyphyletic School during this period.

By the early years of the present century the fossil hominid record had been amplified to such a degree that it was being asked if *Homo sapiens* could be descended from all of the earlier men of the Pleistocene thus far discovered, or was our species descended from some or perhaps from none of these fossils, arising as still another line whose members might yet be undiscovered? If *Homo sapiens* could be shown to have followed a separate evolutionary line, the antiquity of this line could be determined independently of the estimates of the antiquity of the lines for *Pithecanthropus*, Neanderthal, and related fossil hominid forms. During this period there appeared to be some evidence that *Homo sapiens* was more ancient than formerly supposed on the basis of putative *Homo sapiens* fossil specimens from sites that could be dated as earlier than Upper Pleistocene. *Eoanthropus* had already been interpreted as a hominid of great antiquity; its *Homo sapiens* type of cranium was the principle evidence for this decision. Furthermore there was the hesitancy to admit the implications of what man's brute ancestry might have been, an intellectual inhibition that was no less foreign to the sensitivities of dedicated paleoanthropologists of this period than it was to their non–scientifically oriented contemporaries. A separate human line afforded that psychological buffer to the human ego which still found it distasteful to admit the meanness of man's origins. But the presence of certain *sapiens*-like hominid fossils in geological deposits then described as Second Interglacial or earlier was the most significant factor in the query as to whether *Homo sapiens* might not have evolved earlier than the followers of the Unilinear School had supposed. If the *sapiens* line was separate from that which included the Neanderthal and Pithecanthropus forms, then these more primitive hominids could be related only indirectly to modern man. Theirs were phylogenetic lines that withered, while the *sapiens* line flourished and survived. Sir Arthur Keith was the leading voice in support of this "Presapiens School" and the first to draw up a phylogenetic tree to represent the branching off of the *Homo sapiens* from those stems leading to other fossil hominids. Keith differs in his early works from later adherents of the Presapiens School, for he did not set apart particular fossil specimens as representative of direct human ancestors of modern man. Also he relegated *Eoanthropus,* in spite of its *Homo sapiens* skullcap, to a separate evolutionary stem that had become extinct.

The Presapiens School arose in part because of the dissatisfaction of many early twentieth century scholars with the tenets of the Polyphyletic and Unilinear Schools which had been inherited by the discipline from the writings of the previous century. Nor was the Presapiens School the only result of this need to assess the data in a new way in the light of the current amplification of the hominid fossil record. The Unilinear School has sometimes been called the Neanderthal School because of its tenet that the Neanderthal specimens marked a necessary link in the evolutionary sequence of types that led to *Homo sapiens.* This Neanderthalism, or pan-Neanderthal theory, was favored by Dubois, who placed between his *Pithecanthropus* and modern man the Neanderthal specimens then known. Grafton Elliot Smith agreed that *Homo sapiens* shows a number of neanderthaloid traits and that our species of the Late Pleistocene followed in time the European Neanderthals. But Smith differed from his colleagues in the Unilinear School by his interpretation of the popular belief that while all living races today are members of the same genus and species, certain races are more primitive than others. Smith saw these primitive groups as the less evolved representatives of the *Homo sapiens* branch that departed from the main human stem at a period in the Plesistocene prior to the continuation of the Neanderthals into their blind alley of evolution, marked by the "classic" or extremely robust Neanderthals found in western Europe and in the Broken Hill site of Northern Rhodesia. Nor did Smith accept *Pithecanthropus* as the ancestor of Neanderthal Man. This Javanese fossil appeared to him too specialized to be on that main human stem leading from the Miocene apes up to the "Nordic racial group" of modern man. It was primarily Smith's thesis that *Homo sapiens* became divorced from the Neanderthals and evolved separately at some period of the Third Interglacial that became the basic premise of the "Preneanderthal School." The supporters of this theory differ from the Presapiens adherents mainly by placing the origin of the *Homo sapiens* line later in time—namely, within the period of the Third Interglacial—than do their colleagues, who would place this time of species formation at the Second Interglacial or earlier.

By the first quarter of the present century these four ways of interpreting the fossil record had been defined. The results of prehistoric researches suggested that Europe could not be the cradle of human culture any more than it was the home of man's biological progenitors. If only a portion of the prehistoric cultural patterns of the Old World were within the European area, then hominid progenitors might also be forthcoming from Africa and Asia. Yet in 1924 when the first *Australopithecus* was discovered, very few scientists were aware of its significant role in future interpretations of the story of human evolution.

The Place of *Pithecanthropus* in the Genealogical Tree

Marie Eugene Francois Thomas Dubois
1896

In the report on the scientific meeting of the Royal Dublin Society on November 20, in Nature of December 5, 1895, it is stated that I placed Pithecanthropus in the genealogical tree, drawn by Prof. Cunningham, below the point of divarication of the Anthropoid apes from the human line. This indeed I did. But this statement could be misleading as to my real views on the genealogy of Pithecanthropus, such as I stated them already on p. 38 of my original memoir (*"Pithecanthropus erectus,* Eine menschenähnliche Uebergansform aus Java,"* Batavia, 1894), and more fully at the last meeting of the Anthropological Institute of Great Britain and Ireland, on November 25.

It may not be superfluous to explain my views here by means of the accompanying diagram, representing the evolution of the Old World apes from a hypothetical common ancestor, whom I call Procercopithecus.

In Prof. Cunningham's tree, figured in Nature of December 5, p. 116, he regards the left branch as all human, the right one as entirely simian, and he placed Pithecanthropus midway between recent Man and the point of divarication. Now I could find no place for the fossil Javanese form, which I consider as intermediate between Man and Anthropoid apes, many of the branches of *that* tree, only in the third chief line, the main stem, very near to the point of divarication.

Owing to the same circumstances, which indirectly prevented me from explaining my own views on the

"The Place of *'Pithecanthropus'* in the Genealogical Tree." *Nature.* Vol. 53, pp. 245–47. 1896.

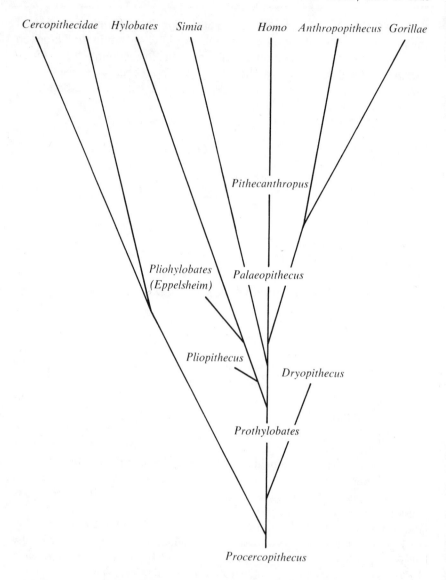

matter at Dublin, I did not then reply to two remarks of Prof. Cunningham, which mission I now wish to repair by the following declaration.

(1) I did not exaggerate the relative height and quality of the cranial arch, which Prof. Cunning-ham had in view (the arch of the glabella-inion part of the calvaria) in Hylobates. The profile outline of the skull of *Hylobates agilis*...is even somewhat higher than that of Pithecanthropus, of which I have an accurate bisected cast before me. In the latter the height of the said

cranial arch is exactly equal to the one-third part of the glabella-inion line, and in the skull of a *Hylobates agilis* it is about 2 mm. higher than the third part of the corresponding line. If in the...diagram in my memoir that line in the gibbon skull were drawn equal in length to that of the fossil calvaria, instead of the natural size, this would be more apparent there than it is even now. The said cranial arch of a *Hylobates syndactylus* in the same diagram is much lower than that of the other gibbon species, and the same arch in the chimpanzee would even be lower than in *Hylobates syndactylus*. It is easy of find skulls of Semnopithecus with a higher "cranial arch" than the chimpanzee has. Further, between different individuals of the same ape species and of man, we find great differences in the height of that arch.

All these facts tend to show that there is no reason for regarding the height *of the suprainial part* of the calvaria as of real importance in our judgment on the place which any human-like being should occupy in the genealogical tree.

(2) In my original memoir, I have already pointed out that the occiput of the fossil skull is very ape-like, especially gibbon-like. But, nevertheless, the inclination of the planum nuchale in the glabella-inion line is very different from that of all the Old World apes. These accord very nearly with one another in the degree of this inclination, whilst the angle in Pithecanthropus approached closely human conditions. I not only compared photographs of the median line of the skulls, but also the bisected skulls with the bisected exact cast of the fossil calvaria. The means which I have taken to determine the degree of this declination are therefore, I believe, entirely calculated to yield trust-worthy results.

A Chapter of Conclusions

Arthur Keith
1915

Those of us who set out some thirty years ago to search for evidence which would throw light on the antiquity of man believed we had to deal with a simple problem. We started under the conviction that there was only one kind of man —man of the modern type. We were certain that he was, like all other living things, subject to the laws of evolution, and that as we traced him, by means of fossil remains, into the remote past, we should find him assuming a more and more primitive shape and structure. The discovery of the remains of Neanderthal man in deposits of a mid-Pleistocene date confirmed us in our beliefs. With his great eyebrow ridges and his numerous simian traits, Neanderthal man was just such a being as we had pictured as our ancestor in the Pleistocene period. Then came the discovery of Pithecanthropus—an older and infinitely more primitive type of human being. He also answered to our expectations, and we adopted him as our late Pliocene or early Pleistocene ancestor. It will be thus seen that we set out prepared to find that man as we know him now was of recent origin, that in the course of a short geological period— one which is estimated at less than half a million of years—a semi-human form of being became endowed with all the attributes of man.

Then came the discoveries of the last ten years. Explorations at Combe Capelle and at Mentone revealed men of the modern type who, if not actually the contemporaries of Neanderthal man, were so closely his successors in point of time that it became impossible to believe that Neanderthal man represented a stage in the evolution of modern man. Further when we came to review critically the facts relating to the earlier discoveries made in England, France, and Italy, we were compelled to admit that men of the modern type had been in existence long before the extinction of the Neanderthal type.

With the recognition of Neanderthal man as a distinct kind or species of human being, our estimate

"A Chapter of Conclusions." *The Antiquity of Man.* Chapter 2, pp. 497–511. Williams and Norgate, London, 1915.

of man's antiquity underwent a profound change. We based our conception of the ancient world of man on the picture which meets our eye when we look abroad at the present time and see a world populated by races which are but variants of one prevailing human type. With such a picture in our minds we peered into the past, expecting to find that the population of every remote geological period was made up of only one type of man. The recognition of the true nature of Neanderthal man compelled us to replace that picture with a different one—one of an ancient population made up of, not mere varieties of one species of mankind as at present, but of totally different species and genera. Amongst this complex of ancient humanity we have to seek for the ancestors of modern man. The problems of man's origin and antiquity are thus less simple than we had anticipated.

We could have avoided our initial mistake if we had kept in mind the condition of things in the anthropoid world. There, amongst the great anthropoids, we find three distinct types, two of them existing side by side in Africa (the gorilla and chimpanzee), while the third (the orang) survives in Sumatra and Borneo. They are so like to man in structure of body that we must, to account for the degree of similarity, regard all of them as collateral descendants of a common stock. We do not hesitate to think that the anthropoids retain, to a much greater degree than man, the structure and manner of living of the ancient stock from which all

four have been evolved. If, therefore, we try to form a picture of the world of ancient and primitive humanity, we must base it on the conditions now existing among anthropoids, not on these which hold for the modern world of mankind. We should expect, then, when we go far enough back, to find humanity broken up into distinct structural groups or genera, each confined to a limited part of the earth. Inside each group we expect to find, as amongst the great anthropoids, a tendency to produce varieties or species. We have seen that many facts relating to ancient man which were formerly obscure or conflicting become easy of comprehension when this interpretation is applied.

Another line of evidence ought to have raised a suspicion that we were underestimating the antiquity of man in our earlier speculations. The anthropologist, when he seeks for an explanation of the evolution and distribution of modern races of mankind, finds it necessary to make a large demand on the bank of time. We all agree that modern human races, however different they may appear, are so alike in the essentials of structure that we must regard them as well-marked varieties of a common species. Let us look at the problem of their evolution in a concrete form, taking as opposite and contrasted types of modern humanity the fair-haired, white-skinned, round-headed European and the woolly-haired, black-skinned, long-headed negro of West Africa. We shall set those two contrasted types side by side and study them from a purely zoological point of view. We must admit that both are highly specialised types; neither represents the ancestral form. Now, in seeking for the ancestral form of our breeds of dogs, of horses, or of cattle, we select one of a generalised and ancient type, such as we conceive might have become modified into various modern breeds. We must apply the same method to the elucidation of human races. If we search the present world for the type of man who is most likely to serve as a common ancestor for both African and European we find the nearest approach to the object of our search in the aboriginal Australian. He is an ancient and generalised type of humanity; he is not the direct ancestor of either African or European, but he has apparently retained the characters of their common ancestor to a greater degree than any other living race. If, then, we accept the Australian native as the nearest approach to the common ancestor of modern mankind, can we form any conception of the length of time which would be required to produce the African on the one hand, and the European on the other, from the Australian type? From what we have seen in Egypt, in Europe, and in North America it is certain that a human type can persist for many thousands of years. A human type changes very slowly. Therefore, we must make a liberal allowance of time for the mere differentiation of the modern type of man into distinct racial forms. Even if we admit that the ancestral type from which all modern races of men have de-

scended was as highly evolved as the Australian native, I do not think that any period less than the whole length of the Pleistocene period, even if we estimate its duration at half a million of years, is more than sufficient to cover the time required for the differentiation and distribution of the modern races of mankind.

The proof that man of a modern build of body was in existence by the close of the Pliocene period is presumptive, not positive. So far, we have no certain trace of the type beyond the middle of the Pleistocene. We presume a greater antiquity in order to obtain a working hypothesis which will explain the facts now at our disposal. The human genealogical tree, given in fig. 1, represents, in a concrete form, the anthropologist's working hypothesis. An inspection of that figure will show the reader how little we know of the ancestry of modern races. Of the fossil predecessors of the Australian native race we know nothing. With the possible exception of the discovery made by Dr Hans Reck, we have not found as yet a single trace of the Pleistocene ancestry of the negro. The discovery reported by Dr Hans Reck, if substantiated, points to the differentiation and existence of a pure negro type in the Pleistocene period. We know nothing of the fossil remains of the Mongolian type in Asia because they have never been sought for. The North American Indian, whom we regard as a derivative of the Mongolian type, was certainly evolved before the close of the Pleistocene period. Indeed, our knowledge of ancestral

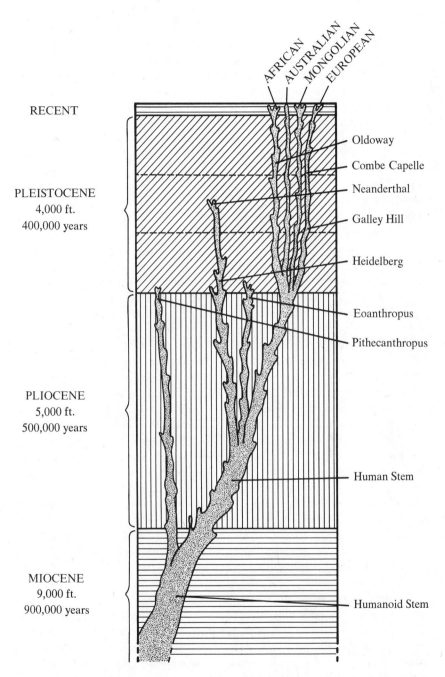

Fig. 1. Genealogical tree of man's ancestry. The depth of the deposits and the duration of the geological periods are based on estimates published by Professor Sollas.

forms is confined to almost a single type—the European. That type, as we have already seen, was in existence by the middle of the Pleistocene period. In some of the ancient Europeans, such as those found at Cromagnon and at Grimaldi, negroid traits can be recognised. At present the Mediterranean forms the boundary line between the European and African types. One can readily believe that in former times the African type may have spread some distance into Europe.

As already said, the genealogical tree depicted in fig. 1 represents a working hypothesis, nothing more. When we try to represent in such a form the structural relationship between existing and extinct human races we again feel the necessity of postulating a great antiquity for man. That becomes evident when we come to fit the phylum of Neanderthal man into the genealogical tree of the human family (fig. 1). He was so different from modern man in every point of structure that, in order to account for his structural peculiarities, we have to represent his phylum as separating from that of the modern human type at an early date. In fig. 1 it will be seen that I have shown the separation as having occurred before the middle of the Pliocene period. My reasons for selecting so early a date are: (1) that we must presume that man of the modern type was evolved by the end of the Pliocene period in order to account for the differentiation and distribution of the present races of mankind; (2) that the discovery of the Heidelberg mandi-

ble indicates the existence of a Neanderthaloid type of man at the commencement of the Pleistocene period. I am thus presuming that before the middle of the Pliocene period there was in existence a type of man sufficiently high to serve as a common ancestor for the Neanderthal and modern species of man.

We have seen that, in mid-Pleistocene times, the brain of Neanderthal man, in point of size, was equal to that of contemporary forms of modern man. His culture, that of the Mousterian age, was not a low one. We might suppose that the common Pliocene ancestor of these two species of man was of a low type, and that after their separation from the common stem each became gradually endowed with a large brain and acquired a separate form of culture. The more feasible explanation, however, is to suppose, not that a large brain was an independent acquisition on the part of Neanderthal and the modern species of man, but that it was a common inheritance from their Pliocene ancestor. That is the most reasonable explanation which is available at the present time—the one which presumes that Pliocene man had already reached a brain standard far beyond that of any simian type of animal.

When we come to fix the place which must be assigned to Eoanthropus in the human phylum, we find further evidence in support of man's great antiquity. We have seen that in the opinion of Mr Charles Dawson the "minimum geological age of the fossil cannot be of later date than the early part of the Pleistocene period." He is also open to the conviction that it may be much older, and on the evidence given in a former chapter we may reasonably presume that Eoanthropus represents a Pliocene type of man.

The problem we have now to solve is this: Does Eoanthropus represent the stage of evolution reached by modern man about the commencement of the Pleistocene period, or does the Piltdown type, like the Neanderthal, represent a separate human species or genus which became extinct and left no progeny? Dr Smith Woodward's answer to this question is given in his original communication to the Geological Society.[1] "It seems reasonable," he writes, "to interpret the Piltdown skull as exhibiting a closer resemblance to the skulls of the truly ancestral mid-Tertiary apes than any human fossil skull hitherto found. If this view be accepted, the Piltdown type has become modified into the later Mousterian (Neanderthal) type by a series of changes similar to those passed through by the early apes, as they evolved into the typical modern apes, and corresponding with the stages in the development of the skull in the existing ape individual. It tends to support the theory that Mousterian man was a degenerate offshoot of early man, and probably became extinct; while surviving man may have arisen directly from the primitive source of which the Piltdown

[1] *Quart. Journ. Geol. Soc.*, 1913, vol. lxix. p. 139.

skull provides the first discovered evidence." Dr Smith Woodward's answer to our question, then, is that Eoanthropus does not necessarily stand in the direct line which leads on to modern man, but represents more closely than any human form yet discovered the common ancestor from which both the Neanderthal and modern types have been derived.

We have seen that Eoanthropus in the size and shape of brain, and in the conformation of the skull, has a very high degree of resemblance to modern man. The characters of the teeth and mandible, on the other hand, were more simian than in any other form of man. The eyebrow ridges, so far as we can judge from the parts preserved, were also peculiar. On the other hand, we find in the skull of Neanderthal man numerous features which are also found in the skulls of anthropoid apes, particularly in the gorilla and chimpanzee. In many ways the Neanderthal skulls and brain casts are more simian, more primitive, than the corresponding Piltdown specimens. In the Neanderthal type of man we find the canine teeth reduced and the chin region of the mandible assuming a non-simian conformation as in the modern type of man. To explain the curious distribution of characters in those three types of man we have to postulate such a generic tree as is shown in fig. 1. There the Pliocene human stem, from which we have derived the Neanderthal and modern types, is also seen to give origin to the Piltdown type.

The common Pliocene ancestor

which gave origin to three such types could not be of a very low form. At least in Eoanthropus, as in Neanderthal man, the brain was equal in size to that of modern man. If we suppose that in an early part of the Pliocene period there was a form of man in which the brain had attained a human size, but in which the mandible, the teeth, and the skull still remained anthropoid in conformation, we have such a type as would serve as a common ancestor for Eoanthropus, modern man, and Neanderthal man. In the course of evolution the first named retained the ancestral form of mandible and teeth; the last preserved the ancestral simian features of the skull. It will thus be seen that I look on Eoanthropus, as on Neanderthal man, as a representative of an extinct form of man.

We come, finally, to an important problem: What status are we to assign to Eoanthropus in the zoological scale of classification? Dr Smith Woodward, in giving Eoanthropus a generic rank, seems to me to have altered the scale we have hitherto applied to the classification of human forms. All admit that Eoanthropus must be regarded as a form of man. A complete analysis of the structural characters of the Piltdown type (so far as they are known to us), of the Neanderthal, and of the modern types of man will show that all are of equal rank, and if we elevate one of them to a generic status we must do the same for the other two. Hitherto all modern races of men have been grouped under one species—*Homo*

sapiens. The varieties of men which belong to the Neanderthal type are placed under the specific name of *Homo neanderthalensis* (*primigenius*). If we apply the same standard of classification to the Piltdown type, then the name ought to be *Homo dawsoni*, not *Eoanthropus dawsoni*. For my part, I would welcome the innovation introduced by Dr Smith Woodward if it could be applied all round. Without doubt distinct varieties of Eoanthropus and of Neanderthal man will be revealed by future discoveries—varieties which are sufficiently characterised to deserve specific names.

We now come to the position which must be assigned to the humanoid form found in Java by Professor Dubois. The thigh bone was shaped as in man, and we presume Pithecanthropus had a body fashioned much like that of modern man. In size of brain and shape of skull, however, this strange form occupies an intermediate position. The stratum in which the remains were found is assigned to a late Pliocene or early Pleistocene date. Clearly, Pithecanthropus represents an early stage in the evolution of the human phylum. The evidence already adduced indicates that certain forms of early man had already attained a high development in the Pliocene period. Therefore in fig. 1 the stem represented by Pithecanthropus is shown as separating from the ancestral phylum of man at a late part of the Miocene period. We can only explain the existence of so primitive a form of human being at the end of the Pliocene period by adopting a hypothesis of this kind.

It is only when we come to draft a genealogical tree, such as that shown in fig. 1, that we realise the true significance of those extinct human types. When we look at the world of men as it exists now, we see that certain races are becoming dominant; others are disappearing. The competition is world-wide and lies between varieties of the same species of man. In the world of fossil man the competition was different; it was local, not universal; it lay between human beings belonging to different species or genera, not varieties of the same species. Out of that welter of fossil forms only one type has survived—that which gives us the modern races of man. Further, we realise that the three or four human types so far discovered represent but a few fossil twigs of the great evolutionary human tree. We may hope to find many more branches.

There is another route by which we may approach the problem of man's antiquity. All who have made a study of the human body are agreed that we must seek for man's origin in an ape-like ancestor. If, therefore, we review the facts which bear on the evolution of the anthropoid apes, we may obtain collateral evidence bearing on the date at which the differentiation of the human body became possible. To save description, I have represented the present state of our knowledge of anthropoid evolution in the form of a genealogical tree (fig. 2). The stems of the three great anthropoids —the gorilla, chimpanzee, and orang

—are seen to join together in the older part of the Pliocene period. We have not many facts to guide us. We know of a late Pliocene anthropoid—Palæopithecus—which shows relationships to both chimpanzee and orang, but was probably not a direct ancestor of either. We know that the great anthropoids were already evolved in the Miocene period. Dryopithecus was alive in that period, and was about the size of the chimpanzee, but more primitive in features of tooth and jaw. We know, too, that the small anthropoids—the gibbons —were already in existence in the Miocene period. So far as our knowledge goes, the Miocene anthropoid apes offer us no form which can serve as a probable human ancestor. The small and large anthropoids were already differentiated, and we may presume that the same was the case with the human form. Hence in fig. 2 the stems of the small anthropoids, of the great anthropoids, and of man are represented as already separated in the Miocene period. The evidence, so far as it goes, justifies us in presuming that the human and anthropoid lines of descent separated in pre-Miocene times.[2]

In fig. 3 the anthropoid and human genealogical trees have been combined. The tree represents a working hypothesis which may require alteration as new facts come to light. It is framed so as to account for the evolution and

[2] For a fuller statement of the case, see *Reports of British Association*, 1912, p. 753 ("Modern Problems relating to the Antiquity of Man").

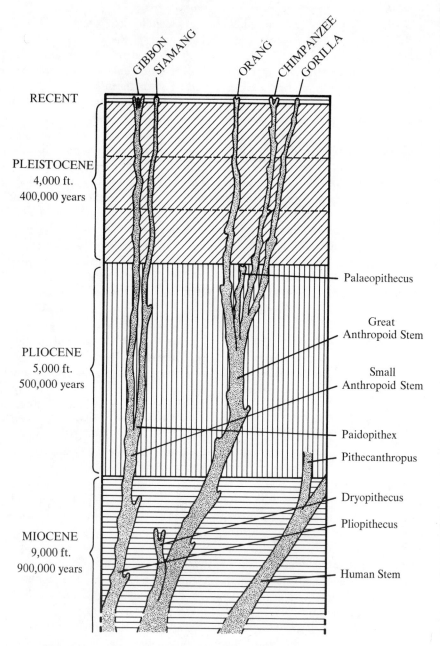

Fig. 2. Genealogical tree, showing the lines of descent of the anthropoid apes.

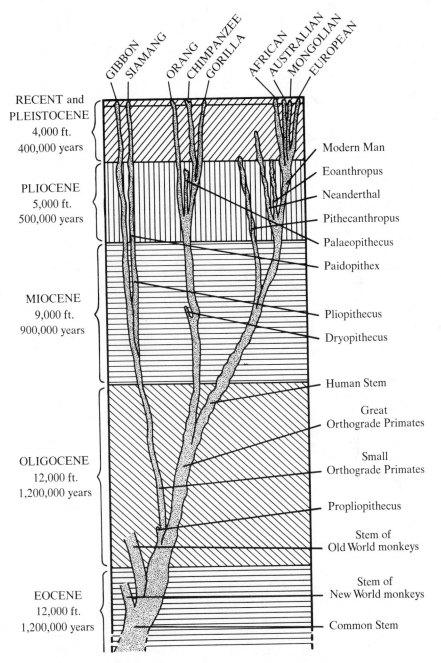

Fig. 3. Genealogical tree, showing the ancestral stems and probable lines of descent of the higher primates.

structural characters of the various forms of ape and man. The discovery of fossil remains of extinct forms gives us some guidance as to the probable date at which various types became evolved. In framing such a genealogical tree it is necessary—at least it seems so to me—to suppose that the separation of the human from the great anthropoid stem dates back to at least the latter part of the Oligocene period (fig. 2). If we mean by the antiquity of man the period which has elapsed since the human stem became differentiated from that which led on to the great anthropoid apes, then it is apparent from fig. 3 that the antiquity of man covers an immense period of time. On the scale of time represented in fig. 3, which is based on estimates published by Professor Sollas,[3] a period of about two million years has elapsed since the separation of the human stem, provided, of course, that the hypothesis represented by fig. 3 is approximately right. That tree probably errs in underestimating rather than overestimating the antiquity of the human stem.

When we speak of the antiquity of man, however, most of us have in mind not the date at which the human lineage separated from that of the great anthropoids, but the period at which the brain of man had reached a human level or standard. We may take the lower limits of the brain capacity in modern living races, say 1000 c.c., as a working standard. If it is arbitrary it is

[3] Sollas (1900).

also convenient. If, then, we propose to estimate the antiquity of man from the appearance of human types with average brain capacities of 1000 c.c. or more, we must still regard man as an ancient form, with a past immeasurably longer than is usually believed. From what we know, and from what we must infer, of the ancestry of Eoanthropus, of Neanderthal man, and of modern man, we have reasonable grounds for presuming that man had reached the human standard in size of brain by the commencement of the Pliocene period. From fig. 3 it will be seen that the Pleistocene and Pliocene periods are estimated to cover a period of about one million years. That period, on the grounds defined above, represents the antiquity of man.

Perhaps the most important and the most convincing source of evidence relating to man's antiquity is one which has been kept unduly in the background throughout this book. We cannot have more certain evidence of man's existence than the implements which he has shaped and used. We have seen how long it took to convince the modern world that the palæoliths in the gravel deposits of Western Europe were shaped by man's hand. Now we marvel that anyone should have denied their human origin. Then came the discovery of Eolithic implements in deposits of Pliocene date —at St Prest, on the Kentish plateau, on the uplands of Belgium, under the Crag deposits of East Anglia. The human origin of eoliths is still being called in question, but the more these shaped flints of Pliocene date are investigated and discussed, the greater becomes the number of those who regard them as the work of the hands and brain of Pliocene man. It is also maintained that flints, similar in shape and chipping, have been discovered in deposits of Miocene and even of Oligocene age. If it be proved that such are of human origin, then we must extend still further the period covered by the antiquity of man. There is not a single fact known to me which makes the existence of a human form in the Miocene period an impossibility.

Studies on the Evolution of the Primates

William King Gregory
1916

1. Phyletic relations of the tertiary and quaternary anthropoids[1]

Parapithecus and Propliothecus. The earliest known member of the anthropoid series, the genus Parapithecus of the Lower Oligocene of Europe, foreshadows the true anthropoids in the fundamental pattern of its pre-molars and molars and appears to be structurally intermediate between an Eocene partly insectivorous anaptomorphoid stage

[1] Until all or nearly all these genera and species are known from both the upper and the lower molars the exact relationships and status of some of them must remain indefinite.

with pointed jaws and small canines and a true anthropoid stage.

Parapithecus must be regarded as a persistent primitive type, for its contemporary *Propliopithecus* is already a true and very primitive anthropoid ape, with a deep jaw and with the highly characteristic dentition, although much smaller and more primitive even than the modern gibbon, as rightly maintained by Dr. Schlosser.

Pliopithecus. This genus of the Upper Miocene and Lower Pliocene of Europe appears to be intermediate between *Propliopithecus* and the modern gibbon. Its jaw is more primitive than that of the latter in its divergent rami, smaller canines,

"Studies on the Evolution of the Primates" *Bulletin of The American Museum of Natural History*. Vol. 35, Article 19, pp. 336–44. 1916.

wider premolars and unreduced third lower molar.

Palœosimia. This genus, from the Upper Miocene of India, so far as known, appears to be ancestral to the orang-utan.

Sivapithecus. This Upper Miocene Indian genus appears to the present writer to be closely related to *Dryopithecus,* as a descendant of a common stem resembling *Propliopithecus.* In another direction it appears to be related to *Palœosimia* and the orang. It approaches man not only in the greater breadth index of the premolars and molars, but also in their fundamental pattern. It retains the high conic canines, which were probably reduced in the Hominidæ. According to the writer's interpretation *Sivapithecus* also exhibited an apelike arrangement of the cheek teeth, in parallel rather than convergent rows. It should therefore be referred, by definition, to the Simiidæ rather than to the Hominidæ.

Dryopithecus. This Upper Miocene and Lower Pliocene genus, which is known from three species in India and three in Europe, retains strong evidence of derivation from a form like *Propliopithecus,* but is much larger and more progressive. Its molars and premolars are ancestral in pattern not only to those of the chimpanzee and gorilla, but also to those of man.

Dryopithecus chinjiensis (of India) may be the remote ancestor of the gorilla line.

Dryopithecus punjabicus (of India) seems to be closely allied or ancestral both to the gorilla and the chimpanzee.

Dryopithecus giganteus (of India) is very much larger than the other species and appears to be closely related to the chimpanzee.

Dryopithecus darwini (of Europe) is known from a third lower molar, which is unusually short and wide and has deep furrows and wrinkles. Its exact relationships are uncertain; perhaps it is related to *Pithecanthropus.*

Dryopithecus fontani (of Europe) is known from lower jaws and teeth, which appear to be allied in many characters to *D. chinjiensis* and to the modern gorilla.

Dryopithecus rhenanus (of Europe) is in some ways more specialized than *D. fontani* and may be intermediate between *D. punjabicus* and the chimpanzee.

Palœopithecus. This genus is known from a palate and upper teeth from the Lower Pliocene of India. It appears to the present writer to be related to the gorilla.

Neopithecus (*"Anthropodus"*). A third lower molar of doubtful relationships, perhaps related to *Dryopithecus rhenanus,* but with a narrow m_3.

Anthropopithecus (*Pan*) *vetus.* An extinct Pleistocene species represented by a lower jaw found near the Piltdown skull. The last survivor of the *Dryopithecus* group in Europe. Teeth and jaw differ greatly from those of the oldest known man, *H. heidelbergensis,* and are not generically separable from the modern *Anthropopithecus* (Pan), as held by Miller.

Pithecanthropus. The two upper molars referred to this genus are of

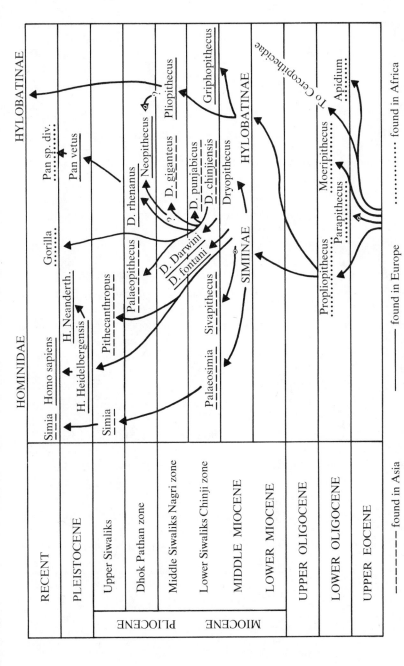

Fig. 1. Geological succession and provisional phylogeny of the Hominidæ and Simiidæ, as interpreted from available evidence by the author.

――――― found in Asia   ――――― found in Europe   .... found in Africa

very large size; in pattern and contour they suggest relationships with the *Dryopithecus*-group as well as with *Sivapithecus* and *Homo*.

2. Origin of the recent anthropoids

The Gibbons. In a recent phylogenetic diagram Dr. Pilgrim (1915) unites the gibbon stem with the human stem in the Upper Oligocene and places a very deep cleft between this gibbon-man trunk and the *Pliopithecus-Dryopithecus* group and its derivatives the modern great apes. This view of the nearer relationship of man to the gibbons rather than to the "giant apes" may be said to be flatly opposed by the anatomical results of many investigators. "The brain of the gibbon," says Keith (1896 p. 372), "is comparatively small and simple, resembling in its form and topography much more the brains of cynomorphous monkeys than those of the three great anthropoids." The brain of the Giant Apes on the other hand in the words of M. Weber (1904, p. 809).... "ist ein vereinfachtes Menschengehirn, dem aber nichts Wesentliches fehlt."

Again, in summarizing the results of his complete dissection of eighty specimens of the higher Primates, Professor Keith gives a tabular analysis (1911, p. 509) of over a thousand characters observed in the gibbon, from which the comparison below is taken.

But these figures hardly convey a correct impression of the relative degrees of affinity of the gibbon to man and to the great apes, since the characters are recorded numerically and are not evaluated according to their phylogenetic importance.

"As to the position of the gibbons in the series of primates," remarks Keith (1896, p. 376), "there is a tendency at present, with which the writer is in sympathy, to remove the gibbons altogether from the company of the anthropoids and place them in a position intermediate between the great apes and the cynomorphous monkeys.... They are really cynomorphous monkeys adapted to locomotion in an upright posture" (1896, p. 376). The present writer, however, regards the Hylobatidæ rather as aberrant Simiidæ, widely removed from the Cercopithecidæ.

In short the dental, osteological and anatomical characters of the gibbons appear to indicate that these apes represent an earlier offshoot of the anthropoid stem, as held by

Total number of characters examined	Common to gibbon and cynomorphs	Common to gibbon and to all other anthropoids and man	Common to gibbon and man alone
over 1000	323	133	84
	Common to chimpanzee and cynomorphs	Common to chimpanzee and to all other anthropoids and man	Common to chimpanzee and man alone
980	172	133	98

most authorities, and that the giant apes and man represent a later radiation. Comparative anatomical evidence sufficiently establishes the fact that the gibbons have been derived from the same brachiating and frugivorous catarrhine apes that gave rise to the whole man-anthropoid series. The derivation of the Gibbons from *Pliopithecus* of the Upper Tertiary of Europe is defended above.

Apart from their primitive anthropoid characters the gibbons resemble man chiefly in the features wherein they have avoided the specializations of the giant apes. The rounding and reduction of the third lower molars are probably secondary characters analogous with similar retrogressive characters in the orang, chimpanzee and man.

The Orang-utan. Professor Keith's vast labors on the anatomy of the anthropoids show: first that from the viewpoint of comparative anatomy the orang stands on a much higher plane than the gibbon, that is it has advanced further on the road toward extreme arboreal, frugivorous adaptation, toward a higher brain and mentality and toward gigantic size; secondly, that it stands well apart from the chimpanzee-gorilla group; and thirdly, that in the majority of its characters the orang is less man-like than the gorilla and chimpanzee.

The possible derivation of the Orang from the Miocene Asiatic genus *Palæosimia* is discussed above.

The Chimpanzee. Many features of the skull and skeleton of the chim-panzee are prophetic of the more specialized conditions in the gorilla. These two apes are indeed so closely allied that until recently both were referred to a single genus *Anthropopithecus*. Certain chimpanzees have exhibited strong resemblances to the gorilla, so that their status as chimpanzees was only determined by careful investigation (Keith, 1899), while on the other hand immature and female gorilla skulls to some extent suggest those of the chimpanzee.

The anatomist Tyson in 1699 published an excellent account of the anatomy of the chimpanzee, which he regarded as a distinct type of man (*Homo sylvestris*), and since then all observers have noted the close relationships of this ape to man in its anatomy, physiology and mental activities.

The derivation of the chimpanzee-gorilla group from one of the Miocene species of *Dryopithecus* is discussed above.

The Gorilla. Morphologists who have had the opportunity of studying the young female gorilla, as well as the gibbons and other anthropoids now or lately living in the New York Zoölogical Park, can hardly fail to be impressed with the superiority of the gorilla's claim to human kinship as compared with that of the other anthropoids, especially the gibbon. This is shown not only in the face, hands and feet and other parts of the body, but in the deep-seated functions of the digestive and reproductive systems. The gorilla, is in fact extremely manlike in many organs of high morphological significance, such as the brain, the sternum, the region of the auditory bulla, the external ear, the genital organs, the mammæ, the heart, and the eye. The musculature of the gorilla also presents many human characterstics. (*Cf.* Duckworth, 1915.)

In adopting a partly terrestrial habit the gorilla has entered upon a line of adaptation which in the forerunners of man resulted in a fully bipedal, cursorial type, capable of invading the plains. But as the gorilla is largely frugivorous and limited to the forests and their neighborhood the only course left for it (apart from its inevitable extinction by man) would have been to go on increasing still further in size until it might have surpassed even the Kodiak bear in bulk. Such a beast might have ambled along on all fours, partly supporting itself upon its knuckles as the gorilla now does.

. . .

3. The origin of man

Most anthropologists have specialized almost exclusively in their own field and have not acquired a practical knowledge of the evolution of the mammals, so far as it is known in many orders and families of mammals throughout the Tertiary and Quaternary Periods. Such specialists are impressed by the great and obvious differences between mankind and the existing anthropoids. They often magnify the phylogenetic importance of these differences, sometimes to the extent of supposing that the derivation of man is still veiled in complete mystery, or that the separation of the Hominidæ from the ancestral primate stock took place even before the differentiation of the Lemuroidea and Anthropoidea.

Many palæontologists, impressed with the vast antiquity of *Homo sapiens* as estimated in years, and with the fact that even the older Pleistocene species of Hominidæ were already widely seperated from the anthropoids in tooth and limb structure, are inclined to push back the point of separation of the Hominidæ and the anthropoids into the early Tertiary.

In the present work the chief conclusions, which appear to be of a conservative character, are as follows:

1. Comparative anatomical (including embryological) evidence alone has shown that man and the anthropoids have been derived from a primitive anthropoid stock and that man's nearest existing relatives are the chimpanzee and gorilla.

2. The chimpanzee and gorilla have retained, with only minor changes, the ancestral habits and habitus in brain, dentition, skull and limbs, while the forerunners of the Hominidæ, through a profound change in function, lost the primitive anthropoid habitus, gave up arboreal frugivorous adaptations and early became terrestrial, bipedal and predatory, using crude flints to cut up and smash the varied food.

3. The ancestral chimpanzee-gorilla-man stock appears to be represented by the Upper Miocene genera *Sivapithecus* and *Dryopithecus* the former more closely allied to, or directly ancestral to, the Hominidæ, the latter to the chimpanzee and gorilla.

4. Many of the differences that separate man from anthropoids of the *Sivapithecus* type are retrogressive changes, following the profound change in food habits above noted. Here belong the retraction of the face and dental arch, the reduction in size of the canines, the reduction of the jaw muscles, the loss of the prehensile character of the hallux. Many other differences are secondary adjustments in relative proportions, connected with the change from semi-arboreal semi-erect and semi-quadrupedal progression to fully terrestrial bipedal progression. The earliest anthropoids being of small size doubtless had slender limbs; later semi-terrestrial semi-erect forms were probably not unlike a very young gorilla, with fairly short legs and not excessively elongate arms. The long legs and short arms of man are due, I believe, to a secondary readjustment of proportions. The very short legs and very long arms of old male gorillas may well be a specialization.

5. At present I know no good evidence for believing that the separation of the Hominidæ from the Simiidæ took place any earlier than the Miocene, and probably the Upper Miocene. The change in structure during this vast interval (two or more million years) is much greater in the Hominidæ than in the conservative anthropoids, but it is not unlikely that during a profound change of life habits evolution sometimes proceeds more rapidly than in the more familiar cases where uninterrupted progressive adaptations proceed in a single direction.

6. *Homo heidelbergensis* appears to be directly ancestral to all the later Hominidæ.

4. On the evolution of human food habits

While all the great apes are prevailingly frugivorous, and even their forerunners in the Lower Oligocene have the teeth well adapted for piercing the tough rinds of fruits and for chewing vegetable food, yet they also appear to have at least a latent capacity for a mixed diet. The digestive tract, especially of the chimpanzee and gorilla, is essentially similar to that of man and at least some captive chimpanzees thrive upon a mixed diet including large quantities of fruits, vegetables and bread and small quantities of meat (Keith 1899). Mr. R. L. Garner who has spent many years in studying the African anthropoids in their wild state, states[2] that "their foods are mainly vegetable, but that flesh is an essential part of their diet." Other observers state[3] that the gorilla and chimpanzee greedily devour young birds, as well as eggs, vermin and small rodents.

[2] Science, vol. XLII, Dec. 10, 1915, p. 843.

[3] Keane, Ethnology, Cambridge 1901, p. 111.

Even the existing anthropoids, although highly conservative both in brain development and general habits, show the beginning of the use of the hands, and trained anthropoids can perform quite elaborate acts. At a time when tough-rinded tubers and fruits were still the main element of the diet the nascent Hominidæ may have sought out the lairs and nesting places of many animals for the purpose of stealing the young and thus they may have learned to fight with and kill the enraged parents. They had also learned to fight in protecting their own nesting places and young. And possibly they killed both by biting, as in carnivores, and by strangling, or, in the case of a small animal, by dashing it violently down.

We may conceive that the Upper Tertiary ape-men in the course of their dispersal from a south central Asiatic centre (Matthew, 1915, pp. 210, 214) entered regions where flint-bearing formations were abundant. In some way they learned perhaps that these "Eolith" flints could be used to smash open the head of a small strangled animal, to crack open tough vegetables, or to mash substances into an edible condition. Much later, after the mental association of hand and flint had been well established, they may have struck at intruders with the flints with which they were preparing their food and in this way they may have learned to use the heavier flints as hand axes and daggers. At a very early date they learned to throw down heavy stones upon an object to smash it, and this led finally to the hurling of flints at men and small game. Very early also they had learned to swing a heavy piece of wood or a heavy bone as a weapon. For all such purposes shorter and stockier arms are more advantageous than the long and slender arms of a semi-quadrupedal ancestral stage and I have argued above that a secondary shortening and thickening of the arms ensued.

One of the first medium-sized animals that the nascent Hominidæ would be successful in killing was the wild boar, which in the Pleistocene had a wide Palæarctic distribution.

From the very first the ape-men were more or less social in habits and learned to hunt in packs. Whether the art of hunting began in south central Asia or in Europe, perhaps one of the first large animals that men learned to kill after they invaded the open country was the horse, because, when a pack of men had surrounded a horse, a single good stroke with a coup-de-poing upon the brain-case might be sufficient to kill it.

I have argued above that the retraction of the dental arch and the reduction of the canines is not inconsistent with the use of meat as food, because men learned to use rough flints, in place of their teeth, to tear the flesh and to puncture the bones, and because the erect incisors, short canines and bicuspids were highly effective in securing a powerful hold upon the tough hide and connective tissue. It must be remembered that with a given muscular power small teeth are more easily forced into meat than large teeth.

After every feast there would be a residuum of hide and bones which would gradually assume economic value. The hides of animals were at first rudely stripped off simply to get at the meat. Small sharp-edged natural flints could be used for this purpose as well as to cut the sinews and flesh. After a time it was found that the furry sides of these hides were useful to cover the body at night or during a storm. Thus the initial stage in the making of clothes may have been a biproduct of the hunting habit.

Dr. Matthew (1915, pp. 211, 212) has well suggested that men may have learned to cover the body with the skins of animals in a cool temperate climate (such as that on the northern slopes of the Himalayas) and that afterward they were able to invade colder regions. The use of rough skins to cover the body must have caused exposure to new sources of annoyance and infection, but we cannot affirm that natural selection was the cause of the reduction of hair on the body and of the many correlated modifications of glandular activity. We can only affirm that a naked race of mammals must surely have had hairy ancestors and that the loss of hair on the body was probably subsequent to the adoption of predatory habits.

The food habits of the early Hominidæ, and thus indirectly the jaws and teeth, were later modified through the use of fire for softening the food. Men had early learned to huddle around the dying embers of forest fires that had been started by lightning, to feed the fire-monster with branches, and to carry about firebrands. They learned eventually that frozen meat could be softened by exposing it to the fire. Thus the broiling and roasting of meat and vegetables might be learned even before the ways of kindling fire through percussion and friction had been discovered. But the full art of cooking and the subsequent stages in the reduction of the jaws and teeth in the higher races probably had to await the development of vessels for holding hot water, perhaps in Neolithic times.

This account of the evolution of the food habits of the Hominidæ will probably be condemned by experimentalists, who have adduced strong evidence for the doctrine that "acquired characters" cannot be inherited. But, whatever the explanation may be, it is a fact that progressive changes in food-habits and correlated changes in structure have occurred in thousands of phyla, the history of which is more or less fully known. Nobody with a practical knowledge of the mechanical interactions of the upper and lower teeth of mammals, or of the progressive changes in the evolution of shearing and grinding teeth, can doubt that the dentition has evolved *pari passu with* changes in food habits. Whether, as commonly supposed, the food habits changed before the dentition, or *vice versa,* the evidence appears to show that the Hominidæ passed through the following stages of evolution:

1. A chiefly frugivorous stage, with large canines and parallel rows of cheek teeth (*cf. Sivapithecus*).
2. A predatory, omnivorous stage, with reduced canines and convergent tooth rows (*cf. Homo heidelbergensis*).
3. A stage in which the food is softened by cooking and the dentition is more or less reduced in size and retrograde in character, as in modernized types of *H. sapiens.*

Conflicting Views on the Problem of Man's Ancestry

Gerrit Smith Miller
1920

Writers who have recently dealt with the problem of man's ancestry have expressed opinions which strikingly contrast with each other. It has seemed of interest to bring together some of the more important of these conflicting views and to add to them a few of my own observations and conjectures.

Incompleteness of the geological record

Paleontology is at present unable to furnish the conclusive direct evidence needed to answer the question: From what particular primate stock did the line of human ancestry take its origin? This failure is the result of the fact that every known fossil which might be expected to supply such evidence represents either: (1) remains that are definitely those of men, (2) remains that are definitely those of apes, or (3) remains whose characters are for various reasons so inconclusive that the systematic position of the creatures to which they belonged has not yet been finally determined. With regard to all this evidence two of the main sources of difficulty are that the bones usually consist of mere fragments, and that the parts of the skeleton most likely to

"Conflicting Views on the Problem of Man's Ancestry." *American Journal of Physical Anthropology.* Vol. 3, No. 2, pp. 213–23, 243–45. 1920.

be preserved through fossilization are those which furnish the least important characters. In the skull the fragile basicranial and facial regions are easily lost, while the calvarium shows relatively great powers of resistance. But the actual processes by which the skull acquired its human structure are to be sought much less in the modelling of the skull cap than in the profound basicranial and facial adjustments by means of which it has been made possible for the head with its enlarged brain to be balanced on top of the upright vertebral column. Similarly with the limbs; the somewhat unimportant long bones may easily be preserved under circumstances which would destroy such essential parts as the hand, foot, wrist and ankle, whose specialization must mark the real course pursued by the early representatives of the human stock in gradually attaining their distinctive structure. The cheekteeth, as might be anticipated, are the parts of the body most frequently found. In all of the higher primates, however, the structural features of the molars are fundamentally uniform, and little removed from the primitive tritubercular type. They are furthermore of a kind which easily leads to the development of similiar crown forms in animals which are not nearly related. Taken alone, therefore, these teeth are of limited value in tracing the direction of evolution.

The fact that the characters shown by a few teeth and fragments of bone do not necessarily furnish a clue to the structure of an entire animal cannot be too strongly emphasized in the present connection.[1] A skull cap, a leg bone, or some molars might possess characters exactly intermediate between those of man and those of a given anthropoid or other primate; but we would have no means of knowing, in the absence of the rest of the skeleton, that the structure of other parts of the animal from which the fragments came had been equally intermediate and that the creature did in fact represent a link in the chain of human evolution. All that can be safely concluded as to the characters of such isolated portions of the skeleton is that they represent plastic stages through which certain human peculiarities could have been derived from certain simian peculiarities. Yet there is a tendency to think, speak, and write of the extinct higher primates as if they were actually known as animals, in the sense that some fossil members of other mammalian families, the horses, for instance, are known. Only in the case of Neanderthal man could such a course be justified. Definite knowledge of the genetic relationships and evolutionary meaning of all the others must await the finding of skeletons sufficiently perfect to include most of the cardinal parts.[2]

[1] A suggestive paper on this general subject has recently been published by B. Petronievics: La loi de l'Evolution non corrélative, *Révue Générale des Sciences,* April 30, 1919, **XXX,** 240–42.

[2] "La solution du problème de nos origines et surtout la détermination précise de notre lignée exigent de nouvelles découvertes de fossiles, de nombreux fossiles!" (Boule).

Until such discoveries are made the incompleteness of the geological record should be kept constantly in mind. The following rough list of the described parts of the fossil primates whose characters might be hoped to aid in solving the problem of man's ancestry may give this phase of the subject some of the prominence which it deserves.

MEN

Heidelberg man—Mandible with its teeth.

Neanderthal man—Most of the skeleton. Exact position not finally determined:

Eoanthropus—Fragments of braincase; squamosal; nasals; one canine tooth; imperfect mandible with first and second molars. Not certainly parts of one animal.[3]

Pithecanthropus—Skull cap; third upper molar; femur. Not certainly parts of one animal[3]

APES

Anthropodus—Jugal; upper incisor.

Dryopithecus—Most of the teeth; maxilla; lower jaw.

Griphopithecus—Third upper molar.

Neopithecus—Third lower molar.

Palæopithecus—Palate and upper teeth (except incisors).

Palæosimia—Third upper molar.

Parapithecus—Mandible with its teeth.

Pliohylobates—Femur.

Pliopithecus—Mandible with its teeth; palate and upper teeth.

Propliopithecus—Mandible with its teeth.

Sivapithecus—Two fragments of lower jaws, one containing three perfect cheekteeth, the other containing the

[3] See Ramström, *Bull. Geol. Inst. Upsala*, 1919, XVI, 12–30.

canine and the roots of two incisors and one premolar; a few cheekteeth, among them the first and second upper molars set in a small piece of the maxilla.

In the presence of so little real information as to be structure of extinct higher primates the treatment of the subject under discussion inevitably resolves itself into the making of hypotheses based chiefly on the facts of comparative anatomy, physiology and embryology of the living members of the group. Speculation as to the early history of the human line cannot therefore do otherwise than lead to widely divergent results.

Simple or multiple origin

By some writers it is asserted that the various living and fossil members of the family *Hominidæ* are not, as usually believed, comparatively recent offshoots from a common stem, but that the uniform general structure of all known men is due less to intimate relationship than to convergence, that is, to the equalizing effect on originally unlike animals of the long action of uniform molding forces. There are two principal forms in which this idea has been expressed.

One is set forth by Klaatsch.[4] After describing and figuring the likenesses which he finds between

[4] "Menschenrassen und Menschenaffen," *Korr.-Blatt Deutsch. Gesellsch. Anthrop. etc.*, July, 1910, XLI, 91–100, Figs. 1–14.

the long bones and the skulls of Neanderthal man and the gorilla on the one hand, and Aurignacian man and the orang on the other, he concludes (p. 97) that it is necessary to assume the existence of two great "streams" of pre-humanity, a western and an eastern, each of which independently gave rise to races of men and to great apes. Neanderthal man and the gorilla are representatives of the western stream, Aurignacian man and the orang are representatives of the eastern. Between these two apes or these two men the relationship is less intimate than that between the ape and the man developed from each stream. To express this relationship he designates the first pair as the "N-G-type," the second as the "A-O-type." The resemblances on which this hypothesis rests are confined to such superficial and unimportant characters, particularly as regards the skull, that it is impossible to regard Klaatsch's conjectures as serious contributions to an understanding of the subject of man's origin. Keith[5] in particular has shown their worthlessness.

The other is elaborately developed by Sergi in various papers, but principally in his two books *Le Origini Umane* 1913, and *L'Evoluzione Organica e le Origini Umane,* 1914. It is based on the general conception that organic evolution is mainly the result of a process which may be described as a succession or superposition of groups (stirpi). The mem-

bers of any group living at a given time have, according to this view, been chiefly derived from equivalent members of a geologically preceding group. The branches of the genealogical tree are therefore mostly parallel. They change their characters as they grow upward, and the branches may subdivide into secondary parallel branches "according to their own vitality and the conditions under which they live," but they do not spread from common centers of radiation. As applied to those of the primates under special discussion that are represented by fossil forms the plan works out as follows. From the unknown predecessors of the primates arose the three independent groups, *Cercopithecidœ* with six independent branches, *Simiidœ* with four branches, and *Hominidœ* with four branches. Each of the four branches of the *Hominidœ* is regarded as a genus: *Eoanthropus, Palœanthropus (heidelbbergensis), Notanthropus* (negro) and *Heoanthropus* (Mongolian) These genera are not derived from a common, earlier, less specialized human type, neither are they connected with the great apes or with other known primates. Each is supposed to have been distinct since the hominid group originated from its hypothetical forerunners. There appears to be small likelihood that the ideas of Sergi will meet with general acceptance. They have been severely and, it seems, justly criticized by Giuffrida-Ruggeri.[6] Yet

---

5 *Nature,* December 15, 1910, LXX-XV, 206, and February, 16, 1911, LXXXV, 509–10.

6 "Unicità del Philum Umano con pluralità dei Centri Specifici," *Rev. Ital. Paleont.,* 1918, XXIV, 3–11.

it must be admitted that they partly rest on two facts or circumstances which are recognized sources of difficulty to the more usual conception of the course of evolutionary history: the Minerva-like manner in which whole faunas suddenly appear in the geological record with complete panoplies of species, genera, and families, and the steadily increasing number of supposedly modern types whose range is being found to extend unexpectedly far into the past.

The known types of men resemble each other so closely in both the generalized and specialized parts of their structure that, as Giuffrida-Ruggeri has remarked, there can be no real basis for speculation as to their origin by polyphyletic or polygenetic types of evolution. Certainly no such ideas would be suggested with regard to any other group of mammals in which an equal degree of uniformity prevailed. Hence there seems to be no reason to abandon the generally accepted opinion that the entire human family is descended from a common ancestry. As to the nature of this ancestral stock and its probable geological history there is little uniformity of opinion. Two main hypotheses, however, represent in a general way the views of most of the more recent writers. They are: (1) that the human line of descent goes back, in relatively late geological time, to a stock that had first become so definitely simian that its representatives would be placed in the same family as the existing great apes, and (2) that the human line took its origin at an early period

from *Tarsius*-like animals and that throughout its subsequent course it has been distinct from the lines of the apes and monkeys.[7] The first may be called the Simian hypothesis, the second the Tarsin hypothesis.

The simian hypothesis

The Simian hypothesis may be considered as the accepted view of the subject. With variations in details it underlies the great mass of recent work. While the evidence on which it rests has been frequently discussed it has probably been most fully and clearly presented in the second part of the "Studies on the Evolution of the Primates," by Dr. William K. Gregory.[8]

"A new synthetic study of the Primates," this author says, "seems timely because of the great additions that have been made during the last two decades to the material or objective side of our knowledge of the Primates. For during this period the Eocene lemuroids have been revised by Osborn (1902), Wortman (1903–1904), Stehlin (1912), and Matthew (1915), while new extinct lemurs of Madagascar have been described by Grandidier (1905), Standing (1908), and others. The fossil anthropoids of Europe have been restudied by Schlosser (1900, 1903),

[7] An intermediate position is taken by Boule (L'Homme fossile de la Chapelle-aux-Saints, 1913, 268). He regards the human line as entirely distinct from that of the great apes, but as having probably originated from the same common primate stock as the apes and monkeys.

[8] "Phylogeny of Recent and Extinct Anthropoids with Special Reference to the Origin of Man," *Bull. Amer. Mus. Nat. Hist.*, June 16, 1916, XXXV, 258–355.

and Abel (1902), and the paleontological history of this group has been recently extended by the discoveries of Pilgrim (1915) in India and of Schlosser (1911) and Stromer in Egypt. Meanwhile great progress has been made in the knowledge of Pleistocene races of man, especially through the labors of Gorjanovic-Kramberger (1906), Schoetensack (1908), Boule (1912), Schwalbe (in numerous studies), Smith Woodward (1913), Keith (1915) and others."

The scope of Doctor Gregory's paper is indicated by its table of contents: I. Introduction; II. Chief adaptive characters of the skull, dentition and limbs of the recent anthropoids and man; III. The Fayûm Oligocene anthropoids (*Parapithecus, Propliopithecus*); IV. The Siwalik Upper Miocene and Lower Pliocene anthropoids (*Palæosimia, Sivapithecus, Dryopithecus, Palæopithecus*); V. The extinct anthropoids and men of Europe; also *Pithecanthropus (Pliopithecus, Dryopithecus, Neopithecus, Pan, Pithecanthropus, Homo)*; VI. Phylogenetic summary and conclusions. Thirty-five text figures give a clear idea of the more important of the fossil remains which form the basis of present knowledge of the extinct anthropoids. The author summarizes his conclusions as follows (pp. 341–342):

1. Comparative anatomical (including embryological) evidence alone has shown that man and the anthropoids have been derived from a primitive anthropoid stock and that man's nearest existing relatives are the chimpanzee and gorilla.

2. The chimpanzee and gorilla have retained, with only minor changes the ancestral habits and habitus in brain, dentition, skull and limbs, while the forerunners of the *Hominidæ*, through a profound change in function, lost the primitive anthropoid habitus, gave up arboreal frugivorous adaptations and early became terrestrial, bipedal and predatory, using crude flints to cut up and smash the varied food.

3. The ancestral chimpanzee-gorilla-man stock appears to be represented by the Upper Miocene genera *Sivapithecus* and *Dryopithecus,* the former more closely allied to, or directly ancestral to, the *Hominidæ,* the latter to chimpanzee and gorilla. On page 327 he adds. "I believe that a concrete and approximately accurate notion of the facts would be given if one were to affirm that the Upper Miocene ancestors of the *Hominidæ* were at least very closely akin to the Upper Miocene common ancestors of the chimpanzee and gorilla, that they were in fact heavy-jawed, stout limbed, tailless and semi-erect anthropoid Catarrhinæ, with quadritubercular second and third upper molars and *Sivapithecus*-like lower molars." In the diagram on page 337 the human line is shown as branching off from the "*Simiidæ.*"

4. Many of the differences that separate man from anthropoids of the *Sivapithecus* type are retrogressive changes, following the profound change in food habits above noted. Here belong the retraction of the face and dental arch, the reduction in size of the canines, the reduction of the jaw muscles, the loss of the prehensile character of the hallux. Many other differences are secon-

dary adjustments in relative proportions, connected with the change from semi-arboreal, semi-erect and semi-quadrupedal progression to fully terrestrial bipedal progression. The earliest anthropoids being of small size doubtless had slender limbs; later semi-terrestrial semi-erect forms were probably not unlike a very young gorilla, with fairly short legs and not excessively elongate arms. The long legs and short arms of man are due, I believe, to a secondary readjustment of proportions. The very short legs and very long arms of old male gorillas may well be a specialization.

5. At present I know no good evidence for believing that the separation of the *Hominidæ* from the *Simiidæ* took place any earlier than the Miocene, and probably the Upper Miocene. The change in structure during this vast interval (two or more million years) is much greater in the *Hominidæ* than in the conservative anthropoids, but it is not unlikely that during a profound change of life habits evolution sometimes proceeds more rapidly than in the more familiar cases where uninterrupted progressive adaptations proceed in a single direction.

6. *Homo heidelbergensis* appears to be directly ancestral to all the later *Hominidæ*.

The tarsian hypothesis

The tarsian hypothesis has been explained by Prof. Frederic Wood-Jones in a pamphlet[9] intended "for

9 The Problem of Man's Ancestry. By Wood-Jones (Frederic), Professor of Anatomy in the University of London. 12°, London, Society for Promoting Christian Knowledge, 1918, pp. 1–48. Price 7d.

a public wider than that represented by those few who attend the meetings of scientific societies." As it is not very generally known I shall give a rather detailed synopsis.

"Before we attempt to follow the story of the evolution of man as a zoölogical type" Professor Wood-Jones remarks, "it is necessary that we follow the evolution of ideas upon the subject. . . ." the first half of the pamphlet is therefore devoted to a rapid survey of the growth of opinion from Aristotle to Gregory. Briefly stated the two main results of this growth are, (a) that man is regarded as a product of evolution, and (b) that while "end-on" evolution, or the direct passage from the highest representatives of a lower type to the lowest representatives of a higher type, is generally discredited as applied to most organisms "we still retain a belief in the 'end-on' evolution of man *via* the stages of the lower quadrupedal mammal, lemur, monkey, and anthropoid ape. It is this belief that determines the modern method of research in comparative anatomy, for if the history of any human structure is sought, its condition of development is examined in the anthropoid apes, in the monkeys of the Old World and of the New World, then in the lemurs, and finally in some common quadruped."

In criticizing this method of study Professor Wood-Jones first eliminates the ordinary quadrupeds from the line of man's descent. "It is enough to study the hand and forearm of man to note the astonishingly primitive arrangement of bones, muscles and joints, to compare them with those of a primitive type of reptile [in which the limbs serve for propulsion but not for support], and to contrast them with those of a quadrupedal mammal, to be certain that at no period has man or his ancestors supported the body weight upon the fore limb, resting upon the surface of the earth.[10] It is therefore hopeless to expect light on man's origin from the study of such an animal as a typical quadrupedal mammal." The lemurs other than *Tarsius* are next considered. As long ago as 1873 Mivart expressed the opinion that it is "in the highest degree improbable that the lemuroids and apes took origin from any common root form not equally a progenitor of other mammalian orders." This idea is now elaborated and brought to the conclusion that "the primitive lemurs and the primitive monkeys resemble each other simply because they are both representatives of exceedingly primitive arboreal mammalian stocks; but here the likeness ends, and the lemur group can certainly not be regarded as belonging to or even ancestral of, the monkey group." Finally as to the monkeys and apes; man differs from these animals in three general directions. "In the first place he does not possess several features which we may term pithecoid or simian specializations. In the second he retains a remarkably large number of very primitive features which have been lost by the

10 This subject has been more fully treated in the author's "Arboreal Man," London, 1916.

monkeys and anthropoid apes. And in the third, he has developed some distinctly human specializations, some of which are dependent upon his upright posture, but some are quite independent of this factor. The features embraced in the first category are not capable of any precise summarization." Those of the second category are more easily dealt with. "Man's retention of astonishingly primitive features is a condition that has not attracted the attention that it deserves.... In the base of the human skull, and upon the sides of the brain case, the bones articulate in an order which is that characteristic of the primitive mammal. In these regions the human skull shows a condition exactly like that of the lemurs. But all the monkeys and anthropoid apes (with one exception) have lost this primitive arrangement and follow an utterly different plan. No monkey or anthropoid ape approaches near to man in the primitive simplicity of the nasal bones. The structure of the back wall of the orbit, the metopic suture, the form of the jugal bone, the condition of the internal pterygoid plate, the teeth, etc., all tell the same story—that the human skull is built upon remarkably primitive mammalian lines which have been departed from in some degree by all monkeys and apes. As for muscles, man is wonderfully distinguished by the retention of primitive features lost in the rest of the Primates." The pectoralis minor, for instance, is attached to the coracoid, while in apes and monkeys it has moved downward toward or to the humerus. "The human tongue is not unlike that of the chimpanzee, but no monkey can show nearly so primitive a mammalian tongue as that typical of man. The human vermiform appendix, although usually regarded as a particularly degenerated rudiment is strangely like that of such simple creatures as some of the pouched animals of Australia, and the very different structure found in the monkeys is most likely a specialization from a primitive condition which is retained in man. The great arteries which arise from the arch of the aorta are of the same number and kind, and are arranged in the same order in man and in such a lowly animal as... *Ornithorhynchus*. In the monkeys and anthropoid apes this arrangement is departed from." Turning to the third category special attention is directed to such features as the absence in man of the premaxilla as a complete bony element though this bone is fully developed in the skull of all the monkeys and apes, the presence in the human leg of the peroneus tertius muscle, also an exclusively human peculiarity, and the structure of the human foot. "The human foot is unique in nature; no other animal has a foot with digits and muscles arranged upon the same plan.... Man's big toe has become dominant, his little toe is becoming a rudiment. In all monkeys and apes the toes are arranged as the fingers, and the third toe like the third finger is the longest." Each of these strictly human characters originates, at a very early embryonic stage, directly, that is

without passing through a stage recalling the condition found in monkeys and apes. After reviewing this evidence "we are left with the unavoidable impression that the search for his [man's] ancestors must be pushed a very long way back. It is difficult to imagine how a being, whose body is replete with features of basal mammalian simplicity, can have sprung from any of those animals in which so much of this simplicity has been lost. It becomes impossible to picture man as being descended from any form at all like the recent monkeys, or anthropoid apes, or from their fossil representatives.... He must have started an independent line of his own, long before the anthropoid apes and the monkeys developed those specializations which shaped their definite evolutionary destinies." Some idea of the stock from which the human line took its origin may be gained from the characters of *Tarsius,* an animal usually included among the lemurs, but here, as by Wortman in 1903, placed definitely with the monkeys and elevated to the rank of a special group. "He is a most highly specialized little creature along his own curious lines and yet he retains with man a host of those astonishingly primitive features that place this odd couple at the base of the Primate stem. He lingers today, a specialized primitive Primate, nearer akin to man than any other animal known to the zoölogist." But even with the truth of this relationship admitted it remains impossible to formulate a definite conception of the original stock, for "no fossil has so far been discovered which throws any real light upon the characters of such a creature." It can only be said that: "The pro-human member of the human stock would probably be a small animal, and we would not venture on a nearer guess than that which anyone is free to make as to the identity of an animal intermediate between a *Tarsius*-like form and man."

. . .

Summary and conclusion

(1) The absence of direct and conclusive paleontological evidence leaves open a wide field for speculation as to the probable course of development followed by the members of that branch of the primates which has produced man. (2) That the family *Hominidæ* comes from a single ancestral line is sufficiently indicated by the essential uniformity of all known men, living and fossil, in both the specialized and generalized parts of their structure. (3) The hypotheses containing the idea that different races originated from different primate stocks are based on features of secondary importance or on evidence which appears to be insufficient. They may therefore be disregarded. (4) Of the various other hypotheses two seem worthy of special attention: (*a*) the "Simian hypothesis" according to which the human line branched off, as the result of a profound change of habits and function, in relatively recent geological time from a stock which had first become so definitely simian

that it would be recognized as coming within the limits of the family which includes the gorilla and chimpanzee, and (*b*) the "Tarsian hypothesis" according to which the human line took its origin from *Tarsius*-like animals at a very remote period without a profound change of habits and function, and that throughout its subsequent course it has been distinct from the line of the apes. (5) Both of these hypotheses in their present form are open to serious objection, the "Tarsian hypothesis" mainly because much of the evidence cited in its support is susceptible of other interpretations, and the "Simian hypothesis" mainly because it is based almost exclusively on morphological characters without full regard to the facts which can be derived from the study of living animals. (6) The hypothesis which now appears to account for the greatest number of facts in the simplest manner may be stated as follows:

The distinctively human line branched off from the generalized primate stock at a point near that at which the line leading to the gorilla and chimpanzee originated and at a time when the great toe had not lost its simply divergent character. The inception of this line was not due to a profound and relatively abrupt alteration of habits and function forced on the animals by environmental change, but to a process the evidence of which may be seen everywhere among mammals living under uniform conditions and of which the primates furnish many striking examples. This is the process known as "local adaptive radiation," or the exploitation by different members of a group of the possibilities offered by different elements of their common environment and common structure. The special "exploitation" in this instance consisted in the development of the grasping powers of the hand rather than those of the foot, while among the ancestors of the great apes the opposite was occurring. Coincidently with the development of the hand terrestrial habits were gradually adopted, through stages such as may be seen among the living Old World primates. The hind foot was thus brought to the ground without the encumbrance of a hallux specialized for grasping, while the hand was so modified that its use as a fore foot was made difficult. This combination of circumstances supplied the structural and functional elements needed for initiating the series of changes which finally produced the essential characters of the human form.

Man's Pedigree

Grafton Elliot-Smith
1924

Before we can attempt to discuss the factors that were responsible for the emergence of the distinctive characters of Man, it is essential that we should make some attempt to reconstruct his pedigree, for it is only when the relationships one to the other of the different races of men and the extinct members of the Human Family are defined that one can begin to consider what were the sequence of changes and what the essential conditions of progress within the Family. Moreover, without some definite scheme of the position in time and the relationship one to the other of the members of the Order Primates, to which Man belongs, it is impossible to form any idea as to the nature of the factors that determined the emergence of the qualities of mind and body that are distinctive of the Human Family.

I have therefore attempted to construct two diagrams to give graphic expression to the present state of our knowledge regarding these

"Man's Pedigree." From *The Evolution of Man* by G. Elliott-Smith, published by Oxford University Press. London, 1924. Pp. 1–15.

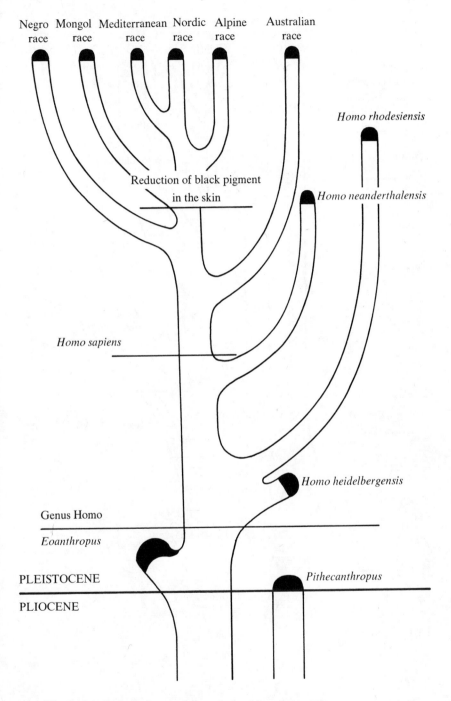

Fig. 1. A tentative scheme of the relationships of the different genera, species, and races of the Human Family.

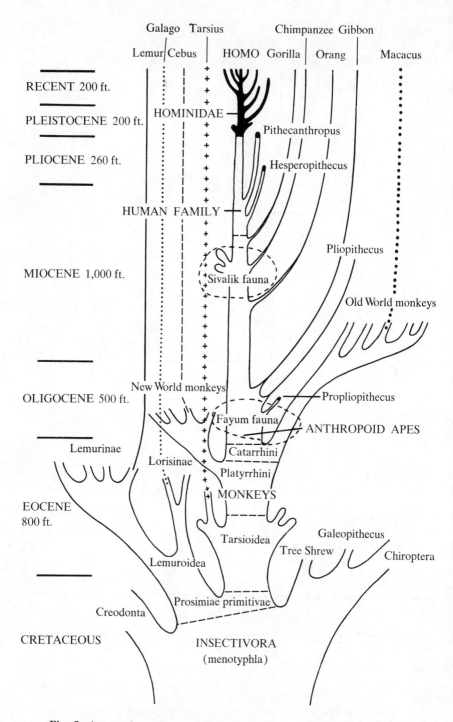

Fig. 2. A tentative scheme of the relationships of the Order Primates.

questions of pedigree. In the first figure the relationships of the Human Family itself have been tentatively plotted out. All of the existing members of the Human Family belong to the species *Homo sapiens*. The most primitive race now living is undoubtedly the Australian, which represents the survival with comparatively slight modifications of perhaps the primitive type of the species. Next in order comes the Negro Race, which is much later and, in some respects, more highly specialized, differing profoundly in many respects from the Australian, but sharing with it the black pigmentation of the skin, which is really an early characteristic of the Human Family that primitive Man shares with the Gorilla and the Chimpanzee. After the Negro separated from the main stem of the Family, the amount of pigment in the skin underwent a sudden and very marked reduction; and the next group that became segregated and underwent its own distinctive specialization was the Mongol Race. After the separation of the Mongol there was a further reduction of pigment in the skin; and from this white division of mankind the Alpine Race first became split off the main stem, which ultimately became separated into the Mediterranean and the Nordic Races, in the latter of which the reduction of pigment was carried a stage further to produce the blondest of all human beings.

There are certain individuals that cannot at present satisfactorily be placed in this scheme. Such, for example, as the men who lived in Europe in the so-called Upper Palaeolithic Age. It is probable that they should be placed in the scheme partly on the stem common to the Nordic and Mediterranean people, and partly lower down at the place where the Negro branched off from the main stem. Before *Homo sapiens* came into existence the ancestors of Neanderthal Man became divergently specialized: in the diagram the attempt has been made roughly to locate in time the epoch to which the actual remains of Neanderthal Man belong, and to contrast it with the time at which this species became separated from the ancestors of *Homo sapiens*.

This necessarily involves a certain amount of conjecture, because it places Neanderthal Man, or rather those members of the species whose bones have been found in Europe, about midway up the stem of *Homo sapiens*, whereas no actual remains of the species *sapiens* have been found except at a period subsequent to the disappearance of Neanderthal Man in Europe. The fact that these earliest known members of our species belong definitely to a higher type than the Australian and the Negro points clearly to the conclusion that these representatives belong to a comparatively late phase in the history of the species, and that they were immigrants into Europe when they displaced representatives of the Neanderthal species.

The skull found in Rhodesia in 1921 represents a species of the genus *Homo* which is definitely more primitive than that of Neanderthal

Man, although the actual bones which were found in the Broken Hill Mine may be actually very much more recent in time than the bones of the Neanderthal species, which have been recovered in Europe. In the diagram the attempt has been made to represent these facts graphically, and to show how the ancestors of Rhodesian Man may have sprung from the main stem at a much earlier period than Neanderthal Man, but survived till a more recent period than the latter. This would not be surprising when one considers that in Africa there have been preserved until the present time representatives of much more ancient genera of mammals whose European representatives became extinct at a vastly more ancient time than that assigned in the diagram to the origin of Rhodesian Man.

In the diagram I have assigned the origin of Rhodesian Man to a place near to Heidelberg Man: but at present it is impossible to define the issue more closely, because the only fragment of Heidelberg Man that we possess consists of a lower jaw, whereas the lower jaw is missing in the case of Rhodesian Man, of whom we possess the skull and some of the limb bones. But the jaw from Heidelberg fits the Rhodesian skull so closely that I have ventured to put the origins of the two species in close apposition, and as we know the date of Heidelberg Man it suggests the time at which the Rhodesian species separated from the main stem of mankind. Heidelberg Man occupies a position at the base of the genus *Homo.* In fact, future

discovery may possibly compel us to exclude the Heidelberg remains from that genus, as Bonarelli suggested some years ago: but at present the available evidence favours the inclusion of these remains definitely within the genus *Homo,* and compels us to locate it right at the base of the stem. Apart from the genus *Homo* two other genera of the Human Family are known from the base of the Pleistocene. These are the Piltdown skull representing the genus *Eoanthropus,* which is very closely related to the main stream which eventually emerged as the genus *Homo,* and the earlier and more primitive, but also more highly specialized, Ape-Man of Java, *Pithecanthropus,* the date of which was formerly assigned to the Upper Pliocene, but is now generally believed to belong to the very commencement of the Pleistocene. So that, although we have no fossil bones generally admitted to be human that can be referred to a period earlier than the Pleistocene, the marked contrast between *Pithecanthropus* and *Eoanthropus,* a separation which is not only structural, but geographical, makes it quite certain that Man must have existed in the Pliocene, and possibly earlier still.

The consideration of this question brings us to the discussion of the remarkable tooth found in Nebraska in 1922, which is referred to the Lower Pliocene Period. This tooth, for the reception of which Professor Henry Fairfield Osborn has created a new genus, *Hesperopithecus,* is regarded by the American palaeontologists as a representative of a hitherto unknown Primate, but so far as its structure is concerned the tooth presents a closer approximation to that of *Pithecanthropus* than to the Anthropoid; and I regard the balance of probability as favouring its identification as a primitive member of the Human Family rather than a new genus of Anthropoid Apes.

The discovery of a single tooth

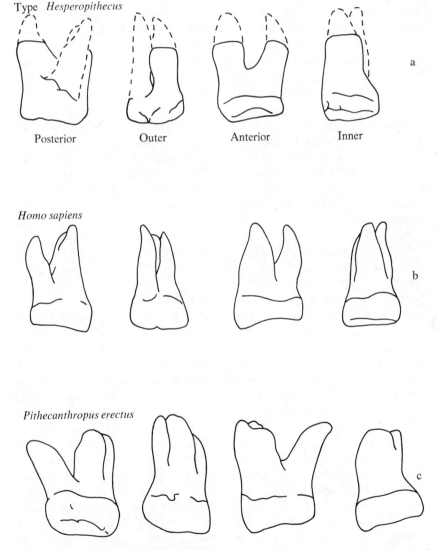

Type *Hesperopithecus*

Posterior   Outer   Anterior   Inner   a

Homo sapiens

b

Pithecanthropus erectus

c

Fig. 3. The Nebraska Tooth compared with those of *Homo sapiens* and *Pithecanthropus*. (After Gregory.)

may seem rather a frail and hazardous basis upon which to build such tremendous and unexpected conclusions; and many, if not most, scientists have grave doubts as to the justification for such an interpretation. But the specimen was discovered by a geologist of wide experience, and its horizon has been satisfactorily established. Moreover, the determination of its affinities and its identification as one of the higher Primates closely akin to the Ape-Man of Java, *Pithecanthropus,* has been made by the most competent authorities on the specific characters of fossilized mammalian teeth, Professor Osborn and Drs. Matthew and Gregory, who not only have had a wider experience of such material than any other palaeontologists, but also are men of exact knowledge and sound judgement. I think the balance of probability is in favour of the view that the tooth found in the Pliocene beds of Nebraska is really that of a primitive member of the Human Family. *Hesperopithecus* is most nearly akin to *Pithecanthropus*; and the fact that the latter was found in what, at the end of the Pliocene Period, was the south-eastern corner of Asia, and the former in North America, which was connected with Eastern Asia by a land bridge enjoying a genial climate, minimizes the difficulty of explaining an identification that at first sight seems to be wholly incredible. For the American palaeontologists have demonstrated that, at the time when the original owner of the Nebraska tooth

was living, certain Antelopes and Rhinoceroses of Asiatic affinities made their way into America, and for this purpose a land bridge and a warm climate were essential.

For many years an experienced geologist, Mr. Harold J. Cook, has been collecting the remains of the extinct fauna that lived in Western Nebraska in Pliocene times; and more than fifteen years ago he collaborated with Dr. W. D. Matthew, the distinguished palaeontologist of the American Museum, and compiled a remarkable inventory of the wonderful collection of mammalian remains found by them and others in a Pliocene deposit, which they then distinguished as the Snake Creek beds. Since then Mr. Cook has continued the work of collecting, and has acquired a thorough knowledge of the stratigraphy and an insight into the circumstances under which fossils are discovered. Hence he is not likely to have been deceived as to the horizon in which a particular fragment was found. When, on February 25, 1922, he wrote to Professor Osborn, President of the American Museum in New York, to say that he had obtained from the Upper, or Hipparion phase, of the Snake Creek beds 'a molar tooth that very closely approaches the human type', the accuracy and reliability of Mr. Cook's identification of its geological age and provenance were not questioned. For he explained that 'it was found associated with the other typical fossils of the Snake Creek, and is mineralized in the same fashion as they are'. His claim that 'whatever it is, it is certainly a contemporary fossil of the Upper Snake Creek horizon, and agrees far more closely with the anthropoid-human molar than that of any other mammal known', has been fully confirmed by the investigations of Professor Osborn and Drs. Matthew and Gregory, who have an unrivalled experience of the scientific study of mammalian fossilized teeth.

Dr. Gregory arrived at the important conclusion that 'on the whole we think its nearest resemblances are with *Pithecanthropus,* and with men rather than with apes'. This conclusion was based upon the study of the features of the tooth; and the claim that it was human was further corroborated by the degree and kind of 'wear', which was unlike that found in any ape, but of the same nature as occurs in the different genera of the Human Family, and especially *Pithecanthropus.*

Elsewhere in this book, I shall have occasion to criticize Dr. Pilgrim's opinion that the form of the teeth of a long extinct Miocene Ape (*Sivapithecus*) found in India is adequate evidence for its inclusion in the Human Family. The ancestors of the Hominidae no doubt exhibited such human traits of teeth and body in the Miocene probably long before they acquired those distinctive characters of brain and mind that alone entitle their descendants to human rank. Hence, even if the resemblances of the teeth of *Sivapithecus* to those of Man were closer

than they are, this would not justify the inclusion of the former in the Human Family. It would merely suggest its kinship to the ancestors of the Family.

The case of *Hesperopithecus* is somewhat different. It is much more recent, Pliocene instead of Miocene; and therefore much more definitely within the range of Man's possible existence. The tooth presents much closer affinities with those of the most primitive members of the Human Family. But the most important consideration of all, when the extreme susceptibility of the Anthropoid Apes to a cold climate and their dependence upon forest conditions is considered,[1] is that a primitive human being is much more likely than an ape to have crossed to America by the northern Pacific bridge.

The full significance and character of this astounding discovery will become more intelligible if we try to put the newly discovered creature into its place in the Human Family, as I have attempted to do in Figure 2.

To the two extinct genera, *Pithecanthropus* and *Eoanthropus,* it is now proposed to add a third, *Hesperopithecus,* the Ape-Man of the Western World. This long-lost cousin is the most surprising member of the Family. For, if the suggestion of his right to human rank should be justified, not only is he the only human being so far discovered who lived in

[1] Henry Fairfield Osborn, *Nature,* August 26, 1922, p. 281.

the remotely distant time of the Pliocene Period, but he or his forbears had already wandered so far from the original home of the Family (in Asia or Africa) as North America.

In the second diagram, which is an attempt to represent the position of the Human Family in the Order Primates, this tentative suggestion with reference to *Hesperopithecus* has been graphically expressed. It must, of course, be understood that with the scanty evidence at our disposal the idea expressed in this diagram is little more than conjecture. But in helping us to understand the nature of the problem at issue it is much more useful to make a concrete proposal that can be criticized and attacked, than merely to play for safety and repress the whole issue as something dangerous that ought to be avoided.

The first diagram, representing the hypothetical family tree of the Human Family, is so arranged as to represent the members that have become specialized as branching away from the main stream, which leads to the highest type, and to give graphic expression to the conception that the attainment of the supreme position is not inconsistent with the retention of primitive characters. Those types which have diverged from the main current have all of them become more or less specialized in structure and lost one or other of their primitive characters. For example, the Negro has lost the primitive characters of the hair which the Nordic Race has preserved.

I should make some explanation of my reasons for putting the Nordic Race at the apex of the main stem. In doing so I am not subscribing to those extravagant claims, so popular at the present moment, in virtue of which blondness is regarded as a character which marks this race as supermen. All that is intended in this scheme is to suggest that those bleaching tendencies, of which several distinct phases are found within the Human Family, are carried furthest in the Nordic Race, which also presents a number of primitive traits that other of the human races have lost. On the other hand, the Mediterranean Race has preserved a number of other primitive characteristics, and especially primitive features of brain, which differentiate it from the Nordic Race. But I have separated it from the main stem mainly on the ground of pigmentation.

Another point I have endeavoured to express by putting upon the right-hand side those branches of the Family in which there is a great development of the eyebrow ridges or, at any rate, a definite tendency in that direction: whereas I have placed upon the left-hand side of the main stem those races which are distinguished either by an absence or a poor development of the eyebrow ridges. This emphasizes the fact that the development of the eyebrow ridge is not of much importance as an index of race. It is neither an exclusively primitive character nor a distinction of a higher race. It is found developed in *Pithecanthropus*, Rhodesian Man, Neanderthal Man, and in the Australian and Alpine Races, whereas a defective development of the ridge is characteristic of *Eoanthropus,* the Negro, the Mongol, and the Mediterranean Races, while the Nordic Race occupies a position between the two extremes.

The second diagram indicates the position of the Human Family in the Primate phylum, but is also intended to represent graphically the position and relations of the whole Order of Primates. Long before the beginning of the Tertiary Period a group of Insectivora had become separated from other mammals, from which they are distinguished by the preservation of features of an extremely primitive character very closely akin to those of the lowlier Marsupials of Australia and America. These creatures, represented today by the Jumping Shrews of Africa and the Tree Shrews of the Malay Archipelago, are known as the Menotyphla, and they are closely akin to the fossil group of Creodonta, from which the Carnivora were derived. On the other side they are closely related to the primitive flying mammal known as *Galeopithecus* and the Chiroptera, consisting of the Bats and the Flying Foxes.

The adoption by some of these Shrews of the habit of living in trees brought about profound changes in the relative proportions of the brain. The sense of vision became enhanced in importance, and the sense of smell correspondingly reduced: but in addition the senses of touch and hearing, and the power of agility of movement, were consid-

erably enhanced. In one of these groups the importance of vision became still further increased, and the result of this was to bring into existence the Order Primates. This happened in the Upper Cretaceous, at the phase represented in the diagram by the Prosimiae primitivae.

Before the beginning of the Tertiary Period these primitive Lemuroids had split into two branches, the Lemuroidea and the Tarsioidea, the fundamental distinction between the two being a further enhancement of the importance of vision, which, in the Tarsioidea, became the dominant sense, definitely usurping the position occupied by smell as the chief guide to the animal, which is found not only in the primitive mammals, but is still retained even in the Lemurs. Of the Tarsioidea one member has survived to the present day with comparatively slight change from the very beginning of the Eocene Period as the Spectral Tarsier which is still found in Borneo, Java, and the Philippines.

Before the close of the Eocene Period one of the Tarsioidea acquired the power of stereoscopic vision and became transformed into a primitive monkey with a very considerable increase in the size of the brain and an enormous enhancement of the power of skilled movement and of intelligence. At this stage in the evolution of the Primates, which occurred somewhere in the neighbourhood of Central America, representatives of all three branches, Lemurs, Tarsioids, and Monkeys, wandered across from the New World to the Old, across

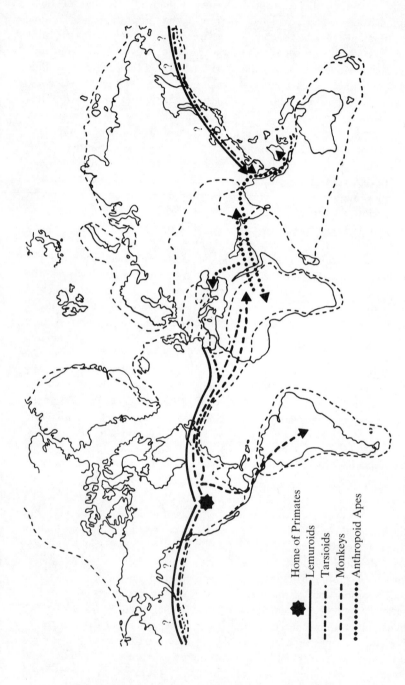

Fig. 4. Map to illustrate the wanderings of the Primates. The Eocene land bridges are shown in accordance with information supplied by Professor D. M. S. Watson, *F.R.S.*

Home of Primates
Lemuroids
Tarsioids
Monkeys
Anthropoid Apes

bridges which stretched from North America to Africa and Europe, and also from North America to Eastern Asia.

The Monkeys which wandered across the Atlantic seem to have undergone a profound change during their journey, for, at the beginning of the Oligocene, we find in the Egyptian Fayum representatives of two new types of monkeys, the tailed Catarrhines of the Old World, and the Anthropoid Apes, represented by a diminutive creature known as *Propliopithecus*. These Anthropoids wandered far and wide in Africa, Europe, and Asia, increasing in size as their power of adaptation increased, and in the middle of the Miocene Period in Northern India a great number of new varieties had come into existence, including the ancestors not only of the Giant Apes, but also of the Human Family.

The object of this diagram, like the previous one, is to indicate the fact that all of these Lemurs, Monkeys, and Apes, which have become specialized in one way or another, should be regarded as having departed from the main stream of development that leads straight up to Man, and by doing so lost something of the primitive structure and plasticity that were necessary for the attainment of the high powers of adaptation which represent one of the most distinctive characteristics of the Human Family.

In the map some idea of the extensive wanderings of the Primates is suggested. Before the beginning of the Tertiary Period members of the Lemuroidea and Tarsioidea were living in North America. In the Eocene Period they wandered across the land bridge to south-western Europe and Africa, but not before some of the latter group had given birth to Platyrrhine monkeys, which found an asylum in South America, where they have persisted until the present day. Of the three groups that wandered across the Atlantic bridge to the Old World—Lemurs, Tarsioids, and Monkeys—the latter underwent the most profound change, and became split up into two divisions—the tailed Catarrhines and the tailless Anthropoid Apes, the diminutive representatives of which have been recovered from the Lower Oligocene beds of the Egyptian Fayum.

Some of the migrations indicated on the map occurred after the Eocene Period when new land connexions were established. The wanderings of Monkeys into South America and from Africa to India fall into this category.

Part Four

In 1925, with the published description by Dr. Raymond Dart of a fossil from Taungs in South Africa, a new type of early hominid entered the record. *Australopithecus africanus*, as represented by the facial bones, mandible, and cranial endocast of a six- or seven-year-old individual, was one of a population whose adult morphology had yet to be determined. Had the australopithecines been known in the Darwinian period they surely would have been greeted as made-to-order "missing links." Indeed, for many paleoanthropologists this fossil filled the hiatus left after the fall from grace of the Haeckelian monster *Pithecanthropus alalus.* Not until the recovery of the adult specimens of australopithecines many years after the finding of the fossil baby from Taungs did a true picture of this South African hominid become discernible. Before then, the major question was whether the Taungs specimen was pongid or hominid. Dart's claim that the australopithecines were hominid was contested by the majority of paleoanthropologists of this period. When Gregory prepared a hominid phylogenetic tree in 1927, he placed *Australopithecus* on a branch together with the African great apes and separate from the hominids. Yet Gregory admitted that of all the anthropoid apes *Australopithecus* was the one nearest in its physical affinity to man. Similarly, in his phylogenetic tree of 1931, Keith included the Taungs discovery. He regarded all of its special features as pongid, and he accounted for its common heritage with the two forms of living African apes by deriving all of them from a common anthropoid stem. Both Gregory and Keith felt that they could amply support the theory of the anthropoid ape

1925
to
1959

241

ancestry of the human stem with evidence from comparative anatomy. They opposed Osborn's theory that the human stem originated with a non-anthropoid progenitor of the Oligocene and was independent of the evolution of the great apes. It is hardly surprising, therefore, that *Eoanthropus* played an important role in Osborn's phylogenetic system. When Wood-Jones produced his work of 1929 in response to Miller's attack on his tarsioid hypothesis of human origins, he was unmoved by the significance of the Taungs specimen, a circumstance that goes far to illustrate the lack of serious attention given the australopithecines at first from many paleoanthropologists.

The increase in the number and variety of other kinds of hominid fossils forced the investigators of early man to appreciate the wide geographical distribution of the pithecanthropine, neanderthaloid, and sapient forms of hominids. Thus, discoveries in the site of Choukoutien near Peking in China confirmed the authenticity of the Mid-Pleistocene hominid fossils from Java and established that the Chinese fossils, by their close morpho-logical similarity to these pithecanthropines, were northern varieties of a type of hominid with a wide geographical dispersion in Asia. The name for the *Sinanthropus* population had been created before the actual excavation of the site. In the region around Choukoutien remains of ancient men had been known since 1921, and on the evidence of a single tooth the anatomist Davidson Black created the genus *Sinanthropus* and the species *pekinensis.* Having committed himself to a special taxonomic category for the skeletal material that began to come from the site during the 'thirties, Black tended to exaggerate the degree of phenotypic difference between the Chinese and Javanese Mid-Pleistocene hominid populations. Boule and his colleagues in Europe, however, tended to stress their similar-ities and to object to the creation of different generic names for what seemed to be closely related phenotypes. Meanwhile additional *Pithecanthropus* specimens were being found in Java by von Koenigswald. One of these bore a close resemblance to the finds of Dubois in 1890–91. But another was sufficiently different from the species *erectus* to have merited a species of its own, *Pithecanthropus robustus.* The calvarium of a young child of two to four years of age was found in a part of Java distant from the location of the specimens discussed thus far. Its presence in a geological deposit pre-dating that of the pithecanthropines led to considerable debate over its possible phylogenetic affinities. This Modjokerto specimen has been described as a neanderthaloid or as a pithecanthropine by various students in the discipline. Finally, in the Upper Pleistocene Ngandong beds of eastern Java, on a terrace of the Solo River, some eleven hominid fossils were recovered between 1931 and 1933. The robusticity and general primitiveness of the specimens suggested to the early describers of the material that here were the lineal descendants of *Pithecanthropus.* Some regarded Solo Man as a precursor of the Neanderthals and as a contemporary of the branch that gave rise to *Homo sapiens* in Europe.

During this period in the history of paleoanthropology the concept of the basic homogeneity of Neanderthal hominids was called into serious question. This was the result of the discovery of a number of specimens recognized as generally neanderthaloid in their morphology but with certain features which were like those of modern man. The dating of these specimens from the deposits at Steinheim and Ehringsdorf in Germany and Saccopastore near Rome is pre-Würm, and the cultural associations are pre-Mousterian. Therefore they are earlier than the Neanderthal specimens from western Europe. This seeming paradox of *sapiens*-like hominids pre-dating the Neanderthals did not agree with the popular dogma that what is earlier in time must consequently be more primitive morphologically. By 1935–36 the occipital and parietal bones of a fossil from Swanscombe, England in association with a Second Interglacial fauna was added to this evidence of the "progressive Neanderthals," as these hominids came to be called in distinction from the later and more robust "classic Neanderthals." This problem was interpreted in very different ways by the members of the Preneanderthal and Presapiens Schools.

Supporters of Preneanderthalism conceived of the later and more robust "classic" Neanderthals as a Late Pleistocene departure from the main human stem. These hominids had become extinct. The earlier and less rugged Neanderthals of the pre-Würm period were representatives of that line along which *Homo sapiens* was evolving. The followers of the Presapiens School agreed that the later Neanderthals were the terminal products of a withered and extinct evolutionary line, but they were reluctant to regard the fossils from Steinheim and Ehringsdorf and the other "Preneanderthals" as ancestral to *Homo sapiens.* Rather they relegated these fossils to the phylogenetic strain that terminated as the classic Neanderthals. For the ancestors of *Homo sapiens* they selected certain specimens in the fossil record in which they could discern no neanderthaloid morphological traits. Thus the occipital and parietal bones of the Swanscombe fossil from the Second Interglacial were frequently placed on the same stem of the phylogenetic tree as *Eoanthropus*, both fossils being representative of the evolutionary forms leading to modern man. When Sir Arthur Keith produced in 1931 the sequel to his opus of 1915 on the fossil evidence for the antiquity of man, he added to this *presapiens* stem the London skull which to him was the type of hominid that had evolved from *Eoanthropus.* During this period the Presapiens School was gaining wide scientific support, and fossils were being found outside Europe which seemed to suggest the early appearance of *Homo sapiens* along a phylogenetic branch that was independent of Neanderthal Man. On the southern shores of Lake Victoria in Africa fragments of a mandible, bones of the cranial vault, and a part of a femur were found in 1932 in circumstances that led the discoverer, L. S. B. Leakey, to refer them to the genus *Homo* and perhaps to the species *sapiens* as well. These Kanam and Kanjera specimens, like other supposed examples of Early and Middle Pleistocene ancestors of modern man, were accorded their phylogenetic status by the Presapiens School on the basis of their morphological similarity to modern *Homo sapiens*, and because they were thought to be of great antiquity. The attacks from supporters of other phylogenetic theories were aimed at demonstrating that these fossils were too fragmentary to support any such phylogenetic interpretation and that the deposits in which they were discovered could not be dated with any definitive accuracy.

Those adopting the Unilinear view allied themselves behind Hrdlička, who was critical of any suggestion that a presapiens population could have been contemporary with a preneanderthal one. In his Huxley Lecture of 1927, the American paleoanthropologist suggested that natural selection had operated on a basically neanderthaloid population during the Würm Glaciation. Those hominids endowed with genetic properties that favored their survival evolved into *Homo sapiens,* while their less fortunate kin, the so-called "classic" Neanderthals, became extinct. Hrdlička rejected the concept of a preneanderthal *Homo sapiens* or any *sapiens*-like precursor of Neanderthal Man; rather Neanderthalism signified a phase of human evolution wherein modern man is the latest and only successful product. This is a classic example of the philosophy of the Unilinear School, in which all the fossils are taken into account as representative of the several stages of human evolution, the individual fossil specimens themselves being better or worse examples of the stage of hominization into which they are grouped. Wilder's phylogenetic tree is a classical representation of this practice. The full significance of Hrdlička's thesis was not appreciated until the appearance of the published description of the neanderthaloid population from Mount Carmel in Palestine in 1939.

Another distinctive trend of this period was the attempt to relate certain Upper Pleistocene fossil specimens to the living races of the continents or regions of continents where the fossils were discovered, a return to the efforts of the latter nineteenth century paleoanthropologists. Thus the Boskop skull from the Transvaal was associated with the Bushman–Hottentot phenotypes. The North African specimens from Afoulou-bou-Rhummel and Asselar became associated with caucasoid and negroid strains respectively. Weidenreich and others found the Pleistocene ancestors of the Australian aborigines in the fossil material from Solo and Wadjak in Java. Weidenreich classified three Upper Pleistocene specimens from the Upper Cave at Choukoutien as reflective of European Cro-Magnon and modern eskimoid and Melanesian phenotypes, nor did he hesitate to suggest the presence of definitive Asian polytypic features in the

Sinanthropus specimens from the Lower Cave deposits at this site. Such comparisons were influenced by geographical considerations as well as by the results of comparisons of superficial morphological features between specimens.

In the paleoanthropological writings before 1939 there is a general lack of agreement on where the cradle of human origins might have been. Africa had been suggested, but few paleoanthropologists were then prepared to see the importance of the discovery at Taungs. The Far East and southern Asia still maintained their hold on the imaginations of scholars seeking to determine the locus of the most ancient fossil hominids, but Hrdlička insisted that at least Neanderthal Man could claim his origins in Europe. The search for Tertiary Man had by now become relegated to a rather restricted aspect of prehistoric archaeology.

For many years cave deposits in Palestine had yielded varied prehistoric artifacts, as well as a few bones of their manufacturers, but with the excavation in the 'thirties of the caves of Skhul and Tabun at Wadi-el-Mughara in the Mount Carmel range, a number of skeletons were discovered which have had a profound effect on subsequent interpretations of the human fossil record. Within prehistoric cultural contexts ascribable to the Levalloiso-Mousterian there were found in the Skhul cave the osseous remains of Cro-Magnon–like individuals, but in the Tabun deposit the skeletons in association with similar cultural artifacts more closely approached the neanderthaloid phenotypic pattern. It was the convincing evidence that these very different specimens shared some phenotypic traits and many cultural associations that favored the hypothesis that they were members of essentially contemporary local populations, if not perhaps of a common lineage. On this question of the temporal affinities of the Mount Carmel fossils to one another depended a very critical issue, namely the genetic integrity of Neanderthal Man, who had heretofore been regarded as a specific division of the genus *Homo* patterned along the confining morphological lines earlier drawn by Boule in his description of La Chapelle-aux-Saints. If Neanderthal Man were of a different species from Cro-Magnon and modern man, then he could not have crossed the lines of specific specialization and successfully bred with the *sapiens* to produce the kind of individuals found at Skhul. Thus argued the scholars who wished to preserve the separate species status of Neanderthal Man. They could not explain the puzzling situation in Palestine on the basis of the zoological tenet that separate species are reproductively isolated. Consequently, many favored the view that at Mount Carmel the paleoanthropologist could observe a point in the evolutionary transformation from *Homo neanderthalensis* to *Homo sapiens*. These explanations, while noted by the describer of the Skhul and Tabun specimens and by his colleague, Sir Arthur Keith, were not the explanations that McCown and Keith favored after they had analyzed the fossils. In the description published in 1939, *The Stone Age of Mount Carmel: the Fossil Human Remains from the Levalloiso-Mousterian*, they suggested that at Mount Carmel there had been a population reflecting both a pre–Cro-Magnon or pre–Caucasoid phenotypic pattern. This population had been actively evolving farther to the east of Palestine, as had a neanderthaloid physical pattern. These two groups covered wide areas of Europe to the west. Thus these ancient Carmelites were not considered the true ancestors of the Cro-Magnon people but "Neanderthaloid collaterals or cousins of the ancestors of that type."

If Neanderthal Man was not phenotypically definable as a member of the genus *Homo,* as had been thought since his discovery in 1856, then his phylogenetic significance was destined to undergo radical reinterpretation. The supporters of the Unilinear School continued to regard Neanderthal Man as the progenitor of *Homo sapiens* since no other fossil group was recognized thus far as being ancestral to modern man. But the separation of the Neanderthals into "classic" and "progressive" types came to be regarded as insignificant in light of the new ideas about the phenotypic variability of this population. The more robust Neanderthals from western Europe were regarded as individuals representing one extreme of the range of morphological variation for the Neanderthal phenotypic pattern. At Mount Carmel the modern form of hominid is also represented in the same basic population, which has its share of members with the "classic' morphology. The Unilinear School therefore conceived of Neanderthal Man as representing a stage of human evolution that followed the *Pithecanthropus* level of human biological history; but that the members of these stages were genetically variable and capable of regional modifications of a sub-specific nature was a point that became stressed in consequence of the discoveries at Mount Carmel. This awareness of the phenotypic variability of Neanderthal Man has been increased with the later discoveries in the 'fifties of neanderthaloid specimens at Shanidar Cave in Iran and at Mapa in South China.

The specimens from these sites influenced such followers of Preneanderthalism as Le Gros Clark, who added the Skhul material to the fossils from Swanscombe, Ehringsdorf, Saccopastore, and Fontéchevade to a pre-Mousterian gene pool that was evolving by the Mid-Pleistocene out of a small-brained pithecanthropine line. From this pre-Mousterian stock evolved the early *Homo sapiens.* While admitting that the pre-Mousterian stock could be graded morphologically within a basic neanderthaloid phenotype, the Preneanderthal School has continued to favor the Mousterian inhabitants of western Europe with the title of "classic" Neanderthals and to regard them as a side branch of human evolution which became extinct. The notion of the dichotomy of the Neanderthals has been continued as a side issue in the theories of the Presapiens School, where all of the so-calld pre-Mousterian specimens as well as the material from

Mount Carmel are assembled together on the same Neanderthal evolutionary stem that branches away from the *Homo sapiens* line to terminate in the Upper Pleistocene as a biological dead end. This circumstance was presumably the result of their competition with the later and better endowed *Homo sapiens*. While the Preneanderthal theorists felt that the Mount Carmel material added support to their contention that Swanscombe was simply another representative of pre-Mousterian man, the followers of the Presapiens School continued to regard the fossil Englishman as their best case for early *Homo sapiens*. With the discovery of a modern-type skull from the Third Interglacial levels of the cave of Fontéchevade in France, they seemed even more confident of their thesis. Here was one more fossil that could be added to the list that by 1953 consisted of *Eoanthropus*, Kanam and Kanjera, the London skull, and of course Swanscombe.

There was a revival of the tenets of the Polyphyletic School during this period. Weidenreich, the describer of the *Sinanthropus* material from China, maintained that man had evolved over a wide Eurasian–African breeding ground. Within this area he suggested that there were several evolutionary centers, from which he sought to trace the affinities of living races to the fossil specimens found in the places of their habitation. Weidenreich's diagram of phylogenetic relationships approaches more closely the form of a chart than of a tree. His groupings of the fossil and living hominids according to their location in the evolutionary sequence were represented by vertical lines. The geographical distribution of the fossils into four groups was indicated by horizontal lines. Cross lines referred to the interchange of genes between populations, a human condition that Weidenreich did not deny but which he did minimize in importance. He conceived of ten stages of hominid evolution which were listed according to the "morphological age" of the specimens. These stages were grouped into the categories that he designated as relevant to the three stages of hominid evolution: a pithecanthropine level, a neanderthaloid level, and a plateau for modern man, *Homo sapiens*. Like others of the Polyphyletic School who preceded him, Weidenreich saw human evolution progressing independently in various parts of the world, the final product being the same at the present limits for all of the lines—the attainment of *Homo sapiens* status. All fossils were accounted for and no hominid line was permitted to become extinct. It is not surprising, then, that he interpreted the fossils from Mount Carmel as evidence that Neanderthal Man was undergoing a direct evolutionary modification into the final stage of this series.

The American physical anthropologist Earnest Hooton accepted many of the principles of this Polyphyletic School, and it is interesting to observe the contrast between his arrangement of the fossils and Weidenreich's. Hooton conceived of a main human stem that led from an unidentified Eocene ancestor directly to *Homo sapiens*, indeed to what he called the "basic White race." The *Pithecanthropus–Sinanthropus*–Neanderthal forms are relegated to side branches, but from these side branches the non-White races originate. Hooton concurred with Weidenreich that the Australians arose directly from the *Pithecanthropus*–Solo–Wadjak line, but he was hesitant to see the mongoloids as the derivatives of *Sinanthropus*. *Eoanthropus* proved useful as a primal ancestor of those mongoloid and negroid groups as well as the precursor of the "basic White race." Hooton's tree is worthy of study for the lesson it teaches about the way the fossils can be manipulated to conform to variations on the major theme of the Polyphyletic School (frontispiece).

The recognition that the neanderthaloid phenotype was present in Asia Minor was supplemented by the discovery in 1953 of a skull from the region of Saldanha Bay on the Atlantic coast of South Africa. Here was a specimen that closely resembled the neanderthaloid skull from Broken Hill in Northern Rhodesia, and the dating of the Saldanha skull suggested that this hominid had occupied southern Africa for a considerable period of time. It preceded Rhodesian Man, to whom it may have been phylogenetically related. The discoveries of hominid fossils made between the years of 1952 and 1958—mainly mandibles and portions of crania from the North African sites of Taforalt, Sidi Abderahman, Ternifine, and Termara—favored the interpretation that the pithecanthropines were not confined to southeast Asia and China during the Middle Pleistocene, but had spread westward where they manufactured an Acheulean cultural industry. But by far the greatest African discoveries of this period were adult specimens of australopithecines described by Dart, Broom, and Robinson from the South African deposits at Kromdraai, Makapansgat, Sterkfontein, and Swartkranz. The recognition of their relevance to the human fossil record has led to Africa's being viewed as the locus of hominization and the place from which fresh evidence on the evolution of our species and its earlier progenitors must be sought. Additional backing for this theory was provided by the discovery of the fossil anthropoid *Proconsul* in 1951 on Rusinga Island in Lake Victoria.

Study of the adult australopithecines convinced many scholars that it was no longer possible to assign their membership to an anthropoid line. Although the various fossils of this group were assigned different generic and specific names by their describers, there was a continuity between all of them that argued strongly for classifying them among the *Hominidae*. Their bipedal locomotor pattern, cranial capacities of 450 to over 600 cc., forward position of the foramen magnum, hominid-type dentition, and many other traits placed them closer to the human line than to the lineage of the anthropoids. But the dating of several of these specimens as Middle Pleistocene suggested to some scholars that they had existed too late to have been the direct ancestors of those hominids whose fossil remains had already been found on three continents of the Old World. Therefore, they came to be recognized as a hominid line that had evolved contemporaneously with the higher types of hominids, before their extinction in the Upper Pleistocene. If was for the ancestors of these australopithecines that the paleoanthropologist must now search to learn the nature of that common stock from which both these fossils and the human stem took their origins. Not all scholars agreed to this theory, however, and the resistance to accepting the South African ape-men into the human family was apparent in certain situations where such an admission would have upset well-entrenched teachings.

By 1950 paleoanthropologists found themselves encumbered with many taxonomic categories for their fossil specimens, each discoverer or describer coining his own generic and specific names to support favored theories of where his specimen might stand in the human phylogenetic tree. This became recognized as a basically unsound procedure according to the taxonomic rules that affect other biotic forms. With the appreciation of some and the criticism of other of his colleagues, the American zoologist Ernst Mayr proposed the following revisions. He classified the specimens of the hominid fossil record into three categories : (1) *Homo transvaalensis*, to which would belong the australopithecines; (2) *Homo erectus*, to include the pithecanthropines with which the fossils from Solo and Wadjak are linked ; and (3) *Homo sapiens*, to cover the hominids of neanderthaloid, Cro-Magnon, and modern types, evidence of their generic conection being seen in the fossils from Mount Carmel. Thus Mayr attempted to simplify the taxonomy of the fossil record by suggesting that the hominids consist of one genus and three species. Of the specific categories, two have become extinct, and sub-specific categories have also occasionally met this fate during the Pleistocene. Only one species of *Homo* has existed at a given time. The point of origin of *Homo* from his nonhuman stock can never be discerned in a single specimen ; thus Mayr retired into oblivion the venerable concept of the missing link. In 1963 Mayr modified his taxonomy to the extent that the australopithecines were assigned their own genus.

The fossil revision of hominid classification was enhanced by the demise of *Eoanthropus* in 1953 as a result of its careful morphological reexamination and biochemical analysis by Sir Wilfred E. Le Gros Clark, Kenneth P. Oakley, and Joseph Weiner. While *Eoanthropus* played a major part in the formulation of phylogenetic theory in the early decades of this century, its significance waned through the years. It was with considerable relief to the scientific community that the discovery of its fraudulency forced its removal from the human family tree. Its loss has grieved no one, but rather has afforded delight to fundamentalist critics of Darwinian evolution.

Summary: the Phylogenetic Tree of the Primates; the Pedigree of the Human Race

Harris Hawthorne Wilder
1926

After the consideration of the living Primates, together with all the available information concerning the Primates of past ages; after the comparison of such important structural details in each as the teeth, the proportions of the cranium, the structure of the brain, and the form of the hands and feet, we are now ready to employ these facts in an attempt to arrange these numerous animals in accordance with their course of development; placing them in such a relation to one another that their various characteristics may be shown in an orderly series, representing the development as nearly as possible as it took place in reality.

Naturally there have been many attempts at making such a phylogenetic arrangement of the various Primate forms, and the diagram expressing this must vary with each attempt, in accordance with the system which for the time being seems of especial importance, or to which the attention of the author has been especially directed. As each attempt thus embodies certain truths

it is well worth while to consider certain of the most authoritative ones, especially those based upon the more recent discoveries in the paleontological field.

The first phylogenetic tree here presented is that of DuBois (1896)[1] constructed soon after his discovery and subsequent study of the Javan link form, *Pithecanthropus,* and based upon a previous diagram of Haeckel.[2] The development starts with an hypothetical form of Eocene date, *Archipithecus.* This form is purely hypothetical, and is not suggested by any of the known Eocene Primates, like *Pelycodus, Notharctus,* or *Tetonius,* since these latter are lemuroid, but is rather the generalized ancestor of the non-lemurine Primates, distinguished in this book as the Sub-Order Anthropoidea. Although not as yet substantiated by actual fossil remains,

[1] DuBois, E. Pithecanthropus erectus, eine Stammform des Menschen. Anat. Anz., Bd. XII, 1896, p. 21.

[2] Haeckel, E. Systematische Phylogenie der Wirbeltiere. Berlin, 1895, p. 601.

"Summary: the Phylogenetic Tree of the Primates; the Pedigree of the Human Race." *The Pedigree of the Human Race.* Pp. 264–72. Henry Holt and Company, New York, 1926.

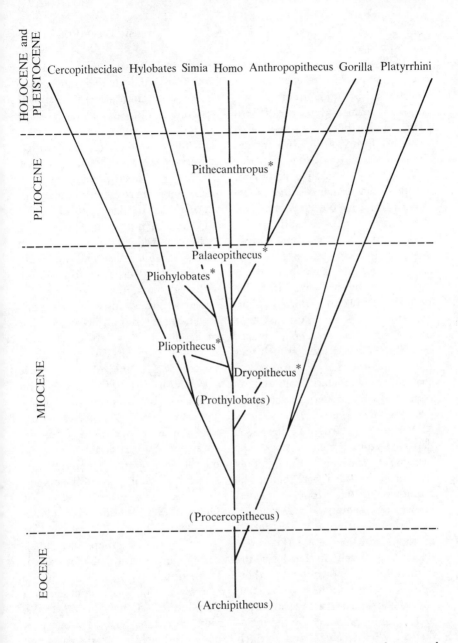

Fig. 1. Phylogenetic tree of the Anthropoidea, based upon the general anatomical structure, and arranged to correspond with the Geological chronology. Hypothetical forms are enclosed in brackets; extinct forms are starred. *Pliohylobates* is based upon the femur from Eppelsheim; *Pliopithecus* comes from Sansan, in the south of France, and *Paleopithecus* from the Sivalik Hills in India. Dr. DuBois studied the remains of this latter in the Museum of Calcutta, and thinks it the immediate ancestor of Pithecanthropus. After DuBois.

this form, *Archipithecus,* assumes the contemporaneous existence, in the Eocene, of both lemuroid and anthropoid forms, already differentiated, and that the generalized ancestral forms of the two modern Sub-Orders existed then side by side.

From this common ancestral anthropoid the branch leading to the American forms, the Platyrrhini, was the first to depart, still in the Eocene, and is here represented by the branch upon the extreme right. This leaves the katarrhine group represented by its generalized, hypothetical, ancestor, *Procercopithecus,* to which we must assign a dental formula with two premolars and three molars, an ossified tube reinforcing the acustic meatus, and the other characters possessed in common by the modern Lasiopygidae and the higher apes. In the early Miocene the true Lasiopygidae departed from the main stock (the branch on the left), leaving only the forms included here under the Simiidae. Of this group the oldest known representative is *Dryopithecus,* from the European oak forests of the Mid-Miocene, and its position not precisely in but near the human line is shown by the short side branch leading to it. The actual ancestor was nearer the recent forms, and is here represented by the hypothetical *Prothylobales,* from which there branched (to the left in the diagram) the modern Genus *Hylobates,* along the line of development indicated by the actual fossils, *Pliopithecus* and *Pliohylobates,* both Miocene in spite of their names. The modern Genera *Simia*

(*Pongo*), *Anthropopithecus* (*Pan*), and *Gorilla* began their differentiation a little later, after the complete separation of *Hylobates; Simia* (*Pongo*) by itself and a little earlier, and the two others together, with a difference between them appearing still later. This left but one line, represented here as the main one, during the development of which the modern human type was gradually assumed through the known forms *Paleopithecus* and *Pithecanthropus,* the one from the Sivalik Hills of India, the other from the island of Java, both tropical Asiatic.

The next diagram presented, that of Schlaginhaufen (1905), is rather a grouping of the living "Anthropoidea" (Hominidae) into their relationships with each other than a general phylogenetic tree of the Primates; but is of especial interest here, since it is derived from the study of the epidermic markings on the sole, a rather unusual anatomical point to use for taxonomic purposes.[3] The two groups of the Old and New World forms, Platyrrhini and Katarrhini, are placed here as two distinct groups, but their derivation from a common source in the distant past is indicated by the convergence of their main stems at the bottom of the diagram. The most important points for our purpose are shown in (1) the early and more complete separation of Hylobates from the Simian stem, a conclusion exactly in accord with the

[3] Schlaginhaufen, O.; Das Hautleistensystem der Primatenplanta, unter Mitberücksichtigung der Palma. Morph. Jahrb., Bd. XXXIII, 1905, p. 119.

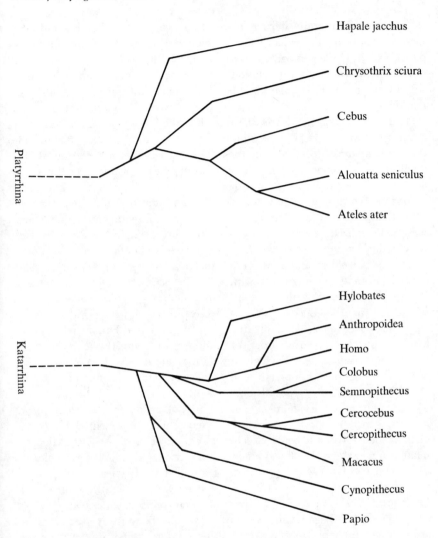

Fig. 2. Phylogenetic tree of the Anthropoidea as based upon the epidermic patterns of the soles. The Platyrrhine and Katarrhine groups are treated as distinct, yet with the suggestion of early relationship suggested by the inclination of the lines at the base of the two. The word "Anthropoidea" is used here in the sense of the Simians. After Schlaginhaufen.

data furnished by other anatomical studies, and (2) the close relation of Man to the chimpanzee, *Pan.* Unfortunately, as the author did not obtain for study any gorilla or orang-utan material, these important forms are lacking. It is also of general interest, although for us a little remote, that the baboons, *Cynopithecus* and *Papio,* which in their general structure depart the most widely from the typical Cercopithecidae (Lasiopygidae), are shown in the same distant relationship by the testimony of the plantar markings.

The last phylogenetic tree here given, prepared especially to illustrate this work, differs from the others more in scope than in ideas, and makes the attempt to include all Primate forms, both living and extinct, and to relate them to the more generalized mammals from which they arose. *Pelycodus* here figures as the oldest and most generalized Primate, or mammal with Primate tendencies, and this is plainly related to the Eocene Insectivora, like *Hyopsodus,* probably the ancestor of the modern Order of this name. *Pelycodus* may have given rise to two lines of development, one of which was a very special one, which reduced the number of incisors, something after the manner of the rodents, without being closely related to them, and developed along the line marked by *Microsyops* and *Mixodectes* into the aye-aye of Madagascar, *Daubentonia (Chromys).* The other began with *Notharctus,* and probaby *Adapis,* from which the group of the modern lemurs took its origin, and from which also through a lost form, *a,* the higher lines of Anthropoidea were to be derived. This form was a small, nocturnal creature, which had large eyes, and developed for their support bony orbital walls at the expense of the nose, the cavities of which became reduced. The face also, owing to the increased activity

of the prehensile hands, and the reduction of the teeth, became flattened, as described above. Still further specialization along the lines thus laid out developed in the direction of *Tetonius* and *Tarsius,* while the more generalized line continued to form *b,* also theoretical. This form somewhat resembled the Callithricidae of modern times, to which it gave rise, but its still generalized descendant, hypothetical form *c,* still with three premolars, gave direct origin to the Cebidae. Form *d* is the first with two premolars, and seems very much like the *"Procercopithecus"* of Haeckel and DuBois, as it is a generalized cercopithecid (lasiopygid), from which the latter Family is derived; and form *e* is already simian, tailless, with reduced ischial callosities, and probably with a flat mesosternum in one piece.

Hypothetical form *e* may have been actually represented by *Dryopithecus,* or at least this Miocene European ape must have closely resembled it. Its near kinship to *e* is here expressed by the shortness of the line connecting the two.

At this point it is possible that three different lines of development were taken, as here indicated, but the records are quite incomplete. It may be generally conceded, however, that at about this point the gibbons, Sub-Family Hylobatinae, separated here from the other hominids, and that consequently form *e,* and undoubtedly *Dryopithecus* also, still retained the small ischial callosities and a few other lasiopygid features. These were soon

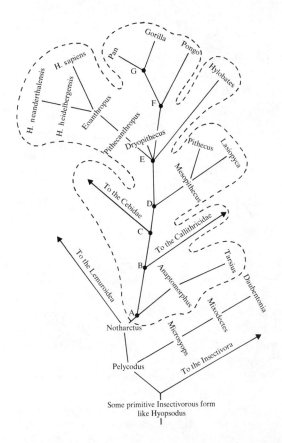

Fig. 3. Phylogenetic tree of the Primates, expressing the ideas of the present author, and largely based upon hypothetical forms.

a. The primordial Anthropoid, much like *Notharctus,* but developed along the line of which *Tetonius* is a more extreme specialization.

b. The point of differentiation of the Callithricidae. The location of this ancestor is highly conjectural. It may have been the *Archipithecus* of DuBois.

c. The last common ancestor of the Cebidae and the Cercopithecidae (Lasiopygidae). Its digits were all furnished with nails and its dental formula was like that of the Cebidae, with three premolars and three molars on each side of each jaw.

d. The primordial Lasiopygid, *Procercopithecus,* much like *c* but with two premolars.

e. The primordial Simian Ape. Here branches the line leading up to the gibbons, *Hylobatinae;* also probably to the *Hominae.*

f. The last common ancestor of the three living anthropoid apes, after taking out the gibbons. Here branch off two lines, the one leading to the Genus *Simia* (= *Pongo*), the other to the hypothetical form *g,* the direct ancestor of the chimpanzee and the gorilla.

The living Anthropoidea are shown as the final lobes of this tree which indicate the modern fauna.

dropped by the main simian line, which, through the forms *f* and *g*, developed into the modern apes of the Genera *Pongo, Pan,* and *Gorilla,* the two last nearer each other than is the first to either.

No one would be willing to say, at the present state of our knowledge, just where the line leading to the Homininae departed from the main stem, but if we include *Pithecanthropus,* as seems probable, it was at least as early as the point designated by form *e,* and possibly a little earlier. The two features especially emphasized by this line of development were the maintenance of an erect position, and the rapid increase in the size and development of a brain and an articulate language, while for a considerable time the jaws remained heavy and ape-like, and the skull was thick and brutal. Within the last thirty years have come the successive discoveries of *Pithecanthropus, Homo heidelbergensis,* and *Eoanthropus,* together with a greatly increased knowledge of the details of *Homo neandertalensis,* and while each has shed much light upon man's immediate pedigree, yet each form found has presented in itself a new problem in establishing its own position relative

to the others. Thus but little reliance can be placed upon any phylogetic diagram of these forms, but one here given will express in a general way that *Pithecanthropus* belongs at the bottom of the human series, that *Eoanthropus* stands, in regard to its jaw, intermediate between it and *Homo heidelbergensis,* but that the cranium of *Eoanthropus* comes nearer the present species of man in some respects than any of the other extinct forms. It is because of this last fact that modern man is here represented as the direct descendant of *Eoanthropus,* while *Homo neandertalensis* is placed on a collateral line, and the hypothesis thus expressed reflects an opinion largely felt at the present time. In this connection the newly discovered skull of *Australopithecus,* recently found in Bechuanaland, South Africa, is of the greatest importance. Broom places it in the main line leading to man, a little lower than *Pithecanthropus,* which, in its turn, leads directly to *Eoanthropus,* while the living apes, *Pan, Pongo,* and *Gorilla,* as well as the two other species of *Homo,* are put along side branches, that is, not directly ancestral to modern Man.

The Neanderthal Phase of Man

Aleš Hrdlička
1927

I. Introductory remarks

In choosing my subject for the Huxley Lecture, it was only natural to reflect what he, in whose honour the lecture is given, would have chosen; and I felt that with his interest, keen mind, and extensive knowledge he would doubtless have preferred some of the most unsettled and difficult problems of man's antiquity and evolution. And he could hardly find to-day one offering more difficulties, and the clearing of which is of more importance to science, than that of Neanderthal man; a subject which, moreover, was one of his first concerns.

Huxley, as early as 1863, published, as one of his essays on the *Evidence as to Man's Place in Nature* (8vo, London), under the sub-title "On Some Fossil Remains of Man" (pp. 118–59), a noteworthy discussion on the Neanderthal skull. In this essay, at that early date, and in opposition to the authority of Rudolf Virchow, Huxley recognized that there was no reason for regarding the skull as pathological; that it unquestionably represented typical race-characters; and that this race was inherently related to man of to-day.

Since Huxley, the Neanderthal skull and Neanderthal man have been written about extensively, but often with but little originality. New finds belonging to the period have become numerous—almost more numerous than legitimate new thoughts. To-day it is no more the question of a single skull, but of a large and important section of man's antiquity, documented ever more geologically, palæontologically, and anthropologically. But the distressing part is, that the more there is the less we seem to know what to do with it. Speculation there has been indeed enough, but the bulk of it so far has not led into the sunlight, but rather into a dark, blind alley from which there appears no exit.

The generalized present doctrine about Neanderthal man may best

"The Neanderthal Phase of Man. The Huxley Memorial Lecture for 1927." *Journal of the Royal Anthropological Institute.* Vol. 57, pp. 249–73. 1927. Reprinted by permission of the Royal Anthropogical Institute of Great Britain and Ireland.

be seen from the following brief quotations, taken from four of the most recent and representative authors, one a palæontologist, one an anatomist, and two prehistorians:

Marcellin Boule (*Fossil Men*, 1923, pp. 242–3): "*Homo neanderthalensis* is an archaic species of man. It was abruptly followed by the Aurignacians, 'who differed from the Mousterians as much in their superior culture as in the superiority or diversity of their physical characters.' "

M. C. Burkitt (*Prehistory*, 1921, p. 90): "The race who made this culture (Mousterian) was of a low type known as the Neanderthal race. This appears to have been a throw-back in the line of evolution of mankind, and this retrograde sport seems to have had no successor."

George Grant MacCurdy (*Human Origins*, 1924, vol, i, pp. 209–10): "During ages long subsequent to the time when the races of Piltdown and Heidelberg lived, there spread over the greater part of Europe the primitive Neanderthal race, of coarse mental and physical fiber.... This race contributed nothing, in fact, save utilitarian artifacts, the so-called Mousterian industry. ...The Aurignacians were a 'new race,' which supplanted completely the archaic Neanderthal race of Mousterian times."

Sir Arthur Keith (*The Antiquity of Man,* vol. i, pp. 198–9): "The most marvellous aspect of the problem raised by the recognition of Neanderthal man as a distinct type is his apparently sudden disappearance. He is replaced, with the dawn of the Aurignacian period, by men of the same type as now occupy Europe.... A more virile form extinguished him.... He was not an ancestor of ours, but a distant cousin."

All these opinions can probably be traced to the authoritative notions arrived at during the earlier years of this century, on material less ample than at present, by one of the foremost students of Neanderthal man, Gustav Schwalbe.

There were, and are, however, also other views. From Huxley and Busk to Karl Pearson; from Fraipont and Lohest, Houzé, Kollmann, and Sergi to Stolyhwo, Gorpanovič-Kramberger, and, most recently, Weidenreich, there have been expressed opinions that Neanderthal man was not a different species, and that he did not completely die out, but became gradually transformed into later human forms, from which in turn developed man of to-day.

The problem of Neanderthal man, as it now exists, presents the following uncertainties: It is not yet properly known just where, when, and how he began, and how far eventually he extended geographically; it is not yet definitely known just who he was and what were his phylogenetic relations to the man that succeeded him; and it is not known plainly just why and how he ended, and whether or not he left any progeny. Besides which there are still but more or less vague notions regarding the exact length of his period, his average physique, his variations and sub-races, the reasons for his relatively large brain, his changes in evolutionary direction. And there are other uncertainties. It thus appears that, notwithstanding his already numerous collected remains, Neanderthal man is still far from being satisfactorily known to us taxonomically, chronologically, and anthropologically.

This state of uncertainties, and of paralyzing notions, concerning one of the main early phases of humanity, is a serious obstacle to further progress, and deserves all possible attention. This even if, without further material, it may be possible to do little more than bring into the subject a greater degree of order and comprehensiveness; to point out here and there facts that have not been sufficiently weighed; and to call attention to some of the inconsistencies in the prevalent assumptions.

The presentation will be as far as possible impersonal; and I wish to acknowledge my deep indebtedness for many of the data to the authors given in the references, as well as to those who in the past, and again during the weeks just passed, have facilitated for me the study of original sites and materials.

II. Neanderthal man

DEFINITION

The only workable definition of Neanderthal man and period seems to be, for the time being, *the man and period of the Mousterian culture*. An approach to a somatological definition would be feasible, but might for the present be rather prejudicial.

GEOGRAPHICAL EXTENT

The territory already known to have been occupied by Neanderthal man was collectively a very large one, including, roughly, all Europe south of a line drawn from southern England to the northern limits of Belgium and thence, with a moderate curve northward over Germany and Poland, to Crimea and possibly the Caucasus, with parts (at least) of northern Africa and of Asia Minor. Whether he reached farther east, south-east, or south, must, notwithstanding some claims, be regarded as still uncertain.

The whole great territory over which his remains have been discovered was doubtless not occupied by Neanderthal man synchronously, or continually, or with equal density. He was evidently not a nomad, though probably more or less of a rover who stayed in a place for a time and then moved away. Some of the deposits he left show up to six different layers of occupation (Grimaldi, Olha, La Quina, Le Moustier, Krapina, etc.). The density of his remains is greatest in France and Belgium, least in the northern limits of his territory and in the mountainous parts, particularly the Alps, Carpathians, and the Balkan peninsula.

The distribution of Neanderthal man in Europe is of much significance, as will be seen later.

LIMITS AND DURATION

The boundaries and duration of the Neanderthal period are those of the Mousterian culture. They may now be delimited with some precision, though not finality, by data of a palæontological, and archæological nature.

PALÆONTOLOGY

Neanderthal man coexisted with a large series of now extinct animals: the question is, how intimately are these forms associated with his coming and going. The Mousterian culture is the culture, essentially, of the earlier times of the mammoth, the woolly rhinoceros, the cave lion, bear, and hyæna, the horse, the old ox, the bison, the reindeer, the stag. There are many other forms, but these are the most characteristic.

The Mousterian culture neither comes in, however, nor ends with any of these large mammals. The mammoth, derived probably from the Trogontherium, is present since at least the Acheulean and lasts to, if not beyond, the end of the Magdalenian. The cave lion, bear, and hyæna, as well as the horse, ox, bison, and even the reindeer, are all there since or before the beginning of the Acheulean, and they last throughout the Mousterian, Aurignacian, Solutrean, and Magdalenian periods, to disappear gradually during the latter, or persist to historic times.

Mousterian man begins during the latter part of the last great interglacial and extends deep into the final glacial time, without perceptible direct relation to the fauna. His remains at Montières, Villefranche, Ehringsdorf, the rock-shelter Olha, some of the Mentone caves, and elsewhere, show still the remains of the *Elephas antiquus*, the Merck's rhinoceros, the large lion, and the panther. On the other hand, various Arctic species (*Ovibos mosch., Gulo bor., Canis lagog., Lepus arct.,*

etc.) come in as the cold advances during the Mousterian period, without, however, marking either its beginning or its end.

There is, therefore, no definite line of faunal demarcation for the beginning and none for the end of the Mousterian period. Neanderthal man did not come in with any fauna, nor did he go out with any—which also are facts of importance.

GEOLOGY

Geological information about the Mousterian period is not as precise or full as is desirable, but it permits of several valuable conclusions.

A survey of the better-known Mousterian sites, from Germany and Belgium southward, shows that fully one-third of them were in the open, while of the remainder quite a few (La Quina, Sergeac, La Ferrassie, etc.) are found in and about shallow rock-shelters that could not have afforded much protection. In Switzerland, moreover, the earlier Mousterian man lived in caverns at a high elevation (Wildkirchli, 4,905 ft.; Drachenberg, 8,028 ft.). All of this indicates that the climate during a considerable part of the Mousterian period was not severe enough generally to drive man into the caves, or even down from the mountains, thus pointing to inter-glacial rather than glacial conditions.

There is no evidence of any critical geological manifestations, either about the beginning or about the end of the Mousterian period.

The cultural remains of the Mousterian in the open stations, as well as those in caves, denote both

The Ice Age; Faunal Relations to Man;
Central and Western Europe

Based on Bayer, Boule, Breuil, Burkitt, Commont, MacCurdy, Obermaier, Capitan and Peyrony

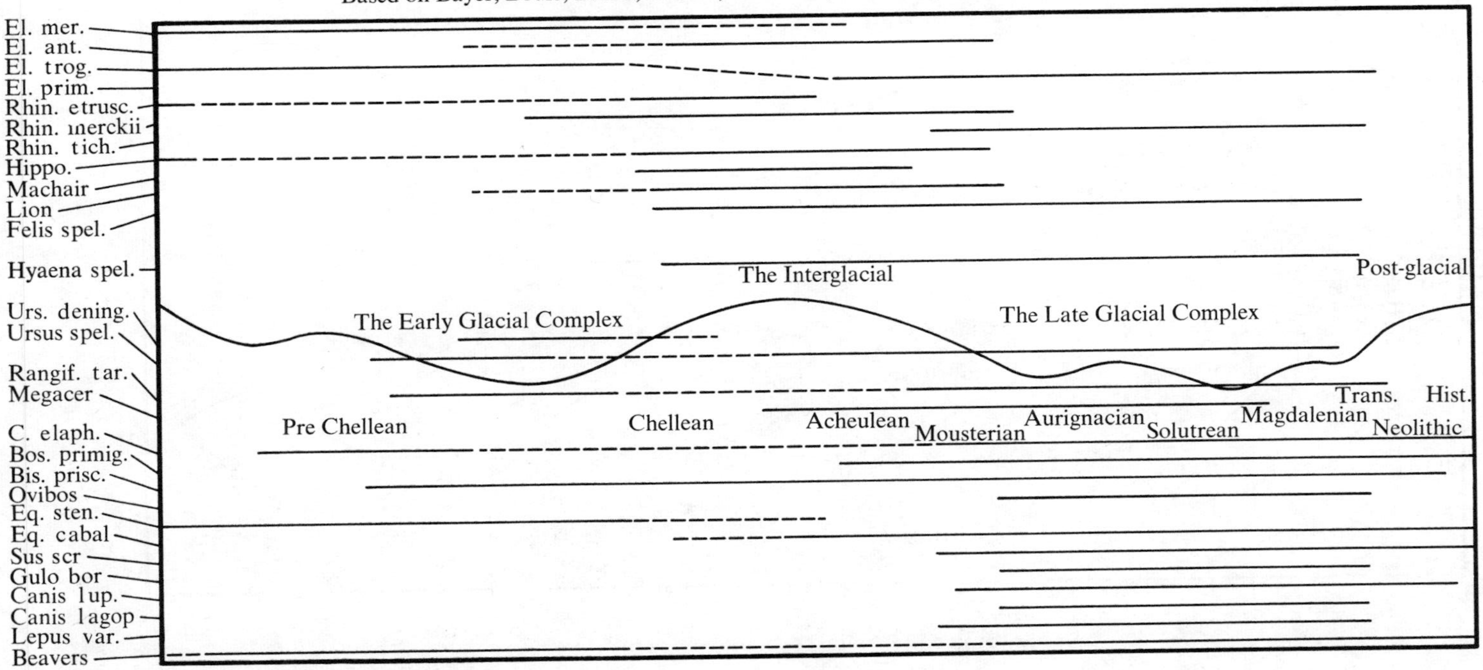

Post-glacial

Hist.
Trans.
Neolithic
Magdalenian
Solutrean
Aurignacian
Mousterian
Acheulean

The Late Glacial Complex

The Interglacial

Chellean

The Early Glacial Complex

Pre Chellean

El. mer.
El. ant.
El. trog.
El. prim.
Rhin. etrusc.
Rhin. merckii
Rhin. tich.
Hippo.
Machair
Lion
Felis spel.

Hyaena spel.
Urs. dening.
Ursus spel.
Rangif. tar.
Megacer

C. elaph.
Bos. primig.
Bis. prisc.
Ovibos
Eq. sten.
Eq. cabal
Sus scr
Gulo bor
Canis lup.
Canis lagop.
Lepus var.
Beavers

Fig. 1.

261

The Ice Age and Man

Approximations According to Different Recent Investigators

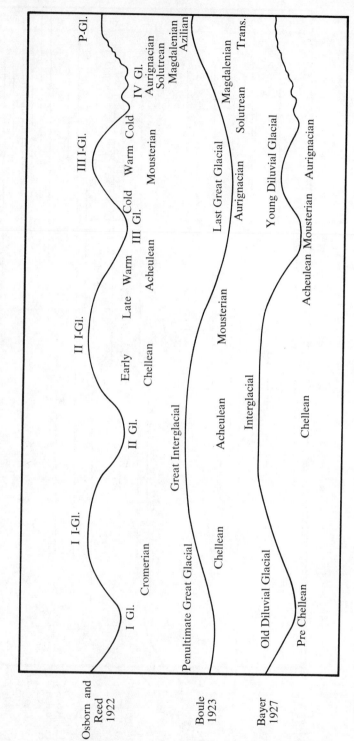

Fig. 2.

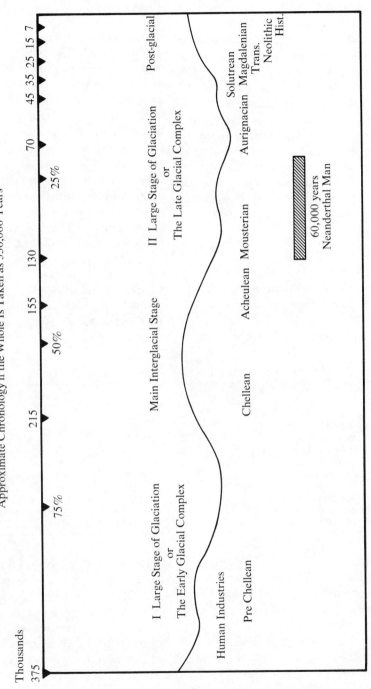

Fig. 3.

considerable age and long duration of the period. In the open the remains lie mostly in old gravels or sand, rarely in clay or loess, or in travertine rock of lacustrine origin. There may be two or three cultural strata or horizons (as at Ste. Walburge, High Lodge, Ipswich, Amiens, etc.), indicating a repeated occupation of the same site after shorter or longer intervals, though there have not been found as many occupational layers as in some of the caves.

ARCHÆOLOGY

Neither palæontology nor geology explain Neanderthal man; perhaps we may learn more from Archæology.

The main archæological ques-

OCCUPATION

The chief activities of man in nature relate to his housing, to the obtaining and preparing of food, and to the manufacture of tools, utensils, and weapons. Let us see briefly how Neanderthal man compared in these respects with his forbears and his followers.

Housing. There is a prevalent idea that Neanderthal man was essentially a cave-dweller, and this idea seems generally to carry with it a sense of inferiority. The records now available throw a different light on this matter. Analysis of 360 better-known palæolithic sites in Europe and the neighbouring regions (from records compiled principally by MacCurdy) gives the following interesting information:

Dwellings in the Open and in Caves during Palæolithic Times

Period	Sites in the Open		Rock-Shelter or Cave	
	No.	Per cent	No.	Per cent
Pre-Chellean	11	100	—	—
Chellean	32	94	2	6
Acheulean	36	78	10	22
Mousterian	45	34	88	66
Aurignacian	24	18	112	82
Solutrean	10	14	62	86
Magdalenian	17	10	148	90
Azilian and Tardenoisian	4	9.5	38	90.5
Accompanying Neolithic	22	22.5	76	77.5

tions are: How does Mousterian man differ in habits and arts from the man that preceded him, and from him that followed? And are the differences, or are they not, substantial enough to brand him as something apart from either his predecessors or his followers?

The figures and chart (Fig. 4) show some curious and important facts. Man begins as a dweller in the open, but since the warm Chellean already he commences also to utilize the rock-shelters and caverns, and then as the climate cools he gradually takes more and more to

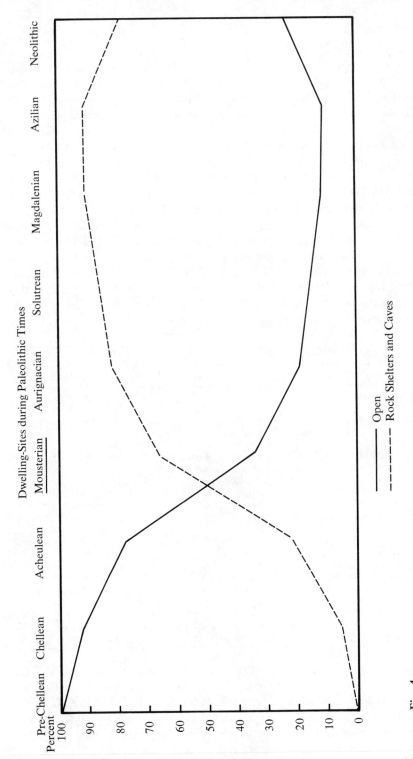

Dwelling-Sites during Paleolithic Times

Open
Rock Shelters and Caves

Fig. 4.

265

the caves. In these phenomena the Mousterian period shows nothing striking, nothing individual. It falls harmoniously into the curve of the progress of cave-dwelling, to be followed equally harmoniously by the Aurignacian and the succeeding periods. Mousterian man occasions no disturbance in the human housing conditions of the time, and what is even more remarkable, no disturbance or change whatsoever is occasioned by the advent of the Aurignacian. Aurignacian man follows in the footsteps of his predecessor without interruption. Like the Neanderthaler, he builds, in the open,

same caves that the latter has used, without introducing any innovation. He, also, like Neanderthal man, leaves here and there a whole series of occupational strata which testify to much the same habits of life. Yet Aurignacian man is represented as a new-comer, of a different species from that of the Neanderthaler, and mentally vastly superior.

Food. Neanderthal man was chiefly a hunter of the larger mammals of his time. He knew fire, but knew not domestication of animals, or agriculture. He compared in these respects with the preceding and following man as follows:

Food, and Habits Relating Thereto

Acheulean Man	*Mousterian Man*	*Aurignacian Man*
Chiefly a hunter.	Chiefly a hunter.	Chiefly a hunter.
Fisher (?).	Fisher (?).	Fisher (probably).
Use of molluscs—no trace.	Use of molluscs—no trace (?).	Use of molluscs (?).
Knew fire.	Knew fire.	Knew fire.
Preparation of food: probably by roasting on fire or coals—no trace of any vessels for boiling.	Preparation of food: probably by roasting on fire or coals—no trace of any vessels for boiling.	Preparation of food: probably by roasting on fire or coals—no trace of any vessels for boiling.
No agriculture.	No agriculture.	No agriculture.
No domestication of animals.	No domestication of animals.	No domestication of animals.
Bones broken for brains and marrow.	Bones broken for brains and marrow.	Bones broken for brains and marrow.
Bones and refuse accumulations in inhabited caves, and in front of them.	Bones and refuse accumulations in inhabited caves and in front of them.	Bones and refuse accumulations in inhabited caves and in front of them.
No trace of storage of food.	No trace of storage of food.	No trace of storage of food.
Pictorial representation of hunted animals—not known.	Pictorial representation of hunted animals—none known yet.	Pictorial representation of hunted animals—gradual development.

huts of perishable materials that leave no trace, and he utilizes the caves exactly as much as, and eventually even more than, Neanderthal man. He continues, in fact, on many of the same sites and in most of the

Evidently, in food and food habits, as in housing, Mousterian man was quite like both the Acheulean man that preceded him, and the *Homo sapiens* that followed.

Clothing. About the clothing of

Neanderthal man we know nothing direct, as is also the case with Acheulean and Aurignacian man. But the cool climate, on the one hand, and the much increased numbers of tools with a cutting-edge, and especially scrapers, on the other hand, indicate extensive preparation of the skins of animals, to be used, doubtless, for clothing and bedding. No sudden change in these connections is observable from the Acheulean to the Aurignacian.

Tools. The Mousterian period is characterized by a definite phase of stone industry, but so are all the periods before and after it. It has no abrupt beginning. It uses flint where this can be had, as do all the other industries; where flint is absent or scarce, it employs quartzite and other stones. The use of bone begins in the Mousterian, to increase henceforward. The period shows three stages of evolution, the lower, middle, and upper, as do also later the Aurignacian and the Magdalenian periods. The implements range from crude to beautifully made (as at La Ferrassie, La Quina, Le Moustier); the technique is partly different from, but in general not inferior to, either the late Acheulean or the earlier Aurignacian, and there are indications that there was no general sudden ending.

On the whole the Mousterian industry, though characteristic, does not provide evidence of something entirely new and strange, intercalated between the Acheulean and the Aurignacian, beginning abruptly by displacing the former or ending suddenly through displacement by

the latter. There is much in fact at either end that may prove to be, more or less, of a transitional nature.

Thus, in H. F. Osborn's opinion (Obermaier, 1924, p. x), the Mousterian "constitutes a further evolution of the two earlier cultures"— the Chellean and the Acheulean. At Ehringsdorf, in the lower travertine, "the technique of the chipping is Acheulean, but the forms are largely Mousterian" (MacCurdy, *Human Origins,* 1924, vol. ii, p. 392). According to Burkitt (*Prehistory,* 1921, p. 27), "...workers in Dordogne find a great difficulty in distinguishing between Upper Acheulean beds and Lower Mousterian beds. In fact, M. Peyrony often only solves the problem by the absence or presence of reindeer." And quotations of similar import could be multiplied. As to the upper limits—at the Cotte de Ste. Brelade, Jersey, excavated by Nicolle, Sinel, and Marett, the upper (fifth) layer gave graceful implements "that may be either upper Mousterian or Aurignacian" (Burkitt). At Le Moustier, the type-station of the Mousterian industry, the upper rock-shelter showed eight layers, "the top one being Aurignacian, the second transitional (Audi), and the rest Mousterian, except the seventh which was sterile." The lower rock-shelter was even more instructive. The section from top to base was: 6. Lower Aurignacian; 5. Transitional (Audi); 4. Typical Mousterian; 3. Mousterian with Audi forms and few *coups-de-poing*; 2. Mousterian with some Audi forms and many *coups-de-*

poing; 1. Some Audi forms, no *coups-de-poing* (Burkitt, 1921, p. 93). But perhaps the best comprehensive statement on this subject is that of MacCurdy, one of the oldest and most cautious students of prehistory. In his *Human Origins*, 1924, vol. i, pp. 161–2, we read: "In certain French stations, a transition from the Mousterian to the Lower Aurignacian occurs, as for example, at Le Moustier (Dordogne), La Verrière (Gironde), and especially at the rock-shelter of Audi in the village of Les Eyzies. In comparison with Mousterian points, those of Audi are more slender and are slightly recurved. The convex margin is rendered blunt by retouching so as not to injure the hand while using the opposite margin for cutting or other purposes. Such a tool, as much a knife, or scraper, as a point, bridges the gap between the Mousterian point or double scaper and the Lower Aurignacian blades of the Châtelperron type. At Audi it is associated with small cleavers and disks, scrapers, spoke-shaves, asymmetric points, and scratchers. The Grotte des Fées at Châtelperron, though distinctly Aurignacian, is so closely related to the transition stage that the chronologic difference must be small. An intermediate stage is recognizable at La Ferrassie (Dordogne)."

The Audi culture is still somewhat controversial. Abbé Breuil (recent letter) regarding it as "degenerate Mousterian." Notwithstanding which, the impression is growing that the more the initial and the terminal stages of the Mousterian industry are becoming known, together with the late Acheulean and the earliest Aurignacian, the less abrupt and striking appear their differences and the greater grows the feeling that they are not absolutely separated. Some interesting things in this connection are now being gathered by Absolon in Moravia.

SEQUENCE OF CULTURE

The sponsors of the view that Aurigancian man was a man of different and superior species to the man of the Mousterian period, conceive him for the most part, apparently, as an invader who came from somewhere outside the Neanderthal area, overwhelmed completely the established less capable species, and annihilated or at least wholly replaced it, over all the great domain over which it once extended. These ideas, however, are never expressed very clearly, and little thought is given to the incongruities they involve.

They would imply, first of all, the invasion of Europe during the height of the last glaciation. This is not in harmony with the main laws of human and biological spread, namely: Movement in the direction of least resistance, and movement in the direction of better material prospect, which are, first of all, climate and food. In the entire history of Europe the movements of men have tended always toward "a place in the sun" and away from the cold.

Such views postulate, next, large

numbers of the new-comers to suffice for the vast task But such large numbers would necessarily mean somewhere near a still larger mother-population, and there is no trace, either in western Asia or northern Africa, the only regions from which such invasions at those times would have been practicable, of any such numerous Aurignacian population.

It is a very serious question whether in palæolithic times, when man was without a tamed animal, without stocks of non-perishable food, dependent wholly on hunting without yet a bow and arrow, and in the imperfect social organization of that

to be explained the fate of the displaced people.

It stands to reason that these great difficulties would have to be satisfactorily explained away before there could be a general intelligent acceptance of an Aurignacian invasion with Mousterian extinction.

Finally, the coming of a distinct and superior species of people ought to have left a very tangible record on the sequence and nature of the cultural levels of the two stocks.

As to sequence, 157 of the better-known and recorded Mousterian sites (as recorded by MacCurdy) give, on analysis, the following conditions:

Sequence of Industries

		Open Stations		Rock-Shelters and Caves	
		No.	Per cent.	No.	Per cent.
Mousterian Topped by:					
(No culture)		(34)	(55.7)	(15)	(18.9)
Neolithic		4	6.6	4	5.1
Magdalenian		3	4.9	9	11.4
Solutrean		2	3.3	10	12.7
"Palæolithic"		1	1.6	2	2.5
Aurignacian		17	27.9	39	49.4
		(61)	——	(79)	——
	MOUSTERIAN				
		(54)	——	(63)	——
Mousterian Reposing on:					
Acheulean		24	44.4	4	6.3
Chellean		5	9.3	3	4.8
(No culture)		(25)	(46.3)	(56)	(88.9)

time, any larger armed invasion would have been feasible. A peaceful extension, on the other hand, would not lead to the annihilation or expulsion of the invaded population, and if small or gradual, would lead to an amalgamation with, rather than the extinction of, the native stock. A complete displacement by any agency is difficult to conceive, and there would remain

The Mousterian culture, in nearly one-half of its stations in the open, follows direct upon the Acheulean; and the Auriganacian, in very nearly one-half of the rock-shelters and caves, and in not far from one-third of the stations in the open, follows upon the Mousterian. It would seem that these figures speak for a rather close relation of these peoples in their habits, and that particularly between the Mousterians and Aurignacians—who should represent two different species of man, one greatly superior to the other.

An objection may here be raised to the effect that the number of available, and especially of the more suitable, caves was limited and, therefore, the same caves that once served the Neanderthalers had to be used also by the shelter-needing Aurignacians; but this point is invalidated by the showing of the Solutreans and Magdalenians, who were even more cave-dwellers than the Aurignacians, yet are found collectively in less than one-fourth of the Mousterian caves.

Another point is, that it is not always the lower or earliest Aurignacian that follows upon the Mousterian. But such a discord is common to all the periods. It may mean a discontinuity, and may also mean a persistence of any given culture in some localities longer than in others. In both cases it would speak against a sudden general displacement of one culture.

There is evidently much here, once more, to be explained by those who conceive of Aurignacian man as very distinct from, and superior to, the Mousterian, and as having suddenly replaced the latter.

ART

The Aurignacian period does not appear to come in full-fledged, as is sometimes taken for granted, but to develop locally, both in industry and art, from humbler beginnings (Breuil, Burkitt, Evans, MacCurdy,

et al.). Also there seems to be more difference in these respects between the lower and the middle Aurignacian than there is between the lower Aurignacian and the upper Mousterian with the Audi and the Châtelperron stages.

It may, moreover, be unjust to assume that Mousterian man was devoid of art-sense. He may not have left any designs in caves (though that is not perhaps absolutely certain), but the same is true of the Neolithic and many other early, as well as later, populations. How many such designs, or other permanent forms of art, for instance, have been left by the prehistoric man of England, or Belgium, or Germany, Moravia, Poland, or Russia? How many have been left more recently by such highly artistic people as the Slovaks and the peoples of the Carpathians and the Balkans? And how many cave designs comparable to those of France and Spain do we find in the whole continent of America, with all its able and highly artistic population, a large part of which—the Lagoa Santa-Algonkin type—may even be related to the Aurignacians? On the other hand, practically a replica of the European cave-art was produced by the lowly Bushmen of South Africa, who certainly were no superior race or species.

That the Mousterians may not have been lacking in artistic sense is indicated by some of their beautiful implements from La Quina and other stations; by the beautiful topaz and then a crystal cleaver found in 1925–6 by the American school at Sergeac; by the decorated bone fragment from La Ferrassie; and possibly by the *pierres-figures* (*e.g.* Roellecourt, Dharvent), and used chunks of manganese oxide, found occasionally in the Mousterian deposits (*e.g.* La Quina, Henri Martin). Sir Arthur Evans tells us that, "When we turn to the most striking features of this whole cultural phase, the primæval arts of sculpture, engraving, and painting, we see a gradual upgrowth and unbroken tradition. From mere outline-figures and simple two-legged profiles of animals we are led on step by step to the full freedom of the Magdalenian artists" ("New Archæological Lights on the Origins of Civilization in Europe," by Sir Arthur Evans, *Science,* 1916, n.s. xliv, No. 1134, p. 406). MacCurdy is even more direct: "The inception, development, and decay of Quaternary art all took place during the upper palæolithic period. The beginnings of sculpture, engraving and fresco are traceable to the Aurignacian epoch" (MacCurdy, *Human Origins,* vol. i, p. 155). And there are some very good words of appreciation of the abilities of Mousterian man in Sir Arthur Keith's recent two volumes (*The Antiquity of Man,* 1925). Thus— Archæology fails also, as did Palæontology and Geology, in isolating Neanderthal man, and in separating him from the succeeding forms of humanity.

III. The skeletal remains

THE SKELETAL MATERIAL

The crucial part of the whole question of Neanderthal man is, however, that of the evidence of the skeletal material, for it is essentially upon this that the separateness and discontinuance of the Neanderthal type of man has been based. It would probably be easy to harmonize all the rest of the differences between Neanderthal and later man with the idea of a simple evolution and transmission, were it not for the obstacle of the Neanderthal man's skulls and bones. These impress one by such marked differences from those of any later man, that bridging over of the gap has, to many, seemed impossible.

Let us glance at what the present skeletal evidence of Neanderthal man consists of. Leaving out of consideration the unimportant and the doubtful specimens, the remains comprise now the following (see pp. 272–74, 276–77).

It will be well in this connection to contrast the Neanderthal remains with those from the Acheulean on one side, and those from the Aurignacian and the following periods on the other. The results are unexpected. There is nothing authentic from Acheulean times; and there is less, in the number of finds, from the Aurignacian than there is from the Mousterian period. Moreover, what there is from the Aurignacian is found, on consulting the details of the discoveries, to be essentially middle and upper, rather than the most needed early Aurignacian. The data leave a strong impression that the material, but especially that from the earlier portion of the Aurignacian period, is still far from sufficient for drawing from it far-reaching inductions.

Neanderthal Remains in Chronological Order of Discovery

Name of Find	Years of Discovery	By Whom Discovered	Find Consists of—	Essential Data of Discovery	Reported by and when (originally)
Gibraltar	1848	Labourers	Adult female skull, damaged (without lower jaw).	Found accidentally, in a crevice during blasting for an emplacement of a battery.	G. Busk, 1868.
Neanderthal	1856	Labourers	Adult male skull-cap, and 13 bones of the skeleton.	Found accidentally in a cave.	C. Fuhlrott, 1857; D. Schaaffhausen, 1858.
La Naulette	1866	E. Dupont	Imperfect lower jaw of a young adult woman.	Excavated from undisturbed deposits in Trou de la Naulette, near Dinant, Belgium, under layers of stalagmite alternating with six layers of earth, the two 12 feet in thickness.	E. Dupont, 1866.
Sipka	1880	Karel J. Maska	Fragment of the frontal part of the lower jaw of a child of about eight years.	Excavated from the "Badger hole," a low lateral extension of the Sipka cave. Lay 1·4 meters deep in undisturbed ash-bed. Freed from a lump of ashes, suffering thereby probably the loss of a tooth and some small pieces of bone (Maska).	Wankel, 1880; Schaaffhausen, 1881 and 1883; R. Virchow, 1882; Maska, 1886.

Neanderthal Remains in Chronological Order of Discovery

Name of Find	Years of Discovery	By Whom Discovered	Find Consists of—	Essential Data of Discovery	Reported by and when (originally)
Spy No. 1 and No. 2	1886	Marcel de Puydt and Maxim Lohest	Two skeletons, males, adult	Excavated from Terrace in front of a cave, 6 and 8 metres distant from entrance, 4 metres deep	J. Fraipont and M. Lohest, 1887.
Bañolas (Gerona, Spain)	1887	Lorenzo Roura	Lower jaw	In hard travertine, about 15 feet from surface.	Cazurro, 1909; Harlé, Pacheco and Obermaier, 1912.
Malarnaud (Ariège)	1889	F. Regnault	Lower jaw, adult female	In ancient clay, with bones of extinct animals, capped by a layer of stalagmite.	H. Filhol, 1889.
Krapina (Croatia)	1895, 1899, and 1905	K. Gorjanović-Kramberger	Parts of over 20 skeletons (adult and subadult, both sexes).	Excavated from the fillings of an old rock-shelter, with remains of fire, bones of extinct animals, and stone implements.	Gorjanović-Kramberger (various dates).
Le Moustier (Dordogne)	1908	O. Hauser	Skeleton of an adolescent male	Excavated from an accumulation of cultural debris of Mousterian age, in lower rock-shelter, at Le Moustier.	O. Hauser and H. Klaatsch, 1909.
La Chapelle (Corrèze)	1908	Abbés A. Bouyssonie, J. Bouyssonie, and L. Bardon	Skeleton (male, middle-aged)	Burial (formal) in a depression dug in the marly soil of the floor of a cave.	A. and J. Bouyssonie and L. Bardon, 1908; M. Boule.

Neanderthal Remains in Chronological Order of Discovery

(continued)

Name of Find	Years of Discovery	By Whom Discovered	Find Consists of—	Essential Data of Discovery	Reported by and when (originally)
Jersey (Channel)	1910	MM. Nicolle and Sinel	13 teeth (from both jaws) of one skeleton.	Cave accumulations, near an ancient hearth.	R. Marett, 1911; A. Keith, 1911.
La Quina (Charente)	1908–21	Henri Martin	Skeleton of an adult (female(?) 1911); lower jaw (1912); skull of a child (1921); fragments of several skeletons (different dates).	Partly in ancient mud-bed of the near-by stream (adult skeleton, etc.); partly in kitchen refuse and debris (child skull, etc.).	H. Martin, 1911–27.
La Ferrassie (Dordogne)	1909, 1910, and 1912	Peyrony	6 skeletons (2 adults—a male, a female—and 4 children).	At base of accumulations in a shallow rock-shelter.	Capitan and Peyrony, 1909, 1912.
Ehringsdorf (Weimar)	1914, 1916 (and later)	Quarrymen	2 lower jaws, remains of a child's skeleton, portion of a thigh-bone.	Deep in hard travertine (and intercalated layer).	G. Schwalbe, 1914; H. Virchow, 1920.
Galilee	1925	F. Turville-Petre	Fragments of the skull of a young adult, including the frontal-bone.	Cave, at the base of undisturbed palæolithic layer, 6½ feet below the modern floor-level.	F. Turville-Petre and Arthur Keith, 1927.
Ehringsdorf (Fischer's Quarry)	1925	Quarrymen	Broken vault of an adult skull.	Deep in hard travertine	F. Widenreich, 1927.
Gibraltar	1926	Miss D. A. E. Garrod	Skull of a child of about ten years of age.	Rock-shelter, with Mousterian culture.	Abbé Breuil (shelter); Miss D. A. E. Garrod (prelim. notes), 1926.

Taking the Neanderthal remains by themselves, we find that, notwithstanding their defects, they constitute a very respectable array of precious material. Let us see what it teaches. If we placed all this material on a table before us, ranged by the date of discovery, we should see a remarkable assembly of more or less deficient or fragmentary skulls, jaws, and bones, with an array of loose teeth, the whole differing widely in colour, weight, state of petrifaction, and in principal morphological characters. We should be struck by the prevailing aspect of inferiority of the material, but the arrangement would soon prove unsatisfactory and we should proceed to another.

As there is not enough for a geographical subdivision, it would be logical to try next an arrangement of the specimens by their antiquity, from the oldest to the latest. The indications are that the Mousterian period was a long one, and of three stages—the inferior, middle, and superior. We should like, therefore, at least to arrange our material by these stages.

But we strike at once great difficulties. The very type-specimen of the lot, the Neanderthal skeleton, lacks direct chronological identification. There were neither animal nor industrial remains with it, or, if there were, they were not saved. Everything indicates that it is very old: physically it is in every one of its parts a prototype of Mousterian man; chronologically it may be even pre-Mousterian. Similar and other difficulties confront us in the case of the first Gibraltar skull and the Bañolas jaw, the important Krapina remains, the Ehringsdorf jaws; and it is not certain just where within the period to place most of the remainder of the specimens. The final conclusion is that, if the eyes are shut to the somatological characters of the remains, a satisfactory chronological grading of them becomes very difficult and uncertain.

The state of preservation or petrifaction of the remains is a question of local geophysics and chemistry, and thus incapable of giving any fair basis for classification. Thus there remain only the somatological characteristics of the skulls and bones themselves, and the endeavour to arrange them on this basis proves of much interest.

The general physical characters of the Neanderthal race have been more or less summed up by a number of eminent anatomists and anthropologists, including especially Schwalbe, Keith, Sollas, and Boule. The main features of the average Neanderthaler are therefore fairly well known. They include a moderate stature, heavy build, and a good-sized, thick, oblong skull, with pronounced supraorbital torus, low forehead, low vault, protruding occiput, large, full upper maxilla, large nose, large teeth, and a large, heavy lower jaw with receding chin. To which may be added stout bones of the skeleton, particularly the ribs and the bones of the lower part of the body, femora and tibiæ with heavy articular extremities, the tibia relatively short and with head more

The More Important and Better Authenticated Remains of Early Man from the Acheulean Period Onward

Acheulean	Mousterian	Aurignacian	Solutrean	Magdalenian
(?) Taubach (teeth).	(1) Gibraltar (skull).	(1) Most (Brüx) (skull).	(1) Laugerie-Haute (skeleton).	(1) La Madeleine (skeleton, fragments of jaws).
(?) Ehringsdorf (2 lower jaws).	(2) Neanderthal (skeleton).	(2) Combe-Capelle (skeleton).	(2) Badagoule (Dordogne) (1 child's skeleton).	(2) Laugerie-Basse (skeleton).
	(3) La Naulette (lower jaw).	(3) La Rochette (parts of skeleton).	(3) Klause, near Neu-Essing (skeleton).	(3) Chancelade (skeleton).
	(4) Šipka (lower jaw).	(4) Camargo (skull).		(4) Cap Blanc (skeleton).
	(5) Spy (2 skeletons).	(5) Castillo (lower jaw).		(5) Duruthy (near Sord Es Landes)—(skeleton).
	(6) Bañolas (lower jaw).	(6) Hohlefel (lower jaw and teeth).		(6) Les Hôteaux (near Rossillon, Ain) (skeleton).
	(7) Malarnaud (lower jaw).	(7) Enzheim (skeleton).		(7) Lussac-le-Château (lower jaw).
	(8) Krapina (parts of over 20 skeletons).	(8) Mentone (8 skeletons).		(8) Grotte-des-Fées (parts of jaws).
	(9) Le Moustier (skeleton).	(9) Paviland (skeleton).		(9) Le Placard (skull and fragments).
	(10) La Chapelle (skeleton).	(10) Ojeów (portion of a skull).		(10) Mas d'Azil (skull).
	(11) Island of Jersey (teeth).			(11) Obercassel (2 skeletons).
	(12) La Quina (skeleton; skull of child, lower jaw, parts of several skeletons).			(12) Freudental (lower jaw and numerous fragments).

The More Important and Better Authenticated Remains of Early Man from the Acheulean Period Onward   (continued)

Acheulean	Mousterian	Aurignacian	Solutrean	Magdalenian
		Aurignacian, probably.		
	(13) La Ferrassie (2 adult skeletons, parts of 4 children's skeletons).	Brno (Brünn) (1 skull, 2 skeletons). Predmost (remains of about 20 individuals, 14 skeletons fairly complete).		(13) Miskolez (child's skull).
	(14) Ehringsdorf (?) (2 lower jaws, child's skeleton, part of a femur).		Solutré (3 skeletons).	
	(15) Near Ehringsdorf (skull).	*Aurignacian or later.*		
	(16) Galilee (skull).	Cro-Magnon (2 skeletons, parts of 3 others)		
	(17) Gibraltar (child's skull).	Halling (1 skeleton).		

than not inclined backward, a peculiar astragalus, and various secondary primitive features.

To this generalized type some of the specimens conform, it is soon seen, much more than others. It is realized that the general conception of the type has been built-up essentially on the Neanderthal, Spy No. 1, and the La Chapelle skulls and skeletons, but that from this generalization there are many aberrations.

An arrangement of the specimens in morphological order, beginning with those that show the most primitive or old features and advancing gradually towards more modern standards, is now in order, and the results are very striking.

The first strong impression is that, with all the seeming riches, there is still not enough material for satisfactory grading. The next appreciation is that it is hard to grade whole lots, but that it is necessary to grade the skulls, jaws, teeth, and bones separately. In one and the same skeleton are found parts and features that are very primitive and far away from man's later types, with parts and features that are almost like the modern; and every skeleton is found to differ in these respects. Here is facing us, evidently, a very noteworthy example of morphological instability, an instability, evidently, of evolutionary nature, leading from old forms to more modern.

The Neanderthal skull and skeleton proper, in all the parts that have been saved, is found to stand at the base of the series. It lacks, regrettably, the lower jaw and the teeth, as well as the sternum, most of the scapulæ, and the ribs, vertebræ, sacrum, the leg, the hand and the foot bones. Of what is present, the farthest from modern type is the skull, the next being the thigh and the leg-bones; the nearest to modern forms, though still somewhat distinct, are the bones of the upper extremity.

The closest in general to the Neanderthal skeleton is Spy No. 1, La Chapelle, and apparently the Le Moustier youth. But Spy No. 1 has almost primitive-modern jaws with practically recent teeth; the La Chapelle shows high cranial capacity, an "ultra-human" nose, and a strongly developed nasal spine; the Le Moustier skull has a higher vault and forehead, with less protrusion of the occiput; while the bones of the upper extremity in all three approach closely the modern types. Thus, even in these most nearly related four specimens, there is in evidence a considerable variability, with more or less advance in various parts in the direction of later man.

These facts deserve, undoubtedly, earnest consideration. But there is much more to be learned. Taking the remainder of the skulls, jaws, and bones attributed to the Neanderthal phase, it is seen that both the variability and the number of characters that tend in the direction of later man increase considerably. The Krapina series, by itself, is probably more variable from the evolutionary point of view than would be any similar series from one locality at the present. This is true in respect to the cranial form, the development of the forehead, the jaws, the teeth, and many of the bones of the skeleton. The additional Neanderthal remains manifest signs of similar instability of type and of tendencies of an evolutionary nature, this being particularly true of Spy No. 2, and of the recently discovered Galilee and Ehringsdorf crania.

In his excellent description of the Galilee specimen, Sir Arthur Keith has shown that it has a fair forehead, with "no suggestion in the vaulting of its frontal bone that the roof of the skull was low and flat, as is usual in Neanderthal skulls." And in his preliminary report on the Ehringsdorf (1925) cranium, F. Weidenreich shows us a specimen with even better developed frontal region, and a vault of good height.

But the most instructive, though most neglected, specimens are the crania of Spy, Belgium. Here the student is confronted with a find in the same terrace and deposits, at the same level, and but 6 feet apart, of two adult male skeletons from the later Mousterian time. One of these skeletons, No. 1, has a skull the vault of which is a replica of that of the Neanderthal cranium, with typically Neanderthal bones of the skeleton. But this same skull is associated with upper and lower jaw and teeth that may be duplicated to-day among the lower races. And the skull of the second skeleton is so superior in size, shape, height of the vault, and height of the forehead, to No. 1, that the morphological distance between the two is greater than that between No. 2 and some of the Aurignacian crania, such as the Most (Brüx) or Brno No. 1 (Brünn) specimens.

About the most distinguishing and important marks of difference of the typical Neanderthaler from later man, are, we may repeat, the flatness of his head, with low receding forehead and a peculiar protruding occiput; heavy, supraorbital torus; heavy, chinless jaw; and, as determined from intracranial casts, a low type of brain. It will be well to see how these characters stand the light of our present knowledge.

Lowness of the vault, low and receding forehead, and projecting occiput, all show in the series of the Neanderthal skulls known to-day a large range of gradation, the lower limits of which are well below, but the upper grades of which are well within, the range of variation of the same characters in later, and even present, man. There exists to-day a whole great stream of humanity, extending from Mongolia deep into America, which is characterized by low vault of the skull (see *Catal. Crania, U. S. Nat. Mus.,* Nos. 1 and 2; also *Bull.* 33, *B.A.E.*). Low foreheads are frequent in prehistoric America (see *Bull.* 33, *B.A.E.,* and *Proc. U. S. Nat. Mus.,* 1908, vol. xxxv, pp. 171–5). The pronounced Neanderthal occiput, such as shown by the La Chapelle, La Quina and La Ferrassie skulls, it would be difficult to fully match in later man, but on the one hand the character is not present or marked in all the Neanderthalers, while on the other hand there are decided approximations to it among recent skulls.

A heavy supraorbital torus, such as is common to the Neanderthal skulls, is not found in later man; but not all the Neanderthalers had the torus equally developed (*e.g.* Gibraltar), and, as has been pointed out by Huxley, Sergi, Stolyhwo, and others, there are later male skulls in which there is a marked approach to the torus. A whole series of specimens may be mentioned (Podkoumok, Brüx, Brno No. 1, Predmost, Obercassel, Alcolea, Djebel-Fartas, two neolithic skulls at Warsaw, the neolithic miner from Strépy at Brussels, etc.) in which the feature is of a distinctly transitional character. Moreover, it is well known that, first, the torus is essentially a sexual (male) and adult feature; second, that a reduction of such characters is easier than that of those which are more deeply rooted; and third, that in the civilized man of to-day a continuance of such reduction is still perceptible. There is less difference in this respect between the Neanderthal and the skulls just mentioned than there is between these and the mean development of the ridges in the highly cultured man—or, for that matter, the ordinary African negro—of the present.

Heavy, large, and receding lower jaws, such as the La Chapelle and some of the Krapina specimens, are among the most striking characters of Neanderthal man. Jaws such as these are not known in later skulls. But with them we have within the Neanderthal group itself specimens very much more advanced morphologically toward the present human type, such as Spy No. 1, La Quina (1912), and the La Ferrassie. Even at Krapina itself some of the jaws are of a less primitive type than others. Let us add to this the various huge, nearly chinless, and even receding jaws that occur now and then in the Australian, Melanesian, Mongolian, American Eskimo, and Indian, and the picture loses much of its discontinuity. Much the same may be said also of the teeth. Teeth of primitive form—incisors, canines (*dents du chien*), molars—occur to this day (see *Am. J. Phys, Anthrop.*, 1922–4), while practically modern teeth may already be observed in Spy No. 1, and more or less also in other jaws of the Neanderthal group.

As to the bones of the skeleton, the conditions are quite as significant as those of the jaws and teeth. There are scales of gradation from forms that stand considerably apart from those of later man (as in Neanderthal, Spy, La Chapelle, Le Moustier) to forms that approach to, or merge with, the modern (many parts of the Krapina, La Ferrassie, La Quina skeletons). To which may be added a word about the brain.

The size and variation of the Neanderthal brain are comparable with those of the Aurignacian, and even the present primitive man. The idea that the Aurignacians were exceptional in this respect is, if due regard be given to the factor of stature, erroneous. The surface conformation of the brain, as shown by intracranial casts, is of a low type in the Gibraltar, La Chapelle, and other specimens. But this does not hold true of the Weimar or the

Galilee brain. The intracranial cast of the Galilee skull shows, in the words of Sir Arthur Keith, that "in its mass and its markings it has reached at least to the level attained by individuals in living races—such as that represented to-day by the aborigines of Australia" (*Report on the Galilee Skull*, p. 106).

IV. Recapitulation

In relation to what perhaps was its most important period, the Mousterian, Prehistory is found to have reached a position approaching dogmatism. But this has only led it into a blind alley, from which so far there has been found no exit, notwithstanding much speculation.

It has been decided, on the weight of a limited initial group of specimens, that Neanderthal man was a man of a different species; that he may possibly have originated from his European predecessors, but that, after a long period of existence and after having spread far and wide, he perished abruptly and completely, without leaving any progeny, on the approach of a superior species, the *Homo sapiens*.

This *H. sapiens* has been assumed to have come from elsewhere, possibly from Africa or Asia; or he was, somehow, cryptically, coeval from far back with the pre-Neanderthaler and the Neanderthaler, eventually to assert himself suddenly and completely, to take over the human burden. He comes on the stage in body and brain largely as he is to-day, and has, since the beginning of

the Aurignacian, undergone but moderate alteration.

A whole line of the foremost workers in prehistory are seen to have become identified with these notions, which obliges every student to give them an earnest and respectful attention. But no notion or dogma can possibly reach the status of a fact before it has been proven to be such through full demonstration.

Owing to scarcity of material, such demonstration has hitherto been impossible; but the more the material remains of early man accumulate and are better understood, the more it is sensed that the whole Neanderthal question is in need of a revision.

If the given assumptions are true, then we are confronted by some strange major phenomena, viz. a long double line of human evolution, either in near-by or the same territories; a sudden extinction of one of the lines; and evolutionary sluggishness or pause in the other. The consideration of these hypotheses brings us into a maze of difficulties and contradictions.

They lead to an outright polygeny —which is undemonstrable and improbable; or they concede the evolution of *H. sapiens* from the same old stock that gave also *H. neanderthalensis*, but deny the possibility of such evolution from Neanderthal man later on; they give us *H. sapiens*, without showing why, or how, and where he developed his superior make-up, and imply that, while he evidently developed much more rapidly at first to reach the status of *H. sapiens,* he then slackened greatly to remain, from the beginning of the post-glacial to this day, at nearly the same evolutionary level.

They place *H. sapiens* in Africa or Asia, without troubling to offer the evidence of his ancient dominion in those regions. Or, if he lived in Europe, coexisting with the Neanderthaler, where are his remains, and why did he not prevail sooner over his inferior cousin? His traces, it will be recalled, never, in Europe or elsewhere, precede or coexist with, but always follow, the Mousterian. And where are there any other examples of a sudden, complete extinction of a whole large group of humanity; or of any wholesale Aurignacian conquest; or of any superior mentality of the *early* Aurignacians? And where are, in fact, in anything like a sufficient number, the undoubted skeletal remains of the early Aurignacians that could be used for comparison? Why did they, a new, superior species, strong and able enough to completely do away with the Neanderthaler, take over the poor Neanderthaler's caves and sites, and live in them exactly, except for technical differences in stone-chipping, as did their crude predecessors? And how shall we explain the anomalous fact of an invasion during the last ice encroachment, an unfavorable period, when man might be expected to move from, rather than into, such a territory?

Valid answers to these and other questions are as yet impossible. There is a need of much further exploration; of much further good fortune

in locating additional skeletal remains of all periods, but particularly of the latest Mousterian and earliest Aurignacian; and of a new generation of able workers, well equipped, and unhampered by tradition.

The *indications,* for the present, seem, however, to be the following:

(1) The Penck-Brückner conception of the Ice Age, as composed of four distinct periods of glaciation with three well-marked inter-glacial periods, does not harmonize with either the palæontological or the human evidence. Both these tend to show but one main inter-glacial interval, from which there is a gradual progression towards an irregular cold period, after which follows an irregular post-glacial. There is no warm fauna that would correspond to the assumed third (Riss-Würm) inter-glacial. And there is evidently no substantial change, such as would necessarily be brought about by a marked alteration in climate, in man's housing and living habits from the Middle Mousterian to the Magdalenian cultural periods.

(2) The Mousterian or Neanderthal phase of man begins towards the end of the warm main inter-glacial. It is essentially the period of the cooling stage of the terminal main ice invasion, reaching to, and probably somewhat beyond, its culmination.

(3) During this period man is brought face to face with great changes of environment. He is gradually confronted with hard winters, which demand more shelter, more clothing, more food, more fire, and storage of provisions; there are

changes in the fauna which call for new adaptations and developments in hunting; and there are growing discomforts with, it may be assumed, increasing respiratory and other diseases, that call for new efforts and seriously hinder the growth of the population.

(4) Such a major change in the principal environmental factors must inevitably have brought about, on the one hand, greater mental as well as physical exertion and, on the other hand, an intensification of natural selection, with the survival of only the more, and perishing of the less, fit. But greater sustained mental and physical exertion, where not over the normal limits, leads inevitably towards greater efficiency attended by further bodily and men-

tal development, which, with the simultaneous elimination of the weak and less fit, are the very essentials of progressive evolution.

Strong evidence that a relatively rapid, progressive change, both mental and physical, was actually taking place during the Neanderthal period, is furnished by the great variability of the skeletal remains from this time.

(5) But such evolution would certainly differ from region to region, as the sum of the factors affecting man differed, reaching a more advanced grade where the conditions in general proved the most favourable; while to many of the less favoured groups disease, famine, and warfare would bring extinction. All these agencies are known to science

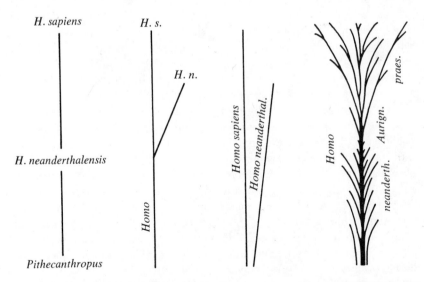

Fig. 5. Various Conceptions as to the Phylogenetic Relation of Neanderthal and Later Man. (Present evidence favours the view represented on the extreme right.)

to-day; only they acted with more freedom of old when social organization and mutual aid were at a low level.

(6) With these processes it is conceivable, if not inevitable, that, towards the height of the glacial invasion, the population decreased in numbers, and that the most fit or able-to-cope-with-the-conditions group or groups eventually alone survived, to carry on.

Here seems to be a relatively simple, natural explanation of the progressive evolution of Neanderthal man, and such evolution would inevitably carry his most advanced forms to those of primitive *H. sapiens*.

(7) The physical differences observable between Neanderthal and later man are essentially those of two categories, namely: (1) Reduction in musculature—that of the jaws as well as that of the body—with consequent changes in the teeth, jaws, face, and vault of the skull; and (2) Changes in the supraorbital torus, of the order known well to morphology as progressive infantilism. For both these categories of changes there are later parallelisms. Further reduction of teeth, jaws, and the facial bones has taken place since Magdalenian times, and is now going on in more highly civilized man, of whatever racial derivation; while infantilism is commonly accepted as an explanation of the differences of the negrillo from the negro, and for the greater average reduction of the supraorbital ridges in the negro than in the whites. It would be illogical to deny

the probable instrumentality of these agencies in men of an earlier period.

(8) Anthropology is thus confronted with the following conditions:

Neanderthal man is of a primitive physique, appears to have ended by a sudden and complete extinction, and to have been replaced by *H. sapiens*.

But there has been discovered no previous home of this *H. sapiens*, nor any remains whatsoever of his ancestors; and, if he coexisted with Neanderthal man, it is impossible to understand why he did not prevail sooner, or why he did not mix, or, above all, why he left no cultural remains of his existence.

On the other hand, this same Neanderthal man is now known to show wide morphological variation, leading in the direction of later man; and there are individuals among later men, even to this day, who show transitional features. This might be explained by an original common parentage of the two strains; or by an intermixture of the Neanderthal stock with the succeeding *H. sapiens;* or by a development, evolution, of the former into the latter.

(9) A critical examination of the known facts does not favour the assumption of a far-back common parentage and early Quaternary separation of *H. neanderthalensis* and *H. sapiens*, for lack of cultural evidence of *H. sapiens* and other great difficulties.

It is equally unable to favour a separate origin of the two stocks with subsequent hybridization, for again there is no evidence of the pre-Aurignacian whereabouts and the doings of *H. sapiens,* there is no trace of his ancestry, and knowing his and his descendants' characteristics, it is impossible, as said already by Karl Pearson, to conceive his origin without a Neanderthal-like stage of development.

There remains but the third alternative—which is the evolution of the Neanderthaler into later man. This proposition is not yet capable of conclusive demonstration. There is not yet enough material to decide it one way or the other. But the thoroughly sifted indications appear to the speaker to favour this assumption.

The great current need of prehistory, it may be accentuated once again, is more exploration and more good fortune in discoveries. Meanwhile there appears to be less justification in the conception of a Neanderthal *species* than there would be in that of a Neanderthal *phase* of Man.[1]

[1] The detailed evidence of the new Gibraltar skull and brain cast, just submitted to the Royal Anthropological Institute (November 1st, 1927), goes far to support this assumption.

Recent Discoveries Relating to the Origin and Antiquity of Man

Henry Fairfield Osborn
1927

In the great drama of the prehistory of man converge many branches of science. In fact, we do not progress very far in this most difficult, as well as most noble, branch of biological research if we pursue pathways which are purely anthropological or purely archæological. It is such specialistic mode of attack which has led more than one generation of man into pitfalls of opinion and of theory from which there is no escape except by direct retreat. In the list of those who have been compelled to reverse engines are the names of many great anthropologists, among them the renowned Hans Virchow, the still more widely known Ernst Haeckel, and no less a name than that of Thomas Henry Huxley. Virchow opposed the recognition of the Neanderthal skull

"Recent Discoveries Relating to the Origin and Antiquity of Man." *Palaeobiologica,* Vol. I, pp. 189–202. 1927.

of 1856 with pathologic and theologic preconceptions. Haeckel also eagerly espoused the ape ancestry hypothesis by ignoring the profound cleft between ape and man. Huxley failed disastrously in rating the Neanderthal man with recent types of man and threw Darwin completely off the track of this veritable missing link. Huxley, too, failed to visit the Foxhall quarry of Ipswich, site of the greatest discovery in modern times, namely, the fireplace and flint tool quarry of Tertiary man. Even Jupiter nods when the purely specialistic pathway is pursued.

In the triumphs of modern astronomy, four sciences converge, namely, mathematics, mechanics, physics and chemistry; but, in the triumphs of anthropology, beginning with its dawn in the mind of Blumenbach, 1796, and reaching a succession of climaxes in 1927, no less than twelve of the major and minor branches of science converge, as follows :[1] The astronomy of Croll (1875) and Wallace (1880); the glaciology of Geikie (1894–1914), of Penck and Brückner (1909), of Leverett (1910); the glaciology and river terraces of Depéret (1918–1921); the paleogeography of Suess (1885), of de Lamothe (1899–1918), of Daly (1920–1926); the clay laminae of De Geer (1910–1921); the loess of Schumacher, of Merzbacher, of Obruchev, and of Soergel (1924–1927). A host of other lines of research conspire to portray the great

successive phases in the environment of man.

These great stepping stones of the Age of Man, of the Quaternary, of the Glacial Period, lead to our modern and greatly extended conceptions of the antiquity of man. Whereas Charles Lyell, in his classic work, "The Antiquity of Man," postulated 400,000 years for the Quaternary Period, we have practically multiplied the Glacial Age of Agassiz by four in the demonstration that there were not one but *four* titanic glaciations during Quaternary time and have thereby reached a minimum estimate of 1,000,000 years for the Age of Man.

But to complete the human prehistoric panorama as it is now painted, we cannot stop with the inorganic sciences. It is necessary to muster the whole galaxy of organic sciences—botany, including paleobotany; zoology, including paleontology; anatomy, including comparative anatomy and embryology; anthropology, including ethnology and archeology. The latest of the biological sciences to make its tribute is psychology, including comparative and physiological psychology; especially, of late (Tilney, 1926–1927), the localization of functions in the brain of *Eoanthropus, Pithecanthropus* and other fossil races of man; and, finally, the latest of the psychic cluster, known as behaviorism. It is our recent studies of the behaviorism of the anthropoid apes as contrasted with the behaviorism of the progenitors of man which compel us to separate the entire ape stock very widely from the human stock.

[1] Osborn-Reeds. Old and New Standards of Pleistocene Division in Relation to the Prehistory of Man in Europe. P. 413. *Bull. Geol. Soc. Amer.*, Vol. 33, pp. 411–90.

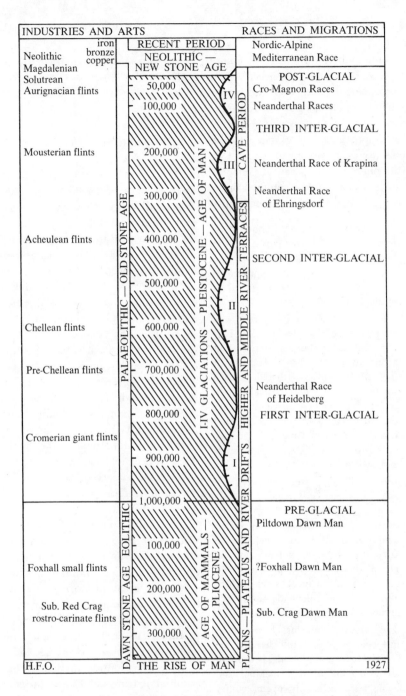

Fig. 1. Conspectus by Osborn of the chronology of man, based upon convergent researches in astronomy, geology, palaeontology, glaciology, palaeogeography and anthropology. This table embraces the recent discoveries of the Tertiary Dawn Men of Piltdown, Foxhall and the sub-Red Crag, but omits the Trinil man, which has been raised recently to Middle Pleistocene time.

While these twelve or more branches of science which bear upon anthropology have been advanced chiefly through the brilliant researches of specialists, it is our privilege and opportunity to gather all the reins and endeavor to present a truly philosophical series of generalizations, which may be summed up in advance under four chief captions:

1. The antiquity of man is now to be reckoned not in thousands, but in hundreds of thousands of years, and we foresee the soon approaching period when it will be reckoned in millions of years.

2. The Age of Man, or Pleistocene, can no longer be regarded as Act I of the phehistoric human drama, but rather as the final act, because at the very beginning of the Pleistocene we find the human race well established and widely distributed over the earth. Act I of the Age of Man is during Tertiary time in what may be known as the "Dawn Man" stage and the "pro-human" stage.

3. While still supported by very able anatomists such as Gregory, the ape-human ancestry theory is, in my opinion, greatly weakened by recent evidence, and I am inclined to advocate an independent line of Dawn Man ancestors, springing from an Oligocene neutral stock, which also gave rise independently to the anthropoid apes.

4. The Dawn Man or *Eoanthropus* line belongs to a distinct family, the *Hominidæ*, ground-living, cursorial, alert, capable of tool making, and living in a relatively open country on the high plateaus and plains of northern Asia.

5. The Anthropoid Ape belongs to a distinct family, the *Simiidæ*, tree living, brachiating, sluggish, incapable of tool making, restricted to the forests of south temperate and tropical countries.

The ape-human theory

The strong resemblance of the apes to man, first seen early in the eighteenth century by native observers, then reported by explorers, noted with hesitation by Buffon and with emphasis by Lamarck, accompanied by deceptive representations of the apes as bipedal, gradually expanded in the course of a hundred and fifty years into what may be called the *ape-human myth*. Apes were depicted by early explorers and artists as walking erect like men and, in the sculptures of Fremiet, as forcibly abducting negresses—in brief, as exhibiting habits and postures very similar to man. By comparative anatomists the many resemblances of the apes to man were closely observed, but the many profound differences were passed by; even as late as the time of the International Zoological Congress at Cambridge Haeckel arranged all the ape skeletons he could find at hand upright in line with human skeletons across the great platform on which he made his final public address. A similar unconscious falsification of posture is to be found in museums and in text books all over the world.

In brief, scientific mythology has accumulated around the anthropoid apes, falsifying and exaggerating their human resemblances, minimizing and ignoring their profound differences from man in habit and gait and in the anatomy and functions of the brain. Small wonder that Charles Darwin in his "Descent of Man" traced the human family back to a branch of the *Simiidæ* and laid for the ape-human theory a scientific foundation which has been greatly expanded by other writers. Three years ago I was myself an advocate of such a theory, being strongly impressed by the remarkable observations of Gregory and Morton on the anatomy, and of Yerkes on the psychology, of the apes. Only recently have I begun to believe that the ape-human theory is without adequate foundation and have begun to advocate a theory of the independence of the human stock from ape stock back to a common ancestor of Oligocene time. I feel quite confident that when the direct Oligocene ancestors of man are discovered they will be found to possess many pro-human traits and characteristics. I recognize all the anatomical resemblances both in the skeleton and in the dentition discovered by my honored colleague Gregory and by other comparative anatomists, but *I now believe that only by the palæontological method of approach can this problem of problems be solved* and that, as in many other cases of phylogeny, we shall find the evidence of embryogeny and of comparative anatomy inadequate.

Let us abandon the ape-human theory

The prologue and the opening acts of the human drama occurred way back 16,000,000 years ago in the Upper Oligocene Period. At this period, or still earlier in Oligocene time, the family of man sprang from a stock neither human nor ape-like, but possessing certain common attributes which have been transmitted over this very long geologic era to variously branching races of human beings on the one hand and to variously branching races of anthropoid apes on the other (Fig. 2).

In this very ancient man-ape stock (*Anthropoidea*) resided the affinity which survives to-day in all blood tests, in peculiar susceptibility to or immunity from certain diseases, in resemblance of the hæmoglobin blood crystals, in the uniform division of the teeth to the number of thirty-two, in the peculiar pattern of the extension of the caudal vertebrae into a tail reversional both in man and apes, and in many psychic characteristics such as curiosity, fear, family protection and courage. It is not surprising that these and other common ape-human characteristics have survived since Oligocene time when we see similar survivals among other animal stocks which we know parted company millions of years ago. Of all substances ever discovered, the heredity or the hereditary germ-plasm on which all these survivals depend is the most stable. The germinal stability which has preserved the earliest Cambrian organisms over a period now estimated at 500,000,000 years is also capable of preserving pro-human anatomical and physiological traits for the relatively brief 16,000,000 years which have elapsed since the close of Oligocene time. As the dog, the horse, the rhinoceros and the tapir acquired their fully modern form and proportions in Oligocene time, is it not theoretically probable that a pro-human type is equally ancient?

Consequently, many of the resemblances between ape and man which have been erroneously cited as proofs of ape-man descent are due either to very remote common inheritance or to the *convergence* of the ape toward the human type. An example of such convergence to the human type is shown in the foot of the gorilla by the recent observations of Akeley, of Morton and of Gregory; the foot of the adult gorilla resembles the human type more strongly than the foot of the infant or young gorilla.

I regard the ape-human theory as totally false and misleading. It should be banished from our speculations and from our literature, not on sentimental grounds but on purely scientific grounds, and we should resolutely set our faces toward the discovery of our actual pro-human ancestors through the methods of vertebrate palæantology rather than of embryology and comparative anatomy. In my opinion, the most likely part of the world in which to discover these "Dawn Men," as we may now call them, is the high plateau region of Asia embraced within the great prominences of Chinese Turkestan, of Tibet and of Mongolia. The great plains area north of the high plateau should also be searched, because we have recently determined that this was probably the home of the primitive horse and, according

to our theory, the home of primitive man should be looked for in the same kind of country in which the primitive horse flourished.

In abandoning the Darwin-Haeckel ape theory which reached its apogee in the fantastic speculation of Klaatsch that different races of anthropoid apes gave rise directly to different races of man, we now give an entirely new frame to the human prototype to separate it sharply from the anthropoid ape type. Reconstructing our pro-human ancestors and endeavoring to assign an adequate date to the origin of the pro-human stock, we depend on the science of phylogeny, which has become in itself one of the finest products of human scientific endeavor. Phylogeny made a brave start in the sciences of comparative anatomy and embryology but it awaited palæontology to place it upon a broad and firm foundation. Most of the recent advances in anthropology have been by palæontologic means and methods.

To build up the unknown human prototype by phylogenetic means we must take advantage of the really marvelous knowledge gained from all the minor and greater steps in the ancestry of the horse, of the rhinoceros, of the tapir and of the titanothere since these animals were first discovered in North America by the great Joseph Leidy, of Philadelphia, in 1856. Our pro-human ancestors through their behavior, their tastes, their habits, and their fondness for travel were the architects of their own destiny, as the horses and titanotheres were the un-

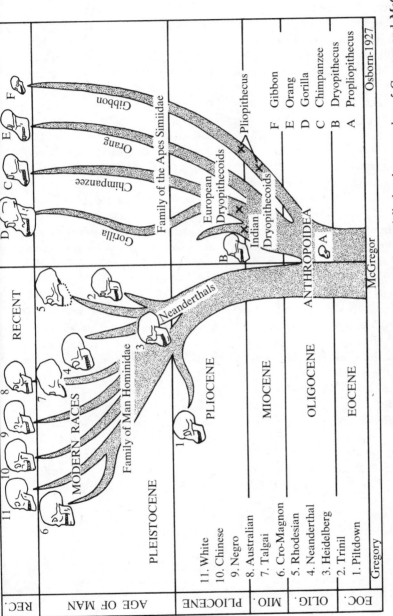

Fig. 2. Osborn's present theory of the ascent and phylogeny of Man, aided especially by the researches of Gregory and McGregor. Left: Family of Man (*Hominidae*), dividing into the Neanderthaloid and modern racial stocks; present geologic location of the Piltdown, Heidelberg, Trinil, Neanderthal and Rhodesian fossil races. Right: Family of the Apes (*Simiidae*), including the Pliocene and Miocene dryopithecoids nearest the ancestral stock of the *Anthropoidea*, also the lines leading to the gorilla, orang, chimpanzee and gibbon. Below: *Anthropoidea*—the common Oligocene ancestors of the *Hominidae* and of the *Simiidae*.

291

conscious architects of their destinies. Moreover, the open country best adapted to the evolution of the horse is also best adapted to the evolution of the higher races of man. Through the findings of the Central Asiatic Expeditions of the American Museum of Natural History we have determined that the primitive horse did not evolve in southern Asia or even in the southerly portions of the high plateau regions of central Asia; the great unexplored plateau and plains region of northern Asia now appears to have been the center of the origin of the family of horses and possibly may have been the center of the origin of the family of man. Certainly, the family of man could not have originated in a densely forested country rich in natural food materials. Man's nomadic wandering instinct, which even in Upper Pliocene time impelled his migrations, is not a forest characteristic but a characteristic of the open country. Almost without exception, precocious human civilizations have been found in open country partly deforested either by secular desiccation or by the severity of the northern steppe climates. Practically the same environmental conditions have favored the precocious development of the finer races of horses.

Secondly, when we at last dis-cover one of our pro-human ancestors in Miocene or even in Upper Oligocene time, the human characteristics will be found plainly stamped on this ancestor, as the horse characteristics are plainly stamped on the Pliohippus, on the Protohippus, on the Mesohippus and even on the Eohippus. It was my observation of the fully evolved single-toed horse of Middle Pliocene time, known as *Pliohipus leidyanus,* which led me to predict to the National Academy of Sciences the discovery of a full-brained pro-man also in Pliocene time; this prediction preceded the recent demonstration that *Eoanthropus dawsoni* of Piltdown is probably of Pliocene age, and also the recognition of J. Reid Moir's wonderful discovery of the sub-Red Crag and Foxhall Dawn Men in the Upper Pliocene of England, a discovery which carries the tool-making ability of man far down into Tertiary time.

This distinctive pro-human stamp will be seen chiefly in certain outstanding characteristics of habit and of structure which were acquired millions of years ago. In contrast with the Simian and pro-Simian stamp, we may clearly present in two columns the chief characteristics of man and of the apes:

HOMINIDAE (FAMILY OF MAN) PRO-HUMAN CHARACTERISTICS	SIMIIDAE (FAMILY OF APES) PRO-APE CHARACTERISTICS
1. Progressive intelligence, rapid development of the forebrain	1. Arrested intelligence and brain size
2. Ground-living bipedal habit—cursorial, adapted to rapid travel and migration over open country	2. Arboreal to hyper-arboreal quadrumanal habit—living chiefly in trees

3. Bipedal habit and development of the walking and running type of foot and big toe

3. Quadrupedal habit when on the ground

4. Shortening arms and lengthening legs

4. Lengthening arms and diminishing legs

5. Development of the tool-making hand, thumb and fingers

5. Loss of the thumb and absence of tool-making power

6. Walking and running power of the foot enhanced by enlargement of the big toe

6. Grasping power of the big toe for climbing purposes, modified when walking

---

In the remarkable discoveries and studies of Boule, of Dubois, and of McGregor on the fossilized limb bones of man and in the complementary studies of Schultz in the embryogeny of man, the ape-arboreal–reminiscent hypothesis has not been strengthened; it has, on the contrary, been somewhat weakened. The thigh-bone of the Neanderthaloid types resembles that of a man rather than that of an ape; it reveals the erect bipedal, rather than the stooping quadrupedal position. The arms of the Neanderthals are not elongated as they should be according to the ape ancestry hypothesis; they are rather short. The legs of the Neanderthals and of the Trinils are not abbreviated as they should be for the ape ancestry hypothesis; they are decidedly long. Similarly, a superb series of embryonic hands and feet of unborn infants assembled by Schultz do not reveal reminiscences of the attenuated ancestral fingers of an ape-arboreal stage, resembling those of gibbons, chimpanzees, or even of gorillas, but they are short and blunt like modern human hands. The embryonic thumb, similarly, is well developed and reveals no symptoms

of recovery from the abbreviated or useless thumb characteristic of all arboreal or brachiating types of primates. Still more, the embryonic big toe, while slightly set apart from the other toes, shows little vestige of former limb-grasping such as is seen in the foot of the anthropoid apes, which is so hand-like as to give the bearer the title *quadrumana,* or four-handed. It is true that the human embryonic big toe is set apart like the toes of *Eocene* lemuroids such as the *Notharctus* of Leidy and Gregory, but the divergent hallux is a common characteristic of all primitive Eocene mammals.

Comparative and human psychology also weakens rather than strengthens the ape-man hypothesis. The geologic rearrangement (Fig. 2) of the Piltdown, the Trinil and the Heidelberg races which we owe to recent geologic discovery renders both the Heidelberg and the Piltdown races far more ancient than we had supposed. All the present evidence points to closing Pliocene age for the Piltdown Dawn Man, appropriately named *Eoanthropus* by Smith Woodward. This Dawn Man has a flat vertical forehead, without brow ridges, like the modern Bushman, a very thick skull, a chimpanzee-like jaw, and a surprising brain capacity of 1240 cubic centimeters. This brain cube equals that of the existing Indian Veddah tribes. As analyzed by Elliot Smith and by Tilney, this Dawn Man has a well convoluted forebrain; in the localization of functions there is space for speech areas and diversified motor areas for the coordinated motions of the fore limbs, of the hands and of the fingers.

Large Tertiary brain capacity; psychology of the Stone Age man

The Heidelberg race, now recognized as of Lower Pleistocene Age, is probably a giant pro-Neanderthaloid, characterized by projecting eyebrows and by a brain which would probably prove to be somewhat inferior in capacity to the more recent Neanderthals. We consequently reach an entirely new estimate of the brain capacity of the human race at the close of Pliocene time and the beginning of Pleistocene time, a period estimated at 1,000,000 to 1,250,000 years before our era.

Brain cube of the Neanderthal and Trinil races

The Trinil man of Java, *Pithecanthropus erectus* of Dubois, was formerly regarded as of Upper Pliocene Age but now it is assigned by Die-

trich and Osborn to a more recent geologic age, namely, Middle Pleistocene, since its fossil remains are found associated with stegodontine elephants (*Stegodon aurorœ*) much more recent in character than those of the Upper Pliocene, such as *Stegodon insignis ganesa*. Meanwhile, the brain of the Trinil man has been shown by Tiley to be distinctly prohuman, with a fairly well-developed forebrain or intelligence area. Consequently, we may now regard *Pithecanthropus erectus* as a case of arrested development, of a very primitive type, possibly related to the Neanderthal stock, surviving in the southern subtropical forests of Asia, with a brain capacity of 940 ccm— not far inferior to that of the native Indian Veddahs with a minimum brain capacity of little more than 1000 ccm.

It required a very long antecedent geologic period to develop the Dawn Man brain capacity and Dawn Man intelligence as demonstrated, in the case of the Piltdown and probably contemporaneous Foxhall races, in the manufacture of many different kinds of small flint implements and in the use of fire. In the case of the Heidelberg race, we observe the manufacture of very large and varied flint implements, such as are found at Cromer on the eastern coast of England and which are believed to be of the same geologic age as the Heidelberg jaw.

Flint tools were, however, by no means the first tools employed by man; they were almost certainly preceded by bone tools of great

	Male	*Female*
Neanderthal Caveman of Western Europe:		
La Chapelle aux Saints	1530	
La Quina, France		1367
Gibraltar, Spain		1280
Trinil Man of Java (*Pithecanthropus erectus*)	940	
Piltdown Man of Sussex, England	1240	
Native Indian Veddahs	1250	1139

variety, and bone tools were in turn preceded by wooden tools. Not improbably there was a very long "age of wood," then a very long "age of wood and bone," followed by a very long "age of flint" preceding the metal ages. During this enormously long period, which we must now reckon in millions of years, tool-designing and tool-making, the adaptation of tools to certain purposes and needs of life, the use of these tools in offense and defense, in the chase, and in the preparation of food and of clothing laid the foundations of the intelligence of mankind.

The listed features of behaviorism are only a fraction of the host of psychic contrasts which might be drawn between the daily behavior of the Dawn Man and the daily behavior of the pro-anthropoid ape. As I have elsewhere summed it up, in the life and conduct of the pro-ape was the potency of the super-apes living to-day—the orang, chimpanzee, gorilla and gibbon—but in the Dawn Man was the potency of modern civilization.

It is true that Darwin used the expression, "Man is derived from some member of the Simiidæ," and that the term "ape-man" is deeply

HOMINIDAE (FAMILY OF MAN) PRO-HUMAN PSYCHOLOGY AND BEHAVIOR	SIMIIDAE (FAMILY OF APES) PRO-APE PSYCHOLOGY AND BEHAVIOR
1. Tool-making capacity of the hands and especially of the thumb	1. Limb-grasping capacity of the hands and loss of the thumb
2. Adaptation and design of implements of many kinds in wood, bone and stone	2. Adaptation of the fore and hind limbs to the art of tree climbing and brachiating
3. Design and invention directed by an intelligent forebrain	3. Design limited to the construction of very primitive tree nests
4. Use of the arms and tools in offense, defense and all the arts of life	4. Use of the arms chiefly for tree-climbing purposes; secondarily for the prehension of food and grasping of the foe
5. Use of the legs for walking, running, travel and escape from enemies	5. Use of legs in tree-climbing and limb-grasping
6. Escape from enemies by vigilance, flight and concealment	6. Escape from enemies by retreat through branches of trees

7. Tree-climbing by embracing the main trunk with the arms and limbs after the manner of the bear	7. Tree-climbing always along branches, never by embracing the main limbs and trunk

engraved in our consciousness, but I claim that it is misleading. The gorilla, chimpanzee and gibbon give us our conception of the ape. I hold that very few of the ape characters were possessed by man in his early stages; they are all characters belonging to an extremely ancient arboreal stage perhaps as ancient as Eocene time. Comparative anatomists find likenesses between apes and man by blood tests, osteology and morphology; these characters are strikingly pro-human, and anatomists have dwelt on them to the exclusion of others not human. Between man and the ape—not only the hands and feet of the ape, but the ape as a whole, including its psychology—you will find more differences than resemblances. In brief, man has a bipedal, dexterous, wide-roaming psychology; the ape has a quadrupedal, brachiating, tree-living psychology.

The term "ape-man" has been forced into our language along a number of lines, and even the term "anthropoid" has come to lose its significance. "Ape-man" has gained prestige through early explorers and travellers who represented the anthropoid apes as walking on their hind feet. We have recently discovered that no anthropoid ape walks upright; the gibbon balances himself awkwardly when he comes down from the trees, but all the other apes are practically quadrupe-

dal in motion, except possibly in defense, when they rear as a horse would rear. So far as the gorilla is concerned, all the mythical evidence as to its erect attitude has been dispelled by the actual observations and photographs by Carl E. Akeley, from which we learn that the gorilla normally progresses on all fours, resting the hands upon the knuckles, and that it rises erect only when aroused to anger, at which time the females and young rapidly retreat to the shelter of the trees. We may therefore eliminate the early descriptions of explorers in forming our notions of the anthropoids. A parallel to the misuse of the word "ape-man" would be this: the horse, ass and zebra are so closely related that unless one examines very carefully one can not tell the skeletons apart; they agree more closely than do the anthropoid apes and man. But when we study the habits of the horse, the ass and the zebra we find that each has a totally different psychology: the horse has a forest psychology, the ass has a desert psychology, the zebra has an open-plains psychology. The horse is a splendid swimmer, whereas the mule—a cross between the horse and the ass—has the ass psychology and is afraid of water. It is no more proper to speak of the common ancestor of the apes and of man as "ape-man" than it is to call the common ancestor of the horse and the ass an "ass-horse."

Another instance of wide psychic difference between like animals is that of the black and the white rhinoceros of Africa, which have a very dissimilar psychology and react differently in every emergency.

Empire of the low-browed Neanderthal races

We may class together as neanderthaloid all the prehistoric races with prominently projecting supraorbital processes; with low, retreating foreheads; with correspondingly low, broad type of brain, especially with low forebrain in contrast with the relatively high forebrain of the Piltdown and of modern races; with massive jaw retreating chin of the Heidelberg and true Neanderthal type. The increasing brain power of these neanderthaloids during Pleistocene time is perhaps measured by contrast between the Trinil brain of 940 cubic centimeters and the most highly developed Neanderthal brain of 1,530 cubic centimeters. The psychology of this race is further revealed by the prevailing type of flint implement, of offense and defense, of the chase and in the preparation of food. The first of these great Neanderthal flint types is found in the Cromer deposits in East Anglia—tremendous flint implements used largely in combat. Over an enormously prolonged period these implements passed through Cromerian, pre-Chellean, Chellean, Acheulean and, finally, Mousterian stages, wherein they begin to show decadence and loss of virility, together with invasion of other types of implements.

The great neanderthaloid race, with its characteristic stone culture, apparently dominated north Africa and all of Europe and extended eastward into the heart of Asia. Its quarries and camping grounds increase in number as Pleistocene time goes on, and an eastward to southward spread may be represented in the recent discoveries of Mousterian camping sites in Ordos, China, and of a neanderthaloid skull, which has been named the Rhodesian skull, at Broken Hill Mine, South Africa. The animal life contemporaneous with this race is well known; it included a large variety of elephants, chiefly of the southern and straight-tusked types, rhinoceroses and, in the lower lands, hippopotami. This is known as a South Temperate fauna adapted to rather fertile lands, river bottoms and abundant forests. In such an environment game was so plentiful that there was relatively little struggle for existence, hence there was little incentive to the development of a diversified flint industry. Superior intelligence was not demanded and it is therefore surprising that under these circumstances the Neanderthal brain attained the dimensions which threw even the genius of Huxley off the track as to the very primitive character of this race. Taken altogether, the widely extending range of the neanderthaloid races is one of the most firmly established facts of prehistory. If our geologic time scale is reliable, it extended over a period of 1,000,000 years, and if our present records of quarry grounds and implements are reliable, the Neanderthals had almost exclusive possession of an enormous territory.

Theory of the north Eurasiatic origin of the high-browed races

It was formerly believed by certain anthropologists that the Neanderthals were the progenitors of the suceeding higher races, but in my opinion we may entirely abandon this theory and substitute a theory of the complete replacement of the Neanderthal empire by invading races that had acquired superior intelligence under entirely different conditions of life. In other words, while the Neanderthals were enjoying exclusive possession of central Europe, Asia and a large part of northern Africa and were spreading southward into Rhodesia, the progenitors of all the modern races were occupying another great area, under conditions of life in which the struggle for existence was much more severe and in which there were far greater demands upon the native wit of man to overcome natural difficulties by invention and resourcefulness.

This unexplored territory, the unknown homeland of the higher races of man, can not be south of the Neanderthal Eurasiatic belt, because to the south conditions of life were less rigorous, food was more easily obtained, and the milder sub-

tropical climate was less stimulating to discovery and invention. In this southern, less stimulating region of Eurasia may have survived the persistent Trinil race of Java and other primitive races still undiscovered. To the south, in Africa, may also have developed Negroid stock under central African conditions of life that must closely parallel those of central and southern Eurasia during the great Neanderthal period.

Consequently, it is to the northern regions of Eurasia that we must look for the unknown homeland of the higher races, to a temperate region which extended along the northern borders of the Neanderthal empire over the high central plateau region of Asia, over the great plains region to the north of the central plateau and, finally, over the confines of eastern Europe. It may be laid down as a fixed principle in the rise of the intelligence of man that only when the struggle for existence is fairly keen does any race progress; when the struggle for existence is too severe the entire life is devoted to physical support, to the exclusion of intellectual and social progress.

The new modern races, pure and blended—Mediterranean longheads, Alpine broad-heads, blended Cro-Magnons, Nordics—apparently moved eastward over this northerly plateau and plains region and finally subdued the entire Central Eurasiatic empire of the Neanderthals. These new races were not only distinguished by large brains and by equal powers of observation, of reasoning, of design, of tool-making, and of social, moral and political

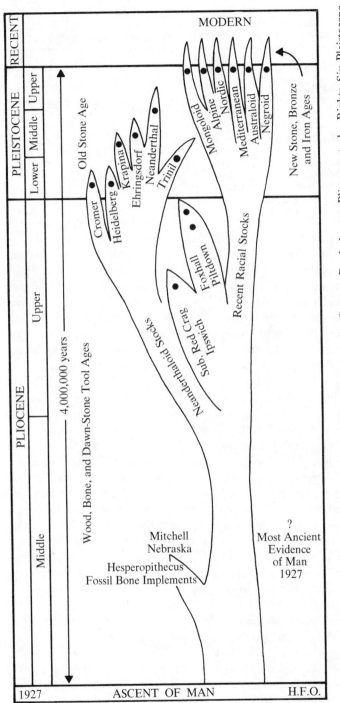

Fig. 3. Prehistoric and recent racial stocks. Left: Neanderthal stocks. Center: Partly known Pliocene stocks. Right: Six Pleistocene and Recent racial stocks. Below: Level of the supposed fossil bone implements of the *Hesperopithecus* quarries in Nebraska—possible evidence of Middle Pliocene bone—tool age in America.

Author's note: Recent exploration has failed either to confirm or disprove that the type superior molar of *Hesperopithecus* belongs to a primate. Similarly, the supposed fossil bone implements still require authentication. The American Museum is still exploring the *Hesperopithecus* quarries in the hope of determining these two much disputed questions.

299

| | *Cube of Brian Capacity* | | |
	Male	*Female*	*Max.*
Cro-Magnon	1550–1590		
Average modern European	1450	1300	
Average modern Swiss	1467 (1200–1660)	1349 (1230–1510)	1660
Upper Palaeolithic broad-head race of Ofnet	1400		
Living broad-head race of Czechoslovakia	1415 (1230–1800)	1266 (1000–1400)	1800
Native Australian race	1310	1154	
Native Indian Veddahs	1250 (1012–1408)	1139 (1037–1217)	1408
Papuans of New Guinea	1236	1125	
Piltdown (latest estimate of McGregor, 1927)	1240		

organization, but were also endowed with higher intellectual, spiritual and creative faculties which gave them both physical and intellectual supremacy over the Neanderthals and led to their entire occupation of western Europe. First, to measure their capacity purely by the cube of their brain, let us place these newly arrived races in order of brain power with the existing races, high and low:

The Cro-Magnons, who have been termed the Palæolithic Greeks, rank extremely high in their cubic brain capacity; they entered Europe side by side with the pure long-headed and broad-headed races, also of high brain power, and are now considered to represent a blend between long-heads and broad-heads. Imagine the enormously long period of time during which this very high modern brain power developed and consider through the astonishing industry and diversified art of these people that every faculty has its cerebral equivalent and ancestry for each of its several coefficients. The extreme accuracy of observation of animal form displayed by the Cro-Magnons is not the result of hundreds of years, but of hundreds of thousands of years.

It is possible that the Piltdown race of Upper Pliocene time with its 1240 ccm. brain cube is an offshoot of the precociously largebrained stock that gave rise to the group of modern races—Australoid, Negroid, Mongoloid, Caucasian. Yet the Piltdown race has a chimpanzee or anthropoid ape type of jaw. It seems a very hazardous prediction, but I am inclined to anticipate the discovery, even in Pliocene time, of a modernized type of jaw with prominent chin. This is against all existing evidence, with the exception of the dubious Foxhall jaw with its prominent chin, for all the known Pliocene and early Pleistocene races have a sloping chin or less remotely resemble the anthropoid ape type.

Conclusion

Let us therefrom conclude with consideration of the ancestry of man according to the modified concept of "dawn men," not "ape-men." In the first place, over an incredibly long period of time the Dawn Men have been tool-makers, of high adaptibility and wonderful technique. We have then a biped, a being with a hand capable of grasping and controlling tools, a tool-maker with as fine a sense of touch as that of any of the present-day etchers, engravers and artists. In my opinion, the pro-man psychology, leaving out the evidence of anatomy and morphology, is certainly that of a Dawn Man and not of an "ape-man." I agree with my colleagues that man passed through an aboreal stage, but I believe that this stage did not progress so far as to carry man into a stage approaching that of the anthropoid apes. Dollo has stated the law of the irreversibility of evolution. The brachiating hand of the ape was used as a hook—apes do not grasp a branch with the fingers and thumb but hook the whole hand over the branch, as trapeze workers do to-day—and the thumb was therefore a grave danger. If man had gone through a prolonged period of brachiating in the branches of trees he would have lost his thumb. I agree to putting our arboreal ancestors back to Eocene time, but I predict that even in Upper Oligocene time we shall find pro-men, and if we find Oligocene pro-man—in Mongolia, for example—that he will have pro-human limbs, not pro-anthropoid ape limbs.

The most welcome gift from anthropology to humanity will be the banishment of the myth and bogie of ape-man ancestry and the substitution of a long line of ancestors of our own at the dividing point which separates the terrestrial from the arboreal lines of primates.

Of all incomprehensible things in the universe man stands in the front rank, and of all incomprehensible things in man the supreme difficulty centers in the human brain, intelligence, memory, aspirations, and powers of discovery, research and the conquest of obstacles. The approach to this unknown field of future human advance—the seat of the human mind and the constitution of the human mind—is along the great paths of human and comparative anatomy and of human and comparative psychology and behavior. Yet this approach will yield only a tentative conclusion; the final solution of this problem of problems —the rise of man—will come only through unremitting exploration and the chance finding somewhere in the Eurasiatic continent of actual fossil remains of the Oligocene pro-man, of the Miocene and Pliocene Dawn Man and, finally, of the early Pleistocene ancestors of the large-brained modern races.

Man's Relationship to the Anthropoid Apes. Conclusion

Frederic Wood Jones
1929

Man's relationship to the anthropoid apes

We are now faced with the problem that appears to be most important of all: What is the relationship of Man to the Anthropoid Apes?

There are three possible answers to the question, and each has been propounded and has been supported by what has been conceived to be sufficient evidence.

(1) Man may be derived from the Anthropoid Ape stock at a stage in which its members had acquired their present characters. It is often maintained that anatomists do not hold such views (see Chapter XI), and that any apparent expression of such a belief in their writings is due merely to their method of phraseology. This may, indeed, be so, and possibly we might so explain the claim of the describer of *Australopithecus,* that it was a form "intermediate between living Anthropoids and Man." But even making this concession, it is difficult to conceive that the creation of a special Family —"*Homo-simiadae*"—for such intermediate forms did not arise in a belief in the existence of a group of "missing links" that showed a blend of the characters of Man and modern Great Apes.

(2) Man may be derived from a common Anthropoid Ape stock that gave rise to him and to the existing Great Apes. This is at present the orthodox view; the only differences apparent in the writings of recent authorities are the degrees of remoteness of this common ancestor. Perhaps the most widely held opinion, or at any rate the one most vigorously and most frequently expressed, is that a common ancestor for Man and the existing Apes may be conceived as being a form not unlike the more generalized members of the *Dryopithecus-Sivapithecus* assemblage of the Siwalik fauna. In this case the "missing link" would be, as Dr Gregory says, "very closely akin to the upper Miocene common ancestors of the Chimpanzees and

"Man's Relationship to the Anthropoid Apes." "Conclusion." *Man's Place Among the Mammals.* Chapter 38, pp. 325–34; Chapter 40, pp. 354–65. E. Arnold and Company, London, 1929. Reprinted by permission of the publisher.

Gorillas." In dealing with the phylogenetic trees that have been published by different authorities we may most readily grasp the essential factor in the author's concept by tracing back the human line to the point of its divergence from other Primate forms, and then noting what the common stock at this point of departure is depicted as having given rise to (see Fig. 1). In this way the human line may be conceived as joining with the other Primate lines at such a point that the common stock gave rise only to the human family and the Gorilla, the Chimpanzee and the other Anthropoids having branched off earlier. This is the scheme depicted by Elliot-Smith (1924). Again, the human line might branch off at such a point that the common stem gave rise to Man, the Gorilla, and the Chimpanzee, the Orang and the Gibbons having been separated earlier. This view appears to be favoured by Gregory, although it is not strictly depicted in his genealogical trees. The more general conception is that Man branched off so that the common stock gave rise to Man, the Gorilla, the Chimpanzee, and the Orang, the Gibbons alone having left the stock previously. This is the concept underlying the varied schemes of Sir Arthur Keith and Dr Gregory. The last variant is that in which the human line joins the Primate line in such a place that the resulting common stock gave rise to all the Anthropoids, including the Gibbons, as well as Man. This supposition is embodied in the genealogical tree drawn up by

Dr W.D. Matthew. It is, therefore, clear that, on the supposition that Man has been derived from an Anthropoid Ape common stock, every possible condition has been claimed by one authority or another as representing the probable parting of the ways of Man from the common stock. The only thing that is common to all these schemes is the hypothesis that the Old World Monkey phylum had separated from the Anthropoid Ape-Human phylum in an earlier and more primitive stage.

(3) Man may not be derived from the stock of the Anthropoids at all. His line in the Primate phylum may be conceived as running back independently of theirs to a more remote ancestor. So thinks Henry Fairfield Osborn, and such an opinion has been advocated by Snell (1863), Hubrecht, Oetteking, Boule, and others.

Which of these three main hypotheses lies nearest to the truth cannot be fully determined by the methods of palaeontology, since the remains of extinct Anthropoids and of extinct Men are far too few and fragmentary to afford any real guide. One day this state of affairs will probably be altered, and the palaeontologist will have sufficient material on which to base a reliable judgment. As things are, it is not fair to expect him to be dogmatic in the matter; and if he is dogmatic it is fair to suspect his conclusions of having insufficient evidence as their basis. The only knowledge that we can use at present, and the only knowledge that we can materially increase by patient research, is knowledge of the comparative anatomy of the existing forms. The fossil record must be used as a check on the findings of comparative anatomy; it can hardly serve further than this. Even now we have a mass of facts that may be used to some purpose. We may at any rate test the three hypotheses by the facts that are already accumulated and attempt to find out which of them appears to fit most nearly with the findings of the comparative anatomy of Man and the Anthropoids. If this be done we shall at once see that in the total anatomy of Man and of the existing Anthropoids there is no warrant for the first supposition. All the existing Anthropoids are far too specialized in their general pithecoid trend, and in their own individual directions for any one of them to have been ancestral to such an animal as Man. So much was at one time freely admitted on all hands, and for the credit of science it is much to be deplored that some recent writers should add fuel to the foolish popular fire by making pronouncements that appear to reveal a belief in Man's origin from the existing Anthropoids.

In dealing with the second hypothesis—that Man arose from a common Anthropoid Ape stem—it is necessary to weigh up the anatomical characters of Man and the Anthropoids, not in the method of Tyson, but by attempting to unravel the primitive features from those that have been definitely modified by a phylogenetic trend. We have seen that there is a very definitely recognizable syndrome of anatomical modifications that constitutes what we have termed a pithecoid trend. This pithecoid trend of anatomical specialization culminates in the African Cynomorphs and in the Macaques, which we are here regarding as end-products of the pithecoid radiation. In all the elements of the pithecoid syndrome the Old World Monkeys show the greatest specialization of their phylum. But we have also seen that certain tailless arboreal forms, characterized by deliberate hand-over-hand climbing, had avoided certain of these pithecoid trends in very varying measure. In so far as these forms had avoided the pithecoid specializations they had remained more primitive. They had acquired their own specializations due to their brachiating orthograde habits; and we have pictured these factors as forming the common bond between the four main types of Anthropoid Ape. But we must remember that, although the hallmark of this group is the variable avoidance of pithecoid tendencies, and the substitution of their own "higher" specializations, no one of the Anthropoids has failed to be branded, and branded very unmistakably, with the mark of the pithecoid trends. Again, we have seen that the key-note of human characteristics is that Man, more than any Anthropoid Ape, has avoided the tendencies of development that culminate in the Cynomorpha. It is this fact that justifies Klaatsch's paradoxical saying that "the less an ape has changed from its original form just so much the more human it appears." We might amplify this dictum by adding that where an

Anthropoid has avoided pithecoid specializations and retained primitive conditions it shows a resemblance to Man. We are dealing solely with simple anatomical facts, such as the fronto-maxillary replacement of the ethmo-lachrymal contact, the fronto-temporal replacement of the spheno-parietal pterion, the frontal intervention between ethmoid and sphenoid in the anterior cranial fossa, and the other features that have been cited in previous chapters. From these facts there are, it seems to me, three, and only three, possible deductions to be drawn as to Man's relations to the Anthropoid Apes.

(1) Man may have arisen from an Anthropoid Ape stem that parted company with the Cynomorph stem before the pithecoid trend had been established in the Primate phylum. In that case, it is easy to understand how Man avoided the pithecoid specializations and retained primitive features in these characters. But as the Anthropoid Apes have developed so many of the pithecoid characters, it is necessary to suppose that they developed them after their separation from, and therefore in independence of, the Cynomorphs. Now it is well-known, as Osborn has repeatedly pointed out, that similar modifications are prone to appear in the two branches descended from a common ancestor. But granting this, we must make unwarrantable demands upon it, and call parallelism to our aid as well, if we are thus to explain the independent development of the whole series of pithecoid specializations in Anthropoids and Cynomorphs alike. It is difficult to imagine that the whole series of identical non-adaptive pithecoid features developed, say, in a Gorilla and a Macaque can possibly have been acquired independently.

(2) Man may have arisen from an Anthropoid Ape stem that parted company with the Cynomorph stem after the pithecoid trend had become stereotyped in the Primate phylum. By this supposition it is easy to explain the pithecoid specializations that are found in varying degrees in the Anthropoids. But we must also suppose that Man originally possessed these specializations, and that he has subsequently lost them, and in these very features reverted to a primitive condition. We know that, with regard to certain structural features, Dollo's Law does not rigidly apply, and that in such things evolutionary trends may be reversed. But it is difficult to imagine that in a whole series of uncorrelated features Man can have passed from primitive to specialized pithecoid, and subsequently have reverted to primitive. No case of structural reversibility of evolution of anything approaching this magnitude is known, and it is, therefore, difficult to conceive it as having occurred in the special case of Man.

(3) Man may not have arisen from an Anthropoid Ape stem at all, his ancestors may have branched off from the Primate phylum before Anthropomorphs and Cynomorphs alike had started on the development of the pithecoid evolutionary trend. By this supposition we can explain the primitive features retained by Man and modified in part or in whole by Anthropoids and Cynomorphs. But we are still left

with a residue of likenesses that exist between Man and the Anthropoids, and which are not shared so fully by the Old World Monkeys. It is here that those who hold altogether different views naturally raise a perfectly legitimate objection to this supposition, for to account for these likenesses we must invoke the action of convergence, and this has previously been rejected as accounting for the development of identical specializations in the Anthropoids and the Cynomorphs. But in our previous rejection we were rejecting wholesale parallelism in uncorrelated and non-adaptive features; in the case of the special likenesses between Man and the Anthropoids we are invoking only a limited homeomorphy of purely adaptive features such as are common to animals that, being once arboreal, have become more or less terrestrial; that are more or less upright in posture, and more or less bulky in their general build.

There is one feature of human and Anthropoid anatomy that probably every anatomist will at first sight regard as being beyond the attainment of even the most perfect homoeomorphy. Dr Gregory has said: "Opponents of the Darwinian view should never refer to the comparison of the brains of Apes and Man, for there is no division of Morphology that so fully testifies to the relatively close kinship of Man to the Gorilla and the Chimpanzee, as the field of comparative neurology" ("The Origin of Man from the Anthropoid Stem—When and Where?" *American Phil. Soc.*

Proc., 1927, p. 461). And Professor Elliot-Smith has declared that those who dissent from the orthodox views "have perforce been driven to repress all reference to the Brain." Despite these warnings I think it is quite legitimate to point out that the undoubted parallel development of the Platyrrhine and Catarrhine brains is a phenomenon far more wonderful than any cerebral parallelism manifested within the Catarrhines themselves.

Taking all the facts of the comparative anatomy of Man and the Apes and Monkeys as we know them, the supposition that Man's remote ancestors had origin from the Primate stem before the pithecoid specializations were stereotyped in its members appears the most reasonable. Ten years ago (*The Origin of Man: Animal Life and Human Progress,* p. 126) the evidence appeared to me to justify the conclusion that "the line of Homo springs from the base of the (nonlemurine) Primate stem and not from from its systematic apex." That Man did not arise from the Anthropoid Apes is also the opinion of Henry Fairfield Osborn, who has declared (*Evolution and Religion in Education,* 1926, p. 136) that the Anthropoids "constitute a separate branch of the great division of the primates, not only inferior to the Hominidae, but totally disconnected from the human family from its earliest infancy," and the pronouncements of Hubrecht, Boule, Oetteking, Haacke, and others, have been very similar.

There are one or two further considerations of this same finding that are worth discussion, even though we are now altogether on the ground of hypothesis. It is well-known to all human anatomists that there are in Man variations which occasionally take the form of the pithecoid specializations that are normal in the Anthropoid Apes. The temporo-frontal pterion occurs in Man; the fronto-maxillary articulation has been recorded in the human orbit; the initiation of the frontal meeting behind the ethmoid in the anterior fossa has been described. In the case of every other pithecoid feature the occasional human occurrence has been noted, with maybe the exception of any simian manifestation in the external genitalia of the male or in the structure of the kidney.

It is also notorious that in the details of their anatomy the Anthropoid Apes are remarkably variable,

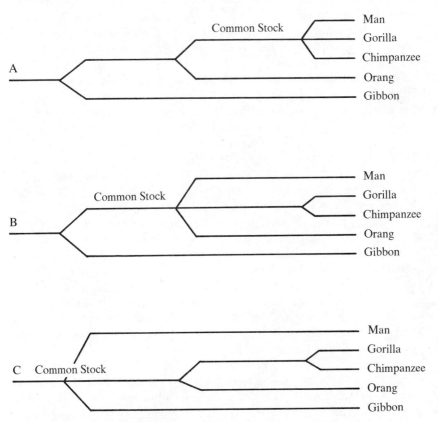

Fig. 1. Diagram to illustrate the common-stock theory of Man and the Anthropoid Apes, and the stage at which the common stock has been postulated by various authorities.

and that the human type of structure at times develops abnormally in certain members of the Anthropomorpha. These facts would seem to show that the separation of the human stock from the remainder of the Primate phylum occurred during a period of phylogenetic plasticity; that the pithecoid trend of evolution was being determined in a stock that was phylogenetically rioting. From the Primate stock in which the pithecoid trend has only recently set in the Asiatic Anthropoids took origin. Despite the opinions of most modern morphologists, and in the face of the trenchant criticisms of Dr. W. K. Gregory, I see no alternative to the supposition that of the Giant Apes it was the Orang stock that differentiated next in succession to the human stock, and, therefore, inherited less of the pithecoid specialization, and retained a greater primitiveness in regard to these characters. It is significant both Dr. Gregory and Sir Arthur Keith agree in assuming that "the Orang was the first to break off from the basal stem of the Giant Primates." This assumption involves for them the belief that therein the Orang is furthest removed from Man; but for us the interpretation would be that as the human stock had already separated, and the Orang was the first member of the Giant Ape stem to take this step, it was therein more closely connected with Man. If the upper molar tooth representing *Paleosimia* is correctly interpreted by palaeontologists, we may assume that the ancestral Orangs were already developed in the Upper Mio-

cene, and the evidence afforded by *Sivapithecus* appears to guarantee this. In Mid-Pliocene members of the existing genus were apparently living in India. As for the Gibbons, they are in some ways almost as much entitled to be termed "living fossils" as are the Tarsiers. The story of *Dryphopithecus, Prophylobates, Pliopithecus* and *Propliopithecus* is generally agreed to carry the palaeontological story of the Gibbons from Pliocene to Lower Oligocene. As Elliot-Smith has said: "In the remote Oligocene, a Catarrhine Ape, nearly akin to the ancestors of the Sacred Monkey, became definitely specialized in structure in adaptation for the assumption of the erect attitude. This type of early Anthropoid has persisted with relatively slight modifications in the Gibbon of the present day" (*Essays on the Evolution of Man,* 1929, p. 37).

The fate of these two tailless brachiators we know well. It has been that of other tailless brachiators, and the Gibbon and the Orang have become no more than persistent types, absorbed by the phylogenetic trend of arm-suspension from the branches of trees. Their affinities are doubtless with the tailed Asiatic Langurs; but during their whole long history of hand-swinging in the jungle they have adopted modifications of their own, so that the Orang especially has become, as Duckworth has well said: "The visible expression of Nature's scorn for those morphologists who ignore physiological considerations."

As for the tailless Chimpanzee and Gorilla, they bear indelibly the marks of having journeyed far with the Guenons, the Macaques, and the Baboons. They are less specialized than the Asiatic Apes as brachiators; and, despite the abundant statements to the contrary, the Chimpanzee is a quadruped habitually, and the Gorilla a biped only very rarely, when descent is made from the trees. The Gorilla is here regarded as the Giant Ape which, showing the maximum of adaptive convergences with human structure, is in its essential features the furthest removed from Man; and this same circumstance would seem in reality to be expressed in the phylogenetic trees of all authorities who depict the Gorilla as a late derivative of the Primate phylum. The ancestors of the Gorilla-Chimpanzee group are by all palaeontologists assumed to be represented in the *Dryopithecus-Paleopithecus* assemblage of the Lower Pliocene.

So much for what the normal anatomy and a certain series of variations in Man and the Great Apes appear to demonstrate. There is another series of human variations that must be considered, and another side to normal human anatomy. It has struck many anatomists that Man is in many ways a very remarkable Mammal. We have got very accustomed to him, we dissect him year in and year out, and we know his structure better than that of any other Mammal, with the possible exception of the white rat and such other creatures that find their apparent utility summed up in the designation "laboratory animals."

The variations of human structure do not only manifest themselves in the display of simian characters, and many distinctive details of normal human anatomy find no parallels in any of the Monkeys and Apes. All anatomists who have devoted attention to human and simian anatomy have remarked upon this general fact, and Schroeder Van der Kolk and Vrolik were among the first who drew attention to the complications that would ensue in the construction of phylogenies if these other—non-simian—characters and variations of Man were given due weight. St George Mivart, in *Man and Apes*, discussed this aspect of the problem with great ingenuity, and the perplexities into which he saw the tracing of these features would inevitably lead are just as real to-day as they were in 1873: "It must be borne in mind that Man is only one of many peculiar forms. The body of the Orang is as exceptional in its way as is that of Man in another. The little Tarsier has even a more exceptional structure than has Man himself. Now, all these exceptional forms show cross relations and complex dependencies as involved and puzzling as does the human structure, so that in each several case we should meet with a similar network of difficulties...." Mivart, in this brief statement, has displayed his usual zoological insight in selecting Man, the Orang and the Tarsier, as being animals, the explanation of whose structure was enmeshed in a network of difficulties if we accept the orthodox phylogenies of the Primates.

One of the most remarkable

analyses of Primate structure and affinities is that to which we have already alluded as being produced by Sir Arthur Keith. In this analysis Keith assesses Man's anatomical characters to be shared among the Primates as follows:

With the Gorilla Man shares 87 characters.
With the Chimpanzee Man shares 98 characters.
With the Orang Man shares 56 characters.
With the Old World Monkey Man shares 53 characters.
With the New World Monkey Man shares 60 characters.

Allowing for all the imperfections of Tyson's method and the eccentricities to which its application in the Primates has led, this must be considered as a remarkable finding. If we accept this evidence, we are faced with the fact that Man has more characters of "morphological worth" in common with the New World Monkeys than he has with either the Old World Monkeys or the Orang. Since by common consent a tarsioid form is the only possible common ancestor of Man and the New World Monkeys, this result must be considered very significant, especially when we take into account Keith's figures for the Anthropoids in regard to their affinities with the Old and New World Monkeys. Man is shown to have 53 characters in common with the Old World Monkeys; but the Gorilla has 144, the Chimpanzee 172, the Orang 213, and the Gibbon 323. But with regard to the New World Monkeys, although

Man shares with them 60 characters, the Gorilla shares only 33, the Chimpanzee 32, the Orang 38, and the Gibbon 76. Obviously, even by Tyson's very imperfect method, Man is revealed in his normal anatomy as a very generalized member of the Primates. In his variations he is even more perplexing. The entepicondylar foramen is present in the Tarsiers and in the New World Monkeys; it is always absent in the Old World Monkeys and Anthropoid Apes, but it occurs as an anomaly in Man.

In discussing such human variations as the development of the entepicondylar foramen, the paramastoid process, and the third trochanter, Thomas Dwight remarked that if we could go back to the Insectivora "it would help a little." The occasional double-rooted canine tooth, the normal presence of the M. pyramidalis, and the M. palmaris brevis, and the common persistence of the metopic suture are other features that display the innate primitive characters either normal, or occurring as variations, in the anatomical structures of Man.

Of the earliest stages of the human radiation we have no palaeontological evidences. We know that Man was existing in his present generic form in the late Pliocene, but his earlier ancestors are unknown. The tarsioid type was in its heyday in the Eocene period, having originated probably during Cretaceous times. A handful of fragments represents its fossil forms in the Eocene of Europe and America, and its history is a blank until we encounter it living in Borneo to-day. A primitive Anthropomorph of the Gibbon type was flourishing in the Oligocene in Africa, having probably arisen from a tarsioid in the Eocene; a few jaws and teeth and a femur represent its progress through the Miocene and into the Pliocene, and we know it again living in South-Eastern Asia. The earliest ancestors of the human line arose also from a tarsioid form—not from any of the definitely pithecoid derivations committed to their own phylogenetic trend. Where it arose and when it arose we do not know. We meet it again when it has already become definitely upright, and with a femur in every way like that of modern Man in the late Pliocene or early Pleistocene of Java, along with the Gibbons and Tarsiers, and next door to the island homes of the Orang. We meet it also in Europe and in the same geological period, and in this case it is already generically *Homo,* even if it is not specifically *sapiens.* We meet it again to-day, spread all over the world, dominant, and having culminated in "the most dangerous and malignant product of creation—the White Man."

.   .   .

It is the criterion of comparative anatomy that we have employed in arriving at our conclusions concerning the relationship of Man to the remaining members of the Primates; but there are other criteria by which this kinship may be measured. Many cognate sciences are interested in the question. Pathologists, physiologists and psychologists have all looked for likenesses between Man and the Anthropoid Apes in their especial fields of inquiry and, naturally, they have found them. It has always been apparent that in a totality of structure these exists the maximum of likenesses between the Anthropoid Apes and Man; no follower of the great John Hunter would ever think of doubting that there were likewise the closest resemblances in function. It is, therefore, necessary that, in accepting the conclusions derived from pathology, physiology or psychology, we should separate conclusions involving a belief in the origin of Man from the Anthropoids from those that merely imply the existence of similarities in structure and function between living Man and living Anthropoids. This process is not always carried out by those instituting these inquiries. Possibly the psychologist, the physiologist and the pathologist are, by their training, less alert to detect the phenomena of convergence than is the comparative anatomist, though, as a fact, the subjects which they have made their own are replete with the most instructive examples of its working.

The zoologist, having consideration for their small numbers and restricted habitat, cannot refrain from deploring the increasing sacrifice of the Great Apes as laboratory animals, and he cannot avoid the suspicion that, in some instances, the investigator makes use of these animals under the belief that they represent Man in the making. It is possible that erroneous deductions may be drawn from investigations carried out on Anthropoids under this misapprehension. If in testing the reactions, mental processes and social behaviors of the Anthropoids the observer is fully aware that he is making test of phylogenetically senile animals, specialized altogether away from human characteristics, all is well with his conclusions, but they can never be of a very far-reaching nature. But if he is under the impression that he is investigating an incipient human stage—a stage through which Man has passed, and which may, therefore, be expected to throw light upon the development of human characteristics, he is likely to be led, and to lead, astray. The findings derived from a specialized and senile end-product of a phylogenetic line must not be accepted as being equivalent to those derived from a primitive and plastic early member of a related stock. The study of morphology is only beginning to free itself from the trammels of such methods of investigation; it is not well that cognate and younger sciences should set out upon the enterprise.

Probably it is concerning the serological reactions of the blood of Man and that of Chimpanzees and Orangs that the findings of science have made most emotional appeal to those who advocate an origin of Man from the Anthropoid Apes. There is a wealth of semi-popular and frankly popular work, purporting to translate orthodox science to the man in the street, that makes much of these serological tests, probably because of the easy transition from the finding of a serological

similarity to the claiming of a blood relationship. The apparent finality of the argument is merely verbal, and it lies wholly within the accepted connotation of the term blood relationship. It is simply because the term "blood relation," in its ordinary hackneyed usage, connotes great intimacy in kinship that the similar serological reactions of Human and Anthropoid Ape blood have so seized upon popular imagination, and one cannot help thinking that this same reason has influenced scientific judgment. We meet with but little surprise when we proclaim the flexor sublimis digitorum muscle of Man to be most nearly matched by that of the Chimpanzee; there is occasion for no more, but rather less, when it is determined that the proteins of the human blood plasma or of the human red blood corpuscles are most nearly akin to those of the Great Apes. The finding that would be surprising is, not that Human and Anthropoid Ape blood sera should exhibit similarities, but that an evolutionary sequence in likeness should be shown in progress from Cynomorpha to Anthropomorpha and to Man. This is exactly the condition that is not demonstrated, but which is definitely contradicted, by serological reactions.

Sir Arthur Keith in a recent publication (*Darwinism and What It Implies,* 1928, p. 49) has said: "Two years ago, Drs. Lansteiner and Miller, of the Rockefeller Institute for Medical Research, carried out a prolonged inquiry into the reactions of human blood by more delicate methods than had been used before.

They wished to verify observations made by previous inquirers, who had declared that the only blood which gave reactions closely similar to that of Man was that of the Great Anthropoid Apes. In summing up the results of their inquiry they state: 'In our studies only the blood of the Anthropoid Apes gave such reactions —a fact attesting to the close relationship with Man.'" This is, of course, perfectly correct. Lansteiner and Miller found, as Professor Nuttall had done a quarter of a century ago, that the serological reactions of human blood were most similar to those given by the blood of the Anthropoid Apes; but it was by no means the most important of their findings. Far more relevant, and in perfect harmony with the deductions from comparative anatomy, is the statement in their summary of results ("Serological Studies on the Blood of the Primates," *Jour. Exper. Medicine,* 1925, Vol. XLII, No. 6, p. 852): "The serological differences between Man and the lower Monkeys appear to be no greater than those between the Anthropoid Apes and the lower Monkeys. These findings confirm the opinion that the Anthropoid Apes do not rank in the genealogical tree between lower Monkeys and Man."

Far from showing that Man has taken origin from the Great Ape group, the serological reactions of his blood demonstrate, as Landsteiner and Miller express it, "that the Catarrhini, Anthropoids and Man have all sprung from a common stock."

It must be by the criteria of comparative anatomy, and by such help as the palaeontological record is capable of providing, that we derive any more precise information concerning this common stock from which the more immediate ancestors of Man and of the Anthropoids diverged. The bulk of the evidence to be derived from comparative anatomy justifies the belief that the proto-human stock separated from the stem of the other members of the Primates before the definite pithecoid specializations had become stereotyped in the Cynomorpha, and, to a lesser degree, in the Anthropomorpha. We are justified in assuming that the proto-human stock arose from a tarsioid form that had not developed the specializations seen in the living Tarsiers; but which possessed all those primitive haplorhine characters which underlie the specializations attained by the modern *Tarsius spectrum.* We are further justified in assuming that there had been a development from this primitive tarsioid stage in the general direction of a primitive Gibbon—a Gibbon that had not achieved any definite pithecoid specializations. The study of the architecture of the skull, and of the foot, would seem to indicate that this stage might tentatively be placed at about the level at which *Propliopithcus* became differentiated on the line of the Anthropoid Apes. We have no palaeontological evidence to guide us here, but the hypothesis which best expresses the facts known at present is that the proto-human stock, the Anthropomorpha stock, and the Cynomorpha stock, are diverging stems which radiated in the Lower Oligocene from a still more primitive tarsioid group.

We have pictured the members of the proto-human stock to be forms which had progressed from a primitive tarsioid stage in the general direction of a primitive Gibbon. From such an hypothesis we could postulate many of the characters that typified the human common stock; but fortunately we need not adopt any method of pure speculation, for we have considerable assurance as to what must have been the condition of much of the bodily make-up of these early forms. It is quite possible to reconstruct some portions of the picture, and the evidence for such a reconstruction is readily available for anyone to examine and weigh, and thus to correct the outline or alter the details as their judgment prompts.

We may have some confidence in assuming that the members of the proto-human stock were distinguished by the following characters:

(1) *They were small animals.*

Such a deduction might be drawn from the fact that, so far as the palaeontological record can inform us, all Primates were small at the period of the separation of the proto-human stock. But there is better evidence than this. As Dr. Dudley Morton has conclusively demonstrated ("Evolution of the Human Foot," *Amer. Jour. Phys, Anthropology,* 1924, Vol. VIII, No. 1, pp. 1–52), the length of the mid-portion of the human tarsus definitely shows that the human stock must have been small and light when it

took to supporting its weight upon its feet. Briefly, in large heavy animals that take to supporting their weight on their feet the mid-portion of the tarsus becomes markedly shortened; in Man it is primitively long. "The mid-tarsal pattern of the Gibbon resembles that of the Monkeys; in the Great Apes it is decidedly shortened, while Man appears with the more primitive pattern...apparently Man could have avoided this shortening only by having separated from the Great Ape stock before it had occurred."

We seem, therefore, to be justified in postulating that the proto-human stock, at the time of its separation, was certainly not larger than the Gibbon, and probably considerably smaller. There is another point, which again has been rightly emphasized by Dr Morton. In all the smaller members of the Primates the head of the third metatarsal is primitively in advance of that of the second: in the larger and heavier forms the head of the second is in advance of that of the third, and this is a derived, specialized condition. As such it is present in the larger, heavier members of both New World and Old World phyla. It is present in the Spider Monkeys (*Ateleus*) and the Woolly Monkeys (*Lagothrix*), and in the Gibbon, and all the Great Apes. It is present also in Man; but in a degree less than that present in the Gibbon. We may, therefore, feel assured that the members of the early proto-human stock were small in body and light in form. From the structure of the foot, and of the leg, we may also be confident of another physical characteristic.

(2) *They were active, agile animals.*

There is no suggestion in human anatomy of descent from the sluggish hand-grasping climbers; and all the anatomical features of foot and leg proclaim human origin from a form with active springy movements of all the segments of the lower limb.

(3) *Their legs were longer than their arms.*

We have discussed this question already, and here it is only necessary to say that in the proto-human stock the leg length probably did not exceed the arm length to anything like the extent that it does in modern Man. It is highly probable that the arm was only a little shorter than the leg—that equality of members was early established in the *Propliopithecus* stock, and that the fatal lengthening of the arm was a gradual development in the Gibbon–Great Ape phylum.

(4) *They were already erect: their movement along the branches was bipedal, and anatomically they were prepared for terrestrial bipedal life.*

Here, again, we may invoke the characters of the foot...with the additional evidence deduced by Dr. Morton from the presence of the primitive mid-tarsal elongation in Man. As Dr. Morton argues, the proto-human must have adapted its foot to the support of its weight whilst it was still small and light; and it must have adapted it in such a way that when the bulk and weight increased it did not suffer mid-tarsal

shortening such as has been effected in all the Great Apes. "This could only have been accomplished by the use of the heel for the transmission of a large portion of the body weight, which in turn would have been possible only with an associated use of the erect posture, whereby the centre of gravity of the body was located at a point perpendicularly between the heads of the metatarsals and the heel." The erectness that had been attained, and that had stereotyped the characters of the tarsus, was an erectness that consisted in maintaining the body erect on the feet with the weight borne largely upon the heels. It was not the erectness determined by brachiating, which later distinguished the perfected Gibbons.

In addition to these features of body size and carriage we may feel confident of some more detailed characters of the head and face.

(5) *They possessed crania that were already enlarged.*

This much may safely be inferred from the fact that, whilst the whole Primate phylum was distinguished by its cranial enlargement we have seen that there is every reason to believe that the proto-human stock was far in advance of the other Primates in this development. The cranial enlargement in our phylum must have set in at a very early stage, since the whole key-note of the large human skull lies in its being an enlarged primitive, and not an enlarged modified, cranium. It is not necessary to point out that the early enlargement of the cranium was merely a consequence of the early enlargement of the brain, and must be considered in association with the erectness of the body and the emancipation of the hand.

(6) *The jaws were small and there was no specialized enlargement, or sexual differentiation of the teeth.*

We have some grounds for inferring so much from the early ontogenetic reduction of the human premaxillae, a fact in human ontogeny that cannot be explained away by any known process of alteration of the ontogenetic sequence. We have further grounds in analogy with the jaws of the known tarsioids, and even with those of the basal forms of the Cynomorpha and Anthropomorpha as displayed in *Parapithecus* and *Propliothecus* respectively.

It is obvious that the proto-human stock had not developed those overwhelming specializations which led to the Tarsiers becoming unprogressive, persistent types. Among the Tarsier specializations that they almost certainly avoided was that of the enormous enlargement of the eyes.

(7) *They possessed only moderately large eyes and orbits, and were, therefore, probably mainly diurnal in habit.*

Concerning this postulate we may feel some assurance when we consider the human retention of the primitively large cartilaginous ethmoid element in the anterior fossa of the skull. When the orbits enlarge greatly in nocturnal and crepuscular forms there is of necessity a tendency for the enlarged orbits to encroach upon the interorbital space. In this way there is produced a narrow interorbital septum, or bridge of the nose, which is so well marked in all large-eyed nocturnal Primates, and which is inherited in all recent forms no matter if their present activities are nocturnal or diurnal. The narrowing of the interorbital septum leads to the reduction of the ethmoid, and to the encroachment of the frontals, and, as we have seen, both these modifications are avoided in the human skull. We have, therefore, every reason to believe that the orbits of the proto-human stock were never greatly enlarged as a part of that correlated growth seen in nocturnal animals. Again, it is of interest to note that, as Winge observed, the Gibbons show a minimum of ethmoid reduction.

With but little sanction from actual palaeontological record, but in conformity with the known facts of anatomical correlation, we may, therefore, postulate that the proto-human stock was represented by small animals that led active arboreal lives, and were probably mainly diurnal in habit. We may further assume that they possessed hind limbs somewhat longer than their fore limbs; that they were erect and bipedal in poise and progression; that the brain and braincase were enlarged, that the jaws and teeth were relatively small, and that the orbits were only moderately enlarged, and were separated by a comparatively wide interorbital space. It is possible that the mandible representing the Oligocene *Propliopithecus* in reality belongs to such a form, and that it may, therefore, be regarded as a relic of the proto-human stock; but in the absence of further evidence regarding this Anthropomorphous Primate it appears most probable that it had already become determined along the phylum of the Gibbons. When we come to *Pliopithecus* of the Miocene there can be but little doubt that we are dealing with a real Gibbon, and not with a proto-human form. By Hoffman *Pliopithecus* was actually placed in the modern genus *Hylobates* along with the living Gibbons, and by all palaeontologists its affinities to the typical Gibbons are considered to be of the closest. Now it is often considered a weakness of any hypothesis which postulates that the human stock did not arise directly from the Anthropoid Apes, that in discarding the known fossil remains of Anthropoid Apes as possible human ancestors, there is revealed an extraordinary blank in the palaeontological record of Man. It is perfectly true that, with the possible exception of *Propliopithecus,* we postulate the absence of any known fossil forms in the human record between the tarsioids of the Eocene and the definitely human remains of the Pleistocene. But this is by no means a singular happening. Of *Tarsius* itself we have no record whatever between the European and American fossils of the Eocene period and the living animal of the Bornean jungle. Of the whole phylum of the New World Primates there is only a single fossil specimen intervening between the Eocene tarsioids, and the numerous existing genera. The palaeontological record of Man is, therefore, in rather better

case than that of the Tarsiers or the Platyrrhines; and, as we have seen, the fossil remains of the Primates as a group are, in common with those of other jungle-haunting creatures, but poorly represented. In the absence of any fossil record, we have to be content with the general knowledge that the small proto-human, having already reaped the enormous advantages of an arboreal life, must have made an early descent into terrestrial activities. It was the obvious merit of the proto-human stock that it never over-specialized in arboreal activities: it took full advantage of all the possibilities of arboreal opportunity, but avoided the pitfall, into which the phylum of the Anthropomorpha fell, of becoming an increasingly specialized arboreal creature. It never became dependent upon a brachiating life among the branches, such as effectively prohibits any possibility of true orthograde bipedal progress when descent is made from the trees.

Why the proto-human stock so early deserted the tree-tops we naturally do not know. It might have been that some environmental change robbed them of the trees—or it might have been that terrestrial enterprises were deliberately entered upon by a phylum fitted to derive advantage from the experiment. What determined the descent we do not know. We do know, however, that an early bipedal uprightness, as evidenced in the conservation of the form of the tarsus, is coupled with an absence of any evidence of extreme arboreal specialization, and there is every reason to believe that, while the pithecoid stock was developing its pithecoid and brachiating trends, the humanoid stock was already a ground-dwelling form. As Boule, Klaatsch, Hubrecht, and other anatomists have conceived it, we may picture it as a creature whose general features might be summed up by terming it a small ground Ape. In the Anthropomorph phylum we know that increase in body size took place during its heyday in the Miocene; we should not be doing violence to palaeontological principles if we postulate that somewhere about the same time a similar increase of size marked the members of the humanoid phylum. We know that *Pithecanthropus* possessed, probably by the end of the Pliocene, a femur which would pass muster among the femora of modern Men; and that in the Heidelberg Man during Mid-Pleistocene the lower jaw and the teeth were already in a form that is essentially human.

It is not proposed to discuss here the remains of early forms of Man; all these have been so adequately dealt with, particularly by Sir Arthur Keith in his *Antiquity of Man.* If we have regard to the phylum of the Anthropoid Apes we may assume, with a high degree of inherent probability, that the human stock underwent what may be termed a period of partial riot, corresponding to the Siwalik period of the Anthropoid Ape phylum, or the Ampasambazimba period of the Lemurs. We know that many forms branched off from the Anthropoid Ape stem and from the Lemur stem;

almost certainly many branched off from the human stem. Of these forms some doubtless ran their phylogenetic course and became extinct; and, therefore, it is by no means essential to consider that every known type of Early Man represents a stage in the evolution of Man as we know him to-day. Were it not that the question of what constitutes a species is fortunately meaningless to-day, we might debate the old problem as to the specific distinctions of the main existing divisions of humanity. Certainly the highly specialized Negro must be regarded as a very distinct side branch of the main stem—if the main stem is egotistically regarded as that leading to the White Man. But these things do not concern us here, and they have a wealth of literature of their own.

In the story of the origin of the proto-human stock, and the subsequent emergence of Man, there is but little legitimate room for most of the fancy portraits with which pseudo-science has been so ready to arrest uninstructed attention. We have all grown used to the picture of the slouching brute, with shaggy hair and elongated arms, that is lumbering into a stage of partial uprightness as it toils along the pathway of the origin of Man. One of the most recent and most sumptuous publications upon the comparative cerebral anatomy of the Primates has shown this progress in a graphic form that renders the ascent the more vivid since it depicts it as taking place up the laborious slopes of a hillside. Here the slouching hairy beast toils lumberingly up- wards, seizing sticks and stones as weapons by the way, and passing from stark hirsute nakedness to the comparative modesty of a skin apron, and ultimately to the decent obscurity of a cave. Were it well attested that Man was derived from the stock of the large brachiating Anthropoid Apes, especially were there any justification for the greatly laboured "Gorilloid heritage" (W. K. Gregory, 1921, p. 98) in Man, these pictures might claim sanction, as do those of the ancestral horses, from the findings of comparative anatomy and palaeontology; but this sanction is wholly lacking. There is no justification for the picture of the slouching, semi-erect, Ape Man, though every investigator who, being imperfectly instructed in human anatomy, attempts an interpreta- tion of the remains of some ancient human skeleton, seeks first to deter- mine evidences of the presence of this character. Probably no more sombre practical joke has ever been played upon a human skeleton than that by which Mr. W. P. Pycraft (*British Museum Report on Rhode- sian Man and Associated Remains,* 1928; and *Man,* December 1928), for want of a little elementary knowledge of the normal anatomy of the human os innominatum, has lately condemned a perfectly upright representative of the genus *Homo* to masquarade as the type of a new genus *Cyanthropus*—since it "walked with a stoop, with the knees turned outwards." The study of this latest claim for the shuffling bentkneed stage of Early Man confirms the opinion, begot by previous ex- periences, that the interpretation of the skeletal remains of Early Man is far better left to the professed human anatomist.

In the case of the Rhodesian Man there is a sufficiency of material by which to arrive at a definite diagnosis as to the actual characters of the type. It is only lack of knowl- edge of human anatomy which per- mits the distortion occasioned by the "reconstruction" of missing parts. When the available material is con- siderably less than in this instance, no amount of anatomical knowledge may justify wide-reaching claims concerning the total anatomy of the animal. There is no justification whatever for the business of con- fidently undertaking the reconstruc- tion of the complete physical features of early types of man from a hand- ful of cranial fragments or even from a peccary's tooth. If physical anthropology is to claim rank as a subject to which the methods of science are applied, we must resist the temptation of making these ter- rible reconstructions either in the impressive solidity of plaster or as fancy illustrations to books dealing with the question of human phy- logeny.

The ordinarily intelligent, but technically uninstructed person who reads books on human origins, or who visits the galleries of museums, does not realize how preposterous are the claims of so-called science in putting forward these "reconstruc- tions." Every physical anthropologist who has tried his hand at the business will agree that to reconstruct the most essential soft parts on a skull, all of whose facial parts are perfectly preserved, is an impossibility when exactness is a criterion of achievement. Even when confronted with an entire skull, and with a series of portraits of a known individual, there must always be an element of uncertainty concerning the positive identification of the skull as being that of the individual. Were this not so the problems that have centred round the supposed crania of Schiller, Raphael, and other well-known men—the latest being Lord Darnley—would have been of easy solution. (See H. von Eggeling, *Physiognomie und Schadel,* 1911).

It was my lot for seven years to share my room with the skeleton of Professor Collimore. As I worked at my desk his skull looked directly towards me, and at the end of the seven years I fancied that I knew very well what manner of face he had, and how his features were formed. It was only then that I managed to obtain a photograph of the living man, and it was at once apparent that the face was utterly different from the one I had reconstructed. This case has been fully dealt with by Lander ("The Examination of a Skeleton of Known Age, Race, and Sex," *Jour. Anat. and Phys.,* 1918, Vol. LII, pp. 282–91), and it is one that should be studied by anyone who would venture to model a face to a cranial fragment of unknown age, race and sex. Lander says: "It seems improbable that anyone examining the skull would postulate a type of face similar to that seen in the photo-

graph," and I venture to supplement this by adding that no living anatomist, nor one that has ever lived, could have achieved this.

Of *Pithecanthropus* there is a skull-cap—there is no hint of any portion of the facial skeleton. This skull-cap has, of course, been used as the basis for a "reconstruction" of every feature of the Java Man. Of this reconstruction Dr W. K. Gregory says ("The Evolution of the Human Face," *Amer. Mus. Jour.,* 1917, pp. 377–388) that it "shows a very wide nose, with the nostrils facing partly forward and partly downward, and with a deep depression above the nose between the eyes; it also has a very thin upper lip and a partly everted lower lip; so that this mingling of human and Apelike characters fully carries out the 'missing-link' idea which is so unmistakably indicated in the excessively low forehead and high brow ridges of this celebrated relic of a prehuman stage." That one should model Ape-like features on a skull-cap which has no skeletal basis for the reconstruction of any facial characters whatever, is to presuppose the possession of a knowledge of correlation which does not exist. Having carried out this purely imaginative work it cannot be claimed as a logical or scientific form of procedure that then urges this fanciful thing, with "a very thin upper lip and a partly everted lower lip" in proof of the preconceived notions concerning the creature that owned the skull-cap.

More than a century ago, the assertions concerning the localization of functions in the cortex of the brain had far outrun any scientific knowledge on the subject. Nevertheless, these assertions had considerable attractions for the general run of educated people who were ignorant of the actual facts of neurology. The false doctrine of cortical localization became fashionable, and many scientific men, not specially conversant with the current knowledge concerning the human brain, eagerly embraced the creed, and gave it out to the general public with the added guarantee of its orthodox scientific nature.

No one who reads the story of the tardy establishment of the modern doctrine of cortical localization can doubt that the extraordinary vogue of the belief in "bumps" materially delayed the progress of true scientific knowledge. One of the unfortunate incidents of the rise and spread of this false doctrine was the very successful attempt to give definition and permanence to the teaching by means of plaster casts to which an extremely deceptive air of scientific accuracy was imparted. In the delay of progress in the discovery and acceptance of the true facts of cortical localization Morgan's Model Busts must take a large share of blame (see *The Skull and Brain: Their Indications of Character and Anatomical Relations,* by Nicholas Morgan, 1875). Morgan's Model Busts were commonly employed in argument in the same manner as are the so-called "reconstructions" of human ancestors. It is to be hoped that the fate of both will be the same, for Morgan's Model Busts passed by a slow transition from the galleries of our museums to the windows of provincial chemists' shops, and so to oblivion. Science gained much in this transition, it would gain still more from a more rapid one in the case of all the "reconstructions" of early human fragments which later human beings have had the ingenuity and the hardihood to produce.

On Australopithecus and Its Affinities

Robert Broom
1937

In 1924 an interesting Primate fossil skull was discovered in a limestone cave at Taungs in Bechuanaland. This was brought to Professor R. A. Dart of the Witwatersrand University, Johannesburg, who at once recognized that it belonged to an interesting new type of anthropoid. With great skill and care he removed all the matrix from the face and teeth, and he found that the face was preserved in almost perfect condition; and the greater part of the brain case was also found to be in a satisfactory state.

Dart briefly described the find under the name *Australopithecus africanus* in "Nature" and he considered it to represent a new type of anthropoid which in a number of respects came closer to man than to the chimpanzee or gorilla, and he suggested that it was probably near to the ape from which man had been descended. Scientists in England were at first inclined to think that Dart claimed too much for his ape and that it was probably only a variety of chimpanzee.

A few weeks after Dart's description had appeared I examined the type, and in the main confirmed Dart's conclusions. I also made a drawing representing the probable appearance of a median section. This I sent to Professor W. J. Sollas of Oxford, and he wrote a short paper on it, also in the main supporting Dart's opinion. Unfortunately the skull is that of a young animal with the milk teeth functional and the first upper and lower molars just coming into use, and thus probably an animal of five years of age; and many held that some at least of the human-like characters are due to the infantile condition, and that an adult would prove to be much more chimpanzee-like and less like man.

A little later Dart removed the lower jaw and fully showed the crowns of both the upper and lower teeth. It then became at once manifest that in structure the milk molars closely resemble those of man and differ very greatly from those of any of the living anthropoids. In

From the book *Early Man* edited by George G. MacCurdy. Copyright, 1937, by The Academy of Natural Sciences. Renewal, ©, 1965 by Mrs. Janet MacCurdy. Reprinted by permission of J. B. Lippincott Company.

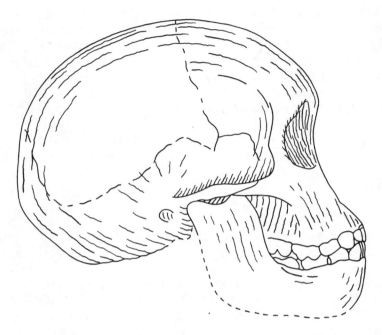

Fig. 1. Side view of skull of *Australopithecus africanus* Dart. One-half natural size.

1928, I wrote a short paper on this milk dentition, and argued that there must be some close affinity between this fossil ape and man, and that it could not be nearly allied to the chimpanzee. Gregory of New York also wrote a paper pointing out that in nearly every character in the dentition *Australopithecus* comes much nearer to man than to the living anthropoids, and Adloff of Königsberg has gone so far as to affirm that it is practically human.

Still there remained a doubt in the minds of many, and it seemed to be advisable, if possible, to secure an adult skull.

In August 1934 I was appointed to a post in the Transvaal Museum. For about two years I was mainly engaged in collecting and describing fossil reptiles, but about the middle of 1936 I thought it would be well to start on the study of the limestone caves of the Transvaal to see if I might find either traces of primitive man or a new specimen of *Australopithecus,* and in any case I was pretty sure to find some new fossil mammals. Mr. G. Von Son of the Transvaal Museum told me that he had seen in a cave at Gladysvale about sixteen miles north of Krugersdorp a jaw that looked like that of man. He had left it in the cave wall hoping to dig it out later, and when he returned he found someone had destroyed it. With Mr. Von Son I visited Gladysvale, and found among some pieces of the bone breccia remains of the horse *Equus capensis,* the fossil pig *Notochoerus meadowsi,* and a new species of *Procavia,* but I could find no trace of man or anthropoid apes.

Mr. Herbert Lang and Dr. A. Roberts told me of another cave at Schurveberg fourteen miles west of Pretoria where there was a good deal of bone breccia lying about near the old lime workings. Here I found much breccia with the jaws and bones of small mammals doubtless brought into a cave by owls. These on examination proved to belong mostly to extinct species of *Cryptomys, Mystromys,* and of a new subgenus allied to *Otomys.* With these rodents there was a new species of elephant shrew which had to be placed in a new genus *Elephantomys,* and a number of specimens of a small shrew which is probably identical with the living *Myosorex tenuis.* There were also the remains of a moderately large cat which I have called *Felis whitei* and parts of a giant baboon which has to be placed in a new genus *Dinopithecus.*

At the beginning of August 1936 two of Professor Dart's students— Mr. H. le Riche and Mr. G. Schepers—came over from Johannesburg to see me. They told me that in a cave at Sterkfontein six miles from Krugersdorp some skulls of a small fossil baboon had been found, and that they had been at

this cave and had also been fortunate in finding some brain casts of this little ape. I immediately arranged to go over to Krugersdorp with them; and at the caves I met Mr. G. Barlow, who is manager of the limeworks there and also caretaker of the caves. A good many years before he had worked at Taungs, and had seen the Taungs ape skull. He told me that many skulls and skeletons of this ape had been thrown into the limekilns, no one apparently taking any interest in the bones, but he added that he fancied a somewhat similar large ape occurred in the caves at Sterkfontein; and curiously enough Mr. Cooper, who owns the caves, in writing a short account of the caves for a little guide book to the places of interest round Johannesburg had written, "Come to Sterkfontein and find the missing-link."

A short examination of one of the caves that has been worked for lime showed portions of small ape skulls in the walls; and I asked Mr. Barlow to keep a sharp lookout for any important bones, and especially for anything that looked like the Taungs ape. I was again at the caves a couple of days later and Mr. Barlow gave me three little fossil baboon skulls and much of the skull of a large carnivore. A hunt in the debris in the cave revealed a good deal more of this large carnivore. On examination it proved to be the skull of a form apparently allied to the sabre tooth tiger *Megantherson,* and I described it as *M. barlowi.* When a better specimen is discovered it may prove not to

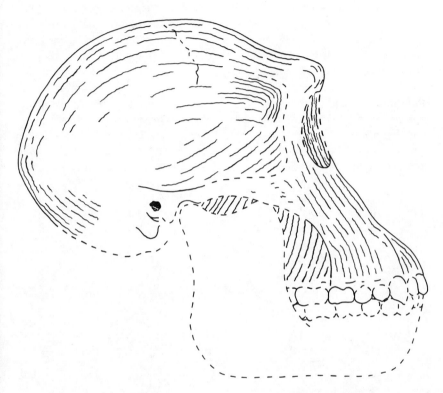

Fig. 2. Side view of skull of *Australopithecus transvaalensis* Broom. One-half natural size.

belong to this genus, but it is certainly a larger felid.

The following week I again visited Sterkfontein when Mr. Barlow presented me with the brain cast of a large anthropoid which had been blasted out a few days previously. I hunted for some hours but could find no other remains among the debris, but I got the cast of the top of the skull in the cave wall. I returned again the following day with Mr. Lang, Mr. Fitz Simons, and Mr. White, and three Kafir boys. A further search resulted in the discovery of the base of the skull, much of the parietals, and part of the occiput. In the matrix that lay on the right side of the brow I discovered, on cleaning it out, the displaced right maxilla with much of the molar and the 2nd premolar and 1st and 2nd molars. The right 3rd molar was also discovered, but quite detached. In the matrix on the left side there was later discovered much of the left maxilla with the beautifully preserved 1st and 2nd premolars and the 1st and 2nd molars. There are also preserved the sockets of the two incisors and of the canine.

It will naturally take months before a full description can be made of the skull, as much careful development must first be done; but something may be said at this stage.

The animal is clearly allied to the Taungs ape, but owing to the one being a child and the other adult, in only a few points can satis-factory comparisons be made. The brain in the Sterkfontein ape has a broader frontal region and is a little smaller than in the Taungs ape. The only teeth that can be compared are the 1st upper molars. They are nearly similar in size but the crown pattern differs in a number of details. As, however, none of the species of mammals associated with the Taungs ape have been found in any of the caves at Sterkfontein, while in at least two cases there are other

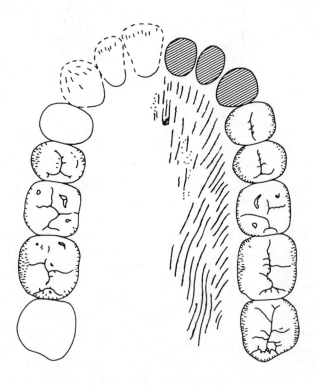

Fig. 3. Upper dentition of *Australopithecus transvaalensis* Broom. Three-fourths natural size. The right incisors and canine have been restored. As the middle line is missing from the back of the palate the palatal width is doubtful.

species of the same or closely allied genera, we may safely assume that the geological ages of the two apes differ considerably and it seems well to place the Sterkfontein ape in a distinct species, and I have called it *Australopithecus transvaalensis*.

There is little doubt that *Australopithecus* must be regarded as an anthropoid ape somewhat allied to the chimpanzee and the gorilla, and only a little larger than the former. In structure the teeth, however, differ very considerably from those of either the chimpanzee or the gorilla, and resemble much more closely those of primitive man— especially those of Mousterian man. They resemble also in a number of characters the teeth of some of the species of dryopithecid apes recently discovered in the Pliocene of the Siwaliks of India.

When we obtain the much fuller evidence that will be afforded by the lower jaw teeth, I think it likely that *Australopithecus* will prove to lie somewhere near the common ancestor of the chimpanzee, the gorilla, and man, and a little higher than the dryopithecoids. Not improbably it will be seen to be a little way along the line that branched off to grow up to man. And there seems no doubt that it is the fossil ape nearest to man's ancestor at present known.

There is one curious fact that may be noted. The teeth of *Australopithecus* resemble more closely in a number of respects those of modern man than do the teeth of the undoubted primitive man *Sinanthropus*. This would seem to indicate that in Pleistocene times there were a considerable number of types of primitive man which had evolved in different ways, and that it was from only one of these types, still unknown, that modern man arose.

Quite possibly before another year is past we will have other skulls and perhaps much of the skeleton of *Australopithecus,* and be able to add much more to our knowledge.

The Relationship of the Fossil People of Mount Carmel to Prehistoric and Modern Types

Theodore Doney McCown and Arthur Keith
1939

Before our readers proceed to study the detailed description of the remains of the fossil people from Mount Carmel which we have given in this work, it will be advantageous for them to know the chief conclusions to which we have come as a result of our prolonged investigation. These conclusions refer (1) to the relationship of one individual to another, and (2) to their relationships to other prehistoric peoples and to the living races of mankind.

In the earlier stages of our investigations we were inclined to believe we had before us the remains of two distinct types or kinds of humanity, the Tabūn and the Skhūl. The Tabūn type, represented by the complete skeleton of a woman (Tabūn I), the mandible of a man (Tabūn II), and some other fossil fragments, comes from the Mugharet et-Tabūn. The Skhūl type is represented by the complete skeletons of two adult males, the complete skeleton of a child, the incomplete skeletons of a male and a female, and

the fragmentary remains of five other individuals. We are persuaded that all the complete and the imperfect skeletons represent deliberate burials. As our investigations proceeded we encountered so many characters which linked the Skhūl to the Tabūn type that we were ultimately obliged to presume that we had before us the remains of a single people, the Skhūl and the Tabūn types being but the extremes of the same series. Yet the range in form, from that represented by Skhūl IV (male) to Tabūn I (female), is unexpectedly great. The Tabūn type possesses many features which link it to the Neanderthal type of Europe while the extreme Skhūl type passes towards a Neanthropic form such as that found at Cromagnon. Between these extremes are intermediate forms. All the members of the group possess certain characters in common, a list of which is given in our final chapter.

The chief consideration which moves us to regard all the specimens

"The Relationship of the Fossil People of Mount Carmel to Prehistoric and Modern Types." *The Stone Age of Mount Carmel. The Fossil Human Remains from the Levalloiso-Mousterian.* Chapter 2, pp. 12–18. The Clarendon Press, Oxford, 1939. Reprinted by permission of the publisher.

from both sites as members of the same species or race are: (1) their dental characters are uniform; we can draw no sharp line between the dentitions of the Tabūn and of the Skhūl people; (2) their cultures are very nearly identical; (3) they lived in the same locality at approximately the same period of time. On strictly anatomical grounds one would presume that the Skhūl was the later type. There is the same difference between the robust mandible of the Tabūn male and that of Skhūl IV or V as there is between the Cromagnon mandible and that of a modern Englishman—almost as great as between the Heidelberg mandible and that of the La Chapelle man. In size of palate the Skhūl men rivalled Neanderthal man, but in the form of their jaws, particularly of the mandible, there is evidence of certain retrograde changes. Miss Dorothea Bate has observed that the fauna represented in the Skhul cave differs in certain details from that recorded for the Tabūn cave.

Relationship to Galilee man

Our knowledge of the Galilean fossil people is based on part of a skull unearthed in 1925 by Mr. Turville Petre during excavations at the Mughāret ez-Zutteiyeh, about thirty-five miles distant from the Wady Mughara. All that was found of the Galilee man (Keith 1927)[1] were three bones of his skull, the

frontal, the right malar, and part of the sphenoid.[2] A close comparison of these parts with the corresponding bones from Mount Carmel has convinced us that the Galilee and the Mount Carmel specimens should be regarded as members of the same group. His place is apparently towards the Tabūn extreme of this group.

The evidence which led us to this conclusion is worth considering by all who are concerned in the classification of extinct races, when only fragmentary fossil remains are available. The Galilean frontal, malar, and sphenoid bones were similar in their chief characters to the same bones of Neanderthal man. There were minor differences—the narrowness of the forehead and the height of the cranial vault. The fossil Galilean was regarded as a member of the species which is represented by Neanderthal man in Europe.

Now our investigations of the Mount Carmel people have shown us that in them it is just the bones found by Mr. Turville Petre, the frontal, malar, and sphenoid, that are most Neanderthaloid in their characterization. In the frontal of the Mount Carmel people we meet with the same narrowness and height as in the Galilee frontal, and we infer that had the rest of his skull and skeleton been found these parts would have possessed a series of characters similar to those of our

[1] See references to literature in the bibliography.

[2] A fuller knowledge of the sex differences in Palaeoanthropic races has led us to ascribe the skull to a man, not to a woman. Hrdlička came to this conclusion in 1930.

Tabūn type. We may presume, provisionally at least, that in mid-Pleistocene times the people of Palestine were of the type or types described in this work.

Variability

We are of the opinion that the variability found amongst the fossil people of Mount Carmel is greater in degree and in kind than is to be observed in any local community of modern times. Had the Mount Carmel people been discovered—not collectively, in one place, but separately, in diverse localities, each excavator would have been convinced that a new and separate form of humanity had been unearthed, so great does one Carmelite individual differ from another.

How are we to explain the structural instability of the Mount Carmel people? Do they represent a people in the throes of an evolutionary transition and therefore unstable and plastic in their genetic constitution? Or is the variability due to hybridity, a mingling of two diverse peoples or races? We shall see that the Mount Carmel people represent a series which can be arranged between a Neanderthal form at one end and a Cromagnon form at the other. Is it possible that Neanderthal and Cromagnon—Palaeoanthropic and Neanthropic—stocks had met on the flanks of Mount Carmel in mid-Pleistocene times and that the fossil bones described here represent the progeny of their union?

We have given the supposition of hybridity our serious consideration and have rejected it. To win support for such a theory we should have to produce the fossil remains of a Neanthropic form of man in Palestine from a level as old, or older, than the Levalloiso-Mousterian of Mount Carmel, as well as the remains of a fully evolved Neanderthal form. We have no such evidence. All who believe in evolution are agreed that Neanderthal man and modern man are descendants of a common human stock. There must have been a time in the history of that ancestral stock when individuals were undergoing differentiation along, at the least, two directions—towards the purely Palaeoanthropic (Neanderthal) type and towards a Neanthropic type represented by the early people of Cromagnon. We regard the tendency of the Mount Carmel people to diverge into two types as being due not to miscegenation but to an evolutionary divergence. We suppose that the Mount Carmel people were in the throes of evolutionary change.

Relationship to other prehistoric types

Readers must not think that we look upon the Mount Carmel people as the actual stock which gave the world its Neanthropic or modern races on the one hand, and its Palaeoanthropic or Neanderthal races on the other. This is not our opinion. We can make our position clear by discussing the place which must be assigned to the Mount

Carmel people among the prehistoric peoples of the Old World. Their relationship to the prehistoric peoples of the East—Sinanthropus and Pithecanthropus—is distant both in space and in time. Between them lies the whole width of Asia. It will be time to discuss how the peoples of the West stand to those of the East when the Pleistocene deposits which lie between Palestine and China have been explored and the cultural history of the intervening peoples has been unravelled. But in the Western world itself we know of at least five groups of prehistoric peoples with whom the Mount Carmel people may claim an evolutionary relationship. These five groups are (1) that found at Krapina in Croatia and so well described by Dr. Karl Gorjanovič-Kramberger (1906); (2) that found near Weimar in Germany and described by Prof. Franz Weidenreich (1928) and by Dr. Hans Virchow (1920).[3] To this group we would add the type described by Dr. H. Weinert (1936) from Steinheim-am-Murr in Württemberg; (3) the western Neanderthal group, found in France and the surrounding countries; the classical monograph on this group is Prof. Marcelin Boule's study of the La Chapelle skeleton (1911);[4] it is probable that this widely spread group was broken up into local types; (4) the Predmost people described by Prof. J. Matiegka (1925, 1929);[5] (5) the Cromagnon people of France

[3] See also Keith 1925, 1931.

[4] See also Boule 1923; Morant 1927, and Hrdlička 1930.

[5] Morant 1930; Keith 1925, 1931.

described by Dr. René Verneau (1906).[6] The Cromagnon and the Predmost groups are Neanthropic in type and are the earliest representatives of the European, white or Caucasian races which have been discovered as yet.

Relationship to the Krapina group

The Mount Carmel people find their nearest affinities among the extinct groups of humanity available for comparison at Krapina. Both peoples—Mount Carmel and Krapina—are assigned to the same geological period, the latter part of the Riss-Würm interglacial epoch. The habitat of the Krapina people is nearer to that of the Palestinians than are the homelands of the other four types. Croatia is 1,400 miles from Palestine as the crow flies. At Krapina no complete skeletons were found, only fragments, but valuable fragments and in great number. There were no people at Krapina of the tall Skhūl type; all are small people, strong in jaw but relatively short and weak in limb. Indeed, in form of limb-bone there is much resemblance between the smaller specimens from Mount Carmel and those of Krapina. Neither at Mount Carmel nor at Krapina were the thick massive femora and tibiae of western Neanderthal man represented. Nor do we find molar teeth of the taurodont type at Mount Carmel, a type so prevalent among the Kra-

[6] See also Morant 1930.

pina people, yet both people possess the same pattern in the crowns of their molar teeth. The crowns of the other teeth, too, are similar if we exclude certain individuals of the Skhūl type. The Krapina people had low-vaulted skulls, whereas the vault in the Mount Carmel people is of medium, even of great, height. The chin was developed to a variable extent in both the Krapina and the Mount Carmel people, but among the former never to the maximum degree shown by some of the Carmel specimens. It is our Tabūn type which makes the nearest approach to that of Krapina. In brief, the Krapina people, although they serve to bridge the gap between the ancient Palestinians and the Neanderthalians of western Europe, have their chief affinities with the latter group.

Relationship to the Ehringsdorf people

The Ehringsdorf group, like that of Mount Carmel and Krapina, is assigned to the Riss-Würm interglacial period and is therefore earlier in date than most members of the Neanderthal group of western Europe. Our knowledge of the group is limited to a skull and two mandibles. The skull is frankly Neanderthal but has three peculiar features which are worthy of note because they are met with in the Mount Carmel people: a relatively high vault, a neanthropic mastoid process, and an incipient external occipital protuberance. Apparently the Ehringsdorf

type will find its closest resemblances with the Neanderthal people of western Europe.

Of the Neanderthaloid skulls of central Europe, that which bears the closest resemblance to the Palestinian type is the Steinheim cranium described by Weinert (1936, 1937). That writer ascribes this fossil specimen, which is one of the most complete of the mid-Pleistocene series yet discovered, to post-Riss times or to an early phase of the Riss-Würm interglacial. It is the skull of a woman and in many points resembles the skull of the Tabūn woman. In the meantime it may be included in the Ehringsdorf group, for it may well be the female form of this group. The molar teeth differ from those of the Tabūn woman. It is a remarkable fact that the Steinheim skull, which seems to be the earliest representative of the Neanderthal type so far discovered in Europe, should show so little of the occipital characterization found in specimens of later date, and should, in its occipital characters, make an approach to the Palestinian type.

Relationship to the Neanderthal group of western Europe

Our conception, hitherto, of the Neanderthal type or species has been based upon the fossil remains found in central and south-western Europe. The man of Düsseldorf and the man of La Chapelle-aux-Saints best represent the male form of this group. They were squat, strongly built men who differed from living types of mankind in almost every detail of bodily structure. Many points in their anatomy recall those found in the anthropoid apes, particularly in the gorilla. This type—the Neanderthal of Europe—is not found among the Mount Carmel people. Our Skhūl men are tall; their lower limbs were long and straight; the long, straight, heavily pilastred Skhūl femur differs altogether from the short, bowed Neanderthal femur, with its massive articular extremities. The feet of the Mount Carmel people were moulded and used as ours are. Like Neanderthal man, the Skhūl men were big-brained, but the moulding of their head and jaws was modern And yet, through the anatomy of the Mount Carmel people there runs a substratum of characters which link them to the Neanderthal type. We have mentioned that the individuals described in this study can be arranged in a series with the Tabūn type, plainly Neanderthaloid, at one extreme and the Skhūl type at the other. Similarly the groups of fossil man just enumerated can be arranged in a series with the Neanderthal group of western Europe at one extreme and the Mount Carmel group at the opposite extreme. It does now seem probable that western Europe, in the middle phases of the Pleistocene period, had become an evolutionary backwater so far as humanity was concerned and that the centres of active evolutionary progress lay much farther to the east, probably in western Asia.

Relationship to the Predmost people

The Predmost people are the earliest representatives of the Neanthropic type of man that have been discovered in central Europe. The men have certain primitive characters, such as their prominent supraorbital ridges, but in general structural characterization they are Caucasian. There are resemblances between them and the Skhūl men which deserve mention. The Predmost man (No. 3) has supra-orbital ridges which, although falling short of the development seen in Skhūl IV, serve as a link between that of Skhūl and of the development found in some modern Europeans. In shape, size, and characterization of their skulls, the Predmost and the Mount Carmel people had many points in common. But the Predmost people are of medium or short stature and are devoid of the Neanderthaloid features of the Skhūl people. Their relationship to the Mount Carmel people is more remote than that of the Neanthropic group we are now to discuss.

Relationship to the Cromagnon group

If only the limb-bones of the Skhūl people had been discovered at the Wady Mughara, we have no doubt of the verdict that anatomists would have passed on them. They would have declared that they were the fossil remains of a Neanthropic race, near akin to the Cromagnon people, the people who appeared in Europe towards the end of the Pleistocene period. Because of their crude characters and seeing how much the Skhūl people ante-date the Cromagnons of Europe, these fossil limb-bones would have been accepted as evidence of the existence of proto-Cromagnons in mid-Pleistocene times. Or let us suppose that only hands, or feet, or the hinder part of the skull, or the auricular region carrying the joint for the mandible, or the lower jaw itself had come to light; the verdict would have been the same. These parts would have been accepted as evidence of the existence of a Neanthropic race. On the other hand, if it had happened, as it did in the case of the Galilee discovery, that only the anterior part of the skull of the Mount Carmel people had been recovered, then the verdict would have been Neanderthal. Most of the teeth, a study of the vertebrae, or of the ribs would have led to the same conclusion: that they must be ascribed to a Neanderthaloid race. Even in the case of the ribs the evidence would have been equivocal for both forms of ribs occur at Mount Carmel, the rounded Neanderthal form and the wide-bladed ribs of Neanthropic man.

Of the early Neanthropic types known to us, there can be no doubt as to the one which comes nearest that of our Skhūl people. It is the Cromagnon type of southern France, the cave-dwellers of the Aurignacian. The Skhūl men, like the male Cromagnons, were tall; their stature ranged from 5 ft. 6.7 in. (1,700 mm.) to 5 ft. 10.3 in. (1,787 mm.). The bones of their lower extremities, from hip-joint to toes, are very similar to those of the Cromagnon men. So it is as regards the bones of the upper extremity, save that those of the Cromagnon males are more robust. But although what we have said of the bones of the upper and lower extremities is true of most of the Skhūl men, it is not true of all. Some have bones exhibiting certain Neanderthal characters to a greater or less degree.

A critical survey of the bones of the pelvis, shoulder, and trunk of the Skhūl males yields a mixed list of characters, Neanderthal, modern, and some which are neither; the latter appear to be peculiar to the Skhūl type. These features of the pelvis and the clavicle are duly described in their respective chapters. An examination of the skull gives the same mixed result. On the whole, characters of a Neanthropic nature are dominant to those of a Neanderthal kind. The Skhūl men had more rugged faces than the Cromagnons. Their brow-ridges formed continuous, prominent, bony ledges above the orbits; their noses were wide, their jaws large, and their chins under-developed to a varying degree. Certainly in the extreme Skhūl form (represented by Skhūl IV) the Cromagnon predominates over the Neanderthal characters.

Dr. Aleš Hrdlička[7] may now claim that the presence of a proto-Cromagnon type among the cave-dwellers of Mount Carmel is a confirmation

[7] Hrdlička 1927.

of the theory he advocated in his Huxley Lecture of 1927, namely, that the Neanderthalians of Europe did not become extinct, but in the course of a rapid evolution became transmuted into modern man. Dr. Hrdlička believes that evolution was speeded up under the pressure of a growing arctic environment. Palestine lay beyond the ice-sheet and we cannot invoke glacial conditions to account for the evolutionary state of the Mount Carmel people.

It might be asserted that the right interpretation of the state of affairs found among the Mount Carmel people is very simple: that Neanderthal man is there being transformed into modern man of the Cromagnon type. This certainly is a simple explanation and a possible one, yet it does not seem to us to be the most probable.

In the first place, it is to be noted that the Neanthropic type which is making its appearance amongst the Skhūl people is a very particular form of modern man, one of the white or European type, for concerning the racial status of Cromagnon man there should be no doubt. All his features are European, Caucasian, or white. Our belief is that at Mount Carmel we have reached a transitional zone which leads from one ancient area of racial differentiation (the Neanderthal or Palaeoanthropic) to another ancient area lying farther to the east, a Neanthropic area where the proto-Caucasian (or proto-Cromagnon) type of man was being evolved. The evidence is now convincing that in mid-Pleistocene times the inhabi-

tants of Europe—of the continent at least—were all Neanderthal in type, but we have seen that the type becomes modified as we proceed from west to east and that in Palestine we find a transitional type leading towards the Neanthropic type. It seems logical to us to assume that when the wide tracts of western Asia of mid-Pleistocene times are entered we shall find ourselves in the homeland of the proto-Caucasian. Eastern Asia we regard as the evolutionary cradle of the proto-Mongols. Our theory therefore assumes that the Mount Carmel people are not the actual ancestors of the Cromagnons but Neanderthaloid collaterals or cousins of the ancestors of that type. We expect that the fossil remains of the real proto-Cromagnons will be discovered still farther to the east.

Our hypothesis helps us to explain many events in the history of mankind in the western part of the Old World. If we assume that a progressive and conquering type of humanity was being evolved in western Asia in the remote times at which the Mount Carmel peoples lived, and that as their tribes increased in numbers and in strength they pushed continually westwards, replacing and extinguishing the native Neanderthalians, then we can give a reasonable explanation of the discoveries made by prehistorians and anthropologists in the late Pleistocene burials of Europe. Before the dawn of history western Asia served as a nursery for Europe, sending out peoples, cultures, and tongues. If our theory is well founded, then we must assume that this relationship between the two continents goes back to the remote times in which the Mount Carmel people lived. In brief, our theory assumes that Europe became the 'Australia' of the ancient world after mid-Pleistocene times and that the people who colonized it and extinguished its Neanderthal inhabitants, as the whites are now ousting the 'blacks' of Australia, were Caucasians evolved in western Asia.

The place of the Mount Carmel people in a scheme of classification

We feel that a knowledge of the mid-Pleistocene races of the western world has now reached a point which makes necessary a revision in the nomenclature and in the scheme of classification of fossil man. The earliest and the most primitive trace of the Neanderthal type in Europe is the Heidelberg mandible. Bonarelli (1909) proposed the generic name Palaeoanthropus for Heidelberg man, and it seems to us advisable to use this name as a generic designation for all forms of humanity which show a predominance of Neanderthal characters. We arrange our specific groups as follows:

1. *Palaeoanthropus heidelbergensis* (Heidelberg Man).
2. *P. ehringsdorfiensis* (represented by the fossil remains found near Weimar).
3. *P. neanderthalensis* (as represented by the Düsseldorf specimen and that of La Chapelle-aux-Saints).
4. *P. krapinensis* (represented by the fossil remains from Croatia).
5. *P. palestinensis* (the Mount Carmel and the Galilee remains).

Facts and Speculations Concerning the Origin of *Homo sapiens*

Franz Weidenreich
1947

The discovery of Sinanthropus and the more recent finds of Pithecanthropus specimens once and for all settled the question of the morphological character of the immediate forerunner of Neanderthal man.

Reproduced by permission of the American Anthropological Association from *American Anthropologist*, Vol. 49, No. 2, 1947.

Both Sinanthropus and Pithecanthropus have been acknowledged by all experts as true hominids, closely related to each other. They represent a phase of human evolution which exhibits more primitive features in number and kind than any of the known types of Neanderthal man. So far as doubts have been entertained, the main reason for the skepticism was the incompleteness of information due to the lack or insufficiency of communication during the years of war. My monograph on the Sinanthropus skull (1943), distributed in 1944 and 1945, may have dissipated some of those scruples. It gave a detailed description and brought forward new facts which earlier were either overlooked or were not fully appreciated.

Some authors were unaware of my monograph but their own studies led them to the same result. It is sufficient to refer to two of these authors. The first is my friend and collaborator, Père Teilhard de Chardin. In a lecture given at the Catholic University of Peking in 1943,[1] that is at a time when we had already been out of contact for two years, as I prepared my monograph in New York, Teilhard made the following statement as to the anatomical character of Sinanthropus:

Seen across a distance of hundreds of thousands of years, we might expect to see man markedly different from what he appears now. Well, in this respect our expectations have almost been surpassed. On the whole, Sinanthropus

[1] Teilhard de Chardin 1943.

decidedly stands, in his anatomical features, on man's side among the primates: face not projecting, brain twice as large as in the largest apes, erect posture, bimanous, etc. But along with those fundamentally human characters, how many deep and significant differences.

Teilhard lists some of these differences and continues:

To a non-anatomist observer these various peculiarities (which, because they occur identically in all the specimens, are certainly not individual anomalies) may at first seem of little value, but to the eyes of an anthropologist they are of utmost significance, for not only does each of them make Sinanthropous different from us, but each brings him closer to the apes. A glance at text figure 3 will be enough to convince the reader that, by the whole architecture of his brain case. ...Sinanthropus stands certainly nearer to the large manlike apes of today than man himself.

With regard to Pithecanthropus, Teilhard states:

Today all doubt is lifted. Pithecanthropus is not an ape but a man; and as a man, he stands approximately at the same evolutionary stage as Sinanthropus, and furthermore: Both Pithecanthropus and Sinanthropus obviously belong...to the same anatomical stage in human evolution; but the Java man looks on the whole more primitive and, besides, he is perhaps geologically older than the Peking man.

The second author to whom I refer is Vittorio Marcozzi. He deals with Sinanthropus in two papers;

in the first, published in 1944,[2] the peculiarities of the temporal bone of Sinanthropus skull Locus E have been described. The results are identical with those at which I arrived in my paper on the same subject in 1932.[3] Marcozzi states that, considering all the facts which the temporal region of Sinanthropus presents, some characteristic features are typically pithecoid, some typically human, and numerous others, human and primitive together. The conclusions of his second paper (1945),[4] which is based chiefly on my earlier publications, read as follows:

From the study of a certain number of Sinanthropus features compared with those of the anthropoids, other fossil hominids and recent man, it appears that Sinanthropus represents a hominid type fairly primitive, or a primate belonging to the human family, but revealing many primitive peculiarities (about half of the ones examined ranged between primitive and intermediate), some pithecoid features (about 26 percent), and about a third human features.

Regarding Pithecanthropus, the author considered him "still more primitive than Sinanthropus." Homo soloensis and Africanthropus (Weinert) are "instead somewhat more developed."

So far as morphologists have been able to advance opinions about the anatomical character of Pithecanthropus and Sinanthropus, they have followed the same line: Pithe-canthropus and Sinanthropus are primitive hominids with typically pithecoid features, but they are undoubtedly members of the human family, more remote from the modern human type than any fossil human forms thus far recovered. The new finds of the Java and China giants (Pithecanthropus robustus, Meganthropus paleojavanicus and Gigantopithecus blacki) (cf. Weidenreich 1945[5]) gave evidence that the hominid line recognizable as such by the incontestably human character of the specimens, can be traced still farther back. Regardless of whether we consider gigantism a general and intrinsic feature of early mankind, or as a regional variation running parallel with the greater primitiveness of those forms, the increase of their body size is obvious. So the human line leads far beyond the stage of the classic Neanderthal man and comes remarkably closer to the supposed common human-anthropoid stem. The name Prehominids or Prehominians given by Boule in order to distinguish the Pithecanthropus-Sinanthropus group from the Neanderthalian is not an appropriate designation, for neither these two types themselves nor their immediate forerunners, the giants, are "pre"-hominids, but already true hominids. Therefore, I have chosen the name Archanthropinae[6] for the so-called "prehominians" group, while I called the Neanderthalian forms Paleoanthropinae, a name which has been applied to this group

2 Marcozzi 1944.
3 Weidenreich 1932.
4 Marcozzi 1945.
5 Weidenreich 1945a.
6 Weidenreich 1946a.

earlier by other authors. Those taxonomists who feel uneasy when the names assigned to hominids fail to come up to the rigid regulations of the zoological nomenclature may be referred to G. G. Simpson.[7] In his recent book on the principles of classification the well-known palaeontologist warns:

All specimens of fossil hominids that differ in any discernible way from Homo sapiens, and some that do not, have at one time or another been placed in different genera. Almost none of the anthropological "genera" has any zoological reason for being. All known hominids, recent and fossil, could well be placed in Homo. At most, Pithecanthropus (with which Sinanthropus is clearly synonymous by zoological criteria)...may be given separate generic rank. Perhaps it would be better for the zoological taxonomist to set apart the family Hominidae and to exclude its nomenclature and classification from his studies.

Although my conception of the state of the Archanthropinae within the line of human evolution met with wide consent so far as the morphological side of the problem is concerned, the same does not apply to my conception of their relationship to the Paleoanthropinae and Neoanthropinae (that is, recent man). I believe that all primate forms recognized as hominids—no matter whether they lived in the past or live today—represent morphologically a unity when compared with other primate forms, and they can be regarded as *one species.* I

[7] Simpson 1945.

arrived at this conclusion by an elaborated anatomical analysis of all particular features, from Pithecanthropus robustus up to modern man of today. *If all hominid types and their varions, regardless of time and space, are taken into consideration, their arrangement in a continuous evolutionary line, leading from the most primitive state to the most advanced, does not meet with any difficulty. Neither any gaps nor deviations are recognizable.* This statement holds good for the entire skeleton, in particular for skull and dentition, and concerns these parts not only as a whole but also their minor structures and special patterns. However, "transitions" are not necessarily found between each regional group in which students may expect them, especially if such a group is represented by only one or a few specimens. Instead they may occur in other, geographically separated groups.

This general continuity is not the only striking phenomenon. It is accompanied by an overlapping of individual features. This means that structures characteristic of a certain phase may extend, nevertheless, to the next one without much change. Those occurrences make it difficult to subdivide the hominids into smaller classificatory units and assign individual specimens to a certain unit. The Heidelberg jaw, for example, is primitive only so far as the character of its bone on the whole is concerned, but the form of its dental arch, its dentition and the pattern of the individual teeth come very close to those of modern man. On the other hand, the Sinanthropus teeth are much more pithecoid than those of the Heidelberg jaw, while the outer side and the inner side of the chin region of Sinanthropus reveal a distinctly more advanced stage than that of the Heidelberg man. The eyebrow ridges of the Galilee skull and the Skhūl skull project much more and are more clearly distinguished from the forehead proper than is the case in the classic Neanderthal skulls, although other features leave no doubt that the Palestine specimens represent a more advanced phase of evolution than the Neanderthalians. The minimum value of the cranial capacity of the normal adult modern man is smaller than that of any of the Neanderthalians and comes close to the minimum capacity of Sinanthropus skulls, although the braincase of Sinanthropus, on the whole and in detail, shows much more primitive features than the braincase of any primitive race of modern mankind. The arrangement of the cusps of the molars of Gigantopithecus and their special patterns resemble those of modern man to such a degree that the description of the human teeth in J. Mummery's textbook can be directly applied to the teeth of Gigantopithecus although they differ widely in size and special features from modern human teeth. These examples are easily multiplied. Gaps in the line of human evolution appear as local occurrences. Gaps like those which exist between the Paleoanthropines and Neanthropines of the Last Glacial Period of Central Europe or

between the Archanthropine Sinanthropus of Choukoutien and the Neoanthropine form of the Upper Cave of the same site do not prove real discontinuity; for the Archanthropines, the Paleoanthropines and the Neoanthropines can be linked by intermediate forms known from other localities. Evolution in man did not proceed in occasional jumps as some students want us to believe. Quite the contrary, the continuity of the line seems amazing when the scarcity of the fossil human material is taken into consideration.

Until recently, it was a general practice to regard *a priori* each newly discovered fossil human form as a side branch of the main stem, which never led to modern man. The "genus" and "species" names freely given those specimens, even before any analysis of the form was possible, favored those interpretations. Lately, however, authors have become more conscious of the fact that not each feature which appears at first glance specific justifies the attribution of those specimens to completely different genetic groups, leading away from the modern human form. For example, not long ago the peculiar spaciousness of the pulp cavity of the lower molars of some of the Neanderthalians ("taurodontism"), especially developed in some molars of the Krapina man, was used to stamp all Neanderthalians as extinct forms. It was claimed that they have not been passed on to modern man because such large spaciousness as found in molars of the Neanderthal man can never be found in modern man.

However, we know now that the statements and the argumentations were wrong, for not all Neanderthalians nor even all the molars of the Krapina man themselves show that peculiarity. In addition, the special spaciousness of the pulp cavity can also occur in racial groups of modern mankind, although some groups may be more affected than others.

My theory claiming morphological unity of all hominids and continuity of the human line regardless of time and space has met with objections from different sides. There are people who are opposed in principle to any "evolution" so far as man is concerned. According to them, "Homo sapiens" never derived from simian-like ancestors. Of course, it is impossible today to deny any existence of fossil human-like creatures with pithecoid features. This fact is admitted, although reluctantly. But those forms are considered as a kind of natural experiment which failed and, in any case, as having nothing in common with "Homo sapiens." Therefore, for these people the origin of "Homo sapiens" is still held in abeyance. Scientists who do not share those ideas are so far in an unfavorable position since in a discussion their opponents prefer to take shelter behind arguments they borrow from those scientists who, although believing in human evolution, disagree with other authors in minor questions.

The most controversial point is the apparent incongruity between the morphological and the chronological sequence of the fossil human remains. I called attention to this fact[8] when I made the attempt to reclassify the hominids only on the basis of their morphological character. The list arranged according to these criteria was then headed by Pithecanthropus erectus as the most primitive hominid and ended with Homo sapiens as the most advanced, while the list arranged on the basis of the chronological sequence was headed by "Homo sapiens" as represented by the Piltdown Man. Koppers,[9] the well-known ethnologist, criticizes my tabulations and calls my attempt to reconcile the seemingly discordant facts "strange nonsense" ("merkwürdige Ungereimtheiten"), although he admits that he is not familiar with biological questions and looks at these problems only as a historian. In the meantime, new finds from Java and South China pushed Pithecanthropus erectus from his leading place on the morphological list to the fourth. The list is now headed by Gigantopithecus blacki, followed in sequence by Meganthropus paleojavanicus and Pithecanthropus robustus, while the leading place in the chronological list is still occupied by "Eoanthropus," the "Homo sapiens" from Piltdown, although everybody now doubts his authenticity.

When I made the chronological list, I was fully aware of the dubiousness of the datings, as shown by my remark: "the geological determination of some of the specimens enumerated...is not above all doubt." Everybody who is familiar with this

8 Weidenreich 1940b.
9 Koppers 1944.

matter will agree with the cautious wording of this objection. But I did not intend at this time to spring the mine. However, I hoped that the obvious falsities exhibited in the chronological tabulation might prompt some geologists to take up the matter and test the data. Instead, I found in F. E. Zeuner's[10] book, recently published, the following statement: "The view that Homo sapiens is a late figure on the human stage is still held by some authors. *The chronological evidence, however, though scanty for the early phases, does not support it.*" (Italics mine.)

The wording of this statement is misleading. Homo sapiens is morphologically without any doubt "a late figure on the human stage." But this really late phase of human evolution may be reached in some regions of the earth earlier than in others and thus give the impression of preceding more primitive forms found in other regions. In any case however, the "evidences" of such an early appearance of Homo sapiens as given by Zeuner are not well grounded. He still considers "Eoanthropus" as the oldest Homo sapiens and places him on his list near to the Pliocene (between Villafranchian and Lower Pleistocene). But at the same time he indicates some doubt about the zoological and geological character of Eoanthropus by setting the name in italics and adding a question mark. In the text itself, Zeuner is more reserved; he states:

From the Lower Pleistocene two fossils are known which might belong to Homo

10 Zeuner 1946.

sapiens in the wider sense. One is Piltdown Man (Eoanthropus dawsoni [Smith Woodward]) whose cranium is remarkably sapiens-like. The mandible, the human character of which is much disputed, and even denied (e.g. Weidenreich, 1936) should be left out of the discussion altogether since it is uncertain whether it belongs to the skull or not. *If the cranium is contemporary with the fauna* (Hopwood, 1935, page 50), Piltdown man would have lived just at the beginning of the Pleistocene and would in fact be the oldest human fossil. *But the geographical conditions in which the finds were made are not unambiguous.* (Italics mine.)

The last sentence of Zeuner's statement is decisive. All the fragments of the Piltdown braincase—only these parts of the recovered bones can be attributed to Homo sapiens and not the mandible—were found, together with other mammalian bones evidently deriving from various geological horizons, in an old river bed which is inundated several months a year even today. Nobody is able to deny the possibility that the modern human bones have been deposited much later than Lower Pleistocene at the different spots from which they have been collected, some even from the surface.[11] In any case,

11 In an obituary of Sir Arthur Woodward signed E. I. W. (White) and published in the quarterly *Journal of the Geological Society of London* (Vol. 101, Parts 3 and 4, p. xiv, 1946) I came across the following remark: "It was always a matter of chagrin to him (Sir Arthur Woodward) that Dawson (who found the Piltdown skull fragments) whom illness had made difficult, never revealed the source of the fragments of the second skull that he had found in the neighborhood." This second

"Eoanthropus" cannot be presented as chronological "evidence" that a true Homo sapiens lived in the Lower Pleistocene or Pliocene.

The second "evidence" of the presence of Homo sapiens in the Lower Pleistocene in Zeuner's list is the Kanam jaw. This name is also set in italics and provided with a question mark. In the text Zeuner says (p. 298): *"Similarly uncertain is the age of the Kanam jaw, the published records on which suggest a lower Pleistocene age."* (Italics mine.) In another place (p. 250) the author states: "A small fragment of a human lower jaw (Homo cf. sapiens) is believed to have come from these beds (Kanam Beds of Lower Pleistocene age), but its exact position could not be ascertained." Indeed, Boswell[12] says that the "geological age of the mandible... is uncertain."

I regret that Zeuner also refers to the Keilor skull, recently found in Australia, in the same uncritical attitude with which he deals with the Piltdown and Kanam fragments. He accepts Mahoney's dating of the skull as belonging to the early part of Last Interglacial, although he makes the reservation, "this recent discovery needs further geological confirmation," and furthermore, "It is most desirable that supplementary

evidence for the geological age be brought forward, either by means of a detailed study of the coastal terrains and the river terraces connected with them, or perhaps on paleontological grounds." I agree with Zeuner's scepticism.[13] Concerning the "paleontological grounds" I[14] was able to show that the Keilor skull is anatomically a mere duplicate of the Wadjak skull II from Java. The age of the latter is not datable with any degree of certainty, but all authors who studied this question agree in the opinion that Wadjak man was much younger than Homo soloensis who has been

[13] How justified my scepticism about the authenticity of the Keilor skull has been is now proved by a new publication which deals with the geology of the Tasmanian River terraces that yielded the Keilor skull. The two Australian authors, R. A. Keble and J. Hope Macpherson (Keble, R. A., and J. Hope Macpherson. The Contemporaneity of the River Terraces of the Maribyrnong River, Victoria, with those of the Upper Pleistocene in Europe. *Mem. Nat. Mus. Vic.*, No. 14, Pt. 2, 1946, pp. 52–68) began their paper with the following comments: "The examination of the terraces of the Maribyrnong River Valley was undertaken to prove the antiquity of what has come to be known as the Keilor skull. *There is now reason for believing that the skeleton may have been a burial, and the age of the terrace in which it was found is not necessarily its age.* Nevertheless...." (Italics mine.)

This is exactly what I expected when I read D. J. Mahony's first report on the Keilor skull. The scantiness of Mahony's argument with regard to the circumstances under which the human bones were discovered was so obvious that the ease with which it was accepted by some English authors was hard to understand. It may be hoped that the Keilor skull will eventually disappear from the list of specimens of Homo sapiens found earlier than Upper Pleistocene.

skull, which consists of some fragments of a recent human braincase and a worn lower molar of allegedly ape-like character, has been and still is referred to as evidence that the fragments of the first Piltdown skull—fragments of a recent human braincase and a simian-like mandible—also belong to the same individual.

[12] Boswell 1935.

[14] Weidenreich 1945b.

attributed to the Last Interglacial or even to a later period (cf. Movius,[15] 1944, Table VI).

Furthermore, Zeuner considers the Swanscombe skull and the Galley Hill man, both from the Thames terrace, as "Homo cf. sapiens" and ascribes them to the Penultimate Interglacial. In these cases too, the skulls were recovered from river terraces and secondary deposits. As to the first find, essential parts of the skull are missing, namely the frontal bone and the entire facial skeleton. We know from other finds (Steinheim, Galilee and Skhūl skulls) how important these parts are to secure a differential diagnosis. For these morphological and geological reasons I continue to set the Swanscombe skull on the list of the dubious cases so far as its classification is concerned.

In spite of all these scruples, I do not and never did deny the possibility that Homo sapiens himself, or a type very close to him, may be found in certain sites of the Old World which are older than Upper Pleistocene. I am even able to boast that I have been one of the first to stress the necessity of revising the generally accepted idea of a necessary coincidence between morphological and chronological sequences of hominids wherever they may be found. I[16] have shown that the skull of Weimar-Ehringsdorf is morphologically a more advanced form than the classic Neanderthal man of Europe although the former is geolog-

ically older than the latter, the first belonging to the Last Interglacial period and the second to the Last Glacial period. But any claim to geological priority for recent human types must be based on incontestable geological facts and not on speculations and conjectures. A more critical attitude, especially on the part of the geologists, would be very useful. As long as uncertainties, as exemplified above, last, the morphological analysis is the only reliable means of tracing the line of human evolution.

Koppers calls me an extreme evolutionist, obsessed with the "principle of primitivity." As a naturalist and morphologist, I believe, indeed, that the modern human type, whenever and wherever it may be found, must have evolved from a less advanced one which preceded it in time. If, for example, a skeleton of Homo sapiens should be dug out from geological layers which, together with the bones, incontestably belong to the Late Pliocene, his paleoanthropine forerunners must have lived somewhere in the earlier Pliocene and his archanthropine forerunner in a still earlier period. Koppers protests against this reasoning; these forerunners, he says, have so far not been discovered and are therefore not factually demonstrable. Koppers is mistaken. Those forms have been found and are available. But they have not been found in exactly the same place as Homo sapiens and not in the Tertiary. However, this failure does not prove that they did not exist elsewhere at such an early period.

15 Movius 1944.
16 Weidenreich 1928.

Be that as it may, what makes me believe that *any* modern type must have had a more primitive forerunner is the fact that all the peculiarities of any skeleton of modern man are the same everywhere except for minor differences which undoubtedly represent individual or racial variations. The mere existence of those structures indicates that they have developed from types which have possessed them, but in a more pronounced form. This is an inference from facts, no less logical than the conclusion that each human skull with permanent teeth must have passed in its infantile phase through a phase with milk teeth.

A normally built modern human skull carries a bulge on the medial side of its frontal bone above the supraorbital arch. The anatomists call this structure the "superciliary ridge." This bulge varies in the degree of its development. In the "primitive" Australian bushman it reaches greater dimensions and projects further than in any individual of the white population. When we go back to the Upper Paleolithic population of Europe we find this bulge still more pronounced and occupying the entire base of the forehead. Nobody has so far questioned that this population has all the characteristics of Homo sapiens and is closely related to the man of today. In the Neanderthalians the "supraorbital ridges" are again heavier than in the Upper Paleolithic man, and in Sinanthropus they appear separated from the forehead proper, forming an independent ledge above nose and orbits. This stage does not differ fundamentally from conditions found in gorilla and chimpanzee. The example can be multiplied *ad libitum*. The occipital torus at the rear of the skull, the mechanical equivalent of the supraorbital ridges, shows a similar transformation.[17] In modern man there is usually no torus but its place is taken by one or two "lines." The center of these formations is occupied by a circumscribed projection—protuberantia occipitalis externa—which varies in the degree of development: in "primitive" races of modern man (Tasmanian, Australian bushman, but also in other groups) a true protuberantia is often absent while the occipital surface between the two "lines" bulges. Early anthropologists called this structure "torus." This "torus"—a very characteristic feature of the Neanderthal man—is still more pronounced in the Archanthropinae (Homo soloensis, Sinanthropus, Pithecanthropus robustus).

Regarding the dentition, it is sufficient to call attention to the fact that in modern man there is a clear tendency to reduce the number of the cusps of the lower molars from five to four. This tendency is especially pronunced in the second molars. In Sinanthropus, six cusps are the rule in the first molar, five cusps prevail in the other molars but four cusps may also occur. On the other hand, the presence of six cusps is a very rare event in modern man.[18]

We know that any peculiarities

17 Weidenreich 1940a.
18 Weidenreich 1937.

of the body can be transferred from the parents, grandparents, great-grandparents, etc., to their offspring. Now I ask historians like Koppers: If modern man did not derive from forms like the Neanderthal man or Sinanthropus or Pithecanthropus, why then does his skeleton show structures which admit of no other interpretation than being "relics" of features which were more developed in the preceding forms? Whence has modern man inherited all these peculiarities if not from his ancestors? Why does the man of today carry around with him "simian stigmata" if he has nothing in common with apes?

No matter from which locality and geological layer a skull may be excavated, it will be recognized as a modern-type human skull by the presence and character of those "relics." For this reason he must have had ancestral types like Neanderthal man, Sinanthropus and Pithecanthropus, even if he lived in the Lower Pleistocene or Pliocene. Although I am not convinced that the evolutionary phase of modern man was already fully developed at those early times, I would not be astonished if we should be confronted one day with such a fact, and if the site of such a discovery were Europe. The presence of "Dryopithecus" teeth—some of them hardly distinguishable from modern chimpanzee—gathered from "Bohnerz" fissures of the Swabian Alb in South Germany proves in any case the existence of specialized anthropoids in the Lower Pliocene of Europe. The femur of Paidopithex rhenanus

Pohlig found in the basin of Mayence gives evidence that a giant gibbon, much larger than any one roaming the forests of Southeast Asia today, inhabited the valley of the Rhine at the same early time. If specialized primates such as chimpanzee and gibbon lived in Central Europe in the Lower Pliocene, the possibility of the occurrence of advanced hominids cannot be denied.

Père Teilhard's point of view as expressed in his recent paper on fossil man[19] has a particular meaning. Morphologically, Sinanthropus as well as Pithecanthropus are designated as "Homo sapiens." In addition, Sinanthropus, says Père Teilhard, was "already far beyond the critical boundary separating the 'reflective' from the 'non-reflective' animals." Pithecanthropus probably "was also an intelligent and reflective being." The Neanderthalians on the whole give "the impression of an archaic human group, the prolongation and survival of some unknown line (?) of Prehominians." Regarding the psychical characters of the Neanderthalians, Père Teilhard states that "they used to bury their dead, a good indication that they had some religious conceptions or feelings." His whole conception of the evolution of man can be gathered from the following sentences:

There, at the first visible appearance of the [human] tree lie the Prehominians with their depressed skull and their rudimentary social aggregation. Here at the terminal stage of today

19 *Loc. cit.*

stands out Homo sapiens, with the uprisen braincase and in such an intensified state of collective organization that he may well seem to approach the critical point of some explosive change. There below, an early man, *only little* —here above, a modern man, *very much* "cerebralized" and "socialized." What does this difference mean?... What the prehistorians have so patiently registered, point after point, during the past eighty years, is nothing less than the trace left by humanity moving persistently toward a higher individual and collective consciousness. What is graphically expressed in Figure 12 [pedigree] is the actual *passing* of reflective intelligence *from a lesser human to a more human condition;* or, if you prefer, it is the *passing of humanity from an embryonic or infantile to on adult age.* (Italics mine.)

In other words, Père Teilhard believes that man passed also phylogenetically from an embryonic (Archanthropines) or infantile age (Paleoanthropines) to an adult age (Neoanthropines). Morphological, psychic and social evidences of such a passage are, according to him, at hand.

So far there seems to be no difference between Père Teilhard's idea and mine. But Père Teilhard considered the three main forms in which the hominids appear—he speaks of "human sheets or leaves" —not as evolutionary phases of one and the same morphological and genetical unit, but as temporarily restricted creatures, each form completely independent from the preceding and the following one. The "sheets" "displace each other rather than to pass into each other directly

...*neither Peking Man, nor Solo Man, nor Neanderthal Man have any direct offspring left today in the living world: they have been swept away by Homo sapiens;* just as the Tasmanians have been and the Australian Bushmen will soon be, replaced by the stronger white or yellow races." (Italics mine.)

Such a concept seems to me to be hardly compatible with the author's before-mentioned statements. There he spoke of an "embryonic, infantile and adult age" of fossil hominids. Such a comparison with the ontogenetic stages of human development is only intelligible if the human form is a unity, and the three fossil stages are phases of the same unit but not different and independent creatures. It is also difficult to understand how Sinanthropus can pass as a "reflecting human being" with the "mental power of Homo sapiens" unless he is connected with Homo sapiens. In addition, races never are completely extinguished. Neither Tasmanians nor the Australian aborigines can be swept away by "superior" races "without leaving direct offspring." A part of the original population will always be amalgamated with members of other races before it "disappears" and will transmit its racial particularities by means of interbreeding. Sinanthropus, Pithecanthropus and Neanderthal man have disappeared only as taxonomic groups, just as Eohippus, Merychippus and Pliohippus, the forerunners of the modern horse, did. But they still "live" in the succeeding phases like parents in their children. In

my book *Apes, Giants and Man*[20]
I showed that evolution (transformation, in close connection with interbreeding) has continually altered the
physical character of mankind from
his beginning, and it does so today.
Therefore inheritable features can
never be eliminated entirely; they
can be gradually "diluted" until
they become invisible. But this does
not mean that even then they have
necessarily gone for good. They may
still reappear in one of the following
generations.

My review of the recently advanced opinions about the origin
of modern man would not be complete if no reference were made to
the ideas advanced in R. Broom's[21]
monograph on the Australopithecinae. The author of Part I of this
book is Broom himself. After an
exhaustive study of the peculiarities
of these very interesting primates, he
lays down his own ideas about the
evolution of the hominids and their
relation to the Australopithecinae.
So far as the latter group is concerned, we can disregard Broom's
views because that group is not the
subject of this essay and Broom
broadly consents to my own views.[22]
As to the relation of the prehominids
and Neanderthal man to modern
man, however, Broom doubts the
human character of Píthecanthropus
because of the small capacity of his
braincase. It is strange that Sinanthropus is not even mentioned in
this connection. As to Neanderthal

man, Broom believes that this group
can be definitely removed from any
place in the ancestry of modern
man; he "probably has arisen from
an Australoid, like the Wadjak man,
by a mutation which led to massiveness, and to be no more worthy of
generic or even specific rank than
the bull dog." This verdict is made
without any evidence whatsoever to
support Broom's idea and without
referring to any of the new discoveries or their discussions in the
last two decades.

Broom's view that a Wadjak
type, that is, a modern human form,
may have been transformed by a leap
or mutation can only be understood
if one is familiar with the ideas of
the author of Part II of Broom's
book, namely Schepers. Schepers
studied the endocasts of the Australopithecinae and draws his conclusions from what he read from the
form and the surface pattern of
their brains. In a special chapter the
author, a neurologist, enlarges on
"the neurological significance of the
endocranial casts." This discussion is
full of generalities and attempts to
interpret the special surface pattern
of the Australopithecinae as an expression of certain higher mental
abilities. As an example I cite the
following passage (p. 253):

These parietal cortices [?], together
with the expansions in the inferior
frontal convolutions, are characteristically human and form the neural basis for
vocal and manual dexterity alike. The
least we can say, therefore, is that
these fossil types were capable of functioning in the erect posture, of using
their hands in a limited sense for

---

20 Weidenreich 1946a.
21 Broom and Schepers 1946.
22 Weidenreich 1943.

skilled movements and not associated with progression, of interpreting their immediately visible, palpable and audible environment in such detail and with such discrimination that they had the subject matter for articulate speech well under control, and of having developed motoric centers for the appropriate application; they were also capable of communicating the acquired information to their families, friends and neighbors, thus establishing one of the first bands of Man's complex social life. With all these attributes they must have been *virtually true human beings, no matter how simian their external appearance may have remained.* (Italics mine.)

For many years I have engaged in studies of the fossil human brain as it appears in endocasts. My study was not restricted to a single small group like the Australopithecinae, consisting of a few specimens, but covered all available groups. I extended it also to endocasts of modern man and higher primates and to what modern comparative neurology has to say about the significance of the convolution system and its relation to the cortex and its function. I have a monograph in preparation; a short summary[23] dealing with some of the problems has been published recently. According to my experience, it is absolutely impossible to read any neural functions, such as described by Schepers, from the impressions that the convolutions of the brain leave on the walls of the cranial cavity, or from the size of the brain and that of its lobes. In this regard

[23] Weidenreich 1946b.

it makes no difference which evolutionary stage the endocasts represent.[24] Therefore I vigorously object to statements such as made by Schepers, especially if the endocasts on which they are based are in such a poor state of preservation as in the Australopithecinae specimens. There is not the slightest justification for such far-reaching conclusions as drawn by Schepers.

In spite of the fact that the size of the brain of the Australopithecinae did not exceed that of an average gorilla—Broom estimates that the cranial capacity varies from 460 cc. to 650 cc.—and that the brains did not differ essentially in their external appearance from those of anthropoids of today. Schepers found that the Australopithecinae are virtually true human beings. This whole argument is in strange contradiction to Broom's own statement. Broom contests, as mentioned above, the human character of Pithecanthropus in spite of his human ap-

[24] A review published recently by W. E. Le Gros Clark (*Nature,* No. 4001, 1946) called my attention to the monograph by Pierre Hirschler (1942) which deals with the endocranial casts of anthropoids and man. As this paper is not accessible to me I quote the following passage from Le Gros Clark's article: "This author [Hirschler] is particularly—and we [Le Gros Clark] think rightly—outspoken about those anatomists who appear to assume that every unevenness of the surface of an endocranial cast must be a fissural imprint; who claim that the relative size of a localized eminence can be taken to signify the possession of such mental qualities as the power of speech. . . . So far as the large anthropoid apes are concerned, Hirschler finds that endocranial casts show extremely few fissural markings which can be identified with certainty."

pearance, although his brain is 100 cc. larger than the maximum value of the gorilla brain, while Schepers claims that the Australopithecinae, with a brain size not exceeding that of the average gorilla, were human beings in spite of their simian appearance. This example adequately shows that Schepers' "neurological" speculations have no scientific basis and cannot, therefore, be accepted as contributions to our knowledge of early man.

I am sorry that I have to say the same about the same author's ideas of the "terminal trends in human and primate evolution." Schepers does not feel at home in "this field of anthropological endeavour," for he introduces himself as a newcomer. Nevertheless he believes himself qualified to subvert all the achievements of experienced students in this field. However, his own theory is nothing but a sort of revival of Bolks' fetalization theory mixed with vague presentiments of gigantism as a general character of early hominids. According to Schepers, the primate stem leads directly from Archaeprimata of the Eocene to Homo sapiens who first appears in the Pliocene age. Intermediate phases of this evolution are Prosimiae primitivae, Paratarsoidea, Anthropomorpha primitivae, Pithecoid homunculi, and Hominidae. So far Schepers' theory does not fundamentally deviate from that of other authors except for the new names he introduces. But the essential point is that all the known fossil and living forms of monkeys, apes and man (except the Pliocene Homo

sapiens) are, according to Schepers, retrogressions toward a "micrencephalic gerontomorphism." Neither Pithecanthropus nor Sinanthropus lies in the line of human evolution; all are degenerated microcephalics. The only group that come close to the human line are the Australopithecinae although they have simian appearance, according to Schepers himself (see above).

Evolution of man in Schepers' version is a cinematographical trick; it is a reversed film: man did not originate from ape-like creatures but apes have originated from man. If this is so, what is the meaning of the "simian stigmata" demonstrable on the skull of Homo sapiens? If they are not relics of the past then they must be "sprouts," foreboding of some future "microcephalic regression."

Any theory of the origin of Homo sapiens has to be based on paleontological facts and only on them. It is a contradiction to logic and scientific reasoning to eliminate first all recovered fossil hominids from the line of man's eventual ancestry and then give play to one's phantasy to build this line again by free invention of new forms. If we hold to the morphological sequence of the fossil human forms, and disregard for a moment its discrepancy with the chronological sequence, ten evolutionary phases can be distinguished as indicated on the depicted Pedigree of the Hominidae. Five of these belong to the Archanthropinae, the most primitive group, three to the Paleoanthropinae, and two to the Neoanthropinae. The latter group

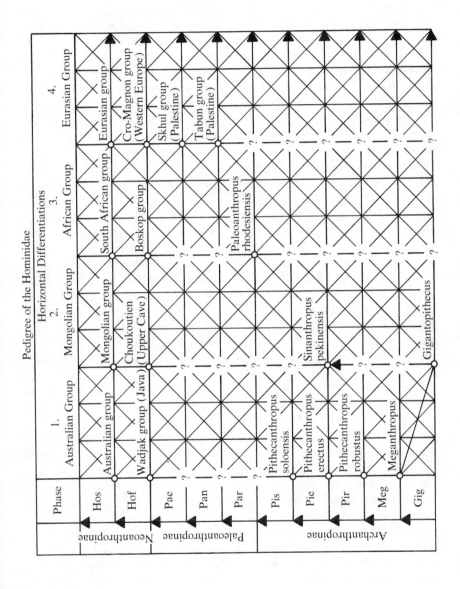

Pedigree of the Hominidae

Horizontal Differentiations

Phase	1. Australian Group	2. Mongolian Group	3. African Group	4. Eurasian Group
Hos	Australian group	Mongolian group	South African group	Eurasian group
Hof	Wadjak group (Java)	Choukoutien (Upper Cave)	Boskop group	Cro-Magnon group (Western Europe)
Pae				Skhul group (Palestine)
Pan				Tabun group (Palestine)
Par			Paleoanthropus rhodesiensis	
Pis	Pithecanthropus soloensis			
Pie	Pithecanthropus erectus	Sinanthropus pekinensis		
Pir	Pithecanthropus robustus			
Meg	Meganthropus			
Gig		Gigantopithecus		

Neoanthropinae
Paleoanthropinae
Archanthropinae

consists of the two Homo sapiens forms, the fossil and the recent ones. The Archanthropinae are so far only known from East Asia: Gigantopithecus (Gig) and Sinanthropus (Pie) and Java. The three phases of the Paleoanthropinae are known from Africa, Asia and Europe: Rhodesian man (Par) represents the most primitive phase, the typical Neanderthalians (Pan) represent the next phase, and the man of Weimar-Ehringsdorf, the man of Galilee or the Skhūl population of Mount Carmel the more advanced group (Pae). The fossil group of the Neoanthropinae (Hof) has been found in Java (Wadjak skull), Australia (Keilor skull), Asia (Upper Cave of Choukoutien), Africa (North, East and South) and in West Central and East Europe. Therefore Paleoanthropinae are missing so far in all those regions where Archanthropinae have been found, while Archanthropinae are missing in those where Paleoanthropinae and fossil Neoanthropinae have been recovered. That these voids in the distribution of the fossil hominids are chiefly due to incomplete exploration is proved by the recent discoveries which brought missing types to light from regions where they were not known before or were even not expected to be found. Those facts, together with the morphological evidences, suggest that man has evolved in different parts of the Old World. The Australian natives have some of their characteristics in common with the fossil Wadjak-Keilor man and with Homo soloensis. Homo soloensis himself appears as an ad-

vanced Pithecanthropus phase. Some of the characteristic features of Sinanthropus reappear in certain Mongolian groups of today. The same relation exists between Rhodesian man and certain fossil South African forms of modern man. The Skhūl group of Palestine presents forms intermediate between the typical Neanderthal man from Tabūn and fossil modern man from Europe.

All this points to an already world-wide distribution of early phases which transmuted into more advanced types by vertical differentiation, while they split into geographical groups by horizontal differentiation. Both processes may have been accelerated or retarded at certain times and in certain places. Changes in the rate of these developments are very common phenomena (cf. Simpson).[25] One can speculate about their causes. They might have been due to general environmental conditions, yet the state of the population as regards its density or scarcity, migration, interbreeding and extermination certainly played a decisive role. In any case, there is no reason to doubt the possibility that the human stem produced more advanced types under favorable circumstances at a certain period and in one place on earth, while it remained stationary in another. Even our days offer examples for those occurrences: seen from the morphological point of view, the Vedda and the Australian bushman are less advanced human forms than the

25 Simpson 1944.

white man; that is, they have preserved more of their simian stigmata.
Whether they have "entered" into
evolution at a later time than the
whites, or their evolution "rested"
or was "retarded" while that of the
whites went on, we do not know,
but it is irrelevant with regard to
their relation to other races of
modern mankind. If the geological
evidence of a very early "premature" development of Homo sapiens
in certain regions of the world
(Piltdown) were incontestable, this
special human branch must have
stopped the expansion of its braincase or even undergone a reduction
of its brain size in the past 500,000
years. It has been calculated that
the cranial capacity of the Piltdown
braincase amounts to about 1300 cc.,
only a little below the average
cranial capacity of the modern European and slightly above the minimum values of the female modern
Europeans (about 1100 cc.). This
is, in any case, not an encouraging

prognostic for those people who consider the increase of the brain size
as a morphological indication of
the augmentation of mental abilities.

The tabulation shown in the
hominid pedigree is an attempt to
present graphically the relation between the different hominid forms
in time and space. It presumes that
they are a unity with the faculty to
pass into other forms and split at
the same time into different racial
groups. The vertical, horizontal and
diagonal lines and the arrows indicate the directions of these differentiations and the possible extent
of their crossing. It is supposed that
main racial groups of today developed in parallel lines from more
primitive human forms. The parallelism of these lines must have
given way to a convergence the
farther down the lines are traced
or the more interbreeding took place.
But all this is more or less speculation. Only new finds can elucidate
this problem as they did in the past.

Part Five

Progress in paleoanthropology within the past decade may be summarized as follows: (1) an impressive increase in the frequency of finds of pre-hominid and proto-hominid fossil specimens, beginning in 1959 with L. S. B. Leakey's discovery of australopithecines at Olduvai Gorge, East Africa; (2) the application of techniques developed by physical scientists to problems of determining the antiquity of fossils, and the use of procedures employed by biochemists and computer mathematicians for the study of primate systematics; (3) an awareness of the relationship of anatomical structures of organisms, and of primates in particular, to functional and behavioral patterns; (4) a sensitivity to the role played by the natural and the socio-cultural environment in relation to man's genetic endowment and his capacity to adapt to changing ecological conditions; (5) a re-evaluation of traditional concepts about biological race.

The recovery of the fossil named *Zinjanthropus* by its discoverer, Louis S. B. Leakey, was the first of a number of exciting fossil finds made in East Africa since 1959. The taxonomic and phylogenetic status of *Australopithecus boisei* (*Zinjanthropus*), *Homo habilis* ("pre-Zinj"), and "George" is currently being argued by Leakey and his colleagues, notably John T. Robinson, Phillip Tobias, and Sir Wilfred E. Le Gros Clark. To this collection of fossil australopithecines may be added others found in the Omo Basin of Ethiopia by teams of French and American paleoanthropologists. The close biological affinities of the Ethiopian specimens to those of Olduvai Gorge and the earlier known sites in South Africa are recognized by F. Clark Howell and Richard Leakey, who

1959 to 1971

355

have been engaged in recent excavations. It is now widely held that certain fossil fragments recovered from Java by R. von Koenigswald around the time of World War II bear a close resemblance to the East and South African australopithecine materials. The same may be said for other specimens found near Lake Tiberius in Israel and in the Sahara in the Republic of Chad. All these australopithecines are associated with deposits dated to the Lower Pleistocene (Villafranchian) and early Mid-Pleistocene.

The recent additions to the fossil record of more advanced hominids are equally impressive. Important discoveries of *Homo erectus* hominids were made at Lantian in China in 1963–64 and at Vertesszollos in Hungary in the following year. Upper Pleistocene *Homo sapiens* fossils have been discovered at many sites of the Eurasian landmass from Mas D'Azil in Spain to the Niah Cave of Borneo. The finding of mandibles and teeth of *Gigantopithecus* from China has led to the recognition of Weidenreich's proto-pithecantropine as a fossil ape which was a contemporary of man during the early Mid-Pleistocene.

Research into the problem of pre-hominids and their evolution as the earliest representatives of the *Hominidae*—the proto-hominids—did not get under way until Elwyn Simons and David Pilbeam began their systematic examination of the many and varied specimens of the Miocene and Pliocene which had been assigned by earlier scholars to the taxonomic limbo of the dryopithecine group. Through careful inspection of collections of teeth and fragments of jaw bones as well as with the discovery of additional specimens from deposits in the Siwalik Hills of South Asia, Simons and Pilbeam concluded that some specimens should be reclassified as belonging to the earliest known hominid—*Ramapithecus punjabicus*. Similar fossils have been collected in China, Europe, and East Africa, of which Leakey's *Kenyapithecus* is one. Simons's recent work in the Fayum of Egypt has been rewarded with the discovery of fossil apes of which some are certainly ancestral to the dryopithecines from which stock the ramapithecines arose.

A developing picture of hominid evolution depicts the earliest members of our family tree—the ramapithecines—arising from an earlier dryopithecine stock and undergoing an adaptive radiation over three continents during Miocene–Pliocene times. By the time of the late Pliocene the australopithecines had emerged from this line, and had adapted to a broad range of ecological conditions over an extensive geographical area. Robinson has effectively pointed out the morphological and metrical differences between the *Paranthropus* (*Australopithecus robustus*) and *africanus taxa* of the australopithecines, which reflect profound differences of ecological adaptation. He regards the *africanus* form as closest to the phylogenetic line to which more advanced hominids are related. Leakey has urged his colleagues to accept the form he calls *Homo habilis* as the earliest known hominid from which modern man can trace a direct line of descent. There is essential agreement among the paleoanthropologists that from one or more of these divisions of the australopithecines arose the Mid-Pleistocene *Homo erectus* hominids, who were ancestral to all modern forms of man, *Homo sapiens sapiens.*

The construction of man's family tree is advanced by the application of recently developed dating techniques which enable the paleoanthropologist to determine the antiquity of specific fossils on the basis of an absolute chronometric scale convertible to solar years. When used as measurement of temporal distance between paleontological specimens, such methods help the paleoanthropologist to estimate degrees of phylogenetic affinity. The radiometric assay of potassium/argon has been especially useful in dating geological contexts with an antiquity of several million years, while radiocarbon (C_{14}) determinations have been improved so that antiquities as great as seventy thousand years can be determined. A wide range of new chronometric procedures for measuring time in relative and absolute scales is now available to the paleoanthropologist, who can apply them to a great variety of dating problems.

A phase of research that has developed recently is associated with the terms *biochemical anthropolgy* and *molecular anthropology.* These are sub-fields of physical anthropology which approach problems of systematics and phylogeny from the study of chemical and subcellular properties of living primates. Vincent Sarich and his colleagues are interested in the degrees of biochemical and genetic affinity between different kinds of primates, be these defined as species or higher *taxa.* Their methods are not directly applicable to the fossil record for obvious reasons, but they are of indirect value with respect to larger problems of primate phylogeny and population genetics.

While the molecular anthropolgist, who works only with living primates and prefers to study characters of known genetic base, may assume that he has transcended the phenotypic level of living organisms, the paleoanthropologist holds some reservations that the answers to many difficult questions about the course of primate evolution lie at the end of the narrow polypeptide path. Skepticism is based on the evidence that natural selection operates on the phenotype in a very direct way. Therefore, an understanding of the morphological and metrical features of a phenotypic character, whether or not its genetic basis is understood, is the means of establishing how it evolved, how it became adaptive, and what are the probabilities that it might disappear from future generations of the species. However, the interests of the molecular anthropologist and the student of the fossil record are not actually opposed, but rather represent different avenues of research in seeking answers to the same question: what is the evolutionary history of particular phenotypic features in man and his infra-human primate kin.

Computers are now widely used in the study of human paleontology. Among the results of programmed research are reconstructions by computers of skeletal structures missing or incomplete in fossils. Growth patterns can be predicted for immature skeletal specimens, and multivariat analysis is now a commonplace procedure. An example of a recent computer analysis of fossil remains is the study of the taxonomic status of the Swanscombe fragments by means of measurements taken on the fossil skull and on the skulls of a large series of ancient human specimens. These measurements were used in the calculation of the "distance functions," which indicate how closely the measurements are related to skulls of modern man—a procedure of only a few minutes in a computer, which indicated to Joseph Weiner and Bernard Campbell that Swanscombe, like Steinheim, is a *Homo sapiens* but of an early form. Similar advanced statistical methods using high-speed computers were applied to the great toe bone found at Olduvai and to an upper arm bone of an australopithecine from Lake Rudolph. Computers are being used for numerical taxonomy as well.

Although Frederick Wood Jones and Sir Solly Zuckerman had written about the functional relationships of the body structures of primates to their behavior patterns, particularly with regard to the evolution of locomotion systems, Sherwood L. Washburn was most successful in emphasizing the value of approaching these problems from the study of free-ranging groups of primates. He and his students have interpreted structural variations in the light of the ecological settings and social behavior of different kinds of primates. Their field studies have demonstrated a great variety of biological and social adaptations within the order, and at the same time have forced anatomists to think of particular corporeal structures as dynamic and highly plastic adaptations.

Primate behavior studies have had the effect of making the paleo-anthropologist aware of the affinity between man's biological adaptations and his behavior as a social primate maintaining traditions of learned behavior. Human ecological adaptations are the products of man's biological and cultural responses to the natural environment as well as to the stresses of his social milieu. Many higher primates form social groups, but only man has evolved that particular adaptation called culture. The questions of how cultural behavior originated and developed within the hominid phylogenetic line and how it has effected man's biological structures and processes are problems of which the paleoanthropologist of this decade has been especially aware. Studies of our fossil progenitors must take into the account the artifactual evidence of cultural variation and change. It is now widely recognized by primate behaviorists, human paleontologists, and prehistorians that the capacity for cultural behavior must have existed with some pre-Pleistocene primates, but evidence of tool manufacture does not appear in the archaeological record until the time of the Lower Pleistocene. With the perfection of a striding bipedal locomotor pattern by some australopithecines of the Lower Pleistocene and with advanced neuro-anatomical changes occurring among hominids of the Mid-and

Upper Pleistocene, man evolved his unique adaptive feature. It is in the anatomical structures of both fossil and living men and in the prehistoric archaeological record that the story of man's ecological adaptations to nature and to society is being read today.

By looking at human evolution through the lenses of ecology and population genetics, physical anthropologists interested in the causes and patterns of biological variation in modern human populations have been questioning traditional classifications and theories of race to the extent that some scholars have denied the scientific validity of the concept. Dissatisfaction with the attempts to define infra-specific classifications was first experienced in the late 'fifties by systematists working with nonhuman organisms. In 1961–62 the journal *Current Anthropopology* carried some provocative articles debating the applicability of race theory to man. The appearance of Carleton Coon's *The Origin of Races* (1962), a polyphyletic approach toward understanding the basis of human variability in the fossil record and in living populations, forced many anthropologists to reexamine venerable theories about race. Ecological studies have demonstrated the high degree of biological plasticity in man, and the rigidity of formal classifications and phylogenetic racial lines is giving way to a study of population variation based on the study of multiple adaptive responses of populations to environmental settings through time. With the passing of the race concept, paleoanthropology loses one of its most venerable and popular topics of inquiry—one of many concepts which have been discussed in this volume which appeared to be irrefutable to one generation of scholars and unacceptable to the next.

New Findings on the Origin of Races

Carleton S. Coon
1962

What is race? A myth, as some popular writers would have us believe, or a rigid division of mankind into superior and inferior groups? A reverse freedom rider northward bound? America's greatest and most divisive unsolved problem? The white, black, yellow, red, and brown races pictured in the school geography books? Or a relatively recent and superficial division of mankind?

No. Re-examined in the light of science and history, race is not exactly any of these. It is not a myth, and races are not, as current theory holds, something that evolved into final form about 30,000 years ago and have remained unchanged ever since. In man as in other animals and in plants, a race is a geographically separate division of a species.

A five-year-long study which I have made of every scrap of bone of every fossil man so far discovered —about one thousand pieces—shows rather that the races of man are as old as man himself. The separation of man into races is the work of geography, acting in the guise of natural selection shaping genetically plastic living material.

Races arose as soon as the primitive ancestors of man had dispersed by migrating from the place where they originated—uncertain but possibly in Africa—into all of the warm parts of the Old World (Eurasia and Africa) which could be reached on foot. These earliest humans were not apes, but close relatives of the Australopithecines, the African apemen with ape-sized brains and essentially manlike bodies.

Between a million and a half-million years ago—in the varied climates and circumstances of regions as widely separated as Morocco and Java—some of the migrants appeared in the form of the oldest known human species, *Homo erectus*. They were already divided into five geographical races and were generally larger of brain, smaller of jaw, and otherwise different in structure from the ape-men.

I. The Australoids. In Java, which was intermittently joined to the Asiatic mainland, *Homo erectus* was already what we now call an Australoid. Later still the Australoids evolved into modern men—*Homo sapiens*—or that part of *Homo sapiens* which includes today's Australian aborigines, Papuans, Melanesians, Negrito dwarfs living from the Philippines to the Andaman Islands, and some of the tribal folk of India.

II. The Mongoloids. In China the early men of the new species, *Homo erectus*, were already Mongoloids. In time they too changed into modern man, siring the numerous peoples of Eastern Asia (except the Ainus) as well as the Polynesians, American Indians, and Eskimos.

III. The Caucasoids. A third race arose somewhere in Western Asia, with the characteristics that were later to be called Caucasoid. By 250,000 years ago some of them had evolved into *Homo sapiens*. From these latter are descended the Europeans and their overseas kin in the Americas and elsewhere; the Middle Eastern whites; most of the people of India; and possibly the Ainus of Japan.

IV. The Capoids. Another race made the transition in North Africa and later, after being pushed south and east, probably evolved into the Bushmen and Hottentots of the race that we call Capoid, after the Cape of Good Hope.

V. The Congoids. A fifth kind of *Homo erectus* appeared in Africa and, as far as we can tell from scanty evidence, it seems to have been related to both Caucasoids and Negroes. I have named it Congoid after the region of the Congo basin.

Very late, at a time not exactly known, these people turned into *Homo sapiens* and the modern Negroes and Pygmies.

Homo erectus, as I have shown in my new book, evolved into *Homo sapiens* (our self-named Wise Man), not once but five times, as each subspecies or race living in its own territory passed a critical threshold from a more brutal to a more sapient state.

That such a seeming miracle of transition could occur even once disturbed the smug beliefs of many people when Charles Darwin presented his theory of evolution more than a hundred years ago. My thesis is at variance with the dogmas of 1962, which insist on a single, relatively recent emergence of man. But it is really nothing new. Zoologists and paleontologists have known for some time that the races of a single species can evolve in concert. Only the self-centered folk who cannot see beyond the problems of our own species need be taken aback by this commonplace of zoology.

Nor am I the first to suggest such an origin of races in man. In the 1930s the late Franz Weidenreich, who was studying the bones of *Homo erectus* found in a onetime cave near Peking—Peking Man—noted their Mongoloid character and suggested that the modern Mongoloid races had descended from Peking Man, or Sinanthropus, as he is also called. The idea was immediately attacked and called an impossibility. Critics pointed out that all living men belong to one species, *Homo sapiens*. On the assumption that *Homo sapiens* had originated only once, it was argued that he then spread around the world from the Arctic to Cape Horn and east to west, conveniently extinguishing all archaic species. Only after this dispersal, the argument continued, could the living races of man have developed, each in its own region, and that would have been not much more than 30,000 years ago.

If this were true, I asked, how does it happen that some peoples, like the Tasmanians and many of the Australian aborigines were still living during the nineteenth century in a manner comparable to that of the Europeans of over 100,000 years ago? This would have entailed some major cultural backsliding which the archaeological record does not show. To me there was something pat, dogmatic, and wrong about the anti-Weidenreich point of view.

Dry land to cross

To test my thesis that human races were ancient and that they evolved early in five different areas, I undertook the study of all available information on all the fossil remains known from more than three hundred sites. But a theoretical foundation also had to be provided for the facts. What forces exerted pressure on that plastic primate man to make him evolve from a crude to a modern state? To satisfy this need I delved into zoogeography, primate behavior, and social anthropology. At the same time I kept in touch with physiolo-

gists studying the mechanisms of adaptation to heat, cold, and altitude, and I went on a field trip with some of them to Chile.

Geography and the rumpled skin of our planet were major shaping elements. From a million to a half-million years ago, the way lay open for the Australopithecine-like ancestors of *Homo erectus* to spread eastward from Africa across the whole range of the Old World tropics. Four of the world's present five continents —Eurasia (Asia and Europe), Africa, and North and South America—were tied together in one fashion or another, but our New world continents were not accessible till later. Low sea levels exposed the Sunda Shelf joining Southeast Asia and the islands of Indonesia. Another now submerged stretch of land, the Sahul Shelf, also stood above the waters to join Australia, Tasmania, New Guinea, and some of the Melanesian Islands. Not only did the shelves serve as dry connections between lands now divided by the seas, but they may also have acted as bellows to suck in and blow out early human populations.

The lesser barriers around the world, such as mountains and deserts, let the dominant animal species, including man, filter through to new territories and favorable breeding grounds. Once there, the populations that had survived the rigors of the journey remained relatively isolated and could evolve in their own ways. New genes brought in from outside, by neighbors or invaders, tended to lose out to those already established by natural selection. However, new genes that were advantageous in all climates and regions, such as those governing higher intelligence, tended to win out everywhere.

In the new lands that the ancestors of the living races reached they encountered many kinds of climate and topography. The newcomers were selected by geographical environment for their ability to resist three kinds of stress in particular—cold, drought, and the thin air of high altitudes. The first entails heat regulation by the human body; the second both heat regulation and the conservation of food and water; and the third, oxygen consumption.

Each race in its own territory independently found its way of surmounting these stresses. The Canoe Indians of Tierra del Fuego at the tip of South America could paddle about without clothing in freezing weather because they have a basal metabolism 160 per cent higher than the norm for whites of the same height and weight. When plunged into cold water, the hands of Alaskan Indians have more blood flow than those of white men.

Selection in another direction enabled the Australian aborigines to take care of cold; they developed insulation in depth of the body core. Members of the Pitjendjera tribe in west central Australia sleep comfortably on the ground in freezing temperatures. They can do this because the outgoing arterial blood in their extremities warms the incoming venous blood.

So far only the Negroes have been shown to possess heat adaptation.

American Negroes can tolerate moist heat better than American whites of the same age and background. And so far only Mongoloids, in the Andes and Tibet, are believed to have shown altitude adaptation, in that they have relatively large hearts and large quantities of blood rich in oxygen-carrying red corpuscles. In general, Europeans seem to have no climatic adaptations, but that is probably partly because we use whites as our standard for comparison in studying other peoples.

Among living races many differences may be found in the biochemical realm, such as the tendency of Negroes to be immune to malaria because of possessing sickle cells in their blood, and the tendency of people with blood groups A and B to resist certain contagious diseases; but we can only speculate about the importance of these factors to *Homo erectus* because all we have of him is teeth and bones.

The basic transition from *Homo erectus* to *Homo sapiens* had nothing *directly* to do with adaptation to climate; all that did was to make it possible for man to live in different places and divide into races. The transition was caused by an increase in intelligence and self-control, both of which were needed as men became hunters, had to live in groups of several families in order to get and share their food, had to plan hunts, teach their children how to behave toward others of different sex and age, and needed speech in order to live. These increases were accompanied by an increase in brain size and probably also by changes in endocrine balance. Only the first of these, brain size, left unmistakable marks on the skeleton. A number of criteria, too technical to be explained here briefly, enable us to divide the skeletons of *Homo erectus* from those of *Homo sapiens* in each of the races where adequate remains have been found to make this distinction.[1]

But two biological problems are central to the question of the origin of races: (1) How did the subspecies or races become differentiated in the first place? This question we have already answered. (2) Why did they not keep on differentiating and become separate species?

The answer to the second question is complicated. In other animals, related species occupying the same territories are kept apart genetically because their members do not feel the desire to breed together, whether or not fertile offspring could be produced if they did. Each has its own set of signals with which it communicates with its kind. In the case of man, we communicate by means of speech, and each group can learn the other's language.

From the earliest times, therefore, there has been gene exchange among groups of people. Wives have been traded or captured, although generally men remain faithful to their own races, at least if their own women are with them. But men traveling alone have no such compunctions, and man is the widest-traveling mammal of them all. So despite racial differences, we are still one species.

One reason why most workers in the fossil man field have failed to realize the vast antiquity of human races is that they have confused two concepts, *grade* and *line*. A grade is an evolutionary level, marked in man by such features as brain size, forehead slope, size of the eyebrow ridges (if any), tooth size, and the presence or absence of a chin. A line is a geographical race, marked by such anatomical details as the shape of the eyebrow ridges, the degree to which the face is either flat or V-shaped, the degree of prominence of the nose, and the structure of the teeth. A skull of any line (race) can belong to any grade (evolutionary level) and vice versa. In most textbooks on human evolution, skulls are lumped together by grade without regard for line, which makes little more sense than confusing bats with birds because both fly.

Inevitably, questions arise as to the modern cultural implications of any discussion of racial differences, but any detailed treatment of this subject will take another book. Briefly, I might say that the Caucasoids and Mongoloids who live today in their homelands and in recently colonized regions, such as North America, did not rise by accident to their present population levels and

---

[1] The designation of a fossil skull as *erectus* or *sapiens* depends on the total configuration, not on brain size alone. But an approximate threshold between the brain-size ranges of *Homo erectus* and *Homo sapiens* can be set at about 1,250 to 1,300 cc, with the expectation that individual differences will occur.

positions of cultural dominance. They achieved this because their ancestors occupied the most favorable of the earth's zoological regions —regions with challenging climates and ample breeding grounds, centrally located within continental land masses. In our times, the success of these groups is being challenged in many parts of the world as other groups who evolved later learn to use their inventions, especially modern means of communication. And evolution is still taking place, particularly natural selection resulting from crowding and stress.

Man on the threshold

The oldest adult human skull yet found belongs to the lowest grade of *Homo erectus,* and to the Australoid line. It is known as Pithecanthropus (Ape-Man) Number 4, because it was the fourth of its kind to be found. All four were unearthed in river banks in central Java. Number 4 is about 700,000 years old, and Numbers 1, 2, and 3 between 600,000 and 500,000. We know this because tektites—small, glassy nodules from outer space—were found in the same beds as the first three, and the beds containing Number 4 lay underneath the tektite bed, along with the bones of a more ancient group of animals. These tektites have been picked up in large numbers in Java, the Philippines, and Australia, where they all fell in a single celestial shower. Their age—approximately 600,000 years—has been accurately measured in several laboratories by nuclear chemical analysis, through the so-called argon-potassium method.

Pithecanthropus Number 4 consists of the back part of a skull and its lower face, palate, and upper teeth. As reconstructed by Weidenreich, it is a brutal-looking skull, with heavy crests behind for powerful neck muscle attachments, a large palate, and large teeth, as in apes. The brain size of this skull was about 900 cubic centimeters; modern human brains range from about 1,000 to 2,000 cc with an average of about 1,450 cc. The brains of apes and Australopithecines are about 350 to 650 cc. So Pithecanthropus Number 4 was intermediate in brain size between apes and living men.

His fragmentary skull was not the only find made in the beds it lay in. Nearby were found the cranial vault of a two-year-old baby, already different from those of living infants, and a piece of chinless adult lower jaw. Two other jaws have been discovered in the same deposits which were much larger than any in the world certainly belonging to *Homo erectus.* They are called Meganthropus (Big Man) and may have belonged to a local kind of Australopithecine, but this is not certain. If so, *Homo erectus* coexisted with, or overlapped, the Australopithecines in Java as well as in South Africa, which implies that man did not originate in either place, but somewhere in between.

The three later Pithecanthropus skulls were all faceless, but essen-

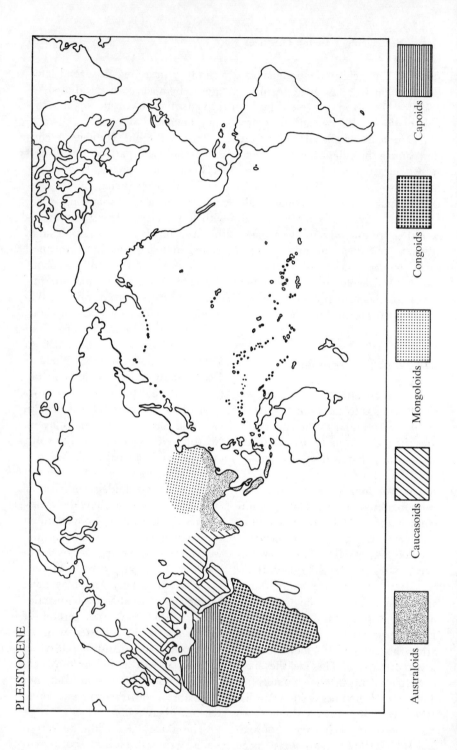

PLEISTOCENE

Australoids Caucasoids Mongoloids Congoids Capoids

EARLY POST-PLEISTOCENE

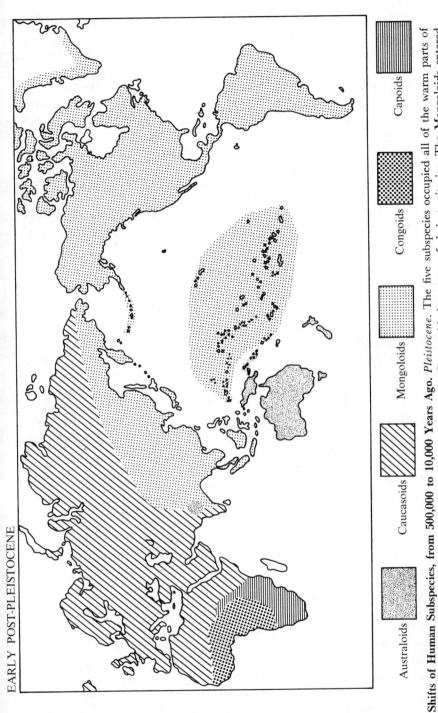

Shifts of Human Subspecies, from 500,000 to 10,000 Years Ago. *Pleistocene.* The five subspecies occupied all of the warm parts of Eurasia and Africa. *Early Post-Pleistocene.* The Mongoloids and Caucasoids burst out of their territories. The Mongoloids entered and inhabited America, Southeast Asia, and Indonesia. The Caucasoids thrust northward and into Africa. The Congoids were much reduced, but later evolved rapidly and spread as Negroes over much of Africa.

Australoids   Caucasoids   Mongoloids   Congoids   Capoids tially similar to Number 4, if a little less brutal, and their brains were no larger. A series of eleven more skulls from the Solo River bank, in the same part of Java, carry on this same evolutionary line, but are larger-brained (1,035 to 1,225 cc). They were probably between 150,000 and 75,000 years old, and were still *erectus,* of a higher grade than their predecessors.

The Australoids had begun to cross the threshold from *erectus* to *sapiens* some 40,000 years ago. We know this from a carbon-14 date given a skull found in a cave in North Borneo. In Java itself, the earliest *sapiens* skulls are a pair found at Wadjak, and dated probably no more than 10,000 years ago. These skulls are identical with those of living Australian aborigines.

What happened in Java occurred also in China to a second major race, the Mongoloid. From a series of rock fissures and caves at Choukoutien, near Peking, pieces of the skulls and jaws of about twenty persons and the loose teeth of at least as many more, have been excavated. These specimens, about 360,000 years old, are what is left of a people called Sinanthropus.

Although definitely *Homo erectus* and equal in evolutionary grade to the much less ancient Solo skulls, they differ from the Javanese specimens racially. Instead of sloping gradually, their foreheads stand out sharply from their eyebrow ridges. These persons had cheekbones and jaws which protruded forward, their eyesockets were shallow, and their faces were flattish. Their teeth were the most peculiar of all known in the races of man, particularly the incisors which were not smooth inside as most of ours are, but shaped like shovels, with raised ridges on either side and lumps and teat-like protuberances on the insides of the crowns. These peculiarities are still seen in Mongoloid teeth, from China to Cape Horn.

A series of less ancient skulls also found in China carries the Mongoloid line of descent from Sinanthropus to the modern Chinese, Indonesians, Siberians, Japanese, and American Indians. The earliest of them known to have crossed the evolutionary threshold between *Homo erectus* and *Homo sapiens* is the Tze-Yang skull from Szechuan, Western China, dated at about 150,000 years old. This skull was discovered in 1951 and described in 1957 in a Communist Chinese periodical which few in this country have seen. All the Mongoloid skulls later than Tze-Yang are *sapiens* also. Thus the first ancestors of the American Indians who crossed the Bering Strait more than 10,000 years ago must also have been *sapiens. Homo erectus* existed only in the Old World.

Maligned Neanderthals

The oldest Caucasoid specimen known is the Heidelberg jaw, about as old as Sinanthropus. Because no braincase was found with it, we do not know whether Heidelberg man was *Homo sapiens* or *Homo erectus* at all. It is chinless, but so are some *sapiens* specimens, and its teeth are of modern size and Caucasoid form.

Two Western European skulls of women, dated at 250,000 years or older, are both *sapiens* and Caucasoid. One is from Swanscombe, England, and the other from Steinheim, Germany. Some of my colleagues have questioned the *sapiens* character of these two skulls, because Swanscombe lacks a face and Steinheim is rather small, and has heavy browridges. But if we are to call all living human beings *Homo sapiens,* then either these ancient women were *sapiens* or else the living Australian aborigines are *erectus,* because Steinheim belonged to the same grade as they do.

From then on all the skulls found in Europe and Western Asia, with one possible exception (Number 5 from the Skhul, cave in Palestine, which could have been Australoid) are both *sapiens* and Caucasoid. This statement includes the famous Neanderthals, a much-maligned group of peoples living all the way from France to Uzbekistan, in small, isolated enclaves, during the extremely cold period which lasted from about 75,000 to 40,000 years ago.

The Neanderthals were not stunted, bent over, nor brutal as commonly claimed. Many of them did, however, suffer from arthritis. One skeleton in France is that of an old man who had lost all but two of his teeth, and was too crippled to move about easily. Someone had fed him soft food for years before his death. Another, in Iraq, had been born with a withered arm, which some Neanderthal surgeon had later amputated with a flint knife. People who care for the crippled and aged are not brutes. Furthermore, the Neanderthals were exaggeratedly Caucasoid, with long, pointed faces and beaky noses. The features in which they differed from other Caucasoids were mostly if not entirely due to local inbreeding and adaptation to cold. In Western Europe the Neanderthals were followed by new invaders from the Near East, men indistinguishable from living Europeans.

Those who fled

In 1939 in a cave near Tangier, Morocco, I came upon the left half of the upper jaw of a child, in a deposit probably 75,000 years or so old. I took it back to our hotel and showed it to a French physician, who said that it was part of an ape. Later, a distinguished Turkish physical anthropologist, M. S. Şenyürek, labeled it Neanderthal. Finally L. Cabot Briggs, an American anthropologist resident in Algeria, stated that the child had belonged to a previously unidentified local North African race. Briggs's insight was upheld by the discovery, a few years later, of three lower jaws as old as Sinanthropus at Ternefine, Algeria. These jaws also resembled those of Sinanthropus, and so did their teeth. Other specimens from the Moroccan coast filled in the time gap between Ternefine and Tangier, but we have yet to find a braincase.

The Ternefine-Tangier line, as I

have called this group of jaws and teeth, resembles the Mongoloid more than any other. Whoever they were, the members of this race were replaced about 10,000 years ago by the Caucasoid ancestors of the living North African Berbers. These invaders came in with an inroad of northern animals—wild cattle, wild sheep, deer, wild boar, and bears— which they had been hunting in Spain or the Near East, and which they pursued into Africa.

Although the evidence is scanty, I believe it likely that the Ternefine-Tangier folk fled into the Sahara and then migrated southward along the East African highlands to the vast paradise of game that was South Africa until the arrival of the Dutch, who began to settle the Cape of Good Hope region about the time that the Pilgrims were landing in Plymouth, Massachusetts. When they first saw the South African natives, the Bushmen and Hottentots, the Dutch thought that they were some kind of Malays or Indonesians, on account of their flat faces and yellowish skins. The Mongoloid features of the Ternefine-Tangier jaws and teeth were thus matched by those of the living Capoids.

Enigma of Negro origins

The fifth major race—the most mysterious of all—is called the Congoid because it includes both the African Negroes and the Pygmies, who share the Congo drainage. The term "Negroid" is to be avoided because it is also used to designate some of the Australoid peoples such as the Melanesians and Negritos. "Negroid" means not a race but a condition (that is, having spiral hair, black skin, etc.), achieved independently in the course of evolution by more than one line of people.

The oldest known Congoid specimen is a skullcap from Olduvai Gorge, Tanganyika, the Grand Canyon of Africa, a rich hunting ground for students of extinct animals as well as for anthropologists. It was found in 1960 by Louis Leakey in a stratum dated at about 400,000 years ago, overlying the layer in which he had previously discovered two kinds of Australopithecines. The Olduvai skullcap is long and relatively narrow, compared to Pithecanthropus, Solo, and Sinanthropus. Unlike these three eastern types, all of which are relatively flat-faced, it has huge eyebrow ridges which sweep backward to either side like bicycle handles. In this respect, and in others, it resembles both the living Caucasoids and Negroes, who have much in common anatomically. This skull clearly belonged to the species *Homo erectus* and probably to the Congoid racial line.

From 400,000 to 40,000 years ago, we have no certain evidence of human evolution in Africa south of the Sahara, although vast quantities of stone implements assure us that people lived there continuously. A skullcap from Saldanha Bay, near Capetown, is probably 40,000 years old or older. It closely resembles the Olduvai specimen. So does a whole skull, minus the lower jaw, from Broken Hill, Northern Rhodesia, which is believed to be no more than 25,000 years old. Sheltered in a cave from death to discovery, it is still in excellent shape. The late Aleš Hrdlička, famed anatomist of the Smithsonian Institution, who was given neither to overstatement nor to displays of unbridled emotion, called it a "comet of man's prehistory" when he saw it in 1930 but, at that time as today, the Rhodesian skull was and remains the only complete specimen of *Homo erectus* yet found, and that may be one reason why it looked so strange. Its brow-ridges, palate, and teeth match in size those of the much earlier Pithecanthropus skulls, but its features are those of Negroes.

After Broken Hill we have no well-dated Negro skulls older than 8,000 to 5,000 years, and these are *sapiens*. Further digging is needed in Africa, particularly in West Africa, whence many Negroes have migrated, both within their own continent and to America, before we will be able to solve the enigma of Negro origins.

But we know, in a general way, the ingredients from which the Negroes may have been blended. One is the old racial line from Olduvai to Broken Hill. A second is the Pygmies of the deep forests, who may be dwarfed descendants of some of the Olduvai-Broken Hill folk. A third is the Capoids, who circled around West Africa and the Congo on their great trek from the Mediterranean to the shores of the Southern Ocean. A fourth is the wave of Caucasoid invaders from North Africa known as the Capsians (after the site of Gafsa in Tunisia) who settled the East African highlands about 5000 B.C., and whose aquiline features may still be seen among the Watussi of Ruanda-Urundi and other spear-brandishing warrior tribes. These four ingredients, combined in varying proportions in different regions and molded by climate and natural selection, probably combined to produce the composite and variable population of black-skinned and curly-haired peoples known as Negroes who, in 1962, figure prominently in the national and international news.

Such, then, is the origin of the five living subspecies of man, our human races, some seen in the broad light of day, others through a dusty glass darkly. I hope to live long enough to see some of the dust swept away, and to know where I was right and where wrong and much more important, where the truth lies.

Quid novi ex Africa?

The Taxonomic Evaluation of Fossil Hominids

Ernst Mayr
1963

Introduction

The concepts and methods on which the classification of hominid taxa is based do not differ in principle from those used for other zoological taxa. Indeed, the classification of living human populations or of samples of fossil hominids is a branch of animal taxonomy. It can only lead to confusion if different standards and terminologies are adopted in the two fields. The reasons for the adoption of a single, uniform language for both fields, and the nature of this language, have been excellently stated by G. G. Simpson in his contribution to this volume.

There is, perhaps, one practical difference between animal and hominid taxonomy. Hominid remains are of such significance that even rather incomplete specimens may be of vital importance. An attempt must sometimes be made to evaluate fragments that a student of dinosaurs or fossil bovids would simply ignore. But, of course, even a rather complete specimen is only a very inadequate representation of the population to which it belongs, and most specimens are separated by large intervals of space and time. Yet, it is the task of the taxonomist to derive from these specimens an internally consistent classification.

The non-taxonomist must be fully aware of two aspects of such a classification: first, that it is usually by no means the only possible classification to be based on the available evidence, so that a taxonomist with a different viewpoint might arrive at a different classification; and second, that every classification based on inadequate material is provisional. A single new discovery may change the picture rather drastically and lead to a considerable revision.

The material of taxonomy consists of zoological objects. These objects are individuals or parts of individuals who, in nature, were members of populations. Our ultimate objective, then, is the classification of popula-

Reprinted from Sherwood L. Washburn, editor, *Classification and Human Evolution* (Chicago: Aldine Publishing Company, 1963); copyright © 1963 by Wenner-Gren Foundation for Anthropological Research, Inc.

tions as represented by the available samples.

Objects versus populations

The statement that we must classify populations rather than objects sounds almost like a platitude in this year 1962. Yet, it is not so many years ago that the study of fossil man was in the hands of strict morphologists who arranged specimens in morphological series and based their classification almost entirely on an interpretation of similarities and differences without regard to any other factor. He who classifies specimens as representatives of populations knows that populations have a concrete distribution in space and time and that this provides a source of information that is not available to the strict morphologist. Any classification that is inconsistent with the known distribution of populations is of lowered validity.

The application of taxonomic principles in concrete cases

There have been several previous attempts (Dobzhansky 1944; Mayr 1944, 1950) to apply the principles of systematic zoology to some of the open problems of hominid classification. A great deal of new evidence has since accumulated and there has been some further clarification of our concepts. The time would seem proper for a new look at some of these problems.

Subspecies or species

The decision whether to rank a given taxon in the category "subspecies" or in the category "species" is often exceedingly difficult in the absence of conclusive evidence. This is as true in the classification of living populations (geographical isolates) as it is for fossils. A typical example as far as the hominids are concerned is the ranking of Neanderthal Man. I have found three interpretations of Neanderthal in the literature.

1. "Neanderthal Man is a more primitive ancestral stage through which *sapiens* has passed." This we might call the classical hypothesis, defended particularly during the period when the interpretation of human evolution was based primarily on the evaluation of morphological series. This classical hypothesis had to be abandoned when it was found to be in conflict with the distribution of classical and primitive Neanderthals and of *sapiens* in space and time.

2. "Neanderthal is an aberrant separate species, a contemporary of early *sapiens* but reproductively isolated from him."

3. "Neanderthal is a subspecies, a geographic race, of early *sapiens*."

What evidence is there that would permit us to come to a decision as to the relative merits of alternatives (2) and (3)? We must begin by defining rigidly what a species is and what a subspecies. As clearly stated by Simpson (1961) and Mayr (1957), degree of morphological difference per se is not a decisive primary criterion. A species is reproductively isolated from other species coexisting in time and space, while a subspecies is a geographic subdivision of a species actually or potentially (in the case of geographical isolates) in gene exchange with other similar subdivisions of the species.

The difficulty in applying these concepts to fossil material is obvious. It can be established only by inference whether two fossil taxa formed a single reproductive community or two reproductively isolated ones. In order to draw the correct inference, we must ask certain questions:

Does the distribution of Neanderthal and *sapiens* indicate that they were reproductively isolated? Not so many years ago Neanderthal was considered by many as a Würm "eskimo," but he is now known to have had an enormous distribution, extending south as far as Gibraltar and North Africa and east as far as Iran and Turkestan. There is no evidence (but see below) that Neanderthal coexisted with *sapiens* anywhere in this wide area. Where did *sapiens* live during the Riss-Würm Interglacial and during the first Würm stadial? No one knows. Ethiopia, India and southeast Asia have been suggested, but these will remain wild guesses until some properly dated new finds are made. All we know is that at the time of the first Würm interstadial Cro-Magnon Man suddenly appeared in Europe and overran it in a relatively short time.

The sapiens *problem*

There has been much talk in the past of the "Neanderthal problem." Now, since the average morphological differences between the classical Neanderthal of the first Würm stadial and the earlier Neanderthals of the Riss-Würm Interglacial have been worked out, and since the distribution of Neanderthal has been mapped, *sapiens sapiens* has become the real problem. Where did he originate and how long did it take for pre-*sapiens* to change into *sapiens?* Where did this change occur?

All we really know is that *s. sapiens,* as Cro-Magnon, suddenly appeared in Europe. Sufficient remains from the preceding period of unmixed Neanderthal in Europe and adjacent parts of Africa and Asia (and a complete absence of any blade culture) prove conclusively that *s. sapiens* did not originate in Europe. The rather wide distribution of types with a strong supraorbital torus (e.g., Rhodesia, Solo-Java) suggests that *s. sapiens* must have originated in a localized area. The sharpness of distinction between Neanderthal and *s. sapiens* (except at Mt. Carmel) further indicates that Neanderthal, as a whole, did not gradually change into *sapiens,* but was replaced by an invader.

There is a suspicion that evolutionary change can occur the faster (up to certain limits), the smaller and more isolated the evolving population is. If *s. sapiens* lost his supra-orbital torus very quickly (and the various other characters it had before becoming *sapiens*) then it can be postulated with a good deal of assurance that *sapiens* evolved in a rather small, peripheral, and presumably well isolated population. Even if we assume that the rate of change was slow and the evolving population large, we must still assume that *sapiens* was rather isolated. Otherwise, one would expect to find more evidence for intergradation with late Neanderthal.

It is obvious that the available evidence is meager. Let us assume, however, for the sake of the argument, that Neanderthal and *sapiens* were strictly allopatric, that is that they replaced each other geographically. Zoologists have interpreted allopatry in the past usually as evidence for conspecificity, because subspecies are always allopatric. We are now a little more cautious because we have discovered in recent years a number of cases where closely related species are allopatric because competitive intolerance seems to preclude their geographical coexistence. The rapidity with which Neanderthal disappeared at the time Cro-Magnon Man appeared on the scene would seem to strengthen the claim for competitive intolerance and consequently for species status of these two entities. Yet, here is clearly a case where it is perhaps not legitimate to apply zoological generalizations to man. The Australian Aborigines and most of the North American Indians disappeared equally or perhaps even more rapidly, and yet no one except for a few racists would consider them different species.

We are thus forced to fall back on the two time-honored criteria of species status, degree of morphological difference and presence or absence of interbreeding. Our inference on the taxonomic ranking of Neanderthal will be based largely on these two sets of criteria, supplemented by a third, available only for man.

1. DEGREE OF MORPHOLOGICAL DIFFERENCE

The amount of difference between the skulls of Neanderthal and *sapiens* is most impressive. There are no two races of modern man that are nearly as different as classical Neanderthal and *sapiens*. And yet one has a feeling that the differences are mostly of a rather superficial nature, such as the size of the supra-orbital and occipital torus and the general shape of skull. The cranial capacity, on the other hand, is remarkably similar in the two forms. The gap between Neanderthal and *sapiens* is to some extent bridged by two populations, Rhodesian Man and Solo Man, which are widely separated geographically from Neanderthal. Although sharing the large supraorbital torus with Neanderthal, these two other populations differ in many details of skull shape and cranial capacity from Neanderthal as well as from *s. sapiens*. Whether or not these peripheral African and

Asiatic types acquired their Neanderthaloid features independently, can be established only after a far more thorough study and the investigation of additional material. It seems quite improbable that they are directly related to Neanderthal. In view of their small cranial capacity they may have to be classified with *H. erectus*.

As it now stands, one must admit that the inference to be drawn from the degree of morphological difference between Neanderthal and *sapiens* is inconclusive.

2. INTERBREEDING BETWEEN NEANDERTHAL AND SAPIENS

Cro-Magnon Man, on his arrival in western Europe, seems to have been remarkably free from admixture with the immediately preceding Neanderthal. There is, however, some evidence of mixture in the material from the two caves of Mt. Carmel in Palestine. Both caves were inhabited early in the Würm glaciation. The older cave (Tabun) was inhabited by almost typical Neanderthals with a slight admixture of modern characters, the younger cave (Skhul) by an essentially *sapiens* population but with distinct Neanderthaloid characters. The date is too late to consider these populations to have belonged to the ancestral stock that gave rise both to Neanderthal and modern man. It seems to me that the differences between Tabun and Skhul are too great to permit us to consider them as samples from a single population coming from the area of geographical inter-

gradation between Neanderthal and modern man, although this could be true for the Skhul population. Hybridization between invading Cro-Magnon Man and Neanderthal remnants is perhaps a more plausible interpretation for the Skhul population, while there is no good reason not to consider Tabun essentially an eastern Neanderthal, particularly in view of its similarity to the Shanidar specimens (Stewart 1960).

Repeated re-examinations of the Mt. Carmel material have thus substantiated the long-standing claims that this material is evidence for interbreeding between Neanderthal and *sapiens*.

3. THE CULTURAL EVIDENCE

As our knowledge of human and hominid artifacts increases, it becomes necessary to include this source of evidence in our considerations. My own personal knowledge of this field is exceedingly slight, but when I look at the implements assigned to Neanderthal and those assigned to Cro-Magnon, I feel the differences are so small that I can not make myself believe they were produced by two different biological species. I realize that the history of human or hominid artifacts goes back much further than we used to think, yet this is not in conflict with my hunch that there was no opportunity for the simultaneous existence of two separate hominid species of advanced tool makers.

I would like to add some incidental comments on tools and human evolution. The history of peoples and tribes is full of incidences of a secondary cultural deterioration, *vide* the Mayas and their modern descendants! Most of the modern native populations with rudimentary material cultures (e.g., certain New Guinea mountain natives) are almost surely the descendants of culturally more advanced ancestors. This must be kept in mind when paleolithic cultures from Africa and western Eurasia are compared with those of southern and eastern Asia. Stone tools and the hunting of large mammals seem to be closely correlated. Could such peoples have lost their tool cultures after they had emigrated into areas poor in large game? Could this be the reason for the absence of stone tools in Javan *Homo erectus?*

Conclusion. The facts that are so far available do not permit a clear-cut decision on the question whether Neanderthal was a subspecies or a separate species. It seems to me, however, that on the whole they are in better agreement with the sub-species hypothesis. It would seem best for the time being to postulate that Neanderthal (*sensu stricto*) was a northern and western subspecies of *Homo sapiens* (*sensu lato*), which was an incipient species but probably never reached species level prior to its extinction.

Polytypic species and evolution

All attempts to trace hominid phylogeny still deal with typological models. "*Australopithecus* gave rise to *Homo erectus*," etc. In reality there were widespread polytypic species with more advanced and more conservative races. One or several of the advanced races gave rise to the next higher grade. It may happen in such a case that the descendant species lives simultaneously (but allopatrically) with the more conservative races of the ancestral species. This is often interpreted to indicate that the ancestral species could not have given rise to the descendant species. *True,* as far as the ancestral species in a typological sense is concerned, but *not* true for the ancestral species as a polytypic whole.

The concept of most polytypic species being descendants of ancestral polytypic species creates at once two formidable difficulties. One of these is caused by unequal rates of evolution of the different races. Let us say that there was an ancestral species 1 with races 1a, 1b, 1c and 1d. Race 1a evolved into species 2, absorbing in the process much of race 1b, and now forms races 2a and 2b. Race 1c became extinct and race 1d persisted in a relic area without changing very drastically. We now have 2 (a and b) and 1 (d) existing at the same time level, even though they represent different evolutionary stages (morphological grades). It is thinkable, for instance, (in part after Coon 1962) that Heidelberg Man was the first population of *Homo erectus* to reach the *sapiens* level, and that as *Homo sapiens heidelbergensis* it was contemporary with *Homo erectus* of Java and China. (This is purely a thought model, as long as only a single mandible of Heidelberg Man is available.) It is possible that *Homo erectus* persisted in Africa as *rhodesiensis* and in Java as *soloensis* at a time when European populations clearly had reached *Homo sapiens* level. Such a possibility is by no means remote; in view of the many polytypic species of Recent animals in which some races are highly advanced and others very primitive.

I am calling attention to this situation to prevent too far a swing of the pendulum. The late Weidenreich arranged fossil hominids into morphological series strictly on the basis of morphology without regard to distribution in space and time (e.g., Neanderthal—Steinheim—*H. sapiens*). Some modern authors tend to swing to the other extreme by classifying fossil hominids entirely on the basis of geological dating without paying any attention to morphology. The unequal rates of evolutionary change in widely dispersed and partially isolated races of polytypic species make it, however, necessary to take morphology and distribution equally into consideration. Even though *Homo sapiens* unquestionably descended from *Homo erectus,* it is quite possible, indeed probable, that some races of *Homo erectus* still persisted when other parts of the earth were already populated by *Homo sapiens.*

The same argument is even more true for genera. The fact that *Homo* and *Australopithecus* have been found to be contemporaries does not in the least invalidate the generally accepted assumption that *Homo* passed through an *Australopithecus* stage. The Australopithecines consisted of several species (or genera, if we recognize the genetic distinction of *Paranthropus*) and each of these species, in turn, was polytypic. Only a segment of this assemblage gave rise to *Homo*. Much of the remainder persisted contemporaneously with *Homo,* for a longer or shorter period, without rising above the Australopithecine grade. The modern concepts of taxonomy and speciation do not require an archetypal transformation (*in toto*) of *Australopithecus* into *Homo*.

The second great difficulty caused by the evolution of polytypic species is a consequence of the first one. It is the difficulty to determine what part (which races) of the ancestral species has contributed to the gene pool of the descendant species. This in turn depends on the amount of gene flow between the races of the ancestral species while it passed from the level of species 1 to the level of species 2. The amount of gene flow is determined by the nature of the interaction between populations in zones of contact. Unfortunately, the situation in the near-human hominids (*Homo erectus* level) was probably different from both the anthropoid condition and the condition in modern man. A number of possibilities are evident in an area of contact between races:

1. Avoidance
2. Extermination of one by the other
3. Killing of the men and absorption of the women

4. Free interbreeding

There is much evidence that all four processes have occurred and it becomes necessary to determine their relative importance in individual cases. The Congo pygmies, the bushmen, and various negritoid pygmies in the eastern tropics illustrate avoidance by retreating into inferior environments. The Tasmanians and some Indian tribes illustrate extermination. The white invaders in North America and Australia absorbed extremely few genes of the native peoples. The frequently made assertion that invaders kill off the men and take the women is often contradicted by the facts. The sharpness of the difference between classical western European Neanderthal and invading Cro-Magnon indicates to me that Cro-Magnon did not absorb many Neanderthal genes (some contrary opinions notwithstanding). Language and cultural differences must have militated at the *Homo erectus* level against too active a gene exchange between different races. The distinctness of the negro, mongoloid, and caucasian races supports this assumption. Gene flow obviously occurred, but against considerable obstacles.

Sympatric species of hominids

When one reads the older anthropological literature with its rich proliferation of generic names, one has the impression of large numbers of species of fossil man and other hominids coexisting with each other. When these finds were properly placed into a multi-dimensional framework of space and time, the extreme rarity of the coexistence of two hominids became at once apparent. We have already discussed the case of Neanderthal and *sapiens,* but there are others in the Middle and early Pleistocene.

At the *Homo erectus* level, we have Java Man and Pekin Man, originally described as two different genera, but so strikingly similar that most current authors agree in treating them as subspecies. Ternifine Man in North Africa may be another representative of this same polytypic species. The existing material is, however, rather fragmentary. A further contemporary is Heidelberg Man, whose massive mandible contains teeth that appear smaller and more "modern" than those of a typical *erectus.* Was this a second species or merely a deviant peripheral isolate? This can only be settled by additional discoveries.

In Africa we find incontrovertible evidence of contemporaneity of several species of hominids. *Australopithecus* and *Paranthropus* apparently differed considerably in their adaptations. Perhaps this is the reason why they are not found together in most South African deposits. Yet the degree of difference between them and the time span of their occurrence leaves no doubt that they must have been contemporaries. Here, then, we have a clear case of the contemporaneity of two species of hominids. The fragments of the small hominid *(Telanthropus)* found

at Swartkrans with *A. robustus,*
which may belong to an Australopithecine or *Homo,* supply additional
proof for the coexistence of two
hominids in South Africa. In Java,
in the Djetis layers, there is also the
possibility of the coexistence of two
hominids, *"Meganthropus"* and
Homo erectus.

By far the most exciting instance
of the coexistence of two hominids
is that established by Leakey in East
Africa. In layer 1 of Olduvai *"Zinjanthropus,"* an unmistakable Australopithecine of the *Paranthropus*
type, is associated with remains of
an advanced hominid, "co-Zinjan-
thropus," that—when better known
—may well turn out to be closer to
Homo than to *Australopithecus.*
Whether the tools of this layer were
made by both hominids or only the
more advanced, can be determined
only when the two types are found
unassociated at other sites. This will
also influence the decision on the
identity of the maker of the Sterkfontein tools in South Africa.

The picture that emerges from all
these new discoveries is that only
one species of hominids seems to
have been in existence during the
Upper Pleistocene, but that there is
much evidence from the Middle and
Lower Pleistocene of several independent lines. Some of these gave
rise to descendant types, others became extinct. The coexisting types
were, so far as known, rather distinct from each other. This is what
one would expect on the basis of
a priori ecological considerations.
The principle of "competitive exclusion" would prevent sympatry if
there were not considerable ecologi-

cal divergence. *Australopithecus* and
Paranthropus, or *Zinjanthropus* and
the associated hominid, "co-Zinjan-
thropus," were able to coexist only
because they utilized the resources
of the environment differently.
Whether one of them was more of
a hunter, the other more of a
gatherer (or hunted), whether one
was more carnivorous, the other
more of a vegetarian, whether one
was more of a forest creature, the
other a savanna inhabitant, all this
still remains to be investigated, when
better evidence becomes available.

It is important to emphasize that
nothing helped more to make us
aware of these problems and to assist
in the reconstruction of evolutionary
pathways than an improvement of
the classification of fossil hominids
both on the generic and on the specific levels. It is here that the application of principles of zoological
taxonomy has been particularly fruitful. Indeed, the earlier morphologists
never appreciated the biological
significance of the problem of coexistence or replacement of closely
related species.

Generic problems

The category "genus" presents
even greater difficulties than that of
the species. There is no non-arbitrary
yardstick available for the genus as
reproductive isolation is for the
species. The genus is normally a collective category, consisting of a
group of species believed to be more
closely related to each other than
they are to other species, Yet, every
large genus includes several groups

of species that are more closely related to each other than to species of other species groups within the same genus. For instance, in the genus *Drosophila* the species belonging to the *virilis* group are more closely related to each other than to those belonging to the *repleta* group, yet both are included in *Drosophila*. They are not separated in different genera because the species groups have not yet reached the degree of evolutionary divergence usually associated with generic rank. As Simpson (1961) has pointed out, the genus usually has also a definite biological significance, indicating or signifying occupation of a somewhat different adaptive niche. Again, this is not an ironclad criterion because even every species occupies a somewhat different niche, and sometimes different genera may occupy the same adaptive zone.

It is particularly important to emphasize again and again that the function of the generic and the specific names in the scientific binomen are different. The specific name stresses the singularity of the species and its unique distinctness. The generic name emphasizes not a greater degree of difference but rather the belonging-together of the species included in the genus. To place every species in a separate genus, as was done by so many of the physical anthropologists of former generations, completely stultifies the advantages of binomial nomenclature. As Simpson has stated correctly in this volume, the recognition of a monotypic genus is justified only when a single isolated known species is so distinctive that

there is a high probability that it belongs to a generic group with no other known ancestral, collateral or descendant species. The isolated nature of *bamboli*, the type species of *Oreopithecus*, justifies the recognition of this monotypic genus.

Of the literally scores of generic names proposed for fossil hominids, very few deserve recognition. More and more students admit, for instance, that the degree of difference between *Homo erectus* and *H. sapiens* is not sufficient to justify the recognition of *Pithecanthropus*.

There are a number of reasons why it would seem unwise to recognize the genus *Pithecanthropus* in formal taxonomy. First of all, *Homo* would then become a monotypic genus and *Pithecanthropus* contain at most two or three species. This is contrary to the concept of the genus as a collective category. More importantly, the name *Pithecanthropus* was first applied to an actual fossil hominid when only a skull cap was known and the reconstruction envisioned a far more anthropoid creature than *erectus* really is. When the teeth and other body parts were discovered (or accepted, like the femur) it was realized that the total difference between *erectus* and *sapiens* was really rather small and certainly less than is normally required for the recognition of a zoological genus. The recognition of *Pithecanthropus* as a genus would lead to an undesirable heterogeneity of the genus category.

The genus *Australopithecus* has already many of the essential characters of *Homo*, such as a largely upright posture, bicuspid premolars, and reduced canines. For this reason I suggested previously (Mayr 1950) that "not even *Australopithecus* has unequivocal claims for generic separation." I now agree with those authors who have since pointed out not only that the upright locomotion was still incomplete and inefficient, but also that the tremendous evolution of the brain since *Australopithecus* permitted man to enter a new niche so completely different that generic separation is fully justified. The extraordinary brain evolution between *Australopithecus* and *Homo* justifies the generic separation of these two taxa, no matter how similar they might be in many other morphological characters. Here, as in other cases, it is important not merely to count characters but to weight them.

Whether or not one wants to recognize only a single genus for all the known Australopithecines or admit a second genus, *Paranthropus,* is largely a matter of taste. The species (*robustus*) found at Swartkrans and Kromdraai is larger and seems to have more pronounced sexual dimorphism than *A. africanus*. Incisors and canines are relatively small, while the molars are very large and there are pronounced bony crests on the skull, particularly in adult males. These differences are no greater than among species in other groups of mammals. *Zinjanthropus* in East Africa seems to belong to the more massive *Paranthropus* group. The two Australopithecines (*africanus* and *robustus*) seem to represent the same "grade" as far as brain evolution is concerned, but the differences

in their dental equipment and facial muscles indicate that they may have occupied different food niches. It may well depend on future finds whether or not we want to recognize *Paranthropus*. The more genuinely different genera of hominids are discovered, the more important it may become to emphasize the close relationship of *Australopithecus* and *Paranthropus* by combining them in a single genus. It depends in each case to what extent one wants to stress relationships. We have a similar situation among the pongids. I have pointed out earlier (Mayr 1950) that gorilla and chimpanzee seem to me so much nearer to each other than either is to man or to the orang or to the gibbons, that degree of relationship would seem to be expressed better if the gorilla were included in the genus *Pan* rather than to be recognized as a separate genus. The decision on generic status is as always based on somewhat arbitrary and subjective criteria. One cannot prove that gorilla and chimpanzee belong to the same genus, but neither can one prove that they belong to different genera.

Diagnostic characters

The collective nature of the categories above the species level show clearly why it is often so difficult to provide an unequivocal diagnosis for taxa belonging to the higher categories. Those who think that "the characters make the genus" have little difficulty in characterizing differences between species and calling them generic differences. It is much easier to characterize the species "chimpanzee" and the species "gorilla" than to find diagnostic characters that clearly distinguish the chimpanzee-gorilla group from man, the orang and the gibbons. Higher categories often can be diagnosed only by a combination of characters, not by a single diagnostic character. The definition of the genus *Homo* presented in this volume is an example of such a combinational diagnosis.

The problem of the relation between taxonomic ranking and diagnostic characters will become increasingly acute as new Pliocene and Miocene fossils are found. Nothing would be more short-sighted than to base the classification of such finds on isolated "diagnostic" characters. We must ask ourselves each time whether relationship will be expressed better by including such new taxa in previously established ones, or by separating them as new taxa. If we combine them with previously established taxa, that is, if we include them in previously recognized genera, subfamilies, or families, we may have to modify the diagnosis of such taxa. We must always remember that the categories above the species are collective categories and subjectively delimited. The pronouncement made by Linnaeus, "It is the genus that gives the characters, and not the characters that make the genus," is true not only for the genus but for the categories at the family level. Diagnostic characters are a convenient tool of the working taxonomist, they should never become a strait jacket.

Nomenclature and communication

Superimposed on all the taxonomic difficulties are some purely nomenclatural ones. Simpson, in this volume, has already pointed out that it is altogether inadmissible to change a scientific name because it is considered inappropriate. A scientific name is, so to speak, merely a formula and its etymological meaning is quite irrelevant. What is important is to avoid arbitrary changes, because the words of a language lose all usefulness if they are shifted around or replaced by new ones. If an anthropologist wants to play around with names, let him concentrate on the vernacular names. No one will care whether he talks of Heidelberg Man or Man of Mauer, or of Pekin Man rather than Man of Choukoutien.

As soon as an anthropologist employs zoological nomenclature that has very definite rules, he must obey these rules. In particular, I would like to call the attention of anthropologists to Article 35b of the Rules of Zoological Nomenclature, which states that the names of families and subfamilies must be based on the name of an included genus. Since there is no genus Euhomo, there can be no family name Euhominidae. If a subfamily is recognized for the Australopithecines, it can only be Australopithecinae. Not only is this system the only valid one, but it also has the advantage of being simple and unambiguous. I should hope that such confusing terms as Praehominidae would soon disappear from the literature.

Those who give names to fossil Hominidae might also be more careful in the choice of specific names. To have several *africanus* and *robustus* in this family is confusing, particularly during this period of rearranging of genera. It would not seem an impossible demand that only such new specific names be given that had not been given previously to other species in the family Hominidae.

The classification of the missing link

Nothing characterized the early study of human evolution as much as the search for the missing link. When one looks at early reconstructions of the missing link, one realizes how strongly the concept was dominated by the ancient idea of the *scala naturae*. If evolution were limited to a single lineage, as thought for instance by Lamarck, the missing link would simply be the halfway stage between the anthropoids and man. Now as we realize that there is no single line of descent but a richly branching phylogenetic tree, the search for the missing link has become somewhat illusory. It is now evident that there is not just one missing link but a whole series of missing links. There is first the species which was at the branching point between the Pongidae and the

Hominidae. On the hominid branch there were those species that first acquired such essentially human traits as making tools, making fire, and possessing speech. There is the first species to be referred to the genus *Homo,* and there is the species that acquired a brain capacity about halfway between the anthropoids and modern man. We may already have representatives satisfying most of these qualifications, and rather than searching for *the* missing link we are now beginning to classify kinds of missing links.

It is now clear that we must distinguish between two essential phenomena. There is on one hand the phylogenetic branching of the hominid line from the pongid line. Yet even after this branching had taken place, which presumably was sometime during the Miocene, there was no sign of Man on the new hominid line. The hominids throughout the Miocene and Pliocene were still apes, and even the Australopithecines of the early Middle Pleistocene can hardly be classified as human. It does appear that *Homo erectus* qualifies better as representative of the stage between prehuman hominids and Man than any other form. It is almost certainly the stage at which the hominids became Man.

The higher categories

The Pleistocene hominids present no problem at the family level. They all clearly belong to the Hominidae. Whether or not to separate the Australopithecines in a subfamily

Australopithecinae is essentially a matter of taste. Matters are more difficult when it comes to Pliocene and Miocene fossils. Not only are most of them known from insufficient fragments, but the criteria on which to base the decision pongid or hominid become increasingly elusive as we go back in time. Furthermore, there is considerable probability of the existence of additional equivalent branches of anthropoids or near-anthropoids which have since become extinct. *Oreopithecus* seems to represent such a branch.

The evidence concerning the branching-off point of the hominid from the pongid line seems on first sight contradictory. Schultz finds that all the great apes agree with each other in very numerous characters of general morphology, in which they differ from Man. Yet, the African apes (*Pan* sensu lato) are closer to Man than to orang or gibbon in hemoglobin structure (Zuckerkandl 1963), in serum proteins (Goodman 1963) and in chromosomal morphology (Klinger 1963). What can be the explanation of this apparent conflict in the evidence? Perhaps the simplest interpretation would be to assume that Man's shift into the niche of the bipedal, tool-making, and speech-using hominid necessitated a drastic reconstruction of his morphology, but that this reconstruction did not, in turn, require a complete revamping of his biochemical system. Different characters and character complexes thus diverged at very different rates. If one assumes this to be correct, one will conclude that the

Homo-line branched from the *Pan*-line well after the line of their common ancestor had separated from the orang (*Pongo*)-line.

Full awareness of mosaic evolution is particularly important for the correct placing of early hominid fossils. As Le Gros Clark (1950) and I (Mayr 1950) have emphasized, the Hominidae are a classical example of mosaic evolution. Every character or set of characters evolved at a different rate. Even Australopithecus is still essentially anthropoid in some characters while having considerably advanced toward the hominid condition in other characters, for instance with respect to upright posture and the general shape of the tooth row. We must furthermore be aware of the fact that evolution is not necessarily irreversible and that temporary specializations may secondarily be lost again. The Pliocene forms *Ramapithecus* from India (Simons 1961) and *Kenyapithecus* from Africa may well belong to the hominid line. Even more difficult is the allocation of Miocene genera. To place them correctly one may have to use "prophetic characters" (a preevolutionary term of Agassiz), that is, characters which foreshadow future evolutionary trends. It is quite certain that the Miocene hominoids lacked some of the characteristic specializations of both the pongid and the hominid lines. They were not the extreme brachiators that some of the modern pongids are, nor had they reached the completeness of upright posture and the special features of dentition of the later hominids. Such seemingly irrelevant characters as the shape of tooth cusps may be more revealing in such forms than the relative size of the canines or the development of a simian shelf. The recent arguments about *Oreopithecus* show how difficult it is to reach an objective evaluation of the evidence.

Conclusions

Fossil hominids are samples of formerly existing populations distributed in space and time. Their classification must be consistent with the generalizations derived from the study of polytypic species in animals.

Whenever the anthropologist uses the terminology of subspecies, species, and genera, such terminology must be consistent with the meaning of these categories as developed in modern systematics (Simpson 1961). Application of the principles of systematics has helped to clarify the formerly bewildering diversity of morphological types. Pleistocene hominids display much geographic variation, but the number of full species coexisting at any one time is not known to have exceeded two. The relatively wide distribution of some of the fossil hominids indicates that there has been a considerable amount of gene flow as early as the lowest Middle Pleistocene.

Facts Instead of Dogmas on Man's Origin

Louis S. B. Leakey
1965

Before I start, I must say two things. First, I cannot fall in with our chairman when he says to keep within a million years, because I think it is important to discuss some aspects of the early Hominidae, which—with *Ramapithecus* and *Kenyapithecus*—go back 12 or 14

million years. Second, I would like to say in public once more how deeply grateful Mary and I and my family are to the National Geographical Society, to the Wenner-Gren Foundation, the Boise Fund at Oxford, the Wicker Foundation and many others who made our field

Reprinted from P. L. DeVore, editor, *The Origin of Man*. Transcript of a Symposium sponsored by the Wenner-Gren Foundation for Anthropological Research, Inc. April 2-4, 1965.

work over the years possible. Without that, we wouldn't have this knowledge to put before you.

As our chairman said, we are desperately out of date. Even since the Darwin Centennial here in Chicago 5–½ years ago, so much has happened that nearly everything in our textbooks, nearly everything in recently written articles, nearly everything that we think even must be updated and brought into relation to the facts as we have them now. And my plea to my colleagues both old and young here is that we in 1965 face the issue that we've got to look at the origin of man and all the problems related to the origin of man with fresh eyes, discarding many things that we have formerly believed to be true.

There is a vast accumulation of new knowledge—new knowledge in the fields of biochemistry, in discoveries of early man and his culture, in discoveries of proto-man back in the Miocene, and new knowledge in relation to the activities of the living great apes. And all this adds up to the need for a complete reassessment of everything we think about where we came from. We've had too many preconceived ideas and theories, which, at the time they were formulated, were entirely justified on the basis of negative evidence. Theories are always desirable but a certain number of them in recent years, have been dressed up and have started to masquerade as facts, when they are not facts at all. And it is this that I am so seriously worried about—this disguising of theories as facts in textbooks and articles which means that we are shutting our eyes to the new knowledge. It is all summed up in phrases like "the missing link" and "up from the ape" and in theories such as: "man went through a brachiating stage when his arms were longer than his legs"; "man once had ape-like canine teeth but lost them somewhere along the way"; "an animal must be bipedal to make or use tools"; and "the Australopithecines represent a stage through which *Homo* passed, even though none of the known specimens is old enough to represent an actual ancestor."

The last theory has become enshrined almost as a dogma, and it's one that I don't believe will hold water today. It's not so very long ago that the textbooks all told us that the super-family Hominoidea, to which we and the apes belong, was only divisible into two families: the Pongidae and the Hominidae. And when Hurzeler produced evidence that *Oreopithecus* had a pelvic girdle and other characters much more like the Hominidae than the Pongidae, he said "This is an early hominid." And others pointed to the molar teeth and other features in the skeleton and said "No, it's clearly pongid." Of course the answer was that it was neither. And I think nearly all my colleagues in this room today agree that we've had to add another full family—Oreopithecidae. They don't all agree, although I think it is almost equally certain, that we should add Hylobatidae. The gibbons, who go back into the remote past, broke away a long time ago and can be shown on biochemical grounds to be far removed from both the great apes and man.

I believe that the *Proconsuls* too, with their entirely different morphology of the mandible—not merely an absence of the simian shelf, but a completely different morphology from either living or fossil pongids—should be given family rank. Because it may well be that it is in that group in the Lower Miocene that the Hominidae started. Le Gros Clark and I, in 1951, did suggest that the *Proconsul* might be the common ancestor of both the Pongidae and the Hominidae, but that was before certain discoveries had been made by Bill Bishop in Uganda and myself in Kenya which show the Pongidae in the stricter sense of the word already present side-by-side with the *Proconsul* in the Lower Miocene.

Then, too, we have a theory—a nice theory once—that *Homo* starts with a brain size of "so many" cc. as a sort of "Rubicon." Rather, we should realize that the important thing is the morphology of the braincase and, above all, its size relative to body-size.

Then again we had the idea that man was a "toolmaker." We decided that man started at the stage of primate evolution when the creature began to make tools to a set "and regular pattern." But that's gone too, because Jane Goodall has shown that chimpanzees in wild conditions make no less than three different kinds of tools to a set and regular pattern. By "tool" I do not mean a natural object picked up and used;

that's a utilized object. A tool, whether it be made of stone, bone, ivory, or some perishable materials, is a natural object or material which has been deliberately modified for a specific purpose. And the chimpanzees do that not only for specific purposes but regularly, making certain tools for two months of the year and then putting away all idea of those tools for ten months. Then they come back and again make that same kind of tool and teach their young how to do it. So the idea that man is uniquely distinguished by his tool-making, won't work.

In the light of a lot of negative evidence, such as the fact that the Australopithecines had a dentition far closer to ours than any of the pongids had, many held to the theory that the Australopithecines were our ancestors. It is also believed that they had a brain size intermediate between that of the great apes and man. As a point of fact, I don't believe they do. *Zinjanthropus,* whose skull is far more complete than most of the *Australopithecus paranthropus crassidens* specimens in South Africa, has yielded us an internal brain cast which can be measured by water displacement and amounts to 530 cc. I believe that the *Zinjanthropus* skull and brain is probably bigger than that of any of the *Paranthropus crassidens;* although skull capacity is very hard to assess. The assessments made by the late Professor Broom and later by Robinson were based on skulls which were crushed. They could never obtain an internal brain cast of the *crassidens* group for more accurate measurement. And I don't believe the brain case or the brain size of the *Australopithecus* ever was very big in view of what we know as a fact—by measurement, not an estimate—for *Zinjanthropus*.

Paleontologists from the beginning of paleontology have always placed a very great deal of faith in dentitions, and within limits, dentitions are certainly very valuable. Teeth fossilize and preserve more easily than bone, so paleontologists usually find themselves with teeth for comparison rather than with jaws or brain-cases or limb bones. But if you've got more than teeth, then you should be careful. Recently my colleague, Phillip Tobias, together with Ralph von Koenigswald, who did considerable work with *Pithecanthropus,* rushed into print, after comparing the teeth of *Homo habilis* type, the juvenile jaw from FLK and the teeth of what we call the paratype, the adult (probably female) jaw from MNK 11 and they found that there were similarities between the teeth of these creatures and those of some of the Pithecanthropines of the Far East. I certainly would not deny this. But they overlooked the fact that these similarities are generic similarities. They were comparing these with each other and contrasting them with the Australopithecines. And I entirely agree that the resemblance between the *Homo habilis* dentition, which is *Homo,* and the Pithecanthropine dentition, which is also *Homo* are infinitely closer to each other than either is to any Australopithecine— a generic and possibly a sub-family

difference. But to conclude from the dentition that the *Homo habilis* paratype is a Pithecanthropine is going far beyond what is legitimate. For we have the exact occipital index of *Homo habilis* and find that it is outside the range of any known Pithecanthropine or Australopithecine that has ever been published and completely within the range of the occipital indices of *Homo sapiens* taken over all races.

As we think about revising our ideas, let us review the last 40 years in ten-year periods just to see what's been happening. In 1925, just before Dart announced the first *Australopithecus* from Taung, there were no Australopithecines anywhere. Although a *Proconsul* specimen had in fact been found by Dr. Gordon, it had not yet appeared in print, and so there were no *Proconsuls.* There was no *Ramapithecus* or *Kenyapithecus,* and very little good information about the Pithecanthropines. And, above all, that ghastly hoax of Piltdown dominated the thoughts of a great many of my colleagues, who, because of it, thought that man had gone through a stage with a human kind of brain size associated with an entirely ape-like mandible.

Let us jump ten years, from 1925 to 1935. Dart, in 1929, had given a great deal of information about *Australopithecus* to his colleagues— at the Johannesburg meeting of the British Association for the Advancement of Science. Almost everyone else said it was a pongid, an ape. And in 1935 the second ten-year period starts with almost every book and almost every scientist saying

Australopithecus is nothing but a near relation of the gorillas and the chimpanzees. *Proconsul* had been published on the basis of some fragmentary jaws—we hadn't any jaw with a symphysis and we didn't know the alignment of the molar–premolar series. It had been published by my colleague, Arthur Hopwood of the British Museum, as well as *Limnopithecus,* the first evidence of a member of the gibbon family south of the Sahara. *Ramapithecus* had been published in 1934, but its significance was completely overlooked, even by its author. It just hadn't sunk in that here *Ramapithecus* was a creature with a molar dentition quite different from the apes, and with a small canine socket. There was nothing yet to tell us that *Oreopithecus* which had been known for a long time from fragments, was not a monkey; as it was then classified. I had noted the Olduvai culture in *Nature* as the first evidence found *in situ* on living floors of a primitive culture antedating the hand axe culture. Even the significance of this was not fully accepted at the time. And still there was no evidence of any Pithecanthropine on the African continent.

Now move to 1945. By this time, thanks to the work of Robinson and Broom and more work by Dart and his colleagues, we knew a great deal more about the Australopithecines. Le Gros Clark had entered the field of battle and began to support Dart and Broom in England and said *Australopithecus* was definitely within the Hominidae. Yet, even then,

nearly every textbook from 1945–46 on puts the Australopithecines in the Pongidae. By that time MacInnes and I had found and published an almost complete jaw of *Proconsul,* as well as parts of the foot of *Proconsul.* We drew attention to the fact that the *Proconsul*—both in the nature of its mandibular condyle and in the alignment of the molar–premolar series, in the nature of the symphyseal region cut through in section and in the nature of its astragalus and calcaneum—had characters closer to the Hominidae than they were to any pongids we could compare them with. But most of that evidence was also bypassed. There was still nothing new on *Oreopithecus.* There was a growing acceptance at last in 1945 of the view that I put forward together with Zuckerman that *Pithecanthropus* and *Sinanthropus* were unquestionably one of the same genus and possibly of the same species. Everybody had said "Impossible" when we first claimed that. But by 1945 it was generally accepted that they were not two separate genera but the same genus and possibly in the same species—still separate from *Homo.* There was still no *Zinjanthropus,* no *Homo habilis,* and still no African *Pithecanthropines,* except possibly my reference a little earlier to the fact that I believed that the Eyasi skull, found by Kohl-Larsen was closer to *Pithecanthropus* than to anything else we then knew. That too was bypassed.

And we go to 1955. By 1955, not so very long before the Darwin Centennial, I think nearly everybody had come to believe that the Australopithecines found by Dart, Broom, Robinson, and others were definitely members of the Hominidae—"near-men" as I call them. Dart by that time was claiming that they made and used certain tools which he called the Osteodontokeratic Culture. Many of us still do not accept everything that he claimed then, but there is no doubt that a proportion of the objects have been utilized. And a very few are tools in the sense that they have been modified. But in 1955 that was being harshly contended.

By 1955 a Pithecanthropine had been found in North Africa, named *Atlanthropus* by my friend Arambourg, with jaws recalling those of Pekin man. But it wasn't a true Far Eastern *Pithecanthropus,* nor would one have expected it to be. It was an African Pithecanthropine, differing in a number of characters from those of the Far East. Because of the widespread belief—a belief that we were brought up to think was true—that you couldn't have two contemporary hominids at one place— Arambourg said that the association of *Altanthropus* Pithecanthropines with hand axes in the Ternifine gravel pit "*proved*" that the hand axe culture was made by Pithecanthropines. It didn't prove it at all but only suggested it. It proved there was a direct association in time between the African *Pithecanthropus* and the hand axe culture but nothing more—a trap I fell into later with the LLK skull.

By this time we had Australopithecines in East Africa. They were not recognized by me as such. I very carefully said that I didn't know what the two teeth from BK II were. I preferred to say simply that they are hominid and milk teeth; while others went further and said that they are milk teeth and are Australopithecine. My friend Robinson was one of those who claimed that very strongly, and I agree with him. But BK II, contrary to what we thought, is at the top of Bed II—not at the base of Bed II. The geologists had mislead us earlier. As a result of fresh and detailed work by my colleague Dick Hay, and as a result of the enormous cuttings that Mary and I have made over the last two years at the BK sites, we know that the BK sites with their very primitive culture that looks as though they were ancestral to hand axes are in fact, way up above a large number of hand axe levels in a channel-filling at the end of Bed II times. And so there is a *Zinjanthropus* type of Australopithecine at the top of Bed II.

There was still, at this time, no evidence of *Kenyapithecus,* no *Zinjanthropus* skull, no *Homo habilis,* nor the Pithecanthropine from site LLK; and there was no trace of the new evidence that I am going to present to you.

By this time we had a great deal more material on *Proconsul,* and Le Gros Clark and I published a big monograph on it. And we had just found but had not yet published a tiny pongid on Rusinga, with a very well developed simian shelf and other pongid characters side-by-side with the *Pronconsuls*. *Telanthropus* was not yet clearly placed. It was a new hominid, bitterly attacked; it was thought simply a variation of the Australopithecines.

And so we come to 1965 and to the need to revise and to review all that has gone before. Why do we have to re-orient our ideas so drastically now and start afresh? There have been most important discoveries by E. L. Simons of Yale in the Oligocene of the Fayum. It's not for me but for him to talk about them. But they throw new light on the beginnings of the Hominoidea, including the beginnings of the *Oreopithecus* group. There is recognition, due to Elwyn Simons, that *Ramapithecus* from India is a hominid, just as *Kenyapithecus* from Kenya is a hominid—a very primitive hominid but with a dentition and a morphology completely unlike the Pongidae. In addition to the small pongid from Rusinga with the simian shelf, very long canine, and very trechant fourth premolar, we have a discovery by Bill Bishop and his colleagues in Uganda of the palate of an immense pongid about the size of a gorilla, which he has provisionally suggested should be cf. *Proconsul major*. I am certain it is not *Proconsul major* and is certainly an ancestral pongid, which could even be ancestral to the gorillas.

Then we have the discovery in the last ten years of *Kenyapithecus*. Of *Kenyapithecus* we have two incomplete maxillae with small canines, not projecting much beyond the molar–premolar series, and this is very important when we consider how often we have talked about man having come through a stage with long canines that he gradually lost. I don't believe he ever had them. And we also have a magnificent upper central incisor of *Kenyapithecus*. Some of my colleagues had this handed to them and said: "A beautiful example of a human shovel-shaped incisor." But it's from the Upper Miocene!

Then we must consider Jane Goodall's work on chimpanzees. She's just finishing her fifth year working down in the Gombe Stream Reserve, and she has completely shattered many of our previous ideas. Chimpanzees living under wild conditions make and shape pieces of wood, creeper, and grass to a "set and regular pattern" and sometimes carry as many as eleven or twelve of them in their hands from as much as a half mile away to where they are going to use them for termiting. When water is short in the dry season and they can't reach water in the boles of trees with their mouths, they make a sponge from the leaves of a particular plant—only one plant has that spongy quality—they take the leaves of that plant and scramble them into a sponge and dip down and sponge the water out. And they've been seen and filmed showing their young how to do it! They occasionally take sticks and go through the forest until they see an ant's nest in a tree and attack it to get at the ants inside. To all of that we would have said five years ago "Impossible! Of course wild chim-

panzees don't do anything like that
—they're only pongids. They've got
a brain capacity far too small." Not
only that, she has seen and recorded
and filmed that chimpanzees hunt,
catch, and kill animals. She has a
film showing them hunting, catching
and killing a red colobus. She has
reported in print their having killed
a young bushbuck. This alters ideas
completely about early man, and
even more so about early prehuman
hominids. I suggest to you, and I
was interested to see that Elwyn
Simons has suggested the same thing,
that we must not be surprised to
find evidence that *Ramapithecus*
and *Kenyapithecus* were tool-makers.
The shape of their muscles and the
nature of their teeth suggest that
they had an omnivorous diet. We've
found the tibia of a Miocene bovid
with as good an example of deliberate smashing while it was green as
any of the smashed-in skulls of the
baboons that Dart found at Makapan and elsewhere. It was in a
matrix where there were no big
stones falling and it suggests that
some hominid—presumably *Kenyapithecus* but not proven—was smashing bones of animals at that site.
We can't prove it, but we've certainly got to keep an open mind.

We have evidence now that the
Australopithecines start way back,
far in the past. Potassium-argon dating puts it somewhere around 1.75–
1.86 million years ago for *Australopithecus [Zinjanthropus] boisei*. Inci-
dentally, in *Science* there is published
a paper by Fleicher, Price, Walker
and myself, on a new dating technique for Olduvai—glass fission-

track dating of fragments of glass
from pelean ash. We find that the
age on the basis of glass fission-
track dating is 2.03 plus or minus
.28 million years—a direct overlap
with the age we had before. And,
of course, the fossil fauna of the
early part of Olduvai Bed I, which
you will find described in part—and
only in part—in the book which is
now available tells the same story—
we're back in the Villafranchian.
We find not only that *Zinjanthropus*
is in Bed I, but the discovery of the
expedition led by my son Richard
and by Glynn Isaac in West Natron
shows that the *Australopithecus
[Zinjanthropus]* type continues into
the Peninj deposits. And last year,
1964, they took another expedition
back there and found magnificent
faunal and cultural evidence that
the Peninj beds are way up in Bed
II—beautiful sites with advanced
hand axes. So *Australopithecus
[Zinjanthropus]* is not only way down
in Bed I but runs right up the series
to the higher part of Bed II, Olduvai, as is before shown by those two
teeth from BK at the top of Bed II.

Homo habilis, which Tobias
Napier and I described in *Nature*
last year, starts at MK I almost sitting on the lava at the bottom of
Bed I with a bit of a mandible with
typical teeth. It goes on into FLK
NN 1, where we had the child's jaw
and the parietals; and it goes on in
my view—in spite of what Koenigswald and Tobias said on the basis of
dentition alone—way above the climatic break in Bed II. *Homo habilis*
is up in a level which in other parts
of the Gorge are yielding hand axes;

although he has not been directly associated with the hand axes as of the moment. There's a lot more work to do at that site. So that gives us a picture of two hominid types living side-by-side right from Bed I up through the top of Bed II.

You may remember that I published a note in *Nature* and elsewhere on a skull which I temporarily and foolishly—I admit my foolishness—called the Chellean skull. It was found at the identical geological level of what we used to call Chellean Stage III. At that time we had no evidence of other cultures or other hominids at that level. And then I fell into the trap that my colleague Arambourg and others have fallen into all over the world, the idea that if you find fossil hominids and stone tools at one and the same geologic horizon at the same level, you may say the tools were made by the type of person which the fossil remains represent. But it's no longer valid—certainaly not at Olduvai, where there are three contemporaneous, co-existent hominids in the upper part of Bed II, the *habilis* type, the *Pithecanthropus* type, and, still continuing, an *Australopithecus* type.

What I called the Chellean skull —I now call, preferably, the LLK skull—though it is certainly not Pithecanthropine in the Java or Pekin sense, is yet morphologically Pithecanthropine rather than a *Homo* of the *Homo sapiens* type. The widest part of the skull is across the temporal bones and the mastoid processes as in Java and Pekin, and not at the parietals above the tem-

porals, as in *Homo sapiens* and *Homo habilis*. So I am now prepared to say to you that this discovery of the LLK specimen in the upper part of Bed II side-by-side with an evolving *Homo habilis* and an *Australopithecus* constitute evidence of three contemporary hominids.

But we've got more to it now. There is a skull which Mary has been working on as a jigsaw puzzle in three dimensions for months and months with occasional help from me and from our colleague Phillip Tobias. It's the skull we mentioned in *Nature* last March and provisionally said might be referable to *Homo habilis*. It was reduced to tiny fragments by Masai cattle as they came down to water in the gorge, and the piecing together of the little fragments into bigger fragments without making any mistakes has been a very lengthy job. But we have now, after several attempts, got a reconstruction with only the left external orbital angle area floating. Otherwise, from the right external orbital angle there are complete, continuous contacts around and over the top of the skull. To me, and to many of my colleagues who have seen it, it is a Pithecanthropine, but it's down on the Bed I–Bed II junction. So here's a third hominid line developing side-by-side with the other two.

Are we to be surprised? We're surprised because of our preconceived ideas that this couldn't happen. I've been in the Congo—the eastern part of the Congo, where in an area of five miles square I saw gorillas and chimpanzees and large numbers of different kinds of monkeys and pygmies and Bantu—and I was there as a white man—all in the same five miles square. If we'd been fossilized together, anthropologists in two thousand years' time— if they still had the same stupid ideas that we had—would say "Impossible, impossible!" I can take you to forests on the coast of East Africa where there are no less than five different kinds of monkeys within a single square mile of forest, and the ecologists say that it is impossible for these different species to be in the same ecology. But they occupy different niches in that forest. In the main, they do not overlap in their food requirements any more than the gorilla and the chimpanzee—any more, I believe, than *Homo habilis* and *Zinjanthropus* competed greatly. One must have been a better toolmaker; the other must have been much more vegetarian. This shows on their teeth in comparing individuals of the same physiological age. In *Zinjanthropus* at Peninj individuals whose third molars are just coming into wear have second molars, first molars and premolars worn right down through the enamel and the dentin exposed. But in the *Homo habilis* of the same physiological age, with the third molars just erupting, the premolars and molars hardly show any wear at all—a comparable condition that you find today in the Masai, the meat eaters, where even at 40 you can find individuals with practically no visible wear on the molar teeth. Obviously these creatures were occupying dif-

ferent ecological niches in the same area.

May I interpose something here which is very important indeed. It arises out of a comment made in one of the papers presented by Simons and Pilbeam and refers to a publication made by two of my colleagues in Great Britain, a publication which I promptly disassociated myself from. It is true that after Napier, Tobias and I published *Homo habilis*, purely on the basis of taxonomical zoology and having no reference whatsoever to any cultural aspects, Napier and Tobias subsequently in some other journal than *Nature* said that this was strengthened by the fact that there was evidence that *Homo habilis* was more likely to be the toolmaker than *Zinjanthropus*. But it's not certain, for they are side-by-side with Oldowan culture. I did a lot of zoological training under Foster Cooper and disassociate myself completely from any suggestion that you can use cultural evidence for any taxonomic purpose. The validity of *Homo habilis* rests entirely and solely on its morphological characters—not on any cultural ones. Let me remind you that down at the base of Bed 1, right down at the MK level within a few inches of the lava, we have a site at DK where there is clear evidence of a stone hut circle, or you can call it stones piled up on each other on a clay floor. These stones were carried there deliberately by men and piled together in little piles in a greater part of a circle. We don't know whether *Homo habilis* was responsible or an earlier form of *Australopithecus*. I don't know how we will ever discover it, as they were undoubtedly contemporary.

So then, we have reached a point in 1965, 40 years after Taung was just about to be discovered, when we must, all of us, try to unmask our theories—the ideas that masqueraded as fact when they weren't fact, the views of our predecessors which we accepted too unthinkingly —and think again. We may come back to some of the same conclusions we had before, but time has definitely come for reassessment of the over-all picture. We can no longer regard the making of tools as a criterion of man, since chimpanzees make tools to a set and regular pattern. We must expect that such creatures like *Ramapithecus* and *Kenyapithecus* may have made tools if chimpanzees with relatively small brains, a non-upright position, large canines, and projecting muzzle make them. We no longer need to exert ourselves in trying to find an explanation of how Nature has reversed the large canines and the small simian shelves of our ancestors to come back to ourselves without either, due to the fact that we know that the earliest hominids don't have the large canines and didn't have the simian shelf. We can no longer imply that an upright position or a nearly upright position is unique to the Hominidae when *Oreopithecus* certainly had a very upright position, as you can judge by his femur and his pelvic girdle. We can no longer say that meat-eating and a change-over from a purely vegetarian diet

to an omnivorous one is a mark of man. Chimpanzees hunt and kill for themselves, and there is strong, suggestive evidence that *Kenyapithecus* may have been doing so some 12 to 14 million years ago. We can no longer argue as was argued by Weidenreich, Aramboung, LeGros Clark, and many since, that we have gone up through four simple stages of evolution, a pongid stage, an Australopithecine stage, a Pithecanthropine stage, and a *Homo* stage. That's much too simple a picture. Man has been behaving as the other mammals have—branching out, with branches disappearing and becoming extinct, others continuing for a time longer, some side-by-side. Eventually one gave rise to us.

Now I want to run through the evidence very quickly to underline the points I've made.* First, *Proconsul* in the Lower Miocene. By contrast to any living pongid, *Proconsul* has a rounded, smooth forehead and a low, rectangular orbit rather than a high, round one. In not just one but many specimens of four species, *Proconsul* is seen to have a relatively small canine with a molar-premolar series converging forward, as opposed to the backward convergence in pongids, including Bill Bishop's fossil pongid from Moroto—a contemporary of *Proconsul*. This fossil pongid and, of course, the living pongids have a simian shelf with the most backward-pro-

* The following discussion of evidence is drawn from Dr. Leakey's comments on a series of slides that were shown from this point to the beginning of the discussion.

jecting part of the mandible right on the bottom; while *Proconsul* is diametrically opposite to this and has the most backward-projecting part in the middle of the symphyseal region, then moving forward again. This is not just a question of a simian shelf but involves the total morphology of the symphyseal region.

Moving to the Upper Miocene, we have *Kenyapithecus,* at this time with a canine tooth which does not project markedly beyond the molar–premolar series. As in hominids, the canine fossa face forward rather than sideways, and the molars have a cusp pattern and crown like that of hominids, with no sign whatsoever of the cingulum. When we found the original *in situ* specimen of an upper central incisor, some of my colleagues, not knowing where it came from, said it was human.

Moving to the Pleistocene for a contrast, I remind you of *Australopithecus* [*Zinjanthropus*], now accepted by me as an Australopithecine. He has a crest along the top of the skull linked functionally to the enormous masticatory muscles coming up over the parietals, and the widest part of the skull is back of the temporals. There is a very exaggerated post-orbital constriction, so that the frontal area is tiny. I am sure that because of this great post-orbital constriction, some of the estimates of brain size based on crushed specimens have been too large. The canines in "*Zinjanthropus*" set in a V-shaped dental arcade are actually large, but they are tiny relative to the premolars. Robinson,

Dahlberg, and I have had a great deal of argument about a huge molar and small canine found at what we used to think was the base of Bed II. But whatever molar it represents, it is Australopithecine. And, most important, Dick Hay has shown that these beds are actually filling a channel almost at the top of Bed II. So we now know that the *Australopithecus* type continues to the end of the Bed II times, as is also shown by the Peninj site.

In *Homo habilis,* on the other hand, you find lower premolars which are elongated anteriorly–posteriorly and narrow bucco–lingually compared to those of Australopithecines, and the dental arcade is rounded instead of V-shaped. The morphology of the roundly-curved occipital bone is completely unlike that of the Pithecanthropines or Australopithecines, but the occipital index fits within the known range of variation of *Homo sapiens* races now living. Again like *Homo sapiens,* the widest part of the *habilis* brain box is on the parietals and not down on the bulging temporals that you get in Pithecanthropines or Australopithecines. Finally, the canine in *habilis* is very large relative to the premolars, which is not the case in the Australopithecines, especially in *Australopithecus paranthropus crassidens.*

Much closer to the Pithecanthropines of the Far East is the LLK skull. It lacks the median keel and has far larger brow ridges than any known Pithecanthropine or *Homo erectus* and differs in a number of other characters; nevertheless, it is

of the same genus and is Pithecanthropine in *sensu lato*. The LLK
skull is bigger in all characters than
Java or Pekin, but it has the same
bulge at the temporals and the same
rather flat dome relative to the total
size of the skull. And it contrasts
markedly with its apparent contemporaries, *Homo habilis* and *Australopithecus* [*Zinjanthropus*]. The small
premolars of *Homo habilis,* for example, are entirely different from
the huge premolars of Australopithecines and fit better with the Pithecanthropine IV of Java.

And now we go to a new and
important find. This is the skull
"George," which was smashed by
Masai cattle into tiny fragments,
some of which are smaller than the
head of a match. With occasional
help from Phillip Tobias and me,
my wife Mary succeeded after seven
months in making a reconstruction
that is approved by all of us. This
skull fits in better with Pithecanthropines, what we now call the
Homo erectus type, than with anything else and looks as though it
might be ancestral both to LLK and
the Far Eastern specimens. This is
also suggested by the fact that it is
near the junction of Bed I and Bed
II and is almost certainly far earlier
than the Pithecanthropines. It is still
in the Upper Villafranchian with a
fauna comparable to that of Omo.

I will only give a resume of the
cultural evidence, and I ask you to
remember that I do not believe in
adducing cultural evidence in taxonomical study. But let's look at cultural evidence as far as we have
it from Olduvai. Way down at the
bottom of Bed I we have what ap-

pears to be a hut circle, a habitation.
So far we only have *Homo habilis*
at this deep level, but I won't say
that *habilis* built the circle. But at
least we have to revise the idea that
appears so often in books to the
effect that earliest man lived out in
the open until he moved into caves.
For this gives us evidence that he
made some kind of a structure.

In the very lowest levels of Bed I
we have very small, simple tools of
the Oldowan type, always associated with utilized flakes and even
trimmed flakes. Whoever made the
earliest part of the Oldowan culture
was capable of making small choppers and flake tools but not many
big choppers. The Oldowan culture
continues through Bed I right to the
top. Whether or not there are minor
modifications I must leave for Mary
to say at a Wenner-Gren conference
later this year.

When you get to the lower part
of Bed II, you find a modified Oldowan culture. It looks like Oldowan,
but it contains more elaborately
trimmed choppers than we ever get
earlier. We once thought we could
classify these as prototypes of hand
axes, but we're not so sure of that
anymore. There are large numbers
of flake tools and of stone balls and
polyhedrals. These latter are not a
common feature in Bed I, if they
occur there at all. We're still un-
packing and studying the materials
from Bed II and don't want to commit ourselves now in detail. But I
will read you an interesting extract
from a letter I received from Mary
two days ago. "I have done EFHR
and TK upper–lower levels, and I
have had a ghastly shock. There

seem to be three, not two, cultures in Bed II." I am not going to elaborate that further, but the situation is obviously far more complex than we had ever dreamed.

When you get up higher in other parts of Bed II and at Peninj, there are well-developed hand axes and quantities of what I call bolas stones. There are those who do not like the idea of a bolas as early as that; yet I do not believe that Nature would put them down as close together that you can almost cover them with your hand, as we have found them on some twelve occasions. I want to stress again that the sites in question, BK and SHK are stratigraphically at the top of Bed II. This puts them far above sites with beautiful hand axes and cleavers; yet in 10,000 or more tool specimens at one upper Bed II site, there were only 23 very crude hand axes, possibly borrowed or imitated.

Bearing in mind the simple, perishable tools that chimpanzees use for fishing about in termitaries and so on, I think we have evidence now that bone was being utilized and even shaped into tools in these early times. For example, we have the utilized rib of a zebra or equid from the bottom of Bed I that has clearly been smoothed and rubbed. Experiment shows that this sort of smoothing results from rubbing a leather thong to make it soft and supple. This fossil rib is more a utilized bone than an actual tool of bone, but it is comparable to some of those that Dart places in the "Osteodontokeratic Culture." There are much clearer examples of this such as the metacarpal of an animal about the size of a gnu or wildebeest from FLK NN 1, near the top of Bed I. The top of the bone is highly polished, and the lower part shows longitudinal striations going down to the point. Again, experiment shows that if you break an antelope metacarpal to a point and use it to dig up roots or rodents, you get exactly the same scratches. I am satisfied that the metacarpal in question was deliberately shaped to a point, and I believe Dart also has some like it. And, surprising to some, we find in Bed II such things as a cleaver chipped from the fresh tusk of *Hippopotamus gorgops* or a crude hand axe chipped from fresh elephant limb bone.

I'm not going to elaborate further on the cultural side, but I'm sure you realize by now that even without evidence from far afield—and there's a mass of evidence coming out of Israel, Hungary, India, China and Baluchistan—we can be certain that we have scarcely begun to touch the evidence of human cultural evolution. I don't say that East Africa is the only area; of course it isn't. Even if the Hominoidea started in Africa, as the evidence of the Oligocene Fayum suggests, there were certainly movements out into Europe and Asia from Miocene times onwards, as shown by the Dryopithecine fossils. We need to stop speculating and get teams out all over the place. Maybe ten years from today we will have another meeting here and will be able to say, "How little we knew, how stupid we were in 1965!"

Some Problems of Hominid Classification

David R. Pilbeam and Elwyn L. Simons
1965

The early 1950's were years of controversy in human paleontology; argument, discussion, and sometimes polemic were focused on the relationship to other primates of the genus *Australopithecus,* primates sometimes called near-men or man-apes. These were known mainly, at that time, from finds made in the Transvaal, South Africa. Although the species of *Australopithecus* are now considered hominid, many students were reluctant at first to accept such a status, believing that small brain volume and "imperfect" adaptation to upright posture prevented their assignment to the Hominidae, the taxonomic family which includes living man. Instead, these creatures were regarded as aberrant apes.

Subsequently, it was realized that it is not possible to exclude species from the Hominidae on account of small brain size; the ancestors of modern man must obviously, at some stage, have had smaller brains. The "imperfections" of the *Australopithecus* pelvis were also overstressed; there is good reason to believe that the species of *Australopithecus* were now habitual and efficient bipeds. The concept that different functional systems may evolve independently and at varying rates (mosaic evolution), has also been assimilated by most anthropologists, and, in addition, it is no longer considered reasonable to discriminate taxa on the basis of a few characters alone.

Another sort of misunderstanding derives from one's reference point in studying hominid evolution. Perhaps we have been looking down the wrong end of the telescope, so to speak, trying to understand the evolution of man by looking backward through time "from the vantage point of the Recent" (Patterson 1954). If *Homo* species evolved from the species *Australopithecus africanus,* as many believe, we should expect that these species would have many features in common. Those characters in which they differ, however, should be regarded as specializations of *Homo,* not as peculiarities of *Australopithecus.* One must not

"Some Problems of Hominid Classification." *American Scientist,* Vol. 53, No. 2, pp. 237–59. 1965.

ask "How *Homo*-like is *Australopithecus?*" but rather the opposite.

Origin of the Hominidae

Washburn has stated recently that "most of the characters of *Homo* seem to have evolved well within the Pleistocene, and there is no need to postulate an early separation of man and ape" (1963:203). But the fossil record, although limited, instead seems to indicate a pre-Pliocene separation. Our Pliocene ancestors evidently were socially and adaptively more like man than great apes. By the early Pleistocene, except in the matter of brain-size, man's relatives (men or near-men) were almost as different morphologically from both living and extinct great apes as are men today. *Australopithecus* in fact resembles *Homo* far more than either resembles the African apes, man's closest living relatives.

Ever since the nineteenth-century inception of human paleontology, the comparison of early man with living apes, the only other well-known hominoids, has been over-emphasized. This tendency has led, on the one hand, to stressing supposedly ape-like features in late forms of fossil man (Boule's classic studies of European Neanderthals, for example). On the other hand, this has led to surprise whenever "advanced" characteristics are found in early forms (for example, the modern looking hominid foot from Bed I at Olduvai Gorge, Tanganyika).

Ramapithecus punjabicus (Fig. 1)

is known from the Siwalik Hills of North India, from Fort Ternan, Kenya, and possibly from the Swabian Alps in Europe (Simons 1964), appearing first in the latest Miocene. This species also occurs in sediments of uncertain age in Keiyuan, Yunnan, China (Simons and Pilbeam 1965). The known morphology of *Ramapithecus* is discussed in Simons (1961, 1964); it is sufficient here to point out that the incisors, canines, and premolars are reduced relative to those of known species of dryopithecines and of present-day apes. In *Ramapithecus,* as in man, internal cingula are absent and molar crowns simple. *Ramapithecus* could have evolved with almost equal probability from a dryopithecine, sometime between early and middle Miocene, or from species more like the Egyptian Oligocene primate *Propliopithecus haeckeli.* Hominoid species evolving respectively in the direction of *Homo* and of *Pan* need not have shared a common ancestor later than early or middle Miocene times.

In our opinion, assignment to Hominidae can reasonably be made for all those species that show evolutionary trends toward modern *Homo,* whenever these trends appear. The evolutionary shift in a major adaptive zone indicated in the case of *Ramapithecus* by its reduced snout and anterior teeth (premolars, canines, and incisors) may well correlate with an increased use of the hands and the incipient development of bipedality, although direct fossil evidence for both these developments is presently lacking.

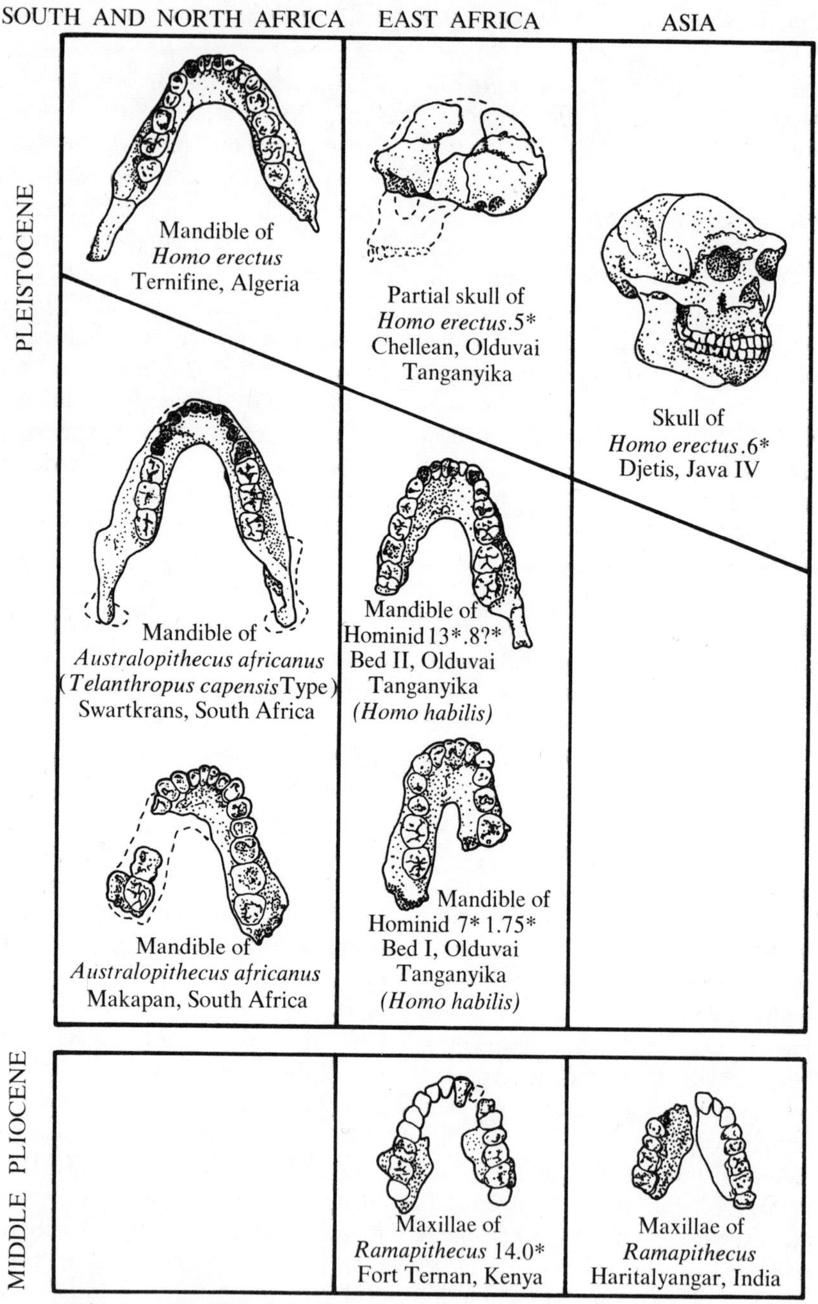

*K/A Ages in millions of years.
The range of error on all dates is of the order of .3 m. yrs. or less.

Fig. 1. Mid-Pliocene and Pleistocene hominids from Asia and Africa with potassium/argon dates. Specimens on the left and right are matched with morphologically similar forms from the K/A-dated East African sequence.

Even if *Ramapithecus* and *Pan* had a more recent common ancestor than either did with the orangutan, the Hominidae are presumably definable in terms of this adaptive shift, as is indicated in Figure 2. Moreover, *Ramapithecus* is presently best regarded as a hominid, not a hominid-like pongid, because it already exhibits the basic dental adaptations of *Homo* and *Australopithecus*. If the other parts of the skeleton, subsequently found, should all be ape-like, this position could require alteration. But why should this be so? Of course, it is quite possible that, if and when cranial and post-cranial remains of *Ramapithecus* are discovered, they will prove to be rather more *Dryopithecus*-like than are those of *Australopithecus*, because *Ramapithecus* lies several million years closer in time to the common ancestor of apes and men. However, the known parts are not ape-like; *Ramapithecus* cannot logically be lumped any longer with the apes.

Fossil ancestors of the living orangutan of Asia are either unknown or unrecognized. Biochemical and serological research underlines the close relationship of modern man to the great apes of Africa. This supports other, mainly paleontological, evidence suggesting that chimpanzee, gorilla, and men are more closely related cladistically, that is, in recency of a common ancestor for all (Harrison and Weiner 1963), than all three are to the orangutan and the Asiatic gibbon. Even if the orangutan and the African apes are patristically related, that is, if all

are more similar in outward (phenotypic or phenetic) morphology than any one of them is to *Homo,* they still could be less similar genetically. However, although the ancestral line leading to the orangutan probably differentiated from an early unknown member of the dryopithecine complex before the hominids did so, the hominids have differentiated more rapidly and now occupy an adaptive niche quite different from that presently filled by the African and Asian apes.

Classification of hominoidea

In comparison with most other superfamilies, too many distinctions of higher taxa have been drawn among hominoids. This is presumably because much of the taxonomic work on these categories has been done by persons unacquainted with the manner in which higher categories have been, or should be, proposed in the light of the new systematics. Most mammalogists would probably now prefer to use three basic principles in justifying the erection or retention of families and subfamilies. Briefly, these principles are: (1) the group which is thought to deserve such status should have had a considerable time duration as a separate stock, (2) the proposed taxon (a formal unit grouping organisms) should show considerable diversity in terms of contained species and genera, (3) the category should be characterized by a reasonably thorough-going structural distinctiveness shared by its members and not like that of related families or subfamilies. Admittedly, criteria of morphological distinctiveness are subjective, but material on which to base such judgments can be derived from comparative anatomy. For instance, one can make an approximate answer to the question: Do members of the families of man and apes differ *more*, or *less*, in total skeletal and dental morphology than do species of other related families within one order, such as Canidae and Felidae?

Because classification should also reflect both the past evolution of given taxa and the morphology and adaptation of the present members of such taxa, a compromise must be reached which reflects both cladistic and patristic relationships (Fig. 1). Consequently, it is preferable in a classification of the superfamily Hominoidea to retain a separate family for the genera *Ramapithecus, Australopithecus,* and *Homo,* a family sustained primarily by the morphological features which indicate the adaptive shift to hominid feeding patterns and habitual bipedalism.

Species of orangutan, chimpanzee, and gorilla, together with those of *Dryopithecus* and *Gigantopithecus,* should be retained in the Pongidae. Dryopithecinae can be justified as a separate subfamily. Although two further subfamilies, Ponginae and Paninae, could be used, these would contain at the most only one or two genera and species, and the distinction would not, in our opinion, be particularly meaningful.

It is even more difficult to justify the division of Hominidae into such subfamilies as Australopithecinae, Homininae, Praehomininae, and the like.

Ecology and adaptation of early hominoids

Modern pongids and hominids are characterized by relative trunk erectness, a feature shared with more "primitive" primate species (Schultz 1961). For example, many prosimians are vertical tree-clingers, like *Indri, Propithecus,* and *Tarsius,* while the New World monkeys *Ateles, Lagothrix,* and *Brachyteles* are partial brachiators (Erikson 1963). Even the more terrestrial Old World monkeys sit erect while feeding, grooming, and resting. Avis (1962) has suggested that the hominoid superfamily differentiated from other primates by becoming arm-swingers confined to a small-branch niche in a forest habitat; in her opinion this differentiation occurred as early as the Eocene. This matter of arm-swinging raises the largely academic question of what is or is not formal "brachiation." (This form of locomotion requires suspension from alternate hands, forward movement being produced by pronation of the arm and trunk around the fixed hand; propulsive force in such locomotion comes entirely from the upper limbs.) *Proconsul africanus, for instance,* is said to have been a "probrachiator" (Napier 1963), and thus in some ways similar morphologically to modern colobine monkeys. *P. africanus* does not exhibit the extreme forelimb elongation characteristic of modern apes (Napier and Davis 1959). Does this mean that *P. africanus* could not have "brachiated" in the formal sense? Perhaps so; perhaps not. Several genera of New World monkeys move through the trees in this manner without showing all the anatomical "brachiating" specializations of the Old World pongids.

Whether "brachiators" or "probrachiators," Miocene apes and their Oligocene ancestors probably showed a high degree of trunk erectness and doubtless spent much time walking and running bipedally, either in the trees or on the ground. As Gregory suggested (1928), some brachiation would probably have been essential for the hominids before they could become habitual bipeds. The structure of the human arm, thorax, and abdomen all suggest that, at some stage, our early Tertiary forerunners may have, on occasion, moved by arm-swinging in the trees.

The idea of the "emancipated forelimb" has been greatly overstressed in discussions of hominid tool-using. Hands have been important throughout all of primate evolution; the higher primates, in particular, use their hands in a wide range of activities such as feeding and grooming. The habit of sitting erect, widespread in primates, insures that the hands are free for these activities. However, in nonhominid primates the hands are typically used in locomotion as well; it is in this respect that hominid forelimb "emancipation" becomes important.

As Kortlandt (1962) and Schultz (1961) have suggested, stone-and branch-throwing in defense were probably important in early hominid behavior before tool-using became widespread. It is also clear from the dentition of *Ramapithecus* that the early hominids could not have fed by stripping vegetable material with the canines and incisors as do the African apes; such feeding behavior requires relatively large front teeth for nipping, tearing, and shredding. It is possible, as a consequence of both these factors, that hominids were *ad hoc* tool-users at least by the early Pliocene (Napier 1963). Once hominids became committed to a terrestrial way of life and some degree of habitual bipedal locomotion, the freeing of their forelimbs would have greatly facilitated tool use.

The earliest hominids may, of course, have functioned fairly well bipedally long before noticeable skeletal alterations increasing the efficiency of this manner of locomotion had become genetically fixed. Such an hypothesis gains strength from observation of the crude walking of the living spider monkey (*Ateles*), gibbon (*Hylobates*), and even some lemurs (*Propithecus*). While it can be debated whether this type of progression should formally be called bipedal, it certainly cannot be written off as quadrupedal movement; none of these primates use the hands habitually to support the forebody during locomotion on the ground. Despite such tendencies toward bipedal walking, however, none of these primates show any man-like skeletal adjustments that make upright walking more efficient.

Selection pressures were doubtless strongly in favor of such trends when the hominids were evolving, but the nature of the ecological readjustments involved in the origin of the hominid line is likely to remain a matter of conjecture. A change in diet also occurred during the course of hominid evolution, but, as Schultz (1961) has pointed out, this shift has been overstressed. The modern great apes are often described as vegetarians, but Schultz suggests that, among the primates, perhaps only the colobine monkeys can be termed truly vegetarian. Most of the other primates tend to supplement their diets with animal protein. However, Miocene apes probably ate mostly vegetable material just as modern baboons, chimpanzees and gorillas do, and the earliest hominids presumably had a similar diet. During the Pliocene, the amount of animal protein in the hominid diet surely would have increased as scavenging and hunting, feeding habits evidently well established by the early Pleistocene, became more widespread in hominid populations. As this dietary shift brought with it increased calorific values, less time would have been required for feeding, and the habit of food-sharing could develop.

Bartholomew and Birdsell (1953) have discussed theoretical concepts of early hominid ecology and believe that the early hominids were wide-ranging, food-sharing, weapon-using omnivores. It has been said that "tool-using and tool-making were

very probably associated with the tendency for early members of the phyletic line leading to man to take to a certain amount of meat-eating" (Robinson 1963a, 393). The reduced canines and incisors of *Ramapithecus punjabicus* suggest that tool-using may have been established by the late Miocene, because smaller front teeth require the use of other means to prepare food, either animal or vegetable.[1] Noback and Moskowitz have emphasized that the increasing dexterity of the hand seems to have played a major role in the evolution of the central nervous system among higher primates, particularly in the case of the Hominidae, and this influence may well have been acting in *Ramapithecus* populations.

Robinson (1962, 1963) has discussed at length the alterations in pelvic anatomy and muscle function consequent to erect bipedalism. Unfortunately, no pelves of Miocene or Pliocene dryopithecines are yet known. It is generally assumed that the pelves of mid-Tertiary higher primates will prove to be similar to those of modern pongids. In this view, the human pelvis is considered to have been derived from an ancestral morphology similar to that of modern apes. It seems more likely, however, that some morphological differentiation has occurred in the

[1] It may be argued that all three *Ramapithecus* maxillary specimens are those of small-canined females. This is not too likely, but, even if true, it would not alter the fact that the premolars and incisors are also smaller relative to molar size than is the case in any pongid.

pongid as well as the hominid line. Indeed, such pieces of evidence as the hominid-like pelvis of *Oreopithecus* and the broad ilia of New World brachiators, taken together with the considerable probability that early pongids were arboreal arm-swingers with erect trunks, suggest that the immediate ancestors of the hominids were actually pre-adapted as brachiators in terms of behavior, and perhaps to bipedal running and walking in terms of anatomy.

Chimpanzees and gorillas have prognathous, that is, projecting faces; their mid-Tertiary ancestors were evidently more orthognathous (straight-faced), and it seems that facial lengthening occurred, at least in part, as a response to demands of ground living, defensive display and vegetarian diet. Baboons and macaques have prognathous faces also. Large teeth and powerful muscles are required in order to chew tough plant food. Considerable sexual dimorphism in canine size is shown among various species of apes and Old World monkeys and, consequently, it is probable that (among other factors) elongated canines are associated with defensive display behavior. Increased stress on olfaction among mainly ground-feeding species such as baboons probably was important in the development of the snout. In contrast, colobine monkeys, New World monkeys, and the erect-postured tree-clinging pro-simians such as *Indri, Propithecus,* and *Tarsius* all have relatively short faces and show less sexual dimorphism. Among fossil forms the small Miocene species *Proconsul africanus*

(Davis and Napier 1963) was also relatively orthognathous as was *Oreopithecus*. New evidence secured by the recent Yale expeditions (Simons 1965) indicates that several of the Egyptian Oligocene hominoids were short-faced too.

Trunk erectness and orthognathism are apparently closely linked. Erect posture is associated with changes in orientation of the cranial base, typically exemplified by downward rotation of the facial axis on the basi-cranial axis (DuBrul 1950; DuBrul and Laskin 1961; Biegert 1963). Mills (1963) has suggested that the assumption of habitual erect posture would cause further flattening of the face. He points out that, in primates with large canines, the lower canines pass behind the upper incisors during chewing. With facial shortening, the canines no longer pass behind, but rather in the plane of, the maxillary incisors. As this happens, selection favors reduction of canine crowns. If tool use (and possible changes in male display behavior as well) had removed the selective advantage of large canines, canine reduction inevitably would have taken place.

Thus, it appears that several anatomical, behavioral, and "cultural" elements—erect posture, orthognathism, changes in diet and display behavior, an increasing use of tools and reduction of the anterior dentition—are here closely linked one to another. Members of the genus *Ramapithecus* have small front teeth and were apparently wide-ranging even in the late Miocene; the dental evidence implies that profound behavioral, dietary, and locomotor changes had already occurred among species of *Ramapithecus* by this time. The commitment to a hominid way of life could conceivably have been made by the late Miocene, and our earliest known probable ancestors, with brains perhaps comparable in size to those of chimpanzees, might have already adopted a way of life distinct from that of their ape contemporaries.

Appearance and speciation of man

Near the beginning of the Pleistocene, hominids are represented in the fossil record by two or more species of *Australopithecus,* a small-brained, large-jawed form similar dentally to *Homo.* Post-cranially, *Australopithecus* is similar to, although not identical with, later men and evidently was an habitual biped. Early Pleistocene sites at Olduvai in Tanganyika have yielded hominid remains, together with crude stone tools (Leakey 1959); stone tools of similar type are known from North Africa (Biberson 1963) and the Jordan valley (Stekelis 1960), and it seems likely that, at about the same time, bone tools were being made in South Africa (Dart 1957). Regular tool-making, utilizing bone, stone, wood, and perhaps other material too, possibly began more than two million years ago.

It has been suggested by many authors that the transition from tool-using to regular tool-making was a step of crucial importance in the evolution of man. This may well be true but, like many generalizations in anthropology, this one has been oversimplified. As Napier has pointed out (1963), tool-making may often have been invented and forgotten in the late Tertiary. During Villafranchian time (that is, during earliest Pleistocene time), some hominids were doubtless tool-makers while others were still only tool-users. Differing environmental demands would produce different behavioral responses. However, the advantages of regular toolmaking are clear and, once invented, the spread of this skill would probably have been fairly rapid.

Speciation in the Hominidae

Simpson (1961:90) remarks:

Supposedly intergeneric hybridization, usually with sterile offspring, is possible among animals, for instance, in mammals, the artificial crosses *Bos* × *Bison, Equus* × *Asinus,* and *Ursus* × *Thalarctos.* In my opinion, however, this might better be taken as basis for uniting the nominal genera. I would not now give generic rank to *Bison, Asinus,* or *Thalarctos.*

There is considerable evidence that the African and Arabian baboons, previously thought to belong to several separate genera, can produce viable hybrids, and may, instead, be classified in perhaps as few as two or three species of a single genus. Hybrid studies, by the Russians and others, suggest that species of *Macaca* (the rhesus monkey) and perhaps of *Cercocebus* (the mangabey), too, should be classified as belonging instead to the baboon genus *Papio*. *Papio* in this sense, can be regarded as a wide-ranging genus with local species populations which show variations in morphology, coloring, and behavior. Freedman's metrical work on cranial variation in *Papio* "species" (1963) lends support to this view. Some of the populations may be sibling species, others may warrant only subspecific rank; only interfertility studies can determine their validity as genetical species. Among members of *Papio*, greater morphological variability is to be seen among samples of adult males than among samples of adult females, particularly in cranial features. This, together with pronounced sexual dimorphism, suggests that differences in mating and display patterns have selected for a great deal of the specific and subspecific morphological differences. The small amount of speciation within the genus is also significant when compared with *Cercopithecus* (guenons) or colobine monkeys, and this is almost certainly a direct reflection of *Papio's* wide-ranging terrestrial way of life. Among these primates, there is apparently a rough correlation between species range size and the degree of speciation within a genus. Highly arboreal primates, such as species of langurs and gibbons, tend to have more restricted ranges and tend to be less mobile as groups; isolation and speciation become more likely under these circumstances.

The earliest hominids probably were at least as wide-ranging and mobile as the baboons, and presumably would have been much more so by middle and late Pliocene time. As noted already, fossil evidence suggests that *Ramapithecus punjabicus* was already present in East Africa, India, China, and possibly Europe, by the early Pliocene; there is no reason to suppose that hominids have not been widely dispersed since then. Man has capitalized on plasticity rather than becoming restricted to narrow morphological and behavioral adaptations. His mobility, his ability to occupy a highly diversified ecological niche, and his apparently slow development of isolating mechanisms (Mayr 1963:644) all tend to reduce speciation. It is a reasonable working hypothesis, therefore, that not more than one genus, and perhaps no more than one or two species of hominid, has existed at any particular time. Like most other mammals, man is polytypic; that is, a number of races are found within the species. We should expect fossil hominid species populations to be polytypic too.

Taxonomy of Australopithecus

Before the student can erect new fossil genera and species he must demonstrate that the new proposed taxon differs significantly from previously described taxa in a number of particular characters. Thus, any diagnosis should take full account of known variability in living related species and genera. Different specific and generic names also imply certain other differences. If two individual fossils or fossil populations have different specific names, this implies that they could not have been members of a single freely interbreeding population; this, in turn, requires a period of reproductive and probably geographic isolation. Different generic names, in their turn, generally imply that the taxa concerned were completely incompatible genetically; to develop such incompatibility would require a long period of isolation. As we have already noted, however, such isolation would probably have been an unusual event during the course of hominid evolution.

Early Pleistocene hominids are known from a number of African localities. The first to be described and discussed was *Australopithecus africanus* from South Africa. It is now fairly generally agreed that two species of this genus are known: *A. africanus* (Fig. 1) from Villafranchian deposits at Taung, Sterkfontein, and Makapansgat, and *A. robustus*, from possibly latest early Pleistocene and middle Pleistocene deposits at Kromdraai and Swartkrans (Robinson 1963). Another form, "*Telanthropus capensis*" (Fig. 1) has been recovered from Swartkrans; its status is equivocal and will be discussed later.[2] Robinson (1963a) discussed these australopithecine forms at length, pointing out that *A. africanus* is, in his opinion, closer to the ancestry of later men than is *A. robustus*.

[2] Invalid or doubtful taxonomic terms are indicated here in quotes on initial citation only.

Definite or probable australopithecines have been reported also from Java, North Africa, Israel, and East Africa. *Meganthropus palaeojavanicus*—represented by finds from the Djetis beds of Java—is said by Robinson to be closely similar to the African form *A. robustus*. Although Clark (1955:86) considers the Java specimen's generic separation from another hominid form, *Homo erectus* (Fig. 1), unjustified in view of the fragmentary nature of the material, the fact is that these jaw fragments do not provide enough information to allow students to draw species distinctions between the Javan and African material.

Coppens (1962) has reported the recovery of an australopithecine skull from Koro-Toro, near Lake Chad south of the Sahara. The associated fauna suggests an early Villafranchian age. Arambourg (1963: 564) states that this fossil is intermediate in morphology between *A. africanus* and *A. robustus* but with perhaps a greater cranial capacity. Robinson (1963b:601) considers it closer to *A. robustus*. No pebble tools are associated, although they are present in later Villafranchian deposits of North Africa (Biberson 1963). "*Meganthropus africanus*" from the Laetolil beds of early Pleistocene age near Lake Eyassi in East Africa has been referred to *Australopithecus* by Robinson (1955). In addition Stekelis (1960) has discovered fragmentary hominid remains of early or middle Pleistocene age associated with a pebble tool culture at Ubeidiya in the Central Jordan valley.

Finally, Leakey has recently described a number of hominid finds in deposits of early and middle Pleistocene age at Olduvai Gorge, Tanganyika (Leakey 1959, 1961, and Leakey, Tobias, and Napier 1964). Two distinct species have been recognized and described, *Australopithecus* (= *Zinjanthropus*) *"boisei"* from Bed I at Olduvai and from possibly middle Pleistocene deposits near Lake Natron, Tanganyika, and *"Homo habilis"* (type, hominid #7) from Bed I and other specimens from Bed II at Olduvai. *A. boisei* is bigger and more robust than *H. habilis* (see Fig. 1) and has larger molars and premolars; we believe that it cannot be distinguished at the specific level from *A. robustus.*

The hominid sites from Bed I have been dated by the potassium-argon method (Leakey, Curtis, and Evernden 1961), the three sites FLK I, FLKNN I, and MK falling between 1.57 and 1.89 million years. The Bed II hominids from FLK II, VEK IV, and MNK II are younger than 1.02 million years, the youngest date for the top of Bed I, and older than 0.49 million years, the date of a post-Chellean II tuff in Bed II (Hay 1963). The *Homo habilis* material therefore falls into two groups, separated by perhaps as much as one million years. Once again, during the period of deposition of the lower parts of Bed II, two distinct taxa appear to have been present, *H. habilis* at Olduvai and *A. boisei* at Lake Natron.

Altogether, then, some half dozen supposedly distinct taxa (both genera

and species) have been proposed for early and early Middle Pleistocene hominids; several of these are based on the most fragmentary and limited material. Schultz has repeatedly stressed the very high level of morphological variability among species of the Hominoidea (see bibliographies in Schultz 1961 and 1963). Nevertheless, small and taxonomically trivial differences in dental, cranial, and postcranial anatomy have still been used to establish or justify specific or generic distinctions among the earlier Pleistocene hominids. What follows is an attempt to bring some taxonomic order to this situation.

At present, *A. robustus* is known from South Africa (Swartkrans, Kromdraai), Olduvai Bed I, Lake Natron, and possibly Java. The other African forms of roughly equivalent age have been referred to three taxa, *A. africanus, Telanthropus capensis,* and *Homo habilis.* The relative dating of the North, East, and South African sites presents a number of problems. Faunally, there are few mammal species as they are presently defined common to all three sites, and those which are common are often unsuitable for purposes of correlation. Cooke (1963) has discussed this problem at length. He believes that the South African sites which have yielded *A. africanus* are broadly contemporaneous with the later Bed I levels at Olduvai. However, he points out that:

Although ecological differences prevent too close a comparison, the faunas suggest strongly that the sequence in East Africa from the Kaiso and the Kanam levels through Omo and Laetolil to Bed I corresponds fairly in time to the sequence Sterkfontein and Makapansgat to Swartkrans and Kromdraai. Although the evidence is extremely tenuous, the Villafranchian (equivalent) fauna of North Africa could well be contemporary with these East Afrian deposits and the ape-man breccias. The occurrence of pebble tools in similar relationships in all three areas may be significant and if the North African beds are truly pre-Cromerian as has been suggested by several authorities this would provide additional grounds for keeping at least the major part of the ape-man deposits within the Villafranchian. (Cooke 1964: 104)

Biberson (1963) considers the Koro-Toro site at Lake Chad contemporary with Kaiso and Kanam in East Africa, and, if this is so, the Chad hominid could well be the oldest *Australopithecus* known. *Telanthropus capensis* from Swartkrans is probably the same age as *Homo habilis* from Olduvai Bed II, while *A. africanus* from Taung, Sterkfontein and Makapansgat and Bed I *H. habilis* are possibly of approximately equivalent age.

The new East African hominids and the South African australopithecines

Known *Homo habilis* material, as already noted, falls into two main groups separated by perhaps as much as a million years. The type specimen of *H. habilis* consists of a juvenile mandible, two parietal fragments, a hand and an upper molar. A foot and clavicle belonging to an older individual (or individuals—associations of all Olduvai individuals are certainly not clear) have been recovered from the same site (FLKNN I). Two other sites in Bed I have yielded teeth, mandibular and skull fragments, and a tibia and fibula belonging either to *H. habilis* or to *Australopithecus (Zinjanthropus) boisei*. Among remains from Bed II are: a complete mandible (with associated maxillae) together with the occipitals and broken parietals and temporals of possibly the same individual, cranial fragments, isolated teeth, and a damaged palate. Although there is insufficient material from which firm inferences can be drawn, the sequence through Bed I to Bed II suggests that teeth and mandibles became progressively reduced during this time, while there was little alteration in cranial capacity. (This seemingly unchanging brain size may correlate with the presence throughout the section of similar crude pebble tools, or the two faunas may be closer in time than K/A–dated horizons appear to indicate.) The juvenile mandible and teeth from FLKNN I in Bed I are some 10 per cent greater in all measurements than the mandible from MNK II in Bed II. Such a small number of mandibles cannot, of course, be regarded as necessarily typical of the populations from which they come, but it is possible that, during this period, jaws and teeth became reduced while cranial capacity remained fairly constant.

A large number of *A. africanus* specimens have been described. Because this taxon is known so well, some have tended to think typologically in terms of an "australopithecine stage" of human evolution during which all hominids would have been morphologically similar to these South African forms. However, if the hominids evolved in the main as a single, widespread, polytypic species, the Transvaal *A. africanus* more likely represents a sample, drawn from a time segment of unknown length, of a peripheral and perhaps aberrant race of this species (Mayr 1963: 640). We should not expect contemporaneous or near contemporaneous races within this same species to be morphologically identical with, or even quite similar to, the South African *A. africanus*. A large number of fossil specimens, say, from a restricted geographic area and from a relatively small segment of time, may well resemble each other more than any one of them resembles a small sample of the same species from a different part of the geographic range and from an earlier or later time. In such a case, however, we must be careful not to regard the large sample as morphologically "typical" of the species. By so doing, we would prevent correct assignment of other specimens of the same taxon. Morphological differences between specimens due to age and sex differences and to geographic and temporal

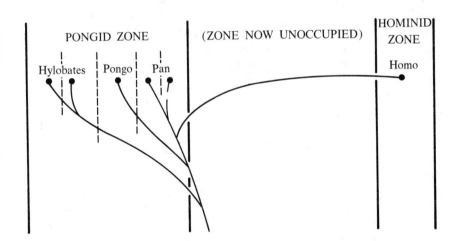

ADAPTIVE AND STRUCTURAL – FUNCTIONAL ZONES

Fig. 2. Diagram showing relative closeness of phylogenetic relationships of living hominoids and their radiation into adaptive–structural–functional zones, from Simpson (1963).

separation, as well as racial variation, must be carefully considered. In erecting new taxa, it is necessary for the discoverer to demonstrate that the new finds are *significantly* different from previously defined taxa.

Thus, when we consider the hominids from Lake Chad and Olduvai Bed I we must ask ourselves, could these represent taxa which are already known? *A. africanus* and *H. habilis* were both habitual bipeds. Unfortunately, we have pelves of the former but not of the latter, whereas we know the foot of the latter but not of the former. It is possible that the *H. habilis* foot from Olduvai Bed I is no more nor less *Homo*-like than is the pelvis of *A. africanus* from S. Africa.

The parietal bones from Olduvai FLKNN I have been reconstructed by Tobias (1964) to indicate a cranial capacity of between 642–724 cc. This volume estimate must be regarded with great caution because of the fragmentary nature of the specimen.[3] Tobias (1963) gives the australopithecine range of cranial capacity as 435–600 cc., this being lower than his estimates for this skull of *Homo habilis*. However, there seems to be no good reason for separating early species of the genera *Australopithecus* and *Homo* on grounds of differences in cranial volume. None of the crania from the

Transvaal breccias or from Olduvai Beds I and II indicate volumes outside the range now known among the single species of living gorilla, and all these crania are distinctly smaller than those of *Homo erectus*.

The teeth and mandible of *H. habilis* from Olduvai Bed I FLKNN I do not differ greatly from specimens of *A. africanus* (Fig. 2 and Dart 1962:268, Fig. 7) in shape or morphology. The molars are similar in size and shape to those of *A. africanus* from Sterkfontein (Robinson 1956). The premolars of *H. habilis* are somewhat narrower than those of the South African forms; but shape, as well as size, of teeth is known to vary greatly in all modern primates, including man, and this seems to be a relatively unimportant character on which to base generic and specific separation of the two forms. Unfortunately, some of the Olduvai specimens are crushed and broken and this limits our ability to make comparisons. Collection of further hominids from the Olduvai beds is thus of the greatest importance; recovery of a more adequate sample should enable students to assess the range of variability within the local population represented at Olduvai, and would allow comparisons of this population with others of approximately equivalent age. *H. habilis* and *A. africanus* may represent nothing more than two variant populations within the same widespread species, but this hypothesis can only be verified or rejected when more information becomes available.

[3] The slightest mis-setting of the two bones at the midline, for instance if flared too much laterally, would markedly increase the brain volume estimate for this individual.

The validity of *Homo habilis,* as any new fossil taxon, depends on the reality and the plausibility of its diagnosis. As Campbell states (1964, 451):

It is here that the hypothesis of the new species must stand or fall;...The diagnosis must support the hypothesis for the species to stand, not in law, but in reality.... (Many examples of this state of affairs could be quoted. The most topical, and one of the most important, concerns the creation of the taxon *Homo habilis.* In their original publication the authors stated that *Telanthropus capensis* "may well prove, on closer comparative investigation, to belong to *Homo habilis*"; thus the effective demonstration of a novel taxon was negated. The name is valid, but the species has not been effectively shown to have existed, as a distinct taxon.)

Telanthropus capensis from Swartkrans is probably broadly contemporaneous with Bed II *Homo habilis.* In spite of its fragmentary nature, some general remarks can be made about *Telanthropus.* The teeth are smaller than those of *A. africanus,* although cusp patterns similar. The mandible is smaller, too, and is said by Robinson (1961) to be reminiscent of other African and Asian hominids of Middle Pleistocene date. This is to be expected for a form transitional in time between the early Pleistocene hominids and middle Pleistocene *Homo erectus.* It is probable that Bed II *H. habilis* and *Telanthropus capensis* represent two populations of a single species or subspecies, but, once again, further material will be required before firm conclusions can be drawn. Both are similar to the mandible of *H. erectus* from the Djetis beds in Java (so-called "*Pithecanthropus* B").

The primitive stone tools associated with *Homo habilis* throughout Bed I and the lower part of Bed II are evidently of uniform type for what may be a very long period of time; this is perhaps correlated with the equally protracted apparent stability of cranial capacity. Tools of similar type are found in Morocco (Biberson 1963) and at Ubeidiya (Stekelis 1961). It should be noted that the early Pleistocene hominid from Chad, found unassociated with tools, has a cranial capacity of the order of that of both *H. habilis* and *A. africanus.* Regular tool-making, as we noted earlier, seems to have been invented during the early Pleistocene, perhaps in Africa, at a time when hominids had already become efficient bipeds. Dates from Olduvai suggest the possibility that a full million years passed after the invention and spread of tool-making during which cranial capacity—and presumably manual dexterity, "intelligence," and hunting skill—remained fairly constant. Some time roughly between one million and five hundred thousand years ago, human brain size increased by more than 50 per cent. Also, during this period, the change from simple pebble chopping tools to hand-axes of Chellean type apparently took place. Elaboration of tool types and expansion in brain size were probably in-

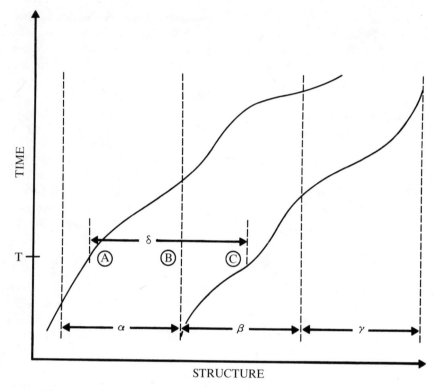

Fig. 3. An attempt to represent Pleistocene hominids as a single genetic continuum, evolving through time. Modified from Simpson (1963).

terrelated, and both, perhaps, were associated with the final anatomical perfection of hand structure. Napier (1962) has suggested that the hand of *Homo habilis* was not as refined structurally and functionally as that of later men. Undoubtedly, limits of both mental ability and hand anatomy affected the form of tools.

The earliest Pleistocene appearance of tool-making, then, seems to have heralded no immediate anatomical changes in the hominid line. Cranial capacity, in particular, remained constant. Jaws, teeth, and faces became reduced during the era of crude pebble tools, but exactly why this was so remains conjectural. Anthropologists have frequently suggested that the appearance of tool-making was causally related to the expansion of the brain. There was never any fossil evidence to support this view, and now we have some evidence to the contrary. Increase in brain size evidently lagged behind the regular making of tools. This skill had altered the lives of early Pleistocene hominids; apparently it did not immediately alter their morphology.

Taxonomy of early African hominids

We have concluded that *A. africanus* and Bed I *Homo habilis* may not be specifically distinct and also that the bulk of Bed II materials and *Telanthropus* may be specifically identical. *Telanthropus* itself is regarded by many students as an invalid genus which should be referred either to *Homo* or to *Australopithecus*. If referred to *Homo* the trivial name *capensis* can no longer be used, since this has already been applied to a Late Paleolithic skull from Boskop (for further discussion of this point see Oakley and Campbell 1964). If the Olduvai Bed I and Bed II *Homo habilis* material is regarded as belonging to a single taxon, it is not unreasonable also to include therein *A. africanus* and the *Telanthropus* material from South Africa. This taxon would extend over a very considerable time period; in fact it would be more than twice as long as the time covered by *H. erectus* and *H. sapiens* combined. Some hominid evolutionary change, particularly trends towards orthognathism and reduced dentition, occurred during this considerable span of time, although the amount of variation within the taxon is probably not greater than that observed in modern mammal species (including man).

If all early Pleistocene hominids ancestral to later men are regarded as members of the genus *Homo*, as the proposal of *H. habilis* by Leakey, Tobias, and Napier suggests, the prior binomial for this taxon would be *Homo africanus*. The evolution of early Pleistocene hominids, first to *Homo erectus*, and finally to *Homo sapiens*, can be shown diagrammatically in Fig. 3 (modified from Simpson 1963, Fig. 3c), which shows a single hominid species evolving through time. A, B, and C are hypothetical contemporaneous individuals, C being more "modern" than B, B more so than A. Simpson (1963: 14) suggests as a possibility that:

...there is only one lineage or evolutionary species and only one genetical species at any one time. In that case, the species would have been highly variable, and even more so during much of past time than *Homo sapiens* is at present. At some time around the middle Pleistocene it might have varied all the way from what in purely morphological (or typological) terms could be called marginal australopithecoid through pithecanthropoid to marginal neanderthaloid. Such variation would be improbable within a single deme or local population. It would be less improbable among geographically separate "allopatric" populations or subspecies. Such geographic semi-isolates would of course be variable in themselves, but some might, for instance, vary about a more australopithecoid modal morphology and others about a more neanderthaloid mode. Discovery that fossil hominids fall into such modally distinct, synchronous but allopatric groups would favor this interpretation. Whether current data do or do not tend to follow such a pattern I leave to the specialists in such matters.

We prefer to accept Simpson's model for the moment.

A, B, and C of Figure 3 are contemporaneous at time T and are members of a single species. However, typologically A and B might be placed in one species α while C is referred to species β. The paradox is imagined rather than real, because the taxa α and β, and the taxon δ are of different types. If the hominids have evolved as a single unitary species, δ will represent a sample of the genetical species which existed at time. T. α, β, and γ are morphospecies, species "established by morphological similarity regardless of other considerations" (Simpson 1961, 155). The problem here is largely one of definition and should not be over-stressed. Nevertheless, this model will be useful in dealing with problems which will appear should "undoubted" (morphological) *Homo* be found contemporaneous with "undoubted" (morphological) *Australopithecus.*

Both *Australopithecus africanus* and *A. robustus* are bipeds, both have greatly reduced canines and incisors, both almost certainly would have been tool-users, and both probably made tools. If tool-making spread by copying within one species of small-brained hominids, it would presumably have been copied by any other species of equally small-brained hominids living in the same area.

Australopithecus robustus is said by Robinson (1961) to have been a vegetarian because of its massive premolars and molars. *A robustus* specimens from Olduvai and Natron exhibit pronounced wear patterns on both upper and lower molars. Such wear patterns are found in certain Australian aboriginal tribes that eat

roots and other vegetable material together with large quantities of sand and grit. In contrast, *Homo habilis* has wear patterns similar to those of meat-eating African tribes such as the Masai (Leakey, personal communication). *A robustus* is said to have been a vegetarian and *A. africanus* (Robinson 1963) and *H. habilis* more exclusively meat-eaters. Although the *A. robustus* wear patterns suggest that gritty vegetable material constituted a large part of the diet, they do not, however, enable us to state categorically that *A. robustus* did *not* eat meat. Nor are we entitled to assume that *A. robustus* and *A. africanus* were at all times vegetarians or omnivores respectively; diet can vary greatly (within contemporary *Homo sapiens* groups for example), and presumably changes with time too. Hominids were successful because they were behaviorally plastic and adaptable; we must take great care before we place ecological limitations on fossil hominids known only in relatively poor detail.

In summary, *Australopithecus robustus,* like *Ramapithecus punjabicus, Homo habilis* and *A. africanus,* has small canines and incisors. This implies that *A. robustus* prepared its food, presumably with tools, and there is no reason to suppose that it could not have eaten prepared animal as well as prepared vegetable food. The diet of modern "primitive" men is varied; could not earlier hominids have been similarly omnivorous? *A. robustus* and *H. habilis* were evidently co-existent in the same general areas for perhaps a million years, if the new dates and stratigraphic-faunal data of Leakey are right. They were, therefore, sympatric species, that is, species occupying the same geographic area. Both were bipeds, both were presumably tool-users and probably tool-makers; their diets might well have been similar at times. As mentioned earlier, there are theoretical difficulties involved in preparing a model of hominid speciation. If we are to distinguish these taxa at a specific level, we need to know far more about geographical barriers during the Pliocene and Pleistocene. Comparative study of closely related pairs of animal species indicates that they must have separate origins in different geographic areas, that is, they must originally be allopatric (Kohn and Orians, 1962). Perhaps one species of hominid evolved in Africa and one in Asia only to mingle at the beginning of the Pleistocene when land connections between Eurasia and Africa presumably became reestablished. The picture as to the number of *Australopithecus* species really indicated by known material is still obscure and the available evidence can be interpreted in a number of ways.

Post-Villafranchian morphological changes

The Pliocene was probably a time of great morphological change in hominid evolution. Locomotor adaptations were being improved and, by middle Pleistocene time at least, the skeletons of hominids were essentially like those of modern man even though the skulls were not. Throughout this time, hominids were getting larger; this size increase was probably associated with increased speed and efficiency in running and walking. Brain size increased in consequence. Some relative increase in brain size also occurred during the early Pleistocene, although the time and extent of this expansion is difficult to assess. The changes in cerebrum and cerebellum which must have taken place are still not satisfactorily documented, nor are the selection pressures that produced them fully understood. These problems are discussed by Garn (1963: 232), who says that:

...human brain size did increase, either because brainier *individuals* were at an adaptive advantage, or because *groups* with larger brains survived and groups with smaller brains did not. It gratifies our ego to believe that selection favored intelligence, that our own ancestral lines came to genetic fulfillment because they were so very smart. But it may be that our vaunted intelligence is merely an indirect product of the kind of brain that can discern meaningful signals in a complex social content generating a heavy static of informational or, rather, misinformational noise.

Ryle (1949) has discussed "intelligence" and "intellect" from the philosopher's viewpoint. He states (p. 26) that:

...both philosophers and laymen tend to treat intellectual operations as the core of mental conduct; that is to say, they tend to define all other mental-conduct concepts in terms of concepts of cognition. They suppose that the primary exercise of mind consists in finding the answer to questions and that their other occupations are merely applications of considered truths or even regrettable distractions from their consideration... (However) there are many activities which directly display qualities of mind, yet are neither themselves intellectual operations nor yet effects of intellectual operations.

Brains expanded as the cultural environment became more and more complex, and larger brains enabled more complex cultures to develop. The actions which we choose, arbitrarily, to term "intelligent," that is those involving theorizing and the manipulation of true propositions or facts, form merely one aspect of our responses to a complex environment.

An increase in adult brain size involves a larger fetal and infantile brain and a prolonged growth period, two of the important trends in higher primate evolution noted by Schultz (1961). Bigger fetal brains require larger maternal pelves, and it is possible that the structural refinements in the hominid pelvis which have evolved since the Villafranchian are, to a large extent, due to the problems posed by the birth of large-brained offspring. During middle Pleistocene times, the brain increased in size with consequent remodeling of the cranial vault (Moss and Young 1960). The facial skeleton and the teeth became reduced, presumably because of further refinements in food preparation and tool-making (Dahlberg 1963). Changes in relative size of the braincase and the jaws and related mus-

cles produced changes in shape and size of the cranium, and in size and form of the supra-orbital ridges. By the late middle Pleistocene, the brain had probably reached approximately its present-day volume, and the morphological evolution of the Hominidae was almost complete.

Conclusions

Earliest hominids known to date are recognizable, in the form of *Ramapithecus punjabicus,* in the late Miocene. This sets back the differentiation of hominids from pongids to the early Miocene or earlier. Circumstantial rather than direct evidence suggests that *R. punjabicus* could have been a tool-using animal and, at least, a partial biped. It was widespread throughout the Old World apparently because of the great mobility in range extension afforded by ground dwelling and/or bipedalism. These factors would have reduced tendencies towards speciation among early Hominidae. Known geographic distribution of *Ramapithecus* (East Africa, India, China) shows that hominids have been wide-ranging, as they are now, at least since late Miocene time.

The early Pleistocene hominids can be classified in *no more than* two species; one of these, *Australopithecus* (or perhaps *Homo*) *africanus,* found in South, East and North Africa, probably inhabited other regions too. The evolution of this species saw the final perfection of the foot and pelvis for habitual bipedal walking, the invention and spread to tool-making and the development of associated refinements in the hand, and finally, late in its history, the rapid expansion of the brain. *Homo erectus,* found throughout the Old World during much of the middle Pleistocene (from 500,000 or 600,000 years ago on), is barely distinguishable taxonomically from *Homo sapiens.*

The Origin and Adaptive Radiation of the Australopithecines

John T. Robinson
1968

Introduction

Understanding of the australopithecines has advanced enormously since the first paper concerning them was published in 1925. At first material of this group was known from South Africa only and scientific opinion was strongly inclined to discount the views of the local workers. This situation has changed greatly: it is now generally agreed that the australopithecines are hominids, not pongids. While by far the greater proportion of the considerable number of specimens now known are South African, there are very encouraging signs that other areas will contribute significantly, to our knowledge. It is greatly to be hoped that these promises are to be ful-filled since, in my opinion at least, australopithecines were spread across the Old World from South Africa to the Far East and it would be very valuable to have specimens from widely separated localities.

The chief purpose of the present paper is to speculate about the nature of the forces which operated to bring the australopithecine group into existence and which controlled its evolution.

Australopithecine taxonomy

Any consideration of the evolution of the australopithecines must first take notice of the taxonomy of this group. This has been dealt with in a number of publications (e. g. Robin-

"The Origin and Adaptive Radiation of the Australopithecines." *Evolution and Hominisation: Papers to the Theory of Evolution as well as Dating, Classification, and Abilities of Human Hominids.* Edited by Gotfried Kurth. Second revised and enlarged edition. Pp. 150–75. Gustav Fischer Verlag, Stuttgart, 1968.

son 1954a, 1954b, 1956 and 1961) but will briefly be referred to here again. The reason for this is that without recognition of taxonomic differentiation within the group, it is futile to consider adaptive radiation within it. Furthermore, it would appear that many authors tend to think of the group as being essentially taxonomically uniform and make statements purporting to refer to all the known australopithecines when this is not the case. As an example may be quoted the statement "...the whole canine-premolar complex is reduced in the australopithecines..." (Washburn and Howell 1960). This hardly does justice to the fact that the whole complex, as listed by these authors, differs very considerably in *Australopithecus* and *Paranthropus*. Furthermore, these differences have far-reaching implications. Or again the same authors in referring to the australopithecine discovery at site FLK in the Olduvai Gorge state, "It affords clear-cut evidence that these primitive hominids (i. e. the australopithecines) were to some extent carnivorous and predaceous...." Now quite apart from the fact that the interpretation here given is one of several which may be drawn from the actual evidence and is therefore not clearcut proof, the evidence concerned refers to one type of australopithecine only. In view of the fact that the dental specialisations of the two main types of australopithecine differ appreciably, it surely is unsafe to generalise from a small amount of information at one site which at the time had yielded only one type of australo-

pithecine. Similarly, discussions about a possible osteodontokeratic culture of australopithecines (in the paper here referred to as well as in the rest of the literature) proceed as though the evidence being debated concerns australopithecines in general. In actual fact most of the evidence so far employed comes from a single site, with some additional information from two others—but all are *Australopithecus* sites. *Paranthropus* may or may not have had such a culture, but whether it did or not cannot be determined from sites which have yielded only *Australopithecus*.

The above point has been dealt with at some length, not in order to attempt to refute the views of the authors concerned, but to stress the need to remember when discussing the australopithecines that at least two types are known which differ considerably in their morphology and apparently also in their ecology and behaviour. If this fact is ignored, discussions are as likely to lead to obfuscation as to clarification of the issues involved.

South African australopithecines

The two types of South African australopithecine are *Australopithecus africanus* Dart and *Paranthropus robustus* Broom (Robinson 1954). Previous to the latter analysis the only taxonomic analysis was that of Broom (1950) who placed the known forms in 5 species of 3 genera—but who thought that a fourth genus should be erected for the Makapan form. Several other schemes have been suggested without being legitimate taxonomic analyses lending legality to the suggested classifications. One may note here in passing that palaeo-anthropologists in general seem to pay very scant, or no, attention to the International Rules govening nomenclature. Mayr (1950) suggested placing the australopithecines and all true men together in the genus *Homo* so that the family Hominidae would contain the one genus alone. Washburn and Patterson (1951) suggested putting all the hominids in two genera, *Australopithecus* and *Homo.* Howell (1959) seems to agree with the latter view except that he would split the genus *Australopithecus* into two subgenera: *A.* (*Australopithecus*) and *A.* (*Paranthropus*).

The practising taxonomist is in the first place primarily concerned with identification and therefore looks for what are generally referred to as good diagnostic characters which enable him to distinguish as easily as possible between closely related forms. The characters adopted are arrived at empirically: that is to say, if observation shows that a particular feature, *taking its range of variation into account,* characterises the group concerned and no others, then it is a good taxonomic character. In some cases it will be found that a single character is so clearly diagnostic that it is not necessary to use others in order to identify accurately the form concerned. Usually however it is necessary to use a group of characters in order to achieve certainty of identification. Where a new form is being dealt with it is always necessary to use a constellation of characters in order to determine its relationships. The level at which a character is useful is again determined by observation. For example, in arthropods the number of bristles on a particular segment of a limb may vary from one species to another but remain constant within any one species. Such a character would be useful only at the species level. But the number of limbs or of wings, for example, are constant over far larger groups than the species and are therefore useless for distinguishing species but are invaluable as characters defining much larger taxonomic groups. Limb number, for instance, is a diagnostic arthropod character at the Class level.

In this practical, workaday taxonomic sense, the characters which distinguish *Australopithecus* and *Paranthropus* are legion since the two can be distinguished by means of almost any bits of skeleton now known in both forms. This in itself is an instructive fact since at low levels of taxonomic distinction general similarity is so great that good diagnostic characters are not common. In general it may be said that taxonomic experience in mammalogy shows that if two forms are readily distinguishable by means of almost any part of the skeleton, then it is highly unlikely that the taxonomic difference between them will be of less than generic magnitude. It does not follow, however, that generically distinct forms will necessarily differ markedly in all skeletal characters. It should be emphasised that this statement is not a theoretical one suggested as a standard for taxonomists, but is a generalisation based on what is found by experience to be the case in mammalian systematics.

There are a number of very good taxonomic characters which distinguish *Australopithecus* and *Paranthropus* according to the known material. For example the first lower deciduous molar not only allows instantaneous recognition (even when very considerably worn) of which group is being dealt with, but serves to distinguish *Paranthropus* from all other hominids in which the tooth is known. Furthermore, this tooth is of the same type in *Australopithecus* as it is in all fossil and living hominines in which its nature is known. Fortunately the deciduous first lower molar is known in Pekin man and also Neanderthal man. Consequently the morphology of dm_1 serves not only to emphasize the distinction between *Paranthropus* and *Australopithecus,* but at the time underlines the similarity between the latter and hominines. The permanent lower canine is another good diagnostic feature. The two australopithecines can be separated

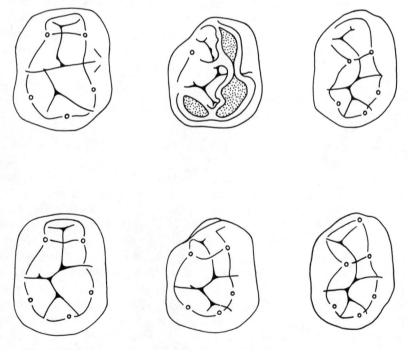

Fig. 1. Upper row: examples of the deciduous first lower molar in *Paranthropus, Australopithecus* and *Homo* (modern Bushman). Lower row: diagrammatic representations of the cusp and fissure patterns of the teeth in upper row. Twice natural size.

at a glance by means of this tooth, which is relatively large and highly asymmetric in crown structure in *Australopithecus* while in *Paranthropus* the crown is small and more symmetrical with little relief on the lingual surface though the root is substantial. The large difference in size between the post-canine teeth and the anterior teeth is also a good diagnostic feature. In *Australopithecus* the canines and incisors are fairly large for a hominid and the postcanine teeth are of proportionate size. In *Paranthropus,* on the other hand, the canines and incisors are appreciably smaller while the postcanine teeth are larger than those of *Australopithecus*. The *Australopithecus* condition fits very well with that found in the hominines, whereas that of *Paranthropus* is quite aberrant and unlike that seen in any other known hominid.

These are some of the most striking diagnostic features distinguishing the two forms, and there are many others: the nasal cavity floor and its relation to the subnasal maxillary surface, the nature and shape of the palate, the shape and structure of the face and of the braincase, etc. However lack of space prohibits detailed discussion of them here.

In contrast to this view, which I have described as the practical, workaday taxonomic approach, there is a larger and more satisfying view which sees the animal not as a series of taxonomic characters, but as an individual which is part of a population in its natural environment. In such a view the isolated characters of the other approach or aspect of systematics are seen as part of an integrated pattern. According to this viewpoint the difference between the two types of australopithecine is even more obvious.

In *Paranthropus* it seems clear that the architecture of the skull and head in general is strongly related to specialisations of the den-

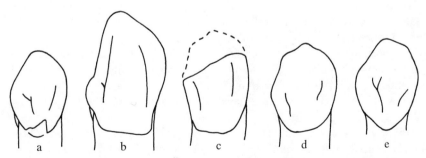

Fig. 2. Mandibular canines of (a) *Paranthropus,* (b) *Australopithecus,* (c) and (d) *Homo* (Pekin man) and (e) *Homo* (modern Bantu). It will be recalled that (a) is from a very robust form while (b) is from a small and lightly built form. (c) and (d) after Weidenreich. Twice natural size.

tition. The small anterior teeth, in the maxilla set in relatively lightly-constructed bone and in the mandible in a more or less vertical symphysial region with no trace of chin, results in a relatively orthognathous face. The massive postcanine teeth with strongly developed root systems are set in massive bone. The areas of support and the channels of dissipation of the forces generated by chewing are well developed. Examples of these are the thickened columns up either side of the nasal aperture, the enormously thickened palate anteriorly (over a centimetre thick in one adolescent where it can be measured opposite M^1), the pterygo-palatine complex and the zygomatic process of the maxilla. The strongly developed musculature required to operate this massive postcanine dental battery has also affected the architecture of the skull in an obvious manner. The temporalis and masseter muscles were manifestly very large. The former was so large as to cover a large portion of the calvarium and more than reach the midline, since all known adults of both sexes with this portion of the skull preserved have a sagittal crest. The origin of the masseter, especially the superficial portion, is very clearly marked and extensive. Similarly the insertion is extensive on the broad and high ramus. The masseter must thus have been large and powerful. The pterygoid muscles were evidently large also as evidenced, for example, by the relatively great development of the lateral pterygoid plate.

The relatively poor development of the anterior teeth reduces maxillary prognathism. The support needed for the relatively massive post-canine dentition has resulted in a strongly stressed, hence completely flat, nasal area. The massive chewing muscles go with a strongly developed zygomatic region—among other things. These factors result in the typically wide, massive, but either flat or actually dished face of *Paranthropus*. The total lack of a true forehead and the relatively great postorbital constriction make the brow ridges seem massive and projecting; though in actual fact they are not especially strongly developed. The well developed postorbital constriction—which is in part at least associated with the great development of the temporalis muscles, the sagittal crest—which is directly due to the relatively great size of the temporalis as compared to the size of the braincase—and the absence of a true forehead result in a braincase shape quite distinct from that seen in all other known hominids. The robust jugal arch and the attachment requirements of massive nuchal muscles result in a mastoid region which projects laterally significantly more than does the braincase above this region.

It is therefore apparent that the effect of the dental specialisations on skull architecture has been far-reaching in *Paranthropus*; more so even than there indicated since only the more obvious features have been mentioned. The result is a skull which bears a considerable superficial resemblance to that of some pongids. However, another important factor has affected skull architecture in the former: erect posture. This has resulted in a very significant lowering of the relative height of the occiput which is quite differently oriented in the erectly bipedal hominids compared to the condition in the quadrupedal pongide or all other terrestrial vertebrates. This clearly distinguishes the skull of both

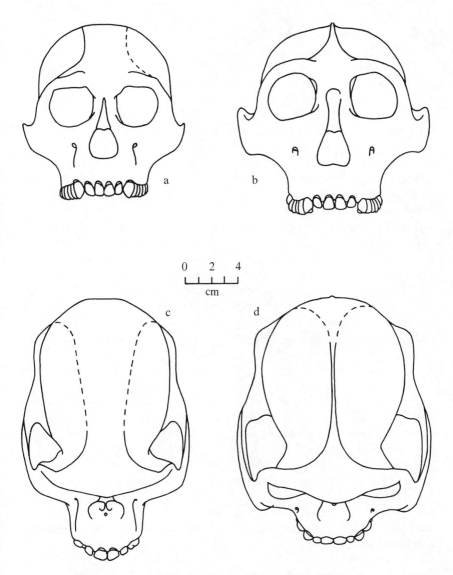

Fig. 3. Facial views of skulls of (a) *Australopithecus* and (b) *Paranthropus*. Top views of skulls of (c) *Australopithecus* and (d) *Paranthropus*. Both skulls are of females.

types of australopithecine from those of pongids, though not from each other, as has been shown by the use of Le Gros Clark's nuchal-area height index (Le Gros Clark 1950; 1955; Ashton and Zuckerman 1951, and Robinson 1958).

In *Australopithecus* the dental picture is quite different from that in *Paranthropus*. The anterior teeth are relatively larger and the posterior teeth relatively smaller than in the latter—a condition which very closely resembles that found in early hominines. Because of the large anterior teeth, the face is more prognathous. Owing to the smaller post-canine dentition the chewing forces were weaker and the musculature less strongly developed. This is shown by such things as the much weaker root systems of the postcanine dentition, less robust bone in which the teeth are set, more slender zygomatic bone and zygomatic processes of maxilla and temporal, as well as lateral pterygoid plate. Furthermore the attachments for muscles are far less obvious than in *Paranthropus*. Besides these points there is normally no trace of sagittal crest since the temporalis muscles do not normally approach the dorsal midline of the calvaria at all closely. However, while the evidence listed above indicates clearly that the temporal muscle was smaller in *Australopithecus* than in *Paranthropus*, the lack of sagittal crest is not entirely due to this fact since another factor is also operative in this case: the braincase is relatively higher. The index devised by Le Gros Clark and called by him the supraorbital

height index, shows clearly (Robinson 1961) that calvaria height above the superior margin of the orbits is very near the hominine condition in *Australopithecus* but of approximately average pongid condition in *Paranthropus*. The usual absence of a sagittal crest in the former is thus due both to reduced temporalis muscle size and increase in relative height of the braincase (see also Robinson 1958).

Both types of australopithecine are hominids, hence the basic similarity of their skulls inherited from a common ancestor. Since both were also erectly bipedal, the modifications of the occiput resulting from this locomotor specialisation are also found in both. Beyond this the two skull types differ sharply. The differences, as I have tried to show, appear to belong in each case to a pattern controlled chiefly by the specialisations of the dentition. Within the context of hominid affinity and morphology, it is very difficult to see how these differences of dental specialisation can be due to anything other than dietary specialisation. The dental specialisations thus at once reflect also ecological and behavioural features of the creatures. As has been argued elsewhere (Robinson 1954, 1956 and 1961), it seems clear that *Paranthropus* was a plant eater. The evidence for the presence of grit in the diet suggests that the plant food included roots and bulbs. On the other hand the very great similarity in the dental and skull morphology of *Australopithecus* and early hominines leads one to suppose that their dietary habits were

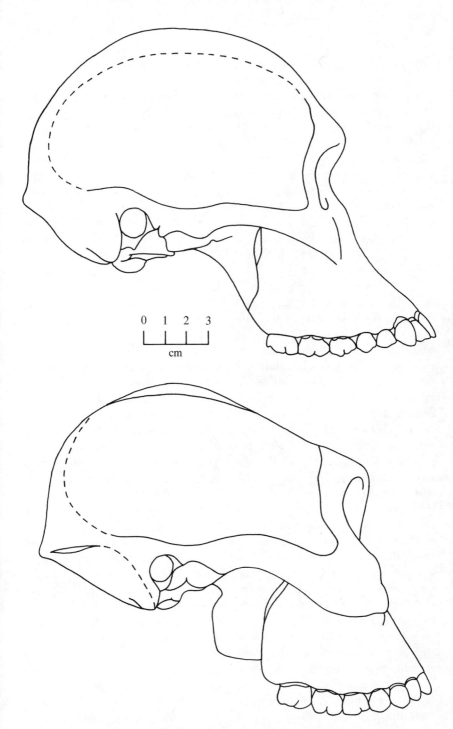

Fig. 4. Side views of female skulls of *Australopithecus* (above) and *Paranthropus*.

similar and included a substantial carnivorous element. Circumstantial support for this view comes from the climatic data which indicates that the vegetarian was present in the Sterkfontein valley in the wetter climatic periods, not the drier ones. One may note that the term 'vegetarian' is used here in the spirit of the Oxford Dictionary definition which is not concerned with what type of plant tissue is eaten but rather with the fact that flesh does not feature in the diet.

If these conclusions are correct—and the morphological differences do not make sense to me if they are not—then they concern a matter of considerable importance since an anatomically specialised vegetarian is far from typical of hominids as we know them. As has already been demonstrated, the morphology of *Australopithecus* links it very closely with hominines; the differences between the latter and it being just the sort of differences normally found between more and less advanced members of a single phyletic sequence. But the morphology of *Paranthropus* is aberrant, no matter with what part of the known *Australopithecus* hominine sequence one compares it. Furthermore, it is aberrant not only in such major adaptive features as the modified size and proportion along the tooth row—reflecting dietary adaptation—but also in such relatively minor features as the modified crown pattern of dm_1. It is difficult to conceive of the latter as being a feature of real adaptive significance. Consequently

both the ecological and behavioural evidence, on the one hand, and the morphological on the other, agree precisely in demonstrating an adaptive difference of considerable magnitude between the *Paranthropus* phyletic line and the *Australopithecus*-hominine one. In effect *Paranthropus* is a pongid-like hominid. Again circumstantial evidence is available which supports this conclusion. At Swartkrans remains of *Paranthropus* and a hominine were found at the same level scattered amongst each other. It must be accepted, therefore, that both forms occurred in the Sterkfontein valley at the same time. In Java the Sangiran site has yielded both "Pithecanthropus" and "Meganthropus" remains. According to von Koenigswald "Pithecanthropus" IV and the type mandible of "Meganthropus" came from the black clay (Putjangan beds) and not far from each other. The 1952 mandible of "Meganthropus" came from the later Kabuh conglomerate of the Sangiran dome, as did "Pithecanthropus" II and III. Evidently, therefore, these two creatures were not merely contemporaneous in this region, but remained so over a substantial period of time. As indicated elsewhere (Robinson 1953, 1955) and later in this paper, "Meganthropus" is fairly clearly a *Paranthropus*. The evidence therefore indicates that an early hominine and *Paranthropus* coexisted in two different places separated by many thousands of miles. This is hardly likely to have occurred if the ecological requirements of the two were virtually identical, but is readily understood if the requirements and behaviour of the two lines were as different as the present analysis indicates. A final point of significance is that all of the australopithecine material so far discovered falls readily into one or other of the two groups—whether found in the Far East, East Africa or the Sterkfontein valley—and are as different when both occur in the same valley as when occuring far apart. This suggests that the two groups are clear-cut and stable, rather than being merely minor modifications of the same thing.

Non-South African australopithecines

Australopithecines are at present known from two areas outside of South Africa: Java and East Africa. The Javanese form was first designated *Meganthropus palaeojavanicus* (Weidenreich 1945), but detailed analysis of the available information resulted in this form being placed in the genus *Paranthropus* (Robinson 1953, 1955). The reason for this is that, with only trivial exceptions, the features of the known specimens fall within the observed range of the known *Paranthropus* material. Among these features are the massive mandible and the combination of small canines and incisors with enormously robust postcanine teeth. Although no incisor crowns are known, roots of both are present in the 1952 mandible and, along with

the roots of the canine and other teeth, reflect the characteristic *Paranthropus* condition.

The conclusion that "Meganthropus" is a *Paranthropus* has been contested by von Koenigswald who has, however, produced no cogent evidence to refute it. A few points from the evidence which has been advanced will here be considered briefly to show that in almost every case the disagreement stems from not taking into account the observed variation in the known material.

It is stated that the anterior fovea of P_2 in "Meganthropus" is "broad" while that in australopithecines is "pit like." The observed range of variation in both sorts of australopithecine actually includes a range from pit-like to broader than that of the Javanese form. The latter form is stated to differ from australopithecines in that the lower permanent molars and dm_3 have uninterrupted connection between protoconid and metaconid, while in the australopithecines this is absent. However, both types of australopithecine have both conditions; i.e. both presence in various degrees, or absence, of a trigonid crest connecting protoconid and metaconid. Such a crest appears to be normal on dm_2 and common on M_1 in *Paranthropus*. Great stress is placed on the observation that the Javanese form has P_3 larger than P_4 (crown) and that the reverse is true of australopithecines. This is a matter of proportion, not absolute size, and can thus be checked on a good cast since shrinkage will not have been strongly differential between two adjacent crowns of similar shape and size on the same cast. Employing the same measuring technique as that used in the monographic study of the australopithecine dentition, it appears that in the 1941 mandible the two teeth are virtually identical in size with P_4 actually slightly the larger. The roots of these teeth in the 1952 mandible suggest that P_4 may have been relatively even larger in that specimen. In which case it would be fair to say that on available evidence the Javan form has P_3 either subequal to P_4 or larger. The proportion between these two teeth actually varies appreciably in the australopithecines, ranging from virtual identity in size to P_4 being considerably larger than P_3. The Javan form is said to differ from the australopithecines in that P_4 is single-rooted in the former and double-rooted in the latter. The 1941 specimen from Java certainly has the buccal face of the root of P_4 single, but the lingual aspect is so much broader that it seems probable that a lingual cleft is present. That is, like the root of P_3 of that specimen, the root is partially divided. On the other hand the 1952 specimen manifestly had a double-rooted P_4 on the left side. The crown of this tooth is gone and two roots with two pulp cavities are clearly visible on the cast kindly made available to me by Dr. Marks. Here again the australopithecines exhibit both of these conditions and both can be demonstrated in *Paranthropus* alone.

From these remarks it will be evident that in each case the charac-

ters of the Javanese "Meganthropus" fall within the observed range of the corresponding features in the far more extensive collections of australopithecine material. Not only is there no valid evidence differentiating "Meganthropus" from the australopithecines, but the former exhibits some features which are diagnostic of *Paranthropus*. It is therefore reasonable to regard "Meganthropus" as a member of the genus *Paranthropus*.

Leakey (1959) has reported the discovery of a good skull of a late adolescent australopithecine from Olduvai. He regards this form as being new and has named it *Zinjanthropus boisei*. It has, however, been shown (Robinson 1960) that the skull and dental characters, and their pattern of specialisation, are typically those of *Paranthropus*. As in the case of "Meganthropus," the morphological differences which are held to validate generic distinction from *Paranthropus* either disappear or become very slight if the *observed* range of variation of these features is taken into account. Hence the proposal that this form be placed in the genus *Paranthropus*.

In 1939 Kohl-Larsen discovered in the Laetolil beds near Lake Eyassi in East Africa, a fragment of maxilla containing P_3 and P_4 as well as an isolated upper molar. These were named *Präanthropus* (a *nomen nudem* since no species name was given) by Hennig (1948) and *Meganthropus africanus* by Weinert (1950, 1951)—a conclusion supported by Remane (1951). This matter has been considered at some length (Robinson 1953, 1955) and the conclusion drawn that (1) since one form is known only by mandibular and the other only by maxillary material, no evidence exists for placing them in the same genus; (2) since the East African specimen exhibits characters which fall within the observed range of the corresponding features of *Australopithecus,* the logical course is to refer the material to the latter genus. This is also the opinion of von Koenigswald (1957).

Very recently *Leakey* (1961) has announced the discovery of further material at Olduvai, including a juvenile mandible from the bottom of Bed I. The mandible appears to have the characteristics of *Australopithecus,* though perhaps not the parietals.

We may conclude, therefore, that:

1. *Paranthropus* is a very well defined genus which includes a somewhat aberrant type of hominid whose morphological, ecological and behavioural adaptions are quite distinct from those of all other known hominids;

2. *Paranthropus* is known from South Africa, East Africa and Java;

3. *Paranthropus* occurs synchronously at the same site, both in Java and South Africa, with an early hominine;

4. *Australopithecus* differs clearly in morphological, ecological and behavioural adaptations from *Paranthropus,* but exhibits very considerable similarity in these respects with hominines;

5. *Australopithecus,* like *Paranthropus,*

is known from both South Africa and East Africa, but not from the Far East—on currently available evidence.

Cultural status of the australopithecines

The cultural status achieved by the australopithecines is also related to the subject of this paper. Since the relationship between the australopithecines and the stone industries found with them in the Sterkfontein Valley and at Olduvai has been discussed elsewhere recently (Robinson 1958, 1960), the argument will not be repeated here. The conclusion was reached that, despite commonly held opinion to the contrary, there is as yet no proof that either form of australopithecine possessed a settled stone culture.

The evidence in fact favours the conclusion that the australopithecines were primarily no more than tool users, employing whatever came conveniently to hand in the form of sticks, stones, bones, etc. This aspect of *Australopithecus* behaviour has been dealt with at considerable length by Dart (e. g. 1957a, 1957b, 1958, 1960). In my opinion the evidence provided is enough to establish that this form was a tool user, though this is disputed by some other authors. For example Mason (1961) holds that since a bone culture (due presumably to *Homo sapiens*) has been found in a Middle Stone Age (end-Pleistocene) deposit and since early hominines were already in existence in australopithecine times, therefore the

Makapan Limewords bone culture should be attributed to a hominine who preyed on *Australopithecus* there. Washburn (1957) has argued against *Australopithecus* having had a bone culture. His argument turns on whether the bones associated with this form represent bone accumulation by the latter or by carnivorous animals such as hyaenids. Washburn and Howell (1960) accept the bone associated with the Olduvai *Paranthropus* as food remains of this vegetarian form and therefore as proof of predatory activity; in the same paragraph they state: "It is very unlikely that the earlier and small-bodied australopithecines (i. e. *Australopithecus*) did much killing, ..." without explaining why associated faunal remains are accepted as food remains of an australopithecine in the one case but not in the other. The logic of this is not clear, especially as the form for which predation is accepted is a specialised vegetarian while the other is not, and both of these authors believe both forms of australopithecine to have had a stone culture.

Tool using is by no means confined to primates, as is very well known. It must be deemed highly probable that primates of the degree of development of the australopithecines and which were erectly bipedal, hence having emancipated front limbs, used tools sometimes. Since later hominines are known to have used bone tools—indeed some still do—the australopithecine cannot be held to be too advanced to use bone. But since many authors believe the australopithecines to have *made* stone tools, these authors at least cannot hold them to have been too primitive to have *used* tools. As much bone is associated with *Australopithecus* as a rule, and as some of it appears to have been altered in a manner suggesting use, it seems entirely resonable to conclude that *Australopithecus* was a tool user. This is supported, but not proved, by the fact that the two main accumulations of *Australopithecus* remains are older than the first definite evidence of the presence of a more advanced hominid in that general geographic region. However, it would seem that the osteodontokeratic prowess of *Australopithecus* has been over-rated. On general grounds it seems probable that *Paranthropus* also used tools, though such activity may have been much more poorly developed in this vegetarian.

The origin of the Australopithecinae

The Subfamily Homininae includes forms broadly distinguished morphologically by having erect bipedal posture and a large brain, and behaviourally by relatively complex cultural activity. The latter feature is largely dependent on the large brain since it appears that intelligence of the hominine calibre is not associated with brains smaller than an ill-defined lower limit in volume of the general order of about 800 cm^3.

The Subfamily Australopithecinae includes forms which have erect posture, but not the large brain, of the hominines. Erect posture is more than adequately proven by the morphology of one virtually complete pelvis with most of the spinal column and a proximal portion of femur; three other adult innominate bones and two juvenile specimens; two proximal ends of femora and two distal ends, as well as a number of skulls showing the structure and orientation of the occiput. The pelvic morphology is very closely similar to that of hominines. There is a short broad innominate with expanded posterior part of the ilium, consequently a well developed, deep, greater sciatic notch, and an iliac crest in the form of a sinusoidal curve when seen from the top; a broad sacrum; distinct lumbar lordosis and femur with a strong lateral lean of the shaft from the vertical when the distal articular surfaces are placed on a flat horizontal surface with the shaft as nearly vertical as possible. The occiput has the near-horizontal disposition found in erect bipeds. Functionally the locomotors mechanism appears to be that of an erect biped. For example the arrangement of the origin and insertion of *gluteus maximus* are such that this muscle must have acted as an extensor of the thigh. *Gluteus medius* must have been an abductor. A well developed anterior inferior iliac spine suggests a powerful *rectus femoris*—and therefore probably *quadriceps* as a whole. This is a very important muscle in erect bipedal locomotion and unsupported standing. A well defined attachment area just below that for the direct head of *rectus femoris,* and a pronounced femoral tubercle, indicate a powerful ilio-femoral ligament strengthened and functioning in the manner of that in hominines and there is even evidence for locking of the knee joint with the leg straight. In function and morphology the locomotor mechanism of australopithecines differed in relatively minor points only from that of hominines.

The Subfamily Australopithecinae must have originated from some more primitive primate group. It is not our aim here to enquire closely into what that group might be. The ancestral form may have been a member of the same early hominoid stock to which *Proconsul* belongs, as is commonly believed, or it may have been part of an independent line already quite distinct at the time the early Miocene East African pongids lived. *Amphipithecus* and *Oreopithecus* suggest that the hominids may have resulted from a line, slow-rate during most of its history, which has been independent since the prosimian stage.

The Australopithecinae would appear to differ from pongids primarily in having erect bipedal posture, a primitive culture and in the nature of the dentition. The main differences between pongid and australopithecine dentitions occur in the anterior teeth, especially in the canines, the incisors and P_3. The reduction in canine size, as was suggested already by Charles Darwin, probably resulted from the use of tools. Effective tool using could only have become possible after erect posture had been acquired. The altered character of the incisors and canines in early hominids may therefore have been a consequence chiefly of changed posture and locomotion. The differences between the pongid and hominid types of P_3 cannot primarily have been due to these changes, however, as is clearly shown by the evidence.

The key feature, then, in the origin of the australopithecines is the change to erect bipedal posture and locomotion. This represents a major adaptive shift which opened up entirely new evolutionary possibilities in this primate line as compared to all known previous ones.

The manner of origin of erect posture is, however, not clear. A critical part of the change centers around the shift in function of *gluteus maximus* from being primarily an abductor of the thigh to an extensor. The power provided by this muscle, especially in the second half of a stride, is largely responsible for the efficacy of upright locomotion; without it the inefficient, shuffling gait seen in pongids walking upright is the best that is possible. Naturally this statement is an oversimplification; but whereas the rest of the pelvic and thigh musculature of pongids and hominids is very similar in function, *gluteus maximus* functions very differently in the two groups and this difference is of great importance in locomition. It is readily apparent that a short, broad innominate—with most of the breadth increase being in the posterior part of the illum—is a major cause of the change in function of

gluteus maximus, since these changes place the origin of the muscle well behind the acetabulum. This, and the fact that the thigh is normally in at least a fairly extended position in erect bipeds, places the main line of action of the muscle behind the hip joint; hence contraction causes extension of the thigh, not abduction.

Higher primates are much given to rearing up on their hind limbs under various circumstances normal to their ways or life. This probably occurs mainly for purposes of getting food, improving visibility or play—though the gibbon often does this in the trees as part of locomotion. It seems reasonable to suppose that members of a population in which the point has been reached where in the erect position *gluteus maximus* functions chiefly as an extensor, would find it easier to use this posture or mode of locomotion and would therefore use it more frequently. This is especially the case if, as seems likely, the population was ground-dwelling and living in broken forest and grass country and avoidance of becoming food for other animals depended on vision and alertness, rather than on speed, large canine teeth, horns, etc.

If erect posture and locomotion came to be used frequently under such circumstances, the nature of selection on the locomotor apparatus would alter considerably. Relatively minor changes only would at that stage be required to adapt fully to erect posture as the normal habit. Rapid adaptation to erect posture could thus be expected. The other important part of this same change, which would make selection favour the new adaptive shift and increase its rate is, of course, the advantage conferred by having freed hands. It is now well recognised that even a small advantage is sufficient to allow selection to operate effectively and in this case the advantage would certainly not be small. Consequently it is very easy to see how natural selection would bring about a rapid re-adaptation of the group in respect of posture and locomotion once the innominate became sufficiently broad and short for the change of function of *gluteus maximus* to occur.

The difficulty—at least for me— is explaining the process which led to the changes in the innominate. Starting from the general sort of pelvis found in the prosimians and arboreal monkeys, it is dificult to see what manner of locomotory specialisation could have brought about the required pelvic changes. Forms specialising in the direction of brachiating seem to acquire a pelvis which is long and narrow. This is the case in the pongids as well as in *Ateles,* which is a New World monkey which brachiates to an appreciable extent. The innominate of the gorilla has a broadened ilium and it could thus be argued that since the gorilla has reached a size too large for it to be a successful brachiator and has become largely a ground-dweller, this could be the answer. That is to say, a brachiator which came down out of the trees would have a broadened innominate, which could have been the starting point for the changes culminating in the hominid pelvis. However, this is clearly not the case. The increase in ilium breadth is entirely in the anterior portion of the bone and related to the stoutness of trunk in this animal. There is no shortening of the pelvis and no expansion of the posterior portion of the ilium. Brachiators, whether modified for ground-dwelling or not, do not appear to offer any suggestion of tendencies in the required direction. Postulating that an arboreal form without brachiating specialisations descended to the ground does not appear to help either. The chacma baboon can be taken as an example. Here again there is no evidence of a tendency for the pelvis to become short and broad in the required manner. The known non-hominid primate locomotory specialisations therefore do not appear to afford any help in explaining how an arboreal primate pelvis could have become modified to the point where changed muscular function could provide a basis for altered selection pressures causing adaptation to erect posture.

Probably the pelvic modifications were associated with changes which were not primarily concerned with locomotion but which rendered the pelvis pre-adaptive for erect posture, though it is not clear what these could have been.

Whatever the reason for the pelvic changes, it is a fact that they did occur and once they had, a new adaptive trend came into being. It would seem that the process occurred in two phases: the first during which it is difficult to see how selection for erect posture as such could have been operating, can in restrospect be regarded as the preadaptive phase; followed by the adaptive phase during which selection pressures were directly concerned with erect posture. This is, of course, typical of instances where a sharp adaptive shift occurs. In this instance the threshold involves the changed function of *gluteus maximus*. Before this, changes in the pelvis represent a prospective adaptation; after the threshold was crossed, adaptation to the new adaptive zone was rapid under the direct control of selection.

In this connection it is of great significance that, according to Schultz (1960), *Oreopithecus* had a somewhat shortened innominate with a relatively broad ilium. Not only this, but the increased breadth is primarily posteriad in the region of the sacro-iliac articulation, judging from an illustration published by Schultz. No other modern fossil pelvis of which I am aware exhibits a clear tendency toward modification in the direction of that of hominids; but that of *Oreopithecus* unmistakably does, judging by Schultz's paper. Since *Oreopithecus* apparently dates from the very early Pliocene (Hürzeler 1958), it would appear to have occurred at an appropriate time to have been an early, pre-bipedal, australopithecine ancestor or a member of a group which provided such an ancestor. This evidence would appear to be very strong support for the opinion of Hürzeler that *Oreopithecus* is related to the known hominids more closely than to pongids or cercopithecoids. What is known of the skull and dental morphology appears to be entirely consistent with such a view. The short face, relatively small canines (still substantial in males), compact tooth row with little or no diastemata, occlusal pattern of the upper molars and vertical chin region, all fit in with the suggested early hominid affinity but do not appear to constitute powerful evidence of such a view. Also the occlusal pattern of the lower molars is not clearly of the dryopithecus pattern type found in hominoids, but this feature is not a serious difficulty with regard to hominid affinity. The strongly bicuspid P_3 does not in any way fit with what is known of either cercopithecoid or pongid dentitions but does suggest hominid affinity.

Apart from *Oreopithecus*, hominids are the only known higher primates which are characterised by having a fully bicuspid P_3. This feature, along with the innominate which shows a tendency to shorten and for the ilium to expand posteriorly, appears to me to suggest a very real possibility that *Oreopithecus* is part of the hominid stream of evolution, though not necessarily a hominid.

In any event, by whatever route and for whatever reason it may have occurred, the adaptive shift in the locomotor apparatus *did* occur and so gave rise to an erectly bipedal primate. This was the first hominid and the ancestor of the known australopithecines. Since vegetarianism in its broadest sense is characteristic of non-hominid higher primates, it is probable that the stock in which this change occurred was also primarily vegetarian. There is no reason to suppose that diet could have been an important factor in the locomotory changes. Furthermore, if hominine carnivorousness had had a very long history, then one could expect to find some clear evidence of dental specialisation for carnivorousness in the later forms. This is not the case. We may assume, therefore, that the first product of the adaptive shift centering around emerging erect posture— that is to say, the first australopithecine—was a predominantly bipedal vegetarian.

Since the conclusion has already been reached that *Paranthropus* is a vegetarian, it is worth enquiring into the possibility that this form could be a little-modified descendant of the early type of australopithecine. As has been seen, erect posture is likely to have led to tool-using and this probably in turn would lead to reduction of canine teeth. One might expect, however, that reduction of canines would proceed more rapidly in a vegetarian tool-user. Until the use of tools had been appreciably refined, substantial canines would be advantageous to a meat eater. *Paranthropus* has much reduced canines and incisors, but large postcanine teeth and thus agrees with expectation. But the skull in some respects is primitive for a hominid. There is no true forehead, the brow ridges are rendered prominent by a well developed postorbital constriction and the vertex rises very little above the level of the supraorbital ridges. This latter

point is well demonstrated by the supraorbital height index of Le Gros Clark (1950). The value of this index for *Australopithecus* (Sts. 5) is 61 (68 according to Le Gros Clark, 74 according to Ashton and Zuckerman [1951]). This approaches the figure for *modern* hominines which, according to Ashton and Zuckerman averages about 70 and ranges from about 63 to about 77. The value for several specimens of Pekin man, determined from illustrations, appears to range from about 63 to 67. On the other hand the three great apes have mean values for this index which range from 49 for the orang to 54 for the gorilla according to Ashton and Zuckerman. The figure obtained for *Paranthropus* from Swartkrans is 50 and that for *Paranthropus* from Olduvai, determined from photographs, appears to be just over 50. It will therefore be seen that this feature (which reflects some aspects of cranial, and presumably also brain, morphology) presents a typically pongid appearance in *Paranthropus* but closely approximates the early—and even modern— hominine condition in *Australopithecus.* If the conclusion that *Australopithecus* was carnivorous to a significant degree is sound, then this is yet a further feature in which this genus is more advanced in the hominine direction than was *Paranthropus.*

The fact that a characteristic feature of the hominine skull— relatively high-domed calvaria—had not yet started to appear in *Paranthropus* but was already well advanced in *Australopithecus,* and the vegetarian specialisation of the former, indicate that it is the more primitive of the two australopithecine types. It would therefore seem probable that *Paranthropus* is a descendant of the earliest australopithecines which retains the same basic adaptational features of that early stock.

If *Paranthropus* represents basically the original australopithecine stock and *Australopithecus* represents an adaptively different line evolving in a different direction, how did the latter line arise?

It seems unlikely that the earliest australopithecines can have been as recent in age as the Pleistocene since the two forms were already well differentiated early in that period. On the other hand it seems logical to suppose that tool-using, tool-making and increased brain size are virtually inevitable consequences of erect posture and that they will have followed the origin of the latter fairly rapidly in terms of the geological time scale. It is therefore likely that australopithecines will have originated in the latter half of the Tertiary; probably in the Pliocene, possibly in the Miocene.

There is reason to believe that most of the Miocene was a period of expanding forests in Africa, but that the late Miocene and Pliocene was a time of desiccation and shrinking forests. The Kalahari sands of central and southern Africa throw some light on this matter. The original Kalahari sands overlie unconformably the Kalahari Limestone plain which resulted from the African

erosion cycle of early to mid-Tertiary times. However they pre-date the cutting of the Kalahari rivers into the Limestone in the Lower Pleistocene. It would therefore seem that between the wetter period of the earlier Miocene and that of the early Pleistocene, considerable desiccation occurred, during which the extensive deposits of Kalahari sand were formed. These extend from fairly far south in South Africa right up into the Congo basin. The studies of botanists and of entomologists studying humicolous faunas support these conclusions in demonstrating marked forest expansion in the Miocene with equally marked recession in the Pliocene, leaving residual forests in a ring round the central Congo basin and in East Africa, and with a certain amount of expansion again in the Pleistocene. (See for example, Mabbutt 1955, 1957; Cahen and Lepersonne 1952. Also private communication from Leleup on humicolous faunas.)

One may conclude from this that suitable habitats for the vegetarian, original australopithecine (*Paranthropus*) line will have become increasingly scarce through the late Tertiary. This will have been as true for other forms requiring forest or broken forest habitat and reasonably moist conditions, hence it could be expected that competition for such environments may have been more severe than usual. On the other hand grass savannah and other more arid environments will have expanded at this time and so provided   increased   opportunity   for animals adapted to, or capable of adapting to, such conditions.

The climatic changes will not have been sudden. Australopithecines living in areas which subsequently became semiarid or arid, will have found that the dry season of the year gradually became longer and drier. Finding food will thus have become more difficult in these times and it is reasonable to suppose that insects, reptiles, small mammals, birds' eggs and nestlings, etc., will have been eaten to supplement their diet. It is known that purely vegetarian primates will eat meat readily in captivity and that baboons, for example, will upon occasion do so in the wild. Taking to a semi-carnivorous diet under environmental pressure could therefore occur fairly easily. As desiccation proceeded such a deme will have found that it had to rely on the seasonal supplement to its normal diet more frequently and to a greater degree. Under these circumstances it could be expected that the population density will have dropped—to vanishing point in some areas. But it is not inconceivable that in at least some areas the creatures will have adapted reasonably well to the altering circumstances and adopted a certain amount of carnivorousness as a normal part of their way of life.

However, with such modifications in their environment, selection pressures will have altered. What may have been at that stage no more than a fairly elementary level of tool-using will have had obvious advantages in the changing food situation. Improved tool-using will have been favoured by selection and any improvements will have made the creatures better adapted to carnivorousness. Similarly, improved intelligence will have had obvious benefits under the circumstances and will therefore certainly have been favoured by selection. Since there appears to be some relationship between intelligence and brain volume with regard to that portion of the range of primate brains between the brain size of the larger pongids and that of the early hominines, it is probable that this part of the process of selection for improved intelligence will have been accompanied by increase in brain volume. Improved intelligence will have led, in turn, to improved tool-using ability and thus to even better adaptation to partially carnivorous diet and general adaptation to a more arid environment.

The changed environmental circumstances resulting from the known desiccation of a substantial part of Africa during the later Tertiary could therefore very easily have led to a second adaptive shift and the establishment of a second phyletic line in the australopithecines in which carnivorousness and an enhanced level of cultural activity were important features. *Australopithecus* is evidently just such a line and it is of interest that this form is present in the Sterkfontein valley in the more arid periods, while *Paranthropus* is present only in the wetter periods (for climatic data see Brain 1958). The canines of *Australopithe-*

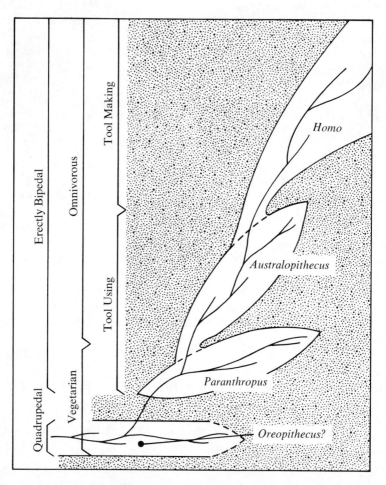

Fig. 5. Diagrammatic representation of the more important adaptive zones occupied by the hominid evolutionary stream. The threshold between the quadrupedal and bipedal stages is a major one between essentially discontinuous zones. The second and third thresholds—change to omnivorous diet and tool manufacture—are of great importance but did not involve clearly discontinuous zones. It should be emphasised that this is not a family tree but an adaptive grid.

cus are appreciably less reduced than those of *Paranthropus;* suggesting that the former genus arose from the *Paranthropus* line well before the reduction of the anterior teeth in the latter had reached the stage found in the known forms. The increase in adaptation to arid or semi-arid conditions and carnivorousness will have kept the canines as large as they originally were or even increased their size slightly.

Naturally, once the line adapting to drier conditions had become established, producing *Australopithecus* as we know it, its evolution would not stop there. The selection pressures operating—and entirely different from those controlling the direction of the *Paranthropus* line—would not cease to operate and therefore it is virtually inevitable that adaptation would be carried well past the *Australopithecus* stage. By this stage it would appear that the cultural situation would be the vital factor. The need for tool-using in successfully adapting to the different way of life would, as indicated, place a high premium on intelligence. As this improved, presumably by an increase in size of the cerebral cortex so as to provide increased correlation and association areas, cultural facility also improved. When the modification of the brain had proceeded to the point where hominine levels of intellectual ability began to appear—apparently when the brain volume reached the order of 750–1000 cm³—facility with tools reached a point where a characteristically hominine phenomenon ap-

peared: the deliberate manufacture of tools for particular purposes. This provided still further scope for development and it appears that increase in brain size now occurred rapidly to approximately the modern volume. At this point it seems that correlation between brain size and intelligence is not especially close. Cultural activity did not improve as rapidly at first, but subsequently the improved use of the cultural capacity occurred with rapidly increasing momentum. "Telanthropus," from Swartkrans, was apparently an early member of this hominine stage. It has now been included in the genus *Homo* (Robinson 1961). From the Sterkfontein valley have come, therefore, members of both the major lines of australopithecine evolution as well as members of both stages of the *Australopithecus-Homo* stream.

It seems to me that the adaptive shift occasioned by increasing aridity and the necessity to use meat as a normal part of the diet was a second critical point in the evolution of hominines. The first was the adaptive shift to erect posture; this provided the possibility of becoming an efficient tool-user. The second point was that of being forced by changing environmental conditions to take to meat-eating, thus placing a heavy premium on tool-using and improved intelligence. The development of the hominine grade of organisation was a natural consequence. The third point or threshold was that where simple cultural activity and increasing intelligence reached a stage where tool-using gave way to tool-making and the typical cultural activity and approach to environmental challenges of man appeared. The potentialities which then came into existence are still being explored and developed.

ACKNOWLEDGEMENTS

It is a pleasure to record here my indebtedness to Dr. J. A. J. Meester, mammalogist at the Transvaal Museum, for valuable discussions and for reading this paper in manuscript; to Mrs. P. Cook for bibliographic assistance and to Mrs. D. Durrant for preparation of this manuscript for publication.

APPENDIX

The genera *Australopithecus* and *Paranthropus* were defined (Robinson 1954a) in terms of the information then available. At present only three genera are recognised by me in the Family Hominidae; the above two and *Homo* (Robinson 1961). These three are defined below. It is recognised that not all of the characters mentioned are independent: in such definitions it is not easy to indicate overall patterns.

Genus Paranthropus. This genus includes vegetarian hominids with an endocranial volume of the order of 450–550 cm^3. Forehead completely absent; supraorbital height index about 50 (about the average for pongids). Bony face either quite flat or actually dished. Distinction between floor of nasal cavity and subnasal maxillary surface totally absent. Zygomatic arch strongly developed; temporal fossa large. Palate appreciably deeper posteriorly than anteriorly. Lateral pterygoid plate strongly developed and large. Sagittal crest normally present in both sexes. Internal mandibular arch contour V-shaped. Ascending ramus vertical and high. Tooth row compact, without diastemata. Anterior teeth very small compared to postcanine teeth. Canine small and wears down from tip. Virtually completely molarised dm_1 with anterior fovea centrally situated and with complete margin. Maxillary canine and incisor sockets in almost straight line across front of palate. Cultural development relatively poor.

Genus Australopithecus. This genus includes omnivorous hominids with an endocranial volume of the order of 450–550 cm^3. Distinct forehead, but never markedly developed; supraorbital height index about 60. Bony face moderately—not completely—flat. Distinction between floor of nasal cavity and subnasal maxillary surface present but poor. Zygomatic arch moderately developed; temporal fossa of medium size. Palate of more or less even depth. Lateral pterygoid plate relatively small. Sagittal crest normally absent—may occur in extreme cases. Internal mandibular arch contour V-shaped. Ascending ramus usually sloping backward and of moderate height. Tooth row compact, no diastemata. Anterior and postcanine teeth harmoniously proportioned. Canine wears down from tip, moderately large in all known cases. Incompletely molarised dm_1, anterior fovea displaced lingualward and open to that side. Maxillary incisor and canine sockets in parabolic curve. Cultural development relatively poor.

Genus Homo. This genus includes omnivorous hominids with an endocranial volume in excess of 750 cm³ and with considerable variability. Distinct forehead always present —may be markedly developed; supraorbital height index above 60. Bony face aquiline to moderately flat. Distinction between floor of nasal cavity and subnasal maxillary surface always sharp. Zygomatic arch moderately to poorly developed; temporal fossa medium to small. Palate of more or less even depth. Lateral pterygoid plate relatively small. Sagittal crest never present. Internal mandibular arch contour U-shaped. Ascending ramus usually sloping and of moderate height but rather variable. Tooth row normally compact and without diastemata— latter present in some early individuals. Anterior and postcanine teeth harmoniously proportioned. Canines wear down from tip; moderately large in early members to small in later forms. Incompletely molarised dm₂, anterior fovea displaced lingualward and usually open to that side. Maxillary incisor and canine sockets in parabolic curve. Cultural development moderate to very strong.

ADDENDUM

The *Australopithecus*-like form from Bed I, Olduvai, referred to in the above paper has now been in-cluded with additional material in a new taxon, Homo "habilis" (Leakey, Tobias & Napier 1964). This step has met with considerable resistance from workers who do not regard it as representing a taxon distinct from ones already known (e. g. Campbell 1964; Le Gros Clark 1964; Oakley & Campbell 1964; Robinson 1965a & b, 1966a & b).

As originally defined the taxon includes material chiefly from the lower levels of Bed I and also from the lower half of Bed II. At the present time Leakey uses the name approximately as it was originally defined; Tobias, however, uses it as applying only to the non-*Paranthropus* hominid material from Bed I.

The nomenclatural validity of this taxon is at best dubious since the original taxonomic description contained a statement to the effect that further investigation might show that it and "Telanthropus" from Swartkrans represent the same taxon. This constitutes conditional proposal of the new taxon as the implication is clear that the new taxon would be valid only if further investigation showed that it was not the same as "Telanthropus." According to the International Code of Zoological Nomenclature, Article 15, names conditionally proposed after 1960 are not valid and available for use.

As I have attempted to show (in papers quoted above, especially 1967), there are quite other reasons for regarding this taxon as invalid as a new species of hominid. Firstly, the Bed I and Bed II specimens do not appear to have exactly the same characteristics; the Bed I material seems to be very similar to the South African material of *Australopithecus* (senus stricto) in its morphology, while the Bed II material appears to represent, as does "Telanthropus" from Swartkrans, an early phase of *Homo erectus*. The taxon, as originally proposed, thus does not appear to include one single, well defined form of hominid.

Secondly, the morphological grounds for distinguishing *H. 'habilis'* appear to be unacceptable in some cases and at best very slender and insecure in others. As an example, a feature which has been stressed as a distinguishing character is the relative narrowness of the post-canine teeth, especially in the mandible. However, it can readily be shown that the ability to distinguish *H. 'habilis'* from *Australopithecus* (sensu stricto) in this respect depends on using the observed range of variation only of the very small samples involved. If estimated standard population ranges of variation (three times the standard deviation on either side of the mean) are used instead, there is extensive overlap. Indeed, study of this character demonstrates beyond question that it completely fails as a diagnostic criterion, both at the species and at the genus levels in hominids and cannot, therefore, be used for distinguishing *H. 'habilis'* taxonomically. This example is representative of the most secure type of distinguishing evidence which has been advanced—and it has been demonstrated to be invalid. Another category of evidence is simply not helpful; such as

the structure of the foot or hand. The former is regarded as being of so advanced nature as to suggest *Homo* affinities. However, this evidence does not assist in distinguishing *H. 'habilis'* from *Australopithecus* (sensu stricto) since neither the hand nor the foot is known in the latter. It has been suggested also that a single estimated value of 680 cm³ for the endocranial capacity of a Bed I individual supports taxonomic distinction from *Australopithecus* (sensu stricto), which appears to have a somewhat smaller endocranial volume. This evidence seems to me to be insecure for three quite distinct reasons. Assuming that the estimate is correct, which is not self-evident since it is based on two incomplete and disarticulated parietals, then one must first take note of the fact that it is a single value, hence its relation to the range of variation in the original population is unknown. Clearly it would make an appreciable difference to a taxonomic assessment if this value is near the lower end of the range of variation or near the upper end. Secondly, there are grounds for believing that the hominine brain expansion had already started in *Australopithecus,* as is indicated by the relatively high-domed brain case referred to in the main body of this paper, whereas in *Paranthropus* this had not begun. If the brain of *Australopithecus* was undergoing expansion, then different demes at about the same time level could differ to some extent with respect to average brain size and it would be very probable that appreciable differences would exist between samples of the lineage taken at different time levels. Thirdly, it seems clear that variation in brain size in modern man and also the African great apes is such that the observed upper limits exceed appreciably, especially in man, the traditional limit set by three times the standard deviation above the mean calculated from samples of substantial size. If this was true also of *Australopithecus* (sensu stricto), then the difference between the single value for *H. 'habilis'* and the small series for *Australopithecus,* need not be significant.

There is yet another difficulty with respect to the arguments used to establish *H. 'habilis';* the taxonomic viewpoint seems to have involved some confusion. This is shown, for example, by the fact that the *species* description in the original taxonomic account is much concerned with distinguishing between the new taxon and taxa believed to be in different *genera.* This demonstrates an insufficiently clear conception of the species as distinct from the genus and the relation between the two. This is a confusion which is not confined to the present case, however, but is characteristic of the whole field of human palaeontology. It seems to me (Robinson 1967) that part of the reason for this type of confusion is an insufficiently clear appreciation *in practice* of the fact that taxa within a single phyletic sequence, which thus has genetic continuity throughout, differ in nature from taxa which are each part of different phyletic sequences and which therefore were parts of

genetic streams which were isolated from each other. Careful analysis from this point of view is therefore required in assessing the taxonomic status of a group of fossils. This becomes especially important in cases, such as the present one, where the new material is not completely isolated in space and time from all the known closely related material.

It would seem that there is a reasonable case to be made out for the view that the Bed I material attributed to *H. 'habilis'* represents an advanced level of *Australopithecus* (sensu stricto) which was already making primitive stone artifacts of an early Oldowan type. Following an appreciable time gap, the Bed II material attributed to *H. 'habilis'* in the original taxonomic description represents this same phyletic sequence but now at a stage where it is manufacturing developed Oldowan artefacts, the general tooth size has reduced, the average massiveness of the corpus mandibulae has reduced and the space between the two halves of the mandible has become relatively wider and more U-shaped rather than having the more primitive V-shape and the braincase has become larger. This seems, in fact, to be an early *H. erectus* stage, which is followed in that area at the level of the top of Bed II by what seems to be a fully developed *H. erectus* in the form of Hominid 9 from LLK II. It is consequently possible that the Olduvai specimens reflect the transformation of *Australopithecus* (sensu stricto) into *H. erectus* and that the material which has been named *H. 'habilis'* is simply a part of this sequence.

A point of considerable interest, which seems to me to be clear from the Oldowan and Peninj material, is that both *Paranthropus* and *Australopithecus* existed in the same region and seem to have done so over a very long period of time— more than a million years, if present dating evidence is even approximately correct. This is consistent with the view that these two forms were not only different in morphology but also in behaviour and ecology and that *Paranthropus* represents a stable adaptation. For example the skull from the lower half of Bed I has all of the diagnostic features of the *Paranthropus* skull as known from South Africa, while the Peninj mandible, which is evidently much later and from upper Bed II time, also agrees very closely indeed with the South African specimens. If the view is correct that the other material from Olduvai represents a single, second lineage, then it was changing steadily through all of the time during which the *Paranthropus* line appears to have been stable. Finally, since fully developed *H. erectus* was already present at about the time the still purely *Paranthropus* Peninj specimen occurs, it would seem very improbable that *Paranthropus* could have been directly in the line of descent of *H. sapiens*. This agrees with the previously known evidence from Swartkrans and Sangiran, in both of which *Paranthropus* and *H. erectus* are coeval. The new material from Olduvai thus is of very great interest

when taken in conjunction with the much more extensive collections from South Africa.

There is another point which should be raised here; I now disagree with much of what I wrote in the main paper on the subject of erect posture. This change of view has resulted chiefly from dissections I have since made on chimpanzee and human cadavers. Further study on a wider range of primate material is being carried out by Mrs. B. Sigmon Storck at this University.

Following Washburn (1950) I accepted the view that *Gluteus Maximus* is an important postural muscle in man, that its function is quite different in man as contrasted with pongids and other quadrupeds, and that the origin of bipedality could easily be explained in terms of this change in function. However, it would appear that these views are not consonant with the facts.

Gluteus Maximus is rather differently arranged in pongids as compared to man but its function appears to be essentially the same in the two. It arises mainly, in the pongids, from the distal end of the sacrum—not from the posterior end of the iliac blade, from the sacrotuberous ligament—and has a very powerful origin, at least in the African great apes, from the ischial tuberosity. The upper portion of the muscle is weakly developed and arises from the gluteal aponeurosis over the powerfully developed *Gluteus Medius*. This portion of the muscle is thus not powerful and its chief function is abduction of the thigh upon the trunk. However, the lower portion of the muscle, especially the very powerful portion arising from the ischial tuberosity, functions virtually as another hamstring as far as the hip joint is concerned, being a very powerful extensor of the thigh on the trunk. It is clear that extension is by far the predominant function of the muscle. Since this is also true for man, there does not seem to be any possibility of postulating a change in function of this muscle from the ape grade of organisation to the hominid grade which could thereafter have been the basis for a different pattern of selection.

Furthermore, there seems to be real doubt about *Gluteus Maximus* being an important muscle in normal bipedal walking in man. According to the work of Joseph (1960) and Basmajian (1962), this muscle is electrically silent during normal bipedal walking or standing at ease. Its main function appears to be to assist the hamstrings, as a reserve supply of power, when extra power is needed in moving the trunk against gravity—as in climbing up stairs, standing up from a crouched position or lifting or lowering the trunk from the hips. The improved efficiency of human bipedality as compared to that of pongids appears to be a consequence of differences in the skeletal architecture of the pelvis and thigh, especially the length of the hamstring moment arm, the length of the femur and the spatial relationship between the two, as well as the angle of the ischium to the horizontal. By the time the femur shaft of a pongid reaches the vertical

during extension of the lower limb on the trunk in bipedal walking, the hamstrings and *Gluteus Maximus* have run out of power. In man, because the moment arm is appreciably shorter and is arranged in a slightly more nearly horizontal position and because the femur shaft is much longer, the hamstrings have not run out of power at that point but can pull the femur a little further back. This, along with the spring action of the foot, give the human stride its power in the closing phases. In the African pongids hamstrings and *Gluteus Maximus* function in the same manner as is true of man but they, especially the hamstrings, are relatively powerful and are more specialised for power than for speed. In the case of man the hamstrings are not especially powerfully developed and their normal action emphasises speed more than power— speed of action, that is, rather than speed over the ground.

The interpretation which has been included in the main body of this paper and others (e. g. Robinson 1962, 1963 and 1964), based on Washburn, was deductive and had some quite elegant aspects such as the change in selection pattern which followed on change of function. But, alas! for the slaying of a beautiful theory by some ugly facts! The situation is different and much more subtle than that—and much more interesting as well. However, this matter and its implications for the early hominids will be discussed at length elsewhere.

Finally, I no longer believe that it is meaningful to distinguish a

genus *Australopithecus* (sensu stricto) from *Homo*. This matter has
been discussed at some length in
Robinson 1967, to which the reader
is referred for details. As is apparent
in the main body of this paper, the
evidence seems to point to the conclusion that the difference between
Australopithecus and *Homo* is of a
quite different sort to that between
either of these and *Paranthropus*.
The Olduvai evidence makes this
even more clear than it already was
on the basis of the South African
evidence. Consequently it seems to
me that *Australopithecus* represents
merely the earlier stages of the establishment of the adaptive pattern
characteristic of *Homo* and therefore does not merit generic distinction if the genus is to be regarded
as a monophyletic category reflecting

a single distinct and distinctive adaptive zone or pattern. This seems
especially the case since it appears
that stone tool making was actually
already in progress at Olduvai at
a time when the brains of the
makers were still within the pongid
size range, so that one of the more
obvious reasons advanced for retain-
ing a generic distinction appears to
have been demolished. Species distinction thus seems the most that
is here called for—though, as I have
noted elsewhere, distinction between
successional taxa in the same lineage
is so completely arbitrary in nature
that it makes little difference what
classification is adopted in such cases
as long as an author explains his
usage if it differs from a commonly
accepted one.

Hominid Origins Revisited: 1971

Vincent M. Sarich
1971

That man had an evolutionary
origin is beyond dispute. The particulars of that origin, though of
pivotal significance in our determining the course of hominid evolution,
remain, however, a subject fraught

with controversy. At the very least
those particulars should include the
identity of man's closest living rela-
tive(s) and the time of our most
recent common ancestry with them.
From T. H. Huxley's time on it

This article was written for inclusion in this collection of papers at the
request of one of the editors (K.A.R.K.).

has generally been agreed that man shares his most recent common ancestry with the African apes—gorillas and chimpanzees—though on this as on any question dealing with man a wide range of alternative opinion is available to the industrious student (e.g., Hurzeler 1968; Genet-Varcin 1963, 1969). The time aspect, however, remains a subject of current and viable controversy with agreement only that origin of the hominid line must antedate the presence of unequivocally hominid fossils; i.e., the at least three million year old australopithecines of sub-Saharan Africa. Beyond that point lie at present major uncertainties rooted in a fragmentary fossil record and disagreements concerning the evolutionary meaning of comparative anatomical and biochemical data. It is the purpose of this brief chapter to attempt a sorting out of a few of the most important, particularly as they relate to the matter of settling this question of time with molecules rather than fossils.

Though the concept of using molecular evidence to elucidate evolutionary relationships goes back to 1902 when Nuttall wrote:

I do not wish these numbers to be taken as final, nevertheless they show the essential correctness of the previous crude results. To obtain a constant it will be necessary to make repeated tests with blood of each species with different dilutions and different proportions of antiserum. I am inclined to believe that with care we shall perhaps be able to "measure species" with this method, for it appears that there are measurable differences in the reactions

obtained with related blood, in other words, to determine degrees of relationship which we may be able to formulate.

and the specific idea of molecular evolutionary clocks at least to Zuckerkandl and Pauling (1962), the first serious application of the molecular clock idea to the solution of a specific problem was contained in the *Science* article: "Immunological Time Scale for Hominid Evolution" (Sarich and Wilson 1967b). In that article, which was the third of a series, we concluded that man, gorilla and chimpanzee share an ancestral species that was still in existence as recently as five million years ago. The logic involved in reaching that conclusion can be summarized as follows:

(1) A single protein—serum albumin—was chosen for the original study. Available evidence would indicate that all modern mammalian albumins are evolutionarily homologous derivatives of a single ancestral albumin presumably present in the common ancestor of all mammals. The unit of albumin evolutionary change is a single amino acid substitution resulting from a single nucleotide substitution in the DNA at the albumin locus. The universal presence of serum albumin and the known unit of change allows a common measure of the difference between any two modern albumin species—a difference which must have developed since the albumins, and presumably the animal species in which they are found, shared a common ancestry. The phylogeny (branching order) of the albumins

is thus necessarily very nearly coincident with that of the species themselves. The same argument can be applied to other appropriate proteins (see Dayhoff 1969) or DNA's (see Kohne 1970) and the remaining problems are basically technical ones such as choosing a molecule whose rate of change is appropriate to the problem at hand and developing and validating adequate techniques for measuring the structural differences between the various protein species and developing such data into the cladistic and temporal dimensions of a single phylogeny (Sarich and Wilson 1966; Wilson and Sarich 1969; Sarich 1969a, 1969b, 1970).

(2) It had been known since Nuttall's time that human and chimpanzee albumins are very similar immunologically and yet the reasons for this remarkable similarity were never seriously investigated. If one accepts a relatively ancient (i.e., at least 15 million years) separation between the two species, then the answer must obviously lie in a slowdown in the rate of evolutionary change in their albumins relative to that found in other primates. Goodman in fact, accepting this conclusion in terms of then (and still) current paleontological opinion, stated:

The fact that the gibbons can be traced as a separate branch of the Hominoidea back into the Oligocene, 30–40 million years ago, highlights the significance of the finding of an extensive correspondence in antigenic structure among hominoid albumins...the fossil record suggests that the family Bovidae first

emerged during the Miocene after extensive branching of the Hominoidea had already occurred. Yet by the immunological plate technique chicken anti-beef albumin sera could detect divergencies even with the subfamily Bovinae, kuda albumin diverging from beef albumin (Goodman 1962b), whereas the anti-human albumin sera failed to show any comparable divergencies among hominoid albumins. Clearly then, albumin evolution has been more rapid in the subfamily Bovinae than in the super-family Hominoidea. This type of finding could be predicted by our theory, for the artiodactyls have an epitheliochorial placenta which, as previously noted minimizes the possibility of transplacental immunizations.

This postulation of an ingenious immune mechanism to account for a phenomenon with no reality of existence was made by Goodman in 1961 and has been steadfastly maintained by him (see, e.g., Goodman *et al.* 1970) since that time.

Thus, Goodman's placentalization hypothesis remains viable (Kirsch 1969; Bauer 1970) even though it was shown, through direct measurement of the amounts of evolutionary change which had occurred in the various primate albumin lineages (Sarich and Wilson 1967a), that ape and human albumins are no less evolved than those of the Old and New World monkeys. In fact anthropoid albumins may, on the average, be somewhat more evolved than those of the prosimians tested (Sarich 1970). The object lesson, and we shall return to it again, is to avoid circularity of reasoning insofar as possible by not converting specifics of paleontological interpretation (e.g., *Propliopithecus* looks hylobatid dentally) into fact (*Propliopithecus* is hylobatid) and then using this "fact" to determine the answer to an immunological question most readily and legitimately dealt with on its own merits and in its own terms.

(3) Given now that conservatism in ape and human albumin evolution was not the explanation for their consistently observed marked immunological similarities (Nuttall 1904; Boyden 1958; Goodman 1961, 1962, 1963, 1970; Hafleigh and Williams 1966; Sarich and Wilson 1966), we were forced to choose the most feasible alternative as a working hypothesis: that the most recent common ancestor of man, chimp, and gorilla lived far more recently than was and still is the prevailing view. Given the finding of regularity in anthropoid albumin evolution (Sarich and Wilson 1967a) one could then apply the molecular clock idea and calculate the relative divergence times within that taxon:

Homo–Pan–Gorilla	1
Hominoidea–Cercopithecoidea	5
Catarrhini–Platyrrhini	8.5

and extrapolating somewhat to the prosimians:

Anthropoidea–Prosimii	~16

Conversion of these relative times into absolute ones required a calibration point and given the generally poor nature of the primate fossil record as it relates to modern forms one had to be careful to get the best overall fit. It was evident even then that the Anthropoidea shared a very long period of common ancestry subsequent to the divergence of any lineage leading to a modern prosimian and in fact more recent work (Sarich 1970) has indicated that more albumin evolution occurred along that ancestral anthropoid lineage than has occurred along an average anthropoid lineage since the platyrrhines and catarrhines became distinct lines. In addition a good deal of albumin evolution is common to the ancestral catarrhine lineage subsequent to the separation of the New World monkey line (Fig. 1). To fit these observations into the 70 million years or so which were then alloted for the whole of primate history meant that it was most difficult to choose a date in excess of 30 million years for the cercopithecoid-hominoid divergence and thus we used this figure as a liberal upper limit calibration point. Subsequently (Sarich 1968) I suggested that a more reasonable figure would be in the area of 20–25 million years. The 5 million year date for the man–chimp–gorilla separation followed directly (Sarich and Wilson 1967b).

It was indicated then, and I repeat now, that this specific date (and the approach in general) was in the nature of a working hypothesis. Hypotheses are of course subject only to disproof, but given the controversial character of this one, one might have expected such disproof to be soon forthcoming. It has not been so. As further data have been developed they have proved to be comfortably interpretable within the framework provided

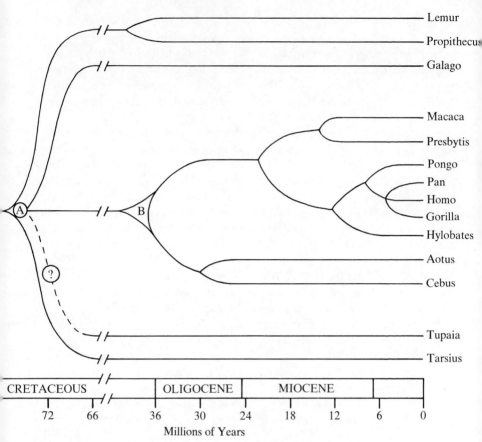

Fig. 1. A primate phylogeny based on the currently available macro-molecular (mainly albumin) evidence. The amount of albumin evolution common to the Anthropoidea (measured as an immunological distance) is about 45 units from time A to time B and only about 30 units along the average catarrhine or platyrrhine lineage since time B. Even when one takes into account the somewhat greater amount of albumin evolution along the average anthropoid compared to the average prosimian lineage, these data still argue that time A must be at least twice time B (i.e., at least 70–75 million years).

by the short time scale albumin picture and not all within any framework requiring man, chimpanzee, and gorilla to represent lineages distinct for at least 15–20 million years (Simons 1969).

Some of these newer data were published as a test of our hypothesis in the *Proceedings of the National Academy of Sciences* (Wilson and Sarich 1969) showing that the hemoglobin, transferrin, and DNA data which had appeared subsequent to the original *Science* article gave human–African ape differences for these macromolecules which were but a small fraction of the human–Old World monkey differences (Table 1). For example, most men and chimpanzees seem to possess

Table 1

Molecule Studied	Homo-Pan Difference	Homo–Macaca Difference	Type of Comparison[a]
Albumin	7	32	immunological
Transferrin	3	30	immunological
Carbonic anhydrase	4	58	immunological
Hemoglobin α and β chains	0	12	sequence analysis
Fibrinopeptides	0	6	sequence analysis
DNA	1.7°C	6.7°C	DNA hybridization

[a]The immunological measurements are made using the MC'F technique and given as immunological distances (100 × log ID). The sequence analyses are given as the number of positions that different amino acids are found in the two species. The DNA data are given as the decrease in thermal stability of the hybrid relative to the native DNA and are linearly proportional to the number of mispaired nucleotides in the hybrids. References are given in the text.

hemoglobin A's of identical primary structure while that of the rhesus monkey differs in 12 positions requiring a minimum of 15 mutational events (in the DNA) to explain. Yet when the human and rhesus monkey sequences are compared to that of horse hemoglobin it is found that they are equally different from it—indicating that since the time the human–chimp and rhesus monkey lineages separated from one another they had undergone equal amounts of hemoglobin evolutionary change. T. H. Jukes (personal communication) has recently added several other non-primate mammalian hemoglobin sequences as reference points and substantiated this conclusion. Thus since the human–chimp–gorilla line separated from that leading to the Old World monkeys eight mutational events resulting in hemoglobin amino acid substitutions occurred along it; since the human–chimp–gorilla divergence, on the other hand, the three lineages have undergone a total of only two such events (both in the gorilla line). Given the general pattern of regularity in vertebrate

hemoglobin evolution (Dayhoff 1969; Kimura 1969) the compatibility with the albumin model becomes apparent.

Since the publication of that 1969 article further data (Table 1) on the fibrinopeptides (Doolittle and Mross 1970), carbonic anhydrases (Nonno *et al.* 1970), and non-repeated DNA sequences (Kohne 1970) have appeared and again the differences found are entirely compatible with the albumin-based picture. For example, one can compare the relative times of divergence for a series of primate taxa calculated on the basis of our most recent albumin data with the DNA hybridization data for the same taxa given by Kohne (Table 2).

Given the implicit and explicit uncertainties in both approaches the concordance shown is heartening. To summarize, then, the protein sequence, immunological, and nucleic acid data available at this time (January 1971) are fully compatible with the suggestion, first made on the basis of the albumin immunological evidence, that man and the African apes share a rather recent

Table 2

Taxa Compared	Most Probable[a] Albumin Time	DNA Timed[d]
Homo-Pan	4	5
Homo-Hylobates	11	12
Homo-{Cercopithecus / macaca}	22	21
Homo-Cebus	36	36
Macaca-Cercopithecus	6	6

[a]The albumin dates are for the most part quite similar to those given earlier (Sarich, 1968). The only significant change is the increase in the hylobatid time of divergence necessitated by our recent observations that the mean hylobatid—other hominoid albumin immunological distance (obtained with a large series of new antisera to *Homo, Pan, Gorilla, Pongo* and *Hylobates* albumins) is 13 units and that the albumin of the gibbon is somewhat less evolved than those of the other hominoids. Each date should be considered a Poissonian mean referred to a stochastic rate of albumin evolution approximating one substitution per million years per lineage.

[b]These times of divergence are calculated in terms of the *Homo-Cebus* date whose development has already been discussed above. For example, Kohne gives the *Homo-Hylobates* difference as 6.2% of their nucleotide pairs and *Homo-Cebus* as 17.4%. The date is then 6.2/17.4 × 36 or 12.8 million years for the human–gibbon separation.

($\sim$4–5 million year old) common ancestor.

Though the internal consistency is impressive our proposal has as yet received little support and rather earnest criticism, and one might reasonably ask why? The answer is that much of this criticism would again appear to have its basis, just as did Goodman's placentalization argument, in an undue reliance on current interpretations of the primate fossil record. In one such case, Read and Lestrel (1970) argued that replacing the relationship log ID=kT given in the 1967 *Science* article with one of the form log (ID-1) α log T (i.e., substituting a log–log function for the exponential one we derived) would allow the calculation of dates more or less compatible with some current paleontological opinion (e.g., Simons 1969). The virtue of the log–log model in terms of paleontological compatibility is

preserved, however, only by ignoring its complete lack of predictive power toward other forms of macromolecular data. One might first consider its immunological inconsistencies.

The log–log model would necessarily predict the MC'F procedure to be extremely insensitive to small differences in protein structure. For example, it would suggest that a MC'F ID of 1.05 (the smallest we have ever seen in the albumin system) would correspond to no less than 20 sequence differences between the two albumin species and that one could never see immunologically differences of fewer than $\sim$15—assuming that about a 30% sequence difference between two proteins will generally abolish their cross-reactivity. Yet a study of a number of different *single* amino acid substitutions in *E. coli* alkaline phosphatase (which is about 60% the size of albumin) showed that 8 of 9 were detectable by the MC'F method with a mean ID of 1.08 (Cocks and Wilson, 1968). Similarly human hemoglobin mutants differing from the wild type by a single amino acid substitution can be readily detected about half the time using the somewhat less sensitive macro-complement fixation procedure (Reichlin 1970). In addition, we have been able to show ID's of 1.09 and 1.15 between three different albumins found in *Aotus trivirgatus* individuals homozygous for those apparently allelic albumins (Sarich, unpublished data). Thus the implications of immunological insensitivity seem totally unfounded.

A further piece of evidence supporting the exponential over the log–log model comes from the fact that Moore and Goodman (1968) showed that the amount of spur formation in the Ouchterlony procedure was proportional to log ID for the same albumin comparisons. As the theory of Ouchterlony analysis (Goodman 1962) would strongly suggest that the degree of spur formation should be linearly related to the number of sequence differences between the protein species being compared, it seems reasonable to use the following logic:

if degree of spur formation α number of sequence differences, then

degree of spur formation α log ID and

$\therefore$ log ID α number of sequence differences.

And as the sequence differences then accumulate as a regular (Pois-

sonian) function of time (Sarich 1968; Wilson and Sarich 1969), the equation log ID α kt follows.

The log–log model (or any model other than the exponential one we originally developed) obviously also shows no compatibility with the hemoglobin, fibrinopetide, trans-ferrin, carbonic anhydrase, and DNA data discussed earlier. It is also of some interest to note that many of these data, so necessary to the testing of the log–log model other than in terms of agreement with certain current views of the meaning of the primate fossil record, were not even considered by Read and Lestrel even though they were available in the literature well before the submission of their manuscript.

The direct paleontological criticisms of our molecular conclusions require a different sort of answering argument. In essence, Simons, Pilbeam, Leakey, and others perceive in the Oligocene and Miocene primate fossils evidence indicating that certain of these fossils can be placed on already separate and distinct lineages represented today by chimps, gorillas, gibbons, man, and the Old World monkeys. The times of divergence given vary with author and publication but the minima would be:

Homo–Pan–Gorilla	15–20 × 10⁶ yrs.
Hylobatids–other hominoids	25–30 × 10⁶ yrs.
Cercopithecoides–Hominoidea	35 × 10⁶ yrs.

We, on the other hand, give these dates as 4–5, 12, and 22 million years, respectively. This discrepancy has recently been commented on in rather vivid terms which deserve quoting:

If the immunological dates of divergence devised by Sarich are correct, then paleontologists have not yet found a single fossil related to the ancestry of any living primate...it is not presently acceptable to assume that all the fossil primates resembling modern forms are only parallelisms, that highly arboreal apes wandered hundreds of miles out of Africa across the Pontian steppes of Eurasia in search of tropical rain forests, or that *Australopithecus* sprang full-blown five million years ago, as Minerva did from Jupiter, from the head of a chimpanzee or gorilla. (Simons 1970: 330)

If Sarich and Wilson had looked more carefully at paleontological investigations, they would have found that their suggestion is unwarranted....If the deductions made from the immunological work cited can be taken as valid, then *Ramapithecus* cannot be a hominid, none of the Dryopithecinae can be ancestral to any living pongids, and *Pliopithecus* and *Limnopithecus* cannot be on the ancestral line of the gibbons...there are some things that cannot be done with molecular data and some things that cannot be done with fossils, and I object to careless assumptions and thoughtless statements about evolutionary processes in some of the conclusions drawn from the immunological data mentioned...Unfortunately there is a growing tendency, which I would like to suppress if possible, to view the molecular approach to primate evolutionary studies as a kind of instant phylogeny. No hard work, no tough intellectual arguments. No fuss, no muss, no dishpan hands.

Just throw some proteins into the laboratory apparatus, shake them up, and bingo!—we have an answer to questions that puzzled us for at least three generations. (Buettner-Janusch 1969: 132–133)

Buettner-Janusch puts it very well and so brings us to the pivotal question of what it is that one can or cannot do with the molecules and what with the fossils? Yet the two sets of data clearly cannot be mutually exclusive. They both developed alone and must therefore be in some fashion interpretable within a single phylogenetic scheme. The point is that one must be very careful in distinguishing between data and interpretation. There are molecular and paleontological and anatomical data, but these data often mean different things to different people—thus there are also molecular, paleontological, and anatomical interpretations for these data. There is, to repeat, but a single evolutionary history or phylogeny for a group of species—and therefore *all* the comparative data must be interpretable within that single context. One cannot legitimately use one phylogeny to explain the molecular data, another for the paleontological, and still a third for the anatomical. Conversely, one cannot legitimately derive three or more phylogenies from three such sets of data. We require that the various lines of evidence be used to place more and more marked constraints upon interpretations from other areas and in this cybernetic fashion to more closely approach evolutionary reality.

Such discordant opinion is hardly unique in the history of scientific developments, and the normal solution involves the formulation of the varying interpretations or points of view into hypotheses which are then tested in terms of their predictive value. It has already been pointed out that when this is done with the five million year date first formulated on the basis of immunological studies of primate albumin evolution, the hypothesis we proposed is fully supported. On the other hand, it might be instructive to reiteratively reflect upon what the paleontological times of divergence would lead us to conclude (and remember that one cannot argue hominoid conservatism in the evolution of any of the macromolecules compared). For the albumins, using a human–chimp divergence time of 20 million years (Simons and Ettel 1970), we should expect about 33 immunological distance units of difference (i.e., an ID of ~2.1). We find 7 (i.e., a mean ID of 1.18). In the case of the fibrinopeptides, where the average rate of substitution is about one substitution per lineage per six million years, we might expect about six sequence differences between man and chimpanzee. We find none. For the hemoglobins (α and β chains combined) the average is about one substitution per vertebrate lineage per 3.5 million years (Kimura 1969). Between man and chimp we might then expect 10 differences in sequence. We find none. In the DNA hybridization studies of Kohne (1970) one might have expected a difference comparable to that shown

between sheep and cow; i.e., about a 10°C difference in the thermal stability of the human–chimp hybrid DNA compared to that of human DNA. In fact Kohne found a difference of only 1.7°C (81.2°C vs. 82.9°C).

Thus it might not be entirely amiss to conclude that much of the argument here is, in large part, an accident of history. It is entirely possible to imagine a situation where the molecular evidence might have come first and the paleontological and comparative anatomical data at some later time. Then, it seems to me, any paleontological suggestions of appreciable antiquity for the African ape–hominid divergence might be greeted with as much skepticism as have been our protein and DNA based conclusions. It is not particularly difficult, it should be pointed out, to interpret the available paleontological and anatomical evidence in terms of the short time scale protein and DNA phylogeny (e.g., Washburn 1968; Lewis 1969; Sarich 1970, 1971) but there is yet to appear a defensible suggestion as to how a 20 million year date for the origin of the hominid line can possibly be used to explain the minimal changes which differentiate the DNA and proteins of man and the African apes. The molecular approach, as Washburn has put it, changes the rules of the evolutionary game by putting marked constraints on the range of interpretations permissible on the basis of the fossil or comparative anatomical data. *Ramapithecus* is a case in point where purely on the basis of minimal dental evidence the hominid line is unhesitatingly extended to an age of at least 12–14 million years (Buettner-Janusch 1969; Simons and Ettel 1970; Leakey 1970). The molecular evidence, and it is the following point that might perhaps be the most difficult for the reader to accept, argues that *Ramapithecus* cannot be a hominid—not because of what it does or does not look like, but because there was no hominid line distinct from those leading to the chimpanzee and gorilla at the period of time *Ramapithecus* lived. The body of protein and DNA data force one to the conclusion that one may no longer have the option of considering any fossil specimen older than 6–8 million years (to put an outside limit on it) a hominid no matter what it looks like. Or to put it into a somewhat more familiar context, anyone seriously arguing the case for an older hominid lineage must be prepared not only to demonstrate a set of uniquely hominid characters in the prospective hominid fossil but also to provide a defensible alternative interpretation of the ever growing body of molecular evidence.

And why, one might ask in closing, is this whole matter so important? Simply stated, the answer is that until we have the phylogeny of a group of species under study we really have nothing; as that phylogeny is the necessary framework upon which we can properly assess the meaning of the evidence we glean from other areas of research. The molecules themselves, at this early stage, still tell us little of their own adaptations but they do allow us to make more meaningful statements about the evolutionary significance of the adaptations found in the organisms containing them—for it is where we have been that tells us what we are and why. Or as an anonymous editorial writer for the *Austin* (Texas) *American* wrote on 29 December 1969:

As if things weren't bad enough for us humans, along comes a new anthropological assessment of man's relationship to the apes.

We're told man and the apes may not be nearly as far apart as has been thought.

Studies conducted at the University of California at Berkeley by two scientists suggest that the time of divergence by man and ape from the common ancestor they're supposed to have shared occurred only five million years ago, and not the 30 million held by some scientists.

Of course, humans actually should not resent too deeply this more intimate cousinship to the ape, for the closer the scientists get man to the trees, the easier it should be to explain why he acts the way he does.

(My thanks to Dr. Charles Laird for bringing this to our attention.)

Summary and Conclusions

The foregoing essays and selected readings have attempted to point out major concepts in the Western intellectual tradition that bear upon the questions of man's place in nature, his origins and affinities to monkeys and apes, and his primitive life. These questions had their earliest known beginnings in pre-Socratic Greece, but this volume has focused on the form they have assumed with the growth during the past three centuries of a scientific study of man.

During the period of the scientific study of man, paleoanthropologists have witnessed the fall of many concepts believed by our forebears to be immutable and necessary. For example, attempts to reconstruct man's "state of nature" based on observations of feral children, primitive peoples, and the anthropoid apes have been abandoned. Today no one assumes that the human condition, as we understand it, was attained through a sudden macromutation within an anthropoid ape stock, nor are seekers of the missing link or of the victims of Noah's Flood in much demand. Providentialism and other varieties of supernaturalism are as out of place in modern human biology as are attempts to refer to Scripture as a manual of geology or anthropology. An evaluation of how modern notions about the primate fossil record and phylogeny are conditioned by older points of view is a far more difficult task than the discernment of the biases of earlier thinkers. Yet this is a critical exercise for the student of any research discipline, and in particular for the student of science, who must observe his own mind and occasionally inquire how his ideas arose. We may now examine some of the precepts held today in the discipline of paleoanthropology.

The Platonic World of Ideas continues to exist in the guise of those prototypes of particular fossils which we accept as representing the "typical" examples of their population. Some specimens have been selected through historical accident as prototypes, for example Boule's description of the fossil from La Chapelle-aux-Saints. This rather aberrant form has been revered as an ideal type of Neanderthal Man; other neanderthaloid specimens are in comparison better or worse representatives. Such a point of view is hardly in keeping with current genetic attitudes about the range of variation possible in each organism's taxonomic group.

That the concept of the missing link was born in the realm of paleoanthropology has been denied often enough by students of fossil man; nevertheless, its ghost frequently haunts their writings. The calculation of how many traits are shared by a given hominid specimen with living and fossil apes and how many with modern human populations reflects a type of reasoning receptive to the concept of a transitional creature in the limbo between ape and man. This concept overlooks the reality that evolutionary changes such as those reflected in morphology are gradual, and that varous physical features are undergoing modifications at different rates and at different times, often independently. A similar gradual process is behind the formation of sub-specific populations of *Homo sapiens*, but a search for the missing link between lightly pigmented Swedes and dark South Indians has not been a source of scientific concern!

The idea of progress is a very obvious intellectual survival in current writings about man and his past. It is present in the very nomenclature of paleoanthropology, as in the taxonomic names of the fossils and in the polyphyletic systems devised to illustrate the relative distance of these specimens from one another and their affinity to man. Blatant or subtle varieties of racist philosophies have frequently converted the doctrine of progress into a political issue.

Closely related to the idea of progress is the belief that if there are gradations of cultural adaptability and success, a hierarchy of biological variations must follow. Within the broad scope of hominid evolution of the past several million years, the fossil record does show a number of major adaptive changes, especially in the evolution of erect bipedalism and the growth of the brain. Many of these biological adaptations are relevant to technological improvements and increasing socio-cultural complexities. But the chain-of-being idea does not suffice as a model of physical and cultural variations between populations of *Homo sapiens* today. A hierarchy of inferior or primitive to superior or advanced races of man is a myth. All populations are a medley of phenotypic characters, some of which are of ancient genetic origin, others of which have been acquired more recently. To select one character, such as the degree of robusticity of the frontal torus, as a primitive feature, is to overlook the total morphological pattern of the population in question and to neglect a search for similar primitive characters in populations which have been set a higher place on the chain of being. Some racial classifications have been based on the well entrenched notion of a natural hierarchy of human populations.

Implicit in scholarly efforts to reconstruct the ancient past is the concept of cycle. To be sure, cyclic cosmology has not been an important philosophical issue since the diffusion of Christianity to the West, but cyclical time has found a refuge in a number of theories in the social sciences, including history and prehistoric studies, and in the geological sciences. The notion that certain events occur periodically and deterministically as a result either of natural processes or of the intervention of supernatural forces has great prestige in pseudo-scientific areas of popular interest. The concept is not unknown in paleoanthropology today. For example, the drama of hominid evolution is viewed against the background of the Pleistocene with its periodic episodes of glacial advances and retreats, pluvial intensities and recessions. Influenced by such geological events were the ancestors of *Homo sapiens,* often described as having been subjected to episodic environmental stresses: isolation and the establishment of gene pools influenced by the mechanism of genetic drift during a glacial phase; and occurrence of gene migration (hybridization) during interglacial periods when movements of peoples were uninhibited. Adaptation to cold during glacial periods altered with adaptation to warmer conditions between glacial maxima. Although these episodes may be applicable to hominids living in particular local areas of the continental landmasses, the implication of this concept of cycle is that such geological events were of world wide scope.

Closely associated with the concept of cycle is the noisy ghost of Catastrophism. Glacial advances are treated as climatological–geological cataclysms that suddenly upset the established ecosystems on a worldwide scale, rather than as gradual alterations. The episodic approach to change is also represented in attempts to account for the disappearance of one fossil hominid *taxon* and for the arrival on the scene of a new group; for example, in much of the literature on the extinction of *Paranthropus* and Neanderthal Man. While Catastrophism has lost its respectablity as a geological and paleontological theory, it continues to be received as marking various episodic stages of man's evolutionary history.

"Ecology," "adaptation," and "behavior" are the most honored words in the vocabulary of modern biology, but the concepts associated with them are flavored by older notions of environmentalism, degenerationism, and the instinct–learning problem. Furthermore, while a Uniformitarian approach to natural history is regarded as self-evident, the charms of cyclical process and Catastrophism continue to lure the unwary. Even the structural–functional orientation to the study of modern anatomy is encumbered with a venerable paradox involving the necessity to explain the existence of every structure in terms of use or function. This has altered our faith in the significance of vestigial organs—one of Darwin's most valued examples of evolution by selection—for there is now no allowance made for so-called "useless parts" in an organism's structure. While the reinterpretation of these anatomical data may prove correct, the researcher is troubled by the present demand to satisfy the long-held notion that structures must be explained entirely within the limits and purposes of their functions.

Paleoanthropology has been suspect by the guardians of tradition, for it appears to be a science that robs man of the qualities of uniqueness that render him eligible for a special place in nature. But that man evolved as did other beasts and that he has for millenia been subject to some of the same stresses as they for survival does not negate man's unusualness. He is the only animal that can discover his own biological history as well as that of the other creatures with whom he shares existence. Man alone can see in the night sky other worlds than his own, and can conceive that the world in which he lives can be altered for the greater benefit of his own species.

Selected References

Abel, O.
    1902   "Zwei neue Menschenaffen aus den Leithakalkbildungen des Wiener Beckens." *Situngsberichte der K. Akademie der Wissenschaften in Wien. Mathematisch-naturwissenschaftliche Klasse* 3, Part 1, pp. 1–37. Vienna: K. K. Hof.

Adloff, P.
    1908   *Das Gebiss des Menschen und der Anthropomorphen.* Berlin: J. Springer.

Agassiz, L.
    1850   "Diversity of origin of the human races." *Christian Examiner* 49: 110–45.
    1854   "Sketch of the natural provinces of the world." In *Types of Mankind,* edited by J. C. Nott and G. R. Gliddon, pp. lvii–lxviii. Philadelphia: Lippincott, Grambo, and Company.

Arambourg, C.
    1963   "Continental vertebrate faunas of the Tertiary of North Africa." In *African Ecology and Human Evolution,* edited by F. C. Howell, pp. 55–64. Chicago: Aldine.

Ashton, E. H., and Zuckerman, S.
    1951   "Some cranial indices of *Plesianthropus* and other primates." *American Journal of Physical Anthropology* 9: 283.

Audebert, J. D.
    1797   *Histoire Naturelle des Singes et des Makis.* Paris: Desray.

Avis, V.
    1962   "Brachiation: the crucial test for man's ancestry." *Southwestern Journal of Anthropology* 18: 119–49.

Bartholomew, G. A., and Birdsell, J. B.
    1953   "Ecology and the proto-hominids." *American Anthropologist* 55: 481–98.

Basmajian, J.
    1962   *Muscles Alive. Their Functions Revealed by Electromyography.* Baltimore: Williams and Wilkins Company.

Bastian, H. C.
    1872   *The Beginnings of Life.* London: Macmillan and Company.

Bauer, K.
    1970   "Cross-reactions between human and animal plasma proteins. III. The relations between ontogenetic and phylogenetic development." *Human Genetics* 10: 8–14.

Bayer, J.
1927 *Das Mensch im Eiszeitalter.* Leipzig and Vienna: F. Deutlicke.

Bendysche, T.
1863 "On the anthropology of Linnaeus." *Memoires of the Anthropological Society* I, pp. 421–58. London: Trübner and Co.

Bertuch, F. J. J., and Vater, J. S.
1808 *Archiv für Ethnographie und Linguistick.* Berlin: Bauer.

Biberson, P.
1963 "Human Evolution in Morocco, in the framework of the paleo-climatic variations of the Atlantic Pleistocene." In *African Ecology and Human Evolution,* edited by F. Clark Howell and Francois Bourliere, p. 417–77. Chicago: Aldine.

Biegert, J.
1963 "The evaluation of characteristics of the skull, hands, and feet for primate taxonomy." In *Classification and Human Evolution,* edited by S. L. Washburn, pp. 116–45. Chicago: Aldine.

Blumenbach, J. F.
1779–1780 "I. Ordn. Bimanus. II. Quadrumana." *Handbuch der Naturgeschichte.* Göttingen: Dietrich.
1795 *De Generis Humani Varietate Nativa.* Göttingen: Vandenhöck.
1796–1810 *Abbildungen Naturhistorischer Gengenstände.* Göttingen: Dietrich.
1806 *Beiträge zur Naturgeschichte,* 2nd edition. Göttingen: Dietrich.
1825 "Order I: Bimanus. II: Quadrumana." *A Manual of the Elements of Natural History.* Translated by R. T. Gore from the 10th German edition, © 1825. Section 4, pp. 34–42. London: W. Simpkin and R. Marshall.

Bontius, J.
1642 *De Medicina Indorum.* Leyden: Hackium.
1658 *Jacobi Bontij Historiae Naturalis et Medicae Indiae Orientalis.* Amsterdam.

Boswell, P. G. H.
1935 "Human remains from Kanam and Kanjera, Kenya Colony." *Nature* 135: 371.

Boule, M.
1911 "L'homme fossile de la Chapelle-aux-Saints." *Annales de Paléontologie* 6: 111–72.
1912 "L'homme fossile de la Chappelle-aux-Saints." *Annales de Paléontologie* 7: 85–190.
1913 "L'homme fossile de la Chapelle-aux-Saints." *Annales de Paléontologie* 8: 1–70.
1923 *Fossil Men. Elements of Human Paleontology.* Edinburgh: Oliver and Boyd.

Boyden, A.
1958 "Comparative serology: aims, methods, and results." In *Serological and Biochemical Comparisons of Proteins,* edited by W. H. Cole. pp. 3–24. New Brunswick, N. J.: Rutgers.

Brain, C. K.
1958 "The Transvaal Ape-Man-bearing cave deposits." *Transvaal Museum Memoir* II.

Breuil, H., and Cartailhac, E.
1906 *Le Caverne d'Altimira a Santillone pres Santander (Espagne).* Monaco: Imp. de Monaco.

Breydenbach, B. von
  1946   *Reyss in das Gelobt Land.* Mainz: Erhart.
Broca, P. P.
  1864   *On the Phenomena of Hybridity in the Genus Homo.* Translated and edited by C. C. Beake. London: Anthropological Society of London.
  1870   "Sur la Transformisme." *Bulletins de la Société d'anthropologie de Paris* 5: 168–239.
Broom, R.
  1937   "On *Australopithecus* and its affinities." In *Early Man,* edited by G. G. MacCurdy, pp. 285–92. London: J. B. Lippincott.
  1950   "The genera and species of the South African fossil ape-man." *American Journal of Physical Anthropology* 8: 1–13.
Broom, R., and Schepers, C. W. H.
  1946   "The South African fossil ape-men: the *Australopithecinae.*" *Transvaal Museum Memoir* 2: 1–272.
Buettner-Janusch, J.
  1969   "The nature and future of physical anthropology." *Transactions of the New York Academy of Sciences* 32: 128–38.
Buffon, G. L., Comte de
  1749–1767   "Nomenclature des singes." *Histoire naturelle générale et particulière.* Paris: Imprimerie Royale.
  1791   "The nomenclature of apes." *Natural History, General and Particular.* Translated by Smellie. London: T. Cadell and M. Davis.
Burkitt, M. C.
  1921   *Prehistory.* Cambridge: University Press.
Burnett, J. (Lord Monboddo)
  1774–1809   *On the Origin and Process of Language.* 6 Vols. Edinburgh: J. Balfour.
  1779–1795   *Antient Metaphysics: or the Science of Universals.* Edinburgh: J. Balfour.
Cadet, J. M.
  1805   *Copie figurée d'un rouleau de papyrus trouvé á Thèbes, dans un tombeau des Rois.* Paris: Schoell and Company.
Cahen, L., and Lepersonne, J.
  1952   "Equivalence entre le Système du Kalahari du Congo Belge et les Kalahari Beds d'Afrique Australe. *Mémoires de la société belge Géologique,* Section 8, Vol. 4, No. 1.
Campbell, B.
  1964   "Just another 'man-ape'?" *Discovery* 25: 37.
  1964   "Science and human evolution." *Nature* 203: 448–51.
Christol, J. de
  1829   *Notice sur les Ossements humaines fossiles des cavernes du département du Gard.* Montpellier: J. Martel.
Church, W. S.
  1861   "On the myology of the Orang-Utang (*Simia Morie*)." *Natural History Review* 1: 510–16.
Clark, W. E. Le Gros
  1930   "The thalamus of *Tarsius.*" *Journal of Anatomy* 64: 371–414.
  1946   "The inside story of the skull." Review of Pierre Hirschler's *Anthropoid and Human Endocranial Casts. Nature* 158: 5.

1950   "New palaeontological evidence bearing on the evolution of the *Hominoidea.*" *Quarterly Journal of the Geological Society* (London) 105 : 225–64.

1955   *The Fossil Evidence for Human Evolution.* Chicago : University of Chicago.

1964   "Letter to Editor." *Discovery* 25, No. 7 : 49.

Cocks, G. T., and Wilson, A. C.
1969   "Immunological detection of single amino acid substitutions in alkaline phosphatase." *Science* 164 : 188–89.

Cooke, H. B. S.
1963   "Pleistocene mammal faunas of Africa, with particular reference to Southern Africa." In *African Ecology and Human Evolution,* edited by F. Clark Howell and Francois Bourliere, pp. 65–116. Chicago : Aldine.

Coon, C. S.
1939   *The Races of Europe.* New York : Macmillan.

1962a   *The Origin of Races.* New York : A. A. Knopf.

1962b   "New Findings on the Origin of Races." *Harper's Magazine* 225, No. 1351 : 65–74.

Coppens, Y.
1962   "Decouverte d'un Australopithecine dans le Villafranchien du Tchad." In *Problèmes Actuels de Paléontologie,* pp. 455–60. Paris : Editions du centre national de la recherche scientifique.

Croll, J.
1875   *Climate and Time in Their Geological Relations.* New York : D. Appleton and Company.

Dahlberg, A. A.
1963   "Dental evolution and culture." *Human Biology* 35 : 237–49.

Daly, R.
1920a   "A recent worldwide sinking of ocean-level." *Geological Magazine* 57 : 246–61.

1920b   "A general sinking of sealevel in recent time." *Proceedings of the National Academy of Sciences* 6, No. 5 : 246–50.

Dapper, P.
1686   *Description de l'Afrique.* Amsterdam : Wolfgang, Waesberge, Broom, and Van Someren.

Dart, R. A.
1957a   "The osteodontokeratic culture of *Australopithecus prometheus.*" *Transvaal Museum Memoir* 10.

1957b   "The Makapansgat australopithecine osteodontokeratic culture." *Proceedings of the 3rd Pan-African Congress on Prehistory, Livingstone,* p. 161. London : Chatto and Windus.

1958   "Bone tools and porcupine gnawing." *American Anthropologist* 60 : 715.

1960   "The bone-tool manufacturing ability of *Australopithecus prometheus.*" *American Anthropologist* 62 : 134.

1962   "A cleft adult mandible and the nine other lower jaw fragments from Makapansgat." *American Journal of Physical Anthropology* 20 : 267–86.

Darwin, C. R.
1839   *Journal of Researches into the Geology and Natural History of the Various Countries Visited by H. M. S. Beagle, under the Command of Captain Fitzroy, R. N. from 1832–1836.* London : H. Coburn.

1871   *The Descent of Man, and Selection in Relation to Sex.* London: John Murray.

1873a *The Descent of Man, and Selection in Relation to Sex.* New York: D. Appleton and Company.

1873b *La Descendence de l'homme et la selection sexuelle.* Translated from the Second Edition by E. Barbier. Paris: C. Reinwald.

1875   *Voyage d'un Naturaliste autour du Monde à bord du Naivre Beagle, du 1831 à 1836.* Translated by E. Barbier. Paris: C. Reinwald.

Dayhoff, M. O.
1969   *Atlas of protein sequence and structure.* Silver Spring, Maryland: National Biomedical Research Foundation.

DeGeer, G.
1910   "Geochronology of the last 12,000 years." *Congres Geologique International. Comptes Rendus.* 11th Session, pp. 241–53. Stockholm: P. A. Norstedt and Sons.

1921   "Correlation of late glacial annual clay-varves in North American with the Swedish time scale." *Geologiska Föreningens i Stockholm Förhandlingar* 43, No. 344, Hafte 1–2: 70–73.

Deperet, C.
1918–1920   'Essai de coordination chronologique générale de temps quaternaires." *Comptes Rendus. Paris: Academie des sciences.* 166: 480–86, 636–41, 884–89; 167: 418–22, 979–84; 168: 868–73; 170: 159–63; 171: 212–18.

1921   "La classification du Quaternaire et sa correlation avec les niveaux prehistoriques." *Comptes Rendus.* Paris: Géologique Société de France. No. 9, pp. 125–27.

Desnoyers, J. de
1831   "Rapport sur les travaux de la société géologique pendant l'année 1831." *Bulletin de la Société géologique de France* 2: 226–327.

Dobzhansky, T. G.
1941   *Genetics and the Origin of Species,* 2nd edition. New York: Columbia University.

1944   "On species and races of living and fossil man." *American Journal of Physical Anthropology* 2: 251–65.

Doolittle, R. F., and Mross, G. A.
1970   "Identity of chimpanzee with human fibrinopeptides." *Nature* 225: 643–44.

Dubois, E. F. T.
1894   *Pithecanthropus erectus. Eine Menschenähnliche Uebergangsform aus Java.* Batavia: Landesdruckerei.

1896a "*Pithecanthropus erectus,* eine Stammform des Menschen." *Anatomischer Anzeiger* 12: 1–22.

1896b "The place of '*Pithecanthropus*' in the genealogical tree." *Nature* 53: 245–47.

Dubrul, E. L.
1950   "Posture, locomotion and the skull in *Lagomorpha.*" *American Journal of Anatomy* 87: 277–313.

Dubrul, E. L., and Laskin, D. M.
1961   "Preadaptive potentialities of the mammalian skull: an experiment in growth and form." *American Journal of Anatomy* 109: 117–32.

Duckworth, W. H. L.
    1915   *Morphology and Anthropology*, 2nd edition. London: Cambridge University.

Eggeling, H. von
    1911   "Physiognomie und Schädel." *Sammlung Anatomischer und Physiologischer: Voträge und Aufsätze* 17.

Erikson, G. E.
    1963   "Brachiation in the New World monkeys and in anthropoid apes." *Symposium of the Geological Society of London*. London: Geological Society of London.

Evans, A.
    1916   "New archaeological lights on the origin of civilization in Europe." *Science* 44, No. 1134: 399–408.

Evernden, J. F.; Savage, E. D.; Curtis, A. E.; and James, J. T.
    1962   "Potassium-Argon dates and the Cenozoic mammalian chronology of North America. *American Journal of Science* 262: 145–98.

Fischer, G.
    1804   *Anatomie der Maki und der ihnen Verwandten Tiere*. Frankfort-am-Main: Andrea.

Fitch, W. M., and Margoliash, E.
    1967   "The construction of phylogenetic trees." *Science* 155: 276–84.

Fleure, H. J.
    1920   "Some early neanthropic types in Europe and their modern representatives." *Journal of the Royal Anthropological Institute of Great Britain and Ireland* 1: 12–40.

Freedman, L.
    1963   "A biometric study of Papio cynocephalus skulls from Northern Rhodesia and Nyasaland." *Journal of Mammology* 44: 24–43.

Fuhlrott, J. C.
    1857   "General meeting of the Natural History Society of Prussian Rhineland and Westphalia, at Bonn; re: location and discovery of cranium of Elberfeld." *Correspondenzblatt No. 2. Vereins der Preussischen Rheinlande und Westphalens* 14: 50. Bonn.

Galen, C.
    1551   *De Anatomicis Administrationibus*. Lugduni: G. Rouillium.

Garn, S. M.
    1963a   "Comments on Newman." *Current Anthropology* 4: 197–98.
    1963b   "Culture and the direction of human evolution." *Human Biology* 35: 221–36.

Garcilasso de la Vega, G.
    1688   *The Royal Commentaries of Peru*. London: M. Flescher.

Gassendus, P.
    1641   *Viri Illustris N. C. Frabricii de Peiresc... Vita*. Paris: S. Cramoisy.

Geikie, J.
    1894   *The Great Ice Age,* 3rd edition. London: Edward Stanford.
    1914   *The Antiquity of Man in Europe*. Edinburgh: Oliver and Boyd.

Genet-Varcin, E.
    1963   *Les singes actuels et fossiles*. Paris: N. Boubée et Cie.
    1969   *Á la recherche du primate ancêtre de l'homme*. Paris: N. Boubée et Cie.

Geoffroy St. Hilaire, I.
  1838   "Sur les ossemens humains provenant de cavernes de Liège et sur les modifications produites dans le pelage des chevaux par un séjour prolangé dans les profundeurs des mers. *Comptes rendus, de l'Academie des sciences de Paris.* 7 : 13–15. Paris : M. Bachelier.

Giuffrida-Ruggeri, V.
  1918   "Unicità del Philum Umano con pluralita dei Centri Specifici." *Revista italiana di paleontologia* 24 : 13–25.

Goodall, J. M.
  1964   "Tool-using and aimed throwing in a community of free-living chimpanzees." *Nature* 201 : 1264–66.

Goodman, M.
  1961   "The role of immunological differences in the phyletic development of human behavior." *Human Biology* 33 : 131–62.
  1962   "Evolution of the immunologic species specificity of human serum proteins." *Human Biology* 34 : 104–50.
  1963a   "Serological analysis of the systematics of recent hominoids." *Human Biology* 35 : 377–436.
  1963b   "Man's place in the phylogeny of the primates as reflected in serum proteins." In *Classification and Human Evolution*, edited by S. L. Washburn, pp. 204–34. Chicago : Aldine.

Goodman, M.; Moore, G. W.; Farris, W.; and Poulik, E.
  1970   "The evidence from genetically informative macromolecules on the phylogenetic relationships of the chimpanzees." In *The Chimpanzee*. Vol. 2, pp. 318–60. Basel : Karger.

Gorjanovic-Kramberger, D. K.
  1900   "Der diluviale Mensch von Krapina." *Anthropologische Gesellschraft in Wien: Mitteilungen* 31 : 190.
  1906   *Der Diluviale Mensch von Krapina in Kroatien. Ein Beitrag zur Paläontologie.* Wiesbaden : C. W. Kreidel.

Grandidier, G.
  1905   "Recherches sur les lemuriens disparus et en particulier sur ceux qui vivaient à Madagascar." *Extraits des nouvelles archives de museum* 7 : 1–142.

Gregory, W. K.
  1916   "Studies on the evolution of the primates. Part 1. The Cope–Osborn theory of the trituberculy and the ancestral molar patterns of the primates. Part 2. Phylogeny of recent and extinct anthropoids with special reference to the origin of man." *Bulletin of the American Museum of Natural History* 35 : 239–355.
  1917   "Evolution of the human face." *The American Museum Journal* 17, No. 6 : 377–88.
  1921   "The origin and evolution of the human dentition : a palaeontological review." *Journal of Dental Research* 3, No. 1 : 87–228.
  1927   "The origin of man from the anthropoid stem. When and where?" *Proceedings of the American Philosophical Society* 66 : 439–63.
  1928   "Were the ancestors of man primitive brachiators?" *Proceedings of the American Philosophical Society* 67 : 129–50.

Gremiackii, A.
  1922   "Podkumskaia cherepnaia kryshka i ieio morfologicheskie osobennosti. (i.e.: "La calotte du crâne de l'homme de Podkoumok et ses caractères morphologiques.")" *Russki Anthropologicheskii Zhurnal* 12 : 92–110.

Haeckel, E. H.
1868a *Naturliche Schöpfungeschichte. Gemeinverständliche wissenschaftliche Vorträge über die Entwicklungslehre im allgemeinen und diejenige von Darwin, Goethe und Lamarck im Besondern.* Chapters 22–23. Berlin: G. Reimer.
1868b "Ueber die Entstenhung und den Stammbaum des Menschengeschlechts; zwei Vortrage." *Sammlung gemeinverständlicher wissenschaftlicher Vorträge.* Vols. 52–53. Berlin: C. G. Luderitz'sche.
1874   *Histoire de la Création des êtres organizés d'après les lois naturelles.* Paris: C. Reinwalf.
1876   *The History of Creation: or, The Development of the Earth and Its Inhabitants by the Action of Natural Causes. A Popular Exposition of the Doctrine of Evolution in General, and that of Darwin, Goethe, Lamarck in Particular.* Translation from the 1st German edition by E. Ray Lankester. New York: D. Appleton.
1895   *Systematische Phylogenie der Wirbeltmere.* Berlin: G. Reimer.

Hafleigh, A., and Williams, C. A.
1966   "Antigenic correspondence of serum albumins among the primates." *Science* 151 : 1530–35.

Harrison, G. A., and Weiner, J. S.
1963   "Some considerations in the formulation of theories of human phylogeny." In *Classification and Human Evolution,* edited by S. L. Washburn, pp. 75–84. Chicago: Aldine.

Hay, R. L.
1963   "Stratigraphy of Beds I through IV, Olduvai Gorge, Tanganyika." *Science* 139 : 829–33.

Heberer, G.
1952   "Fortschritte in der Erforschung der Phylogenie der *Hominoidea.*" *Ergebnisse der Anatomie und Entwicklungeschichte* 34 : 499.
1956   "Die Fossilgeschichte der *Hominoidea.*" *Primatologia* 1 : 379.
1958a "L'Hominization: Selection, Adaptation ou Orthogenese." *Coll. International: Les Processus de l'Hominization* 179.
1958b "Das Tier—Mensch-Ubergangsfeld." *Stud. gen* 11 : 341.
1959   "The descent of man and the present fossil record." *Cold Spring Harbor Symposium of Quantitative Biology* 24 : 235.
1960   "Darwins Urteil über die abstammungsgeschichtliche Herkunft des Menschen und die heutige palaanthropologische Forschung." *Hundert Jahre Evolutionsforschung* 397. Stuttgart.

Hennig, E.
1948   "Quartärfaunen und Urgeschichte Ostafrikas." *Naturwissenschaftliche Rundschau* Jahrg. 1, Heft 5 : 212.

Hirschler, P.
1942   *Anthropoid and Human Endocranial Casts.* Amsterdam: N. V. Noord-Hollandsche Uitgeversmij.

Hooten, E. A.
1946   *Up From The Ape,* 2nd edition. New York: Macmillan and Company.

Howell, F. C.
1951   "The Place of Neanderthal Man in Human Evolution." *American Journal of Physical Anthropology* n.s. 9, No. 4 : 379–416.
1959   "The Villafranchian and human origins." *Science* 130 : 831.

Hrdlička, A.
  1927   "The Neanderthal phase of man." The Huxley Memorial Lecture for 1927. *Journal of the Royal Anthropological Institute of Great Britain and Ireland* 57 : 249–74.
  1930   "The skeletal remains of early man." *Smithsonian Miscellaneous Collection* 83 : 1–79.

Hurzeler, J.
  1958   "*Oreopithecus bambilii* Gervais." *Verhandlungen der natursforschenden Gesellschaft in Basel* 69 : 1.
  1968   "Questions et réflexions sur l'histoire des anthropomorphes." *Annales de Paléontologie* 14 : 195–233.

Huxley, T. H.
  1863   *Evidence as to Man's Place in Nature.* London : Williams and Norgate.

"International Code of Zoological Nomenclature"
  1961   London : International Trust of Zoological Nomenclature.

Jones, F. Wood
  1916   *Arboreal Man.* London : E. Arnold.
  1918   *The Problems of Man's Ancestry.* London : Society for Promoting Christian Knowledge.
  1919   "The origin of man." In *Animal Life and Human Progress*, edited by A. Dendry, chapter 5, pp. 101–31. London : Constable.
  1929   *Man's Place Among the Mammals.* London : E. Arnold

Jonstonus, J.
  1650–1653   *Historiae Naturalis de Quadrupetibus.* Frankfort-am-Main : Heirs of M. Merian.

Joseph, J.
  1960   *Man's Posture and Electromicrograph Studies.* Springfield, Ill. : Thomas.

Keane, A. H.
  1901   *Ethnology.* Cambridge : University Press.

Keble, R. A., and Macpherson, J. H.
  1946   "The contemporaneity of the river terraces of the Maribyrnong River, Victoria, with those of the Upper Pleistocene in Europe." *Memoirs of the National Museum, Victoria.* No. 14, Part 2, pp. 52–68.

Keith, A.
  1896   "An introduction to the study of anthropoid apes." *Natural Science* 9 : 316–26, 372–79.
  1899   "On the chimpanzees and their relationship to the gorilla." *Proceedings of the Zoological Society,* 1899, Part 1, pp. 296–312.
  1911   "Klaatsch's theory of the descent of man." *Nature* 85 : 508–10.
  1912   "Modern problems relating to the antiquity of man." *Report of the British Association for the Advancement of Science.* No 82, pp. 753–59.
  1915   *The Antiquity of Man.* (Second edition 1925.) London : Williams and Norgate.
  1925   "The Taungs skull." *Nature* 116 : 11.
  1927   "Report on the Galilee skull." *Researches in Prehistoric Galilee.* 1925–1926. London : British School of Archaeology in Jerusalem.
  1928   *Darwinism and What It Implies.* London : Watts and Company.
  1931   *New Discoveries Relating to the Antiquity of Man.* New York : W. W. Norton and Company.

Kimura, M.
1969   "The rate of molecular evolution considered from the standpoint of population genetics." *Proceedings of the National Academy of Sciences* 63 : 1181–88.

Kirsch, J. A. W.
1969   "Serological data and phylogenetic inference: the problem of rates of change." *Systematic Zoology* 18 : 296–311.

Klaatsch, H. A. L.
1910   "Menschenrassen und Menschenaffen." *Deutsche Gesellschaft für Anthropologie, Ethnologie, und Urgeschichte.* Korrespondenzblatt 41 : 91–100.

Klinger, H. P.; Hamerton, J. L.; Mutton, D.; and Lang, E. M.
1963   "The Chromosomes of the Hominoidea." In *Classification and Human Evolution*, pp. 235–42. Chicago: Aldine.

Koenigswald, G. H. R. von
1957   "*Meganthropus* and the *Australopithecinae.*" *Proceedings 3rd Pan-African Congress on Prehistory*, Livingstone, p. 158. London: Chatto and Windus.

Kohn, A. J., and Orians, G. H.
1962   "Ecological data in the classification of closely related species." *Systematic Zoology* 11 : 119–26.

Kohne, D. E.
1970   "Evolution of higher-organism DNA." *Quarterly Reviews of Biophysics* 3 : 327–76.

Kolk, S. van der, and Vrolik, W.
1862   "Note sur l'encéphale de l'Orang-outang." *Natural History Review* 2, No. 5 : 111–17.

Koppers, W.
1944   "Urmensch und Urreligion." *Wissen Bekenutris.* Olten: O. Walter.

Kortlandt, A.
1962   "Chimpanzees in the wild." *Scientific American* 206, No. 4 (May) : 2–10.

Lamarck, J. B. P. A. de
1802   *Recherches sur l'Organisation des Corps Vivants et Particulièrement sur son origine, sur la cause de son développement et des progrès de sa composition.* Paris.
1809   *Philosophie Zoologique.* 2 Vols. Paris: Dentu.
1873   *Philosophie Zoologique*, 2nd edition. Paris: Savy.
1914   *Zoological Philosophy.* Translated by H. Elliot. London: Macmillan and Company.

Lamothe, L. de
1899   "Note sur les anciennes plages et terrasses du bassin de l'Isser et de quelques autres bassins de la Côte Algérienne." *Bulletin de la Société geologique de France* 27 : 257–303.
1901   "Sur la rôle des oscillations eustatiques du niveau de base dans la forma-tion des systèmes de terrasses de quelques vallées." *Comptes Rendus. Academie des sciences* 132 : 1428–30. Paris: Gauthier-Villars.
1911   "Les anciennes lignes de rivages du Sahel d'Alger et d'une partie de la Côte Algérienne." *Memoires de la Société geologique de France.* Vol. 1.
1916   "Les anciennes lignes de rivage du bassin de la Somme et leurs concor-

dance avec celles de la Mediterranée Occidentale." *Comtes Rendus Academie des sciences* 162: 948–51. Paris: Gauthier-Villars.

1918 "Les anciennes nappes alluviales et lignes de rivage du bassin de la Somme et leurs rapports avec celles de la Metiterranée Occidentale." *Bulletin de la Société geologique de France* 18: 3–58.

Lander, K. F.
1918 "The examination of a skeleton of known age, race and sex." *Journal of Anatomy and Physiology* 52: 282–91.

Lansteiner, K., and Miller, C. P., Jr.
1925 "Serological studies on the blood of the primates." *Journal of Experimental Medicine* 42, No. 6: 841–72.

Lawrence, W.
1819 *Lectures on the Physiology, Zoology and the Natural History of Man, Delivered at the Royal College of Surgeons.* London: Bohn.

Leakey, L. S. B.
1959 "A new fossil skull from Olduvai." *Nature* 184: 491–93.
1961a "New finds at Olduvai Gorge. *Nature* 189: 649.
1961b "The juvenile mandible from Olduvai." *Nature* 191: 417–18.
1965 "Facts instead of dogmas on man's origin." In *The Origin of Man,* pp. 3–17. New York: Wenner-Gren Foundation for Anthropological Research.
1970 "The relationship of African apes, man, and Old World monkeys." *Proceedings of the National Academy of Sciences* 67: 746–48.

Leakey, L. S. B., Evernden, J. F., and Curtis, G. H.
1961 "Age of Bed 1, Olduvai Gorge, Tanganyika." *Nature* 191: 478–79.

Leakey, L. S. B., Tobias, P. V., and Napier, J. R.
1964 "A new species of the genus *Homo* from Olduvai Gorge." *Nature* 202: 7–9.

Leverett, F.
1910 "Comparison of North American and European glacial deposits." *Zeitschrift für Gletscherkunde.* Vol. 4, Sec. 4: 241–95; Sec. 5: 321–42; Vol. 5, Sec. 4: 315–16.

Lewis, O. J.
1969 "The hominoid wrist joint." *American Journal of Physical Anthropology* 30: 251–68.

Lyell, C.
1830–1833 *Principles of Geology.* 2 Vols. London: John Murray. (9th Edition 1854, D. Appleton, New York.)
1863 *The Geological Evidences of the Antiquity of Man with Remarks on Theories of the Origin of Species by Variation.* London: John Murray.
1865 *Elements of Geology,* 6th edition. London: John Murray.

Mabbutt, J. A.
1955 "Erosion surfaces in Namaqualand and the ages of surface deposits in the south-western Kalahari." *Transactions of the Geological Society of South Africa* 58: 13.
1957 "Physiographic evidence for the age of the Kalahari sands of the south-western Kalahari." *Proceedings 3rd Pan-African Congress on Prehistory,* Livingstone, p. 123. London: Chatto and Windus.

MacCurdy, G. G.
1924 *Human Origins.* New York: D. Appleton and Company.

Malaise, C.
1860   "Notes sur quelques ossements humains fossiles et sur quelques silex
        taillés." *Bulletins de l'académie royale de sciences, des lettres, et des
        beaux-arts de Belgique* 10: 538–46.

Marcozzi, V., S. J.
1944   "Alcune osservazioni sulla regione temporale nel Sinanthropo I Locus E,
        nelle scimmie e nell'uomo recente." *Commentationes Pontifica Accademia
        delle Scienze* 8, No. 9: 107–45.
1945   "Il *Sinanthropus pekinensis*.' D. Black. Observationi anthropologiche."
        Atti, R. Istittuto Veneto Scienze, Lettere, ed Arti 104, Part 2: 499–629.

Mason, R. J.
1961   "The earliest tool-makers in South Africa." *South African Journal of
        Science* 57: 13.

Matiegka, J.
1925   "Les Squelettes provenant de la station de l'homme quaternaire a
        Predmost en Moravie." *Anthropologie* 3: 323–29.
1929   "The skull of the fossil man. Brno III, and the cast of its interior." *Anthro-
        pologie* 7: 90–107.

Matsuda, G.; Tetsuo, M.; Takei, H.; Ota, H.; Yamaguchi, M.; Miyauchi, T.; and Migita,
        M.
1968   "The primary structure of adult hemoglobin from *Macaca mulatta* monkey."
        Journal of Biochemistry 64: 279–82.

Matthew, W. D.
1906   "Hypothetical outlines of the continents in Tertiary times." *Bulletin of the
        American Museum of Natural History* 22: 353–83.
1915a   "Revision of the lower Eocene primates." *Bulletin of the American Museum
        of Natural History* 34: 429–83.
1915b   "A revision of the lower Eocene Wasatch and Wind River faunas." *Bulletin
        of the American Museum of Natural History* 34. Part 1: 1–103; Part 2:
        311–28; Part 3: 329–61; Part 4: 429–83.
1915c   "Climate and evolution." *Annals of the New York Academy of Science*
        24: 171–318.
1928   "The evolution of mammals in the Eocene." In *Proceedings of the
        Zoological Society*, pp. 947–85. London: Zoological Society.

Maupertuis, M. de
1752   *Les Oeuvres de M. de Maupertuis*. Dresden: G. C. Walther.

Mayr, E.
1944   "On the concepts and terminology of vertical subspecies and species."
        National Research Council Bulletin 2: 11–16.
1950   "Taxonomic categories in fossil hominids." *Cold Spring Harbor Symposia
        on Quantitative Biology* 15: 109–17.
1957   "Species concepts and definitions." *The Species Problem. American
        Association for the Advancement of Science Publication* 50: 1–22.
1963   *Animal species and evolution*. Cambridge, Mass.: Harvard University Press.
1963   "The taxonomic evaluation of fossil hominids." In *Classification and
        Human Evolution*, edited by S. L. Washburn, pp. 332–46. Chicago: Aldine.

McCown, T. D. and Keith, A.
1939   "The Stone Age of Mount Carmel." *The Fossil Human Remains from the
        Levallois-Mousterian*. Oxford: Clarendon Press.

Miller, G. S.
1920 "Conflicting views on the problems of man's ancestry." *American Journal of Physical Anthropology* 3, No. 2: 213–23, 243–45.

Mills, J. R. E.
1963 "Occlusion and malocclusion in primates." In *Dental Anthropology*, edited by D. R. Brothwell, pp. 29–52. New York: Pergamon.

Mivart, St. George
1871 *On the Genesis of Species.* London: Macmillan and Company. (2nd edition, 1872.)
1873 *Man and Apes: an Exposition of Structural Resemblances and Differences Bearing upon the Questions of Affinity and Origin.* London: R. Hardwicke.

Moore, G. W., and Goodman, M.
1968 "A set theoretical approach to immunotaxonomy: analysis of species comparisons in modified Ouchterlony plates." *Bulletin of Mathematical Biophysics* 30: 279–89.

Morant, G. M.
1927 "Studies of Paleolithic Man. A biometric study of Neanderthaloid skulls and of their relationships to modern racial types." *Human Genetics* 2: 318–81.
1930 "A biometric study of the Upper Palaeolithic skulls of Europe and of their relationships to earliest and later types." *Human Genetics* 4: 109–214.

Morgan, N.
1875 *The Skull and Brain: Their Indications of Character and Anatomical Relations.* London: Longmans.

Morton, D. J.
1924 "Evolution of the human foot." *American Journal of Physical Anthropology* 8, No. 1: 1–52.

Moss, M. L., and Young, R. W.
1960 "A functional approach to craniology." *American Journal of Physical Anthropology* 18: 281–92.

Movius, H. L., Jr.
1944 "Early man and Pleistocene stratigraphy in eastern Asia." *Papers of the Peabody Museum of American Archaeology and Ethnology* 19: 1–125.

Napier, J. R.
1962 "Fossil hand bones from Olduvai Gorge." *Nature* 196: 409–11.
1963 "The locomotor functions of hominids." In *Classification and Human Evolution*, edited by S. L. Washburn, pp. 178–89. Chicago; Aldine.

Napier, J. R., and Davis, P. R.
1959 "The fore-limb skeleton and associated remains of *Proconsul africanus.*" *Fossil Mammals of Africa* 6.

Noback, C. R. and Moskowitz, N.
1962 "Structural and functional correlates of 'encephalization' in the primate brain." *Annals of the New York Academy of Science* 102: 210–18.
1963 "The primate nervous system: functional and structural aspects in phylogeny." In *Evolutionary and Genetic Biology of the Primates*, pp. 131–78. New York: Academic Press.

Nonno, L. H. Herschman, and Levine, L.
1970 "Serologic comparisons of primate erythrocytes." *Archives of Biochemistry and Biophysics* 136: 361–67.

Nuttall, G. H. F.
1902   "Progress report upon the biological test for blood as applied to over 500 bloods from various sources." *British Medical Journal,* April 5, pp. 825–27.
1904   *Blood Immunity and Blood Relationships.* Cambridge : Cambridge University.

Oakley, K. P., and Campbell, B. G.
1964   "Newly described Olduvai hominid." *Nature* 202 : 732.

Obermeier, H.
1924   *Fossil Man in Spain.* New Haven : Yale University.

Obruchev, V. A.
1926   *Die Metallogenetische Epochen und Gebiete von Siberie.* Halle : W. Knapp.

Osborn, H. F.
1902   "American Eocene primates and the supposed rodent family." *Bulletin of the American Museum of Natural History* 16 : 169–214.
1922a "Old and new standards of Pleistocene division in relation to the prehistory of man in Europe." *Bulletin of the Geological Society of America* 33 : 411–90.
1922b "*Hesperopithecus,* the anthropoid primate of Western Nebraska." *Nature* 110 : 281–83.
1924   "Introduction to H. Obermeier's *Fossil Man in Spain.*" New Haven : Yale University.
1926   *Evolution and Religion in Education.* New York : C. Scribner's Sons.
1927   "Recent discoveries relating to the origin and antiquity of man." *Palaeobiologica* 1 : 189–202.

Osborn, H. F., and Reede C. A.
1930   "Old and new standards of Pleistocene division in relation to the prehistory of man in Europe." *Bulletin of the Geological Society of America* 33 : 411–90.

Patterson, B.
1954   "The geological history of non-hominid primates in the Old World." *Human Biology* 26 : 191–209.

Pearson, K.
1921   "Side lights on the evolution of man." Lecture delivered at the Royal Institution, May 14, 1920. *Galton Laboratory for National Eugenics. Eugenics Lecture Series No 8.* London : University of London.

Penck, A., and Brückner, E.
1907–1909   *Die Alpen im Eiszeitalter.* Leipzig : C. H. Tauchnitz.

Petronievics, B.
1919   "La loi de l'evolution non correlative." *Revue general des sciences* 30 : 240–42.

Picton, J. A.
1870   *New Theories and the Old Faith.* London : Williams and Norgate.

Pidgeon, E.
1830   "The fossil remains of the animal kingom." In *The Animal Kingdom Arranged in Conformity with its Organization by the Baron Cuvier, Member of the Institute of France, etc. etc. etc., with Additional Descriptions of All of the Species Hitherto Named, and of Many not Noticed—by Edward Griffith, F.L.S., A.S. etc., Corresp. Member of the Academy of Natural Sciences of Philadelphia, etc., and Others. Supplementary Volume on the Fossils,* pp. 24–40. London : Whittaker and Co.

Pilgrim, G. E.
  1915 "New Siwalik primates and their bearing on the question of the evolution of man and the *Anthropoidea*." *Records of the Geological Society of India* 45, Part I : 1–74.
Pycraft, W. P.
  1928a *British Museum Report on Rhodesian Man and Associated Remains.* London : British Museum.
  1928b "Some suggestions for the analysis of the os coxa in man." *Man* 28 : 201–5.
Quatrefages de Bréau, J. L. A. de
  1861 *Unité de l'espèce humaine.* Paris : J. Claye.
  1864 "Leçons professées du muséum." *Revue des cours scientifiques de la France et de l'etranger* 2 : 538–812.
  1869 *Rapport sur le Progrès de l'anthropologie.* Paris : Imprimiere imperiale.
Ramstrom, M.
  1919 "Der Piltdown-Fund." *Bulletin of the Geological Institution of the University of Upsala* 16 : 261–303.
Read, D. W. and Lestrel, P. E.
  1970 "Hominid phylogeny and immunology: a critical appraisal." *Science* 168 :578–80.
Reichlin, M.
  1970 "The distribution of specificity in rabbit antisera directed toward human hemoglobin." *Immunochemistry* 7 : 15–28.
Remane, A.
  1951 "Die Zähne des *Meganthropus africanus*." *Zeitschrift für Morphologie und Anthropologie* 42 : 311.
"Review of Darwin's 'The Descent of man, and Selection in Relation to Sex.' "
  1871 *The Quarterly Review* (July) : 47–89.
Robinson, J. T.
  1953 "*Meganthropus,* australopithecines and hominids." *American Journal of Physical Anthropology* 11 : 1.
  1954a "The genera and species of the *Australopithecinae*." *American Journal of Physical Anthropology* 12 : 181.
  1954b "Prehominid dentition and hominid evolution." *Evolution* 8 : 324.
  1955 "Further remarks on the relationship between *Meganthropus* and australopithecines. *American Journal of Physical Anthropology* 13 : 429–45.
  1956 "The dentition of the *Australopithecinae*." *Transvaal Museum Memoirs* 9.
  1958 "Cranial cresting patterns and their significance in the *Hominoidea*." *American Journal of Physical Anthropology* 16 : 397.
  1960 "The affinities of the new Olduvai *Australopithecine*." *Nature* 186 : 456.
  1961a "The australopithecines and their bearing on the origin of man and of stone tool-making." *South African Journal of Science* 57 : 3.
  1961b "The origin and adaptive radiation of the australopithecines." In *Evolution and Hominization,* pp. 120–40. Stuttgart : A. Fischer.
  1963a "Adaptive radiation in the australopithecines and the origin of man." In *African Ecology and Human Evolution,* edited by F. Clark Howell and Francois Bourliere, pp. 385–416. Chicago : Aldine.
  1963b "Australopithecines, culture and phylogeny." *American Journal of Physical Anthropology* 21 : 595–605.
  1964 "Some critical phases in the evolution of man." *South African Archaeological Bulletin* 29, No. 3.

1965a *"Homo 'habilis'* and the australopithecines." *Nature* 205 : 121.
1965b "CA comment on 'New Discoveries in Tanganyika: their bearing on hominid evolution' by P. V. Tobias." *Current Anthropology* 6 : 403.
1966   "The distinctiveness of *Homo habilis.*" *Nature* 209 : 957.
1967   "Variation and the taxonomy of the early hominids." In *Evolutionary Biology,* edited by Theodosius Dobzhansky, Max K. Hecht, and William C. Steere, p. 69. New York : Appleton-Century-Crofts.

Ryle, G.
1949   *The Concept of Mind.* London : Hutchinson.

Saller, K.
1925   "Die Cromagnonrasse und ihre Stellung zu anderen jungpalaeolithischen Langschadelrassen." *Zeitschrift für Abstammungs und Vererbungeslehre* 39 : 191–247.

Sarasin, F.
1924   "Sur les relations des Neo-Caledoniens avec le groupe de l'*Homo neanderthalensis.*" *L'Anthropologie* 34 : 193–227.

Sarich, V. M.
1968   "Hominid origins: an immunological view." In *Perspectives on Human Evolution,* edited by S. L. Washburn and P. C. Jay, pp. 94–121. New York : Holt, Rinehart & Winston.
1969a "Pinniped origins and the rate of evolution of carnivore albumins." *Systematic Zoology* 18 : 286–95.
1969b "Pinniped phylogeny." *Systematic Zoology* 18 : 416–22.
1970   "Primate systematics with special reference to Old World monkeys: A protein perspective." In *Old World Monkeys,* edited by J. R. Napier and P. H. Napier, pp. 175–226. New York : Academic Press.
1971   "A molecular approach to the question of human origins." In *Human Evolution,* edited by P. Dolhinow and V. Sarich. Boston : Little Brown. (In press.)

Sarich, V. M., and Wilson, A. C.
1966   "Quantitative immunochemistry and the evolution of primate albumins." *Science* 154 : 1563–66.
1967a "Rates of albumin evolution in primates." *Proceedings of the National Academy of Sciences* 58 : 142–48.
1967b "Immunological time scale for hominid evolution." *Science* 158 : 1200–1203.

Schaafhausen, D.
1857   Paper read at the meeting of the Lower Rhine Medical and Natural History Society, Feb. 4, 1857. *Verhandlungen des Naturhistorischen Vereins der preussischen Rheinlande und Westphalens* 14 : xxxviii–xlii.
1861   "On the crania of the most ancient races of man." *Natural History Review* 1, No. 2 : 155–76.
1867   "On the relation between the anthropoid apes and man." *Anthropological Review* 5 : 236.

Schlaginhaufin, O.
1905   "Das Hautleistensystem der Primatenplanta unter Mitberucksichtigung der Palma." *Gegenbauers Morphologisches Jahrbuch* 33 : 577–671.

Schlosser, M.
1903   *"Anthropodus* oder *Neopithecus."* *Zentralblatt für Mineralogie, Geologie und Paläontologie.* Referate 4 : 512–13.

1911 "Beiträge zur Kenntniss der Oligozänen Landsäugetiere aus dem Fayum (Agypten)." *Beiträge zur Paläontologie und Geologie Osterreich-Ungarns und des Orients* 24 : 51–167.

Schmerling, P. C.
1833–1834 *Recherches sur les ossements fossiles découverts dans les cavernes de la Province de Liège.* 2 Vols. Liège : P. J. Collardin.

Schoentensack, O.
1908 *Der Unterkiefer des Homo heidelbergensis aus den Sanden von Mauer bei Heidelberge.* Leipzig : W. Engelmann.

Schultz, A. H.
1960 "Einage Beobachtungen und Mas am Skelett von *Oreopithecus.*" *Zeitschrift für Morphologie und Anthropologie* 50 : 136.
1961 "Some factors influencing the social life of primates in general and of early man in particular." In *Social Life of Early Man,* edited by S. L. Washburn, pp. 58–90. Chicago : Aldine.
1963 "Age changes, sex differences, and variability as factors in the classification of primates." In *Classification and Human Evolution,* edited by S. L. Washburn, pp. 85–115. Chicago : Aldine.

Schwalbe, G. A.
1900 "Der Neanderthalschädel." *Bonner Jahrbücher (Verein von altertumsfreunden im Rheinlande)* 106 : 1–72.
1901 "Uber die specifischen Merkmale des Neanderthalschadles." *Verhandl für Anatomie Gesellschaft* (Jena). Erganzungsh., *Anatomischer Anzeiger* 19 : 44–61.
1914 "Kritische Bespreshung von Boule's Werk (L'homme fossile de la Chappelle-aux-Saints') mit eigene Untersuchungen." *Zeitschrift für Morphologie und Anthropolgie* 16 : 527–610.

Simons, E. L.
1961 "The phyletic position of *Ramapithecus.*" *Yale Peabody Museum* 57 :1–9.
1963 "Some fallacies in the study of hominid phylogeny." *Science* 141 : 879–89.
1964 "On the mandible of *Ramapithecus.*" *Proceedings of the National Academy of Science* 51 : 528–35.
1965 "New fossil apes from Egypt and the initial differentiation of *Hominoidea.*" Nature 205 : 135–39.
1967 "The earliest apes." *Scientific American* 217 : 28–35.
1969 "The origin and radiation of the primates." *Annals of the New York Academy of Sciences* 167 : 319–31.

Simons, E. L., and Ettel, P. C.
1970 "Gigantopithecus." *Scientific American* 222 : 76–87.

Simons, E. L., and Pilbeam, D. R.
1965 "Preliminary revision of the *Dryopithecinae (Pongidae, Anthropoidea)." Folia Primatologica* 46 : 1–70.

Simpson, G. G.
1931 "A new classification of mammals." *Bulletin of the American Museum of Natural History* 59 : 672–73.
1944 *Tempo and Mode in Evolution.* New York : Columbia University.
1945 "The principles of classification and the classification of mammals." *Bulletin of the American Museum of Natural History* 85.
1961 *Principles of Animal Taxonomy.* London : Oxford University Press.
1963 "The meaning of taxonomic statements." In *Classification and Human Evolution,* edited by S. L. Washburn, pp. 1–31. Chicago : Aldine.

Smith, G. Elliot
    1924   *The Evolution of Man. Essays.* London: Humphrey Milford. (2nd edition 1927.)

Snell, C.
    1863   *Die Schöpfund des Menschen.* Leipzig: Arnold.

Soergel, W.
    1925   *Die Gliederung und Absolute Zeitsechung des Eisalters.* Berlin: Gebrunder, Born, and Traeger.

Sollas, W. J.
    1900   "Geology." *Nature* 62: 481–98.
    1907   "On the cranial and facial characters of the Neanderthal race." *Philosophical Transactions of the Royal Society of London* 199: 281–339.

Standing, H. F.
    1908   "On recently discovered subfossil primates from Madagascar." *Transactions of the Zoological Society of London* 18, Part 2, No. 1: 59–162.

Stehlin, H. G.
    1912   "Die Saugethiere der Schweizerischen Eocaens." *Abhandlungen der Schweizerische Palaontologische Gesellschaft* 38: 1165–1298.

Stekelis, M.; Picard, L.; Schulman, N.; and Haas, G.
    1960   "Villafranchian deposits near Ubeidiya in the Central Jordan Valley." *Bulletin of the Research Council of Israel* 9G: 175–84.

Stewart, T. D.
    1949   "The development of the concept of morphological dating in connection with early man in America." *Southwestern Journal of Anthropology* 5: 1–16.
    1960   "Form of the pubic bone in Neanderthal man." *Science* 131 :1437–38.

Stolyhwo, K.
    1908a   "*Homo primigenius,* appartient-il à une espèce distincte de *Homo sapiens?*" *L'Anthropologie* 29: 191–216.
    1908b   "Zur Frage der Existenz von Uberganzformen zwischen *Homo primigenius* und *Homo sapiens.*" *Globus* 94, No. 23: 363–64.
    1908c   "Le Crâne de Nowosiolka considere comme preuve de l'existence a l'époque historique de fromes apparentées a *H. primigenius.*" *Bulletin International de l'Académie des Sciences de Cracovie,* 1908. Pp. 103–26.

Suess, E.
    1885   *Das Antlitz der Erde.* 3 Vols. Wien: F. Tempsky.

Szombathy. J.
    1926   "Die menschenrassen im oberen Palaolithicum, insbesondere die Brux-Rasse." *Mitteilungen der Anthropologische Gesellschaft* (Wien) 55: 202–19.

Teilhard de Chardin, P.
    1943   *Fossil Man. Recent Discoveries and Present Problems.* Peking: Henri Vetch.

Thevet, A.
    1558   *Les singularitez de la France antarctiques autrement nommee Amerique et de plusieurs terres et isles decouvertes de nostre temps.* Paris: Les heriteurs de M. de La Porte.

Tilney, F.
    1928   *The Brain from Ape to Man.* New York: D. B. Harber.

Tobias, P. V.
   1963   "Cranial capacity of *Zinjanthropus* and other australopithecines." *Nature*
          197: 743–46.
   1964   "The Olduvai Bed I hominine with special reference to its cranial capacity."
          Nature 202: 3–4.

Topinard, P.
   1876   *L'Anthropologie.* Paris: C. Reinwald.
   1890   *Anthropology.* London: Chapman and Hall.

Tournal, M.
   1828   "Note sur deux cavernes à ossements découvertes à Bize, dans les environs
          de Narbonne." *Annales des sciences naturelles* 15: 348–50.
   1833   "Considerations générales sur le phenomène des cavernes à ossements."
          Annales de chimie et de physique 52: 161–81.

Tyson, E.
   1699   *Orang-outang: or the Anatomy of a Pygmy Compared with that of a
          Monkey, an Ape and a Man. To which is Added a Philosophical Essay
          Concerning the Pygmies, the Cynocephalie, the Satyrs, and the Sphinges
          of the Ancients. Wherein it will Appear that They are All either Apes or
          Monkeys and not Men, as Formerly Pretended.* London: Printed for T.
          Bennet.

Ulloa, A. de
   1748   *Relacion Historica del Viage a la America Meridional.* Madrid: A. Marin.

Verneau, R.
   1906   "Les Grottes de Grimaldi." *Anthropologie* 2, Fasc. 1. Berlin: Friedlander.

Vesalius, A.
   1543   *And. Vesalius de Corporis Humani Fabrica. Libri Septem.* Basle: Johannes
          Oporinus.

Virchow, H.
   1920   *Die Menschlichen Skelettreste aus dem Kämpferschen Bruch im Travertin
          von Ehringsdorf bei Weimar.* Jena: G. Fischer.

Vogt, C.
   1863   *Lectures on Man: His Place in Creation, and in the History of the Earth.*
          London: Longman, Green, Longman, and Roberts.
   1863   *Vorlesungen über den Menschen, seine Stellung in der Schöpfung und in
          der Geschichte der Erde.* Giessen: Ricker.

Wallace, A. R.
   1870   *Contributions to the Theory of Natural Selection.* New York and London:
          Macmillan and Company.
   1876   *The Geographical Distribution of Animals.* New York: Harper and
          Brothers.
   1880   *Island Life.* London: Macmillan.
   1887   "The antiquity of man in North America." *The Nineteenth Century* 22:
          667–79.
   1889   *Darwinism.* London and New York: Macmillan and Company.

Wang, A. C.; Shuster, J.; Epstein, A.; and Fudenberg, H. H.
   1968   "Evolution of antigenic determinants of transferrin and other serum proteins
          in primates." *Biochemical Genetics* 1: 347–58.

Washburn, S. L.
1950   "The analysis of primate evolution, with particular reference to the origin
         of man." *Cold Spring Harbor Symposium on Quantitative Biology* 15 : 67.
1957   "Australopithecines : the hunters or the hunted ?" *American Anthropologist*
         59 : 612.
1963   "Behavior and Human Evolution." *Classification and Human Evolution,*
         edited by S. L. Washburn, pp. 190–203. Chicago : Aldine.
1968   *The Study of Human Evolution.* Eugene, Ore. : University of Oregon.

Washburn, S. L., and Howell, F. C.
1960   "Human evolution and culture." *Evolution after Darwin* 2 : 33. Chicago :
         University of Chicago.

Washburn, S. L., and Patterson, B.
1951   "Evolutionary importance of the South African man-apes." *Nature* 167 :
         650.

Weber, M.
1904   *Die Saugetiere.* Jena : G. Fischer.

Weidenreich, F.
1927   "Der Schädel von Weimar-Ehringsdorf." *Verhandlungen der Deutsche
         Gesellschaft für Rassenforschung. (Gesellschaft für physische Anthro-
         pologie* 2 : 34–41.
1928   *Der Schädelfund von Weimar-Ehringsdorf.* Jena : G. Fischer.
1932   "Ueber pithekoide Merkmale bei *Sinanthropus pekinensis* und seine
         stammesgeschichteliche Beurteilung." *Zeitschrift für Anatomie und
         Entwicklungsgeschichte* 99 : 212–53.
1937   "The dentition of *Sinanthropus pekinensis.*" *Palaeontologica Sinica* 101 :
         1–180.
1940a "The torus occipitalis and related structures and their transformation in
         the course of human evolution." *Bulletin of the Geological Society of
         China* 19 : 480–558.
1940b "Some problems dealing with ancient man." *American Anthropologist*
         42 : 375–83.
1943a "The Neanderthal Man and the ancestors of '*Homo sapiens.*'" *American
         Anthropologist* n.s. 45 : 39–48.
1943b "The skull of *Sinanthropus pekinensis:* a comparative study of a primitive
         hominoid skull." *Palaeontologica Sinica* 127 : 1–484.
1945a "Giant early man from Java and South China." *Anthropological Papers
         of the American Museum of Natural History,* Part 1, pp. 1–34.
1945b "The Keilor skull : a Wadjak type from southeast Australia." *American
         Journal of Physical Anthropology* 3 : 21–32.
1946a *Apes, Giants, and Man.* Chicago : University of Chicago.
1946b "Size, special form and pattern of the human brain in the light of evolution."
         Cleveland Anatomical Record 94, Sec. 3 : 59.
1947   "Facts and speculations concerning the origins of *Homo sapiens.*"
         American Anthropologist 49 : 187–203.

Weinert, H.
1936   "Der Urmenschenschädel von Steinheim." *Zeitschrift für Morphologie
         und Anthropologie* 35 : 463–518.
1950   "Ueber die neuen Vor- und Fruhmenschenfunde aus Africa, Java, China
         und Frankreich." *Zeitschrift für Morphologie und Anthropologie* 43 : 73.
1951   "Uber die Vielgestaltikeit der Summoprimaten von der Menscheuerdung."
         Zeitschrift für Morphologie und Anthropologie 43 : 73.

Weisbach, A.
1867 "Reise der Osterreichischen Fregatte 'Novara.'" *Anthropologischer Teil.* Vienna: Gerold's.

Whitworth, T.
1958 "Miocene ruminants of East Africa." British Museum of Natural History, *Fossil Mammals of Africa* 15: 1–50.

Wilder, H. H.
1926 *The Pedigree of the Human Race.* New York: Henry Holt and Co.

Willis, T.
1664 *Cerebri Anatomae, Cui Accessit Nervorum Descriptio et Usus.* London: Jo. Martyn and Ja. Allestry.

Wilson, A. C., and Sarich, V. M.
1969 "A molecular time scale for human evolution." *Proceedings National Academy of Sciences* 68: 1088–93.

Woodward, A. Smith
1913 "Description of the human skull and mandible and the associated mammalian remains." *Quarterly Journal of the Geological Society of London* 69: 124–51.

Wortman, J. L.
1903–1904 "Studies of Eocene mammalia in the Marsh Collection, Peabody Museum. Part 2. Primates." *American Journal of Science* 16: 368; 17: 23–33.

Wright, C.
1870 "Limits of natural selection." *North American Review* 3: 295–311.

Zeuner, F. E.
1946 *Dating the Past.* London: Methuen and Company.

Zuckerkandl, E.
1963 "Perspectives in molecular anthropology." In *Classification and Human Evolution,* edited by S. L. Washburn, pp. 243–72. Chicago: Aldine.

Zuckerkandl, E., and Pauling, L.
1962 "Molecular disease, evolution, and genic heterogeneity." In *Horizons in Biochemistry,* edited by M. Kasha and B. Pullman, pp. 189–225. New York: Academic Press.